God's Diplomats

God's Diplomats

Pope Francis, Vatican Diplomacy, and America's Armageddon

Victor Gaetan

ROWMAN & LITTLEFIELD
Lanham • Boulder • New York • London

Published by Rowman & Littlefield
An imprint of The Rowman & Littlefield Publishing Group, Inc.
4501 Forbes Boulevard, Suite 200, Lanham, Maryland 20706
www.rowman.com

86-90 Paul Street, London EC2A 4NE

Copyright © 2021 by The Rowman & Littlefield Publishing Group, Inc.

Preface Copyright © 2023 by The Rowman & Littlefield Publishing Group, Inc.

All rights reserved. No part of this book may be reproduced in any form or by any electronic or mechanical means, including information storage and retrieval systems, without written permission from the publisher, except by a reviewer who may quote passages in a review.

British Library Cataloguing in Publication Information Available

Library of Congress Cataloging-in-Publication Data

ISBN 978-1-5381-5014-6 (cloth)
ISBN 978-1-5381-8461-5 (paperback)
ISBN 978-1-5381-8467-7 (electronic)

∞™ The paper used in this publication meets the minimum requirements of American National Standard for Information Sciences—Permanence of Paper for Printed Library Materials, ANSI/NISO Z39.48-1992.

The true strength of the Church is in our work, so often hidden.
—Pope Francis, December 21, 2018[1]

Contents

Preface ix

Part I

Introduction: What Does Washington Fear about
Pope Francis and Vatican Diplomacy? 1

1 An Adaptable Network, Willing to Bleed 15

2 Mission beyond Religion 43

3 Education of a Diplomat 67

4 Sovereignty Is the Ticket to the International System 93

5 Diplomatic Classics, Rules of Thumb, and Modus Operandi 117

Part II

Introduction: The Mustard Seed: Jorge Bergoglio as
Manager, Missionary, and Mystic 145

6 Stifling War in Ukraine: Prioritizing Peace with Russia 155

   2013 protests in Ukraine lead to a war that threatened over two decades of relationship building between Rome and Moscow.

7	Mediating Cold War Quarrels: Cuba and the United States	181
	2014 marks normalization of relations between the United States and Cuba, a landmark agreement brokered by Rome.	
8	Diminishing Division: Kenya	205
	2015 finds Pope Francis in Kenya, where he shares a simple gesture.	
9	Letting War's Victims Lead: Colombia	219
	2016 clinches a peace deal signed by government and guerillas after over fifty years of fighting; the Catholic Church helps define the agreement's core concern.	
10	Piecing Together the Middle East: Lebanon, Syria, Iran, and Saudi Arabia	245
	2017 brings political crisis in Lebanon that cardinal-patriarch works to untie.	
11	Unifying the "Religion of the Lord of Heaven": China	271
	2018 achieves agreement between Vatican and Beijing on bishop selection.	
12	Piercing Gestures: South Sudan	299
	2019 witnesses a pope on his knees kissing the feet of warlords.	
Acknowledgments		317
Notes		323
Bibliography		441
Index		451
About the Author		467

Preface

In the two years since *God's Diplomats* was published, Pope Francis' practice of pastoral diplomacy continues to define his pontificate in a chaotic global context. Francis seeks opportunities for dialogue and encounter with "peripheral" places, other religious leaders, and people on the margins to catalyze reconciliation of all sorts. Behind the scenes, he deploys the Vatican's diplomatic network to produce concrete results, often small steps designed to build trust. It's a process of endless *nudging* as Francis acts in counterpose to an undeclared, piecemeal world war, laid bare by the tragic Russian invasion of Ukraine, which he describes as "cruel and absurd."

One arena in which Francis has been quietly successful—with crucial support from the Dicastery for Interreligious Dialogue and scant attention from the West—is in strengthening relations with the Muslim world. It's a priority that underscores the Vatican's independence from a Western worldview. Unlike his predecessor, Francis is far more interested in the Middle East, Africa, and Asia (where Catholics comprise two-thirds of the 1.3 billion global faithful) than with the tediously self-obsessed West where Christianity is in precipitous decline.

IRAQ, BAHRAIN, AND SUNNI-SHIA DIALOGUE

Against advisers preoccupied with his security, Francis insisted on making Iraq his first destination outside Italy after the pandemic. As usual, the trip had multiple goals: to highlight the common roots of Christianity, Islam, and Judaism by participating in an interfaith prayer in Ur, Abraham's biblical birthplace; to encourage hope against extremism, by standing in the rubble of Mosel; to make an act of penance for US-led destruction of the country;

to encourage remaining Christians whose faith faces obliteration as numbers fall from 1.5 million in 2003 to under 300,000 today; and to meet one man, Shiite leader Grand Ayatollah Ali al-Sistani, at his modest home in Najaf, the world's most sacred and influential Shiite center.

Francis thanked Sistani for his help protecting Christians in Iraq; Sistani insisted that Iraqi Christians are citizens with "full constitutional rights." Sistani's statement after their meeting showed how closely aligned these two moral authorities are in calling for the rejection of violence and the "language of war" in favor of focus on poverty, social justice, and human dignity. (It is worth noting that al-Sistani refused to meet any US official following the 2003 invasion.) Through this encounter, Francis sought to offer an embrace to Shia Islam, representing about 15 percent of the Prophet's followers. According to Vatican diplomats, this was no "check the box" meeting; it was a central *purpose* of the pilgrimage. At the time, Iraq's prime minister was facilitating negotiations between Sunni-majority Saudi Arabia and Shia-majority Iran, which the Pope wanted to encourage.

Why was this so important? Because conflict in the Middle East has been enflamed by Sunni–Shia tension for over 40 years—since the 1979 revolution in Iran. The devastating eight-years-long Iran–Iraq war, conflict in Lebanon, the emergence of ISIS, Saudi Arabia's invasion of Yemen—all were exacerbated by Sunni–Shia rivalry. Francis reached out to Sunni leaders early in his pontificate, at the height of ravaging religious violence in the Middle East. He developed a friendship with Sheikh Ahmad al-Tayeb, the grand imam of Al-Azhar mosque in Cairo, memorialized in the United Arab Emirates (UAE) as explored on pages 133-34.

In November 2022, Francis made another maiden voyage to a Gulf state: the small island nation of Bahrain, where most Catholics are guest workers from the Philippines, India, or the Middle East. At an inter-faith forum with the Pope, al-Tayeb called for reconciliation between Shia and Sunni, which Francis later told him was "very courageous." It was the first such public call from a prominent Sunni leader; it was also a fruit of Francis and al-Tayeb's extended dialogue. While in Bahrain, Francis met with the Muslim Council of Elders, an al-Tayeb brainchild created with Vatican help. The landing page of its website features both men. This year, the Holy See established diplomatic relations with Oman, another Sunni Gulf country, making it the 184th nation with which the Vatican has formal ties.

THIRD PROVISIONAL AGREEMENT WITH CHINA

In March 2023, Iran and Saudi Arabia reestablished diplomatic relations in a landmark agreement ultimately brokered by China. Vatican diplomats were impressed to see China playing this constructive role: The Holy See favors a multipolar world in which all nations prioritize peacemaking, especially those aspiring to regional and international leadership. Despite Western detractors such as the *Wall Street Journal* throwing darts at Francis's commitment to rapprochement with Beijing, the Holy See renewed its provisional agreement on the selection of bishops again in 2022. As outlined in chapter 11, and emphatically ignored by his critics, Francis achieved a goal pursued by the Holy See for some 45 years. The Vatican will continue fostering unity among Chinese believers while preserving the apostolic succession of bishops, crucial for priestly ordinations and the provision of sacraments.

What detractors miss is the Holy See's ability to hold two thoughts in mind at the same time: Yes, the Chinese Communist Party (CCP) is autocratic. It discourages Christianity. At the same time, the Church bravely exists and persists in China. Political regimes wax and wane; Christ's bride will prevail. Rome's ongoing negotiations to produce Chinese bishops acceptable to the CCP is a *modus vivendi* in Vatican parlance, a centuries-old diplomatic practice—a way to stay in the game. As a Vatican diplomat explained, "We support the politics of small steps. We believe that each result, even if it is not striking, even if it is not showy, even if at the beginning it doesn't appear to give great results, is, however, a step forward toward greater religious liberty."[1]

RECONCILING WARLORDS

When we left South Sudan in chapter 12, President Salva Kiir and Vice President Riek Machar, protagonists in a civil war, had created a unity government, inspired by their experience together at a 2019 Vatican retreat where Francis memorably kissed their feet. This government has held. In March, the pope kept his promise to visit the country as part of a historic first: an ecumenical pilgrimage with the Archbishop of Canterbury and the moderator of the Church of Scotland. Catholics make up the country's largest faith coordinating actively with other Christians through the South Sudan Council of Churches, which first requested Francis's engagement at a 2016 meeting in Rome.

The pope's moving visit to the world's newest—and poorest—nation, showed a crucial dimension of Vatican diplomacy: top-down meets bottom-up peace building. In the Vatican's service to a broken world, Rome is well aware it sometimes breaks bread with murderers as it negotiates with politicians. The mantra is, never give up on an individual, a place, or a situation. Meanwhile, the pope's presence often creates space for the local Church to show its best face. People such as 46-year-old Bishop Christian Carlassare, who led a 9-day peace pilgrimage of 60 youth and 24 supporting staff on foot from Rumbek to Juba (comparable to New York City to Washington, DC) to see the Pope and inspire citizens along the way. It was a vision of the Church that Francis hopes to build, a synodal Church, walking together.

"MARTYRED" UKRAINE

For the Vatican, war in Ukraine represents failed secular diplomacy—or an unwillingness to even respect diplomacy's capacity to settle differences without yielding winners and losers. Of the case studies in this book, a chapter 6 epilogue would have to report dramatic deviation from the course Pope Francis pursued: war was not stifled; the Vatican's relationship with the Russian Orthodox Church (ROC), cultivated for decades, has thus suffered.

In the conflict's first months, Francis suggested that NATO had provoked Russia, describing the Western alliance as "barking on Russia's border." But he has repeatedly condemned the invasion since, even comparing Putin's tactics against civilians to Stalin's forced famine of 1932–1933. Regarding ROC Patriarch Kirill, once called "brother," the pope warned him by phone not to be "Putin's altar boy." (Although Francis has tried to mediate for Kirill by asking Kyiv not to expel Russian Orthodox monks from historic Lavra monastery.)

Invited to Kyiv, Francis says he will only visit Ukraine if he can go to Moscow too. Meanwhile, the Pope thinks wars are inevitable because the arms trade, utterly normalized, is booming: "No peace is possible where instruments of death are proliferating" he told diplomats in Rome. And while he curbed criticism of the West (advisers tell me pressure on the Pope to trash talk Russia is fierce), Francis is leery of US sanctions (about one-third of world population suffers under US economic sanctions) and military flexing—the United States maintains some 750 foreign military bases.

HUNGARY AND MONGOLIA IN 2023

One country the Holy See is closer to since the Ukraine war is Hungary, which refused to send weapons to Kyiv or let weapons transit its territory. In addition to that, the Pope's views converge with those of Prime Minister Viktor Orbán's on Western excesses such as gender ideology. According to Francis, "Some interests, perhaps not European ones, try to use the EU for ideological colonization and this is not good. The EU must be independent for itself and for all countries at the same level inspired by the dream of the founding fathers." The Pope visits Hungary for a second time this year.

Elevated in 2022, the Church's youngest cardinal is Bishop Giorgio Marengo, age 48, a missionary to Mongolia cultivating a small young Catholic community, fully engaged with the majority Buddhist faith. He is a humble, open-hearted priest, an apt spiritual son of Francis. The Pope's anticipated visit to this country will be another first. Although peripheral in being unknown and overlooked, Mongolia's location, completely embraced by China and Russia, has strategic importance which fascinates Francis, a cartophile.

PRAEDICATE EVANGELIUM

Chapter 1 outlines the pope's governing instruments, the various offices of the Roman curia that help him manage the universal Church. In 2022, the Holy See promulgated a much-anticipated apostolic constitution, *Praedicate Evangelium* (Preach the Gospel). In terms of diplomatic functionality, the Secretariat of State retains its centrality although its financial responsibilities moved to the Secretariat for the Economy. Departments known as "congregations" or "councils" all became dicasteries. The whole apparatus is now supposed to, more explicitly, serve the worldwide bishops and uplift evangelization as the central mission as discussed on pages 29–30.

CONCLUSION

Having outlived his historic shadow, Pope Emeritus Benedict XVI (who Francis referred to as a "wise grandfather" although the German was only 9 years older) as well as some well-placed closet critics, such as Cardinal George Pell, Pope Francis is freer today than he was when elected in 2013. The internal reforms he was elected to start are under way. He knows which closets hide what skeletons and where far-flung colleagues are producing results. What he needs is more time. So, he recently called his throne a job "for life," despite lauding Benedict for resigning.

In his diplomatic prowess, Francis reminds us of two predecessors: John XXIII (1958–1963) functioned across cultures and deeply appreciated other religious traditions. Sainted in 2014 by Francis, John innovated in international affairs up to his death as discussed on pages 84–86. The other kindred pontiff is Leo XXIII (1878–1903), whose extraordinary work ethic included 86 encyclicals. Trained at the Holy See's storied diplomatic school, Leo ushered in the modern papacy, elaborated modern Catholic social teaching, and improved relations with all the great powers of his time. Regarding the

United States, he protested its use of military might to annex the Philippines, upending local culture. Leo lived and reigned until age 93—the oldest sitting pope ever.

God's Diplomats spells out how the Holy See mediates conflict including the strategies used and diplomatic playbook deployed. It explains why a state smaller than New York's Central Park has diplomatic relations with 184 countries (more than the United States) and functions within the United Nations. There is no country big or small *not* of interest to the Holy See. With no military, no trade interests, and a miniscule economy, the Vatican is respected, in turn, for its discretion and reliability. This book highlights why the pope is the best-informed man on the planet. At a time when diplomacy too often seems to be a lost art, it is good to recall what it takes to avoid war, expand peace, and advance the common good. *God's Diplomats* is that reminder.

Victor Gaetan
March 2023

1

Introduction

What Does Washington Fear about Pope Francis and Vatican Diplomacy?

The US government has long kept an eagle eye on the world's smallest sovereign, Vatican City, which covers less ground than the Pentagon and its parking lot. More precisely, Washington warily watches the Vatican's supranational ruler, *Pontifex Maximus*, the greatest priest, and his governing apparatus, the Holy See. Despite phases of coordination, such as Ronald Reagan's relationship with Pope John Paul II to cultivate the anti-Soviet Solidarity movement in Poland, the modern norm—arguably since the United States bought the Catholic-majority Philippines for $20 million in 1898—is mutual skepticism between empires with deeply divergent worldviews.[1] Mainly at odds when Rome refuses to defer to the American view of reality, the relationship has been punctuated by blowups.

Popes have consistently opposed US wars. President Franklin Roosevelt went ballistic when Pope Pius XII awarded full diplomatic recognition to Japan just months after the attack on Pearl Harbor, although later he thanked Vatican diplomats for visiting American POWs in Japanese camps. The Vatican was horrified when the Pentagon unleashed nuclear mayhem on civilians in Hiroshima and Nagasaki (the bomb, which destroyed the largest Catholic cathedral in Asia, was a direct hit on the nation's most historic Catholic district,[2] founded by St. Francis Xavier, SJ, in the sixteenth century), especially since Vatican emissaries informed the US military throughout the war about the location of military targets. Despite extensive pressure from Harry Truman's White House, the notoriously anti-Communist Pius XII refused to endorse the US crusade against Soviet power on the Korean Peninsula.[3]

A CIA director flew to Rome to reprimand a dying Pope John XXIII for opening a dialogue with Soviet premier Nikita Khrushchev. The American warned him that it was dangerous "to dicker with the Kremlin," to which the pope responded that the Church would talk to everyone to achieve urgent tasks.[4] The pope's secretary, Cardinal Loris Capovilla, was there. He recalled, "After the war, the US expected us [the Holy See] to be an annex," but the pope was undeterred.[5] Four years later, it was Pope Paul VI who slammed his hand on his desk in anger over bombing raids on North Vietnam—in a meeting with President Lyndon Johnson.[6]

More recently, Middle East policy has been the source of dire disagreement. John Paul II tried to dissuade President George W. Bush from attacking Iraq on the eve of the invasion, sending Cardinal Pio Laghi to the Oval Office with the Holy See's case against it.[7] Laghi was a Bush family friend. He played tennis and drank cappuccino with Vice President George H. W. Bush as a neighbor, living across the street while serving as the Vatican's representative to the United States from 1980 to 1990.[8] When President Bush sent his elderly father to Rome to placate the pope three days before the United States began bombing Afghanistan in 2001, Laghi and Bush 41 reconnected.

But personal ties were worthless in the face of the younger Bush's determination to hammer Iraq under what proved to be a false accusation. The cardinal, who had also been a diplomat in Jerusalem, warned that invasion would yield countless casualties, sectarian conflict between Shiites and Sunnis, and long-term regional turmoil including the scapegoating of Christian communities. In response, the president told Laghi that reason—and Jesus—were on his side. Bush explained that "Jesus saved him from alcoholism" and was guiding him. "He spoke and behaved as though he was divinely inspired and seemed genuinely to believe that it was a war of right against wrong," the diplomat recounted in Italy months later.[9]

Accompanying Laghi was the nuncio (Vaticanese for ambassador) to the United States, Archbishop Gabriel Montalvo, and a young Vatican diplomat, Joseph Marino, a native of Birmingham, Alabama, who recalled, "We met first with Ms. [Condoleezza] Rice in the White House and then with the president in the Oval Office. Both meetings lasted around 45 minutes. The next day, we met with Secretary of State Colin Powell at the State Department." Other religious leaders had requested meetings with the president to plead for peace, but only the pope's three-man delegation was given this opportunity.

Today, Archbishop Marino is president of the Vatican's diplomatic school, the Pontifical Ecclesiastical Academy, known as the *Accademia*. An important lesson is the one Marino lived: American arrogance in the face of Vatican wisdom. The Alabaman summarizes crisply, "Historians have already affirmed, and events have already proved, that the Holy See's position was verified in the years following the war."[10]

In fact, new information indicates that the Vatican delegation was too late. The decision was already made. Episcopalian Bishop John Bryce Chane revealed to me that Christian leaders were given a preview of the Bush administration's plans in November 2002. According to Chane, who led Washington National Cathedral at the time, he was summoned to the Pentagon for a top secret briefing on Afghanistan. Instead, the topic was a US plan "to liberate" Iraq, which the group learned as soon as Secretary of Defense Donald Rumsfeld arrived by helicopter from the White House.

Chane told me, Rumsfeld "explained that using intensive pinpoint bombing on Iraq will minimize civilian casualties and we will then put boots on the ground and our troops will be received as liberators, and we will begin the process of supporting and sustaining the rise of a democratic movement in Iraq which will have a positive impact on the region and stabilize it. We were told we could not share the intel with anyone. I left that meeting knowing the decision had pretty much been made."

Why did Rumsfeld, together with his deputy, Paul Wolfowitz, gather faith leaders? "It was a matter of bringing religious leaders onboard to know the strategy so they could be supportive if and when it was carried out," said Chane, who was appalled. Baltimore Cardinal William Keller was silent. Others, such as evangelical Chuck Colson, were enthusiastic. Trusted columnist and Catholic convert Robert Novak said little.

The confrontation regarding Iraq crystallized Vatican dismay at the US tendency to militarize foreign policy after the Cold War, while discounting the cost of bellicose problem solving. When they met a year later, Bush told the Polish pontiff, "Your Holiness, we just want security!" John Paul retorted, "At the feet of this idol that you call security, you want to sacrifice all human dignity."[11]

Pope Benedict XVI's papacy carried the same critique: frustration with the militarized nature of American foreign policy. He lamented on Easter 2007, "In the Middle East . . . unfortunately, nothing positive comes from Iraq, torn apart by continual slaughter as the civil population flees."[12] (However, the Holy See refused to pull its own nuncio from Bagdad during the war.) The United States officially protested the pope's word choice, but as usual, antagonism was contained behind the scenes.[13]

A new fault line opened up: As Benedict normalized relations with Vladimir Putin, a German speaker and Germanophile,[14] hostility grew between the United States and Russia. The United States increasingly used NATO to isolate Moscow from neighbors and potential allies.[15] The German pope's unexpected move to establish diplomatic relations with Russia and his increasingly respectful exchanges with the Russian Orthodox patriarchate, were challenges to American rule. As a result, the hegemon took measures to preempt another uncontrollable pontiff. Italian media reported evidence that US intelligence spied on the conclave that elected Jorge Mario Bergoglio, now Francis, to the papacy in 2013—and allegedly started surveilling the Argentinian cardinal years before.[16] (Information compiled on the papal sweepstakes was allegedly organized into four categories: leadership dynamics; foreign policy objectives; finances; and human rights.)

And it was not surprising that a longtime Bergoglio antagonist, with US ties, Horacio Verbitsky, popped up immediately. As Eugene Ionesco, the renowned theater-of-the-absurd playwright, said, "How strange, how bizarre, and what a coincidence" that a sinister individual who was associated, by turns, with left-wing terrorists, two right-wing military juntas, the US embassy, and American pass-through organizations (the Ford Foundation, the National Endowment for Democracy, and the Open Society Foundation) launched attacks against Jorge Bergoglio, a prelate the intelligence community appeared to have ongoing interest in.[17]

For the first four years of Francis's pontificate, relations with President Barack Obama's administration were largely respectful. Pope Francis successfully discouraged the United States from bombing Syria. The Vatican and the US Conference of Catholic Bishops enthusiastically supported the nuclear agreement with Iran. Francis's divergent assessment of politics in Ukraine, the topic of chapter 6, was balanced by his ready assistance to reconcile Washington and Havana—a diplomatic tour de force we will explore in chapter 7. The US-Cuba deal merged a classic papal function (impartial mediation) with Bergoglio's personal identity as Argentinian and thus independent of long-standing East-West political battles regarding the island.

Then President Donald Trump happened . . .

Pope Francis has been subjected to a relentless campaign of innuendo, a constant multiplication of accusations mainly traceable to American interests.[18] After surging to unimaginable global popularity, including a wildly popular visit to the United States in 2015, he's suddenly St. Sebastian, withstanding relentless arrows, including accusations for not handling clerical sex abusers whose offenses occurred on his predecessors' watch.

Pope Francis's main offense is, apparently, standing up to American foreign policy in multiple theaters, especially against endless wars. The US establishment generally loathes being contradicted, certainly not by a character whose very modus operandi suggests Washington is doing something wrong. From his position on climate change to confronting the adverse consequences of unlimited weapons sales, from challenging the ethics of the global financial system to opposing border walls, Pope Francis has gone toe-to-toe with the world's leading superpower—and it does *not* appreciate his advice. In September 2020, on the eve of a visit to Rome, Secretary of State Mike Pompeo bluntly and undiplomatically challenged the Vatican regarding its ongoing negotiations with China where some 12 million Catholic faithful live. Profoundly unimpressed, Francis simply ignored the US official while his top advisers publicly reminded Pompeo that the Sino-Vatican deal "is a matter that has nothing to do with American politics. This is a matter between Churches and should not be used for this type of end."[19]

It is not as though American leaders did not, once upon a time, recognize the truths Francis highlights. President Dwight Eisenhower, a Presbyterian, saw the direct relationship between poverty and spending billions on war. Early in his presidency, the five-star general said,

> Every gun that is made, every warship launched, every rocket fired signifies . . . a theft from those who hunger and are not fed, those who are cold and are not clothed. . . . The cost of one modern heavy bomber is this: a modern brick school in more than 30 cities. . . . We pay for a single fighter plane with a half million bushels of wheat. . . . This is not a way of life at all, in any true sense. Under the cloud of threatening war, it is humanity hanging from a cross of iron.[20]

With a sense of unfinished mission, after eight years in the White House, Eisenhower included a warning in his January 1961 farewell address. He told the American public that the nation's freedom could be undermined by the "total influence—economic, political, even spiritual" of the US military, with political interests everywhere it is based, combined with the financial drive of US weapons' manufacturers. He dubbed the fusion of interests the "military industrial complex."[21]

It's not just what Francis says but what he has allowed to unfold. Francis never openly endorsed Syrian president Bashar al-Assad, but he empowered a phalanx of Catholic regional leaders who defended the Alawite leader as the only reliable protector of Christians—and welcomed Russian military engagement. The pope has continued a respectful relationship with the Shia leadership in Iran, as he established new bridges to Sunni Muslim leaders and nations, including Bangladesh, Egypt, Morocco, and the United Arab Emirates (UAE). While in the Holy Lands, Francis spontaneously climbed out of his popemobile to pray on the Palestinian side of the giant Israeli barrier wall, next to graffiti in red proclaiming, "Free Palestine."[22] Quelle horreur! Rome aligned with much of the world to oppose designating Jerusalem as the capital of Israel, then joined the European Union, Russia, and the UN to oppose Israel's plan to annex some 30 percent of the West Bank in 2020—both positions against the US side.[23]

Building on ground laid by his predecessors, Francis has drawn closer to Russia and the Russian Orthodox Church even as a Western, US-led coalition hammers the Orthodox power with sanctions. The pope refused to affirm Ukraine's version of events in its contest with Russia: instead of an invasion, he describes the conflict as "fratricide" between Christians.

In Asia, Francis negotiated with the Chinese government for four years, which led to a provisional agreement regarding the appointment of bishops as announced in 2018. The deal flows from John Paul II's analysis that two Catholic communities exist in China, one functioning officially, the other avoiding registration with the state, yet both loyal to the Holy See. Despite the fact that the topic is largely an internal ecclesiastic matter, and the text is not even public, former White House adviser and Trump campaign strategist Steve Bannon waltzed between European luxury hotels using the China deal to flog Pope Francis and his secretary of state, Cardinal Pietro Parolin.

Bannon told a journalist, "What the Church has done is made a pact with the devil. Actually, they're hurting the Chinese people. The Chinese people hate this deal. . . . They've [Francis and Parolin] jeopardized the lives of living saints, the living saints of the underground Catholic Church. They're putting all religious believers in jeopardy by giving a false cover to a murderous regime."[24] This is a very harsh critique—and substantially inaccurate as we will see in chapter 11.

Deploying a classic American scheme—using attention-getting rhetoric and agitation to fund-raise and self-enrich—Bannon said he raised $100 million from Chinese expatriate billionaires.[25] Some of that was earmarked to discredit Pope Francis and his diplomats. The fast-talking Bannon toured European capitals promising to convert a monastery into a "gladiator school for culture warriors." This thrice-divorced recovering alcoholic, former Wall Street investment banker, film producer, Trump campaign strategist, and, briefly, White House operative was obviously more Catholic than the pope.

For about two years, he even seemed to have a few well-placed supporters in high Vatican echelons. But the unnatural construction unraveled in Italy and the United States over the course of a year. First, he lost the veneer of orthodoxy he gained through association with a few traditionalist churchmen. Cardinal Renato Maria Martino warned the Dignitatis Humanae Institute, Bannon's collaborator, to respect Catholic doctrine and maintain a nonpolitical program, challenging Bannon and friends' bombastic plans for a "gladiator school" in an old Carthusian monastery.[26]

In June 2019, the Italian Ministry of Culture revoked the institute's permits due to bidding irregularities and insufficient evidence that it had expertise in managing historical sites.[27] Then conservative American Cardinal Raymond Burke denounced Bannon's plans and ended his relationship with Dignitatis

Humanae.[28] Meanwhile, European politicians on the right distanced themselves one after another. According to a *New Yorker* account, an Alternative for Germany party representative said Bannon did not understand European politics. French populist Marine Le Pen said, "[He] isn't from a European country." An Italian representative from the League political party was most blunt, speculating to Politico that Bannon "looks like he's going after money."[29]

But Bannon's coup de grâce came on Long Island Sound, off the Connecticut coast, with his spectacular arrest on a luxurious yacht owned by one of his controversial Chinese financiers, said to be the source of some of his anti-Francis shenanigans.[30] The charges? Conspiracy to commit multimillion-dollar fraud and money laundering. It seems Steve Bannon's allegiance was to money, power, and over-the-top luxury, mainstays of gluttony and vanity so repulsive to Catholic doctrine and Francis. In his last days in office, Trump pardoned Bannon, yet his legal problems seem not to be over.

President Joe Biden is just the second Catholic to hold the nation's highest office, following John F. Kennedy. As vice president, he led the US delegation to Francis' 2013 inauguration and the two men have met several times since. On the campaign trail, Biden referred frequently to his faith and quoted with approval the most recent papal encyclical, *Fratelli Tutti* (Brothers All, 2020). Are the president's personal beliefs assertive enough to redirect a longstanding clash in worldviews between the US and Holy See? Probably not. His foreign policy advisers draw from the same well that delivered destruction to the Balkans, Iraq, Libya, and Syria. Russia is still in the State Department's crosshairs even if Iran probably is not.

The Soviet Union targeted the Holy See as an enemy, too; eventually its role was sussed out. Priests sent to infiltrate Catholic institutions in Rome typically unmasked themselves after acting like ignorant pagans. A play demonizing Pope Pius XII's decisions during World War II, *The Deputy*, was ultimately revealed as the work of a left-wing agent supported by Moscow.[31] The triggerman who nearly assassinated Pope John Paul II might have been Turkish, but his ties to Bulgarian intelligence, then controlled by the USSR, were revealed by an Italian parliamentary commission.[32]

So close in time to the Sturm und Drang, it's difficult to know the extent to which an intelligence "deep state" is behind the relentless attacks on Francis. But there are indisputable connections between the Argentinian character Horacio Verbitsky, who fomented the first, most persistent, and most egregious character assassinations against Bergoglio, and a network of US and British entities carrying out initiatives abroad without much accountability for their activities.

Soon after Bergoglio became archbishop of Buenos Aires in 1998, a sinister coalition emerged against the future pope. Horacio Verbitsky published the shocking accusation that the prelate was complicit in the kidnapping and torture of two Jesuit priests in 1976 while Bergoglio was provincial (director) of the Society of Jesus and Argentina lived under a military dictatorship, an oppressive period known as the Dirty War (1976–1983). Bergoglio defended himself as innocent, as did others, but Verbitsky hardly seemed interested. He forged ahead with a book, expanding the slanderous story into an indictment of the Catholic Church. *The Silence: From Paul VI to Bergoglio, the Secret Relations of the Church with ESMA*[33] (ESMA is a military detention center where five thousand people were tortured under the regime) was published in March 2005, as John Paul II was dying. Then, just three days before the conclave that almost elected the Argentinian, an activist from Verbitsky's circle, Myriam Bergman, member of the Socialist Workers' Party, filed a lawsuit against Bergoglio alleging his involvement in the 1976 abduction of two Jesuits based on material provided by Verbitsky's book.[34] Quickly, the big lie was whispered during the 2005 conclave. Had Bergoglio been elected, the most prominent news about him would have been this bogus claim.

In his most recent incarnation, Verbitsky has been president of the *Centro de Estudios Legales y Sociales* (Center for Legal and Social Studies, CELS) since 2000. CELS received $4.5 million from the Ford Foundation between 2000 and 2012. Between 2003 and 2005, it received grants from the taxpayer-funded National Endowment for Democracy (NED),[35] criticized for various unorthodox operations in the name of democracy since it was founded in 1983.[36] George Soros's Open Society Foundation and the British Council are also on the CELS list of donors.

When Bergoglio was elected in 2013, within one hour, news circled around Verbitsky's big lie. The BBC, CNN, *Time* magazine, the *Guardian*, and the *Washington Post* all had a version of the *New York Times*' headline, "Starting a Papacy amid Echoes of a Dirty War." My editors at the *National Catholic Register* asked me to tackle the rumor; I wrote about Verbitsky's campaign in "Anatomy of a Lie: The Assault on Pope Francis' Reputation."[37] What I discovered about the ties between the unethical Argentinian "journalist" and US entities reminded me of an important observation made by General William Odom, director of the National Security Agency under Ronald Reagan. He told me that a major mistake made by the intelligence community was the accelerated use of civil society fronts and so-called democracy advocates and movements to execute political goals: "It undermines democracy and advances conspiracy!"[38] Odom was an unusually independent mind. He was one of the few military leaders to openly call the Iraq invasion "the greatest strategic disaster in United States history."[39]

More recently, based on handwritten documents found among the papers of an Argentinian military junta leader, it emerged in 2015 that Verbitsky was a double agent, working for a Leftist terrorist group, the Monteneros, and the despised military junta, responsible for the Dirty War, at the same time. The account is laid out by investigative journalist Gabriel Levinas in *Doble Agente: La Biografía Inesperada de Horacio Verbitsky* (Double Agent: The Unexpected Biography of Horacio Verbitsky).[40]

According to evidence provided by Levinas, Verbitsky helped to execute a campaign in major news magazines agitating for a military coup, which brought to power General Juan Onganía's four-year dictatorship in 1966. Levinas told me that *Confirmado* magazine, where Verbitsky was a young editorial assistant, was created specifically to incite a coup d'état.[41] I asked Levinas, "Did Verbitsky receive money from General Onganía before and after the coup?" His answer: "Si, positivamente recibio dinero de Onganía, antes y despues del golpe de estado!" My translation: "Yes, absolutely, he received money from Onganía before and after the coup d'état!"[42]

In light of this revelation, Verbitsky's admission that he belonged to the Monteneros in the 1970s is astonishing. Their radical activities led to another military coup in 1976 and the Dirty War repression. While Verbitsky was a ghost writer for the junta (receiving $5,000 per month between 1978 and 1982), other terrorists were kidnapped, tortured, or disappeared. In the 1990s, Verbitsky, still under indictment for terrorism, became an American asset, according to Levinas. The US ambassador fed Verbitsky compromising information, which led to the resignation of several ministers. Next, Verbitsky emerged as a national human rights and anticorruption star with an evident anti-Bergoglio mission. He was also a recipient of US funds through CELS. Did the NED know about Verbitsky's past as a double agent? In sum, Pope Francis's relentless accuser appears to have been a paid destabilizer for decades with multiple ties to the United States.

US intelligence has certainly been involved in outlandish campaigns to boost US prestige and undercut opponents. Think of the CIA's postwar strategy to portray American abstract expressionist painters as the heroic future of modern art. This "cultural cold war" used a "long leash" technique: various nongovernmental fronts (foundations, galleries, magazines, and private citizens) were engaged to promote artists, curators, and museum exhibits that were designed to show New York as the world's cultural center and its painters as paradigms of freedom and creativity. One purpose was to portray Soviet realism as stodgy; another was to promote a counterpoint to Communism's appeal to intellectuals and turn New York into the world's cultural epicenter.[43]

The Museum of Modern Art, with support from the Rockefeller Brothers Fund, launched a massive international program to project abstract expressionism—and painters such as Willem de Kooning, Robert Motherwell, Mark Rothko, Jackson Pollock, and others, most of them members of the American Committee for Cultural Freedom—as evidence that nonconformity could only be secured by democracy.[44] Former Marxists from the arts, literature, and journalism were favored. They were called the "non-Communist Left." Because the American people and Congress would have opposed financing them, it had to be done secretly. The CIA's involvement and funding source went undetected for decades.[45] In his diary, President Harry Truman recounts his many early-morning visits to the National Gallery of Art just blocks from the White House. In an entry from 1948, after peering at Rembrandts and Holbeins, he notes: "It's a pleasure to look at perfection and then think of the lazy, nutty moderns. It is like comparing Christ with Lenin." Even Truman seemed not to be aware of the CIA's art project![46] In Part II's introduction, we will see that Truman was not aware that Nagasaki, Japan, would be bombed either.

Nor was the hand of the CIA seen in the publication and distribution of a Russian-language edition of *Doctor Zhivago*. Using a Dutch publishing house and the Vatican's pavilion at the 1958 Brussels world's fair, US intelligence challenged the Soviet worldview via a humanistic novel. The scheme even involved a step-by-step strategy for getting the author a Nobel Prize for Literature.[47] Later, the book was turned into a five-Oscar award-winning film starring Omar Sharif and Julie Christie.

After the fall of the Soviet Bloc, a bellicose approach quickly became associated with the United States, beginning with the US invasion of Panama, as we will see in chapter 1. The United States has seemed bent on generating worldwide chaos: from destroying Iraq and Libya, to supporting a humanitarian disaster in Yemen, to strong-arming traditional nations over "gender theory." Henry Kissinger's magnum opus *Diplomacy* talks about how different societies produce unique ways of conducting foreign policy. In his view, the American approach was based on idealism.[48] No more.

As former president Jimmy Carter told the *New York Times*, "The US has been the dominant character in the whole world and now we are not anymore. And we're not going to be. Russia's coming back and India and China are coming forward."[49] It's not just that these nations matured; it's also that the United States stopped exercising its significant reservoir of soft power, including moral influence as a country striving to calm nerves, encourage liberal order, and facilitate peace. The question is whether Joe Biden, marinated for decades in the assumptions of US exceptionalism and military problem solving, can drastically shift gears to engage diplomatically with nations the US disagrees with along the lines that Pope Francis, his spiritual leader, models. Can Biden press on his foreign policy apparatus the need to settle disputes justly, without revenge, without seeking to "win" or to make another nation suffer for disagreeing?

Between America's loss of prestige and the multiplication of conflicts around the world, there are fewer disinterested actors aiming to defuse conflict and more space for alternative solutions. This is the arena into which Pope Francis is deliberately steering the Holy See, as we will see in these pages. US foreign policy titans such as former Secretary of State George Schultz recognized the gap the Vatican seeks to fill: In a 75th commemoration of the nuclear attacks on Hiroshima and Nagasaki, he singled out dialogue between the Holy See and the Russian Orthodox Church as a hopeful sign.[50] The Vatican is certainly not the only entity that sees the necessity of reframing inter-state relations in terms of transformational dialogue,[51] but it has a peerless status in international law, which allows the pope and his diplomatic corps to positively influence the world order from within the inter-state system.

As the world's only transnational absolute monarch, the leader of the Catholic Church has extensive discretion to choose his priorities. Naturally, every pontificate is shaped by a pope's personal story and passion. Karol Wojtyła, whose entire priesthood was exercised under an atheistic regime in Poland, was a dogged anti-Communist as Pope John Paul II. The brilliant German theologian Joseph Ratzinger, who considered radical secularism to be a spiritual ailment crippling Western Europe, sought close relations with the Russian Orthodox Church as Pope Benedict XVI, aiming to ally with that faith's post-Communist renaissance in order to counter Western European decadence and the expansion of religious extremism.

Little in Jorge Bergoglio's personal history before 2013 marked him as a man set to make geopolitics his signature arena as bishop of Rome. Yet from his first half year in office, Pope Francis exercised skill and persistence as a diplomat. Eight years after his inauguration on March 15, 2013, it is now possible to dissect what animates his diplomatic approach and assess the functionality of Vatican diplomacy under his direction. The hallmarks of Francis's approach are three: commitment to the centrality of personal encounters in problem solving, respect for local perception, and patience.

Before becoming Pope Francis, Jorge Bergoglio honed these characteristics primarily in three ways: through his Jesuit education, one of the most rigorous courses of personal spiritual development in Catholicism; through his role as a priest, who take seriously the need to offer pastoral care to the faithful, which includes helping people through their most trying personal decisions; and through his regional leadership of the Latin American Episcopal Conference (CELAM).

Pope Francis owes much to the tradition preceding him. His muscular version of nonviolence is grounded in Catholic doctrine going back thousands of years. His confidence that Christ-inspired statesmanship is relevant everywhere and his willingness to act on behalf of the common good rather than particular interests are codified in documents of the Second Vatican Council, yet they can be found in the work of all the landless popes—pegging contemporary papal history to the 1870 loss of the Papal States, including Rome.

Jorge Bergoglio's emergence from the Southern Hemisphere and his charismatic personal authenticity make him the first pope truly independent of the twentieth century's ideological battles. *God's Diplomats: Pope Francis, Vatican Diplomacy, and America's Armageddon* takes stock of the Argentinian's international practice: his priorities, his achievements, and the techniques he uses on the world stage.

Francis is standing on the shoulders of giants. Despite some misguided attempts to paint the pope as a rogue operator, his diplomacy is squarely built on the priorities and pragmatism of Pope John Paul II and Pope Benedict XVI. And Francis's pastoral approach reaches back to Pope John XXIII. Unlike political office holders, potentially bringing different platforms to the task, each pope inherits the same mantle of teaching and tradition. In turn, each opts to highlight various facets of the multicolored coat. In terms of doctrine, continuity underlies stylistic difference in successive papacies.

Finally, the well-informed, discrete nature of the Catholic Church's global diplomatic network gives each pope a flexible and responsive institutional capacity that goes far in explaining how the ancient bones of the Catholic Church remain so agile.

Some of the Holy See's most startling accomplishments come in the field of international diplomacy, shrouded in secrecy—executed by actors who have vowed silence. I will employ historical accounts of specific events to demonstrate the high degree of functionality operative in the Catholic Church's global diplomatic network and to introduce its key players: the pope; his ambassadors, called nuncios (from the Latin word *nuntius*, messenger); religious orders of sisters and brothers; lay faithful organized in special movements; and bishops and cardinals at work in every national context, sometimes deployed by the pontiff for special international assignments.

It is in this behind-the-scenes arena that Pope Francis has been especially adept, although the discreet nature of the work means too few appreciate the success of Francis's diplomacy of encounter.

Introduction 13

A note about names: *Holy See* refers to the government of the Catholic Church, while *Vatican City* is the territory occupied by the Holy See. Born of a treaty signed in 1929 with the Italian government, Vatican City gives the Holy See essential independence, but it is the Holy See that is the unique sovereign entity seated at the United Nations as I will elucidate in chapter 4. Diplomats from around the world are accredited to the Holy See, not to the Vatican City microstate. So, while I use the terms *Holy See* and *Vatican* synonymously, the former is the power, and the latter is the place.

Pope Benedict XVI stepped down from the throne of St. Peter on February 13, 2013—the first in 598 years to do so—admitting that his "strengths . . . are no longer suited to an adequate exercise of the Petrine ministry."[52] Catholics were dumbstruck. Although most analysts focused on his age as the main explanation, it emerged that he made the final decision following a grueling trip to Mexico and Cuba, while contemplating the need to travel to Brazil for World Youth Day—an inadvisable trip according to the papal doctor.[53]

Thus, Benedict's prophetic decision was directly tied to the pope's international role—although there was certainly more to it than that. (According to Gianluigi Nuzzi's *Merchants in the Temple*, intractable financial corruption convinced Benedict to facilitate a clean sweep by stepping aside.) These times require a leader who can function in a multipolar world, where regional leaders are as influential as once-invincible world powers. These times require a vicar of Christ willing to dine with sinners and work miracles on the Sabbath—a shepherd with the "smell of the sheep," as Pope Francis perceives and lives.[54]

What the US government wants from the supreme pontiff is something else—a yes-man. Francis is constitutionally unable to comply because he's a fearless truth teller and the first pope to grow up in the Global South. From his perspective as a citizen of Latin America, Bergoglio is wary of both the overall American narrative of the necessity of force and of the United States' unscrupulous tendency to support any strongman willing to do its bidding.

For this, American hubris will crucify him—but for naught, because the Holy See's diplomatic network and theory of the diplomatic arts will survive long past any one successor of St. Peter. In this book, I explore the flexibility and authority of this network as well as the specific greatness of Pope Francis's diplomatic achievements in order to portray what the American Goliath fears.

1

An Adaptable Network, Willing to Bleed

> One has to come to Rome to realize that the Vatican goes everywhere and knows everything.
>
> —Anne O'Hare McCormick, *New York Times*, July 24, 1921[1]

On Christmas Eve in 1989, Archbishop José Sebastián Laboa, apostolic nuncio to Panama, got a phone call. As nuncio, he was the pope's personal representative to the Panamanian government. When he picked up, he immediately recognized the voice of *La Piña*, Pineapple Face, General Manuel Noriega. For years, the dictator had harassed Laboa by phone when political opponents trying to evade Noriega's heavy-handed regime took refuge in the nunciature, the Vatican's embassy.

This time, the tables were turned. Noriega gave the archbishop ten minutes to decide if he would let the strongman himself take residence on Vatican property. A massive military force of over twenty-seven thousand soldiers under orders from President George H. W. Bush had bombed twenty-seven targets, toppled Noriega's government, and then turned Panama City inside out to find him. Noriega was a former CIA operative, now accused of cocaine trafficking, laundering drug money, and upending democracy.[2] Although Noriega narrowly escaped capture, he had a $1 million bounty on his head.

Pineapple Face warned the nuncio that if barred from entry, he and his men would flee to the jungle and launch a violent insurgency.

Afraid of the real possibility of bloodshed, Laboa reluctantly opened the iron gate to let Noriega's car inside. A bodyguard and three aides arrived too. US troops soon surrounded the nunciature, and helicopters hovered overhead; but diplomatic immunity protected everyone inside, including the fugitives. Laboa tried to get Noriega to tape a message telling his allies to surrender, but he wouldn't do it. Instead, the fugitive fell asleep for eighteen hours.[3]

That night in Rome, St. Peter's Basilica was full of believers celebrating Christmas Eve Mass. Pope John Paul II was on the high altar, directly under a dome designed by Michelangelo. American chargé d'affaires Jim Creagan was there, too, until an aide crept up to his pew to say he was needed at the embassy for an urgent call on a secure line. As the top US diplomat to the Holy See, the Catholic Church's global governing structure, he was first in line to get instructions from the State Department: don't let Rome give Noriega asylum! Creagan returned to St. Peter's and tiptoed up to the Holy See's undersecretary for relations with states—the equivalent of a deputy foreign minister—to give him Washington's curt message regarding events in Panama.

Msgr. Jean-Louis Tauran was unfazed. He noted that the key decision makers, the pope and the cardinal secretary of state praying nearby, were occupied. He warned Creagan, "Tell [President George] Bush and [Secretary of State James] Baker they have about three hours to think, and don't go in to get Noriega."[4] Like the nuncio in Panama, Tauran was neither intimidated about going toe-to-toe with the US government nor uncertain about the Holy See's position: protect Noriega while figuring out the best path to resolution.[5]

FINDING COMMON GROUND

The Holy See was not impressed by the American show of force and considered the invasion of Panama a violation of international law. Territorial sovereignty is a core concept for the interstate system. The Church would not turn Noriega over to what its top diplomats termed "the occupying power" without Noriega's own agreement. The nuncio said he assured Noriega he could stay: "I told him up to the last minute: 'You can stay here. We will never throw you out.'"

But with guidance from Rome,[6] Laboa also took many small steps to make the stay less than comfortable: the air-conditioning was turned off; the TV in Noriega's bedroom was left broken; and resident nuns removed wine and served regular fare, not the vegetarian specialties Noriega preferred. The nuncio later explained that he sought to "create a psychological environment" leading Noriega to the conclusion that the best option was to turn himself over to the United States. Guidance for Laboa's actions came straight from Rome—from the Secretariat of State, the Holy See's command center for foreign relations.

At first, the US secretary of state tried to pressure the Vatican to hand over Noriega, asserting that as a criminal, he had no right to sanctuary. But the Holy See's position that the United States violated international law by invading Panama argued that Noriega could not be turned over to the United States involuntarily.

On Christmas morning, the Vatican's secretary for relations with states (equivalent to foreign minister) Archbishop Angelo Sodano met with American diplomats in his apartment behind St. Peter's Basilica. He told Creagan that the case should not become contentious. Having Noriega in the nunciature was in fact a "peace dividend" because it meant the deposed leader could not stir up trouble. The American diplomat noted that President Bush was pleased Noriega was in the hands of the Church's "diplomatic authorities." Sodano mentioned the possibility of a third country taking Noriega, meaning the nunciature could serve as a temporary "parking lot." Creagan remembers explaining that that plan was unacceptable to Washington. So Laboa's strategy of harboring the human hot potato was the only game.[7]

From day one, US diplomats met with their Holy See colleagues to negotiate a peaceful way out. They met every day, ten hours a day.

When Archbishop Laboa complained to superiors that the US military psyops strategy of blasting rock music at the compound 24/7 while shining klieg lights into his windows was preventing his sleep—while not being particularly annoying to Noriega—negotiators in Rome made it stop.[8] Among higher-order agreements reached that week, the United States conceded that if Noriega stood trial in the United States, capital punishment was off the table, because the Catholic Church opposes it.

Within the Church itself, there were cross pressures: Rome was well aware that the Panamanian bishops had often clashed with the dictator. They were not keen to see him protected for long: the bishops feared that the Church's local reputation would suffer if the public perceived that the Holy See was harboring a notorious criminal who had brutalized believers.

In the end, the general gave in. It happened on a day when thousands of anti-Noriega Panamanians demonstrated outside the gates—a scenario, the nuncio explained to Noriega, that could lead to a mob swarming the compound, giving the Americans an excuse to strike. At morning Mass, with the general sitting in the last pew (nominally Catholic by baptism, he reportedly consulted a Brazilian witch doctor for spiritual advice), Laboa gave a homily on how loyalties shift but God is constant.[9]

Noriega took Communion. A few hours later, the dictator put on his uniform and told the nuncio he was ready to go. He asked to keep his Bible.[10] He walked with three priests across the nunciature's front yard to the front gate, where he surrendered and ended the immediate crisis.

Operation "Nifty Package," the sophomoric US label for its plot to snag Noriega—a character who, in the 1970s and 1980s, served as a key CIA asset[11]—was part of what was then the biggest US military invasion since the Vietnam War. Some 27,500 soldiers swarmed Panama in a forty-two-day campaign, ostensibly to protect Americans living in the small nation, but more likely to eliminate Noriega, an obstreperous regional menace who knew too much. As a result of the ensuing violence, the US military killed six hundred Panamanians, and twenty-three Americans died, while causing $2 billion in economic damage.

The international community castigated the United States for its "flagrant" disregard of international law. Both the UN General Assembly and the Organization of American States condemned the invasion. The US response? Laughably, it claimed self-defense.

Meanwhile, halfway across the globe, as the US military was flexing in Panama, people were dying in the streets of Bucharest as Communism collapsed and the Cold War came to a crashing close in the last weeks of 1989. Like Manuel Noriega, Romania's dictator, Nicolae Ceaușescu (once used by the US government and pumped up as an anti-Soviet maverick), had outlived his usefulness. Ceaușescu and his wife were executed on Christmas Day by a kangaroo court. By January 1990, Central and Eastern European countries were no longer Communist. The Soviet Union was one year away from its dissolution—a failed and tragic ideological experiment.

Vatican analysts perceived the two phenomena as related: by deploying an exaggerated show of military force to bring a small country to heel, Washington gave an early preview of what its exercise of power in a unipolar world would look like. The Panama invasion marked the beginning of a new era: military dominance by the American hegemon.

MASTERFUL PATIENCE AND VATICAN NEUTRALITY YIELDED BLOODLESS RESOLUTION

By all accounts, Archbishop Laboa, the face of Rome, was masterful in managing the 1989 Panama crisis. Although he was not trained at the Vatican's boot camp for diplomats, the Pontifical Ecclesiastical Academy (*Pontificia Accademia Ecclesiastica* in Italian), universally known as the *Accademia*, his example is a textbook case—literally—for how Vatican diplomacy works.

Teachers at the *Accademia* extract several lessons from the Panama case, say former students. First, the Holy See takes no sides in political (or military) disputes and works to preserve its neutrality. The nuncio remained equidistant vis-à-vis his local interlocutors: Manuel Noriega and his small band, the new Panamanian authorities, and the US government.

Second, the nuncio's main weapon was verbal persuasion. He had long discussions with Noriega about his options. He war-gamed potential scenarios with him and helped him see the best way to move forward. He also actively ministered to the man, preaching homilies as well as reminding Noriega about Christian virtues. Basically, Laboa pastored the fugitive.

Another exemplary aspect of the case is Laboa's decisiveness. Under pressure, with little time to consult superiors, the nuncio made a moral decision to protect the individual, a man whom he had reason to detest. This is a key thing to understand about the Catholic Church's way of interacting with foreign leaders. They are seen as human beings: both sinful, as we all are, and capable of redemption, as we all are.[12]

Strategically, the situation involved multiple levels of Church engagement: the nuncio handled the situation on the ground, while numerous Vatican offices were engaged in simultaneous, related activity in Rome, Washington, and various Latin American capitals where negotiations unfolded regarding the future of Noriega's wife and three daughters. (They initially took refuge in the Cuban embassy but were relocated to the Dominican Republic, with US agreement, when Noriega turned himself in.)

Throughout the week, the Vatican secretary of state, Cardinal Agostino Casaroli, followed each step of the Panama saga, advising Laboa through encrypted cables. As the ultimate decider, Pope John Paul II approved the gist of the guidance but was not engaged in daily decision making. Ten years before, Casaroli had taken charge of the Secretariat of State at John Paul II's request, so by the time General Noriega came on stage, the two men had faced innumerable international puzzles together.

DIPLOMATS TAKE VOW OF SILENCE

An unusual aspect of the Panama mediation was Archbishop Laboa's willingness to talk about it. Usually it is very difficult to get a papal diplomat to discuss his work on the record. Some open up over time or will offer familiar faces insight on deep background, but generally this is a remarkably tight-lipped crew. They prefer action to be the mark of accomplishment—an attitude with biblical support. These men await "the just judgment of God, who will repay everyone according to his works."[13]

Each diplomat takes an oath to maintain the secrets of the Holy See,[14] and most take that rule quite literally. These are hard nuts to crack. American Cardinal James Harvey served as prefect of the papal household (1998–2012) under Pope John Paul II and Pope Emeritus Benedict XVI. The job required managing the pope's public and private schedule and receiving heads of state when they arrived for meetings. Few are as personally up close to the intimate reality of a pope as the prefect of the papal household. So, perhaps unsurprisingly, Harvey is notoriously tight lipped. He told me he burned all his papers related to the years he served John Paul II and Benedict XVI. Why? "No need," he cryptically replied.[15] I silently wondered, why take two decades' worth of notes only to torch them?

Insight into how some governments mistakenly perceive the workings of the Vatican comes from former Israeli prime minister Golda Meir. In a 1972 cabinet meeting, Meir said she was happy to receive a long-awaited response from Pope Paul VI confirming a private meeting at the Vatican. To convince cabinet members who doubted that anything valuable could come out of it, she outlined what mesmerized her about the unique attributes of the Holy See. According to Gordon Thomas (a British author with privileged Israeli intelligence sources), she noted the "Marxist structuralism of the papacy. First it has financial power which is almost unprecedented. Then it operates without political parties or trade unions. The whole apparatus is organized for control. The Roman curia controls the bishops, the bishops control the clergy, and the clergy control the laity. With its multitude of secretariats, commissions and structures, *it is a system tailor-made for spying and information*."[16]

To assess characteristics of Holy See diplomats, colleagues who have served with them, open-source material, and personal interviews reveal five attributes in particular: collegiality, efficiency, discretion, deep knowledge, and dedication.

COLLEGIALITY

Evidence of Vatican collegiality is recognized in the 1961 Vienna Convention on Diplomatic Relations. Article 16 confirms a practice of some countries, especially majority-Catholic ones, to designate the nuncio as the "dean" of diplomats serving in a host country, regardless of when he arrives.[17] In that role, the dean might host or open gatherings attended by all diplomats in-post. This special status was first codified in the 1815 Vienna Convention and is based on the Holy See's historical identity as a progenitor of diplomatic practice and the even older concept of the pontiff's superiority to all civil authorities.[18]

Collegiality includes a commitment to work with other diplomats, especially to share information and perspectives. US State Department cables released via WikiLeaks demonstrate extensive, frequent collaboration between the two governments on a wide range of topics. Vatican diplomats seem to go out of their way to share their point of view, rather than specific intelligence. Their tone remains respectful, even when major differences are discussed.

For example, while serving under Pope Benedict XVI as deputy foreign minister, Msgr. Pietro Parolin was the main point of contact for US diplomats in Rome. Two classified US diplomatic cables, leaked by WikiLeaks, provide an excellent window on Parolin's collegial modus operandi. Both documents summarize meetings between Parolin and American officials. In February 2006, the Vatican diplomat discussed nuclear arms in Iran, then a month later he shared the Church's perspective on US nuclear arms policy vis-à-vis India and Iran. The context was this: the board of the International Atomic Energy Agency (IAEA) had referred Iran to the UN Security Council for violating rules governing nuclear nonproliferation[19] amid escalating rumors that the United States was considering military intervention in Iran.

In the first meeting, Parolin noted that Iran had the right to develop nuclear energy for peaceful use but assured the United States that the Holy See was pressing Iran to cooperate with the IAEA. Parolin calmly reminded the United States that Iran is a "very proud nation" and "hinted that perhaps they need more opportunities for a face-saving solution." Parolin challenged American democracy promotion programs as problematic because democracy "must come in response to popular will, rather than being imposed from outside—otherwise it won't work." Yet the cable described Parolin as only "mildly critical." It suggested that Parolin offered to facilitate better communication with Iran's leadership because the Vatican maintained relations with Tehran for over fifty years. As Parolin explained, "We never break relations with anyone."[20] He was presented as honest and helpful, even as he delivered, in fact, a strong critique of how the United States does business.

A month later, Parolin met with US ambassador Francis Rooney to criticize the US-India nuclear cooperation agreement as an "unhelpful signal" because it created a double standard compared with the American attitude toward Iran. A cable reporting back to the State Department summarized Parolin's main points: "The entire international community should work together; there should be no attempt to humiliate Iran."[21]

Parolin mused that conflict, such as air strikes, would be truly terrible in Iran. Don't isolate Iran, he urged; open a dialogue. The ambassador agreed. It is a fascinating document because it shows the Holy See frankly calling out policies it perceives as hypocritical yet delivering that message constructively. Today, Parolin is the cardinal secretary of state, Pope Francis's right hand on all diplomatic endeavors. At the heart of Francis's approach to the world is personal encounter and dialogue: exactly what Parolin was urging on the United States as described in the 2006 cables. Dialogue is the Holy See's favored tactic, not a proposition Francis invented.

It's almost too obvious to mention yet remarkably significant: the Holy See has neither economic nor military interests. It's easier to be helpful to foreign colleagues when no material competition exists. A Norwegian state secretary wrote, "There is no leverage that any other actor has over the Holy See. This in itself is a major power resource."[22]

EFFICIENCY

Efficiency is a crucial requirement for an institution with limited human resources. As former British ambassador to the Holy See Nigel Baker pointed out, "There are in fact only 50 or so people working on what we would recognize as 'foreign policy' within the Secretariat of State in Rome, on top of the 300 or so staff in nunciatures around the world, compared with the 4,000 British and 10,000 local staff employed by the British Foreign Office."[23] The obvious downside of this arrangement is that when key positions are vacant, mistakes can be made. Pope Benedict XVI inflamed the Muslim world in 2006 with a speech perceived as insulting the Prophet Muhammad. Some insiders blame the fact that the Vatican's top specialist on Islam, Archbishop Michael Fitzgerald, secretary (1987–2002) then president (2002–2006) of the Pontifical Council on Interreligious Dialogue, had been sent to Cairo, Egypt, as nuncio six months before.[24] The controversy also occurred during the transition between two secretaries of state—an additional moment of administrative weakness.

As an American diplomat who has served with Vatican diplomats in five countries told me, "A nuncio is efficient because he has to be. He has no time to waste except on the most valuable contacts in a country and the most significant sources of information because each nunciature runs with so few people."

When one considers the geographic assignments handled by some of God's diplomats, you have to imagine they are efficient managers of work and time—or they would go mad. Tanzanian-born Archbishop Novatus Rugambwa serves as apostolic nuncio to New Zealand as well as to ten islands in Oceania, including Fiji, Samoa, and the Federated States of Micronesia[25]—all full members of the United Nations. Covering so many places, he must travel often and manage many communities of faith. When a cloistered convent of Carmelite nuns in Guam realized a local bishop had misused a $2 million donation, the women religious sent detailed evidence to Rugambwa's predecessor for him to investigate.[26] A nuncio is the Holy See's eyes and ears on a nation, helping the pope to screen and select new ones, while serving as the Vatican's face to a country's government and its political institutions.

Rugambwa was posted to the Pacific in 2019 following a three-year assignment in Honduras. Meanwhile, Archbishop Martin Krebs, who served in Oceania for five years, moved on to Uruguay. A lifetime in the Vatican diplomatic service can entail years spent on several continents; regional specialty is not the norm.

Spanish Archbishop Pedro López Quintana is now nuncio to Austria following five years as nuncio to Estonia, Latvia, and Lithuania, with residence in Vilnius, the capital of Lithuania, where some 75 percent of the people are Catholic.[27] He handled quite a different demographic picture in Estonia, where only 1 percent follows Rome. Yet all three Baltic nations fondly recall Vatican support in 1918 for their independence from the Russian Empire, an interlude crushed in 1940 when the Soviet Union reoccupied the small nations. A nuncio engages with bishops' conferences and governments to plan various landmark events. In the Baltics, 2018, the year of centenary celebrations, included a visit from Pope Francis. For any nuncio, a landing by the Holy Father assures several months of near sleeplessness, as so much coordination falls on his office.

After managing Francis's Baltic pilgrimage, López Quintana earned a historical post in Vienna, which has seen a resident papal envoy since 1630. Because numerous specialized United Nations entities are based there, Rome also accredits a diplomat to serve as permanent observer to the UN office in Vienna.[28] Polish native Msgr. Janusz Urbańczyk has held that position since 2015.[29] Urbańczyk is also permanent representative to the Vienna-based Organization for Security and Co-operation in Europe (OSCE). Quintana and Urbańczyk live in a palatial three-story nunciature completed just months before World War I erupted.

Church diplomats often wear multiple miters: Archbishop Eugene Nugent serves as apostolic nuncio to Kuwait, Bahrain, the United Arab Emirates, Yemen, and Qatar, while carrying the title of apostolic delegate to the Arabian Peninsula[30] because the Holy See has no diplomatic relations with Saudi Arabia. The nuncio is based in Kuwait, which established bilateral relations with the Holy See in 1968, the second Gulf state to do so, following Iraq in 1966. The number of Catholic guest workers in the region is increasing, so the nuncio moves between the fabulously wealthy royal elite and the poor, vulnerable migrant workers, many Catholic, who are often denied time to worship because they work on Sundays. Securing religious freedom is a key task in any nuncio's portfolio.

American Archbishop Peter Wells serves as apostolic nuncio to South Africa, Botswana, Lesotho, Namibia, and Swaziland. After fourteen years in

Rome working in the Secretariat of State, he was thrilled to get back to "direct ministry," where his priority activities are helping to alleviate poverty, build bridges, and promote peace[31]—a naturally "Francis" list, given that he was appointed nuncio by the pope in 2016.

In interviews, which most nuncios are loath to give, Wells puts an accent on his mission to represent everyone. He explains, "I am here for the people of this country, for all of them, Catholics and non-Catholics, to hear their sufferings and joys, and to take them back to the Holy Father as his interlocutor."[32] From one pope to another, doctrine does not change, but the diplomatic corps follows the direction of the pope in terms of priorities and message—and not surprisingly his appointees tend to sound like him.

What these priestly diplomats from around the world— born in Tanzania, Germany, Spain, Poland, Ireland, and the United States—have in common, besides a calling to serve God through the Catholic Church, is one school: all are alumni of the *Accademia*, a shared education we will explore in chapter 3.

DISCRETION

It is astonishing that the Vatican's foreign service is as small as it is. Yet it's one way the Holy See protects its reputation for maximum discretion. As a former Western ambassador said, "the nuncios I worked with were professional secret keepers. Nothing I discussed was ever repeated. They build great trust among diplomats around the world that way. I think it is a skill they have as a result of hearing confession," since the Catholic sacrament of penance is protected under a seal of confidentiality.

Some diplomats have assignments that mean they cover multiple sides of a geographic conflict or rivalry. Italian Archbishop Leopoldo Girelli is the apostolic nuncio to Israel, a post created when Israel and the Vatican recognized each other in 1994. It took several decades for the two to hammer out an agreement over the status of Catholic Church properties on Israeli territory and taxation. To this day, neither side is entirely content.

Girelli also serves as the apostolic delegate to Jerusalem and Palestine,[33] underscoring the Holy See's position that Jerusalem should be considered an international city with special status because it has sites sacred to three world religions: Christianity, Islam, and Judaism. The nuncio has stepped in on occasion to mediate between the Palestinian community (including Muslims and Christians) and Israeli authorities. As if this diplomat isn't busy enough, he serves as nuncio to Cyprus, thus monitoring another major conflict zone. Turkey invaded Northern Cyprus in 1974 and has occupied it ever since; the island is divided ethnically, with occasional flare-ups, most recently over offshore natural gas assets.[34]

If Girelli was not a man known for his discretion and ability to listen hard, weighing all the versions of complex, historical situations, in no way could he carry out his job.

KNOWLEDGE

The "knowledge" component of the Holy See's diplomatic profile is the lynchpin of its institutional identity: because these diplomats are knowledgeable, they are relevant and sought after by colleagues. Because the Holy See strives to remain neutral vis-à-vis politics, its information is framed not to benefit particular interests but, ideally, to reflect the truths of a place.

Since the end of World War II, the majority of nuncios and apostolic delegates—the most common title given to diplomats working in countries where the Holy See has no formal diplomatic relations—are graduates of the *Accademia*, where a rigorous program of history, geography, international law, and language study shapes a highly educated cadre.[35] The knowledge they possess—and share with the home office in Rome—is also a function of one of the most important characteristics of Vatican diplomacy: a wide and deep network, which also proves to be efficient.

"Nobody can beat us in info gathering and grassroots operations," declared Archbishop Bernardito Auza, apostolic nuncio to Spain. The Filipino diplomat offered a good example of the functionality of this network. Following graduation from the *Accademia*, his first assignment was to Madagascar. While at a party, he ran into a colleague from a powerful embassy with a large staff. She told Auza that her ambassador would soon be inaugurating a new dam and irrigation system in Madagascar, financed by her government.[36]

Auza asked his colleague if she knew who owned the land on which the dam was being built. She did not. So the priest told her that the speaker of the parliament owned the land, a fact that revealed a potential corruption scheme and one the embassy and its staff of hundreds had missed. Although he didn't tell his "shocked" colleague where he got his information, years later, Auza revealed that his source was a community of "nosy nuns" living near the project. Auza said he thanked his religious "intelligence operatives" when he next saw them.[37]

As a French diplomat told me, "They're respected because they're often right. Vatican diplomats are powerful analysts. Here's just one example: all the misery that flowed from the US invasion of Iraq was anticipated by the Holy See. Not even one intelligence service saw that so clearly."

DEDICATION

By the nature of their calling—remember, the Holy See's career diplomats, with rare exception, are priests—nuncios and apostolic representatives are exceptionally dedicated people. Their secular colleagues often note that, without immediate family responsibilities, they tend to be wholly focused on their work. All foreign service officers assume personal risk by living in places or being close to political situations that might not be stable. Many examples demonstrate that God's diplomats try to stay put long after most secular governments have pulled diplomatic assets out.

The credo of Holy See personnel is that living within the truth of a situation, or striving to maintain a moral posture there, might require physical sacrifice. In modern Vatican history, Msgr. Achille Ratti is well remembered for exemplifying the humble heroism expected of its diplomats. Pope Benedict XV named Ratti apostolic visitor to Poland in April 1918, before the country was independent. A year later, Benedict named him the first nuncio to the Republic of Poland.

When war broke out between Poland and the Soviet Union a year later, Ratti refused to leave. He was the only foreign diplomat to remain in Warsaw as the Bolshevists marched on the city. Incredibly, on the verge of defeat in 1920, Polish forces ousted the Soviets in the Battle of Warsaw, known to Catholics as the Miracle on the Vistula. The victory prevented the advance of Communism further west and protected Poland's autonomy—for twenty-five more years.

Besides recognizing an excellent general, Poles credit the intercession of the Virgin Mary with the victory because it occurred during the August 15 Feast of the Assumption. Ratti had called for universal prayers for Poland, and all the churches were filled as the battle shaped up just outside the city limits.[38] Ratti's faith and leadership were heralded, although Polish clergy cooled on him after his insistence that clerics avoid political activity. He left Poland in 1921 with a sterling reputation. A year later, he was elected pope, taking the name Pius XI.[39]

With the assumption of risk, of course, comes the possibility of the ultimate sacrifice. The most recent nuncio to be murdered was Irish-born Archbishop Michael Courtney, who served in Burundi. His car, flying the yellow-and-white Vatican flag, was ambushed on December 29, 2003, while driving through territory controlled by rebels who had not yet signed a peace agreement[40] with the new government—an accord Courtney was involved in negotiating. In fact, Courtney had stayed in Burundi rather than leave for the holidays because he thought a breakthrough was possible in the process of settling the civil war. He was one of the few diplomats who had talked to the Hutu faction[41] suspected of killing him.

Rather than treating Burundi—one of the world's poorest counties, suffering chronic ethnic conflict—as a backwater post, the Holy See had sent one of its best: Courtney spoke more than ten languages and had served all over the world, including five years as special envoy to the Council of Europe in Strasbourg.[42] And upon his assassination, Rome sent another top dog, Archbishop Paul Gallagher, a British graduate of the *Accademia*, who had also succeeded Courtney at the Council of Europe.

In 2014, Pope Francis appointed Gallagher foreign minister (formally, secretary for relations with states), the Vatican's number-two diplomatic slot, just below secretary of state. Until 2013, Gallagher had never met Jorge Bergoglio, but the Brit worked closely with Pietro Parolin between 1995 and 2000; Parolin and Gallagher are widely considered like-minded pragmatists, similarly knowledgeable, phlegmatic, and disinterested in personal power.[43]

Pope Francis demonstrated in an unusual way his thanks for a diplomat who has embraced risk: in 2016, he elevated to the College of Cardinals *Accademia* alum Mario Zenari, nuncio to Syria, where he has lived since 2008.[44] It's almost unheard of to turn a nuncio into a cardinal. The pope said he was honoring Zenari's service to that "beloved and martyred" country.[45] Reflecting on his job, the nuncio said, "At times, I feel as if I am dressed like a simple soldier in military fatigues uniform . . . using the weapons of charity and truth. Spiritually, I feel that I take orders from the 'Commander in Chief,' Jesus Christ, and his lieutenant, the Pope, who tells me: 'Go there!' and I go; 'Come here' and I come; 'Stay there!' and I stay."[46]

VATICAN DIPLOMATIC ORGANIZATION IS DECEPTIVELY SIMPLE

There are a million books on organizational theory, but it doesn't take the Wharton School to conclude that a small organization with a relatively straightforward reporting chain has a good chance of excelling, especially if it has a clear governance structure, strong leadership, shared goals, sustained resources, efficient internal and external communication channels, and access to influence. The Holy See has those attributes—especially under Pope Francis, for whom diplomacy *and* its mechanisms of execution are a priority.

To understand how the Holy See organizes diplomatic resources, we will look at its command and reporting structures. It is an exercise that highlights key institutional actors repeatedly encountered in accounts of diplomatic engagement—including many of the players who figured in the story of Vatican mediation in Panama that opened this chapter.

THE SUPREME PONTIFF MUST IMITATE CHRIST

The Holy See is organized as an absolute monarchy. That means all roads lead to the supreme pontiff (a title Francis rarely uses). The Catholic Church has no branches of government. The pope controls executive and judicial authority, and there is no legislature. Every member of the Vatican diplomatic corps today has the same boss: Pope Francis.[47] In the book *Church, Ecumenism, and Politics: New Endeavors in Ecclesiology*, Cardinal Joseph Ratzinger, the future Pope Benedict XVI, offers an interesting "martyrological" explanation for why ultimate Church authority must be located in an individual.

God came to earth as one man, Jesus Christ, who gathered disciples by name and was personally condemned to death unjustly. Christ founded the Church in the name of one apostle, Simon, whom Jesus renamed Peter (Petros, "rock" in Greek).[48] Peter "becomes the institution that goes through history . . . yet in such a way that this institution can exist only as a person and in particular and personal responsibility," Ratzinger writes.[49]

Each pope is called to imitate Christ, with a dedication of love to the point of martyrdom, in obedience to God. The theology of primacy requires the personal liability of one man willing to die—in counterpose to worldly power—and only an individual human can be martyred, not a council or a parliament. This theology is echoed in diplomacy: an apostolic nuncio serves as the pope's single representative before a secular power, assuming responsibility, including the risk of death.

Defending the sanctity of the Church unto death isn't just a romantic, theoretical notion. French troops led by Napoleon Bonaparte swept through Italy in the late eighteenth century. When Pope Pius VI (1775–1799) refused to renounce his authority over the Papal States—territory in the midsection of the Italian "boot" including Rome, stretching from sea to sea[50]—he was taken prisoner, shipped to Siena, then stashed in a monastery outside Florence. Months later, he was smuggled overland in a carriage to France, where he died in captivity after a handful of weeks. His heart was buried in Valance while his body was eventually shipped back to Rome.[51]

Although the pope is their boss, papal nuncios are in regular touch with the offices that exist to support him in the Herculean task of preserving faith and maintaining unity. Dating back to the sixteenth century, these offices comprise the Roman Curia.

KEY ORGANIZATIONAL ACTORS

First in prestige and power is the Secretariat of State (SOS), which has direct responsibility for diplomacy and so much more. Thomas Reese, SJ, describes it as a combination State Department and White House staff.[52] Rather than employing thousands of people, though, the SOS employed 197 people in 2019, virtually the same number as worked there in 2012, Pope Benedict XVI's last full year.[53] The secretary of state, who heads the office, is the pope's lead collaborator. His role is often compared to a prime minister. Pietro Parolin, Francis's wingman, worked for both of the pope's predecessors. He is considered a "consummate, talented Vatican diplomat" in the words of former US ambassador to the Holy See Francis Rooney, who worked closely with him.[54]

The secretariat is organized into three sections, in constant communication. Apostolic nuncios routinely report to the first section dedicated to "general affairs," which manages all documents and correspondence for the pope, both external and internal, and is organized by language. The *sostituto* (substitute) who leads the section functions as the pope's chief of staff, seeing the pontiff daily. He is often described as the second most powerful functionary after the cardinal secretary of state. Supporting the *sostituto* is the assessor, another key post.[55]

The second section is dedicated to relations with states. It manages all communication with heads of state and foreign leaders. Led by the secretary for relations with states, supported by an undersecretary, it is organized into country desks. The staff is so small that each expert covers several countries. When Cardinal Parolin worked in the second section (1992–2002), he covered Andorra, Italy, San Marino, and Spain—switching constantly between Italian and Spanish. Papal nuncios are the local subject matter experts serving these "desk officers" as they communicate with foreign governments on behalf of the pope. In 2017, Pope Francis announced the creation of a new third division for the professional needs of diplomatic staff. It is dedicated to the recruitment, formation, promotion, and support of papal representatives abroad—more evidence of the value the pope puts on diplomacy.

The SOS is also the coordinating body for most other curial offices: three dicasteries, nine congregations, three tribunals, five pontifical councils, and seven pontifical commissions are among the fifty-five entities listed by the Vatican as comprising the Roman Curia, a partridge-in-a-pear-tree assemblage.[56] Pope Francis is overseeing a reorganization of this web of departments, many with overlapping functions;[57] some of his streamlining efforts have already been implemented.[58] The pope's organizational reforms for the curia are included in a new apostolic constitution titled *Praedicate Evangelium* (Preach the Gospel). A draft, circulating since June 2019, describes a new vision of the curia: rather than consolidating power on behalf of the pope alone, Francis wants the C-suite in Rome to be more of a help desk, serving bishops and the global Church.[59]

DIPLOMATIC DICASTERIES

One of the changes outlined in *Praedicate Evangelium* is the creation and elevation of a new Dicastery of Evangelization. To Francis, the Church at every level should be engaged in the work of imitating Christ and preaching the Gospel, a central message in his first papal document, *Evangelii Gaudium* (The Joy of the Gospel, 2013). As he explained in the first paragraph, "I wish to encourage the Christian faithful to embark upon a new chapter of evangelization." Speaking to curial officials during an annual Christmas audience, he summarized his reform objective in three words: "A missionary outlook."[60]

That's a task he gives his diplomats, who regularly engage with one of the offices expected to merge into the evangelization dicastery: the Congregation for the Evangelization of Peoples, which was founded in 1622 as the Congregation for the Propagation of the Faith, *Propaganda Fide*, or the Propaganda for short.[61] (People still regularly refer to it by its old Latin name.) It was established to spread the faith in non-Catholic countries. From helping to select bishops and establish schools, to coordinating with missionary religious orders and providing translations of catechism materials into local languages—typically printed in Rome—this congregation was so powerful that its prefect (director) was called the "red pope," red for the color of the robes worn by the cardinal who led it. The Propaganda's geographic area of responsibility includes Africa, Asia, and India. Until 1908, its "mission territory" also comprised Protestant-majority countries such as England, the Netherlands, and the United States.

Francis thinks the division between historically non-Catholic and Catholic countries is irrelevant. He told the curia bluntly that *Propaganda Fide* was

> established in an age when it was easier to distinguish between two rather well-defined realities: a Christian world and a world yet to be evangelized. That situation no longer exists today. People who have not yet received the Gospel message do not live only in non-Western continents; they live everywhere, particularly in vast urban concentrations that call for a specific pastoral outreach. . . . Brothers and sisters, *Christendom no longer exists!*[62]

This insight informs the organizational changes he intends to make. It also inspired a change Francis made to the requirements for diplomatic training: as part of the *Accademia*'s program, a year of missionary work is now obligatory.[63]

Three other curial offices that diplomats often deal with are important to recognize: the Congregation for the Oriental Churches, the Pontifical Council for Christian Unity, and the Pontifical Council for Interreligious Dialogue. The Congregation for the Oriental Churches is responsible for the well-being of twenty-three ancient and modern Eastern Catholic, or "Oriental Catholic," sister Churches practicing a divine liturgy akin to the Orthodox Christian tradition—including vestments, chants, and sacred imagery—while in full communion with Rome. These branches of Catholicism recognize the pope as the supreme pontiff; each took a slightly different path to unity with the Holy See. Most Eastern-rite believers have traditionally been located in the Middle East, West Africa, Eastern Europe, and India.

The Eastern Catholic Church leadership (most with the title "patriarch" or "major archbishop") are automatic members of the congregation, which has a geographic assignment as well. In collaboration with the SOS, it has "exclusive authority" over Egypt, Northern Ethiopia, Eritrea, Southern Albania, Bulgaria, Cyprus, Greece, Iran, Iraq, Jordan, Lebanon, Palestine, the Sinai Peninsula, Syria, and Turkey—some of the hottest hot spots of this century.[64] Fortunately, this office, like *Propaganda Fide*, has a robust budget for programming, church maintenance, and local operations to provide support to its constituents.

A dicastery that has been especially prominent under the last three popes is the Pontifical Council for Christian Unity, which has emerged as one of the most successful nontraditional instruments of Holy See diplomacy. The council helped the Holy See draw closer to Orthodox Churches and to several Protestant denominations, especially the Lutherans.[65] Pope Francis has deployed council members and staff in nonstop engagement. At a weeklong synod of Orthodox Churches on the island of Crete in 2016, I ran into Swiss Cardinal Kurt Koch, who has led the council since 2010, and his number two, Bishop Brian Farrell. The two men were told they were not welcome at daily sessions, although they could attend opening and closing ceremonies of the much-anticipated event. I asked the cardinal if he was insulted or disappointed. "Of course not!" he replied. "Our God is a God of surprises. In large and small matters, we give thanks." He also said he was happy to have extra time to get some work done while the Orthodox bishops met.[66]

Another dicastery playing a significant diplomatic role is the one dedicated to interfaith dialogue. In 1964, Pope Paul VI created a Secretariat for Non-Christians, renamed by Pope John Paul II as the Pontifical Council for Interreligious Dialogue. The contemporary impetus for this engagement is the Second Vatican Council's encyclical *Nostra Aetate*, which presents a more positive image of all world religions by seeing the work of God in them. It compels Christians to reach out to other people of faith and breaks new ground by describing what Christians and Muslims have in common, especially faith in one God. Pope Francis has energetically encouraged the council's work, led by his friend, French Cardinal Jean-Louis Tauran, from 2007 until his death in 2018. It is now led by Spanish Cardinal Miguel Ángel

Ayuso Guixot, MCCJ, an expert on Islamic history who spent many years in Egypt and Sudan. He is a member of the religious order the Comboni Missionaries of the Heart of Jesus (*Missionarii Comboniani Cordis Iesu*, MCCI, in Latin).

Curial offices engaged in diplomatic activities are, in each case, led by a member of the College of Cardinals. Papal nuncios regularly work with these offices and collaborate often with cardinals, especially those in curial leadership roles, because the pope frequently deploys them on foreign assignments. Another pattern in Church service is this: many cardinal prefects and presidents are drawn from the diplomatic service and served as nuncios who attended the *Accademia*.

CARDINALS ARE POWER PLAYERS, INCREASINGLY FROM THE PERIPHERY

After the pope, the College of Cardinals is the Church's second most powerful governing body because it has the power to select a new supreme pontiff in a solemn gathering termed a conclave. Cardinals alone have performed the honor since 1059.[67] Pope Paul VI implemented administrative reforms including a rule that cardinals could not vote after reaching age eighty.[68] He also revived the practice of consulting them as advisers,[69] an idea Francis advanced when he appointed nine to serve as his "kitchen cabinet." In a letter formally establishing the group as the Council of Cardinals, Francis refers to it as a "further expression of episcopal communion," assisting in the governance of the universal Church.[70] Francis often deploys cardinals on small missions to represent him, as we will see. From the start, Francis has explored ways to widen collegial responsibility for running things, but he remains the peerless chief.

The College of Cardinals manages the Church during the *sede vacante* ("vacant seat" in Latin): the interregnum after a pope dies or resigns and before a new one is selected. Since 1917, to be appointed a cardinal must be a priest, and with few exceptions he is selected from the ranks of archbishops and bishops.[71] A cardinal derives power from the prestige of the position, especially in his home country, and as a result of the offices some lead in Rome.[72] The total number of cardinals and "cardinal electors" fluctuates as they die or age beyond the eighty-year-old cutoff.

Pope Francis has most dramatically changed the complexion of the College of Cardinals by broadening its international reach. Cardinals from forty-eight nations participated in the synod that elevated the Argentinian Jorge Bergoglio. Today, cardinals hail from six continents and ninety nations, while cardinal electors are from seventy.[73] Francis has awarded 101 red hats to date. He has used his choices to communicate his priorities. He often picks men who live off the beaten track, at the "peripheries," a leitmotif for this papacy. He has rewarded priests especially known for humility and loyalty to their people, and he has favored ones who minister with a strong pastoral spirit. We will see how this practice has implications for diplomacy.

APOSTOLIC NUNCIOS

The apostolic nuncios engage with the pope through the Secretariat of State. The pope spends part of every morning reading reports from around the world written by the nuncios. Nuncios representing mission countries also report to the Congregation for the Evangelization of Peoples and, if an Eastern Catholic Church is active in his country, to the Congregation for the Oriental Churches as well.

What are the field diplomats reporting on? As the eyes and ears of the Holy See, the apostolic nuncios concentrate on two things: (1) the government and politics of the host country, and (2) the health of the local Catholic Church. On the political side, Vatican diplomats are attuned to issues impacting Catholics and to broader issues, especially those related to human rights (including religious freedom and the rights of the unborn), social justice (especially poverty), economic inequality, war and peace, and the environment.

The pope personally selects each nuncio (from a list of names provided by the secretariat's third section, approved by the cardinal secretary of state) to serve a specific country. Sometimes a pope asserts a strong preference for a certain pairing. Francis, for example, was keen to move Archbishop Christophe Pierre into the nunciature in Washington after seeing the French-born prelate in action as nuncio to Mexico, where he served for nine years. Among the achievements of "Don Christophe" was helping to build greater unity among a very divided bishops' conference, which went on to successfully advocate for constitutional reform in 2013—the addition of religious freedom as a protected right for Mexican citizens.[74] Just two months after the pope's five-day visit to Mexico in 2016, which Pierre helped organize, the Vatican announced that he would be the next nuncio to the United States.[75] Asked about his priorities in the United States, he laughed and told me, "For one thing, I'm finding I have to explain Pope Francis to America!"[76]

Even when the Holy See does not have formal relations with a country, the Church will sometimes post a representative there, in which case he is an apostolic delegate, with no diplomatic status.[77] (Only accredited diplomats are covered by the Vienna Convention of 1961, which outlines the rights and responsibilities of mutually recognized bilateral representatives, offering a degree of protection.) Currently, the Holy See assigns delegates to Jerusalem, Laos, and Puerto Rico, for example.

Angelo Roncalli, who became Pope John XXIII in 1958, was apostolic delegate to Turkey for ten years. The first thing he did upon arriving in Istanbul was to register with the local police to get a visa and residency permit. He won respect from local officials by informing them of his comings and goings and by acknowledging the limits on his authority—and freedom.[78] When the government passed a law banning clergy from wearing religious garb in public, Roncalli assembled his priests in suits and posed them for a photo outside a major church. Representatives of the Holy See are not rebels.

Bishops Are Much More Than "Franchise Operators"

Fr. Reese cautions readers not to think of the Catholic Church hierarchy as Burger King, where the pope serves as CEO and the bishops are franchise operators, following orders from headquarters.[79] As presented in the Church's dogmatic constitution, *Lumen Gentium*, and codified in canon law, the legal code that undergirds the Catholic Church, bishops have extensive responsibility for the "daily care" of believers in the diocese they are charged with governing.[80] Bishops represent God. They aren't local papal stand-ins. The idea that the pope as successor to St. Peter and the bishops as successors to the apostles should govern the Church together is an idea found squarely in Second Vatican Council documents. Recentralizing tendencies characterized the papacies of John Paul II and Benedict XVI. Francis, on the other hand, enthusiastically promotes more power sharing with bishops, an approach termed collegiality or "synodality," which in Church parlance means walking together and can include laity.[81]

Cardinals, archbishops, and bishops often have tremendous local stature. Thus, it is not uncommon to find them in roles hovering between politics and diplomacy without assignment or portfolio. Take, for example, Cardinal Jaime Sin, archbishop of Manila (1974–2003). He was instrumental in ending President Ferdinand Marcos's regime in 1986 when he called the faithful into the streets to support an uprising aimed at the autocratic leader. Over one million Filipinos protested against Marcos, many praying the rosary as they marched. Marcos fled the country into the arms of the United States. Miraculously, no one was killed in the street protests. Although Sin supposedly defied the Vatican to mobilize citizens in the Catholic-majority country, it is hard to believe John Paul II was not aware of Sin's calculations and rationale.

The Second Vatican Council (Vatican II) emphasized the authority of the bishops and the spirit of collegiality that should mark Church governance, while reasserting the primacy of the pope. As a result of Vatican II, national bishops' conferences gained importance.[82] These conferences often interact with a nation's government and therefore coordinate regularly with the papal nuncio. A nuncio who ignores the preferences or positions taken by an episcopal conference is sure to suffer backlash, because bishops are key constituents.

A recent example of a nuncio being ousted after getting on the wrong side of key local bishops—as well as the pope—came in 2015. One of the only sour notes during Pope Francis's pilgrimage to the United States was a media storm, a week after his visit, provoked by news that the pontiff had met with a controversial Republican local official while he was at the nunciature. Indeed, Archbishop Carlo Maria Viganò, the nuncio, had arranged a short, private exchange between Kentucky county clerk Kim Davis, a Protestant fundamentalist, and the pope, who had little idea who she was. At the time, Davis was a contentious political figure who had flouted a federal court order and denied marriage licenses to same-sex couples in her locality—incurring jail time as a result of pressuring other officials to follow her lead—a month before Francis arrived.

Pope Francis was furious about the impropriety—the Holy See steers clear of partisan politics—especially upon his discovery, as he said to Viganò, "You never told me she had four husbands!"[83] As well, it later emerged that the nuncio had ignored advice from Archbishop Joseph Kurtz of Louisville, Kentucky, president of the US Conference of Catholic Bishops, and Cardinal Archbishop Donald Wuerl of Washington, DC. Both prelates recommended against such a meeting.[84] Some believe this incident contributed to the pope's decision to replace Viganò with Archbishop Pierre.[85] Viganò did not go quietly, though; in August 2018 he released a bombshell letter against the pope, then went into hiding.

HOLY SEE DIPLOMACY COMPRISES A FLEXIBLE NETWORK

Although God's diplomats have a simple chain of command—they report to the pope through the Secretariat of State—they function in a system with other stakeholders, most prominently local bishops, but many others as well. Through the bishops, connections run down to parishes and priests and spread locally through schools, charities, and lay organizations. Laterally, a nunciature communicates with religious orders (which have their own global command and control structures running to Rome), as well as with Catholic universities, seminaries, and the media. In many developing nations, missionaries working in remote locations comprise reliable sources of information even where the Catholic faithful are not numerous. Thus, Vatican diplomats do not function in a closed or isolated system. On the contrary, they gather information, and energy, from a variety of interlocking organizations that share the same ethos. Ambassador Rooney makes the valuable point that the Holy See has more impact than the UN because "it is part of local culture, not imposed on local culture."[86]

The Church body, in terms of religious personnel, has a global network with over one million nodes—over 5,300 bishops, 414,000 priests, 50,500 brothers, and 641,500 women religious[87]—linked, through an array of offices in Rome, to their spiritual leader. So, it is a top-down *and* bottom-up system.

In his book on networks, *The Square and the Tower*, historian Niall Ferguson contrasts rigid power hierarchies (including the Catholic Church) with new social networks, which are flexible, adaptable, and capable of assimilating and circulating information with great economy.[88] But as one peers into the interactions at work in the Vatican's diplomatic problem solving, the clichéd image of the Church as a fixed pyramid with the pope as pharaoh, perched on the top, is less and less satisfactory for explaining the functionality of its diplomacy. For this system also functions as a distributed network. Nodes such as the nuncio have high "degree" (more edges, or relationships) and high "betweenness centrality," facilitating maximum network traffic in information.[89]

What gives the Holy See its true power is a network of relationships more like an organic body of capillaries and nerve endings than a static structure of building blocks. The Church as the Body of Christ is far more evocative as a social network—and that's an image we come back to in accounts of diplomacy.

TALENTED AND DEDICATED, MISSIONARIES OFTEN PLAY SPECIAL DIPLOMATIC ROLES

One "class" of Catholic actors who sometimes figure as diplomatic players are men and women religious, the brothers and sisters who belong to religious orders. The best known of these—such as the Order of Preachers (Dominicans), the Order of Friars Minor (Franciscans), or Mother Teresa's Missionaries of Charity (MC)—are transnational, sprawling across the globe. Each has a central office, typically in Rome, although MC is still headquartered in Kolkata, India. Communities such as the Society of Jesus (the Jesuits), formally recognized in 1540, and the Maryknoll Fathers and Brothers, an American order founded in 1911, were created with the express purpose of preaching the Gospel in new lands, effectively making them ambassadors of the faith without portfolio.[90]

A Catholic missionary has the opposite career path compared to a diplomat for the Holy See, who moves around the world on assignments averaging three years at the lower rungs of the ladder. Historically, a missionary assigned to a faraway location went out into the world and never came back. If a missionary returns to his or her home country, it's usually to retire or for a very rare visit. These religious effectively serve as diplomats and support the ones with the title.

Texas-raised Jesuit Fr. Anthony Corcoran helped rebuild the Catholic Church in the vast Siberian region in the late 1990s, meeting families for whom faith was preserved by prayerful grandmothers. He returned home to visit his own family for Thanksgiving—21 years later. Today he serves as apostolic administrator in Muslim-majority Kyrgyzstan in Central Asia bordering China, routinely representing the Church before officialdom, especially considering the nuncio, based in neighboring Kazakhstan, covers oner one million square miles of territory. I asked the priest what wise advise had helped him in his remote ministry. He replied: "An old Jesuit missionary told me, 'Every day pray for two things. Pray that you fall in love, absolutely love, the people you are there to serve, and pray that you love the language.' I remember being surprised by both. He explained, 'You don't have to love a government, you don't have to love a culture, but if you don't love people, concrete people, what are you doing there? Who do you think you are?' Love is the only thing that changes anything, and that's what a missionary does."[91]

When nunciatures seek local talent to serve as "collaborators," missionaries are among the most sensible picks. Fr. Gerard Hammond (better known as Fr. Ham Je Do, his Korean name) is a Maryknoll priest who has lived in Korea since 1960, when he arrived by ship and soon found himself caring for refugees from the North, displaced by the Korean War. It is the nature of this work to become deeply embedded in local communities.

Fr. Ham Je Do explains: "As a missionary, it is essential to devote our whole lives—especially minds and hearts and even our physical abilities—to the people we came to serve." His spoken Korean is flawless; he is widely loved and respected in the Korean Catholic community, the fastest-growing Catholic Church in East Asia.[92] So it was no surprise that Archbishop Osvaldo Padilla, nuncio from 2008 to 2017, tapped the missionary for help with the nunciature's workload.

What did he do? "Anything the nuncio needed! Call people. Send emails. Translate. Explain the country," the jovial priest replied. Was it a bit disconcerting to be pulled from his existing assignments? "Heavens, no! The Church is my mother and my bride. If she needed me in the nunciature, I was eager to serve."[93] With commitment like that at its fingertips, one sees how much more capacious the Holy See's diplomatic community really is. Pope Francis honored an eighty-five-year-old nun he met in the Central African Republic, who arrived at the papal event in a canoe. She spent sixty years as a midwife, delivering thousands of babies in the Congo.[94] Francis described missionaries as "consuming" their lives in service, without ever making news—yet always available to guide Catholic diplomats who come and go.

As Niall Ferguson explains, "many networks are complex adaptive systems that are constantly shifting shape."[95] In the Church, a significant process of adaption is the substitution of lay missionaries for religious ones: as the number of people enrolled in religious orders (especially men) has decreased,[96] the number of laypeople organized in analogous transnational networks has increased. Lay groups share faith, a common worldview, and a commitment to evangelization while cultivating distinct interests.[97]

There are major lay movements with different core concerns, including family and culture (Communion and Liberation, founded in 1954, with some 90,000 members in 23 countries);[98] peace and poverty (the Community of Sant'Egidio,[99] founded in Rome in 1968, with 50,000 members in over 70 countries); interreligious dialogue (the Focolare Movement, founded in 1943, with over 140,000 core members in 180 countries);[100] and revitalizing parish life (the Neocatechumenal Way, founded in 1964 in Madrid, which reportedly has over 1 million members).[101] The Church has even invented new structures for these twentieth-century formations: Pope St. John Paul II made Opus Dei (founded in Spain in 1928, with over 90,000 members today) a "personal prelature," the only one of its kind to date.

Laypeople associated with Catholic charitable groups have played diplomatic roles too. Caritas Internationalis, founded in 1951, is a Rome-based confederation of over 160 national member organizations on every continent. Caritas chapters run food/school/medical programs for refugees, manage hospice/rehabilitation/AIDs/elderly centers worldwide, and furnish disaster relief wherever earthquakes, floods, cyclones, or tsunamis strike. Caritas shows up to tackle a mind-boggling range of humanitarian problems. The first national-level Caritas was established in Germany in 1897; Caritas Internationalis is a well-respected, highly competent network of networks.[102] These lay-dominated groups (many with some formal clerical component) collaborate with the Vatican's diplomatic chain of command informally. Caritas chapters are official partners of episcopal conferences.

One more potential diplomatic actor should be recognized: individual members of the faith often make contributions to the Church's diplomatic activity.

SANT'EGIDIO SHEPHERDS PEACE IN MOZAMBIQUE

A captivating example of a Catholic lay movement playing a pivotal role in diplomatic engagement can be found in Mozambique, an East African colony of Portugal for almost five hundred years (1498–1975). The country's road to self-sufficiency was violent and bloody. Some ten thousand Mozambicans died in a ten-year war of independence between the Portuguese military and the Mozambique Liberation Front (FRELIMO), which triumphed in 1975.

Unfortunately for the country's ten million people, the first FRELIMO president, Samora Machel, was a hard-line Marxist. Just a year after one war ended, another began. The new power was challenged by an anti-Communist insurgency led by the Mozambican National Resistance (RENAMO). Over the next sixteen years, 1 million people died and 4.5 million were displaced. Drought and famine multiplied the misery, turning the country into the world's poorest place.[103] Although the ruling party imposed a harsh, anti-Church strategy, it failed, and Christian institutions stepped in to provide some of the only social services available to the people.

When Machel's presidential plane crashed in 1986, many saw a chance to initiate peace talks. The Holy See had no diplomatic relationship with Mozambique, but Catholic bishops had been calling for negotiations for several years.[104] They teamed up with Anglican bishops to coax the new president, a more conciliatory character, to the peace table. John Paul II even visited Mozambique in 1988 to try to get a new spirit flowing. While there, the pope encouraged Archbishop Jaime Gonçalves of Beira to take a leadership role in exploring new paths. A popular prelate among the faithful, Gonçalves had studied in Rome where he became friendly with lay Catholics active in the Community of Sant'Egidio. During the civil war, Sant'Egidio shipped and airlifted food, medicine, and other supplies to Mozambique.

Despite efforts by the governments of Kenya, Italy, and the United States to get the two warring opponents into the same room, plans kept collapsing over where to meet. The government wanted any face-to-face negotiations to occur outside the country. Finally, Sant'Egidio cofounder Andrea Riccardi offered his organization's headquarters in Rome as a neutral site, with approval from Pope John Paul II as well as the Italian prime minister, who promised material support.

In July 1990, the first meeting in Rome brought together both sides, with no formal mediators but four "observers": Riccardi and a Sant'Egidio priest, Archbishop Gonçalves,[105] and a socialist member of the Italian parliament with Foreign Ministry experience regarding Africa.[106] Opening the meeting, Riccardi observed, "An expression of the great Pope John XXIII, which was also his working method, comes to mind: 'Let us strive to find that which unites rather than that which divides.'"[107] Although the Secretariat of State was hardly involved, the pope was regularly briefed on the progress of negotiations.

It took twelve rounds of talks across twenty-seven months. Ten foreign governments were engaged at one point or another.[108] In October 1992, a comprehensive peace agreement, known as the Rome Accords, was signed calling for a cease-fire, policed by UN peacekeeping forces, with a two-year transition to democracy and multiparty elections in 1994.[109]

Lasting Lessons from Mozambique's Peace

As summarized in a *Harvard International Review* article titled "Divine Intervention," the lay movement served as a catalyst: "The mediation work of Sant'Egidio in Mozambique illustrates how savvy religious organizations, building on their neutrality and compassion and utilizing the skills of other institutions, can bring feuding parties together and perhaps help end civil wars."[110] Many credit the way the peace was achieved—focusing on what united both sides, producing a compromise without a winner and a loser, and multiplying the number of stakeholders, which were all guidelines provided by the Catholic mediators—as contributing to its success.

Remarkably, both sides respected the terms of the agreement. Democratic elections were held. One of sub-Saharan Africa's largest repatriations ever unfolded: within three years of the peace agreement, 1.7 million refugees returned to Mozambique from neighboring countries. Another 4 million displaced domestically returned to their homes. The government's focus shifted to economic and social policies to benefit the whole nation. Between 1993 and 2009, its economy was the fastest growing of any non–oil producer in the region.[111]

The Holy See established formal relations with Mozambique in 1995. Sant'Egidio deepened its involvement in the country, establishing Peace Houses nationwide run entirely by local people. The community also extended its reach across Africa, providing health care, education, work with the poor, and engagement in conflict resolution. Reflecting on the lay movement's relationship with Pope John Paul II, Riccardi mused, "He knows what we do. Perhaps, he's pushed us to pass from Rome to the rest of the world, not as an order, but a kind of stimulus . . . a geopolitical spirituality."[112] Today, Sant'Egidio is a favorite of Pope Francis's because its charism, "prayer, poor, and peace,"[113] aligns so closely with his most fundamental vision for the Church.

While the Community of Sant'Egidio is widely credited with the peace accomplishment, the lay organization is synonymous with the Catholic Church:

its standing in Mozambique was highly dependent on the success of national bishops in positioning the Church as impartial, neither allied with government nor insurgency, after independence and throughout the war. Archbishop Jaime Gonçalves's role was critical. He was the human link that brought together three elements: the suffering Mozambican people, a government ready for talks but leery of legitimizing its enemy, and external resources willing to provide (and pay for) neutral ground. As one of twelve bishops, he was obviously a member of the Mozambican elite. Yet his role as head of the Church in Beira, a major port city with half a million people, put him close to the misery of the war. Thousands of homeless and displaced people occupied the city. With no functional social services, the Church was the main source of charity.

What we see in this successful example of Catholic diplomacy defined as encompassing a range of potential actors is the extraordinary adaptability of the Holy See's network *across time*. Consider this: Catholicism was associated with Portugal, the colonial overlord. Yet, in the postcolonial Church, Mozambican priests were promoted to positions of power because most foreign clerics left the country. Jaime Gonçalves was ordained bishop in 1976. He and his peers consciously adopted a pastoral model, ministering close to the people, intentionally setting the Church apart from politics.

Ultimately, this strategy allowed the Church to serve as the channel for peace. As two historians explain, "indeed, it is the high level of differentiation in the relation between church and state that led the Catholic Church to be perceived as sufficiently independent from both the Mozambican state and RENAMO to act as an impartial mediator."[114] In its self-understanding, the Church sees this agility as evidence of grace—a gift from the Holy Spirit to the people of God.

2

Mission beyond Religion

> When there is question of saving souls, or preventing greater harm to souls, we feel the courage to treat with the devil in person.
>
> —Pope Pius XI, speech to students at Mondragone College, May 14, 1929[1]

The duality of Vatican diplomacy—representing a state, serving a religion—is at the heart of its mission, not dissimilar to a duality that characterizes the Church. Like light, which is both a particle and a wave, or Jesus, both divine and human, the Catholic Church is simultaneously one thing and another. This double nature creates a tension between the ideal (imitation of Christ, who models perfection) and the real: the quotidian scrappiness of interstate relations, which valorizes compromise. Well balanced, this complex identity is the source of what Pope Francis has called the "special power" of his diplomats.[2] It's also key to appreciating why the Holy See sometimes makes decisions that baffle national governments—and Catholic constituents, too.[3]

One diplomatic clash at the height of World War II in particular—between the Church on the one hand and the United States and Great Britain on the other—illustrates the Church's mission within the global interstate system and makes clear how its goals often differ from those of temporal sovereigns.

BUCKING PRESSURE, POPE PIUS XII DRAWS CLOSER TO JAPAN

Less than two months after the cataclysmic Japanese air attack on Pearl Harbor, Hawaii, in December 1941, which killed over 2,400 American citizens (including an entire crew of sailors who drowned when their battleship, the

USS *Arizona*, sank[4]), Pope Pius XII agreed to Japan's request that it send an "extraordinary envoy" to the Holy See.[5] It took just a few weeks to work out the details: Tokyo would assign a resident diplomat exclusively to the Holy See, with the intention of upgrading his status to ambassador as soon as Japanese political conditions allowed. With that agreement, Japan became the first Asian country to establish formal diplomatic ties to the Holy See, although the Church had maintained an apostolic delegate in Tokyo for decades.[6]

When the secretary of state, Cardinal Luigi Maglione (1939–1944), informed American and British diplomats that the Holy See and Japan would formalize diplomatic relations, they warned the cardinal that their governments would be very unhappy.[7] Indeed, Allied officials howled in protest. Britain's foreign minister wrote a note to the pope charging, "His Holiness has again deferred to pressure from the Governments of the Axis Powers." US Undersecretary of State Sumner Welles called Pope Pius XII's decision "deplorable." President Roosevelt found it, simply, "unbelievable."[8] The president assumed that public opinion would see the decision as a victory for the Japanese. American officials even convinced themselves that they had persuaded the Holy See's apostolic delegate in Washington that recognizing Japan so respectfully was unjustified.[9]

It didn't help that, as these arrangements were being made, Japanese troops occupying the Philippines were reportedly desecrating Christian churches to advance the imperial policy of eliminating foreign influence from Asia. In that light, the Holy See's timing was, at the very least, surprising. But if one is familiar with how the Vatican conducts diplomacy, the gesture was comprehensible.

The recognition came after a history of fits and starts. In 1919, the Holy See requested that Tokyo accept a resident apostolic delegate, which it did. Since then, the two governments had discussed formalizing relations at several junctures, but Buddhists in the Land of the Rising Sun had consistently lobbied against any formal agreement.[10] Interstate diplomacy is an essential way the Catholic Church protects its believers and advances its spiritual mission, so the Church takes every opportunity to establish bilateral ties. When the emperor's envoys approached Rome in 1942 with a proposal Rome had long sought, the Church pragmatically agreed.

As the American chargé d'affaires Harold Tittmann Jr. pressed for more information to share with his government, he consulted Archbishop Giovanni Montini, Pius XII's *sostituto*, who would become Pope Paul VI. Montini and a colleague offered two more explanations: by strengthening bilateral relations with Japan, the Holy See might have a positive influence on the empire, possibly even mediating between the parties at war on some delicate issues. But that was an aspiration. Pragmatically, the Holy See had no choice but to engage with the Japanese because the empire's advancing military was bringing more and more Catholics under its control. Protecting the spiritual interests of some twenty million Catholics in Japanese-occupied territory was a fundamental responsibility, because Catholic believers are akin to citizens of the Holy See's spiritual domain.[11]

Pope Pius XII summarized the Holy See's reasoning in a message to President Franklin Roosevelt, underscoring the obvious point that initiating diplomatic relations never means approving all the actions of a foreign interlocutor.[12]

Having allowed an acrimonious debate to unfold for almost two months, the Holy See finally turned its back on protests and accepted Ken Harada as special envoy with the rank of ambassador. Harada was a career diplomat who moved from Paris to Rome. The following week, President Roosevelt told reporters that the Vatican had convinced him that, considering Church interests in Asia, the pope had no choice but to accept Japan's request for recognition. For example, with 33 percent of American troops being Catholic, the Holy See could be helpful in resolving issues around prisoners of war held by the Japanese. Indeed, a year later, the Vatican delegate began visiting American and British prisoners of war held in Japanese camps, checking on their well-being and bringing food and books.[13]

WILLING TO DEAL "WITH THE DEVIL IN PERSON"

This case brings to mind an observation attributed to Pope Pius XI: "When there is question of saving souls, or preventing greater harm to souls, we feel the courage to treat with the devil in person."[14] The Holy See's view of diplomacy as a forum for ministry to a broken world is often unappreciated by both secular and religious commentators who assume the Church should not compromise its spiritual values by engaging with immoral actors. Yet, in Pius XII's view—as supreme pontiffs before and since have concluded—the only way to influence a malevolent regime is to engage it directly. This drive to exert Christian influence in earthly contests frequently underlies Vatican diplomacy, a tacit motivation more often understood than explicitly declared.

Pope Pius XII himself was eager to negotiate with the government of Prime Minister Hideki Tojo, a man eventually tried for war crimes and executed by hanging. The pope and his small team of advisers were undeterred by pressure from the Allies. This example highlights key aspects of the Holy See's diplomatic mission.

The simple act of exchanging envoys created a real relationship between the Holy See and Tokyo, sanctified by international law and codified by international treaty.[15] It allowed dialogue on the status of the small Catholic community in Japan. *Representation* is the fundamental purpose of diplomacy and a key activity for its envoys, as it facilitates direct communication between representatives of heads of state or sovereign entities; it's the primary way the Catholic Church interacts with Caesar's agents.[16]

Within that elevated world, the Holy See carefully preserves its impartiality vis-à-vis political disputes. Notice the pope's fearlessness facing demands from Britain and the United States. Papal diplomats prefer to remain equidistant to warring parties. This allows the Church to play a useful role through *mediation*, another important element of its diplomacy. The Church's capacity to mediate agreements is rooted in its longevity and how history shaped its institutional identity.

The Holy See often negotiates with secular governments on behalf of local Catholic communities to secure religious freedom or to improve church-state relations. In these cases, the Church's mission is the *preservation* of the faith. Pius XII's team was laying the ground to protect Catholics—not only the small number in Japan, but also those in Japanese-occupied Asia—fully aware that the faithful were literally under the gun. Using the space provided by international diplomacy is an efficiency uniquely available to this world religion alone, as it seeks to advocate for the well-being of its members, citizens in every land.

In addition to representation, mediation, and preservation, *evangelization* is at the core of all Church activity, for it was given by Jesus Christ: after He rose from the dead, Christ summoned His eleven remaining apostles to Galilee and directed them to "make disciples of every nation."[17] This task is known as the Great Commission. As successors of the apostles, Catholic bishops, including the preeminent bishop of Rome, trace a central mission back to this assignment.

These four activities are such core aspects of the Holy See's diplomatic pursuit that each concept, together with its crucial historical context, deserves examination in turn. As we will see in chapter 3, the Church's intellectual foundation, especially the natural law tradition, assumes the ability of the Church to advance the good of all. So its mission involves protecting the flock and the common good at the same time.

ORIGINS OF PAPAL DIPLOMACY AND ITS CONTINUOUS MISSION

Representation

In its most basic manifestation, diplomacy is the sending and receiving of envoys in order to extend the eyes, ears, and goodwill of one worldly power to another. The Catholic Church certainly did not invent this practice. Original credit might go to the system of communication and negotiation developed some 3,300 years ago linking societies in Egypt, Mesopotamia, Assyria, and Hatti, with Egypt as the hub. This thriving network shares features with the contemporary diplomatic regime according to recent research.[18]

Notwithstanding these ancient antecedents, the origins of papal diplomacy came one thousand years before the emergence of residential ambassadors representing Italian city-states in the fifteenth century, which historians often describe as the starting point of modern diplomacy.[19]

First Papal Envoys Sent from Rome to Constantinople

With the Edict of Milan in the year 313, Emperor Constantine made Christianity legal, allowing Christians to be openly active and the Church hierarchy to play more constructive public roles. Soon after Constantine moved his imperial court to the banks of the Bosporus, he convened a council of bishops in 325 to settle questions around the identity of Jesus Christ. Pope Sylvester I sent two legates, both priests, to represent him at the Council of Nicaea,[20] which was an especially remarkable convocation because it signified the emperor's belief that Christian unity was directly related to imperial unity.[21] Based on the reporting he received, Sylvester approved the council's decisions. These legates are considered the earliest papal diplomats;[22] a papal representative to the Byzantine court was called an *apocrisiarius*.[23]

When Pope Leo the Great sent a team to represent him at the Council of Chalcedon in 451, the group included Julian, bishop of Cos, fluent in Greek as well as Latin. From the council, Julian was next sent to the court of Emperor Marcian in Constantinople as the papal *apocrisiarius*—probably the first sent to live there long term. A letter from Leo to Julian in 453 outlined Julian's tasks: to defend Christianity against heresy, to report to the pope on various conflicts within and between communities of faith, and to translate (from Greek to Latin) and manage documents that would aid papal decision making, all duties that Julian's diplomatic descendants continue to this day.

Latin popes continued sending *apocrisiarii* to the Byzantine court for three hundred years. Between 537 and 752, when the emperor had the right to approve each bishop of Rome, seven *apocrisiarii* became pope, including St. Gregory the Great (590–604). Gregory's six years as the pope's ambassador to Constantinople convinced him that Rome could not rely on the Eastern empire for protection.

The Medieval Emergence of a Diplomatic System to Unify Christendom

As the most powerful institution in medieval Europe, the Catholic Church was a political, judicial, and spiritual authority rolled into one. The pope was compelled to manage political alliances, intervene in the seemingly endless conflicts between rival powers, and interject his opinion in succession struggles. With so many demands for attention—and interventions to make—medieval popes beginning with Gregory VII (1073–1085) deputized special envoys, termed *legati missi* (legates sent) to distinguish them from *legati nati* (residential bishops), representing Rome in important locations such as Canterbury, Cologne, Reims, and Toledo. The most important type of *legatus missus* was a class of representative sent "from the pope's side," (*legatus a latere*), typically a cardinal. All these assignments were temporary and mission specific.[24]

The range of political engagement of an ambitious, late medieval pope such as Innocent III (1198–1216) was tremendous. He settled disputes between brothers fighting over a throne in Hungary. He wrote the rules for selecting a king in the Holy Roman Empire, giving himself veto authority. He issued an interdict against King John of England, preventing Catholic clergy from giving sacraments, burying the dead, or ringing church bells to pressure the king to accept the pope's choice for archbishop of Canterbury. When John resisted, Innocent excommunicated him; the king caved. He wrote a letter of concession to the pope, basically putting England and Ireland under Innocent's control.

Innocent crowned princes of Armenia, Bohemia, and Bulgaria. He served as guardian for a four-year-old child-king of Sicily until he came of age (the pope selected his wife too). Meanwhile, the pope plotted a (disastrous) crusade to regain Jerusalem and convened medieval Europe's most important Church council, the Fourth Lateran Council.

Innocent III's papacy exemplifies the increased use of special agents, with specific instructions, for political and ecclesiastical assignments of varying lengths of time. It was a legate who delivered the excommunication notice to King John; a cardinal serving as legate assessed the Hungarian power struggle; first a cardinal, then an abbot, mediated conflict between France and England for the pope—at least five times.[25] Most legates were clerics, including monks from religious orders. The 1208 murder of a legate and Cistercian monk, Pierre de Castelnau, in the south of France angered Innocent. He declared Pierre a martyr and ordered a military campaign against Catharism, the heresy the monk had been assigned to investigate. The war continued for some twenty years and annihilated the Cathar community.[26]

Beginning in the fourteenth century, papal *nuntii*, collectors or fiscal agents, were sent to secure taxes earmarked for Rome or for the crusades. The network covered Europe, from the northern kingdoms of Sweden and

Norway, west to Portugal, through Germany, and south to Sicily. The agents interacted with local authorities and occasionally conducted business for the pope besides counting receipts. The title *nuntius*, meaning messenger or envoy in Latin, came to be applied to officials on diplomatic assignment in the fourteenth and fifteenth centuries.[27]

Thus the Holy See developed a diplomatic system to serve the requirements of governing Christendom, the society of medieval Europe having shared religious and cultural norms united by belief in God. The diplomatic tools were especially aimed at preserving unity. The Church and Christian doctrine were thoroughly integrated into the social fabric, while Rome in the person of the supreme pontiff was perceived as the ultimate authority and adjudicator, deploying agents to preserve the peace.

The coherence of the medieval worldview is beautifully depicted by a huge map created around 1300 on one giant sheet of vellum, housed in England's Hereford Cathedral. At the center of the circular rendering of the known world stands Jerusalem—central because the death and resurrection of Jesus Christ was the defining event in human history for this civilization. The second most prominent place on the map is Rome, as the seat of Christ's earthly vicar. Paris is the third major place of the 420 cities and towns depicted because it is the font of learning in theology and philosophy. Biblical places including Eden, the Red Sea, Babylon, and the Tower of Babel are also located on the densely decorated document. Above the map and outside the earthly circle is Christ enthroned, governing all.

The Shift to Permanent Embassies in the Renaissance

By the late 1400s, Rome was not only mobilizing legates to serve abroad; the city was itself a cosmopolitan center of political activity and elite information exchange. From European royal and imperial courts, from Christian Africa, from the city-states dotting the Italian Peninsula, and, less often, from the East, envoys converged on the papal court. They came to submit petitions for the pope's consideration, to view relics and religious treasures, and to learn what was happening across Europe. While in the Eternal City, embassies and envoys also consulted with each other, sharing information on alliances and the progress of various conflicts.[28] Rome was a magnetic destination because it was a religious and spiritual center as well as a crossroads for worldly interests.[29]

Garrett Mattingly, an erudite scholar on the subject of early modern diplomacy, attributes to Rome not only a role in helping to spread the practice of residential diplomacy; he also sees the first signs of professionalism emerging there:

[T]he importance of Rome in the establishment of permanent diplomacy both in Italy and throughout Europe was enormous. . . . Probably at no other court in Europe were so many distinguished diplomats collected. . . . Rome began to be what it remained for centuries, the chief training school of diplomacy. . . . And here the *corps diplomatique* first began to develop a professional spirit, to codify their mutual relations, and to act together in a crisis.[30]

Even before it *had* a school, Rome *was* a school for the art of international collaboration.

Mediation

Personal Papal Mediation since the Fall of Rome

Mediation, especially the practice of attempting to reconcile parties at odds over territory, has been the pontiff's preferred method of engaging the external world throughout history. In 410, Pope Innocent I persuaded an early band of Visigoths descending on Rome not to overrun the city's principal churches where people were sheltering. Although unsuccessful, the pope even travelled to Ravenna, the Roman capital since 402, as part of a delegation to Emperor Honorius in order to find a peace settlement satisfactory to the Visigoth leader, King Alaric, a former Roman commander.[31]

A century later, legendary aggressor Attila the Hun was encamped with his warriors in Northern Italy threatening full-scale invasion of the peninsula. It was Pope Leo who trekked to Attila's settlement near Mantua in 542. According to Jesuit historian Hartmann Grisar, the nomadic leader was impressed to see the illustrious head of the Church in person. He assured Leo he would try to make peace with the Romans and moved his warriors north of the Danube River.[32] A year later, Attila died. Pope Leo's purported encounter three years later with King Genseric, a Visigoth strongman from North Africa, was less successful.[33] Meeting just outside Rome's walls, the pontiff managed to negotiate several important limits on banditry, including a ban on torching the city, protection for treasures brought to churches, and a two-week limit on plunder.[34]

These widely reported fifth- and sixth-century examples of papal mediation on behalf of the Roman population (including Christians and non-Christians) were formative in depicting the pope as willing to assume risk in order to protect whole communities from harm.

Other Catholic Leaders Recruited as High-Stakes Mediators

Over time, a reputation for risk taking, rationality, and commitment to finding peaceful solutions became associated with other leading clerics besides the pope. Secular rulers recruited bishops as diplomats as early as the fourth century: Rome's imperial court asked St. Ambrose, Milan's popular bishop, to negotiate with a Spanish-born Roman commander, Magnus Maximus, who had declared himself emperor in 383, after a battlefield victory near Paris.[35]

St. Ambrose is credited with traveling to his birthplace, Trier, a major city in Gaul, where he persuaded Maximus to stay out of Italy.[36] In exchange, Maximus was declared co-emperor of Britain and Gaul. But Ambrose's second attempt to negotiate with Maximus a year later was unsuccessful, as the "usurper" marched on Italy in 388. He was defeated (and executed) by troops employed by Theodosius, emperor of the East.[37]

Ambrose's moral authority over secular rulers was poignantly captured when he excommunicated Emperor Theodosius and refused to celebrate Mass with him in attendance. The emperor's crime? He had ordered the massacre of some seven thousand spectators at a huge hippodrome in Thessalonica, a major city in Roman-controlled Greece. Murder violated the Fifth Commandment, and murder as revenge—the emperor felt he was paying back the local population for a mob attack on the Roman garrison—was particularly unchristian.

To do penance for the massacre, Theodosius, garbed in civilian clothes, prostrated himself on the Milan Cathedral's marble floor, asking forgiveness and praying the psalms.[38] Policy-wise, the emperor also agreed to establish a thirty-day "cooling-off" period between a death order and its execution. By Christmas, Ambrose restored Theodosius to communion. St. Ambrose's legacy includes Latin Catholicism's early assertion of independence from the state: he opposed a variety of imperial policies and refused to bring the Church community into compliance with political demands. He modeled Christ's imperative to "repay to Caesar what belongs to Caesar and to God what belongs to God."[39]

Renaissance Reaches of Papal Power

A diplomatic episode from the Renaissance illustrates what papal power was like at its height, when the pope had authority to divide the world.

Christopher Columbus returned from his first transatlantic journey with pineapples and parrots, tobacco, and eight captive humans to entice his royal sponsors, King Ferdinand and Queen Isabella. He was angling for more funds to return to the New World, having left thirty-nine men back in Hispaniola. The power couple, in turn, wanted assurance that they could keep what he found. Spain was vying with Portugal for new lands. In fact, Columbus learned everything he knew as a member of the Portuguese merchant marine. Since Portugal, too, was led by a Catholic monarch, Ferdinand and Isabella turned in 1493 to the king of kings, Pope Alexander VI, to secure rights to territory they anticipated Columbus would conquer.

In response, Pope Alexander VI drew a north–south line, from pole to pole, down the middle of the Atlantic Ocean, one hundred leagues (320 miles) west of the Cape Verde Islands off the coast of Northwest Africa, an archipelago already claimed by Portugal. In the papal bull *Inter Caetera*, Spain was granted rights to explore the ocean and take possession of all lands west of the demarcation line. Portugal could have territory east of the line. Although the two monarchs negotiated with each other a year later to amend the papal rule, nudging the imaginary line further west to allow Portugal's possession of the South American "bulge" that is today Brazil, the pope's declaration established the origin of Spanish claims to much of the New World while Portugal concentrated on colonizing West Africa.

Pope John Paul II Steps in to Prevent War in South America

Fast-forward some five hundred years, and we find Pope John Paul II playing a similarly activist role as a mediator settling a century-old territorial dispute involving neighboring countries (both Catholic) and a watery divide. In late 1978, Argentina readied warships against Chile to capture three small islands, mainly inhabited by sheep, in the Beagle Channel, a strategic waterway linking the Atlantic and Pacific Oceans at the southern tip of South America. Chile put forty-five thousand forces on alert for engagement. Coming upon Christmas, the two sides "were militarized. They were sending troops to the border. Actually, they were on the brink of war," recalled a diplomat from the region.[40]

At the last hour, John Paul II announced that he was sending a personal envoy, based on a private agreement between the two governments that the pope was the only acceptable mediator. Argentina's president had confided to the apostolic nuncio that an invasion was scheduled—and US satellite images confirmed for Rome that troops were massing—so it was objectively known that war was imminent.[41] Declassified cables confirm that the US government shared extensive intelligence with the Vatican and virtually begged the new pope, just two months in office, to play this critical role. The main holdup was the Vatican's strict rule that both sides of a dispute must request its assistance. While Chile was eager for the pope's engagement, Argentina took its time to make the request but finally did.[42] On Christmas Day, John Paul II sent an emissary. Spanish-speaking Cardinal Antonio Samorè, chief of the Vatican Library, flew to Buenos Aires. A specialist on Latin America, he was former president of the Pontifical Commission for Latin America and former nuncio to Colombia—with a special devotion to Our Lady of Guadalupe.[43]

Samorè spent two weeks shuttling between Buenos Aires and Santiago. In the midst of these events, he told journalists, "This is a different diplomacy; one of the Pope with his children."[44] His objective, bringing the near belligerents to a concrete first step,[45] was achieved when the three parties (Argentina, Chile, and the Vatican) signed the Act of Montevideo in neutral Uruguay, renouncing force, pulling troops away from borders, and formally requesting Vatican mediation. Nearly six years later at the Vatican, foreign ministers representing the two protagonists, together with Vatican Secretary of State Agostino Casaroli, signed a Treaty of Peace and Friendship, awarding the three contested islands to Chile but limiting its rights beyond the islands to just thirty miles[46] and conceding to Argentina navigation rights in Chilean waters.[47] The settlement included a signature Holy See element: it resulted in no winner or loser, and yet it allowed both countries to claim success.[48]

How was it that both Argentina and Chile deferred to a brand new Polish pope in the heated buildup toward war? Granted, both countries are predominantly Catholic, but in neither place were Catholic bishops close to the respective military regimes. On the contrary, bishops in both nations had criticized them for using repressive tactics against political opponents and workers. There was no standing alliance between either the Argentinian Catholic bishops and President Jorge Rafael Videla (1976–1981) or the Chilean bishops and General Augusto Pinochet, president of the Government Junta of Chile (1973–1990). Both men took power via a coup d'état.

The Holy See's success in settling the Beagle Channel dispute demonstrates that it retains attributes that made it a global power broker five hundred years ago: respect for the papacy and its status as an impartial authority and confidence in the Holy See's ability to facilitate a just agreement—one that could stick. When dealing with Catholic-majority countries, there is also the spiritual dimension that commands deference apart from any military or commercial might. As Thomas Princen wrote, "[T]he mere presence of a papal envoy in a Catholic country meant the leaders had to talk. . . . Whereas an invasion would have rallied public support [for the Argentinian government] without a papal intervention, it became unthinkable in the presence of a papal envoy."[49]

It is also proof that God's diplomats deploy an approach that works. Negotiators produced a remarkably detailed agreement that required tremendous patience, and almost six years, to achieve. The Vatican used that time to help working-level officials from the two sides build and deepen relationships with each other. Negotiations became a crucible for long-term implementation. Despite innumerable setbacks—including war between Argentina and England over the Falkland Islands/*Islas Malvinas*—Vatican mediators were able to hold the antagonists at the table until domestic politics were ripe for a conclusive solution.

In the Beagle Channel mediation, Pope John Paul II left most of the work to his diplomats.[50] As supreme pontiff, he was considered the only human who could get the process started, but once underway, a relatively small group kept it moving. Samorè gave his life to the effort. He died of a heart attack in Rome in 1983, at age seventy-eight, in the midst of negotiations. A major mountain pass through the southern Andes on the Argentina-Chile border was renamed after him.[51]

Preservation

Preservation under Duress: The Church Survives War, Persecution, and Suppression

The Church has, in every century, sought to ameliorate the harsh impact of war and political persecution against Catholics and others. Maintaining and extending religious freedom is a basic principle of Rome's engagement with the world. This requirement responds to the inevitable, persistent tension between church and state, a reality confronting the faith ever since a Roman governor condemned Jesus Christ to death. The Church is concerned to protect two dimensions of its life: the institution, including the sacraments and ministry, and the internal, or spiritual, health of the faith.

One key diplomatic instrument developed to formalize the relationship between the Catholic Church and other sovereigns, especially to settle disagreement or conflict, is the concordat, a treaty backed by international law. Because Catholicism is the only world religion with a "sovereign personality," it's the only one with access to such a tool. The most dramatic medieval use of this approach was in the twelfth century (the Concordat of Worms of 1122) to settle a dispute between Rome and the Holy Roman Empire over who had the authority to name bishops and Church officials.[52] In modern history, the first major deployment of this type of agreement to halt a political campaign of dechristianization was in France in 1801.

Dealing with Napoleon to Save the Post-Revolution Church

One of the most extreme eras of pressure—in fact, terror—against the Catholic Church unfolded during the French Revolution. The Church became a major target, mainly for its wealth and proximity to the much-despised ancien régime, the monarchy and nobility. What began as a financial shakedown of Catholic assets—the Church owned about 6 percent of all national property—evolved into a brutal purge of the institution ranging from the forced expulsion of nuns from convents and the takeover of all ecclesiastical property to the conversion of churches into warehouses and the forced marriage, deportation, trial, or killing of clerics. The revolutionary assault on the Church, which began in 1789 and escalated until 1799, aimed to abolish it.

Yet, by 1801, First Consul Napoleon initiated negotiations for a concordat. He was an opportunist, motivated by the prospect of consolidating his rule and getting the Church back into the business of providing education and health services. The French leader considered it expedient to control Catholicism instead of trying to decimate it, as it proved impossible to suppress, especially in the countryside. The concordat he negotiated with Secretary of State Cardinal Ercole Consalvi over the course of eight intense months restored some traditional liberties to the Church and affirmed it as the faith of the majority of French citizens. The government reopened many churches. On the downside, priests became civil employees who had to swear allegiance to the constitution, the state assumed the authority to appoint bishops, and all Church claims for expropriated land were canceled. Most important, the Church was resurrected as a result of the 1801 concordat, which remained in force for over one hundred years.[53]

Martyrdom of Patience: Coping with Communism

When Vladimir Lenin decreed the separation of church and state in Russia, he unleashed a terror against the majority Orthodox Church and other Christians across the country. In comparison, Catholics constituted a small community in Russia. But as the Soviet Union's orbit increased to include countries with significant Catholic populations after World War II, the Vatican was invariably drawn into conflicts between the atheists in power and the faithful struggling to survive. In most countries where the Communist Party took over, Christian denominations suffered a fierce onslaught of persecution, ranging from the expropriation of property and the slaughter of clergy to bans on the practice of religion and efforts to create new national church structures independent of the Vatican.

In Catholic-majority countries such as Poland, Croatia, and Hungary, as well as in places where Catholics were few, such as Bulgaria, and where Catholic communities were regionally specific (Albania, Czechoslovakia, Romania, and Ukraine), worship went partially or entirely underground. In many countries, during the first few years of the Communist takeover, local Church leaders encouraged believers to fight back; bishops and priests were often engaged in resistance. Cardinal József Mindszenty, who took refuge in the American legation in Budapest for fifteen years after Soviet troops crushed the 1956 uprising, became the best known.

Under John XXIII, a new approach took shape, implemented under Paul VI. Not surprisingly, it centered on strategic, pragmatic diplomacy—and required extensive concessions from the Church. Known as the Vatican's version of Ostpolitik (a term first applied to West Germany's opening toward East Germany), its initial gesture came in 1964 when a Vatican representative, Msgr. Agostino Casaroli, entered Hungary from Austria, visited Cardinal Mindszenty at the US legation,[54] and a year later signed a partial accord with the Hungarian government following secret negotiations.[55]

Across the Eastern bloc, a cadre of Vatican diplomats discreetly opened lines of communication with Communist officialdom, not signing treaties everywhere, but finding a variety of ways to deal with the devil in the interest of preserving the institutional Church. As the guiding light of this effort, first for Paul VI and then for John Paul II, Casaroli negotiated a treaty with Yugoslavia in 1966, then full relations with the country in 1970. Between 1979 and 1990, Casaroli, by then a cardinal, served as John Paul II's secretary of state. He was the first Vatican official to visit the Soviet Union in forty-seven years and the first to step foot on the island of Cuba after the 1959 revolution. In 1989, he arranged the historic meeting between Russian president Mikhail Gorbachev and John Paul II at the Vatican.[56] Casaroli was fond of quoting John XXIII, who said, "There are enemies of the Church, but the Church has no enemies."

To date, Ostpolitik is controversial. Debate surrounds the question, did the strategy concede too much to an immoral force, or did it protect and preserve the Church, assuring its post-Communist survival?[57] Casaroli's memoir, *The Martyrdom of Patience*, published after his death, reveals that he knew all along what motivated the ideologues he dealt with: self-interest. Communist bureaucrats were keen to quiet the Church and its pope, to confuse international appeals for human rights, and to mislead their own people. But they never abandoned their intent to crush Christianity, and the concessions they offered were hardly meaningful in the diplomat's view. And yet it worked. The Catholic Church thrives across the former Communist landscape, where the dictatorship wound up in the dustbin of history.

A contemporary challenge comes from transnational efforts—including programs sponsored by the UN—to dictate norms to countries that uphold traditional values. The Church has long defended the right of national cultures to define themselves, an idea known as subsidiarity, or just sovereignty. Pope John XXIII made this point in *Mater et Magistra* (Mother and Teacher, 1961). Pope Francis makes this point whenever he rejects "ideological colonization."[58]

Evangelization

The flip side of the Catholic Church's fundamental mission of preserving the faith is to spread that faith anew: to evangelize and bring the message of Jesus Christ, who is the way, the truth, and the life,[59] to all corners of the earth. This means that any earthly priority or diplomatic objective not coherent with Sacred Scripture and Church teachings over time (the cumulative treasure known as the magisterium) is one that should probably be nixed. It is a universal, not national, Church. Because charity is a core Christian value, it is a necessary aspect of the Church's diplomatic activity too. In times of war, for example, it is sometimes the only way to manifest Christ's presence.

Diplomats Form a Priestly Cadre

A fundamental way the Catholic Church assures that its diplomatic initiatives are faithful is by requiring that all accredited diplomats be priests and by raising apostolic nuncios, delegates, and visitors—all titles for papal diplomatic representatives—up to the highest priestly rank: archbishop. Because each bishop is assigned a specific jurisdiction, archbishops in the diplomatic corps are assigned "titular sees" to govern, Church districts that no longer exist due to the vagaries of history. For example, Archbishop Christophe Pierre, nuncio to the United States, is titular archbishop of Gunela, an ancient Roman-Berber town in what is Tunisia today.

For the Vatican, diplomacy is a calling, not just a job or function. Theology related to sacerdotal authority considers all priests—each having been ordained by a bishop—to have a sacred power shared with Christ Himself, meaning that priests and bishops have identical authority when they act, as the catechism says, *in persona Christi capitis* (in the person of Christ the head), consecrating bread and wine into the body and blood, the Real Presence, of Jesus Christ in the sacrament of the Eucharist.

These details on priesthood are necessary to help explain three characteristics of Vatican diplomacy: the shared fellowship and identical sense of mission among its agents, the network's flexibility and power to incorporate important contributions from outside its cadre of trained personnel, and the relevance of a pastoral approach. Not only are virtually all Vatican diplomats priests, chosen for this ministry, but their shared education, ordination, and sense of mission give them a certain uniformity of purpose that strengthens the corps itself. Missionary priests, notably the Jesuits but other orders too, play a significant supportive role.

Shared formation means the entire clergy—from the College of Cardinals, who select a pope and, since 1917, must be priests before appointment; to the College of Bishops, the geographically assigned governors of the global Church; to regular priests, whether assigned to a parish or pledged to a religious order—might be called on to contribute to diplomatic goals, not just the nuncios and *monsignori* trained at the *Accademia*.

A recent case of successful diplomacy to moderate Zimbabwe's 2017 political crisis turned on the involvement of a priest not specially trained for the role. It helps illustrate how evangelization functions within the settlement of political conflict or tension—the meat and potatoes of diplomatic problem solving. This situation also offers an excellent example of how priests can become "interchangeable" parts in Catholic diplomacy, which helps explain the network's flexibility and elasticity.

A President Refuses to Leave and a Priest Gently Ushers Him Out the Door

After leading the country of Zimbabwe for thirty-seven years and crashing its economy during his tenure, President Robert Mugabe, age ninety-three, sparked nationwide panic by firing his vice president and longtime protégé Emmerson Mnangagwa in November 2017. What the president seemed to be plotting was the installation of his unpopular wife, known as "Gucci Grace," as the elderly head of state's successor.[60] Forty-one years younger than her husband, Grace's behavior and statements—at a rally days before the crisis, she gave a speech calling the vice president a "coup plotter"—suggested she was in on a plan to take charge.[61] Mnangagwa took refuge in South Africa, having received death threats.[62] In response to the odd events and mad rumors, Zimbabwe's army drove tanks into the capital city, Harare, and put Robert Mugabe under house arrest. The British and American governments warned embassy personnel to stay indoors until the situation stabilized.[63]

Over fifty thousand citizens filled the streets. Mugabe's own political party disowned him. Yet the president was defiant. Hoping to avoid violence, the generals running the country contacted Fr. Fidelis Mukonori, SJ, age seventy. They asked him to personally explain to Mugabe the military's grievances with the president, a baptized Catholic (although apparently lapsed, since he married Grace while his first wife was dying of kidney failure), and his ruling party.[64] Thus began the priest's role as the key negotiator between president and army. He also arranged for Mugabe and the former vice president, known as "Crocodile," to make peace by phone. The Jesuit had known Mugabe since the struggle for independence against minority-white rule and the colonial government of Rhodesia in the 1970s.[65] Mugabe was the first postcolonial prime minister, then president—running the country from 1980 on.

Catholic bishops were among the most vocal opponents of Mugabe's brutish policies over many years. Bishops publicly decried the regime for a murderous campaign against the Ndebele people in western Zimbabwe—the Gukurahundi massacres aimed at eliminating potential opponents of a one-party state.[66] Fr. Mukonori helped white farmers threatened with expropriation in the 1970s and Mugabe's political opponents in 2008 to find power-sharing solutions, so the Jesuit was hardly an uncritical actor.[67]

Calling on pastoral training and long friendship with the president's family, Fr. Mukonori was key in concluding the crisis by shuttling between the army and Mugabe's home for a week.[68] (Every night, he returned to Chishawasha mission, the Jesuit parish he led, some forty minutes outside Harare.) It took several days to convince the old man that a peaceful resignation was the best way to save his reputation, allow him to die in his homeland, and even keep him from jail. The priest negotiated an agreement that gave Mugabe immunity and a comfortable life in exchange for immediate resignation.[69] The calm conclusion led to Mnangagwa's return and his immediate succession as the next president.

Publicly, the priest portrayed resignation as a "success" for the longtime politician, even a relief for him.[70] What opened Mugabe to this religious intervention was clearly his personal faith story. He was born in Katuma, a Jesuit mission station, to a single mother who brought her son to Mass every morning. She enrolled him in a Jesuit school, where an Irish priest encouraged him to attend college and become a teacher.[71] According to Fr. Mukonori, the president always carried a rosary from his mother in his pocket. He also attended the funeral Mass of Pope John Paul II in Rome in 2005.

But it was the priest's intuitive diplomatic skill that was the crucial factor. His focus was on a solution that satisfied the need to find what Catholic doctrine calls the "common good" for all. In Fr. Mukonori's words, "I look for what I believe is just for individuals and the nation of Zimbabwe."[72]

Secular media widely credited the Jesuit with convincing Mugabe to resign;[73] the main Vatican news report on the transfer of power did not.[74] One might read the omission of Fr. Mukonori's role as indirect criticism. More likely, from the Church's perspective, the Jesuit was playing a normal pastoral role that all priests play, the role of helping someone in trouble, which is always a situation to treat with discretion, not a feat to use as public relations. Indeed, a Tanzanian book reviewer writing about Fr. Mukonori's 2017 memoir remarks on "the author's unmatched capacity to bring friend and foe to the negotiating table and to midwife common solutions."[75] This is exactly what the priest sees as his most important role: "My business is to get people together and to get them talking. . . . I engage government, I engage parties and I engage individuals—the president included."[76]

Pastoral Priority for All Priests

What Fr. Mukonori contributed in Zimbabwe was a form of pastoral diplomacy. Pastoral work is the bread and butter of a good priest's ministry. The word evokes pastures and fields for a reason: the Latin word *pastoralis* means "relating to a shepherd." Remember Psalm 23? "The Lord is my shepherd; / there is nothing I lack. / In green pastures He makes me lie down; / to still waters he leads me; / he restores my soul. / He guides me along right paths / for the sake of His name."[77]

In his pastoral responsibility, a priest, too, guides as the Lord does. This role does not entail dictating answers or telling people what to do. Rather, it involves awakening people to their own participation in God's truth—the power of love, the pointlessness of violence, the existence of objective moral reality, and the idea that suffering is shared with Christ on the cross. Some of these ideas don't sit well with contemporary Western culture, built to avoid suffering at all cost. A whole set of skills learned by Catholic clergy relates to "holding up the image of Christ in a healing way."[78]

Pastoral ministry is not just a contemporary face of Catholic theology; Church Fathers emphasized the idea of priests as spiritual doctors. St. John Chrysostom wrote a six-volume treatise on the priesthood in the fourth century. In book 4, he writes,

> [T]here is but one method and way of healing appointed, after we have gone wrong, and that is, the powerful application of the Word. This is the one instrument, the only diet, the finest atmosphere . . . with this we both rouse the soul when it sleeps, and reduce it when it is inflamed; with this we cut off excesses, and fill up defects, and perform all manner of other operations which are requisite for the soul's health.[79]

Priests patiently facilitate a process of bringing souls closer to the truth, to improve understanding or correct behavior. These skills are relevant to the talking and guiding and exhorting done by God's diplomats—and this is no imaginative stretch. Papal statements in the modern era regarding the purpose of training at the Pontifical Ecclesiastical Academy consistently sound the refrain: diplomacy is a pastoral ministry, and the most important skills to refine are the ones related to priesthood.

EXCELLENT DIPLOMATS MUST BE PROVEN PASTORS

Pope Paul VI graduated from the *Accademia* in 1926 and in 1931–1937 taught history there. As a Vatican diplomat, he spent seventeen years working in the Secretariat of State, mainly under Pius XII. Perhaps his greatest diplomatic accomplishment transpired inside the Church: he guided the Second Vatican Council to significant consensus, including a barrel of final documents that will shape the Church's life long into the future. Even before the council's curtains closed, he seized its call to meet the world by visiting Jerusalem and New York, the first pope to fly out of Rome—kicking off a style of papal diplomacy practiced to this day.

The most important attribute for God's diplomats in Paul's view was authentic faith. At a visit to the *Accademia*, he advised, "[U]se this period intensively for your moral and spiritual formation, to gain intimacy with Christ, to establish a living contact with Him which, far from slackening, will become more and more deep and consolidated."[80]

Thirty years later, Pope John Paul II (ordained by a Polish graduate of the *Accademia*, Cardinal Adam Sapieha, archbishop of Kraków[81]) made the connection between priest and diplomat even more explicit:

> If . . . the Gospel is present and firmly rooted in your lives it will tend to give a very precise content to your action in the complex field of international relations. In the midst of a world permeated by material interests that are often contradictory, you must be men of the spirit in the search for harmony, heralds of dialogue, the most convinced and tenacious builders of peace. Although the Church is present in the symphony of nations, she pursues only one concern: to make herself the echo of God's Word in the world in the defense and protection of the human person. . . . The world that awaits you is thirsting for God even when it is not aware of it.[82]

In his first papal talk to the students of the *Accademia*, Benedict XVI confirmed, "It is a unique mission that demands, as does every form of priestly ministry, the faithful following of Christ." But he highlighted the relevance of this stance to all people, not just Catholics: "[T]he witness of Pope John Paul II awakened a profound 'echo' in non-Christians too. . . . This confirms that when Christ is proclaimed by a consistent life, it speaks to the heart of all, even the brothers and sisters of other religious traditions."[83]

Always colorful, echoing Christ's promise to make his apostles "fishers of men," Pope Francis told aspiring diplomats assembled in the Apostolic Palace, "[D]o not fish in aquariums or farms, but have the courage to move away from the safety of what is already known and cast your nets and fishing rods out into less predictable places. Don't grow used to eating packaged fish." In moving, prophetic language, Francis also specified the "secret power" of the Church of Rome and why its mission is necessary:

> The charity of Christ is the true authority of the Church of Rome, there is no other. This is the only strength that renders her universal and credible to mankind and the world; this is the heart of her truth, which does not erect walls of division and exclusion, but makes herself a bridge that builds communion and calls the human race to unity; this is her secret power, which nourishes her tenacious hope, invincible despite momentary defeats.[84]

For four of the last five popes—those given sufficient time to accomplish meaningful diplomatic breakthroughs—the primary requirement they laid down for diplomats-in-training was to deepen their identity as priests. Why? To properly execute assignments that entail more ministry than profession, to avoid worldly temptations, and to serve as worthy peers and role models for brother bishops in host countries.

A HOLY DIPLOMAT TO HIS CORE: POPE JOHN XXIII

There's no better modern example of what the Church's "secret power" looks like in the field of diplomacy than the career of Angelo Roncalli, who became Pope John XXIII (1958–1963). He is the twentieth-century pope with the most extensive field experience in diplomacy (although he did not attend the *Accademia*), and his experience includes examples of representation, mediation, preservation, and evangelization. Fr. Roncalli's first step toward diplomacy came in 1921 when Pope Benedict XV called him to Rome to work in the Sacred Congregation for the Propagation of the Faith, coordinating various national efforts to support missionaries.[85]

Modeling Unity in Bulgaria

His first appointment as a papal envoy abroad came in 1925, when Pope Pius XI assigned him to Orthodox-majority Bulgaria to serve as apostolic visitor. Although the title sounds temporary, before leaving Rome, the forty-four-year old priest was consecrated archbishop[86] and posted to Sophia, where he remained for ten years. He shepherded a flock of some sixty-two thousand Catholics, often visiting their poor, remote villages on the back of a mule, and he built a thick network of connections for the Catholic Church with the Orthodox Church. He implemented the pope's goal of cultivating local clerical talent (he started a seminary where both Latin and Oriental Catholic priests were trained, in two sections), weaning the Catholic community from reliance on and deference to outside leadership, especially from the French.

Nine days before Roncalli arrived in Sophia, a bomb exploded in the Orthodox cathedral during the prime minister's funeral—he had been assassinated—resulting in 150 deaths and hundreds injured. These were hairy days in the Balkans, with various external powers seeking to fill the void left by the retreat of the Ottoman Empire. As an apostolic visitor, Roncalli had no diplomatic status—he was just the first personal papal envoy in hundreds of years, arriving at a particularly tense historical moment. He immediately established his orientation toward unity and caring: Sophia's leading hospital was a Latin Catholic one. Roncalli and the women religious staffing the hospital offered medical and financial care to everyone, including Orthodox priests. He visited the wounded across the city. He quickly established the Church's identity with those in need. He represented the Church by living as a witness to God's love.

Mediating Blockade in Greece

His next appointment was as apostolic delegate to Turkey and Greece, based in Istanbul. Again, he did not have diplomatic immunity because the Holy See had no formal relations with either country, but his responsibilities were all those of a nuncio. Roncalli used his office to protect the most persecuted people. With wit, reason, and temerity, this diplomat exhibited skills grounded in pragmatism, a Vatican hallmark when coping with evil. He also exemplified mediation in negotiating a humanitarian response for people suffering a severe military blockade.

Following the invasion of Greece by Italy and then Germany in 1941, the British navy set up a naval blockade to pressure its enemies, but the blockade quickly led to famine in a country dependent on food imports. Roncalli pressed Italian and German ambassadors in Ankara to allow medicine and food into the country. Then he drove to Sophia and flew to Athens where he collaborated with Orthodox metropolitan Damaskinos of Athens—no minor thing since the Catholic and Orthodox Churches still functioned under mutual excommunication. Damaskinos gave Roncalli a letter for Pius XII requesting his intervention with the British government to allow wheat, food, and fuel through the blockade. The metropolitan's archives reveal that Roncalli also transmitted letters to the Greek government in exile, detailing the crisis and activating worldwide charitable efforts.[87] So well respected by the nation, Damaskinos was appointed regent of Greece when it was liberated in 1944. The wartime collaboration between Roncalli and the Greek Orthodox leader contributed to improved relations between the two Churches.

Protecting Jews in Istanbul and in Transit

Roncalli's other assignment was Turkey. Neutral during the war, Istanbul and Ankara were cities of great wartime intrigue; Istanbul was also an important base for groups trying to help Jews escape Nazi-occupied Europe. Roncalli became deeply involved in these efforts. Using Vatican diplomatic couriers, he transferred immigration certificates for Palestine (given to him by the Jewish Agency of Palestine's local office) to Catholic contacts in Budapest, mainly Archbishop Angelo Rotta, apostolic nuncio to Hungary

(1930–1945),[88] and the Sisters of Zion, a religious order founded by Jewish converts to Catholicism with convents in both Turkey and Hungary.

The future pope also collected blank baptismal certificates from sympathetic priests and sent them to Hungary. These documents were secretly distributed to Hungarian Jews to help them flee or to protect them from being shipped to death camps. By his own count, he saved, minimally, twenty-four thousand people through these measures.[89]

Roncalli used the relationships he had built up over decades to protect Jewish people. Some Hungarian Jews made it to Bulgaria, which was occupied by Germany. Hitler ordered the king to send them back to Hungary. Roncalli beseeched his friend, King Boris III, to resist. Boris's wife, Giovanna, was an Italian Catholic, daughter of King Victor Emmanuel III, and Roncalli had helped the couple get papal permission for a mixed marriage.[90] As well, Roncalli had been posted in Bulgaria for ten years before his Turkish assignment, so he knew them personally. While the royals were disposed to protect the fifty thousand Bulgarian Jews, the priest helped stiffen their resolve regarding the Hungarian refugees. Roncalli's office then completed transit visas allowing the refugees safe passage to Palestine.[91]

In another case, when a ship crossing the Black Sea from Constanța, Romania, with 739 Jewish refugees (including 250 orphans) was stopped by the Turkish navy for return to Romania, it was Roncalli who coached the Romanian ambassador to get permission from Ankara in order to free the ship and let it proceed to Palestine.[92] With the Holy See's permission, Roncalli appealed to political leaders on behalf of Jews in Bulgaria, Croatia, France, Germany, Greece, Italy, Romania, Slovakia, and Transnistria, according to the International Raoul Wallenberg Foundation in its "Roncalli Dossier."[93] Presented in 2011 to Yad Vashem (Israel's official memorial to Holocaust victims), the investigation concluded that the Catholic "was one of the most remarkable rescuers of the 20th century."[94] It recommended him for the title "Righteous Among the Nations," reserved for those who personally intervened to save Jews.

One of the most interesting stories about Angelo Roncalli's extensive record of personal charity is not in the Roncalli Dossier because it involves Hitler's ambassador to Turkey, Franz von Papen. As a Catholic, von Papen attended Archbishop Roncalli's Sunday Mass; they became friendly. Both feared that if Turkey joined the Axis powers, the Soviet Union would invade. When Hitler provided money to von Papen to entice Turkey to side with the Nazi cause, the ambassador passed the money to Roncalli instead. And twice a week the archbishop donated it to a newspaper editor who was providing food to Jewish refugees living in Istanbul. The priest who interviewed von Papen as part of the detailed research for Pope John's sainthood cause observed, "That was the sort of diplomat Roncalli was,"[95] capable of subverting enemy dollars to pay for victims' needs. None of Roncalli's activities are imaginable without approval from Rome.

Practicing the Diplomacy of the Priesthood

In December 1944, Roncalli was abruptly uprooted from Istanbul and assigned to serve as apostolic nuncio to France. It was an unexpected elevation, after the nuncio in Buenos Aires, Argentina, declined. Roncalli was compelled to rush to Paris in time to appear on January 1, when the dean of the diplomatic corps, by tradition the nuncio, had to deliver a New Year's message to all the ambassadors accredited to France, in front of the nation's leader. Roncalli arrived on the last day of December and delivered the January 1 greeting in front of General Charles de Gaulle. American troops had liberated Paris in August 1944. Had Roncalli missed the event, the Soviet ambassador was next in line based on seniority; the Holy See was not going to let the Soviets have that honor.

Roncalli's assignment entailed relentless conflict resolution as postwar France tried to recover its equilibrium following Nazi occupation. An atmosphere of accusation made the peacemaker's job especially valuable. His own notes show he was self-aware that his humility was an asset: "To be 'meek and lowly of heart' [Matthew 11:29] is still the brightest glory of a bishop and a papal representative. I leave to everyone else the superabundant cunning and so-called skill of the diplomat and continue to be satisfied with my own *bonhomie* and simplicity of feeling, word, and behavior. In the end, all turns out for the good of those who are faithful to the teaching and example of the Lord."[96]

In France, Roncalli again acted to serve the most despised, this time on the German side. Two years after the German surrender, 250,000 German prisoners of war were still held in French camps. The nuncio pointed out to the government the "sacred rights" of incarcerated soldiers. He encouraged French bishops to protest too. Finally, the government relented when a pastoral letter portrayed the issue as a matter of conscience for all French Catholics.[97] Having successfully healed divisions within the postwar French Catholic community, the Italian prelate was called home. Nine years had passed since he rushed from Istanbul to Paris. At age seventy-two, Roncalli was given a cardinal's hat and the watery See of Venice. He assumed this was his last, beautiful assignment.

Talking to a fellow priest in Venice, Cardinal Roncalli summed up his attitude toward the twenty-eight years he had spent representing Rome in distant lands: "They say I am a diplomat," he mused. "The Church's only diplomacy is that of the priesthood. This is the diplomacy that I have always practiced."[98]

Pope Francis Points Diplomats toward John XXIII

Two months into office, Francis assembled students and professors from the *Accademia* to discuss their ministry, then met for the first time with papal nuncios from around the world. To both audiences, he described Pope John XXIII as an exemplary diplomat mainly because he avoided "spiritual worldliness"—a self-serving orientation toward recognition—cultivating instead "inner freedom" through prayer and daily devotion to Christ.[99] Francis quoted with admiration from the memoir *Journey of a Soul*, drawn from Roncalli's journals, in which he wrote, "I have always held that for clerics the so-called 'diplomacy!' must always be imbued with a pastoral spirit; otherwise it counts for nothing, and makes a holy mission ridiculous."[100]

Both elected in their late seventies, the most fundamental similarity between Francis and John XXIII is this characteristic: Angelo Roncalli brought a pastoral spirit to diplomacy, then to Rome; Jorge Bergoglio, too, is a pastor first and foremost.[101]

Roncalli's diplomatic background made him especially sensitive to the idea that since the Church's mission is universal, it does not identify with any one culture. Everywhere he went, his ability to solve problems based on Gospel truth was welcomed. Yet, paradoxically, the mission also adheres in respect for the importance of local culture. In 1936, Roncalli said Christmas Mass in Turkish; he was an early proponent of using vernacular in the liturgy to communicate better with the faithful—a practice spread universally as a result of the Second Vatican Council.

By convening the council just three months into his pontificate, Pope John planted in the Church's heart the wisdom he had gained based on twenty-eight years in Orthodox, Muslim, and Catholic national settings: the insight that what people have in common is so much greater than what divides us; that pluralism is a given, and ecumenical cooperation is a fruitful way to protect peaceful coexistence; that the Church must serve the world from a position of mercy through love and charity;[102] and that humanity is threatened by the malignant obsession with power, which everywhere drives a military reflex. These understandings are upheld by Pope Francis.

3

Education of a Diplomat

The world that awaits you is thirsting for God even when it is not aware of it.

—Pope St. John Paul II, address to the community of the Pontifical Ecclesiastical Academy, April 26, 2001[1]

A BLOODY CENTURY CALLED FORTH A DIPLOMATIC SCHOOL

It is a bloody hinge that swings modern Europe into sight: a sprawling, savage conflict, the Thirty Years' War (1618–1648). The war—more than eight million died as a result of fighting, famine, and disease, including 20 percent of the German population[2]—got its start in slapstick: Lutherans gathered at Prague Castle and, angry at the Catholic emperor's denial of their right to build new churches, tossed three imperial emissaries out a window.

The defenestrated officials survived (saved, it seems, by a mound of manure), but the feud crystallized a widespread sensibility: Protestant strongholds and ministates, mainly in Central Europe and Germany, did not want to be controlled within the sprawling, fractured Holy Roman Empire, loosely ruled by the Catholic Austrian Habsburg dynasty. The Protestants gained support from the Dutch Republic, Denmark, and Great Britain. Emperor Ferdinand II turned to Catholic allies, mainly Bavaria, Spain, and the papacy.

Decades of mass destruction finally led to peace talks involving 109 parties, but belligerents refused to stay in the same place. So Catholic delegates congregated in Munster while Protestants based themselves in Osnabrück, two towns in the Duchy of Westphalia. Intermediaries conveyed proposals between the towns by horseback. No surprise, it took four years to conclude two treaties.

France emerged as the critical actor and, in a sense, the ultimate victor—under the guidance of two turncoat cardinals running Bourbon foreign policy, Cardinal Armand Jean du Plessis, first Duke of Richelieu (the legendary Cardinal Richelieu), and his protégé, Cardinal Jules Mazarin (born in Italy as Giulio Raimondo Mazzarino). The two, who aggressively promoted France's national interest, shared the conviction that central government should have strong authority over its territory and allied France with Protestant powers to keep Austria on its heels.

The Catholic Church lost all property in Protestant-majority regions. Most "free cities" in the Holy Roman Empire were permanently ceded too. Calvinism was now legal.[3] Worst of all, secular negotiators made decisions about the disposition of archbishoprics, bishoprics, and abbeys, which in the Church's view they had no business discussing. Some of the jurisdictions had functioned as ecclesiastical states![4]

A heightened investment in diplomacy helped the Holy See continue its influence after the Westphalian treaties kick-started a world of sovereign fiefs in 1648.

A NEW FORM OF ARMY: PRECISION DIPLOMATS

The Peace of Westphalia represented landmark accomplishments: it slowed a barbaric state of perpetual war in Europe and eventually produced a stable state system of independent powers that frames international reality to this day. For Rome, it highlighted a trend to curb and needs to fill. First, the pope needed to restrain rogue prelates, such as Cardinal Mazarin, who proved a boon to the four-year-old king he advised[5] but disloyal to the Holy See—the patron who sent him to Paris as a nuncio in the first place. Second, with new state entities, more competition, and, invariably, emerging challenges around Church property and prerogatives, the Holy See had to deploy more papal representatives.

The Holy See's response to the ruination and new world order ushered in by the Peace of Westphalia was a new diplomatic school, the Pontifical Academy of Ecclesiastical Nobles, the world's oldest training institute for professional diplomats, established in 1701 (and renamed in 1939). Pope Clement XI (1700–1722) authorized Abbot Pietro Garagni to establish the academy and asked him to draft regulations. The rules reveal a highly selective school prioritizing history, languages, and Catholic ministry, much like the school today. Prospective students had to be at least twenty-one years old, with fine reputations and good manners. Despite the school's name, admission was not restricted to aristocrats: candidates had to be "of noble birth or at least qualified of some ecclesiastical dignity."

The school could not have launched without papal support, and Pope Clement XI, born Giovanni Francesco Albani, was an enthusiastic booster.[6] He assumed the papacy with two major interests well formed: scholarship and diplomacy. His Jesuit education gave him early—and sustained—exposure to the way faith, united with reason, propels a search for order in the universe. For thirteen years, Albani served as secretary of papal briefs, managing sensitive communication with foreign leaders, so he had a keen sense of the accomplishments—and idiosyncrasies—of Vatican diplomacy. His personal experience alone made the inauguration of a Vatican diplomatic school appealing.

Unfortunately, the *Accademia*'s birth years coincided with the outbreak of another pan-European war, the War of Spanish Succession, embroiling the Holy See in fierce political machinations. Buffeted by international affairs he could hardly influence let alone control, Pope Clement XI continued to foster the new diplomatic school. He shepherded the endeavor by bestowing money, providing spiritual leadership, and assuring space.

Evidence of the *Accademia*'s universality was baked into its nature: more than half the class of students entering in 1706 came from beyond Italy. They represented some of the major belligerents in the ongoing war: Austria, England, France, Ireland, Poland, and Portugal. One fundamental metric reflects how consistent the *Accademia*'s profile has been. In the first twenty years (1701–1721), 196 students graduated, and the average class size was ten; in the first twenty years of Pope John Paul II's pontificate (1978–1998), 195 students were educated at the school, with an average class size of ten.

In that first generation of graduates was one future pope: Carlo della Torre di Rezzonico of Venice, who arrived in Rome to attend the *Accademia* at age twenty-one. Like many graduates, he was sent to govern jurisdictions in the Papal States. As Pope Clement XIII (1758–1769) he was famously generous, distributing a personal fortune to the poor. Unfortunately, the pope closed the school due to precarious funding. For eleven years it was virtually abandoned, with tenants, then random pilgrims, taking occupancy—and removing everything of value down to the lead pipes and floorboards. The school revived in 1775 but was again forced to close in 1798 when French troops overran Rome and kidnapped Pius VI who died abroad. Fortunately, the school bounced back five years later.

WHO GOES THERE? EDUCATING HOLY SEE DIPLOMATS

The school's glory days would not come until after the 1870 reunification of Italy, which stripped Rome from the Holy See and made the pope a self-designated prisoner of the Apostolic Palace. Fortuitously, the first pope to cope with dispossession and landlessness for his entire pontificate was an *Accademia* graduate. Leo XIII (1878–1903) understood diplomacy's potential as he sought to reshape the Church's global mission. Unwilling even to travel across town to the Basilica of St. John Lateran, where the pope presides as bishop of Rome, Leo and his successors rediscovered the value of a cadre of anointed representatives.

Leo actively cultivated the best and brightest as a way to, literally, extend his reach. He cemented the contemporary importance of the Vatican diplomatic corps as the infrastructure of papal influence not only to secular governments but also to far-flung Catholic parishes throughout the world. A student he cultivated wrote one of the few memoirs recounting the typical experience of a student at the *Accademia*.[7]

In 1885, Francis MacNutt, an American from the midwestern heartland, was brought before Pope Leo XIII's throne. Questioning in French the Harvard graduate who was kneeling at his feet, the pope sized the young man up as a potential *Accademia* candidate. Leo concluded that he needed Italian instruction before he was ready, if he was ready, for admission. Two years later, with papal approval secured, MacNutt entered the school, located in a fourteenth-century palazzo adjacent to the Pantheon. MacNutt joined a class of eight students,[8] just the third American in the school's storied history. Most of his colleagues were already priests.

To this day, priests selected for the *Accademia* are referred by bishops and others close to the Roman Curia. "We want candidates to be thoroughly presented by people who know them, not someone who is simply attracted to this way of life and decides, 'I want to spend my life traveling,'" explained Cardinal Justin Rigali, a 1966 graduate of the *Accademia* who served as its president from 1985 to 1989.[9]

Even though he lacked ambition for the very career he was being groomed for, Francis MacNutt possessed two other traits that remain critical attributes for admission to the school today: a high degree of self-direction in faith and a personality at once worldly and humble. Raised in a Presbyterian family, MacNutt wandered alone into a Catholic Church at age six and sought instruction for the next fourteen years, eventually receiving First Communion at age twenty on Easter Sunday in the Sistine Chapel. Second, he was comfortable in the world, talented with languages, and culturally curious, yet he was satisfied to let older mentors propel him into unusual scenes and elite circles. In three words: competent yet deferential.

Despite possessing the right stuff, Francis MacNutt abandoned the *Accademia* after two years when he realized he lacked a priestly vocation—a calling to dedicate his life to the Church. Sent back to Pope Leo XIII, kneeling before the same throne, MacNutt easily convinced the pope to release him, but Leo was concerned to protect the young man, and the school, from the appearance of failure. To facilitate a scandal-free exit from Rome, MacNutt was entrusted with packages to deliver to Paris and Brussels. After serving as a messenger, he made his way back to the United States.[10]

BUILDING A VATICAN DIPLOMAT: INTERNATIONAL LAW, HISTORY, LANGUAGES, AND NEGOTIATING SKILLS

Depending on the credentials a matriculating student has when he enters the *Accademia*, his course of study usually lasts two years, although it can take up to four. All are ordained priests. That means they arrive with a degree in theology and a tremendous amount of shared knowledge, from familiarity with Latin to training in how to console the dying.

The *Accademia*'s specialized program covers international law, including treaties and conventions; diplomatic history, especially the role the Church has played; multilateral institutions; contemporary economic and social questions in the context of Catholic teaching; techniques of negotiation; and diplomatic style and writing. Information technology is required, minimally because Vatican communication is digitally encrypted.

Two new courses were added for the 2020–2021 academic year: (1) the pathology of pedophilia, its social and ecclesial impact, and relevant canonical norms, and (2) the plight of migrants and their impact on Church life in various parts of the world.[11] The big news for matriculating students in 2020 was the addition of a required "missionary year" as part of each diplomat's formation. Four months into the job, Archbishop Joseph Marino from Birmingham, Alabama, told Vatican News that Francis gave him the directive in an audience, with details regarding the assignment process to be worked out. As Marino explained, the missionary experience is a spiritual one that tracks with Francis's vision of a Church going outside itself. Since his diplomats are his eyes and ears, they should experience the pope's "dream of a missionary Church," said the American prelate, who expects the plan will yield "even more enthusiastic diplomats for the Holy See."[12]

Major emphasis is placed on language fluency. Besides a native language plus Italian, graduates master two additional languages, typically English, French, German, or Spanish, but increasing emphasis is given to Asian languages, Arabic, and the tongues of Eastern Europe. To complete the program, candidates must pass an oral and written exam that takes the form of a written report on a specific subject, then a verbal defense of the analysis.[13]

But it is impossible to understand the school based on a course list, explains Cardinal Rigali. "The preparation in the *Accademia* isn't just a matter of curriculum. It is, above all, preparation for a life that is very intense, very involved." The dual nature of the nuncio's assignment makes it especially demanding: the nuncio is the Holy See's representative to the government and to the local Church. In the face of the government, the Holy See's representative must "make known, relay, and communicate the Church's position on all aspects of the social doctrine," explained Rigali, who said Vatican diplomats often face secular representatives with no clue about Church positions.

"To educate [authorities] well, you have to be well educated. At the *Accademia*, preparation involves reading, learning, penetrating the teachings of the Church on social questions—whether religious freedom or the importance of maternal and child health—and seeing how intimately related to the Gospel these doctrines are," he went on.[14]

Synthesizing information is a key function for every papal representative. Preparing reports on political trends and church-state relations on the one hand, then on internal Church issues and briefs on bishop candidates on the other, means the job is writing intensive. Rigali taught the course "*Stylo Diplomatico*," diplomatic style, which aims to "make sure you tell the Holy See what the Holy See wants to know. What is the Holy See interested in? Many, many things. What is going on in the country, of course, but also what the bishops are doing, the priorities of the local Church, missionary activity—the local Churches have to be understood" by Rome, especially when it comes to appointing new bishops, who constitute Church leadership in each country.

The pope closely guards this prerogative, although historically many compromises have been made to allow involvement by secular government in the selection process.[15] The nuncio plays a key screening and research role, preparing files on candidates for consideration. Being concise is one attribute of diplomatic style. Nunciatures generally submit a "short report" followed by a more analytical "long report" on any significant topic.[16]

Ideally, as many Vatican diplomats are quick to point out, the nuncio or apostolic delegate is constantly working in concert with the Secretariat of State, as well as with the relevant curia dicasteries. "They [nuncios] aren't making this up as they go along," Rigali reminded me. "They are constantly instructed and constantly informing the Holy See about what is unfolding." Sometimes, though, politics is a wild horse that jumps the harness, as we saw in the example of the standoff in Panama between the US military and the nunciature in chapter 1. As Cardinal Rigali emphasized, deep knowledge of Church diplomatic history *and* the history of church-state relations in the host country is essential.

At the *Accademia*, instructors use case studies—positive and negative examples of negotiation and representation in action—to exemplify valuable principles and techniques. To illustrate how case studies are employed in the curricula, I summarize four examples in order to demonstrate the lessons drawn out by *Accademia* professors.

DIPLOMATIC CASE STUDIES: FORESTALLING CONFLICT AND ADVANCING CHRISTIAN VISION . . . OR NOT

1. Peace at the China-Russia Border: Treaty of Nerchinsk, 1689

Priests and missionaries have been recruited to advise temporal authorities through the ages because they are well educated and typically disinterested in power or wealth per se. This was certainly true in China, where Jesuits, beginning with Fr. Matteo Ricci in 1601, became the first Westerners invited to the imperial court. Ricci shared knowledge, especially on astronomy, science, and geography. An unlikely example of successful faith-inspired negotiations emerged from this relationship. Far from the European spotlight, two enterprising Jesuit missionaries, mathematicians working in the Forbidden City, were given a task by the Kangxi Emperor (1661–1722): he asked them to negotiate an agreement with Russia to settle China's northeastern border.

Russia had been expanding east across Siberia, and by 1665 traders built a fort on the Amur River, replete with an Orthodox monastery. Twenty years later, the Qing dynasty, which considered the region part of Manchuria its ancestral lands, used force to oust the Russians—who simply returned to the settlement within a year. The emperor wrote to Moscow demanding the Russians leave the Amur River area and negotiate. Talks were scheduled for summer 1689.

The emperor sent several thousand soldiers but no mandarins. Instead, he assigned the Jesuits, Frs. Thomas Pereira and Jean-François Gerbillon.[17] The major reason was to have a common language with the Russians: Latin. On the other side, an adviser to Peter the Great led the Russian team, supported by detailed instructions from Moscow, 500 regular soldiers backed by 1,500 Cossacks, an Orthodox priest, and a Polish Russian speaker to serve as a Latin translator.[18]

The two sides practiced humility to set an atmosphere of mutual respect. To signify the sense that neither side was more important than the other, they lived in tents side by side during negotiations. They honed in on core objectives, not mutually exclusive. Discussions uncovered trade as the common ground. For their part, the Russians had concluded that the Amur River settlements were virtually indefensible. So, in exchange for a point in the treaty confirming that the Chinese were willing to exchange goods, the Russians gave up territory north of the Amur River and agreed to destroy the embattled settlement.

The six-paragraph agreement (in Latin, Russian, and Manchu) established the Sino-Russian border along natural geographic markers. Its success can be measured in its longevity: it was respected for the next 170 years. The straightforward treaty was the first between the two powers, even, it seems, the first between a European nation and an Asian one. As a sign of his esteem for this and other contributions, the emperor rewarded Gerbillon with an edict granting Christians religious freedom in the kingdom.[19]

The 1689 Treaty of Nerchinsk is a positive example of Christian negotiations. First, it is an elegant solution to a political conflict that had already entailed military engagement (and death as a result). By precisely focusing on a specific, beneficial relationship—land for trade—the Jesuit negotiators were able to gain a major concession from the Russians, evacuation of disputed territory, which satisfied the main objective of their Chinese patron. Second, they used the encounter to strengthen relations between the two sides, who were both able to return to their respective governments and report success. Finally, they used Christian principles in key ways—for example, stipulating that all prior issues that divided the countries be forgotten, that is, forgiven—therefore remaining faithful to their calling.

The ultimate upshot of the treaty was peace, a just Christian goal. It also gained points for the Jesuits toward their longer-term objective of achieving imperial acceptance for Catholic Christianity.

Lessons

- Jesus teaches that all people are sons and daughters of God, so Christian negotiators emphasize equal standing rather than framing conflict as national competition.
- The willingness of priests to help settle a border dispute—a conflict that provoked military clashes and death—reflects the biblical commitment to peacemaking. It also shows the Church's comfort with political authority per se. Political authority is divinely sanctioned by God, responsible for advancing the common good. So it is rational for Christians to aid these positive government efforts.
- The treaty itself is short and to the point, with clear description of a process for resolving disputes in the future. It conforms to classic rules on diplomatic practice.
- Although not trained at the *Accademia*, the missionaries who negotiated the Treaty of Nerchinsk exemplify how seminary and the Jesuit charism are excellent preparation for diplomacy.

2. From No Cards to Royal Flush: A Secretary of State at the Congress of Vienna, 1814–1815

A momentous accomplishment in modern Vatican diplomatic history was the performance of Secretary of State Cardinal Ercole Consalvi at the legendary Congress of Vienna. Consalvi, who spent six years at the *Accademia*, served two popes, Pius VI (1775–1799), well known for condemning the French Revolution, and Pius VII (1800–1823). Incredibly, both were kidnapped (in 1798 and 1809, respectively) by troops under Napoleon Bonaparte's command. Pius VI died in exile, just six weeks after arriving in France; Pius VII, a monk, survived a five-year sojourn, returning triumphantly to Rome when Napoleon was finally defeated in 1814 by British and Prussian forces.

The Bourbon dynasty was restored to the throne, and Napoleon was sequestered on the Isle of Elba. The treaty ending hostilities was generous because other major powers did not want an unstable France. Because the Holy See was not a party to the negotiations, it lost out: Avignon, long a papal property, was simply awarded to the Bourbons. By the time Consalvi got to Paris, the gifting of Avignon was a fait accompli.

But a peace congress with a wider scope was scheduled later that year in Vienna. Consalvi immediately began lobbying for the Holy See's main goal: restoration of the Papal States. These lands were considered an existential necessity because receipts from their economic activity underwrote Rome's budget and assured Church independence. Regaining the land would be an uphill battle. Next to the four major victors—the Russian and Austrian Empires, England, and Prussia—the Holy See had few chips besides respect for the pope. Of the four powers, only one was Catholic, the Austrian Empire, and its foreign minister was rumored to covet the richest part of papal land for his sovereign or an ally.[20]

Consalvi's personality was a benefit to his mission. A refined, personable man with tremendous curiosity and few material needs, he was, among other things, an Anglophile and Anglophone, at a time when few Italians spoke English. After making contact with all the principal negotiators in Paris, he obtained a passport to London and became the first Roman cardinal to visit the United Kingdom in over two hundred years. He bonded with the nation's ruler, the prince regent,[21] who recognized that the papacy had gone out on a limb to protect the rights of British ships. The secretary of state left London confident of British support. In exchange, he committed the Holy See to advancing the cause of abolition by pressuring Spain and Portugal, the two most active European slave traders.[22]

In Vienna, Consalvi continued his strategy of meeting one-on-one with government principals. He met personally with the tsar of Russia, who said he admired the pope, wanted to visit Rome, and felt papal lands should return to papal hands. Another breakthrough for Rome came when Austria's foreign minister, Prince Klemens von Metternich, concluded that having the Holy See manage Italy's midsection was a stabilizing influence.

Not flagging as he was winning, Consalvi sent an Italian archivist and a famous sculptor to Paris to identify valuables stolen by Napoleon and deposited in various French institutions. On the sidelines of the congress and later from Rome, the cardinal successfully gained release of almost all the treasures with support from Austria, Prussia, and England. His new best friend, the British government, offered free shipping.[23]

The Final Act of the Congress of Vienna was signed on June 9, 1815. It awarded the Papal States to the Holy See but confirmed France's possession of Avignon.[24] Consalvi was not a signatory, in protest over Avignon, but he was satisfied with the results. Who did the cardinal credit with his achievements after a solid year of negotiations?[25] Pope Pius VII, of course. The diplomat wrote home, "Without the immense personal reputation of the Holy Father—and the view that is held about his sanctity and his character—it would have been useless . . . I repeat, useless, to have made claim and negotiated, and cajoled; or at least we should have gained very little."[26]

Lessons

- Consalvi was persistent. Despite being greeted with a loss at the start, he redoubled his efforts. Overall, his comportment reflected the four cardinal virtues given in the Bible: fortitude, justice, prudence, and temperance.
- His style of personal, one-on-one diplomacy allowed confidences. It was a priestly method, endorsed by classic diplomatic texts studied at the *Accademia*, especially François de Callières's *On the Manner of Negotiating with Princes*.
- He did not bargain as a political protagonist to benefit Catholic-majority entities such as Poland. He bargained to preserve what the pope considered essential for the Church's independence and respect. One rule in diplomacy is not to overreach.
- The overall effort represented by the Final Agreement was to limit war by creating a balance of power, especially hemming in France without humiliating or antagonizing its people.[27] Such an outcome is considered just—and thus Christian.

3. An "Unchristian" Settlement: Treaty of Versailles, 1919

Not all case studies examined at the *Accademia* feature the Catholic Church as a protagonist. Despite playing a significant humanitarian role in the Great War (as World War I was known)—including setting up a massive transnational communication system for prisoners of war on both sides of the conflict—the Vatican was locked out of the 1919 peace conference at Versailles for one main reason: Italy.

Italy entered the war in 1915 on the side of the Triple Entente (England, France, and the Russian Empire) based on a promise of gaining coveted territory if victorious. In the secret pact formalizing its commitments, the Italian government insisted on a clause blocking papal participation in any end-of-conflict negotiations.[28] The king feared the Vatican could take back Rome in any broad postwar agreement. The Church lobbied England and looked for support from smaller Catholic powers such as Spain and Belgium, but alas, Pope Benedict XV (1914–1922) was frustrated in his efforts to overtly influence the conditions of peace.

The Versailles final settlement struck the Holy See as fundamentally unchristian because it enshrined revenge.[29] The agreement humiliated Germany especially, in misguided and harmful ways.[30] First, it imposed massive financial reparations. Germany was obligated to pay $63 billion, or $995 billion in 2021 dollars.[31] It was forced to give up territory to Belgium, Denmark, France, Lithuania, and Poland. Colonies in Africa, Asia, and the Pacific were divided up among the victors.

The Vatican was especially perturbed at the inclusion of a "war guilt" clause, Article 231, blaming the conflict on "Germany and her allies." The premise was historically dubious and strategically counterproductive. Regarding the forced breakup of the Austrian Empire, leaving Germany unchecked on its Eastern border, the Vatican worried that the new, small successor states were vulnerable to intimidation by the Soviet Union.[32] Another fundamental flaw with the 1919 agreement was that it was written without the participation of Germany or its allies. German negotiators were faced with a fait accompli when they arrived in Paris. When they objected to specifics, the victors threatened to resume hostilities. The Holy See thought international ambition motivated the United States—not considered an admirable or moral stance.[33]

Benedict issued an encyclical less than a year later warning, "[T]here can be no stable peace or lasting treaties, though made after long and difficult negotiations and duly signed, unless there be a return of mutual charity to appease hate and banish enmity."[34] His words proved prophetic. Scholarly consensus today regards the punitive nature of the 1919 treaty as having sown the seeds for Germany's return to aggression twenty years later.[35]

Lessons

- Pope Benedict's objections were grounded in the Gospel, which replaces the logic of "an eye for an eye" with Christ's injunction to "love your enemies." Revenge should not be enshrined in a "peace" agreement. Dispute resolution requires forgiveness, again following Jesus. Neither compassion nor mercy was reflected at Versailles.
- The Holy See also saw the process of writing the treaty without participation of the defeated countries as unjust—a key concept in the Bible, the writings of Church Fathers, the magisterium, and Vatican II documents.
- The treaty's scope was too broad. It almost entirely redesigned Europe, multiplying instability instead of reducing it. This was not prudential, a highly valued Catholic intellectual and moral virtue.
- With a total of 440 articles, the text itself was too long. It triggered innumerable unintended negative consequences, thus violating common diplomatic practice and classic guidance.

4. Contemporary Battles: International Conference on Population and Development, Cairo, Egypt, 1994

In 1994, the United Nations convened an international conference in Cairo, Egypt, to set future strategy against global overpopulation, under the auspices of the United Nations Fund for Population Activities (UNFPA).[36] In the five years of pre-event meetings held around the world, this International Conference on Population and Development (ICPD) was clearly shaping up as the Woodstock of UN gatherings—big, left leaning, and era defining. The political Left has long dominated, and defined, the issue of "population control." In fact, the first world population conference was organized in 1927 by the League of Nations and Margaret Sanger, the American activist, eugenics booster, and socialist who founded the first American birth-control clinic.

The Cairo ICPD was perceived by the Holy See as moving toward a wide legitimization of abortion—even a new "right" to abortion—under the guise of improving health outcomes for women. It was part of a policy trajectory that had been evolving for at least twenty-five years.[37]

The pro-life position is pivotal in Catholic doctrine: life begins at conception, and the unborn child has dignity—and deserves protection—from the start. Sexuality is viewed in the context of marriage and family. Marriage is an institution created by God, as described in the book of Genesis: "God created man in his own image, in the image of God he created him; male and female he created them. And God blessed them, and God said to them, 'Be fruitful and multiply, and fill the earth and subdue it.'"[38] From this passage also flows the centrality of family, called the "original cell of social life" in the catechism.[39] So families have a God-given right to self-definition against state attempts to impose rules on size or beliefs.

To counter efforts by Western governments and nongovernmental organizations (NGOs), mainly from Europe and the United States, Cardinal Renato Martino and the Secretariat of State, with the personal engagement of Pope John Paul II,[40] developed a three-pronged strategy against objectionable language in ICPD draft documents. Church diplomats persuaded governments in more traditional countries of Latin America and Africa to side with the Vatican. They also approached both governments and religious entities in the Muslim world to make common cause in Cairo. One result was a lawsuit filed by Muslim lawyers against the Egyptian government for hosting a conference that abrogated Islamic moral principles.

Rome asked episcopal conferences for help identifying political allies who could be counted on to listen to Church arguments, at least to temper the provisions sought by more extreme delegates. The pope wrote to UN secretary general Boutros Boutros-Ghali, appealing to his Christian identity, to flag risks in the ICPD's direction. The pope even lobbied President Bill Clinton, who ultimately named Vice President Al Gore to head the US delegation, with guidance to collaborate with the Vatican, regardless of State Department negativity.[41]

The Church broadcast its objections publicly rather than relying on diplomatic back channels—a new approach. Rome was convinced that most governments, and most people, did not support extremist views. Thus, unusual public declarations were heard from Rome: the president of the Pontifical Council for the Family declared that the ICPD would provoke "the most disastrous massacre in history" if it legitimized abortion.[42] Holy See activism was widely, and negatively, noted by Western NGOs and media. The *New York Times*, for example, claimed the Holy See was bartering with extremists in Iran and Libya regarding the Cairo language.[43]

The result? At the biggest-ever world population conference,[44] the Vatican and its allies gained inclusion of thirteen hard-fought words in the twenty-year Program of Action: "In no case should abortion be promoted as a method of family planning," reads the first sentence of paragraph 8.25, a statement even the UN summary noted was key to consensus on other priorities. The Vatican found plenty of passages and assumptions morally corrupting, so it registered reservations, noted in the final text.[45] Alliances with some Muslim countries did not prove ironclad; countries such as Indonesia, Pakistan, and Egypt broke ranks on some contraception-related issues.[46] However, the principle of rejecting abortion as an acceptable form of family planning, let alone a "right," has been maintained by the UN ever since.

Lessons

- When it comes to defending fundamental principles, the Catholic Church will not defer to "friends." In fact, it is a mistake to imagine permanent alliances existing with any temporal government.
- Collaborating with other religions to block materialistic norms is smart strategy. The Second Vatican Council, in particular, recommended more openness toward Islam—a key to the 1994 Cairo outcome.
- Engagement of national and regional bishops' conferences in political goals such as influencing an international forum is effective—a practice only common since Cardinal Jean-Louis Tauran, an *Accademia* graduate, became secretary for relations with states (1990–2003).[47]
- Liberalism's commitment to a reading of individual freedom as endless personal choice is at odds with the Catholic doctrine of freedom to do good, a clash that will continue to surface, at the UN and elsewhere. The Left can be expected to challenge the Catholic Church's participation as a sovereign member of the UN community, as it did in the wake of this meeting.

SOURCES OF DIPLOMATIC PRINCIPLES

As the case studies illustrate, every diplomatic situation entails unique circumstances and requires an original assessment. That's why the Catholic diplomatic tradition has no one school or stock theory from which responses are readily drawn. Instead, five fundamental sources guide Vatican diplomats. Four are uniquely Catholic: Sacred Scripture, natural law, Catholic social thought, and the magisterium, prominently including key documents from the Second Vatican Council. The fifth source, classic diplomatic texts, I'll discuss in chapter 5.

Sacred Scripture

Diplomacy is encoded in Sacred Scripture, first, in Christ's specific attention to nations. The risen Lord directs his eleven remaining apostles to "make disciples of all nations . . . teaching them to observe all that I have commanded you."[48] The Holy Spirit's gift of speech "in different tongues" allows the disciples to communicate with people "from every nation under Heaven" on Pentecost,[49] an image for the universality of Christ's message and the absence of barriers for capable envoys. Describing God's judgment, Christ explains that He will examine "all the nations," not just individuals, for their service to the least among us.[50] Again, Christ establishes the relevance of his message for nations as well as individuals; both should adopt Christlike comportment.

Think of this: In the "judgment" scene of Jesus's passion as described in John's Gospel, Pontius Pilate, a Roman governor—a temporal tyrant, vested with civil authority—asks Christ if he is king of the Jews. The two have a civil exchange. Christ confirms he does have a kingdom, just not in "this world," setting up parallel authorities for believers to negotiate for millennia. As the two men part, Christ identifies Himself with truth while the governor walks away asking, "What is truth?" Truth, then, is what Christian diplomats help states to see.[51]

Perhaps more important than simply introducing public diplomacy as a legitimate activity for Christians, the Gospels give tips to mediators, reconcilers, and peacemakers. What to do when that proverbial "violent storm" swamps your position? Stay quiet. Remain in the ark of faith![52] Should hypocrites (with logs in their eyes) point out fault in others (with mere splinters in theirs)? No![53] One of the most moving diplomatic moments is when Christ stops a gang from stoning an adulterous woman. How does he defend her? By shifting the antagonists' focus from the woman who infuriates them to the ground, where Christ is drawing. He forces a pause in the conflict, redirecting attention to a larger question of justice, changing the dynamic by stepping into it, and thereby turning a passionate clash over passion into reflection.[54] That is diplomacy in a nutshell. The Bible provides tactics and constructive analogies in addition to moral positions.

Natural Law

While only those of the Christian faith consider the Gospels holy documents, the beauty of natural law for Vatican diplomacy is its status as Catholic and universal at once. It is undoubtedly a central strand in Church thought—developed in greatest detail by St. Thomas Aquinas following Aristotle—while providing an account of morality and the state, applicable to all cultures, all people, and all nations, everywhere and at all times. We find St. Paul anticipating the central idea of natural law in Romans:

> When the Gentiles, who do not have the law, by nature observe the prescriptions of the law . . . they show that the demands of the law are written in their hearts.[55]

According to St. Thomas Aquinas, God created the world, animated by an eternal law not entirely knowable by human beings. God imprinted men and women with reason and an ability to discern right from wrong. It is a moral compass, "written in their hearts," that flows from eternal law. Regardless of when people live or under what political regime, they know that being truthful, seeking God, and creating families are all rational goods. They know that killing, lying, and adultery are not. These are all examples of natural law.

People living together in any society require order, imposed by authority. St. Paul counsels the Romans to obey imperial authorities because "there is no authority except from God and those that exist have been established by God."[56] So God authorizes political power. In turn, the ruling authority is responsible for maintaining order and peace by governing justly. However, the state, and the variety of political forms it can take, is a manifestation of natural law because it is the product of human society's natural need for organization.

Aquinas explains:

> For where there are many men together and each one is looking after his own interest, the multitude would be broken up and scattered unless there were also an agency to take care of what appertains to the common weal.[57]

God's creation requires this arrangement. Tyrants, however, let private interests guide them; Aquinas is loath to invite revolution, but he recognizes the need to curb tyrants.[58]

While love of Christ should be the ultimate motivation for God's diplomats, their political assessments and solutions usually rest on the foundation of natural law, which applies to believers and nonbelievers equally.

Catholic Social Thought

The range of social issues considered legitimate for Vatican diplomats to worry about expanded with the pontificate of Pope Leo XIII (1878–1903). Responding to workplace inequality and reforms proposed by socialism, Pope Leo XIII released *Rerum Novarum* (Of New Things, 1891), outlining the Church's vision of employment and the workplace. The document is a key text, evoked by every pope since.

Rerum Novarum captures key principles of Catholic social teaching. Fundamental is the idea that each human being has fundamental dignity and deserves respect because each is created in the image of God and is capable of self-knowledge and freedom. The Church's work on behalf of justice and peace is aimed at protecting and promoting human dignity. The individual also has God-given rights—to education, sufficient food, health care, security, religious freedom, and to the fruits of his or her labor, interpreted as living wages and decent work conditions. If wealth is in the hands of a few, workers are reduced to slavery. For their part, workers must perform duties as well as possible, never injuring the employer's property or using violence to make a point.

Another axiomatic belief of Catholic thought is that human beings are social. Nothing should interfere with the families, faith communities, or associations that people are called to create. Private possessions, including property, allow individuals and their families to plan for the future and pass on inheritance. *Rerum Novarum* describes private property as preceding the existence of a state, and thus the state generally has no right to deprive people of property. That would be theft, violating God's commandments.

In a talk to Fortune 500 leaders, Pope Francis emphasized that each decision made by a corporate entity should be analyzed for its impact on individuals in order to "promote the centrality and dignity of the human person within our institutions and economic models." By focusing less on corporate profits and more on humanity's common good, business leaders will allow "each person to share in the resources of this world and to have the same opportunities to realize his or her potential."[59] Nothing in Pope Francis's message deviated from Leo XIII's writing some 125 years ago. Every pope since Leo has built on his legacy of social engagement. Beginning in World War I, diplomats were given assignments that tracked with this expanded interpretation of the Church's core concerns.

VATICAN II'S MISSIONARY IMPULSE AND CORE IDEAS

As explored in chapter 2, Angelo Roncalli's twenty-eight-year diplomatic career, and his unflagging ministry to all—Orthodox victims of famine, Jewish targets of genocide, and warehoused German prisoners, most of them Protestant—make more intelligible important aspects of the international Catholic assembly he announced just sixteen weeks after becoming Pope John XXIII. In convening the Second Vatican Council, Pope John had no interest in changing Church doctrine but in renewing its commitment to reach out to the entire world, advancing the truth of the Lord in a pastoral spirit.

The pope's goals are eloquently outlined in his opening address to the council. He begins by promoting unity—within the Church, between Christians, and among nations, on behalf of humanity. One passage in particular finds an uncanny echo in the stance of Pope Francis: "The Spouse of Christ [the Catholic Church] prefers to make use of the medicine of mercy rather than that of severity. She considers that she meets the needs of the present day by demonstrating the validity of her teaching rather than by condemnations."[60]

In the East and in the West, Roncalli encountered a miserable, aggressive, heartless world riven with division. He had personally done what he could, but he wanted the whole Church to have a response that was both confident regarding the validity and relevance of its wisdom and humble about the exclusivity of its answers. For the Church to pursue its transformative mission in the world, it needed all hands on deck: Vatican II repictured Church membership from a hierarchy of obedience to a communion of faithful, all called to holiness, all participating, including lay members.[61]

The ideas, themes, and spirit of evangelization that emerged from Vatican II had a profound impact on how Rome's diplomats perceived their mission.[62] *Gaudium et Spes* (The Church in the Modern World, 1965), the council's final document, depicts a Church serving the world, not standing apart and judging it.[63] This spirit immediately influenced papal practice too. Before the council even concluded, Pope Paul VI inaugurated international travel as a method of pastoral outreach by visiting the Holy Lands in 1964 and the United Nations in 1965.[64] (He was the first modern pope to leave Italy and quickly became known as the "Traveling Pope," visiting twenty countries—including the Philippines, where a deranged Bolivian artist dressed as a priest stabbed him in the chest at the airport—between 1964 and 1970.)

But the papal text from the Vatican II era most important to diplomacy is *Pacem in Terris* (Peace on Earth, 1963), the encyclical that Jesuit scholar Fr. Drew Christiansen called "the lynchpin of modern Vatican diplomacy."[65] *Pacem in Terris* was the direct product of a little-known diplomatic encounter: Pope John XXIII would not have written it if he had not played a role in the Cuban missile crisis the year before. The encyclical, and the events that inspired it, go a long way toward exemplifying how Holy See diplomacy infused with the spirit of the council should work.

THE POPE SPEAKS TO KENNEDY AND KHRUSHCHEV—THROUGH THE RADIO

Soon after Pope John set the council in motion, the fast-moving crisis over Soviet-installed missiles on the island of Cuba reached the Vatican. According to the pope's biographer, on October 23, 1962, after imposing a blockade to prevent Soviet ships from landing on the island, President John F. Kennedy asked his friend Norman Cousins, editor of the *Saturday Review*, to make contact with the Vatican.[66] That week, Cousins was attending a conference in Massachusetts with Soviet writers and scientists. Fortuitously, an acquaintance of Cousins, Fr. Felix Morlion, a Belgian Dominican priest with friends in the Apostolic Palace, was also at the conference. The priest contacted Rome after verifying with the Soviet visitors that the pope's engagement might be helpful.[67]

Pope John quickly responded to the request for a public intervention, urged negotiations, and began drafting a message, which was first delivered to the Soviet embassy in Rome, then as a message to the world via Vatican Radio:

"I beg heads of state not to remain insensitive to the cry of humanity: peace, peace. Let them do all that is in their power to save peace."[68] The value of the message was in allowing Khrushchev to look like a "lover of peace," rather than a coward for backing down. Six weeks later, Cousins met with President Kennedy, then flew to Rome to deliver a letter from Kennedy to Pope John, then flew to Moscow to meet with Khrushchev. It was the Soviet leader who confirmed the value of the Good Pope's involvement. He told a journalist, "During that week of the Cuban crisis the pope's appeal was a real ray of light. I was grateful for it."[69]

The pontiff's personal secretary, Monsignor Loris Capovilla, who was with the pontiff as the high-stakes intervention unfolded, says Pope John decided to write an encyclical on peace while he was working on the radio intervention, designed mainly for Khrushchev.[70] At the time, the pope was already gravely ill. In fact, he knew he was dying. "His old diplomatic habits began to operate once more: when you sense an opening, hasten to exploit it. . . . So keep up the pressure for peace," explains the pope's biographer, Peter Hebblethwaite.

Using Cousins as a messenger again, the pope even sent an advance copy of the encyclical translated into Russian to Khrushchev.[71] Pope John XXIII issued *Pacem in Terris* just two months before he died. It was received eagerly beyond the Church and published full length in secular newspapers around the world, including the Soviet newspapers *Izvestia* and *Pravda*. The council expanded on *Pacem*'s core ideas in longer documents released as products of Vatican II, for example on religious freedom.[72]

Not everyone was delighted with the encyclical, though. The US Central Intelligence Agency (CIA), for example, considered *Pacem in Terris* to be too conciliatory toward the Soviets. CIA director John McCone flew to Rome to meet with the pope to put him on notice. McCone said he was personally representing President Kennedy with the message: Communists can't be trusted, and the Vatican was playing with fire by dealing with them. Author and intelligence expert Gordon Thomas reports that American intelligence believed the Vatican was considering establishing diplomatic relations with the Soviet Union—that's why McCone was so charged up and spoke in a "blunt manner" for ten minutes straight in the deathly ill pontiff's face.[73]

When Pope John tried to explain his assumption that it is wise to talk to those in power, including Soviet leadership, the CIA director retorted that he was not in the Apostolic Palace to debate. Later, according to Thomas, McCone told colleagues Pope John was "softer on Communism than any of his predecessors."[74] Yet, President Eisenhower, Great Britain, France and the same Soviet leader were able to successfully negotiate the permanent neutrality of Austria in 1955, removing all troops occupying the country for ten years. Sergei Khrushchev, told me, in 2018, his father wanted to concentrate on economic reforms at home and complete the destalinization process.

One June morning in 2014, I was honored to attend Mass with Cardinal Capovilla and a few nuns who helped him in Sotto il Monte Giovanni XXIII, Italy—Angelo Roncalli's hometown, which changed its name to honor him. The gentle priest had been given the red hat five months before in an utterly unexpected, and unusual, gesture by Francis. It was interpreted as a selection honoring those who quietly serve, in a year that would witness the canonization to sainthood of Pope John, whom Capovilla served as personal secretary from 1953 to 1963. Although age ninety-eight at the time, the slender priest gave a vibrant homily to the twenty or so of us in the small chapel adjacent to his simple home.

After Mass, he invited me to his study to chat. Capovilla confirmed that the CIA director's warning in 1963 was surprisingly pushy and insistent, but he said Pope John was unmoved and calm. The pope simply replied that he did not share the US government's worldview. The priest told me in French, "After the war [World War II], the US expected the Holy See to behave as an annex, but the Holy Father dramatically changed the policy of non-dialogue with the Soviet Union."[75] The cardinal also said John refused to name American priests (with no diplomatic training) to diplomatic posts with US strategic interests—something Pope Pius XII did willingly immediately after World War II. (Three Americans were named as nuncios to Germany, Romania, and Yugoslavia, respectively, by John's predecessor. The US government pressed these priests into service and expected them to follow American direction. However, they remained faithful to Catholic teachings, and all three became critical of US foreign policy. Pope John even made one of them, Bishop Aloisius Muench, a cardinal.[76])

Pacem in Terris is addressed not just to Catholic priests and faithful, but to "men of goodwill." The text crystallizes key ideas, both ancient and modern, that provide enduring guidance for God's diplomats. It situates human rights in natural law, which states are obligated to respect. Pope John's final encyclical, together with the documents produced by the Second Vatican Council, reconceptualize the Church's engagement with the world in ways that directly relate to modern Vatican diplomacy. It renewed how the Church advances the core concepts of Catholic doctrine, concepts that the Holy See under Francis continues to advance today.

FUNDAMENTAL CATHOLIC PRINCIPLES RELEVANT TO DIPLOMACY

Political Authority as a Moral Force

Most know the famous injunction from Jesus Christ, "Render unto Caesar what belongs to Caesar and to God what belongs to God," a pithy description of the Christian's relation to the state.[77] The individual is obligated to respect and conform to legitimate civil authority, yet political order has obligations too. For one thing, as St. Thomas declares (echoing Aristotle), "[t]he chief concern of the ruler . . . is to procure the unity of peace."[78]

Political regimes must be held accountable to a higher law. According to the Catholic catechism, political authority must guarantee a well-ordered community without usurping individual freedom. It should be guided by moral law, which is transcendent, universal, absolute, and equally binding on all and which has its source in God. The state is obligated to enforce just laws that correspond to the dignity of the human being. The state should serve as a neutral arbiter, reconciling the interests of social groups, remedying injustice, and providing for the least among us. Its main responsibility is to promote the common good. The catechism even provides guidance on a citizen's right to conscientious objection and the right to resist.[79] Although theologians over time have declared certain political regimes preferable—St. Thomas Aquinas claimed, "[G]overnment of a king is the best"—no particular regime is considered superior apart from the concrete conditions it delivers. Vatican diplomats sometimes perceive their role vis-à-vis temporal government as nudging leadership to listen to their better angels.

Human Dignity

Fundamental to Catholic thought is a conception of human dignity flowing from the belief that each person is created by God in His image and is capable of self-knowledge and freedom—freedom to pursue truth, to enter into relationships, and to love God and others. The Church's work on behalf of justice and peace is aimed at protecting and promoting the dignity of each person. The individual also has God-given rights: to life and bodily integrity, to respect and freedom to investigate the truth, and to worship and marriage, as well as economic rights such as to the fruits of his or her labor, interpreted as living wages and decent work conditions, and to private ownership of property. The Church considers these "natural rights" granted to each by a divine moral order. Political authority has no right to prevent individuals from exercising those rights, since they are God given. It should be clear from this short explanation that, far from being an invention of the late twentieth century, the very idea of universal human rights is grounded in Christian theology. And human rights jurisprudence is built on the foundation of natural law.

Solidarity and Subsidiarity

Another axiomatic belief is that human beings are social. Nothing should interfere with the families, faith communities, or workplace cooperatives, for example, that people are called to create. The solidarity of people living and working together is an essential, meaning-producing activity that is also at the heart of worship. The Catholic Church developed the related principle of subsidiarity for the idea that activities should be done by the smallest, most decentralized unit possible, as opposed to large, complex organizations. Subsidiarity is a principle supporting local decision making, limited government, and personal freedom. The term was first used in Pope Pius XI's encyclical *Quadragesimo Anno* (On Reconstruction of the Social Order, 1931).[80]

Within the Church structure itself, parish communities have significant authority to shape their own activities, and the local bishop is vested with extensive decision-making power—contrary to the picture of the Catholic Church as a highly centralized hierarchy. John XXIII updated the application of subsidiarity in *Pacem in Terris*, explaining that although an entity such as the United Nations is necessary to help solve some universal problems, it should not take responsibilities away from an individual state or limit its sphere of activity.

Common Good

The Catholic principle of the "common good" says that individuals naturally aspire to participate in communities and contribute to a social whole—known as the common good. If the parts of the whole are harmed or hurting, then the whole is damaged and vice versa. This means that if any group within society is ostracized or discriminated against, society itself suffers. Attaining the common good, with material and spiritual dimensions, is the main purpose of civil authority, and attention to justice is the main way to get there. Pope John Paul II said quite bluntly to the diplomatic corps in Nairobi, "The state . . . must never lose sight of its principal objective, which is the common good of all the citizens without any distinction, and not simply the well-being of a group or a particular category."[81] The original formulation of these ideas was in *Rerum Novarum* (1891). It, too, rests on principles of natural law and moral order, requiring employers and employees to cooperate in defining a more humane work life. Limited state power is assumed in this moral order.

God's Hand Guiding History

Catholic theology sees God working through history. The Supreme Being did not kick things off and step away—Deism's watchmaker God. Implications of God's ongoing engagement in human events is a Catholic doctrine explored by Joseph Ratzinger, Pope Benedict XVI, who wrote his doctoral thesis on the matter. In his 1968 classic *Introduction to Christianity*, the great theologian explains:

> Christian belief is not merely concerned with the eternal, the "totally other." . . . On the contrary, it is much more concerned with God in history, with God as man. By thus seeming to bridge the gulf between eternal and temporal, between visible and invisible, by making us meet God as man, the eternal as the temporal, as one of us, it knows itself as revelation.[82]

This less appreciated idea has important implications for Vatican envoys— and really, for the pope himself. First, a diplomat's witness and interventions can advance God's plan, and he must do his best to discern God's will, but human limits prevent him from comprehending His infinite scope. So the inability to control outcomes is a fact of life.

Further, evil too is relentlessly operating in earthly affairs; this reality calls God's people to engage in temporal struggles on the political plane. This does not mean the Church should thrash out policy details or impose its vision of particular civil solutions. Lay Catholics can engage in specifics, while the Church and its diplomats function to defend human dignity and the common good, religious freedom and interfaith collaboration.

RELIGIOUS FREEDOM

A central biblical theme is that God is the Father of all, despite status or belief, gender or age—despite even sinfulness. Pope John XXIII particularly appreciated the godliness of all people regardless of religion. Spending nineteen years in Orthodox and Muslim countries honed his appreciation. He often spoke in admiration of Turkish Muslim fishermen he saw at dawn by the Bosporus saying morning prayers on the beach. "We were all made in God's image, and thus, we are all Godly alike," he explained.[83] The right to worship God according to one's conscience is a major category of human rights, highlighted in *Pacem in Terris* as specifically including worship in both public and private settings. The Second Vatican Council expanded this idea in the encyclical *Dignitatis Humanae* (On the Right of the Person and of Communities to Social and Civil Freedom in Matters Religious, 1965).[84]

INTERFAITH RESPECT AND COLLABORATION

The real-world implications of advancing religious freedom are explored in *Nostra Aetate* (In Our Times, 1965), on the relations between Catholics and non-Christian religions, issued by Pope Paul VI. The text is a milestone for Catholic-Jewish relations because it recognizes the Jewish identity of Jesus and the apostles and recovers the centrality of spiritual ties between the two religions. It explicitly rejects anti-Semitism and reminds the world that discrimination is "foreign to the mind of Christ." Regarding Islam, the document asserts that Christians and Muslims worship the same God. It virtually orders the faithful to turn from past prejudices in order to see Islam in a new, positive way:

> Upon the Moslems, too, the Church looks with esteem. They adore one God, living and enduring, merciful and all-powerful, Maker of heaven and earth and Speaker to men. Although in the course of the centuries many quarrels and hostilities have arisen between Christians and Moslems, this most sacred Synod urges all to forget the past and to strive sincerely for mutual understanding.[85]

Ecumenism

One of the council's key documents, *Unitatis Redintegratio* (Restoration of Unity, 1964), identified Christian unity as a key long-term goal. The document describes baptized Christians who profess faith in another church as "separated brethren," not as "heretics," the term commonly used for centuries. Pope Paul VI made this concrete in 1964 when he left the Vatican Council during its third year of deliberations to meet Ecumenical Patriarch Athenagoras in a pilgrimage to the Mount of Olives in East Jerusalem.[86] The next year, the Roman Catholic Church and the Eastern Orthodox Church canceled mutual excommunications dating back to 1054,[87] thereby allowing ecumenical dialogue to begin.

FROM JUST WAR TO JUST PEACE

Pope Benedict XV considered World War I unjustified. Combatants had not exhausted all options short of war and weren't fighting to address a specific wrong—rather, material interests drove the conflict. The Catholic Church has recognized, since the third century, the principle of legitimate self-defense and thus the idea that sometimes war is justified. Known as "just war theory," it is a social doctrine that helps to discern when conflict is necessary, as well as the proper conduct in war. Traditionally, distinguishing between combatants and noncombatants is a key requirement of prosecuting a just war. Yet, as Benedict XV saw, modern techniques of aerial bombardment almost assure civilian death, thereby compromising military ethics.

Twentieth-century popes followed Benedict XV's lead in applying strict criteria to determine if a conflict was just, persistently tried to find diplomatic solutions to conflict, and put the Church to work in humanitarian service. In fact, during World War II, the much-maligned Pope Pius XII in many ways simply followed the course set by Benedict XV: hewing to impartiality, concentrating on providing material aid and comfort for innocent civilians, and using back channels, including German Catholics in positions of authority, to negotiate certain protections or concessions.[88]

The Second Vatican Council's "pastoral constitution," *Gaudium et Spes*, largely closes the door on the prospect that a just war could be theologically rationalized besides by pure self-defense. No one who heard Pope Paul VI's emotional appeal in French to the United Nations, "*Jamais plus la guerre!*" (Never again war!), could mistake the Catholic Church for an institution keen to find loopholes rationalizing violent conflict.[89] Paul VI also became a major proponent of economic and human development as keys to justice, a precondition for peace.[90]

OPERATIONALIZING A NEW DIPLOMACY

Within the text of *Pacem in Terris* are seeded prophetic thoughts on the future of diplomacy, especially relevant to Rome's dealings with non-Christian states. These come toward the end of the document as a few tactical observations flowing from the Catholic worldview—and the pope's personal experience. What was on the pope's mind in his dying months was the encounter he had with Soviet leaders; he sought to transmit lessons from that experience. Mainly, Pope John was convinced that dialogue was essential.[91]

After noting that the logic of fear is what sustains the arms race, he offers "mutual trust" as the attitude that ideally should replace fear in relations between nations. How to get there? By "establish[ing] contact" and then pursuing a "policy of negotiation," protagonists are more likely to discover common ties that can form the basis of a new relationship. But this shift is not a quick one. Because "[i]t is the law of nature that all things must be of gradual growth," breakthroughs in reorienting international relations are more likely to occur as the result of a step-by-step, methodical effort. Embracing the opposite approach, political revolution, is bound to undermine justice. Here we see Pope Francis's theory of diplomatic encounter shining through.

In a thinly veiled reference to the criticism Pope John XXIII got for engaging with Premier Nikita Khrushchev after the Cuban missile crisis,[92] the encyclical explains that when Catholics collaborate with unbelievers "to achieve some external good," they do so recognizing the inherent dignity possessed by all people. Besides, that encounter could inspire a "conversion to the truth" for the one with little faith, an assumption underlying most Christian missionary endeavors—and the work of God's diplomats.

4

Sovereignty Is the Ticket to the International System

> The Pope, as a temporal sovereign, has a diplomatic service as formerly he had an army.
>
> —Jacques Maritain, *The Things That Are Not Caesar's*, 1931[1]

The story of Vatican diplomacy is bound up in the story of how the Holy See gained its contemporary place in the world. When speaking about what the pope actually presides over, and the key to the Church's place in the international system, it's important to be precise. Vatican City State is a place you can visit—a land island in the middle of Rome.[2] But the Holy See is the governing body of a transnational religion. The two are intrinsically related, which causes confusion. Many people assume that having territory (albeit, territory the size of the San Diego Zoo) gives the Catholic Church her unique ability to function as a state. Not true.

It's the Holy See that sends diplomats around the world and receives them. The Holy See signs international instruments, whether on preventing torture, protecting refugees, controlling psychotropic drugs, or eliminating nuclear weapons.[3] The Holy See participates in General Assembly debates at the United Nations as a permanent observer—a status it chose over full membership.[4] A clear sign of which entity has more clout is found in the UN directory of country names, where you find guidance to use "Holy See" for all documents unless referring to telecommunications and postal issues, when "Vatican City State" is appropriate.[5] The International Law Commission has observed that treaties between the Church and foreign governments are "entered into not by reason of territorial sovereignty over the Vatican State, but on behalf of the Holy See, which exists separately from that state [VCS]."[6] Even the faithful stumble on this point. The question worth exploring here is, Why is the Catholic Church[7] the only world religion that has the same diplomatic rights as a state?[8]

Keep in mind, the United Nations, which has emerged as the main arbiter of sovereignty and the status of international actors, is clear that Church authority does *not* derive from the pinprick of territory upon which the Holy See sits. I'll explore at least four reasons why: (1) its historical legacy as a spiritual *and* political actor in the modern—and pre-modern!—interstate system; (2) recognition from other states even when the Vatican was landless; (3) the Church's track record as a useful, impartial member of the world order; and (4) the conclusive 1929 treaty signed with Italy, creating the world's smallest state, in order to give the Catholic Church independence.

MODERN STATES ESCAPE PAPAL AUTHORITY

Unlike other world religions, the Catholic Church has a legacy as both a spiritual and political actor in the modern interstate system. Indeed, it was the Church that developed Europe's first *system* of diplomacy, when the pope deployed representatives to communicate with political leaders—and, crucially, to promote peace between them—in the medieval period, as discussed in chapter 2. The concept of national sovereignty, meaning the independent authority of a territorially distinct state, emerged in the sixteenth century as monarchs asserted themselves against Rome. Political scientist Robert Jackson explains:

> The rulers of early modern Europe initially came up with the idea in their repudiation of the overarching authority of the pope. . . . Their successful assertion of sovereignty was a way of escape from papal authority, an act of secession. They also asserted their sovereign authority in relation to rival authorities.[9]

A quintessential move of this sort came in 1534 when randy King Henry VIII pressured his parliament to name him supreme head of the Church of England—only after he spent six years lobbying the pope. Henry deployed special envoys and utilized an Italian-born ambassador to wrangle an annulment from Pope Clement VII so he could dump his first wife and marry another.[10] The king did not set out intending to break with the Church but concluded—when his second wife was already pregnant—that it was the most expedient way to achieve his personal and political goals.

Jesuit father Francisco Suárez, a Spanish theologian, looked back at the split some eighty years later to assess the error of Anglicanism, at the pope's request. This progenitor of international law explained, based on the natural law tradition, that no temporal ruler can dominate spiritual matters. However, he concedes to political leaders' control of the temporal realm, as long as they rule justly.[11] Suárez laid conceptual grounds for viewing international relations as a system of equal states, with the papacy categorized as a special case: superior as a religious authority but equivalent in terms of political power, and sovereign as a result.

After the Thirty Years' War concluded with the 1648 Peace of Westphalia —rejected by the pope because the treaty permanently sealed the loss of land, property, and ecclesiastical sees while reducing Church prestige—a diplomatic rupture opened between Rome and most Protestant powers that lasted for some 150 years. The animosity was mutual. Prussian leaders regarded the pope as the Antichrist. British law penalized anyone who dared reference papal authority over anything Christian.[12]

But diplomacy evolves to solve problems.[13] Thus, the Holy See and Protestant-majority European states made amends in the face of pragmatic questions. The first Protestant minister accredited to the Vatican was Wilhelm von Humboldt, sent to represent Prussia in 1802, especially to settle ecclesiastical questions relevant to Catholic communities within the kingdom.[14] When he joined other diplomats at the Congress of Vienna twelve years later, he was one of Rome's biggest supporters.

It is there, in Vienna, where we find the Holy See fully integrated in the firmament of independent states. These were momentous multilateral deliberations, intended to contain French ambition, after Napoleon Bonaparte wreaked havoc across the continent. The pope was awarded a sweet territorial prize (return of the Papal States) with essential support from three non-Catholic delegations: Anglican England, Orthodox Russia, and Protestant Prussia, whose delegation to the talks was headed by Humboldt. The Congress's Final Act also produced a dull-sounding but important declaration,[15] a "Regulation concerning the Precedence of Diplomatic Agents." In it, the Holy See's separate-but-equal diplomatic status is codified. In Article 1, three types of "first rank" diplomatic representatives are recognized: "full ambassadors, legates, and *nuncii*," using the Vatican-exclusive term for diplomatic agents, *nuncii*, the Latin plural of *nuncio*.

SOVEREIGN BECAUSE . . . REASON #1: THOROUGHLY INTEGRATED AND ASSIMILATED

Rather than using the Church's defeat at Napoleon's hands, and its total loss of property, to eliminate it from Europe's political map for good, the plural powers of Austria, France, Great Britain, Portugal, Prussia, Russia, Spain, and Sweden reaffirmed the Catholic Church's sovereign status by integrating its diplomats into the modern world order in 1815 as reviewed in chapter 3. So, the first reason the Catholic Church has the status of a sovereign entity is her historic legacy: the Holy See was assimilated into the European power structure by convention and custom. This recognition is inscribed in international law.

Jesuit lawyer Robert Araujo affirms the importance of viewing the Catholic Church's contemporary global status through the prism of its past: "History plays an essential role in comprehending the participation and evolution of the Holy See in international affairs and relations."[16] He explains that the Holy See has an international personality with the power to exercise sovereignty —including the authority to enter treaties with other sovereigns and to send and receive accredited diplomats—mainly on the basis of established state practice, custom, and the Church's long legacy of negotiating agreements with worldly regimes.[17] What's past is prologue, as Shakespeare wrote.

Paradise Lost

The story of how the Catholic Church lost (definitely, this time) the Papal States, including the city of Rome, in 1870 is the saga of a military noose that tightened around the neck of Pope Pius IX (1846–1878) over the course of twenty-two years. Pio Nono, as he was known, took office with a flourish of liberal gestures. He freed thousands of political prisoners, endorsed a more independent press, announced plans to illuminate streets at night and build a railroad, and appointed a municipal council for the city of Rome.[18] Patriotic Italians were led to believe Pius supported the liberation of Northern Italy from Austrian occupation as a crucial step toward unifying the country. But he didn't. At least, his position was subtle—too careful to satisfy a mob: "The pontiff wished to see the peninsula free, but he was opposed to war."[19]

Radical elements quickly turned on the pope and his court. On his way to a parliamentary meeting, the Vatican's lay prime minister was stabbed in the neck by a dagger-wielding assassin and killed instantly.[20] No one even tried to detain the murderer.[21] It was the opening foray of a violent regime. Extremists attacked the pope's residence. Ambassadors from Bavaria, France, Portugal, Russia, and Spain physically came to the pontiff's defense. Days later, in November 1848, Spanish and Bavarian officials helped Pio Nono sneak out of Rome incognito (unimaginatively disguised as an ordinary priest) by carriage to Gaeta, south of Rome on the Mediterranean coast, while revolutionaries announced the creation of the Republic of Rome.[22] Scornfully, they lit up St. Peter's Square with a fireworks celebration on Good Friday and trashed St. Peter's on Easter. Pio Nono excommunicated them all.

The pontiff returned to Rome seventeen months later under the protection of a foreign force: Napoleon III, France's first elected president,[23] ordered troops to occupy the city and suppress the new republic, shielding the Holy See from the vicissitudes of Italian politics for the next twenty years. But the nationalist tide could not be restrained forever.[24] By 1860, Risorgimento forces swept through the Papal States and controlled all but Rome—an accomplishment tacitly supported by Napoleon, who played a double game balancing devotion to the papacy with sympathy for Italian territorial goals.[25]

Ten years later, French troops withdrew from Rome abruptly, being required back home to battle Prussia. Astonishingly, not only did the French military lose, but Napoleon III was captured, and a new government rushed into office in Paris in early September 1870. Realizing the emperor was out of the picture, King Victor Emmanuel immediately planned a strike against Rome. The king sent a letter to the pope offering guarantees such as protection of his person and property around St. Peter's Basilica, but the pope would not negotiate, seeing no compromise when it came to his authority over the city. Pius appealed to Catholic powers in Madrid, Munich, Paris, and Vienna for help. They sent only condolences.[26]

Fully aware that Rome would soon be captured by the Kingdom of Italy, on September 20, foreign diplomats accredited to the Holy See arrived at the Apostolic Palace "in full dress and in gala carriages" for morning Mass offered by Pius IX.[27] The German ambassador assured Pius they would protect him physically. Soon, Italian cannons could be heard assaulting the Porta Pia, a gate designed by Michelangelo, so the pope ordered a white flag of surrender to be hoisted.[28] He did not want anyone hurt, but he also wanted it known that Italian forces had initiated an armed aggression against the Holy See. The battle ended within three hours; sixty-eight soldiers died—forty-nine Italian regulars and nineteen papal *zouaves*, a French-speaking volunteer defense unit.

King Victor Emmanuel declared from his palace in Florence, "As King and Catholic, I guarantee liberty to the Church, unity to Italy, and independence to the Pontificate."[29] Roman citizens proved to be with the king: they voted overwhelmingly to incorporate the city into the kingdom. With an eye toward placating foreign governments as well as the pope, the Italian parliament passed the "Law of Guarantees" eight months later. Article 1 identified Church sovereignty with the pope himself: "The person of the Sovereign Pontiff is sacred and inviolable." It granted immunity and legal protection to the pope equal to the king, assured freedom for all spiritual activity, and confirmed the Holy See's right to send and receive diplomats.[30] Overall, the Italian government politely fenced off the defiant pope and his curia, treating them as autonomous, while unilaterally enforcing the protective law despite nonrecognition from the Vatican.

SOVEREIGN BECAUSE . . . REASON #2:
DIPLOMATIC RECOGNITION IN SPITE OF BEING LANDLESS

Staunchly unwilling to negotiate his status—or Rome's—with the "usurpers," as he called Italian officialdom, Pius IX retreated into the Apostolic Palace adjacent to St. Peter's Basilica. He declared himself a prisoner, setting a precedent followed by each of the next four popes. No genius diplomat could fix the problem as Consalvi did in 1815, because both sides believed in its absolute right to possess Rome. The Catholic Church was literally backed into a corner for the next six decades.

Except something extraordinary happened during this period: the Vatican's status as a diplomatic actor increased. When Pio Nono took the throne, the Holy See had bilateral relations with eighteen countries. That number climbed to twenty-seven by the time the Lateran Treaty was signed in 1929, a 50 percent increase in accredited ambassadors.[31] During the interregnum, while the "Roman Question" remained an unsolved puzzle, the Holy See negotiated sixty-two concordats with foreign governments regarding various aspects of church-state relations.[32]

Why? Mainly because the "captive popes" did a brilliant job of redefining Church power, centralizing it in the figure of the pope and forging new roles valued by other sovereign actors. For our purposes, what matters is that the very act of recognizing the Holy See and engaging the Church diplomatically, regardless of her lack of physical territory, confirmed her sovereignty under mainstream legal definitions.

As one of international law's most important modern theorists, L. F. L. Oppenheim wrote, "[a] State is, and becomes, an International Person through recognition only and exclusively."[33] Oppenheim elaborated this position, known as constitutive theory, in his 1905 classic *International Law: A Treatise*, in which he explains that global jurisprudence should be based on customs, practices, and specific agreements respected by nations, not on untested theories.[34]

Territory is rarely why states engage with the Vatican. More often, countries respect the Vatican's long history of temperate problem solving while considering the practical reality that Catholics invariably live within their borders. So, the loss of papal land did not undermine international recognition, because states are keen to engage with the Holy See, the government of the Catholic Church, regardless of its physical footprint. Recent scholarship finds that the global order's ability to accommodate an entity such as the Holy See, based on the Church's unique history and contributions, proves that the modern diplomatic order is more robust—and resistant to change—than much contemporary academic literature on diplomacy assumes.[35]

Even in the midst of that painful dispossession of 1870, some had clarity regarding what it ultimately meant for the Holy See to lose temporal power. The *New York Post* presciently reported,

> The possession of authority not purely spiritual has added nothing to its strength. . . . Indeed, it has weakened the influence of the Church by reason of the lack of vigor and progress with which the temporal power was directed and enforced. It was, in a certain sense, a scandal to the Church, and the loss of its temporal power at Rome will revert to the advantage of the Church in all other parts of the world.[36]

Captive Popes Redefine Papal Power and Increase Value of Recognition

The five "captive popes" each adapted unique ways to project the Holy See's global relevance in light of its humiliating loss of property and prestige. Their coping strategies together came to define modern Catholicism and the multifaceted nature of papal authority. Especially the four twentieth-century captives—three of the four being experienced diplomats—provided positive reasons for states to welcome Church engagement in the world system. Each in his own way built the internationalization of the papacy and its centralization in the papal throne; each strengthened the Holy See's claim to sovereignty. Their contributions were so unique and complementary that it's hard not to credit the Holy Spirit with a good share in their success.

Pope Pius IX (1846–1878): Mobilizing Mass Catholic Support

Pope Pius IX is best known for convening the First Vatican Council (Vatican I), which assigned to the pontiff a dramatic attribute, infallibility, when pronouncing matters of doctrine. What few remember is the strategic rationale for this edict. The idea for the council emerged at celebrations for the three hundredth anniversary of the Council of Trent in 1863. Just as Trent served to revitalize the Church in response to the Protestant challenge, Vatican I was an opportunity to highlight papal power in the face of Italian threats to the Holy See's worldly status. Usurpers could take land, but they could never steal his spiritual authority, reasoned Pio Nono.[37] The council convened in December 1869 and voted on infallibility seven months later.

In the midst of a massive thunderstorm, the council affirmed that the supreme pontiff's doctrinal pronouncements regarding faith and morals are truth, as though delivered by God, and thus unerring.[38] The council stopped short of an assertion the Italian government feared: formally defining temporal power as a dogmatic condition of spiritual infallibility.[39] Church fathers dispersed for summer and low and behold, on September 20 Italian troops seized Rome. The bronze doors at the Apostolic Palace's entrance were locked tight, sequestering the pope inside for the rest of his life.

Pio Nono did not rest long on his elevated spiritual laurels. Europe's rulers might have abandoned him, but regular believers were ready to act on behalf of the "prisoner pope." He mobilized international Catholic sentiment in support of papal independence. Catholics petitioned their governments. Around the world, Catholic organizations and newspapers multiplied. Delegations were sent to Rome to express support, then to bring messages home. Euro-Catholic aristocrats played roles behind the scenes, lobbying political elites and raising money for the Holy See.

Astutely, the pope revived a medieval almsgiving vehicle, "Peter's Pence," and launched perhaps the world's first successful international fund-raising effort. Money raised from the faithful worldwide replaced funds once generated by the Papal States.[40] Vincent Viaene explains the reorientation facilitated by Pio Nono and his curia as transformative: "Replacing the Papal States with the Catholic peoples, it gave a new legitimacy, a new financial base, and a new guarantee to papal sovereignty."[41]

Leo XIII (1878–1903): Reaching Out to the World, Creating New "Social Content"

Trained at the *Accademia*, Pope Leo XIII capably expanded Pio Nono's external opening while creating new "Catholic content" for diplomats and laypeople alike. Just as his predecessor's contemporary notoriety is pegged to papal infallibility, Leo is mainly known for one accomplishment, the encyclical *Rerum Novarum*, which Pope John XXIII called the "Magna Carta of Catholic Social Thought."[42] What few today remember is how that document, and the spirit of social engagement it encouraged, functioned to benefit a Church under extraordinary political—even physical—pressure. Leo carefully cultivated three advantageous fields in which to renew the Church's power: diplomacy, theology, and social justice. With a pontificate that lasted over 25 years, Leo achieved significant progress in each arena.

When he took the papal throne, relations between the Holy See and most European powers were badly frayed. An immediate foreign policy challenge was the accelerated suppression of the Catholic community in Prussia. After winning the Franco-Prussian War and unifying the Protestant-majority German state, Chancellor Otto von Bismarck turned on the Catholic Church as a potential enemy within. Based on anger over the papacy's declaration of infallibility (perceived as overtly anti-Protestant), the *Kulturkampf*, or "culture struggle," resulted in the expulsion of religious orders, state control of Catholic schools and many ecclesiastical appointments, and the requirement of civil marriage. By the late 1880s, Leo had calmed the waters with German leadership, and most of the punitive laws were rolled back.[43] In fact, Bismarck requested that Leo arbitrate a dispute between Germany and Spain over the Caroline Islands, a disagreement amicably solved with the pope's help in 1885.[44]

As relations with Prussia were smoothed out, tension with France heated up. For most of his papacy, Leo kept a close eye on France as it implemented a variety of anticlerical initiatives. Rather than siding with Catholic monarchists, though, the pope put out a pacific message: live with the republican government.[45]

In 1886, the Chinese emperor reached out to the pope, interested in opening direct diplomatic relations. Although France put a kibosh on the relationship, a comment in a Chinese newspaper at the time illuminates what made the Vatican attractive: "As the pope has no troops and no territory, but is merely a kind of Dalai Lama, there is no danger to China from opening direct relations with him. The affairs of the missionaries can then be dealt with in an open and straightforward manner, as no fear of political traps will lurk behind."[46] Even Tsar Nicholas II, who had a representative at the papal court, appealed to the Holy See for help with the 1898 Hague Peace Congress.[47]

It's in the world of ideas that Leo really made his most creative contributions. In the encyclical *Aeterni Patris* (On the Restoration of Christian Philosophy, 1879), Leo famously restored the prestige of St. Thomas Aquinas, making the angelic doctor's theology and philosophy the touchstone—and normative measuring stick—for modern Catholic thought. With Thomism officially elevated and endorsed, the Church regained access to a vast store of wisdom and a flexible interpretative key for many social dilemmas.[48]

Pope Leo issued an astonishing eighty-five encyclicals during his twenty-five-year papacy.[49] Many utilize the thought of St. Thomas Aquinas, as though the pope—certainly with the help of his brother, a Jesuit scholar and Aquinas expert, who became a cardinal under Leo—was preparing the Church for his most daring document, *Rerum Novarum*,[50] analyzing relations between owners and workers since industrialization.

Rerum Novarum demonstrates great sympathy for the plight of the working poor, without advocating for either socialism or unfettered capitalism. It also maintains an activist stance, urging Catholics to get involved in efforts against injustice. Jesuit philosopher Joseph Koterski thinks the loss of the Papal States is a crucial factor in understanding Pope Leo's ability to deal frankly with these timely issues. Koterski believes the pope restored Aquinas's relevance twelve years earlier as the essential theological foundation for his landmark text.[51] *Rerum Novarum* provided relevant references for the legion of Catholic organizations inspired by Pio Nono; Catholic social thought provides the Church with tools to analyze and respond to contemporary political dilemmas.

Pius X (1903–1914): Unifying Canon Law Means Centralizing Roman Authority

Leo was succeeded by Giuseppe Sarto, who took the name Pius X. As heir to Peter, Pius was known as a staunch conservative, mostly concerned with liturgy, sacred music, and ecclesiastical matters. During his eleven-year papacy, of the four traditional "first-class nunciatures," three were closed or hardly functioning at some point in his tenure: Paris, Lisbon, and Madrid.[52] Diplomacy per se was not his forte.[53]

A demonstration of how ineffective hard-nosed papal diplomacy was with the big powers came in the first year of his papacy. When the president of France visited the Italian king—the first Catholic head of state to do so since 1870, the year Italy took Rome—the Holy See complained to the French government. Paris's response? It called its Vatican envoy home to Paris.[54]

Yet Pius X, too, advanced a particularly valuable initiative that strengthened the Holy See, despite being sequestered in political limbo vis-à-vis Italy. It was under Pius that the Church unified canon law, the Church's legal code written in Latin. The project required reconciling some ten thousand norms, developed across hundreds of years, and condensing them into one volume. It took thirteen years and was ultimately completed by Pope Benedict XV. But it was Pius X's deep concern for good internal order that inspired the effort, which served to further centralize decision making and reinforce papal authority.

Benedict XV (1914–1922): World War I and the Humanitarian Response

Less than a month after the Great War's outbreak in July 1914, Pius X died of a heart attack. Catholics were on both sides of the war; cardinals entered a tense conclave and opted for a pope with foreign policy experience. They chose Giacomo della Chiesa, an *Accademia* graduate. As Benedict XV, he spent most of the war trying to end it. In August 1917, the pope proposed a seven-point peace note, twisting the arm of his cardinal in Baltimore to get the proposal in front of President Woodrow Wilson—who politely dismissed it as naive.[55] Just five months later, Wilson's Fourteen Points speech to Congress echoed concepts found in Benedict's proposal. Not that the pope wanted credit; he really just wanted to end the senseless "ruin and slaughter."[56]

During the war, Benedict protected the Church as a neutral actor and saw the war from the ground up.[57] Though mostly unsuccessful, the Holy See tirelessly used private channels and careful, secret negotiations with rulers to prevent the war from spreading. Meanwhile, he oriented the Church's perspective to the nonpowerful: soldiers and civilians. For example, a papal nuncio successfully deterred German soldiers occupying Belgium from deporting local citizens—and victims of war of all sorts. He explained, "The Pope must actually place himself among the combatants instead of keeping away and preaching peace and concord from a distance."[58]

The pope and Secretary of State Pietro Gasparri (a cardinal secretary who did not attend the *Accademia*) mainly focused on activities no one else prioritized.[59] The Vatican managed an international postal system for POWs and their families that eventually processed over six hundred thousand pieces of correspondence, including forty thousand regarding repatriating sick and injured soldiers. It arranged medical care for POWs with tuberculosis in Switzerland, which helped twenty-six thousand POWs and three thousand civilian detainees.[60] Benedict XV ran down the Holy See's treasury[61] as a result of its humanitarian commitments at a time when the war caused a great reduction in donations, but the Church's selflessness contributed immeasurably in restoring prestige to the Holy See.[62] Benedict's charity created new fields of intervention embraced by the Church ever since.

Meanwhile, the war crippled the Church's global missionary work. From China to the Congo, young missionaries, especially from France, the mother country of nineteenth-century missions, were fighting and dying rather than preaching and ministering to fledgling Catholic communities. After the war, France and Great Britain were especially harsh in restricting German missionaries from taking up their old places—not only in former German colonies now controlled by the victors but also in countries such as China.[63] In response, Pope Benedict renewed Church commitment to fostering indigenous clergy, especially in Africa and Asia. His apostolic letter *Maximum Illud* (On the Propagation of the Faith throughout the World, 1919) prioritized the cultivation of local missionaries.[64] It also invested authority for evangelization in the Holy See.[65]

Pope Benedict XV successfully patched up relations with the French government, in part by using the Holy See's expressive power—evocative symbolism and ritual—to bind the faithful. He canonized beloved St. Joan of Arc in May 1920. Church and state reestablished diplomatic relations a year later.

SOVEREIGN BECAUSE . . . REASON #3: THE HOLY SEE MAKES VALUABLE, UNIQUE CONTRIBUTIONS

In the eyes of the international order, throughout World War I the Holy See made valuable contributions, especially to the sick, wounded, and displaced on both sides of the conflict. The Church proved her unique ability to function transnationally, impartially, and beneficially. A contributor to the *New York Times* reported, "The Italy that in the secret pact of London excluded him from the Peace Conference came home from Paris chastened and disillusioned to seek the friendship of the Vatican. 'It is a pity we could not have sent the Pope to Paris,' said one embittered Italian statesman. 'He is turning out to be the only diplomat we have.'"[66]

South African legal scholar Tiyanjana Maluwa argues that the Holy See's international personality is based on objective factors, beyond interstate recognition alone.[67] He is unconvinced by the many occasions (especially in the field of international law) that the Holy See is categorized as a sui generis sovereign entity, considering this status a kind of cop-out if not interrogated more deeply. He develops a "social need" theory that considers the Holy See's international standing to be the result of "the usefulness of the functions which the entity claims to serve."[68]

Although he does not interpret the nature of this usefulness, the author circles back to the concept of recognition, since the extent to which an entity is successful in fulfilling its mission depends on approval by other states. Mainly, states have signaled satisfaction with the Holy See by accepting Rome's right to make treaties and to exchange diplomats, two functions "traditionally . . . regarded as the touchstones of sovereignty and therefore of international legal personality."[69] One of the source documents affirming the Holy See's functional contributions to the world, according to Maluwa, is the text that finally set the Church free: the Lateran Treaty of 1929.

Pius XI (1922–1939): Paradise Regained

In the end, diplomacy did indeed come to the rescue. The impasse with Italy ended as a result of thirty months of bargaining, although the two sides had approached each other quietly, floating variations of a solution, even on the sidelines of the 1919 Paris Peace Conference. Having waited for decades, the Church was prepared to seize an optimal opening when Italian political conditions were ripe, as they were in the late 1920s. It was Pius XI who cut the Gordian knot with Prime Minister Benito Mussolini, a figure few in Church leadership liked or trusted.

The conflict was long frozen over two seemingly irreconcilable claims: Italy's strong national pride would never let go of Rome as its capital, while the Holy See's long legacy meant it would never accept dependence on any other state. By the early 1920s, Church leaders could see that recovering Rome was a pipe dream. But political scandal such as the violent overthrow of the Romanov family in Russia, for example, did little to convince the

Vatican to put itself at the mercy of any secular government, even a relatively protective one such as the Italian constitutional monarchy. From the perspective of the Church, time was on its side; there was little pressure to resolve the stalemate. "Italy needs the Church more than the Church needs Italy," said Pope Benedict XV a year before he died.[70]

Yet the divisiveness it created for Italian Catholics, pitting their Italianness against their Catholic identity, contradicted Christ's call for unity. As well, radical elements in the growing Fascist movement made ominous statements, as exemplified by this disdainful declaration in its newspaper: "[T]here is only one possible revision of the Law of Guarantees and that is its abolition, followed by a firm invitation to his Holiness to quit Rome."[71]

One Italian politician saw political value in resolving the Roman Question: Benito Mussolini. Starting his political career as a revolutionary socialist, Mussolini was brought up by an anti-Catholic father and a devout mother.[72] In 1915, he ditched the socialists to advocate Italy's entry into World War I, creating the Fascist Revolutionary Party. By 1922, Mussolini was Italy's prime minister, and the (rebranded) National Fascist Party was growing quickly. A megalomaniac with dreams of re-creating the Roman Empire, Mussolini's anticlerical hoodlums harassed the Church on the local level—even murdering a parish priest for rejecting a Fascist youth club in favor of a Catholic scout troop[73]—but the ambitious leader sought to make amends personally. He baptized his children, introduced religious instruction in elementary schools, and restored the crucifix to courtrooms and classrooms[74] as part of a "boldly opportunistic policy."[75]

Communication between the pope's team and Mussolini's inner circle increased as Mussolini consolidated power throughout the 1920s, despite evidence that Fascism was a destructive variant of totalitarianism, not unlike movements in Russia and Germany.[76] Secret negotiations to settle the issue of Holy See sovereignty, and church-state relations, began in earnest in August 1926,[77] led by the pope's legal adviser, Francesco Pacelli, brother of Msgr. Eugenio Pacelli, who was serving as nuncio to Germany. To tamp down rabid antireligious influences in his ranks, Mussolini portrayed Catholicism as synonymous with Roman civilization, explaining its staying power as a function of Roman identity.[78]

Negotiations moved quickly on two components of the pact, a treaty settling the Holy See's legal status and a financial settlement. It took more time to nail down elements of a third document, a concordat normalizing overall relations between Italy and the Church.[79] In the last phase of talks, Prime Minister Mussolini personally led negotiations.[80] His hands-on engagement sealed the impression that the treaty was a personal achievement.

The Roman Question Finally Resolved

On February 7, 1929, Cardinal Gasparri assembled the ambassadors to the Holy See to reveal the still-secret accord. The next day, Mussolini telegrammed Italian ambassadors around the world with the same news. Three days later, Mussolini (acting as foreign minister as well) and his undersecretary drove across town to the Lateran Palace, the seat of the bishop of Rome. No pope had entered the place in fifty-nine years. Gasparri and the prime minister signed the accords privately in the Hall of the Council. Public jubilation followed. Most Italians were astonished, unaware that the settlement was in the works, because so few people had accomplished this historic feat.

Mussolini was credited by his followers as being a genius and by the curia —including the pope—as being a gift from God.[81] Although there were quiet dissenters on both sides, they mainly held their fire. One of the most circumspect observations came from someone who had reason to be angry: Alcide de Gasperi, a fierce Fascist critic, brilliant intellectual, founder of a Catholic political party forced to dissolve, and future postwar prime minister. His attitude, written in a private letter the day after the treaty signing, reveals how a prudent Catholic saw the event on a very long horizon:

> [W]ith Mussolini knocking hard at the Bronze Door, the pope had to open the door, and once the conversation was underway and an area of accord had been found, his own broad sense of responsibility . . . led him to conclude an agreement. Today, the outcome is viewed in Italy as a success for the regime, but as seen in history and in the world, it is a liberation for the Church and a blessing for the Italian nation.[82]

The glee and appreciation for Il Duce proved short lived. Two years later, the pope issued an encyclical denouncing "a regime based on an ideology which clearly resolves itself into a true, real pagan worship of the State."[83] The inevitable rupture between the Church and the lead Fascist did not abrogate the treaty. On the contrary, it was absorbed into the Italian postwar constitution of 1948.

SOVEREIGN BECAUSE . . . REASON #4: LATERAN TREATY GRANTS SOVEREIGNTY AS "INHERENT"

The most important aspect of the Lateran Accords is the treaty establishing the Holy See's international status.[84] Article 2 includes this pithy definition:

> Italy recognizes the sovereignty of the Holy See in the international realm as an attribute inherent in its nature in conformity with its tradition and with the requirements of its mission to the world.[85]

In other words, the treaty treats the Holy See as sovereign because it was historically embedded in the interstate system, but even before that, the Church was incarnated as a transnational authority—an invisible kingdom of God, if you will—with a valued mission to proclaim peace and neighborly love.

Article 3 creates a new microstate[86] in order to guarantee the Holy See's independence. The language explicitly describes Vatican City as dependent on the Holy See:

> Italy recognizes the full ownership and the exclusive and absolute power and jurisdiction of the Holy See over the Vatican as it is presently constituted . . . creating in this matter Vatican City for the special purposes and conditions given in this treaty.

It's as though the Italians created a kind of physical pedestal for the government of the Catholic Church, with an implied caveat that if, God forbid, the Catholic Church ceased to exist, the beautiful park would revert back to Italy, since the conditions giving rise to the treaty would no longer obtain. A detailed map specifying Vatican City's boundaries was attached, including the open plaza of St. Peter's Square—to be supervised by Italian police, whose authority ended at the steps of the basilica, as specifically noted.[87]

Thus, the Pentagon-sized plot of land[88] functions as a guarantor of the Holy See's "absolute and visible independence," in the treaty's words, securing sovereignty for an entity that transcends property.[89] As Timothy Byrnes writes, "Rule over a micro-state in Rome is not the source of the Pope's diplomatic standing. But rule over that micro-state is the necessary condition for the endurance of that legal and diplomatic standing."[90]

Proof of the exact risk popes from Pius IX through Pius XI were determined to avoid emerged in World War II when Germany occupied Rome. Because Vatican City was sovereign, German tanks could only surround the perimeter of its borders. Joachim von Ribbentrop, Nazi foreign minister, approved a declaration given to Secretary of State Cardinal Luigi Maglione stating, "On the German side, it is affirmed that the sovereignty and territorial integrity of the Vatican will be respected and that the German troops in Rome will behave accordingly."[91] Its independent status also protected the Vatican's ability to harbor thousands of Jewish civilians inside religious properties and palaces and to hide Allied soldiers on the run.[92]

Article 24 of the treaty requires the Holy See and Vatican City to remain neutral, beyond worldly rivalries, unless "contending parties make a mutual appeal to its mission of peace." That's a solid description of the unique mediation and arbitration role the pope has assumed directly and through the offices of the Holy See to the present day.

Although his name did not appear on the treaty, a Pius XI "signature element" was the fact that he used treaty negotiations as a chance to conclude a concordat with Italy, privileging the Church's relationship with the state. The concordat affirmed Catholicism as the state religion. It allowed religious instruction in public schools and gave bishops the power to select instructors and textbooks, but it also required bishops to swear an oath of loyalty to the king and government. A principle that satisfied both parties (for different reasons) was Article 1, describing Rome as the "center of the Catholic world and place of pilgrimage."[93] Mussolini hoped to use the Church in his pitch for Italian global greatness; the Vatican saw in the language a recognition of the reality it had long defended.

Concordats were the pope's go-to diplomatic instruments;[94] a total of eighteen were signed under his watch. In fact, evidence that the Catholic Church's sovereignty preceded the Lateran Treaty can be seen in the concordats concluded during Pius XI's papacy before and after the pact: the governments of Latvia (1922), Poland (1925), Romania (1927), and Lithuania (1927) signed formal agreements with the Holy See before the momentous treaty, while concordats were signed with Prussia (1929), Austria (1933), and Germany (1933) afterward. They all have the same legal standing regardless of when the Holy See got the keys to its own kingdom.

CLASSIC TECHNIQUES AND EXPRESSIVE POWER USED TO CLINCH THE DEAL

Resolving the "Roman Question" was considered an existential necessity by three generations of supreme pontiffs. Yet the pope and his advisers used standard diplomatic techniques to conclude the treaty.

First, the Holy See approached the dilemma with an element of pragmatism behind the scenes, even as each captive pope upheld Pope Pius IX's stern, nonnegotiable standard: territorial independence. Pio Nono himself bent the rules of nonengagement with the Italian government. He permitted his nemesis King Victor Emmanuel II's burial in the Pantheon, despite having excommunicated the king.[95] Pope Pius X modified the *non expedit* (Latin for "it is not expedient") forbidding Catholics from voting in Italian elections when it looked like the ban might benefit radical political elements.[96] It was annulled in 1918. These accommodations allowed the two sides to function "cordially" despite the long stalemate and can be considered trust-building steps while the Church waited for a more propitious political atmosphere.

Practicing the art of patience was critical. The Holy See, as always, played a long game in order to let time—and God—create better circumstances. An improved context emerged under a regime that most in the Church considered toxic. Benito Mussolini did not conceal his disdain for Catholicism as he grew in power. No one around Pius XI had illusions that the prime minister was a radically new man as negotiations unfolded. But that did not matter. The man held power, and the Church shows respect to temporal leaders. From the Holy See's perspective, Il Duce was like all politicians—a man with interests. And when his interests dovetailed with those of the Church, the pope's advisers were ready to get the best deal possible.

Such a high-stakes puzzle required utmost secrecy as the two sides tested options, floated proposals, and exchanged drafts. Fewer than ten people were always up to speed on the status of the negotiations. When his most trusted surrogate died, Mussolini took the role of lead negotiator himself. At that point, even the king was irregularly informed about progress. A fortress of confidentiality surrounded the proceedings, allowing the greatest freedom for those inside. Papal diplomacy has always placed a premium on discretion. Another practice much valued is precision. The Lateran Treaty is concise. It says what it needs to say and not much more. In less than 3,500 words and 27 articles, the document births a state[97] and restores familial relations between Italy and the Catholic Church.

CATHOLIC EXPRESSIVE POWER ENVELOPING THE TREATY

In the field of international relations, a common construct contrasts hard power, referring to military prowess and economic might, with soft power, a term coined by Joseph Nye to include, for example, culture, which can have a persuasive impact on foreign relations.[98] In this schema, the only power the Vatican has is soft—and plenty of commentators have used the phrase to characterize the Holy See's diplomatic arsenal. I prefer a different descriptor for what the Holy See possesses, a term used by Eric Hanson to describe the Catholic Church: *expressive power*.[99]

Expressive power captures the Church's artistry, imagery, gesture, pageantry, color, sensuousness, and its tremendous use of nonverbal, symbolic cues, including numerology and a religious calendar with special feast days and seasons. For example, symbols allow ordinary events to be filled with theological references, creating layers of meaning.

Looking at the events surrounding the Lateran Treaty, one discerns ample use of theological references to frame the document and the event. Start with something as seemingly minor as the number of articles, twenty-seven, outlining the treaty's major points. The number twenty-seven is the number of books in the New Testament. It is equivalent to $3 \times 3 \times 3$, or three times the Trinitarian three, a sacred number with special meaning within the Christian narrative. Three is the Trinity, the Holy Family, and the number of days between Christ's crucifixion and resurrection.

The size of Vatican City can be interpreted in terms of biblical numerology. VCS's total land area is 44 hectares (or 0.44 sq km). In Revelations 21:16, the City of God is laid out as a square with dimensions that are multiples of 4. Four also symbolizes creation.[100]

Regarding the initial signing, it was held in the palace adjacent to the Basilica of St. John Lateran, signifying a restoration of papal power. The Lateran is the oldest basilica in Rome and came into Church patrimony in 311 from Constantine. It is the pope's cathedral as bishop of Rome. An adjacent palace was the papal residence for about one thousand years—from the fourth to the fourteenth century. Bringing Mussolini to the Lateran to finalize the agreement allows the entire history of the institutional Church to be evoked—in one building. The location presented the Catholic Church as fully restored to its pre-1870 authority—despite the permanent loss of most of Rome.

The treaty was signed on February 11, which might seem a blasé date until you look at the Catholic calendar: it is the feast day of Our Lady of Lourdes, commemorating the visitation of the Blessed Virgin Mary to a peasant girl in France in 1858 during Pius IX's reign. He authorized the veneration of Mary at Lourdes and provided a "canonical coronation" for the holy image—Our Lady of the Rosary, a statue in white, blue, and gold—installed at the grotto where she first appeared. Symbolically evoking the pope who suffered through the physical loss of Rome (and whose decisive refusal to negotiate is admired in retrospect) is a classic Catholic gesture few nonbelievers would recognize.

On June 7, an Italian delegation headed by Mussolini drove to the Apostolic Palace to deliver parliament's ratification and to receive the pope's signed copy. They also brought a check for 750 million lira (equivalent today to $1.4 billion).[101] To mark this finale, Pope Pius XI, a devotee of science, used a new symbol of Vatican independence, the telegraph service.[102] He dispatched the first telegram to King Victor Emmanuel III, blessing him, his family, the Italian people, and the world.[103] Using expressive power, the Church projected the message that an incarnated Holy See was back—ready to deploy her timeless message with new tools. Vatican City promptly exercised its status as an entity comparable to other independent states by joining the International Telegraph Union (ITU) and the Universal Postal Union (UPU).[104]

THE HOLY SEE AND THE UNITED NATIONS

The Holy See's relationship with the United Nations both cemented the Lateran Treaty and preserved its unique status in the international system.

A tremendous amount of international business has transpired within the United Nations over the last seventy years. How effective the UN has been is debatable, but the Holy See's support for the endeavor—"from the very beginning," as John Paul II said[105]—is indisputable. Nothing automatic, no explicit process, yielded Rome's integration into the UN system. The history of this accommodation reflects again the unusual nature of the Catholic Church's place in the world order. Neither fish nor fowl, both a part of and apart from the family of nations, the Holy See continues to grow its engagement with the UN, despite clashing more frequently with some of its most powerful members.

The Holy See's sovereignty was clinched with the Lateran Treaty, but some actors in the world system were not keen to accept its peer status too quickly. Diplomats at the Secretariat of State queried the US government in 1944 regarding the prospect of UN membership. Secretary of State Cordell Hull replied, "As a diminutive state the Vatican would not be capable of fulfilling all the responsibilities of membership in an organization whose primary purpose is the maintenance of international peace and security."[106] Indeed, preparatory meetings that year conceptualized the United Nations as a security-oriented peacekeeping system dependent on the Allied powers.[107]

Yet the Vatican saw strong convergence between the transnational mission of the Church and the UN—to promote peace and cooperation between states—and was never going to remain aloof while postwar civilization built new institutions to temper humanity's worst impulses.[108]

The Church had a significant intellectual asset helping to shape the UN's mission statement. French philosopher Jacques Maritain was among a small circle of thinkers preparing the ground for the Universal Declaration of Human Rights through a select committee established in Paris in 1946. Maritain was one of its most active members,[109] while serving as France's ambassador to the Holy See (1945–1948). He was in regular touch with two Vatican diplomats, both future popes: Archbishop Angelo Roncalli, the papal nuncio to France, and Archbishop Giovanni Montini, *sostituto* at the Secretariat of State. Through Maritain's contributions, some of the Church's key assumptions about the very purpose of a state can be found in the masterful declaration.

Maritain, of course, believed that human rights are rooted in natural law, an idea we find in the final declaration, approved in December 1948 as the UN's guiding light. Some Christian critics complained that the document does not mention God. However, the text anchors human rights in the concept of human dignity, highlighted in the first line of the preamble—"Whereas recognition of the inherent dignity and of the equal and inalienable rights of all members of the human family is the foundation of freedom, justice and peace in the world"—as well as in Article 1: "All human beings are born free and equal in dignity and rights." In Catholic doctrine, God plants this universal notion of human dignity in us, so the prominence of the term is shorthand for His will.

Meanwhile, the Church gained entrée through its territorial identity: the UN invited the ITU to become its first "special agency" in 1947. As an ITU member, Vatican City thus became part of the system. A year later, the UN added the UPU and its membership roster to the list of special agencies, again including Vatican City State.[110]

THE HOLY SEE GAINS ENTRÉE THROUGH SPECIAL AGENCIES

It was also through invitations to participate in special agencies with issue-specific mandates that the Holy See gained access to the UN system. The Food and Agriculture Organization (FAO) was created in 1945 to address world hunger and starvation. A Catholic priest and agricultural expert, Msgr. Luigi Ligutti, was involved in helping define FAO's mission and encouraged the Holy See to join as a permanent observer, based on Rome's war relief food programs. The Vatican wrote to the group, which found no rules preventing such a title. By a vote of 41–1, the FAO approved the request in November 1948, marking the first time the Holy See assumed this designation.[111]

While Maritain worked with the United Nations Educational, Scientific and Cultural Organization (UNESCO) at an elite level, the Holy See established a liaison committee to formalize collaboration with the education-oriented group. Over the next few years, the organization defined a new category of participation, "permanent observers of nonmember states," which could join by invitation only. In 1952, when the director general invited the Holy See to appoint a permanent observer, Pope Pius XII turned to his nuncio, Archbishop Roncalli.[112] A different route made the Holy See a member of the International Atomic Energy Agency (IAEA). Invited to join a 1955 conference on the peaceful uses of atomic energy, the Vatican wound up involved in negotiations to create, by statute, the new entity, which became an agency of the UN two years later.

Because the Holy See and Vatican City State were active in different arenas within the UN—sprawling as it was from the start—a moment of confusion emerged in 1957, leading to an exchange of notes between the secretary general's office and the Secretariat of State, clarifying that it's the Holy

See carrying the primary relationship with the UN. Secretary General Dag Hammarskjöld (1953–1961) set the tone for resolving this juridical question, observing, "When I request an audience from the Vatican, I do not go to see the King of Vatican City but the head of the Catholic Church."[113]

U THANT FACILITATED PERMANENT OBSERVER STATUS

Two developments in the early 1960s cemented the Holy See's integration into the UN system. First, Rome was a party to the 1961 Vienna Convention on Diplomatic Relations, which regulated diplomatic exchanges, privileges, and immunities—updated for the first time since the 1815 Congress of Vienna. Once again, the Holy See preserved its place in the diplomatic firmament, including a nuncio's right to be automatically designated dean of the corps wherever a host country favored this tradition.

Second, Secretary General U Thant, a practicing Buddhist, proved to be a key advocate for the Holy See and for Pope Paul VI personally. Catapulted to power unexpectedly when Hammarskjöld died in a plane crash, Thant was elected as a compromise candidate, acceptable to both the West and the Soviet Union. As Burma's representative to the UN (1957–1961), he was active in the Non-Aligned Movement of developing nations trying to find a middle path between the superpowers. He believed communities of faith should be UN allies,[114] an attitude that benefited Rome. He also admired the stance of impartiality taken by the Holy See, an attitude personified by Pope John XXIII's role during the Cuban missile crisis, which Thant was in the thick of settling.[115]

John XXIII already had his eye on the UN. He thought the first papal trip to the United States should be to the UN's New York headquarters. Unfortunately, he was dying. So he sent a cardinal to explain his new encyclical, *Pacem in Terris*, to UN delegates, which yielded a working relationship with U Thant.[116] Less than a month after Paul VI took office, the secretary general visited him at the Vatican. In his remarks, Paul VI praised the UN as the fruit of Christian principles and poetically described a kinship between the two: "The universality proper to the Catholic Church, with its pulsing heart here in Rome, seems . . . to be reflected from the spiritual sphere into the temporal sphere of the United Nations."[117]

In private talks, the two former diplomats discussed Thant's commitment to postcolonial nations joining the UN as newly independent countries with great socioeconomic challenges. A specific problem on which they focused was opposition to the war in Vietnam, "the cruel, bloody, senseless conflict" that obsessed the Burmese leader.[118] This shared viewpoint led to ongoing collaboration between the two men and their organizations—with a lasting impact on the Holy See's status.[119]

Eight months later, the cardinal secretary of state wrote to Thant requesting "more stable relations with the United Nations."[120] The secretary general responded quickly, offering the Holy See permanent observer status,[121] a role five countries had at the time.[122] He took the decision on his own. Indeed, the UN's first three leaders acted with great autonomy, their latitude being constrained later.[123]

Impressed by Pope Paul's comportment during a December 1964 pilgrimage to India[124]—the first pope to journey there, Paul believed the Church's future was in Asia and Africa—the secretary general extended an invitation for him to address the General Assembly, against the advice of some advisers. Told that he might be criticized for not consulting the General Assembly, Thant brushed the concern aside: "No impartial observer could accuse a Buddhist secretary-general of prejudice in inviting the head of the Roman Catholic Church to the UN."[125]

When Paul VI landed at JFK airport on October 4, 1965, it was Thant who boarded the Alitalia jet to escort the pope to American soil. The pope's whirlwind fourteen-hour visit included a meeting with President Lyndon Johnson and Mass for one hundred thousand at Yankee Stadium; but the high point was his encounter with the UN, where he gave "the speech of his life,"[126] best remembered for his exclamation in French, "Never again war!"[127] (Some credit it with boosting domestic mobilization against the Vietnam War.[128]) The audience of some four thousand people gave the pope a ten-minute standing ovation.

Another ovation met him the next afternoon as he strode into St. Peter's Basilica where the Second Vatican Council was in its last session, about to discuss the last section of *Gaudium et Spes*, concerned with the international community.[129]

Over the last fifty years, the *Accademia* has added material on multilateral diplomacy as more graduates are called to do this work. When a nuncio serves in a city where a multilateral entity is based, he typically covers that organization as well. The nuncio in Kenya, for example, who also serves as nuncio to South Sudan, is permanent observer to the United Nations Environment Programme (UNEP) and the UN Center for Human Settlements (UN-HABITAT), both based in Nairobi.[130] At The Hague in the Netherlands, the nuncio does double duty as papal envoy to the Organisation for the Prohibition of Chemical Weapons (OPCW), a UN family member based in the Dutch seat of government.

Multilateral diplomacy has been a growth field for the Secretariat of State since the creation of the UN, although this added workload is only slightly reflected in its employment stats. In January 2020, Pope Francis created a new position within the Secretariat of State: a second undersecretary for relations with states dedicated to multilateral relations. He gave the position to a woman—the first woman to hold a managerial position in the secretariat.[131]

TOUGH CALL: JOHN PAUL II OPTS FOR OBSERVER STATUS, NOT MEMBERSHIP

Swiss voters elected to make their country a full member of the UN in 2002, the first time a member state joined by popular referendum.[132] The only other permanent observer at the time was the Holy See. Secretary General Kofi Annan asked Archbishop Celestino Migliore, the pope's representative, if Rome would consider applying for full membership.[133] After extensive consultation and reflection, John Paul II concluded that full membership put the Holy See's impartiality at risk, since it would plunge the Vatican into the competition and horse-trading found in every legislative body. However, he decided it was time to formalize the permanent observer role, premised for decades on U Thant's letter of welcome. (Under John Paul II, between his enthusiasm for travel, personal outreach, and diplomacy and the birth of new states, the number of countries with which the Holy See had bilateral relations increased 27 percent—from 151 nations in 1978 to 183 in 2005.[134])

On July 1, 2004, the General Assembly unanimously approved a resolution outlining the Holy See's contributions while expanding its privileges.[135] One UN diplomat explained the new status as akin to being a "full member state, just without the vote." What Migliore hurried to explain was that the Church could revisit the issue down the road, if it wanted: "The Holy See has the requirements defined by the UN statute to be a member state," he said. "If in the future it wished to be so, this resolution would not impede it from requesting it."[136] The vote, which proved noncontroversial (completed in less than ten minutes) was a comeuppance to nongovernmental organizations on the left dogging the Vatican—and challenging its sovereign status—since the infamous contests over population control, abortion, and women's rights in the mid-1990s.[137]

But the Catholic Church's acceptance as a high-functioning member of the UN network does not depend on what resentful NGOs think. In 2004, as in 1964—and in 1815, for that matter—the Holy See's integration in the transnational system turned on respect from its peers—other governments and the world's diplomats—not the international media. Not even Catholic pew sitters around the world are the Holy See's audience. As Cardinal Parolin writes, "One cannot function in the framework of intergovernmental institutions without the necessary expertise, technical capacity, and true professionalism."[138]

Discretion is one of the hallmarks of professionalism in this world. Prudence has a downside, though: the Holy See is involved in myriad admirable initiatives for which it gets little credit. Who knows that under Pope Francis, Vatican diplomats have questioned the ethics of weaponized drones, challenged pharmaceutical companies for claiming intellectual property rights that prevent the poor from accessing medicine, or defended indigenous people losing land and resources to extractive industries such as mining?

One who is well aware of these efforts is UN secretary general António Manuel de Oliveira Guterres. A former prime minister of Portugal and a practicing Catholic, appointed to lead the UN in 2017, he welcomes the Holy See's constructive role, describing it quite simply as "renewing the moral dimension in international relations."[139]

5

Diplomatic Classics, Rules of Thumb, and Modus Operandi

> For whoever is begotten by God conquers the world. And the victory that conquers the world is our faith.
>
> —1 John 5:4

As the world prepared to celebrate Easter in 2018, it looked as though years of discreet talks under a quarantine of secrecy had finally led Rome and Beijing to a breakthrough: The two sides were poised to sign a historic agreement in Rome. For the first time in seventy years, the Chinese government would recognize the pope as chief decider for the selection of mainland Chinese bishops—monumental for a regime that categorically rejects foreign influence in domestic matters—a goal long pursued by the Vatican.

The complex political background is crucial. A painful split in the Catholic community developed after Mao took power. The Communist Party created a new Chinese Catholic Patriotic Association under government control. Priests and bishops who refused to register with the government through this association were ostracized, jailed, or just disappeared. But entire parishes turned their backs on this national entity and worshipped without official approval; they became known as the underground Church. During the Cultural Revolution, the Vatican had no idea if the Church even survived. With the early 1980s opening,[1] Rome was overjoyed to discover not only that the Church was alive but that communities continued to say Mass, typically in Latin, since Vatican II changes were never introduced! The underground Church quickly developed a quiet relationship with Rome, which became more open with time. Meanwhile, Catholic members of the patriotic association, especially bishops, also strengthened ties to Rome—often covertly.

By Easter 2018, a short text was ready for signature, and a brief ceremonial event was planned at the Urbaniana, a pontifical university run by the Congregation for the Evangelization of Peoples, which oversees the Church in mission lands, including the Middle Kingdom. But at the last minute Beijing balked. The Foreign Ministry blamed an "underground" bishop in Mindong for offering a Chrism Mass on his own, rather than together with a "patriotic" bishop in the same province. The offense briefly landed the prelate in jail—again. In the government's view, the misstep proved that Francis could not control his people.[2]

For Cardinal Pietro Parolin, secretary of state, the Chinese change of heart was no shock. In 2009, after leading negotiations with Beijing for four years under Pope Benedict XVI, the diplomat flew to Beijing with a text in his briefcase, crafted by both sides and approved by the pontiff. But the Chinese got cold feet, and the bilateral effort was buried. Parolin was sent as nuncio to Venezuela a few months later. It was this stillbirth that Bergoglio revived with his pontificate.

Although Pope Francis was disappointed that the breakthrough—scheduled to mark Divine Mercy Sunday, no less—was a no go, his commitment to accord with Beijing did not waver. According to collaborators in China, the pope outlined three concrete goals to be overseen by Parolin: keep channels open with the Foreign Ministry, get the two Mindong bishops in the same room, and intensify focus on joint cultural projects, including an art exhibit and horticulture show. Meanwhile, the pope personally reached out to interlocutors, including President Xi Jinping and the Chinese ambassador to Italy, minimizing the significance of the Mindong misunderstanding.

As a result of a private dinner between Mindong's two bishops—Bishop Vincent Guo Xijin, the popular unregistered prelate with a flock eight times the size of government-approved Bishop Vincenzo Zhan Silu's community—the two men agreed to implement Francis's request for concrete steps to unify their communities as Christ prayed, "so that they be one" (John 17:22). It was a triumph for Francis's fundamental conviction that through sincere personal encounter, we find Christ with us, making unexpected transformation possible and restoring dignity to our mutual relations.[3] Tempers at the Chinese Foreign Ministry calmed, too.

And just like that, the fruit of three pontificates was ripe.

FORTY YEARS IN THE MAKING: BEIJING BREAKTHROUGH

On September 22, 2018, Msgr. Antoine Camilleri, undersecretary for relations with states (an *Accademia* graduate from Malta) and Deputy Foreign

Minister Wang Chao[4] (born in Hebei Province,[5] a Catholic stronghold where one million believers live) sat at a standard wooden conference table in the Foreign Ministry's swank Chaoyang District office. With little fanfare, they signed a provisional agreement structuring the collaborative selection of Catholic bishops, lifting the excommunication of seven sitting bishops, and creating a new diocese in China, the first step in updating the Church's territorial organization. Neither side publicly released the document, set to expire in two years—and no bootleg copies were circulating even years later.[6]

The only Beijing media outlet that anticipated the event was the *Global Times*, an online news site close to power, which reported on September 18 that a Vatican delegation was expected later in the month. The article confirmed the pope's superior role in designating bishops because, it reported, he will issue letters of appointment to new bishops.[7]

Securing the elusive agreement with China over bishops was almost forty years in the making, as we will explore in chapter 11. In the Vatican's long view, this is just the first step in renewing a Sino-Catholic relationship marked by persecution since the Communists took power in 1949.

Pope Francis's instinctive response to the Easter setback, a response that set the stage for the eventual agreement signing, demonstrates two key aspects of his international success. First, he showed mastery of his office's diplomatic instrument panel. The directive to his collaborators was consistent with classic Vatican insight on the art of diplomacy: keep talking. As Cardinal Armand Jean du Plessis, Duke of Richelieu—better known as Cardinal Richelieu—explained in a seventeenth-century memo for King Louis XIII, optimal diplomatic results require "continuous negotiation."[8] The legendary early modern statesman urged envoys to build relationships with government counterparts through ongoing discussion:

> Whoever is constantly negotiating will ultimately find the right moment to achieve his end, and even if it does not come, there was no harm in trying, and by his negotiations he will be keeping up on what is going on in the world, which is of no small importance.[9]

In Richelieu's view, the technique allowed diplomats to foresee potential problems rather than parachuting into a crisis, with neither contacts nor local knowledge to turn problems around.[10]

The second thing we see in Pope Francis's ability to put the China deal back on course is the powerful pastoral and theological wisdom he brings to each political task. He has drive and confidence. As noted in chapter 2, it's always an institutional priority to preserve Catholic communities in distress. Add to this task Bergoglio's vision of the Church as an agent of reconciliation, employing processes of personal encounter, and you begin to see diplomacy as an occasion for evangelization too.

As a Jesuit who has spent a lifetime discerning God's will, as a pastor who has guided human beings toward the light, and as a Christian intellectual who loves the world, believes in the devil, and favors concrete action, Jorge Bergoglio brought a distinct approach to his job as *Pontifex Maximus*, the great bridge builder. It's a proactive style especially valid for the bumptious give-and-take of today's highly contentious world order.

Much as Pope Francis inherited an adept network of capable collaborators (chapter 1) and an international legal personality that gives the Holy See sovereign status (chapter 4), he gained a tradition of diplomatic practice honed for hundreds of years into a mighty art. It is valuable to review elements of this classic tradition, still practiced today. Then I will outline how this practice is summarized in five primary rules of thumb imbued by students at the *Accademia*, practiced at every post, and advanced by the Secretariat of State under the pope's guidance.

THE ART OF DIPLOMACY IN CLASSIC EXPRESSION

Undoubtedly, the most famous treatise on politics and diplomacy penned by a Catholic practitioner is *The Prince* by Niccolò Machiavelli. Written in 1513, its ends-justify-means advice to leaders who want to retain power is a product of its time: he represented the small but mighty Republic of Florence on missions to France, Germany, and Rome while the infamously corrupt pope Alexander VI sat on Peter's throne. Instability and persistent war plagued Northern Italy. Machiavelli even witnessed murderous acts committed by the pope's . . . son.

But the Florentine has had little impact on papal diplomats with their own canon of classic guides.[11] A Catholic worldview produced Europe's first diplomatic handbook: *Ambaxiator Brevilogus* (*Short treatise on ambassadors*), written in 1436 by Bernard du Rosier, papal legate to the Court of Castile in Spain and later archbishop of Toulouse, France. Rosier explained that for diplomacy to be truly divine, to be God's work, it should advance the common good, which requires peace. On the basis of this special, sacred task, the author makes the case that an ambassador needs freedom of access and transit, security from violence, and exemption from local taxes. He also explained that since diplomats function on behalf of all Christendom, it is sacrilegious to murder them—not an uncommon tragedy in medieval Europe. The sanctity Rosier assigns to God's agents and the protections they need are the first attempt to define diplomatic immunity. These ideas form the basis of immunities formally assigned to accredited diplomats at the 1815 Congress of Vienna.

FRANÇOIS DE CALLIÈRES

As discussed in previous chapters, there was perhaps no more famous—or infamous—practitioner of diplomacy in his day than Cardinal Richelieu, whose wisdom was captured in the *Testament Politique*, compiled and circulated after his death. The treatise that really popularized Richelieu's ideas, though, was *On the Manner of Negotiating with Princes* by François de Callières, published in 1716. Not only was it *the* go-to textbook in the eighteenth century regarding ideal conduct and methods, but its influence was revived in the twentieth century when scholar Ernest Satow quoted it extensively in his seminal *Guide to Diplomatic Practice* (1917), and Harold Nicolson, a British diplomat and masterful commentator, called it "the best manual of diplomatic method ever written."[12]

At the Pontifical Ecclesiastical Academy, Callières's guide has long been required reading. In the Frenchman's points, one recognizes a description of Vatican practice to this day. It comprises a set of principles to follow, dependent on the envoy being a moral person.

Callières gives diplomats a dual aim: to build durable relations with a host government while discovering the designs of others. Peace is the overall goal.[13] Envoys should be fluent in several languages, including Latin. They must know regional and local history. They should debrief predecessors, reading past dispatches to understand the network of relationships informing the court and linking neighboring countries. With colleagues, it is smart to share information and maintain a collaborative demeanor, although, when it comes to negotiating agreements, "secrecy is the very soul of diplomacy."[14] The pursuit should never be left to amateurs; ideally, each country should develop a diplomatic school, although requisite good judgment is innate, not taught.[15]

Honesty is an essential personal attribute and approach in negotiations: deception can be lethal—"a lie always leaves a drop of poison behind"[16]— and misunderstandings should immediately be corrected. To maintain independence, gifts should not be accepted. To keep the home office informed, written reports should give complete accounts, and dispatches should be sent almost daily. In Callières's ideal world, the home office is in constant contact with envoys, and credit for success can be shared fifty-fifty since the front line and distant perspectives combine for the best decision making.[17]

What's especially eye catching is to find in this three-hundred-year-old treatise ideas advanced constantly by Pope Francis. The Frenchman valorizes empathy, the ability to see problems from the other's perspective. So does Francis. Callières describes negotiation as seeking to "harmonize the interests"[18] of both sovereigns. For Francis this is essential because neither side should have to capitulate to find common ground. He describes the best way to come to agreement as making "not so much a synthesis, as a harmony . . . because harmony is the work of the Holy Spirit."[19] Francis refers to harmonizing diversity,[20] or "reconciled diversity"[21] (a term first used by a Lutheran theologian), as an appropriate goal for achieving agreement or peace without imposing a false unity.

Both men share an attitude toward time and the value of patience: Trust is established gradually, so decisions should not be forced. In light of this reality, it is best to set out step by step to achieve concrete tasks rather than giant goals. Callières offers an explanation for this strategy that Francis would surely affirm:

> [T]he majority of men will never enter upon a vast undertaking, even though advantageous to themselves, without they can see beforehand the whole length of the journey upon which they are asked to embark. Its magnitude will deter them. But if they can be brought to take successfully one step after another they will find themselves at the end of the journey almost unawares.[22]

Even the Frenchman's modest definition of what this endeavor is all about finds resonance with Francis's practice: diplomacy "is the attempt to find a basis of common action or agreement."[23]

On the Manner of Negotiating with Princes distills the elements of French diplomacy originated by Richelieu and practiced across Europe from the Peace of Westphalia until about World War I, when new constituencies and ideas broke consensus regarding the conduct of interstate relations.[24] The Holy See was not subject to the same pressures that challenged "old diplomacy" in other places (democratic pressure or intervention from nonstate actors), so it has maintained many practices found in this classic text. More important, Gospel values remain unchanged, as does the Catholic Church's commitment to natural law as an appropriate basis for international intervention. These sources of inspiration—and motivation—make peace the raison d'être of God's diplomacy.

LONG-STANDING DIPLOMATIC RULES OF THUMB

1. Avoid Creating Winners and Losers

The Treaty of Versailles, which ended World War I in 1919, came with a sober lesson: don't create triumphalist winners and resentful losers if you want peace to last. As explored in chapter 3, Pope Benedict XV and the Holy See were excluded from negotiations as a result of a secret clause Italy demanded when it joined the Allies in 1915. (Italy feared that Vatican influence in negotiations might translate into property gains in Rome.) Pope Benedict XV had no way to directly influence the Paris agreement. But as soon as he reviewed it, the pope foresaw violent fallout, which descended on Europe some twenty years later.

The Holy See objected to the punitive treatment of Germany and to the Wilsonian mantra of "national self-determination." First, the treaty "humiliated Germany," as the Jesuit journal *La Civiltà Cattolica*[25] wrote. Pope Benedict XV feared that the huge reparations bill imposed on Germany would lead to economic instability and prevent German recovery. Second, the Vatican worried that the new, small successor states created on the principle of self-determination would continue to fight over borders and minority rights. Rome didn't believe those states would be strong enough to resist takeover by Communist forces to the east. On this, Vatican worries proved especially prescient.

Rome had similar fears some thirty years later when World War II ended with the unconditional surrender of Germany and Japan. Though there was no treaty to critique, the Vatican was concerned that the organization of the United Nations enshrined the winners (China,[26] France, Russia, the United Kingdom, and the United States) as a permanent class: the five winners comprised the Security Council's permanent members, each with veto power. The idea that political settlements should not create winners and losers flows from fundamental Christian concepts of human dignity, equality, and forgiveness—scaled up to apply to nations.

2. Remain Impartial in the Face of Conflict

Tightly bound up with the idea of not creating winners and losers is to remain impartial in the face of conflict—another long-standing Vatican practice. Consider that once the Vatican lost its geographic footprint in 1870, Pope Leo XIII utilized neutrality to demonstrate the Church's unique ability to mediate conflict.[27] As discussed in chapter 4, despite his frustration over not finding a role in mediating peace during the Great War, Pope Benedict XV used neutrality to great purpose in providing humanitarian assistance, communications networks, and medical care, especially to prisoners of war (POWs) and their families. The 1929 Lateran Treaty stipulates that both the Holy See, in its actions, and Vatican City, in its geographic attributes, remain neutral.[28]

Benedict XV's stance had a lifelong impact on a talented *Accademia*-educated diplomat in his secretariat: Eugenio Pacelli, future Pope Pius XII. Pacelli served numerous functions during World War I, most related to managing relief programs and maintaining a registry of POWs. In 1917, Benedict sent him to Bavaria as nuncio. Three years later, he was named nuncio to Germany. Since there was no Vatican representative in Moscow, he also ran food and relief shipments to the Soviet Union, despite its persecution of Christians.[29]

As Pope Pius XII, Eugenio Pacelli has been castigated relentlessly for not publicly denouncing the Nazi terror. His implementation of papal neutrality under Benedict XV probably contributed to his strategy during World War II. As Rabbi David Dalin has demonstrated, there's no doubt that Pacelli was personally convinced of the evil embodied in National Socialism, having witnessed its growth.[30] However, he was convinced the Vatican could not take a public position regarding the war, with Catholics living in every country involved in the conflict and the possibility that his public comments would put them—as well as people the Church was already protecting—at greater risk.

More recently, one sees the prophetic fruits of neutrality in Pope John Paul II's effort to prevent the US invasion of Iraq. The pope was engaged in numerous Middle East peace efforts, so he knew how volatile the region is. In Damascus, Syria, in 2001, he became the first pope to visit a mosque. As he entered the Umayyad Mosque—also the site of St. John the Baptist's tomb—the pope kissed a Quran as a sign of respect for Islam and its people, a theme captured in his address when he used a family metaphor to describe relations between the two faith groups.[31]

Out of this experience, John Paul II was sure that a US-led invasion of Iraq would backfire badly. He and his foreign policy team believed an invasion would destabilize the region, putting its two-thousand-year-old Christian communities at existential risk and provoking Islamic extremism. And so it came to pass: brutal instability across the Middle East and North Africa, Christian genocide, and Islamic radicalization. The practice of neutrality has given the Church tragic powers of prediction.

3. Refrain from Partisan Politics

Practicing true diplomatic neutrality is impossible without avoiding the pitfalls of partisan politics. Pope Francis has warned nuncios to avoid politics even as he encouraged laypeople to jump in,[32] to advocate for the common good, regardless of "getting your hands or heart a little dirty."[33] Benedict XVI was emphatic regarding the Church's distance from politics. The Church, he wrote, "does not have any specific answers to concrete political questions.... She points out paths for reason to follow."[34]

Being wary of secular power goes very far back. It was a politician, of course, a Roman governor, who ordered the execution of Jesus Christ. In modern history—and certainly since the loss of Rome in 1870, when Italian politicians enthusiastically sacrificed the Church's independence for national unity—each pope has been skeptical of tainting spiritual goals with political ones. At the same time, protecting the faithful and advancing a vision of human dignity, especially since Vatican II, requires the Church to engage in dialogue with national governments. To thread this needle, the Church often works behind the scenes, building trust with secular authorities regardless of political leanings.

Vietnam is a good example of where the Vatican worked quietly for decades to strengthen the local Church and increase its autonomy by gaining the trust of political leaders. After the Communist Party took power and reunified the country in 1975 (following the chaotic retreat of US troops), the Church was suppressed. No priests were ordained between 1976 and 1990,[35] but atheism couldn't eliminate an institution with roots in the seventeenth century and millions of devoted followers. In 1989, Pope John Paul II sent Cardinal Roger Etchegaray, president of the Pontifical Council for Justice and Peace, to visit Hanoi and establish parameters for cooperation with the government.[36]

Gradually, local Church groups reemerged. The Daughters of Mary Immaculate started a small health clinic in an ad hoc motherhouse in 1992; they expanded the clinic when the government returned their expropriated convent.[37] Over the next fourteen years, Vatican delegations visited Vietnam some twelve times.

When Undersecretary of State for Relations with States Pietro Parolin led a delegation there in 2004, the group was allowed to visit the country's largest diocese, Xuan Loc (where over 30 percent of the people are Catholic), for the first time since 1975.[38] As a result of years of discussion, prior visits, and, most important, the reality of Catholic Vietnamese communities as indisputably law abiding, the government was sufficiently convinced that Catholics weren't a destabilizing force.

On the contrary, as Parolin told local reporters, the Church "asks only to be able to exercise its mission freely, placing itself at the service of the country and its people."[39] A year later, the government approved a new ordinance on religion, allowing the Church to implement charitable activities. It also agreed to let the Hanoi seminary expand and enroll annual classes.[40] By 2010, the Vietnam–Holy See Joint Working Group agreed that the pope would appoint a nonresident representative to Vietnam, allowing a bilateral relationship just short of full recognition.[41] Eventually the government agreed to a hybrid plan for the selection of bishops, allowing local bishops in consultation with the government to compile a list of three candidates submitted to Rome, which announces the bishop's appointment.[42] The main problem emerged when, on occasion, vacancies languished as the government simply failed to act.

Overall, this diplomacy of patience with Vietnam has paid off. The Catholic Church continues to grow in membership, vocations, and the number of schools it manages.[43] New churches are built, even in remote mountainous regions, financed mainly by parishioners.[44] The Church collaborates well with Vietnam's largest religion, Buddhism, especially in caring for HIV/AIDS patients and other charitable work.[45] During an invitation-only press opportunity, a Catholic journalist from Vietnam looked surprised when Cardinal Joseph Zen (who said he was recently back from a visit to Vietnam) told her, "Congratulations, you succeeded in Vietnam!"[46] referring, ironically, to achievements engineered by Cardinal Parolin, Zen's nemesis when it comes to negotiations with China. Meanwhile, political activism is the domain of lay Catholics: the faithful push the envelope with demonstrations against corruption, restricted freedom of speech, and environmental mismanagement.

4. Pursue Dialogue . . . with Everyone

Not favoring one political ideology over another, not involving itself in political fights of the day—these make the Vatican a less threatening actor. On his visit to Damascus, John Paul II offered a poignant picture of what dialogue is, in words and actions. He said, "In Syria, Christians and Muslims have lived side by side for centuries, and a rich dialogue of life has gone on unceasingly. Every individual and every family knows moments of harmony and other moments when dialogue has broken down. The positive experiences must strengthen our communities in the hope of peace; and the negative experiences should not be allowed to undermine that hope."[47]

At a different stop on the visit, the pope recited the Apostles' Creed together with an Orthodox patriarch of Antioch, demonstrating deep bonds between Catholics and Orthodox, especially those living in Muslim-majority countries. John Paul II even prayed at a decimated Greek Orthodox church in Quneitra, a town in the Golan Heights destroyed by Israel during the wars of 1967 and 1973, proclaiming, "May all believers find the courage to forgive one another, so that the wounds of the past may be healed and not be a pretext for further suffering in the present."[48]

What the pope demonstrated is the conviction that all religious divides—between Catholics and Orthodox, Christians and Muslims, Arabs and Jews—can be overcome through forgiveness and diligent efforts at dialogue, premised on mutual respect. As simple as that idea is, the Church meets plenty of secular audiences for whom the notion remains foreign. An example revealed by WikiLeaks describing Parolin in discussions with US officials cogently demonstrates the Vatican's conviction that dialogue is always an appropriate course.

In 2006, Parolin met with a group of US congressional representatives as part of an open-ended discussion:

> Parolin discussed the Holy See's philosophy of dialogue . . . expressing the Vatican's well-known principle that such interaction was the best way to attempt to change aberrant behavior. . . . Parolin said, ". . . the Holy See would not refuse an approach for talks from Hamas. . . . We will not seek contact, but neither will we refuse it if approached," he said.[49]

Hamas, an acronym for the Islamic Resistance Movement, is designated a terrorist organization by the US State Department.[50] A Sunni affiliate that grew out of Egypt's Muslim Brotherhood, it is "untouchable" to the United States, but the Vatican has no such verboten list. The Americans must have been puzzled at Parolin's nonchalant attitude toward a group American foreign policy demonizes.

5. Walk the Talk: Show Faith through Charity

Charity is an essential component in Christian life, and it plays an essential role in Vatican diplomacy too. Innumerable examples of Catholic aid being used to beneficial effect could be mentioned, but especially interesting is when charity is the only form of Catholic outreach to a place, or when it is the first or early manifestation of Church presence. These cases most exemplify humanitarian diplomacy.

After the 2010 earthquake in Haiti, for example, the US government quickly engaged with Rome regarding local conditions, aid delivery, and political risks. The Church in Haiti is large; before the disaster, there were eighteen bishops in ten dioceses. About 70 percent of the population of ten million is Catholic. A high-profile casualty was the archbishop of Port-au-Prince, thrown to his death from a balcony at the nunciature.

The Church quickly pledged over $50 million in assistance and raised another $14 million in donations. Summarizing actions the United States and the Holy See were taking together, an American official wrote, "Normally contemplative and deliberately slow to act in political crises, the Vatican and Church-related organizations are responsive and effective when dealing with humanitarian disasters. Its global network of aid organizations and local Church entities provide a well-organized and reasonably well-funded structure to deliver assistance."[51]

A captivating example unveiled by WikiLeaks was how Vatican charities work with regimes in China, North Korea, and Myanmar. A priest working as an Asia desk officer at Caritas Internationalis revealed that Caritas workers disguised as tourists flew every two weeks from Thailand to Myanmar to provide medical assistance to needy patients. In North Korea, the Church paid for the construction of a hospital that Caritas staffed and trained local people to run. In China in 2009, Caritas worked with government-registered churches, as well as with unregistered underground Catholic communities. Because HIV/AIDS was a growing problem, Caritas increased its prevention work while providing antiretroviral medication. According to the source, Chinese officials were well aware that Caritas worked with the underground Church but turned a blind eye.[52]

In all three countries, what caused the unfriendly regimes to allow Catholic charity to continue was, first, the Church's policy of maintaining a low profile and not seeking publicity for its contributions and, second, Caritas's efficiency in delivering much-needed services to vulnerable and disabled people.

Although Vietnam was not as politically closed as China before 1990, it too was a place where humanitarian assistance established an early bridge to wider Church presence. The US embassy to the Holy See accurately concluded, "Caritas clearly believes that its mission of assisting the needy in repressive countries must come ahead of condemnation of the governments doing the repressing. In this sense, it reflects the priorities at the Vatican itself. Embassy therefore expects that Caritas will continue to seek quiet accommodation even with the most repressive regimes, as long as such accommodations allow its life-saving work to continue."[53]

Pope Francis continues these policies centering charity and dialogue in the framework of an evangelizing, outward-looking Church. As he wrote in his first doctrinal text, *Evangelii Gaudium* (On the Proclamation of the Gospel in Today's World, 2013),

> An evangelizing community gets involved by word and deed in people's daily lives; it bridges distances, it is willing to abase itself if necessary, and it embraces human life, touching the suffering flesh of Christ in others. . . . Evangelization consists mostly of patience and disregard for constraints of time. Faithful to the Lord's gift, it also bears fruit. An evangelizing community is always concerned with fruit, because the Lord wants her to be fruitful. It cares for the grain and does not grow impatient at the weeds. The sower, when he sees weeds sprouting among the grain does not grumble or overreact. He or she finds a way to let the word take flesh in a particular situation and bear fruits of new life, however imperfect or incomplete these may appear.[54]

In the pope's prioritization of a mission-oriented Church, one sees how charity and diplomacy are two faces of the same effort: Charity is not just a tactic, or tip of the spear for diplomatic machination. No. Both are ways to proclaim the Gospel message, in different ways. The Catholic Church is an eminently expressive institution. This is its main power. In political science terms, the Church is sometimes described as maximizing its "soft power" rather than coercive force.[55] But as Pope Francis's statement makes clear, the Church's goals are immaterial, almost utopian: not to manipulate in order to gain, but to restore, renew, reveal, rejoice. Francis sets a high task for God's diplomats.

INCARNATING DIPLOMACY THROUGH A CULTURE OF ENCOUNTER

In *Evangelii Gaudium*, Francis lists four principles that he believes should shape the thinking and behavior of those who seek to advance peace and the common good: time is greater than space, unity prevails over conflict, reality is more important than ideas, and the whole is greater than the parts.[56] Although abstract at first glance, the rules genuinely summarize his strategy and reflect his desire to avoid the divisiveness and competition that characterize interstate (and, too often, interpersonal) relations. He goes so far as to assert that "their application can be a genuine path to peace within each nation and in the entire world."[57] In chapter 6, I will show how these principles help explain Francis's response to war in Ukraine.

The same section of *Evangelii Gaudium* that highlights the four principles evokes a related concept: the culture of encounter.[58] Austin Ivereigh describes it as one of Bergoglio's "big themes" when he was archbishop of Buenos Aires—the others being politics as service, the preferential option for the poor, solidarity, and the common good.[59] What the culture of encounter represents is an attitude of openheartedness toward others, including rivals or opponents. It includes the pope's call to "go to the margins" and serve people on social and geographic peripheries. Here's what's critical: the culture of encounter is meant to describe *real* encounters with *real* people. It's a program of action, not theory. (As one of the principles says, reality first.)

This approach flows from Christianity itself. At the heart of Catholic faith is the incarnation of God as man; the torture and murder of that innocent man, Jesus Christ; and each believer's encounter with His life and resurrection through the sacraments, through Scripture, and through the teaching authority of the Church. The reality of God entering human history is not abstract, and the impact of His sacrifice should not be theoretical for the faithful. Besides that, the Jesuit order has a special charism for Christ crucified—the unjustly persecuted, humiliated, reviled figure of God hanging on a cross.

Francis himself summarized the pivotal notion of encounter with Christ as the trope for all meaningful encounter when he described one of his favorite paintings, *The Calling of St. Matthew* by Baroque master Caravaggio. Located in a side chapel of the Church of St. Louis of the French in the center of Rome, it shows Jesus pointing directly at a tax collector, calling him to follow. In response, a shocked St. Matthew points to himself as he touches coins with his other hand. Personal encounter changes lives. Francis says he felt like Matthew when he was selected by the conclave to lead the Church: "It is the gesture of Matthew that strikes me: he holds on to his money as if to say, 'No, not me! No, this money is mine.' Here, this is me, a sinner on whom the Lord has turned his gaze. And this is what I said when they asked me if I would accept my election as pontiff."[60]

It is helpful to think of the culture of encounter as a pastoral style Francis applies to diplomacy. It's also an updating version of the Good Samaritan parable. Asked by a fellow Jew to explain who is the "neighbor" that God expects us to love "as yourself," Jesus tells an unexpected story.[61] First a priest (assumed to be a rabbi), then a member of a religious community, a Levite, cross the narrow road to avoid helping a traveler who is "half dead," beaten and stripped by robbers. Along comes a Samaritan. (Key fact: in first-century Judea, Jews and Samaritans were enemies.) The Samaritan binds the victim's wounds, puts him on a donkey, brings him to an inn, and pays for his care. The Samaritan is the quintessential neighbor. Jesus is pointing to the erasure of prejudice when people encounter each other with empathy and the irrelevance of social status to God.

A diplomat who served as Francis's permanent observer at the United Nations, Archbishop Bernardito Auza, an *Accademia* graduate, called the culture of encounter the "golden thread" tying all the pope's "words and actions" together.[62]

Through his papal documents and many verbal pronouncements, Francis has given the faithful action-oriented assignments to get out of church buildings, go to the margins, serve others, evangelize, and work to save the environment, even to the point of causing "a mess" in his words to Argentinian youth during World Youth Day in Rio de Janeiro. The pope continued, "I want to see the church get closer to the people. I want to get rid of clericalism, the mundane, this closing ourselves off within ourselves, in our parishes, schools or structures. Because these need to get out!"[63] Reoccurring in his public—and private—statements, Francis offers his own rules of thumb. This guidance is valuable for diplomats as well as pew sitters called to manifest the culture of encounter.

In a sense, Francis's rules of thumb are simply tips for putting Christian values into practice. Anyone can benefit, not just the *Accademia*'s elite. I've listed five of Francis's rules that we will see in the cases studies of Part II. Since the pope's advice builds on existing principles, I've continued the numbering from above.

6. Start Processes (That God Can Finish)

So often we fail to take initiative because we aren't sure how the effort will turn out. Francis urges us to overcome debilitating fears because no one can ever control outcomes—and shouldn't even try. Christians have a liberating reason to embrace risk: God can step into the space you create by beginning something new. As the pope reassures the faithful, "Trust what God is doing through you."

Once again, we find this idea living in *Evangelii Gaudium* in Francis's discussion of unity over conflict. When looking at conflict, the pope explains that some people ignore it, while others get sucked into it, but imagine a third way: face the problem head on and make it the start of a new process.[64] It's not always easy. In Nicaragua, the *Accademia*-trained Polish nuncio and Managua's popular archbishop, Cardinal Leopoldo Brenes, were high-profile advocates for social reconciliation, even out in the street beginning in 2018.[65] They tried various tactics to mediate between a trigger-happy government and opposition groups protesting arbitrary rule—and illegal detention of some eight hundred political prisoners—including getting the Organization of American States involved and working with the regional conference of Jesuits. Having risked engagement, escalating violence targeted the Church: leaders blame terrorism for an August 2020 petrol bomb attack against a four-hundred-year-old wooden crucifix, a centerpiece of worship for the country's faithful in Managua's cathedral.[66]

Implementing the culture of encounter applies beyond conflict. The Good Samaritan gave the victim a helping hand although he had no time to stay with him and passed his care to the innkeeper. Start something good and good will follow. This advice is related to the Christian requirement not to seek credit for good deeds. Francis has a go-to recommendation for anyone who asks him how to live. He points to two sources, both in Matthew's Gospel, where charity acts without concern for recognition or reward. Serving as a peacemaker, feeding the hungry, and visiting those in prison all involve initiating a relationship, advancing the culture of encounter—and simply manifesting Christian faith:

What must we do, Father? Look, read the Beatitudes: that will do you good. If you want to know what you actually have to do, read Matthew Chapter 25, which is the standard by which we will be judged. With these two things you have the action plan: the Beatitudes and Matthew 25. You do not need to read anything else.[67]

7. Initiate Encounters with Humility and Respect

Pope Francis's humility is legendary. He rejected a chauffeured limousine in favor of public transportation as archbishop. He refused the sumptuous papal apartment to live among guests served upscale cafeteria style at Casa Marta. He sports a black Swatch watch, wears black orthopedic shoes, and carries a standard black briefcase when he boards for foreign trips. Adult beverage of choice? Whiskey.

This personal preference extends to his diplomatic style. Deference is both natural and a savvy long-term strategy when courting foreign leaders, especially non-Christians. One of the countries with which Francis initiated diplomatic relations was Myanmar in 2017,[68] country number 183 on the Vatican's list of mutuals. Six months after the breakthrough, he became the first pope to visit the country.

Although his interest in visiting the region was strongly propelled by his concern for the Rohingya people (a Muslim minority hounded and brutalized by the state and forced into exile in neighboring Muslim-majority Bangladesh, despite the community's longtime presence in Myanmar), the pope did not mention the Rohingya by name when he met with military and political leaders. For that, he was chastised by the international media.[69] But had he insulted the country's leadership, would he have advanced the situation of the Rohingya? No, he would merely score rhetorical points against the regime.

On his next stop in Bangladesh, Francis met with refugees, acknowledged their pain, and said their name: "The presence of God today is also called Rohingya,"[70] he assured them. The culture of encounter requires direct personal action, but diplomats should never weaponize a tragedy to score points against a government, no matter how misguided the regime is.

Humility has an interesting role in one of Francis's favorite books, *The End of the Modern World* by Jesuit philosopher and theologian Romano Guardini, the subject of Bergoglio's unfinished PhD dissertation. Guardini presents humility as the "decisive characteristic" of the Christian message, especially for our time. He sees it as the most authentic response to the obsession with power found in contemporary society.[71]

8. Proceed through Concrete Steps and Gestures

The Burmese military junta released activist Aung San Suu Kyi in 2010, a Nobel Prize winner held under house arrest for fifteen years—one of the world's best-known political prisoners, sequestered again in 2021. Francis met Suu Kyi at the Vatican in 2013 and 2017, which helped normalize relations. According to Burmese diplomats, though, another factor that spurred parliament to approve Vatican recognition was Francis's appointment of the country's first cardinal, Archbishop Charles Bo of Yangon, a much-respected peacemaker.[72] Naming a cardinal from a small Catholic community in what is considered a peripheral place represents a concrete form of recognition with the power to help open a wider relationship—as it did.

Appointing a cardinal to signal the importance of a place is a traditional gesture. A far more novel one was Francis's invitation to twelve Syrian Muslims (three families), refugees he met on the island of Lesbos in a detention center, to immigrate to Italy via the papal plane. Once in Rome, the Vatican cared for the families through the Sant'Egidio lay Catholic community.[73]

Francis's motive was to highlight the message that everyone should help support migrants who flocked by the millions to Europe from places of war and poverty beginning in the fall of 2015. Rather than give another speech, he took some people in. "It's a drop of water in the sea. But after this drop, the sea will never be the same," explained Francis, quoting Mother Teresa.[74] The pope communicates regularly through gestures like these, as we will see in Part II.

9. Allow Mutual Respect to Grow Step by Step

An outstanding example of how the diplomacy of encounter proceeds, over time and step by step, is the relationship between Pope Francis and the grand imam of Al-Azhar, Ahmed al-Tayeb, one of Sunni Islam's most esteemed leaders. He's also past president of Al-Azhar University in Cairo, the country's oldest university, a center of Islamic culture and authority. Relations between the Holy See and the grand imam hit a low in 2011 when al-Tayeb broke off communications, including annual meetings begun by John Paul II. The Muslim leader was upset over a statement about terrorism in Egypt that he inferred from one of Benedict XVI's Sunday Angelus prayers.

Fast-forward eight years to find Francis and al-Tayeb together on a futuristic stage in Abu Dhabi signing a landmark pledge of fraternity between the two world religions united against religious extremism and the political manipulation of religion. It was the historic first papal trip to the Sunni Muslim heartland, the Arabian Peninsula, and the first public Mass there.

To get to that moment took innumerable small steps and concrete gestures, especially these: Francis sent his trusted French adviser Cardinal Tauran to probe the situation on al-Tayeb's home turf in 2015, apologizing for any misunderstanding. Six months later, the scholar was at the Vatican meeting with the pope. Institutional dialogue resumed. A year later, Francis visited Cairo where, incidentally, he began each talk, including the Mass, with the Arabic phrase *As-salamu alaykum!* (*Peace be with you*!), a sign of respect in the Muslim world. The two religious leaders signed a joint statement declaring violence and faith incompatible. Francis believes, as he said, "the future principally relies on the dialogue between all religions."[75]

According to a priest working at the Council on Interreligious Dialogue, the visit evinced a personal rapport between the two men. As a result, they explored widening the reach of the 2017 document, which grew into the United Arab Emirates conference—deepening their bond further. Now these two powerful men of faith are in regular contact. In April 2020, on the eve of the month of Ramadan, Francis phoned al-Tayeb to offer a greeting.[76] Undoubtedly, unknown fruits have grown from the relationship, and the process remains open ended.

Cardinal Fitzgerald, an Islam expert, considers this relationship to be especially significant. He points out that the Vatican has long supported interreligious dialogue (see, for example, the 1984 Vatican document "Dialogue and Mission"), but Francis models *how* and emphasizes the task of "serving humanity together."

"Pope Francis has given—as he has in his teachings generally, *Laudato si'*, *Evangelii Gaudium*—a more practical way of living out our Christian life. And living out the Christian life means to be related to people who are not Christians too and to be working together with them," Fitzgerald told the *National Catholic Register*.[77]

Contrast that spirit with the reflection of a high-profile adviser to successive US administrations on military strategy and geopolitics, Romanian-born Professor Edward Luttwak, who told the *Guardian*, "You know, I never gave George W. Bush enough credit for what he's done in the Middle East. . . . I failed to appreciate at the time that he was a strategic genius far beyond Bismarck. He ignited a religious war between Shiites and Sunnis that will occupy the region for the next 1,000 years. It was a pure stroke of brilliance!"[78]

10. Find Common Ground and Build Agreement from That Point

What Francis and al-Tayeb (and their advisers) especially honed in on between 2017 and 2019 was a shared commitment to combating extremism. That was the common ground, and it became the locus of discussion. This focus and engagement had immediate ancillary benefits. For example, the outdoor Mass in Abu Dhabi, which drew Catholics from all over the region and was a source of profound joy for the UAE's Catholic faithful (over one million strong, mainly foreign workers), was possible *because* the regime wanted to please the pope. Francis quite candidly noted this himself. On the plane ride home, he mused, "What did I find here? A welcome so great that they wanted to do everything, little things and great things, because they felt that the Pope's visit was a good thing . . . and they wanted to make known that I was welcome."[79] In chapter 6, we will see how protecting Christians in the Middle East became the common ground for a breakthrough between the Holy See and the Russian Orthodox Church even in the midst of a war pitting Ukrainian Greek Catholics against Ukrainian Orthodox.

Something worth noting is how Francis's rules of thumb and the openheartedness of the process he recommends contribute to a perspective markedly different from the cynical outlook that marks many worldviews these days. For example, assessing the geopolitical situation on the Korean Peninsula, Archbishop Paul Gallagher sees a "crisis of communication." What a contrast to an American president who taunted the North Korean leader as "little rocket man."[80] Start with empathy and you will see very different things.

A PASSION FOR PEACE IN KOREA

Before turning to case studies in Part II, where each chapter highlights a specific agreement, historical meeting, or act of reconciliation achieved, I want to train a light on the pope's method in medias res, in the middle of the story, by looking at Korea.

Mobilizing a SWAT Team for Diplomacy

The pope is highly engaged behind the scenes with Korea, especially after he made it his first destination in Asia in 2014. The overall goal on the peninsula is reconciliation between North and South. To get there, the Vatican encouraged President Moon Jae-in, local officials, Church leaders, and its own diplomats on the ground. On a visit to Seoul in late 2017, I attended the second annual Korean Peninsula Peace-Sharing Forum, hosted by the Seoul archdiocese's Institute on Peace Sharing and sponsored by the Korean Ministry of Culture, Sport, and Tourism, thus a church-state partnership. Arriving at the event's venue on the campus of the Catholic University of Korea, the country's oldest university, I was surprised to see three Church luminaries from Latin America: Salvadoran Cardinal Gregorio Rosa Chávez;

Cardinal Odilo Pedro Scherer of São Paulo, Brazil; and Archbishop Carlos Garfias Merlos from Morelia, Mexico. The Holy See's Secretariat of State had encouraged them to share war stories—often literally about war—from their home countries in order to inspire Koreans facing a major political challenge.

Circulating solemnly among assembled student leaders, priests, journalists, and government officials, Salvadoran Rosa Chávez distributed tiny *ex indumentis* relics of Blessed Óscar Romero attached to Mass cards. He did not include a message with the cards, which were laminated to include small fragments of the assassinated archbishop's clothing. He did not ask us to pray for El Salvador or Korea, for that matter. Quietly, he merely bestowed grace.

Rosa Chávez exemplifies the kind of priests Francis has elevated to the College of Cardinals. He has rewarded humble men and he has elevated clerics who minister with a strong pastoral spirit—often in places not given much attention. The modest Salvadoran fits all three categories. The first cardinal in his nation's history, he's also the first auxiliary bishop ever to be raised to the college.[81] Ordained an auxiliary or "assistant" bishop in 1982, he was reportedly passed over for promotion on numerous occasions by Pope John Paul II and Benedict XVI because he was close to Romero, a pastor of the people, who denounced rural poverty, violence against community leaders, and atrocities committed by the Left and the Right in the escalating civil conflict of the 1970s and 1980s.

While saying Mass in the chapel of a cancer hospital, Romero was murdered in March 1980 by a state-sanctioned death squad determined to silence regime opponents.[82] At Romero's funeral, police opened fire on mourners, killing dozens.[83] Rosa Chávez, who was a seminarian when he met Romero, led the archbishop's communications office for three years before the assassination. Afterward, he humbly dedicated himself to Romero's legacy as an unassuming, tireless priest promoting peace. He participated in negotiations between the Salvadoran government and the main opposition group, the Farabundo Martí National Liberation Front, from 1984 to 1989.

When Rosa Chávez received news of his appointment in June 2017, he responded by going to Romero's grave where he said Mass, explaining to the Catholic News Agency that his mentor "shed his blood, like a true cardinal. He shed his blood for Christ, for the Church."[84] The bishop told others that he felt he was being elevated on behalf of Romero, whom Pope Francis canonized in October 2018.

To encourage others, the El Salvadoran cardinal traveled to Seoul, where he talked about his experience mediating peace talks in El Salvador.[85] The trip could be considered a function of Rosa Chávez's assignment to the Dicastery for Promoting Integral Human Development,[86] but it is also a way the pope signals his personal interest and solidarity with the Church of Korea as it faces the daunting task of negotiating peace with the North.

Cardinals serve as a sort of SWAT team for papal diplomacy, even without being told what to do. Cardinal Rosa Chávez visited Salvadoran immigrant communities in the United States soon after his promotion to demonstrate the Church's closeness to people under pressure, celebrating Mass in Spanish with Salvadoran communities on Long Island and even visiting a prison. People were ecstatic to meet him, as he mirrored Pope Francis's stance on the pastoral needs of hardworking immigrants who remain tied to home in their hearts.[87]

As Rosa Chávez was distributing relics in Seoul, Brazilian Cardinal Odilo Pedro Scherer jovially stood for pictures with middle-aged Catholic volunteers wearing sumptuous traditional dresses with skirts like big bells in bright colors. The visiting cardinals wore a version of traditional dress as well: long black cassocks trimmed in scarlet, a scarlet watered-silk sash, scarlet piping, thirty-three scarlet buttons down the front signifying Christ's age when He was crucified, and five buttons on the cuffs signifying Christ's wounds when nailed to the cross. Scarlet is the color symbolizing Christ's blood and martyrdom. Scherer is considered an intellectual with great command of finance and economics. In the lead-up to the 2013 conclave, he was counted as *papabili*, a papal contender, and he got some votes in the first round.

Pope Benedict XVI made him a cardinal in 2008, but he got to know Jorge Bergoglio well the year before when they shared an experience crucial for understanding Francis's weltanschauung: the Latin American Episcopal Conference (CELAM) meeting at the Marian shrine in Aparecida, Brazil. Pope Benedict XVI opened the gathering, and Cardinal Bergoglio was chosen to finalize a report summarizing the assembly's conclusions on how to enliven the Gospel message. Written as a road map for Latin America, it applies as well to the whole world.

The Aparecida text pictures a Church in perpetual outward movement that is continually renewing itself: encouraging personal encounter with Jesus; coaxing the faithful to live more simply and humbly as Christ taught; centering the poor, disabled, displaced, spiritually confused, and lonely at the heart of Christian ministry; picturing the earth as a common home, with social justice considered an ecological issue, not just a political one; and endorsing traditional, popular devotions.[88]

In his capacity as cardinal and as a member of the dicastery devoted to evangelization, Cardinal Scherer is another roving diplomat serving as the eyes and ears of Pope Francis, capable of transmitting and circulating messages to the curia on the hot-button issues of the day. The College of

Cardinals is a trusted, discreet vertical and horizontal network of information connecting Rome and the world, with an especially quick-response capacity to fly the yellow-and-white Vatican flag at key moments, in key places.

Rosa Chávez is an eminently spiritual man; Scherer is on the bookish side. An excellent third was a scrappy streetwise priest, comfortable in a pub or in a chapel or library: Mexican Archbishop Carlos Garfias Merlos, a solid rock of a man with a PhD in psychotherapy. Built like a boxer with a bulldog face, he looks like he's working a side job as his own bodyguard. Maybe his tough-guy look helps tame the devil out of bad actors in Latin America, because he emerged as a leader unafraid to confront drug and gang violence in Acapulco between 2010 and 2016.

He didn't hesitate to keep Rome aware of the metastasizing violence in Mexico either, by sharing his experiences via membership in various dicasteries. In 2016, Pope Francis visited Morelia, a picturesque colonial city in central Mexico, where organized crime groups have battled for control over methamphetamine production, using extortion, kidnapping, and murder to eliminate rivals and intimidate authorities from intervening. The pope decided to relocate Garfias to this new version of a war zone.

Peace Sharing in Seoul

In Seoul, the three special guests sat on a panel moderated by Professor Thomas Hong-Soon Han, former Korean ambassador to the Holy See, exploring reconciliation and healing as a way of life modeled by Jesus. In turn, each Church leader echoed solutions favored by Pope Francis as well as his predecessors. Rosa described the civil war that engulfed El Salvador from 1979 to 1992: "Oppressed under a military dictatorship, we started to arm ourselves as part of the right to defense, but we realized violence only begets violence. Instead, we followed Archbishop Romero, who exemplified mercy, and St. John Paul II, who urged us toward dialogue," recalled the prelate in Spanish. He was the only Salvadoran to participate in every meeting between the government and opposition guerrilla forces, leading to a peace treaty that ended the war in 1992.

Scherer discussed the conflict between Brazil and Argentina when both were under a military dictatorship. It was an especially threatening period because each country was in the process of developing nuclear weapons against the other. Warning that governments often promote "manipulated truth or false truth," the Brazilian cardinal explained that Church teaching allows us to appreciate the "seeds of faith" in the other side's perspective, which opens a path for dialogue.

In his country, three approaches advocated by the Church helped the two countries overcome decades of suspicion to ultimately sign a 1990 accord renouncing atomic weapons while agreeing to share equipment and facilities for nuclear power: commitment to the truth, willingness to forgive, and patience. The third requirement, patience, is crucial because reconciliation can only be premised on trust and collaboration, which take time, explained the prelate. "If you are impatient, you might destroy the opportunity to achieve reconciliation," warned Cardinal Scherer.

Garfias described problems in some Mexican states involving violence, organized crime, and social breakdown. He said the Church has had to develop multiple ways to refocus all parties on a common good in order to build peace. It is a work in progress, but it shows the Church's ability to mediate seemingly intractable social problems.

Yet So Different?

The event's host was Seoul's archbishop, Cardinal Andrew Yeom Soo-jung, who opted for a priest's version of business casual, a black suit with a white Roman collar, identical to the outfits of other clerics at the event, except for a cardinal's ring given personally by Pope Francis. Underscoring what is unique to the Korean conflict, Yeom brought Rosa Chávez and Garfias to the Demilitarized Zone (DMZ), a strip of land about 260 miles long and 2.5 miles wide that splits the Korean Peninsula in half. The DMZ was created in 1953 by the truce that stopped the North-South conflict—a cease-fire still in force that never yielded a formal peace treaty.[89] Unlike the Argentina-Brazil case study, in which both countries were majority Catholic living under similar political regimes, or the examples from El Salvador, Mexico, and Colombia, where protagonists were all living in the same national space, the seventy-year-old Korean conflict cleaved a nation and spun its halves in radically opposite directions.

To the DMZ's south, Catholicism is more dynamic than anywhere else in East Asia.[90] Liberal democracy has produced prosperity, stability, and civic engagement so efficient that a corrupt president was ousted and replaced in 2017 without a shot being fired or a downturn in the gross domestic product (GDP). And so loathing of war is the Republic of Korea that President Moon Jae-in constantly affirms his refusal to develop or accept nuclear weapons on its territory.[91] In the upside-down world to the DMZ's north, not one Catholic priest is known to be offering the sacraments—that's how thoroughly and oppressively atheistic the one-party Marxist regime is, despite its historical identity as the "Jerusalem of Asia."[92]

In many ways, political scientists might say, the situations faced in Latin America and on the Korean Peninsula are incomparable because the circumstances are so different. The Church, however, is less interested in political typologies than in truths about human nature, the potential for goodness and agreement to prevail, and the efficacy of tactics it has deployed in multiple situations.

Nunciature and Government

What is the purpose of bringing people from around the world to Seoul? According to the chargé d'affaires in Seoul, Msgr. Marco Sprizzi, an *Accademia* graduate from Sicily, Pope Francis is following events in Korea very closely, and he wants the Korean Church to feel richly supported by people and communities around the world that have successfully found new models of reconciliation. Meanwhile, Sprizzi was compelled to hold down the nunciature (covering Mongolia, too) for eight months, a period including the Winter Olympics, because one nuncio retired in September, and his replacement, Archbishop Alfred Xuereb from Malta, did not arrive until May.

On both dimensions of a nuncio's main responsibilities—recommending new bishops for appointment by the Holy See and engaging with the host government—the position in Korea is demanding in a good way. The country is producing a surplus of vocations, parishes are active, and membership has inched upward steadily since 2005. In 2019, 11 percent of the Korean population was Catholic; there were 5,522 priests (an increase over the year before) and 146 working abroad as missionaries. A total of 1,209 seminarians were in training.[93] The country's forty-two bishops, including two cardinals, are active, respected, and unified in their dedication to seeing one country on the Korean Peninsula in their lifetimes.

Korea's democratic government has been eager for accompaniment by the Catholic Church. President Moon Jae-in was elected in May 2017 to fill an unexpected vacancy left when his predecessor was impeached for corruption. He is a practicing Catholic and a famously humble person.[94] One of his first postelectoral initiatives was to send Archbishop Hyginus Kim Hee-jong, president of the Korean Catholic Bishops' Conference, to Rome as a presidential envoy to request the pope's ongoing engagement.

Archbishop Kim met with the pope twice and with Parolin as well. The archbishop explained, "The majority of people want to improve South-North relations. As an envoy of the president, I explained the situation on the Korean Peninsula and President Moon Jae-in's policy for peace at the meetings with Pope Francis and Cardinal Parolin."[95] It's clear the archbishop and the president are close allies: "President Moon is a highly credible leader whose principles and commitment to justice transcend today's conflicts and confrontations," Kim passionately told me.[96]

The president has indeed hewed close to the Catholic Church's position on war and reconciliation since he was elected, even when it put him at odds with its powerful military protector, the United States, and neighboring nations. For example, Moon refused to accept any nuclear weapons on South Korean soil, considering it a destabilizing step, a position also maintained by the Church. As well, President Moon went ahead in providing $8 million for food and medicine to impoverished hospitals in the North through UN programs, despite complaints from Japan that this aid violates the spirit of severe sanctions against North Korea imposed after Kim Jong-un fired nuclear test missiles in 2017.[97] Moon's explanation was a morally centered response: "In principle, giving support for infants and small children and pregnant women should be handled separately from politics."[98]

Moon Jae-in is a human rights lawyer who is no novice in national politics. He served as chief of staff under the first Korean Catholic president, Kim Dae-jung (1998–2003). As a student, he was an activist against military dictatorship, a social and political movement supported by the Church.[99] Some analysts believe Catholicism is so respected (the most respected religion according to one 2015 poll) because priests and lay leaders fearlessly aligned themselves with student demonstrators, and churches became sanctuaries for regime opponents. The Church is also associated with nonviolent efforts to achieve normalcy with the North.[100]

"The Catholic Church was the first to speak out with a united voice in Korean society on the need for national reconciliation in the early 1990s, when the word 'reconciliation' was unpopular. The mind-set of confrontation prevailed," Ambassador Han told me.[101] He also described Pope Francis's trip to Korea in 2014 as "providential." An astonishing eight hundred thousand people attended a Mass celebrated by Francis for the canonization of 124 Korean martyrs from the nineteenth and twentieth centuries.

Pope Francis also held a Mass for peace and reconciliation in Seoul's Cathedral of Myeong-dong, where he reminded the faithful, "What appears, from a human perspective, to be impossible, impractical . . . He makes possible and fruitful through the infinite power of His cross. The cross of Christ reveals the power of God to bridge every division, to heal every wound and to re-establish the original bonds of brotherly love. . . . Let us pray, then, for the emergence of new opportunities for dialogue, encounter, and the resolution of differences."[102] Every Tuesday evening for the past twenty-five years, a Mass for reconciliation between North and South Korea has been offered in the cathedral. According to Cardinal Yeom, the gathered faithful also pray for the fifty-seven Catholic parishes that were active in the North before the country was divided.

Xuereb and Sprizzi have had their hands full reporting to the Secretariat of State on the fast-moving events in Korea. Xuereb has the advantage of being very familiar with the curia and how it works, since he was an insider for three papal administrations, holding various posts since 1997. He was named Pope Benedict XVI's second private secretary in 2007. When Pope Francis took office, Msgr. Xuereb became the pontiff's first private secretary. By the end of the year, he was given responsibility for reporting directly to the pope on economic reform efforts undertaken by the Pontifical Commission for the Organization of the Holy See's Administrative-Economic Structure. A year later, Pope Francis appointed Xuereb to a leadership position in the newly formed Secretariat for the Economy.

At an evening Mass on the Feast of St. Joseph in 2018, Pope Francis elevated three new archbishops being sent out as nuncios, including Xuereb. During the episcopal ordination, the pope offered advice, reminding the three to avoid the temptation of becoming princes and to respond to requests from priests within twenty-four hours whenever possible. Francis also reminded the men that they had been selected "not for business, not for high society, not for politics." Instead, they must pray, preach, and serve rather than dominate others.[103]

Peace Puppies

Meanwhile, as a son of the Church, President Moon has worked his heart out to further the spirit of reconciliation that has seemed tantalizingly close at hand at several points over the last few years. What he has done, step by step, is build trust with the North Korean leadership through concrete initiatives—essentially implementing a "culture of encounter," a term used so often by Pope Francis. It is a vision of diplomacy premised on building personal relationships, which is particularly in sync with Asian cultural norms.

The apex of recent Korean diplomacy came in September 2018 when Moon spent three days in Pyongyang, meeting for the third time with Kim Jong-un and North Korean officials. He even addressed 150,000 citizens at an annual gymnastics festival. (They gave him a standing ovation.) A Catholic bishop was a member of the presidential entourage. Moon brought home a tangible document: the Pyongyang Joint Declaration commits North Korea to permanently shut down nuclear facilities and make the peninsula free of nuclear weapons. It also commits to shutting down the main missile test site. Kim promised to visit South Korea "soon."[104] Restarting cross-border railroads and opening family-reunification centers are key nonmilitary commitments.

Evidence that the two men established personal rapport could be seen in a series of gifts the two exchanged. Kim sent Moon crates of pine mushrooms and two North Korean hunting dogs. The female gave birth to six "peace puppies," seen on the presidential Twitter feed.[105] In thanks, Moon sent tons of South Korean tangerines via military planes to the northern neighbor. These are all examples of concrete steps that result in humanizing former enemies and making reconciliation natural and more authentic—strategies recommended by the pope.

In late 2018, on a nine-day trip to European capitals to generate support for peace—and commitments to easing sanctions on Pyongyang—Moon and his wife stopped in Rome, where he met Pope Francis and participated in a Mass celebrated by Cardinal Parolin.[106] At the Vatican, Moon conveyed Kim's intention to welcome the pope in the Hermit Kingdom. Francis said he would happily respond to an official invitation.

This account of the Holy See's diplomatic efforts in Korea is inconclusive. Yet, indisputably, the Church accompanies those in the theater, including the nation's president, who seek peace, probing any opportunity to advance beyond threats and the logic of revenge. Privately, God's diplomats worried that the erratic policies on Korea flowing from the Trump administration flooded the zone with uncertainty, a counterproductive atmosphere, undermining that critical ingredient: trust.

Source: Photo by Joseph O'Connell, 1945; reproduced with the permission of his wife Kimiko Sakai

On August 9, 1945, the US military dropped an atomic bomb on the city of Nagasaki, the center of Catholicism in Japan, with a seminary, schools, hospitals, and homes for orphans and the homeless. It was a direct hit on Urakami Cathedral, the largest in Asia, pulverizing the building and two priests saying confession at 11:01 in the morning. Over 80,000 civilians were killed.

Declassified Pentagon documents reveal that President Harry Truman was unaware of the target. Nagasaki was not on the priority list. Allied commander David Eisenhower opposed its use. It was mysteriously added in handwriting, on an official strike order as revealed by historian Alex Wellerstein. Shocked, Truman ordered that no more attacks be carried out without his approval.

Pope Francis printed cards of a young boy carrying his dead brother to a Nagasaki crematorium, a picture taken by a US Army photographer. On the back, Francis included the message "The Fruits of War," and signed his name. He distributes it to emphasize the concrete reality of Armageddon, delivered by the US to a city with no military installations. Some suspect the bomb was directed at the Church as well as Japan because the Vatican established diplomatic relations with Japan in 1941, over US opposition.

The allies rationalized revenge, not only against Japan but against Italy even after the Fascists were gone. Bombings in 1943–1944 killed thousands, destroying homes, sacred places, and infrastructure unnecessarily.

II

Introduction
The Mustard Seed: Jorge Bergoglio as Manager, Missionary, and Mystic

As archbishop of Buenos Aires, Jorge Mario Bergoglio avoided travel abroad because it kept him away from *mi esposa*, "my wife," as he referred to his diocese.[1] When compelled to attend Church business outside Argentina, he kept trips short and precise, never traveling with staff and rarely tacking on a scenic excursion. The committed pastor was especially leery of time spent in Rome, telling friends, "It's bad for my faith."[2]

Becoming Pope Francis might have been an anguishing stretch for Jorge Bergoglio. Between 1914 and 1978, every pope had served as a Vatican diplomat, and those skills profoundly shaped the exercise of papal leadership in the twentieth century. Although Pope John Paul II was not trained as a diplomat, he traveled extensively as archbishop, and his personal gifts—a charismatic actor with geopolitical insight—were well suited for the role he designed, that of a global pilgrim. For his successor Benedict XVI, the international dimension of the job proved especially taxing—and was one of the factors that contributed to his retreat via resignation. When he left, the Vatican was embroiled in a series of financial and sexual scandals, bureaucratic quarrels, and harmful leaks of classified documents. Benedict's decision to step down meant a clean slate for his successor who would be able to reconstitute the team of top decision makers, including the all-important position of secretary of state.[3]

Then along came Bergoglio. Not only were his international credentials sketchy, but he was known to rush home for dinner to avoid tiresome evenings socializing as archbishop of Buenos Aires. Given his background, how was it even possible to catapult into a role requiring constant engagement?

POPE FRANCIS'S GIFTS: MANAGER, MISSIONARY, MYSTIC

In Part I, I've presented several institutional assets of the Catholic Church that give the pope a ready-made identity as a world leader: its network, mission, diplomatic school, sovereign status, and praxis. The Church is a capillary network of diplomats, at once horizontally arrayed across earth as priests and religious and dedicated laypeople, while also vertically linked to a central command in Rome. The network has a unified and unifying mission: to spread the Gospel message, which can be boiled down to "Love God and neighbor!"

Like no other religion, the Catholic Church is itself a sovereign. The status of sovereignty gives the Church unusual political access and mobility. Yet its lack of material interests—with a tiny geographic footprint and fewer than one thousand residents, the Holy See has no economy or military—allows it to focus on immaterial goals such as peace, human development, and the common good. Finally, the Church has been practicing diplomacy for centuries; its envoys are widely considered among the best in the business. All this helps explain Pope Francis's ability to ascend the throne of St. Peter and immediately function as an international leader.

But it turns out Bergoglio had experience and insights especially suited for the deft management of international affairs. Appreciating three aspects of his identity—as manager, missionary, and mystic—characteristics and sensitivities that emerged early in his priestly life, it is far easier to understand his diplomatic success as supreme pontiff, described in Part II's case studies.

MANAGER

What Francis demonstrated right out of the box was administrative prowess, a skill set neither of his two papal predecessors brought to the job. The conclave that selected this outsider was well aware that the curia had devolved into dysfunction after thirty-five years of weak papal management.[4] Being able to manage reform was a top priority for the cardinals who elected Bergoglio. According to people who know him, the pope has a prodigious capacity for managing information, an excellent memory, and an authoritative decision-making style—overall "a talent for government"—and he doesn't take vacations.[5]

His diplomatic approach has been influenced by certain management experiences in particular: his tenure as provincial of Argentina's Society of Jesus (1973–1979), a period coinciding with a military coup d'état; appointment as bishop (1992–1998), then archbishop of Buenos Aires (1998–2013); and leadership at the 2007 CELAM meeting in Aparecida, Brazil.

Bergoglio was selected to lead the entire Argentine Jesuit community at age thirty-six. Facing a double crisis—national political chaos and an ideological divide within the Society of Jesus—he was an unusual choice to replace a provincial superior forced out for being too supportive of radical politics.[6] In an extremely politicized atmosphere, Bergoglio avoided being associated with any faction or ideology, liberal, conservative, or socialist. Instead, he emphasized Christian hope and, within the order, a renewal of Ignatian spirituality.[7]

His tenure as the country's Jesuit leader went from being tense to nightmarish during a military dictatorship known as the Dirty War, when "the Church was itself a theatre of war," with priests, religious, and lay activists among those arrested, kidnapped, disappeared, and even murdered—all suspected of being Communist sympathizers.[8] The deeply spiritual man suddenly had to protect confreres while defending potential victims, hiding dozens in the Jesuit college while helping other targets get out of the country. He showed little fear. A student who realized the provincial was hiding refugees among Catholics on retreat called him "an eel," with an "amazing ability to maneuver in that environment."[9]

Despite the unstable national setting, as provincial Bergoglio managed to introduce innovations that depoliticized the order and focused members on more missionary objectives. He created Jesuit teams to minister in remote areas as well as the slums and even sent priests to Ecuador where the Society had some troubled ministries.[10] Against any political ideology, he focused the Jesuit community on the concrete needs of real people, especially those on the periphery.[11]

URBAN BISHOP

Bergoglio might not have enjoyed being away from his hometown, but early on in his career he knew the Church's global power structure. As a provincial, he took his place within an efficient network connecting Jesuits worldwide. Once appointed auxiliary bishop in Buenos Aires, he became part of the international college of bishops, another global network reporting up the chain to Rome. As president of the country's bishops' conference for six years (2005–2011), he was point man for innumerable public policy issues that meant wrangling with the secular state. Then in 2001, when John Paul II made Bergoglio cardinal, he was assigned to several dicasteries,[12] topical departments of the Roman Curia. As a member of the Pontifical Commission for Latin America, the Argentinian participated in a forum meant to serve as a bridge between Rome and Latin America, where some 40 percent of all Catholics live.[13]

The pope knows intimately the operations of a Church on the national scale, a microcosm of the universal Church. His twenty-one years in episcopal leadership entailed managing budgets and property, priests and teachers, government relations and interfaith dialogue, doctrinal disagreements and media firestorms—most important to him, it involved teaching the Gospel, deploying charity, and calling on God's mercy for the people of faith. Throughout his tenure as archbishop, Bergoglio worked on organizational improvements. He created new parishes, restructured the archdiocese's administrative office, and institutionalized initiatives on subjects such as the right to life and divorce.[14] A major undertaking was building the Church's presence in urban slums known as *villas miserias* (places of misery), where he spent part of every week, gaining the moniker "slum bishop." He doubled the number of priests assigned to these neighborhoods.[15]

Importantly, he introduced financial accountability. When Bergoglio took over the archdiocese, it was broke. Part owner in several banks, the Church could get loans on special terms, which made financial mismanagement chronic. According to Federico Wals, a layman who served as the archbishop's spokesman for six years, "It was a black hole, so there were basically no limits on what we could spend."[16] Bergoglio sold off the ownership stake in local banks and opened regular accounts with international banks. This simple reform forced the Church to be more disciplined because borrowing and spending were officially tracked. Wals told the *National Catholic Reporter* that it also spared the Church embarrassment down the road.

Francis has used the coronavirus pandemic's quarantine—and the necessity of coping with related income decline—to tackle financial reorganization dealing with corruption untouched by six popes. Vaticanista John Allen documented the pope's productivity on this front throughout 2020, from breaking up a secretive network of Swiss real estate holding companies to moving an accounting division out from under the entity it was supposed to audit.[17] He even stripped his former *sostituto*, Cardinal Angelo Becciu, of prerogatives and evicted him from the curia when nepotistic financial payments came to light—one of the most decisive actions taken against a senior churchman in the last century. Another corruption-related reform announced in 2019 addressed the devastating sexual abuse gangrene. Francis canceled the so-called pontifical secret, approved by Joseph Ratzinger and John Paul II in 2001, which blocked civil authorities from getting documentation against priests under investigation for sexual abuse.[18]

REGIONAL LEADER

Latin America has the strongest explicitly regional identity in the Church. Pope Pius XII encouraged the creation of a regional bishops' conference, CELEM, created in 1955. Its periodic meetings are important signposts of the greater institutional well-being of the Church. While living through a military dictatorship helped prepare Jorge Bergoglio for the worst imaginable situations, participating in CELEM's fifth episcopal conference, held at Aparecida, the world's largest Marian shrine, gave him a positive experience of how much spiritual wisdom lives at the Church's "lower" levels.

Bergoglio was selected by his peers to edit the meeting's concluding document, drawn from hundreds of local submissions and meeting notes. (As pope, he highlighted the value of that participatory process.) The text is masterful as an evangelical vision of Church renewal based on personal encounter with the Lord Jesus and missionary discipleship. It shows the Latin American Church's insight and vigor, grounded in recognition that popular piety—the faith of regular people—is the basis of both tradition and a future path.

Other concepts that would define the Francis pontificate are found in the document, including the need to focus on the poor and to perform "concrete" works of charity. In the spirited Aparecida proposal, we find a blueprint for Francis's papacy overall and the foundation of his first apostolic exhortation, *Evangelii Gaudium*, which describes evangelization as the universal Church mission.[19]

MISSIONARY

As a Jesuit, Jorge Bergoglio spent years refining his power to *discern*, a decision-making technique devised by the order's Spanish founder, Ignatius of Loyola, in the sixteenth century and outlined in his *Spiritual Exercises*. From the start, Ignatius's society was dedicated to contemplation *and* action. A soldier and nobleman turned ascetic on the model of St. Francis of Assisi, Ignatius discovered God while recovering from cannonball wounds in his father's castle.

Similarly, Bergoglio decided to join the Church's most intellectually rigorous religious order while recovering from surgery, which removed part of one lung. At age twenty-one, Bergoglio was left with physical limits—no heavy lifting, no soccer—but an expansive view of how to pursue God in the world: the Ignatian way, "done in the presence of the Lord, looking at the signs, listening to the things that happen, the feelings of people, especially the poor," as he explained.[20]

One way his missionary disposition has expressed itself is in his appointment of cardinals for the task of choosing his successor. Pope Francis has selected new cardinals once each year since 2014–2019 of them the very first from their nations.[21] Pope Francis uses his choices to communicate priorities, such as elevating bishops who live in the "peripheries," regions that get less attention because they are neither wealthy nor powerful.[22] He has rewarded men known for great humility and loyalty, and he has favored clerics who minister with a strong pastoral spirit.

For example, in 2015, Archbishop Charles Maung Bo of Yangon, Myanmar, was given a red hat, the first Burmese prelate to receive the honor. The Holy See did not even have diplomatic relations with the government at the time. Two years later, Francis and Burmese state councilor Aung San Suu Kyi met in Rome and announced formal bilateral recognition as well as the pope's plan to visit. A small 1 percent (about 750,000) of the nation is Catholic, yet the Church has a disproportionate impact, in part through the schools it runs. (Bo is a Salesian priest, a teaching order with schools and youth ministry around the world.)

Months before the pope's visit, the Myanmar military's brutal treatment of the Rohingya people, a Muslim minority being systematically forced across Myanmar's border with Bangladesh, drew fierce international criticism. Instead of postponing, the pope decided to visit both countries, meeting with military leaders in Myanmar and some of the stateless exiles in Bangladesh. After the visit, Cardinal Bo was able to follow up more effectively with both national leaders and the Rohingya community because his status as a cardinal signaled his close relationship to the pope.[23] Bo was elected president of the Federation of Asian Bishops' Conferences—a regional coordinating council modeled on CELAM—and took charge in 2019, exemplifying how Francis's people are evangelical too.

Francis's travel choices similarly emphasize peripheries. It was his idea to arrive in the United States from Cuba in 2015 and to hold a Mass right on the Mexican-American border during the 2016 US presidential election season.[24] His first trip outside Rome was to the Italian island of Lampedusa, where African and Middle Eastern migrants trying to get to Europe across the Mediterranean often land—unless they drown on the way.

Even within Europe, his first trip abroad was to Albania, not exactly a garden spot. He was especially keen to highlight a country where Catholics, Orthodox Christians, and Muslims have solid, positive relations. In Tirana, Francis met an old priest, age eighty-five, with snowy white hair. Fr. Ernest Simoni was ordained secretly in 1956, when the Church was illegal. He was arrested, tortured, jailed for eighteen years, and sent to hard labor in mines. When he was finally released in 1981, Simoni was forced to work in city sewers. With the collapse of Communism, the priest was happiest in the confessional, offering the sacrament for hours.[25] So moved was he to hear this testimony, the pope made the dedicated priest a cardinal.[26]

While Pope John Paul II's innumerable adventures abroad are especially remembered as pastoral visits to inspire, reactivate, or congratulate Catholic communities, Pope Francis is more intent on visiting places that need special attention, whether Catholic or not. Again, it's his missionary spirit. But the emphasis on viewing the world from peripheries is more than a matter of charity: from this vantage one sees and appreciates the great diversity of peoples and cultures—a pluralism threatened, in the pope's vivid view, by uniformity imposed by consumerist forms of globalization.[27]

A core idea of missionary work is that *all* need to hear the Gospel messages, whether on salvation or on justice as a precursor to peace. Throughout his 2015 pastoral trip to the United States where Francis addressed a joint session of Congress, the UN General Assembly, and more than 1.5 million people in Philadelphia, Francis urged audiences to be better and do more (for the poor, for the climate, and for each other), yet he never came off as a tedious scold.[28] He appeals even to audiences that have no obligation to listen, such as global business leaders.

Just one example of Francis's unusual outreach demonstrates his faith in the universal relevance of Christ's message. The Vatican cosponsored a forum with *Fortune* and *Time* magazines titled "How CEO's Can Be 'Partners with God.'"[29] Some one hundred participants listened to this Christian message: "Our great challenge is to respond to global levels of injustice by promoting a local and even personal sense of responsibility so that no one is excluded from participating in society"[30]—not typical boardroom fare.

Inspired by Francis and Catholic social teaching, at the end of two days' work the conference divided into discussion panels. These groups included some of the world's most influential business leaders. They produced an encouraging action report. After reading it, Francis said,

> Our world today is marked by great unrest. Inequality between peoples continues to rise, and many communities are impacted directly by war and poverty, or the migration and displacement which flow from them. . . . Your very presence here today is a sign of hope, because it shows that you recognize the issues before us and the imperative to act decisively.[31]

The report lays out some twenty solutions (that track with Francis's economic priorities) to be pioneered by the transnational private sector.[32] Its objective is to end poverty.

MYSTIC

Believers seek the will of God in specific situations. What others might call "coincidence," discerning Catholics—especially ones like Pope Francis, Benedict XVI, and John Paul II, who spend hours each day meditating before the crucifix despite the pileup of mortal business—read signs of God's presence. As a practitioner of St. Ignatius of Loyola's particular approach, Pope Francis is adept at delving into an interior, spiritual world and orienting his prayerful perceptions toward action. This really is a special charism of the Society of Jesus—from the start—a constructive tension between contemplating and actualizing, navigating back and forth between God's infinite horizon and the local particularity of real, concrete situations.

Italian philosopher Massimo Borghesi convincingly describes Pope Francis's thought as flowing from a conviction that Catholicism allows opposing thoughts to be held together in tension: the universal and the particular, God and man, grace and freedom. These are meaningful and simultaneously true, without one concept erasing or triumphing over the other, as would occur in a Hegelian-style synthesis.[33]

When Francis promotes a culture of encounter, he is suggesting a process through which people, in good faith, can share ideas and find agreement without losing or giving up their own identity. He sometimes refers to this as "reconciled diversity." In a homily delivered to the indigenous Mapuche people in Chile, at an airport that served as a torture center during Augusto Pinochet's military dictatorship, Francis explained:

> Unity can never be a stifling uniformity imposed by the powerful, or a segregation that does not value the goodness of others. The unity sought and offered by Jesus acknowledges what each people and each culture are called to contribute to this land of blessings. Unity is a reconciled diversity, for it will not allow personal or community wrongs to be perpetrated in its name. We need the riches that each people has to offer, and we must abandon the notion that there are superior or inferior cultures.[34]

In a sense, this is Francis's update of the classic diplomatic rule of thumb, "no winners or losers," with greater attention to culture and the significant role played by ethnic and religious identity in contemporary conflicts.

Another implication of Pope Francis's mystical outlook is his perception of history and the extent to which anyone can control outcomes. Simply put, we can't. God works through human history. People can begin processes, but it is the Holy Spirit who brings our actions to fruition. Therefore, dialogue and bridge building are essential for initiating processes that *might* lead to greater mutual respect and eventually trust, which *could* lead to reconciliation and deeper understanding—or not. We are compelled only to begin the journey, something Francis presses on his diplomats all the time.

This relates directly to his principle "time is greater than space." What at first seems rather abstract is an insight with real-world implications for diplomacy. By letting a process unfold, participants allow best outcomes to emerge:

> This principle enables us to work slowly but surely, without being obsessed with immediate results. It helps us patiently to endure difficult and adverse situations, or inevitable changes in our plans. It invites us to accept the tension between fullness and limitation, and to give a priority to time. One of the faults which we occasionally observe in sociopolitical activity is that spaces and power are preferred to time and processes. Giving priority to space means madly attempting to keep everything together in the present, trying to possess all the spaces of power and of self-assertion.[35]

Here, Bergoglio's ideas enhance classic diplomacy's valorization of patience.

Of course, dialogue over time risks devolving into endless "kumbaya" peace seeking, cynics might say. Possibly, but Francis balances abstraction with insistence on concrete steps and real, flesh-and-blood acts of mercy. As rector of a Jesuit college in the 1980s, he reorganized the philosophy and theology curricula; he also used the school's fallow land to set up a farm with sheds and barns for livestock (including twenty cows), vegetable gardens, and beehives. The farm fed the students and the nearby poor. Everyone worked on it. A student who became a nun remembered Bergoglio's enthusiasm for farm labor: "He took me outside to where the community kept sheep and pigs. He told me this was a good place to pray and that God is to be found in the lowliest of things."[36]

INDEPENDENCE

A mystic in this day and age would also be a man set apart. As a function of spiritual discipline and his birth south of the equator, Jorge Bergoglio is unusually independent. His assessment of international politics reflects this independence. As pope, Francis practices diplomacy for a multipolar world. He doesn't consider Russian imperialism any more dangerous than American imperialism. So he dares to offer a critique of Western foreign policy practices and failures, such as the perpetually churning war machines; arrogant ideas like gender ideology and other products of radical individualism being brusquely imposed on traditional, communitarian cultures; and consumerist indifference that sees many as "throwaway" people, such as the elderly and the preborn.

Although it's rare to find him making a bald political assessment, he bluntly condemned NATO's choices in Libya by observing, "Before there was one Qaddafi, today there are 50. The West should be self-critical. On this topic, in part, the Holy See and Russia have a convergence of analysis. In part, it's best not to exaggerate because Russia has its own interests."[37] What differentiates the Holy See from virtually every other sovereign entity is that it has no material interests. In Francis's view, at the root of political conflict is always a clash of interests related to power. Thus, the godly position is equidistance to all sides, which opens the door for constructive and self-giving diplomacy.

Independence is a form of freedom, allowing Francis to speak truth to power, sometimes in expressive ways. As just one example, the pope printed cards with a macabre photograph taken in 1945 of a stoic Japanese boy, maybe ten years old, standing in line at a Nagasaki crematorium. Strapped to the boy's back is his dead baby brother, killed in the inhumane destruction wrought by the American bombing of a residential area, which happened to be the "heart and soul of Catholicism in Japan since the sixteenth century."[38] On the back of the card, the pope wrote three words, "Fruits of War," and signed his name. On a flight to Latin America in 2018, he circulated among the traveling press corps and gave each a card, pressing them to worry about war.

6

Stifling War in Ukraine
Prioritizing Peace with Russia

> FRANCIS: Brother . . . Finally!
> KIRILL: Now things are easier.
>
> —Pope Francis and Russian Orthodox Patriarch Kirill meeting for the first time, Havana, Cuba, February 13, 2016[1]

> The Society [of Jesus] was saved by a German Protestant, who then became Orthodox—a great woman, Catherine II.
>
> —Pope Francis with Dominique Wolton, July 2016[2]

Although the war in Syria was one that Francis inherited, war in Ukraine, on the country's eastern border with Russia, began on Pope Francis's watch in April 2014. His response demonstrated that even friends could not predict his actions on the international stage. It's a case study in which we see principles of diplomacy favored by Francis at work to advance objectives pursued by each pope since the mid-1960s.

In *Evangelii Gaudium*, his first papal exhortation, Francis outlined four principles that order the "tensions present in every social reality."[3] These ideas are keys to his diplomatic method: that the whole is greater than the parts, reality is more important than ideas, unity prevails over conflict, and time is greater than space. Although abstract at first glance, the rules can be seen in his strategic choices and reflect his intent to remain neutral among competing geopolitical powers. This neutrality, in turn, has helped restore the Holy See to its status as a major diplomatic player.[4]

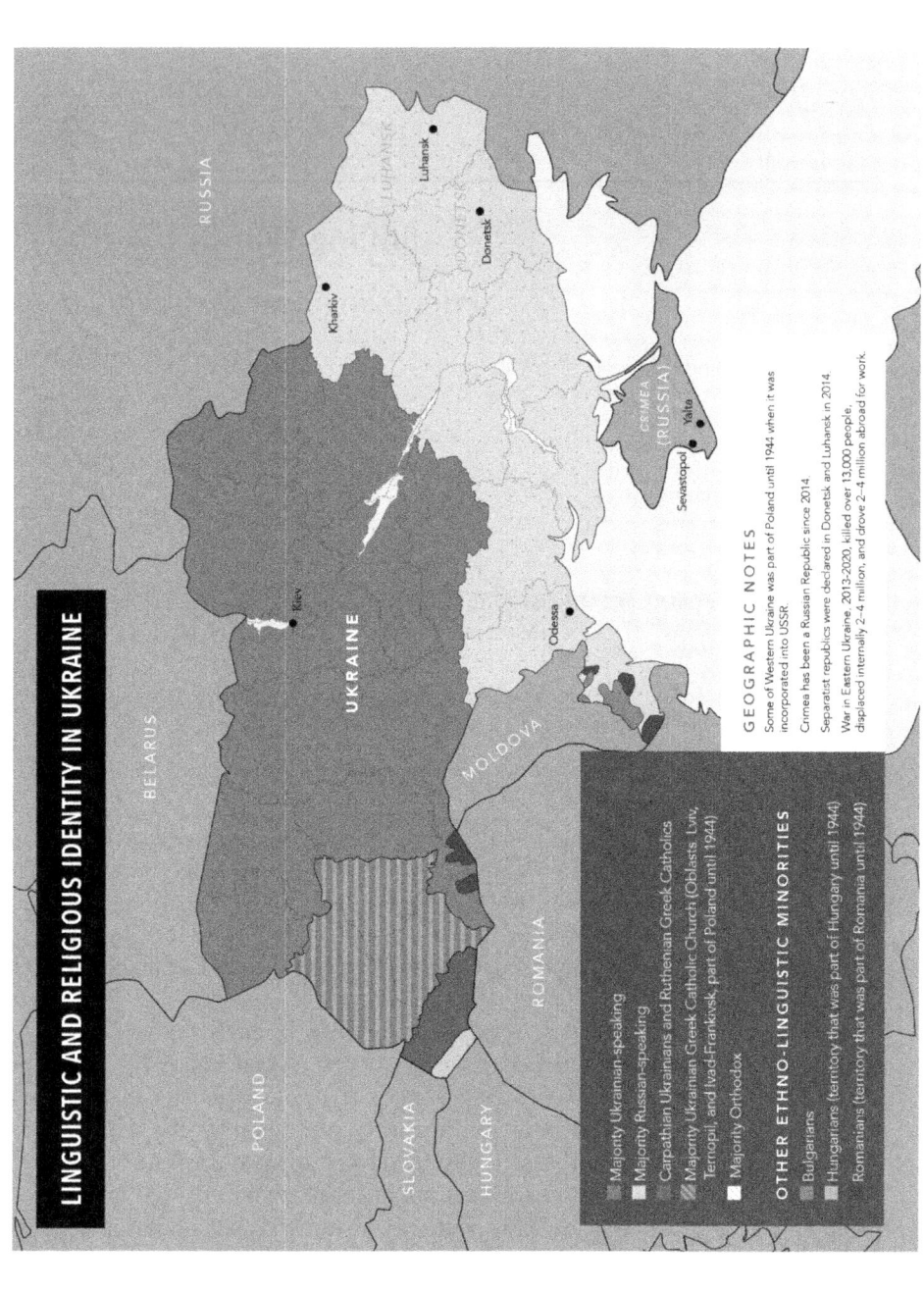

POPULAR REVOLT OR COUP D'ÉTAT?

The seeds of conflict were sown on November 21, 2013, when Ukrainian president Viktor Yanukovych unexpectedly announced his decision to walk away from an expansive partnership agreement with the European Union (EU)—just a week before it was to be signed. This triggered the takeover of Independence Square (*Maidan Nezalezhnosti*) in the capital city of Kyiv[5] by a few hundred opponents protesting the government's volte-face regarding the EU deal, which had come to symbolize a path toward a more stable, less corrupt society, especially for those living in Western Ukraine—where most of the country's Catholics live.

"For several years, Ukraine was preparing to sign an Association Agreement with the EU. It was the government's official policy," explained Serhii Plokhii, professor of Ukrainian history at Harvard University. "Europe and European values became a dominant discourse in Ukrainian politics—a big hope."[6]

The government's announcement that it had changed its mind, now finding economic difficulties with the deal, represented an abrupt turn in policy. "The protests show Ukraine is a democratic state and the government can't do what it pleases as a result of a backroom deal," Plokhii explained at the time. "What we see is the result of the Ukrainian economy being completely mismanaged by the Yanukovych government, which was looking for an emergency bailout. Apparently, they received one from Russia."[7] Russia offered Ukraine a deal worth $15 billion in financing and a 33 percent discount on natural gas—an immediate solution, while the EU agreement only promised future financial rewards.

To disappointed Ukrainians, it was like salt on a wound when nearby Georgia and Moldova went ahead and inked accords with the EU in late November. The next day, crowds swelled to ten thousand people in Kyiv's Maidan Square. In response, riot police with tear gas and truncheons attacked, scattering the protesters and injuring over seventy-five people.

The Maidan protests continued for three months, dramatically triggering the collapse of the Ukrainian government on February 22, 2014. President Yanukovych fled to Russia after a furious conflagration in downtown streets ended with over fifty protesters and three police officers dead.[8]

The US government was actively involved in helping to select and boost Ukraine's caretaker government pending national elections. Even before Yanukovych's ouster, the Russians released a hacked phone conversation between US assistant secretary of state Victoria Nuland and US ambassador to Ukraine Geoffrey Pyatt, revealing the extent to which Washington was involved in internal Ukrainian politics, literally helping to select the next prime minister.[9] The new president, Petro Poroshenko, was also backed by the West.[10]

Moscow saw the Obama administration's high-profile involvement with Maidan and the creation of the 2014 Kyiv government as a coup d'état, not the fulfillment of popular demands. In Russia's view, the United States was violating an agreement that dated back to negotiations with Mikhail Gorbachev over German reunification in 1990–1991: the British, French, German, and American governments assured Gorbachev that if he removed Soviet troops from Eastern Europe, the West would not exploit the decision and step into the space.[11] US support for democracy promotion activities in former Soviet countries and regime change in the Middle East were two other US foreign policy practices that President Vladimir Putin and the Russian government had long discerned and resented. Some fifteen years of US-Russia distrust thus came to a head in Ukraine that season.[12]

In response to the collapse of the Ukrainian regime, the Russian military quickly moved into Crimea, a large peninsula in the country's southeast jutting into the Black Sea. The majority of the 2.2 million people living in Crimea in 2014 considered themselves ethnic Russians.[13] Crimea is prime waterfront real estate, giving Moscow access to the Mediterranean Sea. The Russian Black Sea Fleet has been stationed at Sevastopol since the late eighteenth century. Ukraine only took possession of the territory in 1954 after Soviet premier Nikita Khrushchev initiated two energy projects that local officials convinced him were more efficiently managed in Kyiv—when Ukraine was part of the Soviet Union.[14]

Putin ordered the annexation of Crimea, popularly approved via referendum in March 2014, out of fear that Russia would lose the strategic port as an upshot of chaos (and Western influence) in Western Ukraine, more than as a preplanned imperialistic strategy sprung on the country when it was suddenly leaderless.[15] Western governments, led by the United States, responded immediately by slapping sanctions on Russia. Indeed, the seizure of Crimea violated the 1994 Budapest Memorandum, which promised no use of force against Ukraine, Belarus, or Kazakhstan. Signed by the Russian Federation, the United Kingdom, and the United States, the agreement facilitated the successful removal of nuclear stockpiles from the three former Soviet-controlled republics.

FRIENDSHIP NOT A FACTOR

The local Catholic Church had an early stake in the crisis because of its involvement in the Maidan protests. The country's most powerful Catholic entity is the Ukrainian Greek Catholic Church (UGCC), a Byzantine-rite branch of the Church in full communion with the Holy See. It was founded in 1596 when a group of Orthodox bishops agreed to recognize Rome as long as they could maintain the Byzantine-rite liturgy. The UGCC uses a style of ritual, chant, and clerical garb more mystical than the Latin Church but the two are identical in doctrine.[16] Today, the UGCC is the biggest Eastern Catholic Church in the world. Under Soviet rule, it was banned.

A brutal campaign was launched against the Church in 1945: bishops were exiled and murdered, clergy driven underground, and property transferred to the Orthodox Church. "We were one generation away from extinction," American-born, Harvard-educated UGCC Archbishop Borys Gudziak explained to me. "In 1949, Ukrainian Greek Catholics had about 3,000 priests. In 1989, we emerged from the catacombs with only 300 priests—a 90 percent reduction, with an average age close to 70 years."[17]

With help from a far-flung diaspora, the Church rebuilt itself. By 2014, some 5.4 million believers animated a dynamic faith community in Ukraine, while an increasing number joined abroad. The resurgence of the UGCC over the last thirty years has been one of the Catholic Church's most dramatic success stories. Especially given the history of repression, it makes sense that the Church emerged from the underground as a powerful proponent of the Ukrainian nation. Most of its faithful favor strong relations with the West, including membership in the EU.

Many Catholics in Western Ukraine assumed Pope Francis would side with them in the confrontation with Russia. They knew Major Archbishop Sviatoslav Shevchuk, the UGCC's energetic leader based in Kyiv, was an old friend of the pope. As archbishop of Buenos Aires, Jorge Bergoglio had authority over the UGCC diaspora community. He came to know Shevchuk as a young bishop assigned to the city.[18]

But the pope did not side with Kyiv. Instead, he bemoaned a war he called "fratricidal" because it pitted Christians against Christians. He warned Shevchuk not to become enmeshed in politics. The Secretariat of State—invariably with Francis's approval—replaced the Vatican's nuncio (an American citizen) for being too critical of Moscow. To understand Francis's management of the Ukrainian crisis is to penetrate his larger worldview and perception of the Church's geopolitical role. And to understand how disappointing his decision was to local Catholic leaders especially, you have to recognize why the Maidan experience was special.

REVOLUTION OF DIGNITY: MAIDAN

During the Maidan protests, Christian clergy and believers together created a utopian encampment, although that wasn't their goal. Fr. Mykola Buryadnyk, pastor of Chicago's St. Joseph the Betrothed Ukrainian Catholic Church, was itching to participate in Maidan as he watched events unfold in his homeland. So, the thirty-something priest flew to Ukraine and spent a week in the heart of "a new nation transformed," as he described it.[19]

"When you approached Maidan Square, it looked very scary from the outside because of huge homemade barricades," he recounted. "There were strict controls to get inside, with former soldiers and 'defense experts' guarding the Maidan perimeter, checking people for weapons, and excluding anyone who had been drinking. Inside, it was a joyful place, with many people in their twenties. Everything was very well organized, with teams responsible for food, medical aid, media, clothes, defense scheduling. People registered and did duty."

Buryadnyk described the "great role" of the Ukrainian Greek Catholic Church. There was a chapel in the middle of the square providing daily Mass, confession, and counseling. He was especially impressed by the ecumenical spirit at Maidan: "The Orthodox Church of Kyiv was very active, but also priests from the Autocephalous Church and the Moscow Patriarchate, too. We all looked the same, our vestments, and no one asked each other, 'What church are you with?' because it was not appropriate."[20]

Archbishop Gudziak credited Pope Francis with making it logical for clergy to be involved so unabashedly: "Pope Francis has encouraged us clergy to be pastors—to have the smell of the sheep. That is why our religious are in the square with the people." The Catholic Church in Ukraine represents about 10 percent of the population nationwide but over 30 percent in Western oblasts centered around the city of Lviv.

PRIESTS AT THE BARRICADE

Early on December 11, riot police attacked Maidan Square again. To alert the public, a graduate student at a nearby theology academy next to Mikhailovsky Cathedral began ringing the sacred bells, which could be heard for miles, from 2 to 5 a.m.[21] Fr. Buryadnyk joined other priests in cassocks and armed with crosses, taking up positions between the riot police and the demonstrators.

Gudziak was also at Maidan that night. "We spoke directly to the storm troopers—special forces dressed in Darth Vader suits. I told them the sin of Cain, of killing a brother, is a terrible one. They should not bring shame to their families," he recalled.[22] "You could absolutely see they didn't want to be there. You could see—we could see their faces we were so close!—that they were under orders. They didn't relish beating their own citizens," he said.[23]

He considered it a miracle that the events on December 11 didn't result in casualties. He told me, "The fact that peace has prevailed even when the crowd swelled to eight hundred thousand—that there was so much peace, levity, and humor in Maidan—all of this is not natural, it is supernatural. And we believe that the grace of God is inspiring people to claim their human dignity."

Although Gudziak was not shy to describe "the Putin government" as the "principal troublemaker in this situation," he was also quick to describe a positive evolution in relations between Catholics and Orthodox, not a simplistic West versus Russia split. For example, a Maidan rally on December 15 opened with an ecumenical prayer in which priests from each of Ukraine's three Orthodox churches participated alongside Catholics (both Eastern and Latin rite) and evangelical Christians.[24]

Those who participated in the Maidan community adamantly saw it as the chrysalis of a new Ukraine, coining the term "Revolution of Dignity." Archbishop Stefan Soroka, a Church leader from Canada, told me it was essential to understand events at Maidan in a historical context. "This is a fight for all the countries in the East, that we don't return to the repression we experienced. Everyone is saying, 'Let's not go back to a bygone era.' What is developing is not East versus West, but an authentic *duch* [spirit], wanting a nation to progress out of this path of ongoing conflict."[25]

Buryadnyk optimistically predicted that Maidan "is a place from which Christianity will spread."

WEAPONIZING THE UGCC AND A NUNCIO GETS AXED

But the Christian spirit of the Maidan moment was soon shattered. Fighting erupted on Ukraine's eastern border in May 2014 when Russian-backed separatist forces in Donetsk and Luhansk (provinces with overwhelmingly Russian Orthodox populations) declared independent "people's republics" and the poorly equipped Ukrainian military, including newly drafted men, were mobilized to fight the insurgents. The UGCC and Orthodox Church–Kyiv Patriarchate were not shy about blessing the troops, even accompanying them to the front in some cases. Blogs circulated images of rockets and military vehicles painted with Christian symbols. Intense national patriotism against a perceived aggressor was certainly the main sentiment in Western Ukraine, fomented by clergy as much as by the faithful.

The UGCC, which enthusiastically supported Ukraine's closer alliance with Western institutions, was clear about the situation: Russia was an aggressor against Ukraine and must be repelled at all costs. In his earliest statements on military activity in Eastern Ukraine, as he traveled the world raising awareness—and money—for the national cause, Archbishop Shevchuk called it an invasion of one neighbor against another.[26]

I met the American-born nuncio to Ukraine, Archbishop Thomas Gullickson, in Kyiv.[27] Posted to the country in 2011, he offered a smart assessment on the divergent worldviews of Ukrainian and Russian elite. He openly considered Moscow the aggressor, referring to its "propaganda machine," which portrayed the UGCC as fomenting war. His candor got him in trouble, it seems.

Three months later, I called Gullickson to get an update on the situation. He described himself as "a guy whose days are numbered." On December 6, the Italian newspaper *Corriere della Sera* ran a front-page headline reporting rumors that the nuncio to Ukraine would be removed due to anti-Russian sentiments. The nuncio thought he might have stung some sensitive Russian clerics when he gave a frank talk in Germany about the human tragedy on Ukraine's eastern front. A Russian online site, Interfax, covered the talk. Gullickson added that he heard personally from Archbishop Becciu, the *sostituto*, that "Russians" had complained about him. "I'm just waiting for when they move me out of here," he told me.[28] By September, he was gone, assigned to cover Switzerland and Lichtenstein—nuncio, to be sure, but a sleepy assignment.

FRANCIS STEPS IN

The Holy See was dead set against provoking a new Cold War—a "religious Cold War" in the words of author and academic Massimo Franco—pitting Catholics and Orthodox against each other. Specifically, Pope Francis wanted to block a conflict in which Christians from Western Ukraine, many Greek Catholics, would fight Christians in the Donbas region, where most people belong to the Ukrainian Orthodox Church canonically allied with Moscow. In early February 2015, Pope Francis referred to "this horrible fratricidal violence" in Ukraine, adding, "Think: This is a war among Christians! You all share one baptism! You are fighting with Christians. Think about this scandal."

Soon after, Pope Francis met with the Catholic bishops of Ukraine at the conclusion of their weeklong *ad limina* visit—a five-year "check-up" for the Holy Father to take the pulse of a nation's Catholic leadership. Francis warned the bishops, both the Greek Catholics and the Latin Catholics—who did not meet together with the Holy Father because of tension between them[29]—not to politicize the Church in public discourse in the heat of Ukraine's crisis. "I know the historical problems that have marked your land and are still present in the collective memory. They are questions that, in part, have a political basis, and to which you are not called to give a direct response."[30]

Francis's first guiding principle—that the whole is greater than the parts—can be seen in his reluctance to take sides in Ukraine's religious conflict. For Francis, all conflict can be traced to interests, whether military, economic, or those related to national pride. But he is no more suspicious of Russian imperialism than of what he sees as US imperialism—both Moscow and Washington, in his view, are equally self-interested and capable of being destructive. He therefore refuses to prioritize one group of Christians over another. The whole of Christianity is sacred, so peace must be found among its warring parts.

Instead, the pope advised clerics to focus on "human dramas that await your direct and positive contribution," adding, "What is important in such circumstances is to listen carefully to the voices that come from the land, where the people live who are entrusted to your pastoral care." The pope's analysis focused on the suffering of the entire Ukrainian population, which was under severe stress from a bankrupt economy, endemic corruption, and a humanitarian crisis caused by war.[31]

A witness to the UGCC's February 20, 2015, meeting recounts, with eyes wide open, a moment when Shevchuk evoked what he considered a priority item: that he be recognized by Rome as "patriarch" rather than his current title. "I attributed his chutzpah to youth and his close relationship with Francis," my source recalled. "Of course, this is not the way to do business in the Vatican!" There are Catholic patriarchs among the Eastern-rite leaders, including Cardinal Béchara Raï, Maronite Catholic Patriarch of Antioch, featured in chapter 10. These titles are historic. In any event, if you attend a UGCC liturgy, you will hear Shevchuk referred to as patriarch in the prayers of the faithful. To date, Rome still counts him as a major archbishop.

ALTERNATIVE APPROACHES

A second principle for discerning the correct course in any worldly situation is that reality is more important than ideas. Living through Argentina's "Dirty War," Francis grew to despise ideology. He applied this outlook in Ukraine, where he prefers to address the realities of poverty and war weariness rather than insert himself into a blame game that requires adjudicating competing claims.

Between 2016 and 2018, the pope raised $18 million for some nine hundred thousand Ukrainians, most of them Orthodox, who either resided in the conflict zone or had been displaced from their homes. Food, medicine, social services to treat posttraumatic stress disorder (PTSD), and renovations to winterize homes and install boilers were the main expenditures.[32] The aid was delivered directly to desperate people and supervised by the papal nuncio who succeeded Gullickson, Archbishop Claudio Gugerotti. According to the nuncio, Francis told him his role should be more charitable than political.[33]

Former ambassador Charles Freeman, a widely respected American diplomat, thoroughly objective about Francis's choices in Ukraine, considers the pope's approach "sensible, geopolitically, because the problem with Ukraine is not fundamentally external but internal. This is a society that has yet to establish itself as a viable state. It is highly corrupt. It is divided linguistically and religiously. There is no consensus on Ukraine joining the EU or NATO, quite the contrary."[34]

"I suppose the pope would like to see Ukraine emerge as a viable, prosperous, democratic, at least well-governed, state," Freeman said. "My own view is simple: Ukraine cannot be a member of either the European or Russian bloc. It must be both a bridge and a buffer between them. In order to do that, it needs to become a viable country. It needs to develop an economy that works. In fact, the Ukrainian economy is very closely tied to Russia, and that can't be undone."

He suggests a relevant example from recent history: the Austrian State Treaty of 1955. "At the height of the Cold War, the Soviet Union, Britain, France, and the United States agreed to withdraw from Austria, enabling it to emerge, for the first time, as a German-dominated independent state. But they did it in such a way that allowed the ethnic minorities to be treated fairly and given a measure of autonomy. If we could do that at the height of the Cold War, why can't we do something like that in Ukraine?"

"By not taking sides in the manner that he has done, the pope has not prejudiced the possibility of a prosperous, peaceful Ukraine," the diplomat concluded.[35]

Besides seeing pragmatic alternatives to self-interested conflict, Pope Francis and his right hand on all foreign policy matters, Cardinal Parolin, made it clear that protecting Catholic–Russian Orthodox dialogue, over fifty years in the making, was a higher priority than egging on internecine aggression in Ukraine. And Patriarch Kirill took public notice of their attitude: speaking to the Russian Ministry of Foreign Affairs' Diplomatic Academy, he praised Francis and Parolin for "avoiding unilateral assessments and calling for an end to the fratricidal war" in Ukraine.[36]

The Vatican leadership believes Russia is a valuable ally for Europe: it sees relentlessly negative depictions of Vladimir Putin as peculiarly shortsighted. Indeed, Rome's approach directly contradicts the American and Western European effort to isolate Russia.

By keeping some distance from the largest Catholic community in Ukraine, Pope Francis earned credit from the Russian government as well as Patriarch Kirill, leader of the Russian Orthodox Church (ROC). But the Vatican's position goes beyond mere geopolitics. The Holy See sees in the Russian Orthodox Church a potential force for good, and in Russia a better model for Christianity's beneficial public role than found almost anywhere else. Moreover, pursuit of Christian unity is one of Francis's prime objectives; in his engagement with the ROC, he is continuing an ecumenical effort that began more than half a century ago after the Second Vatican Council, according to staff at the Pontifical Council for Promoting Christian Unity (loath to be quoted by name).

BREATHING WITH TWO LUNGS

Since the Second Vatican Council, it has been a Catholic priority to achieve closer relations with other Christians. One of Vatican II's key documents, *Unitatis Redintegratio* (Restoration of Unity, 1964), describes "restoration of unity among all Christians" as a key long-term goal.[37] Evidence of this dramatic new outlook is reflected in the document's term for baptized Christians professing faith in another church: "separated brethren" replaced "heretics."

To calm a contentious divorce between the two branches of Christianity that split in 1054, Pope Paul VI and Ecumenical Patriarch Athenagoras canceled mutual excommunications of Latin Catholic and Eastern Orthodox Church leaders in simultaneous ceremonies held in 1965 (following their 1964 meeting in Jerusalem), thereby allowing interchurch dialogue to begin in the modern era.[38]

Pope John Paul II fully embraced the ecumenical objective. In a turn of phrase so simple and memorable it sounds like something Pope Francis might say, the Polish pope wrote in *Ut Unum Sint* (On Commitment to Ecumenism, 1995) that the Church must breathe with two lungs, meaning that, to fully live, Christianity requires the Latin *and* Orthodox traditions.[39]

The pope explained that during Christianity's first one thousand years, the two lungs were located in Rome and Constantinople respectively. Then, in the year 988, baptism was conferred on the pagan leader of Kyiv, now known as St. Vladimir, because he consolidated Christianity in today's Ukraine, Russia, and Belarus and evangelized as far as Alaska. Thus, in *Ut Unum Sint*, John Paul II honors the Orthodox world's two main actors: the ecumenical patriarch of Constantinople, considered "first among equals" based on the see's historical legacy, and the Russian Orthodox patriarch, the most powerful Orthodox Church demographically and financially.[40]

But on the Russian side, there is an old idea going back to the sixteenth century that history has anointed the Russian Orthodox Church as a spiritual successor to Rome: "Two Romes have fallen, a third stands, and a fourth there shall not be" is the phrase attributed to a ROC monk. It was an idea that helped consolidate Russian independence. It also captures an underlying conviction among the Orthodox that Orthodox Christianity is superior to Catholicism.

STUMBLING BLOCKS

John Paul II became the first pope to visit a majority-Orthodox country, Romania, in 1999, where Romanian Orthodox patriarch Teoctist accompanied him for three days, and the pope wowed the country by speaking its language and expressing knowledgeable sympathy for its wrenching experience of Communism.[41] Later he went to Orthodox Armenia, Bulgaria, Georgia, Greece, and Ukraine. But he was never able to achieve his dream of a personal meeting with Russian Orthodox patriarch Alexy II, who took office in 1990.

Despite years of negotiations and a variety of trial balloons on location options and meeting configurations floated by the Vatican, Alexy resisted John Paul II's charm, even after the fall of the Soviet Union. Five major areas of tension between Catholics and Orthodox conspired to lock the pontiff out: (1) Catholic property claims against the Russian state, which had brutally expropriated, repurposed, or destroyed churches, monasteries, and ecclesiastical buildings during the Soviet era, in some cases turning Catholic properties over to the Orthodox Church; (2) Orthodox fears that Catholics and other missionary churches would sweep into Russia to woo believers; (3) centuries of Polish-Russian rivalry; (4) missteps at the Vatican in how it structured new Catholic administrative units in Russia; and (5) for the first decade after the Soviet Union was dissolved, under President Boris Yeltsin (a former Soviet apparatchik), the Russian Federation fell into economic and social chaos, which affected the rebuilding of the Orthodox Church, devastated under Communism, and created suspicion of outsiders.

Relations between the Catholic Church and the ROC reached a real low in 2002 when Russia barred Catholic Bishop Jerzy Mazur from returning to Russia from his native Poland. Four other priests were expelled. Mazur had been revitalizing—and governing—Catholicism in Siberia, the biggest diocese in the world by land area. Several other Catholic priests were kicked out or barred as well. The Vatican's apostolic administrator for European Russia, Archbishop Tadeusz Kondrusiewicz (an ethnic Pole from Belarus), complained, "An organized campaign is being waged against the Catholic Church in Russia."

Confirming that things were bad, the *Economist* called it an "ugly and bitter feud" and observed, "Relations between the Vatican and the Orthodox hierarchy, always tense, are going from bad to worse."[42] A key dispute pertained to proselytism. The ROC was seemingly preoccupied with the idea that any Catholic religious coming to post-Communist Russia was there to poach believers.

Another stumbling block foiling collaboration (especially in the first two decades of democratic Russia) was the common perception that the Catholic Church is somehow "foreign." The overwhelming presence of Polish clergy and religious seemed to bear this out. An American priest told me that once a Russian woman stopped by a Jesuit residence in Novosibirsk, a city in Siberia, and asked if she could pray in the chapel, which was designed by a Pole. She entered the small sacred room but seemed ill at ease because of its foreign appearance. Finally she asked, "Is it permitted to pray here?"

Catholic institutions have too often been deemed "foreign" by laws passed by the Duma. A law on foreign NGOs is especially harsh. To undercut Catholic outreach efforts, local officials often make it difficult for missionary churches to get permits for anything related to construction or repair. A house of Mother Teresa's Missionaries of Charity on the eastern periphery of Moscow offered very useful services to the homeless and prisoners newly released from jail, almost all of whom suffered from tuberculosis. The house was summarily shut down by state authorities for "lack of applicable permits," according to priests who lived in Moscow.

Early on, after the fall of the Soviet Union, numerous Catholic groups offered a wide variety of caritative services in Russia. The ROC, in the midst of an enormous reorganization, was not able to provide many of those services. The Catholics thought they could step in where the ROC and the new Russian state needed assistance, but the Orthodox Church reacted negatively from the outset, especially with the opening of Catholic-sponsored orphanages. New legislation, backed by cries of "proselytism" from Orthodox entities, resulted in the closing of most of the homes after a short time.

JOHN PAUL II'S GIFT, DELIVERED WITHOUT HIM

But John Paul II thought he could work miracles if only he could get there. One story in particular demonstrates how intensely Pope John Paul II hoped to visit Russia. For years, John Paul kept on a wall in his private study the Mother of God of Kazan icon, a wonder-working masterpiece stolen by the

Bolsheviks from a Russian basilica and sold in the West to a British noble. The aristocrat in turn sold it to the Catholic Blue Army of Our Lady of Fatima, which put the icon in a small chapel in Portugal, where it remained during the 1970s and 1980s. After the Soviet Union dissolved, Pope John Paul II asked the nuncio in Lisbon to request that the icon be brought to Rome; the spiritual treasure was delivered to him in 1993, and he kept it close, waiting for the moment when he could carry it to Mother Russia by hand.

Meanwhile, author and publisher Robert Moynihan, president of the Urbi et Orbi Foundation (created to improve East-West Christian relations), had been asked by the Orthodox Church in Kazan to help find this icon, lost somewhere in the West. Moynihan learned quickly from journalists in Rome where the icon lived—in the Apostolic Palace. "I went and talked to the pope's secretary, Bishop Stanisław Dziwisz. We ended up in the pope's study, and I saw the icon. The face of Our Lady was splendidly beautiful. I felt she was speaking to me. The secretary said, 'She is saying, she wants to return to Russia, but we aren't sure how.'"[43] The pope's hope to deliver the icon personally did not seem likely.

Moynihan had contacts in the ROC's Department for External Church Relations, comparable to its Foreign Ministry, in Moscow, so he started exploring possibilities for the icon's return in a way that would benefit relations between the two churches. At one point an Orthodox bishop said, "We know all about the icon, we don't want it to come. We believe it is a forgery, not authentic, and we aren't interested." The bishop opened the door and ushered Moynihan out, only to call him back a minute later. He said, "Sit down again. We care, but we can't beg for it. It is against our sense of dignity to beg for the icon from Rome. If they give it to us freely and generously, we would receive it in return, but we can't exchange a papal visit for the icon."[44]

Moynihan returned to Pope John Paul II's secretary and told him the story. John Paul II decided to entrust the Mother of God to German Cardinal Walter Kasper, president of the Pontifical Council for Promoting Christian Unity at the time. In August 2004, the cardinal and a small delegation carried her back to Moscow.

In the Kremlin's Assumption Cathedral, Kasper kissed the icon as a sign of veneration and handed it to Patriarch Alexy II, who venerated it too. Then the men kissed each other three times on alternating cheeks, a sign of respect.[45] Kasper handed a letter to Alexy in which the pope wrote, "Divine Providence made it possible for the people and the church in Russia to recover their freedom, and for the wall separating Eastern Europe from Western Europe to fall. . . . Despite the divisions which sadly still persist between Christians, this sacred icon appears as a symbol of unity."[46]

Three months later, Ecumenical Patriarch Bartholomew I, leader of the Orthodox Church of Constantinople, traveled to St. Peter's Basilica for a ceremony at which Pope John Paul II presented relics of two saints who lived before the schism. Both were precious to the Orthodox Church.[47] Rome had obtained bones of the patriarchs St. John Chrysostom and St. Gregory Nazianzen from the eighth century.

Sitting next to the patriarch, the pope, just five months away from death, was too weak to read his own remarks, so an assistant read of the pope's hope to "purify our wounded memories" and "strengthen our path of reconciliation."[48] The Holy See's main Orthodox interlocutor since 1964 was the ecumenical patriarch, in large part because Communism created a squid-like ink cloud concealing Orthodox reality, thus preventing authentic relations from developing with the ROC.

The return of icons to the Russian Orthodox Church and the Orthodox Church of Constantinople were concrete steps in the Holy See's goal of closer relations with the Orthodox world. The fact that the gifts were given in the last year of Pope John Paul II's life signals the importance to him of Catholic-Orthodox closeness.

But what significantly repaired Christian division, especially between Moscow and Rome, was the ascension of Benedict XVI in April 2005.

BENEDICT TAKES OVER

Against expectation, Pope Benedict XVI achieved diplomatic breakthroughs impossible for his predecessor, especially in relations with Russia and the ROC. Benedict's authority as a renowned theologian, his sapient personality, and the happenstance of his German birth combined to make him an unusually effective advocate for Christian unity—quite a legacy for a pope pegged as the "guardian of orthodoxy" when he was elected.

Two very different trends comprise the pragmatic (as opposed to spiritual) motives for ecumenism: a secularizing trend that tends to marginalize, diminish, or even deny Christianity's relevance, on the one hand, and a marked increase in violence against Christian churches and believers, on the other. Pope John Paul II was well aware of the first trend and feared the second. Pope Benedict XVI governed as both negative realities, in the Church's eyes, settled onto the world, compelling a coordinated response. In his first papal message to his former peers, assembled in the Sistine Chapel, Benedict (speaking in the third person) announced,

> [T]he current Successor assumes as his primary commitment that of working tirelessly towards the reconstitution of the full and visible unity of all Christ's

followers. This is his ambition, this is his compelling duty. He is aware that to do so, expressions of good feelings are not enough.[49]

On his first papal trip abroad, to a group of religious leaders in Germany, Benedict offered his most specific vision of what ecumenism looks like, rejecting the idea that institutions are the focal point of dialogue or that it requires denying one's own faith history. He explained that ecumenism "does not mean uniformity in all expressions of theology and spirituality, in liturgical forms and in discipline. Unity in multiplicity, and multiplicity in unity. . . . It is obvious that this dialogue can develop only in a context of sincere and committed spirituality."

The pope ended his talk with a picturesque observation, "Now let us all go along this path in the awareness that walking together is a form of unity."[50] It was as though Benedict the inquisitor had thrown off the doctrinal cape he had to wear as leader of the Congregation for the Doctrine of the Faith (charged with policing issues ranging from polygamy[51] to exorcism) to reveal his authentic self, Benedict the mystic and theologian.

ORTHODOX OUTPOST IN ISTANBUL

The main purpose of Benedict's first papal visit to a majority-Muslim country, Turkey, in late November 2006 was to meet with Bartholomew for the Feast of St. Andrew—the apostle who by tradition founded Eastern Christianity over two thousand years ago. Many counseled Benedict to cancel the trip due to Muslim anger over a speech he gave in Regensburg, Germany—interpreted by many Islamic clerics as insulting—that continued to produce violent protests. Just two days before Benedict arrived in Istanbul, twenty-five thousand people demonstrated against him.

Benedict met with the patriarch under tight Turkish police security. In a glittering evening prayer service at the modest Church of St. George—a church not marked by a cross due to Turkish restrictions on religion—Bartholomew greeted the pontiff as a "beloved brother," and Benedict framed his response with the psalm, "Behold, how good and pleasant it is when brothers dwell in unity."[52] The two spoke at length about the ecumenical mission, mainly to promote peace through love. Together, they prayed before the relics of St. John Chrysostom and St. Gregory of Nazianzen, returned to Bartholomew by John Paul II.

The next day they signed a common statement. They appeared together with clasped hands held aloft. Although Bartholomew presides over a minute, beleaguered local Orthodox community in Istanbul with fewer than three thousand believers—and the Turkish government padlocked the country's only seminary in 1971, making it impossible to cultivate young leaders[53]—the patriarch of Constantinople is a towering symbol of Eastern Orthodox spirituality. He is considered "first among equals" among the leaders of Eastern Orthodoxy's autocephalous (self-governing) Churches, making this picture of unity set in Byzantium a dramatic sign of progress.

As Cardinal Kurt Koch, president of the Pontifical Council for the Promotion of Christian Unity, explained to me, after the fall of Communism, Orthodox churches in many newly liberated countries were skeptical about working with the Catholic Church.[54] As mentioned, they feared that Catholics aimed to evangelize Orthodox believers. Patriarch Bartholomew worked hard to help restore Catholic-Orthodox relations, especially because Catholic communities survived everywhere from Albania to Uzbekistan, and it was essential to have open lines of communication between the two.

Bartholomew visited Rome several times after Benedict came to the Phanar, the patriarchal residence in the historic Greek quarter of Istanbul. Each occasion marked a step toward greater reconciliation. In June 2008, the patriarch participated in a Mass at St. Peter's Basilica, where the two men recited the Nicene Creed together in Greek, leaving out a three-word phrase ("and the Son") known as the "Filioque clause" that the Orthodox do not accept. This theological dispute, pertaining to the Holy Spirit, dates back to the eighth century. Benedict showed that Catholics can overcome a doctrinal point as a living act—even before any paperwork is signed.

The most significant development in the deepening East-West dialogue, though, was the elevation of a new Russian Orthodox leader, Patriarch Kirill, in January 2009 and the opening of bilateral relations between the Russia Federation and the Holy See at the end of the year.[55]

RELATIONS WITH RUSSIA

Upon the death of Alexy II, a synod of bishops elected Metropolitan Kirill as ROC patriarch.[56] For twenty years, he had served as chairman of its Department for External Church Relations (DECR), which made him the Vatican's main post-Communist interlocutor. Kirill, born in 1946, is a sophisticated man and a third-generation priest, following his father and grandfather, who was arrested in 1933 for capitalizing the word "God."[57] Kirill's father was a priest and theology teacher; his mother was a German-language teacher. In 1971, Kirill was posted to Geneva to serve as the ROC representative to the World Council of Churches, the global ecumenical forum founded in 1948, with some 350 Christian members, though not the Catholic Church.

Kirill and Benedict share an analysis of the risks threatening the West. They believe that Western culture depends on its Christian foundation for the precepts of virtue, which guarantees freedom. For these men who lived through totalitarianism, rampant secularism and moral collapse signal a dangerous instability that can invite new forms of tyranny. They are also wary of radical Islam and its threat to small Christian populations around the world.

Patriarch Kirill advances his ideas from a position of strength: the Russian Orthodox Church is ascendant. In 1917, just before the Russian Revolution, the ROC had over fifty-five thousand churches and about sixty-six thousand priests. After brutal persecution, in just twenty years, those numbers sank to three hundred churches and three hundred priests. Following the breakup of the Soviet Union, the ROC emerged as one of Russia's only trusted institutions. The percentage of people describing themselves as Orthodox surged from 37 percent in 1991 to 71 percent in 2015.[58] Following a construction and restoration boom, in 2017 there were over thirty-four thousand active ROC churches in Russia and approximately thirty-five thousand priests.[59]

The ROC is also closely allied with political power, giving the Church muscle and relevance. Under Putin, Russia and the ROC have achieved a cooperative relationship reminiscent of the Byzantine ideal of church-state harmony known as *symphonia*. Elaborated under Emperor Justinian, *symphonia* assumes that since both patriarch and emperor work to achieve heaven on earth in complementary ways, there's no need to define sharply different roles. One can argue that the mutuality evident in the relationship between Patriarch Kirill and President Putin exemplifies this model.[60]

Russian scholar Nicolai Petro confirms that one of the primary successes of the post-Communist ROC has been "to transform relations with the state from subordination to meaningful partnership by reasserting the concept of *symphonia* in church-state relations."[61] The partnership also promotes Russian interests abroad. The ROC envisions a meaningful role for religion in foreign policy, and Putin has encouraged Orthodox engagement. Kirill has taken major international trips to every part of the world, promoting Russian culture, spirituality, and the value of cooperation. (In 2013, Kirill visited Beijing and met with President Xi; two years later, while in Moscow, Xi sat down with the patriarch for a one-on-one meeting—in the Kremlin.[62])

As cooperation began to flourish under Benedict and Kirill—the Vatican sponsored a "Day of Russian Culture and Spirituality," and the Orthodox countered by organizing a concert dedicated to the pontiff—political relations between the Russian Federation and the Holy See gained ground. In 2010, for the first time since the Bolshevik Revolution, Russia and the Vatican exchanged ambassadors based on full diplomatic recognition. Not only did warmth between the Churches facilitate this agreement, but cordial relations between President Putin and Pope Benedict paved the way.

The two men met at the Vatican in March 2007, conversing in the pontiff's native language. Putin speaks German fluently; he learned it at home and lived in Dresden for several years while working for the KGB. During the visit, according to a US embassy cable released through WikiLeaks, Putin pledged that his government would "do all it can to favor dialogue between the two churches."[63] Putin is himself Orthodox.

The ROC also has an engaging "foreign minister" who has very effectively cultivated relationships in Rome. Metropolitan Hilarion of Volokolamsk has been chairman of the ROC's Department of External Church Relations since 2009—appointed when he was just forty-three years old. Widely considered a wunderkind, he has many friends and admirers in Rome, including Pope Benedict, who sat next to Hilarion at a concert of Russian spiritual music offered by Patriarch Kirill to mark Benedict's birthday and the fifth year of his pontificate.

At the concert, the pope, obviously moved, said, "Let us return to the vision of a Europe that breathes with both lungs, to restore the spirit not only of believers, but to all the peoples of the Continent, thus promoting trust and hope by rooting them in the age-old experience of Christian faith!"[64] Benedict's fundamental assumptions—that Europe includes Russia and that Christianity is whole only when Catholics and Orthodox collaborate—are shared by Pope Francis and animate his diplomacy, as it did that of his two predecessors.

FRANCIS'S PRIORITIES

Ecumenical Patriarch Bartholomew's decision to attend Jorge Bergoglio's installation Mass as Pope Francis was widely noted as the first such gesture since the Great Schism.[65] In fact, it was probably the first time in history that a bishop of Constantinople attended the elevation of a bishop of Rome.[66] Bartholomew came to underscore the importance of continuing the collaboration that had developed under Popes John Paul II and, especially, Benedict.[67] Francis and Bartholomew quickly established a relationship that found them meeting so frequently between 2013 and 2014 that the *Washington Post* headlined, "Pope Francis and Patriarch Bartholomew: A Budding Bromance?"[68] The two have prayed together at the Holy Sepulcher in Jerusalem, planted a tree in the Vatican Gardens, prayed together at the Cathedral of St. George in Istanbul, visited the Greek island of Lesbos, prayed together at St. Francis's birthplace in Assisi, and exchanged scores of greetings and messages. The pope especially admires Bartholomew, known as the "Green Patriarch" for his pathbreaking advocacy for the environment. Curial staff say the two are real friends.

As comfortable as Francis is with his brother Bartholomew, he also has a special place in his heart for Russia, and for Catherine the Great in particular, who is credited with helping to save the Society of Jesus, better known as the Jesuits, from extinction. The Jesuit order experienced a Calvary rarely remembered today. In the eighteenth century, it was expelled from Portugal, France, Spain, and the Austro-Hungarian Empire for opposing slavery and the reckless plunder of riches in the Americas by Spanish and Portuguese powers. Being independent—financially and politically—was also perceived as an offense. (The 1986 film *The Mission* is a moving portrayal of the clash between the institutional Church and Jesuit missionaries.) All Jesuit schools, universities, and hospitals were closed, properties confiscated, libraries dispersed, and many members jailed. Pope Clement XIV was pressured to endorse this suppression in a decree, *Dominus ac Redemptor* (1773), that forbade novices, thus condemning the order to death.

It was Catherine the Great of Russia who "saved the Society."[69] She protected over two hundred Jesuits present in Russia, as well as four colleges and other cultural entities ministering on her territory. She ignored protests from rulers in Western Europe and diplomatically persuaded Pius VI to grant permission for a novitiate to train young members of the order. Pius VI conveyed his verbal approval through Catherine's envoy in Rome. The tsarina's successor, Paul I, continued support. Thus the Society of Jesus survived. Finally, in 1814, Pope Pius VII decreed the Jesuit order fully restored. Most members, including Pope Francis, respect Russia for assuring Jesuit survival—when even Rome suppressed them.[70]

PRESERVING ORTHODOX DIALOGUE

As a sovereign head of state with far more influence than his thimble-sized kingdom would normally garner, the pope meets regularly with political leaders. At the height of the Russian-American standoff, Pope Francis met with Vladimir Putin in June 2015 at Moscow's request.[71] Considering the intractability of the conflict in Ukraine, Francis considers dialogue to be a moral requirement. He also supports multilateral engagement to solve international problems. Francis kept close tabs on progress made by the Organization for Security and Co-operation in Europe (OSCE) and European leaders negotiating two versions of a peace plan for Ukraine and Russia.[72]

During a visit to Sarajevo a few weeks before his audience with Putin, the pope said, "We need to communicate with each other, to discover the gifts of each person, to promote that which unites us, and to regard our differences as an opportunity to grow in mutual respect." It's a sentiment that could seem banal, except Pope Francis has elevated the notion of personal encounter into a central precept of his papacy.[73] Another principle of life and diplomacy is that the Holy Spirit can "harmonize every diversity," as mentioned in *Evangelii Gaudium*, which the pope handed to Putin when they met.

To the packed stadium in Sarajevo, where he celebrated Mass, the pontiff also evoked his antiwar theme: "[I]n the context of global communications, we sense an atmosphere of war. Some wish to incite and foment this atmosphere deliberately, mainly those who speculate on wars for the purpose of selling arms." Besides objecting to the reliance on military force for regional problem solving, the Vatican resents strategies designed to punish opponents—a practice that has become a default tool in the American diplomatic toolbox, in Rome's view.

During their fifty minutes together, Francis told Putin it would take "a sincere and great effort" to bring peace to the Ukraine-Russia border and urged him to comply with the Minsk agreements.[74] The pope also asked for support facilitating humanitarian aid. Sources in the secretariat say Francis was well aware that the Group of Seven industrial countries (G7) had met just days before to turn the sanctions screws tighter on Russia; Francis does not believe those tactics are productive, as the Church opposed sanctions against Cuba and, more recently, Iran.

Significantly, Putin told the pontiff he would do what he could to advance collaboration between his Church and Francis's—a pledge that bore fruit very soon.

HISTORICAL SUMMIT IN AN AIRPORT VIP LOUNGE

Eight months later, on February 12, 2016, Pope Francis and Patriarch Kirill sat together in an airport lounge outside Havana, the first-ever face-to-face meeting of Catholic and Russian Orthodox Church leaders. The event, announced via a joint press release just a week before, was a very well-kept secret, arranged by fewer than ten people on both sides, according to a Vatican diplomat.[75] Pope Francis's plane diverted slightly to Cuba on his way to Mexico; the neutral location was selected by the ROC because the island was Kirill's first stop on his own Latin American itinerary.[76] It is worth noting, though, that the site's proximity to Washington was considered a plus—

allowing the meeting to be read as conveying the message, "No, you do not control the world."

At 2:00 p.m., Francis's Alitalia flight landed at the old orange-and-blue José Martí International Airport. Although neither was involved in arranging the historic event, President Raúl Castro and Cardinal Jaime Ortega escorted the pontiff to an airport hangar where, upon meeting Kirill, Francis's first word was, "Finally." Pope and patriarch spent the next two hours chatting in a nondescript presidential lounge with faux wood paneling, accompanied by translators and a few key advisers, including Metropolitan Hilarion and Cardinal Koch. Exchanging gifts, Kirill gave Francis a small copy of the Icon of Kazan; the pope gave the Russian a chalice and a relic of St. Cyril, revered by Catholics and Orthodox alike.

The two signed a thirty-point joint declaration, which highlighted a major point of common purpose: the plight of Middle East Christians, together struggling to survive religious extremism. The two leaders appealed to the international community to stop the killing, condemning violence committed in the name of God as against the very nature of God. Their litany of concerns included "secularist ideology," consumerism, the crisis of the family, reproductive technology, and euthanasia. Addressing a ROC preoccupation, they even renounced "proselytism" because "we are not competitors but brothers."[77]

Three points were devoted to the conflict in Ukraine. The holy men deplored ongoing hostility and "invite our Churches to work toward social harmony." They referenced the schism within the Ukrainian Orthodox Church, and Francis sided with the ROC by calling on "canonical norms" as the proper standard. Kirill gave a little too: he recognized the UGCC's "right to exist," since it emerged in a certain historical circumstance, and acknowledged the need to find "forms of coexistence" between Orthodox and UGCC to advance reconciliation. No surprise, the UGCC was not very content to witness this discussion occurring over its head.[78]

Media coverage emphasized the historical aspect of the meeting as overcoming a legendary East-West breach. However, another prominent Orthodox patriarch, Bartholomew, is a frequent visitor to Rome. He and Benedict signed a common declaration in 2006 renewing "our commitment to move towards full communion."[79] He and Pope Francis are bosom buddies. So, hadn't the Catholic-Orthodox rupture already been addressed? What made the meeting between Pope Francis and Patriarch Kirill momentous was not what it said about the past but what it said about Christianity and the complementary role Church leaders now see themselves playing in international relations.

For the Holy See, Russia's post-Communist cultural and spiritual resurgence is glorious evidence of the Holy Spirit moving among us. Christ could not be buried despite a seventy-plus-year effort by Soviet atheists. As a function of its global perspective, the Holy See sees Russia as an ally against secularism and Islamic radicalism. The part of Francis that resents American militarism and hypocrisy relishes the counternarrative presented by a Rome-Moscow unity posture—the way the meeting foiled Western isolation of Russia was intentional. And his willingness to hold the meeting on Communist Cuban territory is another way to say that non-American worldviews are just as legitimate as the US Goliath's perspective.[80]

This independent outlook is based on the Holy See's view that Western culture is fundamentally Christian and thus stretches from Europe east to Eurasia and west to North and South America, wherever Christian communities are found, especially as a majority. Rather than conceding to a "clash of civilizations" culture war, Holy See diplomats have for generations slowly worked to heal the "scandal to the world" of East-West division, as Pope Benedict termed it, to allow Christ's church to "breathe with her two lungs," in John Paul II's famous phrase.[81]

John XXIII, who convened Vatican II, was a lifelong proponent of ecumenical dialogue. In 1926 he wrote, "Catholics and Orthodox are not enemies, but brothers. We have the same faith; we share the same sacraments, and especially the Eucharist. We are divided by some disagreements concerning the divine constitution of the Church of Jesus Christ. The persons who were the cause of these disagreements have been dead for centuries. . . . Let us abandon the old disputes."[82] This commitment was confirmed by his ten years of service as Vatican representative to Orthodox Bulgaria and partially explains why he convoked an ecumenical council.[83]

Pope Francis echoed the saint he so admires when he described to *La Stampa* his attitude toward Orthodox bishops: "I felt like their brother. They have the apostolic succession; I received them as brother bishops. It is painful that we are not yet able to celebrate the Eucharist together, but there is friendship. I believe that the way forward is this: friendship, common work, and prayer for unity. We blessed each other; one brother blesses the other."[84]

This is an example of the unity that forms Francis's third principle of diplomacy and problem solving: by prioritizing ecumenical unity over conflict, he managed to achieve a historic breakthrough, which can hopefully contribute to solving the real conflict still unfolding in Ukraine.

CHURCHES SHARE A MORAL AGENDA

As the joint declaration signed in Cuba laid out, beyond personalities, collaboration between the Catholic and Orthodox Churches flows from a shared diagnosis of contemporary threats to Christianity itself: Christian persecution and Islamic fundamentalism, on the one hand, and secularism and moral relativism on the other. A secularizing trend that tends to marginalize, diminish, or even deny Christianity's relevance, especially in Western culture, is a force for ecumenical unity.

It's not just faith in Jesus Christ that traditional Catholics and the Russian Orthodox share; it is an attitude toward a range of social issues, from protecting life in the womb to opposing same-sex marriage, from rejecting the crass materialism of consumer culture to supporting the Church's role in the public square. The primary sticking point between the two Churches is the primacy of the Latin pope, yet even that has been minimized by Pope Francis—at least symbolically.

Fr. James McCann, SJ, described how Pope Francis changed the Vatican's *Annuario Pontificio*, its comprehensive annual directory: The cover typically featured the papal coat of arms, and the first page had the pope's name with his many titles. Pope Francis kept the cover, but on the first page he listed only Francis, bishop of Rome. "I've never been so excited to see an almost blank page," remembered the Jesuit, a fluent Russian speaker who served as rector of the Pontifical Oriental Institute and worked with many Orthodox scholars. "I knew the Russian Orthodox Patriarchate would be responsive to that humility."[85]

Francis's humility is a catalyst for positive response because his self-denial opens space for the other. For example, I was told by a diplomat working in Moscow that one of the boldest strokes that advanced the ROC's willingness to meet with Francis was the pope's offhand comment during an in-flight press conference: "With Patriarch Kirill, I let him know of my wish for us to meet, and he's in agreement. But I said, 'I will go where you wish, if you call me I will come.'"[86] This deference allows the interlocutor to posit himself as the chief decider in the process. It is Francis's expression of confidence in the process itself, without insistence that anyone can control where it ends up.

What has emerged in the Catholic–Russian Orthodox dialogue is agreement to focus on common morality and mutual respect as the basis for shared action, letting the Joint Commission on Theological Dialogue work in the background at its gradual pace. As Metropolitan Hilarion told AsiaNews in 2013, "I am convinced that at the moment our joint work in the field of promoting moral and social values is much more effective. I believe that the elaboration of a common position on various social and moral issues has helped us to move ahead."[87] Add to Hilarion's perception the existential need to band together to defend Christians in the Middle East (equal parts Catholic and Orthodox, all facing liquidation), which emerged dramatically in 2014 with the genocide fomented by ISIS, and you get a strong motivation to set aside differences and focus on common goals.

Francis made clear what he thinks about dialogue with the Russian Orthodox Church on a flight from Istanbul to Rome in December 2014, combining the elements of shared journey and shared sacrifice, a process that evolves over time:

> I believe that we are on the journey with the Orthodox. They have the sacraments, they have the Apostolic Succession. We are family. But we must wait still for the theologians to reach agreement; that day will never arrive, I assure you; I am skeptical.
>
> Unity is a journey that must be made, a journey that must be made together, and this is spiritual communion: to pray together, to work together, so many works of charity, so much work together, to teach together, to go forward together. There is the spiritual communion, and then there is the communion of blood. . . . When they kill Christians, so many martyrs that we have, they [the killers] did not say, "You are Catholic, you are Anglican, you are Christian?" and so the blood is mixed. This is the ecumenism of blood. Our martyrs are shouting to us, we are one, we have a unity in the spirit and in blood.[88]

War in Ukraine risked paralyzing the relationship between the Holy See and Moscow, but Pope Francis prioritized ecumenical dialogue and made clear he would not take sides in a dispute between Christian brothers, namely, Greek Catholics in Western Ukraine and Orthodox Christians in Eastern Ukraine.[89] This decision was grounded in two decades of "relationship building" between the Holy See and the Russian Orthodox Church. Open channels between Rome and Moscow allowed the two Churches to continue communication and consultation even as the headlong rush of political events risked swamping the trust that the two faith centers had painstakingly built.

UNITY IS A JOURNEY

With patience and persistence, good things evolve over time. This conviction—that time is greater than space—is the fourth principle shaping the Holy See's diplomacy. In Francis's view, politics is preoccupied with taking positions, gaining advantage, and occupying space in a manner that mimics military action. He prefers to advance slowly, through personal encounters that gradually build love and mutual respect. Francis believes that his job is to encourage reconciliation without trying to control the outcome.

The pope's neutral line on Ukraine is the latest example of how Catholic doctrine and Vatican diplomacy have diverged from US foreign policy preferences since the end of the Cold War. Pope John Paul II, for instance, sent top diplomats to personally dissuade US president George W. Bush from invading Iraq, prophetically warning Bush that the war would lead to countless casualties and long-term regional turmoil, including the scapegoating and repression of Christian communities.

In the Vatican's view, the United States' post–Cold War foreign policy has been overly militaristic and dismissive of the benefits of peaceful diplomacy. There have been notable exceptions—Rome strongly supported the Obama administration's nuclear deal with Iran and its rapprochement with Cuba. In general, however, the Holy See is concerned that the United States has stopped exercising its once significant moral influence as a country striving to calm nerves, encourage liberal order, and facilitate peace, opting instead for counterproductive bellicosity.

Yet US aggression has opened up space for the Vatican. With more conflicts around the world and fewer mediators to settle them, room exists for new approaches—even ones based on old truths. This is the void into which Francis quietly steps.

7

Mediating Cold War Quarrels
Cuba and the United States

> I want to thank His Holiness Pope Francis, whose moral example shows us the importance of pursuing the world as it should be, rather than simply settling for the world as it is.
>
> —President Barack Obama, announcing normalization of relations between the United States and Cuba, December 17, 2014[1]

> For some months now, we have witnessed an event, which fills us with hope: the process of normalizing relations between two peoples following years of estrangement. It is a process, a sign of the victory of the culture of encounter and dialogue. . . . The world needs reconciliation in this climate of a piecemeal third world war in which we are living.
>
> —Pope Francis, Welcome Ceremony, José Martí International Airport, Havana, Cuba, September 19, 2015[2]

As Francis has consciously tried to keep tensions between Russia and Ukraine from escalating into a new Cold War, he had a considerable role in healing divisions left over from the old Cold War—namely, a half-century standoff between the United States and Cuba.

In 2014, Pope Francis helped Havana and Washington overcome distrust in order to conclude a prisoner swap and normalize Cuban-US diplomatic relations. The story has two distinct parts. When secret negotiations between the countries reached an impasse, the Obama administration and a handful of congressional allies turned to a pope with a proven ability to untie knots. Francis's independence vis-à-vis Western powers, his status as a Latin American "favorite son," and his popularity with the American public (believers and nonbelievers alike) allowed him to serve as a bridge between the two sides—and a broker who could guarantee that both sides honored their part of the bargain.

When that breakthrough did come, however, it rested on Vatican efforts stretching back over fifty years. The Church in Cuba has carefully cultivated a modus operandi with the regime that led to its emergence as the only independent institution on the island. Cardinal Jaime Ortega of Havana managed the evolution of the church-state relationship from 1981 until his death in 2019. He also played a key role engaging the three parties—Cuba, the United States, and the Holy See—after Francis met personally with President Barack Obama in March 2014.

Yet Ortega's status as a mediator on behalf of the Castros in a variety of situations before the US-Cuba negotiations includes painful elements—always true when the Church deals with tyrants. The Cuban diaspora, especially Cuban Americans, were enraged by Ortega's strategy (endorsed by successive popes) of maintaining friendly relations with a regime far more pernicious, even deadly, than portrayed abroad.

The Cuba case study demonstrates the geopolitical benefit to the Holy See of Francis's birthright, namely, his status as the first Latin American pope. It shows Francis and his advisers functioning as an effective team. At the same time, the pontiff relied on institutional attributes of Holy See diplomacy that have nothing to do with his biography. Most important, what Francis helped the United States and Cuba accomplish was grounded in policy he inherited from his predecessors. It was a fruit of the legendary "martyrdom of patience," Agostino Casaroli's poignant description of bargaining with dictators.[3]

HOPE AND CHANGE—FOILED

During his 2008 presidential campaign, Obama blasted the "failed policies of the past," including the longtime US strategy of isolating Cuba.[4] He told a Florida audience convened by the Cuban American National Foundation that it was "time to pursue direct diplomacy" with the island nation; he promised Cuban Americans he would make it easier to send money home to relatives, and he would lift a ban on family travel.[5] In his first year in office, the president made good on several reforms, but his hope for a policy reset was foiled in December 2009 when the Communist regime arrested Alan Gross, a sixty-year-old American development specialist accused of crimes against the state. Gross was sentenced to fifteen years for bringing illegal communications equipment to the island—including a computer chip not freely available on any open market.

Gross was a US Agency for International Development (USAID) subcontractor specializing in setting up internet access. He was part of a big shift in USAID's democracy promotion efforts on the island: away from traditional political activism, toward creating digital space for nascent opposition. The Cuban government was antagonized by democracy activities supported by USAID. In 2003, some seventy-five democratic dissidents were jailed,[6] effectively shutting down one of the most effective local opposition efforts since 1959.

By 2009, USAID had largely turned its support to technology-driven programs (including a secret social media platform).[7] Digital space has the potential to link thousands of people. Democracy advocates around the world used social media to mobilize opposition movements; USAID deployed those techniques in Egypt and Ukraine. As well, USAID needs activity to burn budgets—$45 million for Cuba in 2008—but it was getting harder to devise programming in a country with so little civil society space. One benefit of technology from the perspective of a development agency is that it's expensive.

The regime worked hard to control access to information in order to keep citizens in the dark. The Communist Party's Department of Revolutionary Orientation oversees the press. Internet access is limited. Independent radio signals are jammed. Freedom of information is a huge threat. It was into this maw that Alan Gross traveled to Cuba on tourist visas five times in 2009, employed by a USAID contractor. His assignment (for which he received $500,000 and, eventually, a $3.2 million settlement from the US government[8]) was to set up satellite internet service for three Jewish communities.

Although small, the Jewish community in Cuba is historical.[9] An estimated fourteen thousand Jews fled Cuba after the revolution, so the existence of a solid community of some fifteen hundred believers maintaining three synagogues in Havana attracts wide support.[10] For his USAID assignment, Gross identified himself as part of a Jewish humanitarian group and gave other American Jews some of the equipment to transport in carry-on bags.[11]

No one claimed anti-Semitism motivated Gross's arrest or retribution against the Jewish community, which is not persecuted, according to Jewish Americans.[12] Travel was blocked for average Cubans under Fidel Castro (Raúl Castro loosened the ban starting in January 2013), but Jews who wanted to visit Israel got permission.[13] Raúl Castro even attended Hanukkah at Havana's Bet Shalom synagogue wearing a yarmulke in 2010.[14] More likely, say Cuba watchers, Alan Gross was targeted because his Jewish connections made him a more valuable asset in efforts to win concessions from the United States, especially to gain the release of five Cuban intelligence officers serving long sentences in American jails.[15]

HILLARY CLINTON AND POPE BENEDICT'S EFFORTS FOUNDER

Secretary of State Hillary Clinton saw an opportunity to try negotiating with the Cuban government in 2010 as a result of unusual cooperation between the two countries for post-earthquake disaster relief in Haiti, located just ninety miles to the east of Cuba. Clinton assigned her chief of staff and a high-level State Department expert on Latin America to initiate secret meetings with the Cuban Ministry of Foreign Relations.[16]

For over two years, the two met with the top echelon of ministry officialdom, in Port-au-Prince, Manhattan, and Santo Domingo. What began as a broad review of issues dividing the two countries, including the impact of the US embargo and the Cuban desire to shut down a US naval base at Guantanamo Bay, evolved into a focus on Alan Gross and the "Cuban Five."[17] Washington was adamant that a swap was impossible because Gross was not classified as a spy, while the Cuban side would not budge from this demand. Clinton's effort capsized on the shoals of this impasse.

What the two sides did accomplish was agreement to let the wives visit their incarcerated husbands: two Cuban women were quietly given visas to travel to a maximum-security prison in Texas, while Judy Gross was allowed to see Alan in the Carlos J. Finlay Military Hospital where his cell was. In her memoir, Hillary Clinton called the lack of progress in talks with Cuba a major regret, especially because the bad relationship inhibited American goals across Latin America.[18] A Cuban deal was not in the cards for Clinton for two reasons: (1) Obama was not going to let her have that sweet cake, and (2) Jorge Bergoglio was still in Buenos Aires.

This problem became especially clear in April 2012 at the Sixth Summit of the Americas, held in Cartagena, Colombia, when regional heads of state complained they might not come back if the United States continued to exclude Cuba. Colombian president Juan Manuel Santos seemed to speak for other leaders when he called the US embargo against Cuba "anachronistic" and "ineffective."[19]

In Rome, it was the American Jewish Committee that brought Gross's situation to the attention of the Vatican's Secretariat of State.[20] Pope Benedict XVI evoked the plight of Alan Gross to President Raúl Castro when they met on March 27, 2012. The pope framed his intervention as a humanitarian issue considering Gross's deteriorating health.

In fact, perhaps as the Cuban government expected, Jewish organizations mobilized globally on behalf of Gross, who belonged to a synagogue in suburban Washington, DC. That the work he was jailed for was designed to help Cuban Jews also galvanized the community. The American Jewish Committee, the Anti-Defamation League, B'nai B'rith International, the Jewish Community Relations Council, and the Orthodox Union all played a role.

His team—including a law firm, a well-connected PR firm working pro bono, and a fleet of volunteers—activated over five hundred rabbis from around the world.[21] A rabbi led weekly vigils for Gross outside the Cuban Interest Section in Washington. A senior B'nai B'rith official told me how he met the president of Panama to discuss Gross's case as part of a regional strategy to pressure Havana.[22]

SECOND-TERM PRIORITIES

President Obama made reconciliation with Cuba a top priority for his second term in office, which began in January 2013. He pulled the subject back from the State Department and lodged it with a balanced two-man team. Deputy National Security Adviser Ben Rhodes was one of the president's closest advisers. Those in the inner circle said they had a father-son bond, so Rhodes was an impressive sign of the president's real commitment to what he called the Cuba "project." Rhodes was paired with the White House's Cuba expert, Ricardo Zúñiga, senior director for Western Hemisphere affairs at the National Security Council.

Born in Honduras in 1970 to an illustrious family, Zúñiga's father was murdered in 1985, a victim of political intrigue; his American-born mother educated him in the United States. He joined the US Foreign Service in 1993 and spent two years in Havana as a human rights officer.[23] Zúñiga briefly led the State Department's Office of Cuban Affairs. He served at embassies in Brazil, Spain, Mexico, and Portugal. Bottom line: the diplomat had spent his life preparing to help recalibrate the US-Cuba relationship.

In May 2013, the White House proposed to the Cuban government a dialogue on two subjects, Alan Gross and counterterrorism. The response came just a few days later, and it was a bingo: Colonel Alejandro Castro Espín, Raúl Castro's only son (thus Fidel's nephew), would lead the delegation. Although he keeps a low profile, Alejandro Castro is a powerful member of the Cuban ruling elite, with revolutionary street cred because he lost an eye in an accident in Angola during Castro's military intervention.[24] His degrees are in engineering and international relations.

The Americans requested help from the Canadians in arranging a safe house where the two small delegations could meet without anyone discovering the endeavor. Rhodes and Zúñiga, joined by a counterterrorism expert, flew to Ottawa, where a Canadian official picked them up at the airport and hustled them to a remote lakeside house with conference rooms and sound-jamming capability to block potential eavesdroppers.[25]

The Cuban delegation of four included Castro, age forty-eight at the time; Juana, a translator who worked for Fidel Castro for decades; and two men from intelligence services. After some filibustering from Castro on the long history of American efforts to undermine the regime, the two sides explored how wide or narrow their scope should be. Over lunch, Castro relaxed and talked deep-sea fishing.

Describing the achievement, Ben Rhodes wrote, "The rest of the day we circled around our agenda. There was the occasional tense moment—when they attacked our democracy programs and we defended the right of Cuban people to protest. But just the fact that we sat there for six hours talking, back and forth, without descending into argument, felt like an achievement. We'd accomplished our minimal objectives for the meeting—establishing a channel, building a relationship, agreeing that we would meet in a few weeks."[26] The way the talks started, as an encounter to explore where the two sides could locate common ground, is an excellent example of what Pope Francis means when he urges us to build a "culture of encounter."

This "culture of encounter" as a motif for Francis's diplomacy—as well as his papacy—is a broad and reoccurring idea. Intellectually, Austen Ivereigh and Massimo Borghesi locate a crucial source of Francis's inspiration in the writings of Romano Guardini, an Italian-German priest and philosopher who was also a favorite of Pope Benedict.[27] Of course, the notion of personal encounter yielding truth is embedded in the New Testament: Christ teaches through personal interaction, not lectures.

In Argentina, Jorge Bergoglio's culture of encounter meant hosting meetings of leaders from different political groups to encourage trust, friendship, and a shared sense of the common good. In Francis's apostolic exhortation *Evangelii Gaudium* (The Joy of the Gospel, 2014), he writes, "[T]he Gospel tells us constantly to run the risk of a face-to-face encounter with others, with their physical presence, which challenges us, with their pain and their pleas, with their joy, which infects us in our close and continuous interaction."[28] This is why he meets often with Ecumenical Patriarch Bartholomew and why he was so keen to meet Russian Patriarch Kirill. It's why the pope flew to Lampedusa to meet refugees in Italy and Lesbos to meet refugees in Greece. It's why he urged Cuba and the United States to embrace risk when they turned to him for guidance.

SECRECY AND TRUST BUILDING THROUGH BIOTECHNOLOGY

The Americans were especially concerned to keep the meetings under wraps to prevent congressional hard-liners from derailing the talks before they even got off the ground.

Yet there was a core group of officeholders pushing the White House to do more for Alan Gross. Senators Patrick Leahy (D-VT), Dick Durbin (D-IL), and Carl Levin (D-MI) met with National Security Adviser Susan Rice, Zúñiga's boss, to express frustration. The president's chief of staff, Denis McDonough, was also in the September 26 meeting. They wanted Gross freed, and they put the problem in the context of recalibrating the bilateral relationship.

As chairman or ranking member of the Appropriations Subcommittee funding the State Department for decades, Senator Leahy had long opposed the type of programs Gross was implementing when he got caught. During the meeting, Senator Durbin, who is Catholic, suggested the White House engage Pope Francis to help find a path for Gross's release. Another liberal Catholic in the meeting, Leahy, thought it was a good idea. Not only is Francis respected in Latin America, their reasoning went, but his involvement might mollify anti-Castro Catholics in the Senate: Senator Bob Menendez (D-NJ) and Senator Marco Rubio (R-FL), for example, both Cuban Americans.[29]

The White House did not reveal to Senate allies that they had already developed a back channel to Cuba; with Ricardo Zúñiga in the meeting, he could have given a firsthand report. But the entire "encounter with Cuba" could be undone if it leaked, so the president decided to keep it top secret, meaning no sharing even with political friends.

Senator Leahy had opposed the trade embargo and the travel ban since 1975. He was aggressively engaged in efforts to normalize relations with the island nation, and the incarceration of Gross stood in the way of progress. The senator brought colleagues to Cuba where they met with Raúl Castro and Gross in February 2012 and February 2013. In November 2013, Leahy got sixty-six members of the Senate to sign a letter asking President Obama to take every necessary step to free the American captive.

TIME TO TAP ROME

Leahy decided to reach out to several cardinals he knew, including Jaime Ortega in Havana. Striving to limit the number of people involved, Leahy's staff activated Julia Sweig, a Cuba expert and scholar who knew Ortega. She carried a message to him from Leahy asking Ortega to engage Francis in US-Cuba reconciliation. The cardinal was positive but wanted something concrete to give to the pope. Sweig asked Leahy's people to draft a letter Ortega could take to Rome.

Unbeknownst to Leahy, the White House was also eyeing Vatican involvement. Secretary of State John Kerry sat down with Cardinal Parolin in Rome on January 14, 2014. The former senator had served as an altar boy. He had his first marriage annulled so he could continue to receive the Eucharist despite being divorced.[30] Kerry had never visited the Holy See and was mesmerized by the art, grandeur, and especially the Sistine Chapel, according to witnesses in the Secretariat of State. At the unusually long meeting, Kerry requested the Holy See's help with Gross.[31]

Kerry was reportedly very impressed with Parolin's range of knowledge and sensitivity to US perception. Parolin served as nuncio to Venezuela, Cuba's closest ally, from 2009 to 2013. He knew the Gross case and was highly disposed to support rectifying the dysfunctional US-Cuba relationship. Together with most Catholic leaders in Latin America, he considered the bilateral stalemate harmful to the region; with others, he was convinced the embargo was politically and economically counterproductive. The Catholic Church has opposed the US blockade for decades as a blunt tactic punishing regular people more than the elite.

Sitting as he does at the apex of a tremendous global network, all submitting information up the chain to the pope and cardinal secretary, Parolin was also aware that many Jewish groups had brought Gross's case to the attention of Vatican offices for several years. Under Pope Francis, fostering interfaith relations is a primary goal. So, between Secretary Kerry's request, petitions from Jewish groups, and his own disposition, Secretary Parolin was poised to prioritize Alan Gross. Coincidentally, the pope's chief of staff at the time, Archbishop Becciu, had served as nuncio to Cuba. He knew Raúl Castro well.[32]

Parolin and Kerry discussed a meeting between the president and the pontiff, set for March 27 and publicly announced, which created a new flurry of activity on behalf of Gross. In Boston, a group of Obama's financial donors, allies, and his former lawyer, Greg Craig, sat down with Cardinal Seán O'Malley in early March to persuade him to brief the pope on how Gross's incarceration blocked a new relationship with Cuba.

Craig carried a letter from Senator Leahy to O'Malley asking him to help focus the pope's attention on the matter. The cardinal hardly needed much convincing: he is a Spanish-speaking Capuchin friar, devoted to the region, who has visited Cuba dozens of times and opposed the US embargo. As a member of the pope's kitchen cabinet, the G9, the Boston cardinal had ready access to the pontiff.

When President Obama met with Pope Francis, although it wasn't mentioned in accounts at the time, the subject the two men spent the most time discussing was Cuba: "He was very supportive," explained President Obama. "He said he'd be helpful in any way he could." But when Rhodes pressed the president for details on *how* the Holy Father would get involved, the president responded, "He's the pope. He approaches things from a pretty high level."[33]

US GOVERNMENT'S TOP CATHOLIC ADVISER: TED MCCARRICK

When Rhodes and Zúñiga next met the Cuban delegation in May, they needed a way to shake things up because "the actual negotiations had reached an impasse."[34] On the US side, the Americans had not agreed to release Gerardo Hernández, the most culpable spy of the Cuban Five. And the Cubans were unwilling to release their most valuable catch: Rolando Sarraff Trujillo, a major US intelligence asset imprisoned on the island for nineteen years. So the Americans floated the idea of giving the Holy See a formal role. At first cautious, Castro reminded the room, "Papa Francisco is a son of Latin America"; he agreed to move forward with Vatican involvement.

To decide *how* to use Rome, Denis McDonough contacted the US government's favorite American churchman, retired Archbishop Theodore McCarrick, conveniently living in the Washington area. McDonough grew up in an Irish Catholic family with ten siblings. One of his brothers is a priest. He was more than comfortable engaging the Catholic Church in a White House foreign policy capacity. Regarding McCarrick, he became involved with politics and power brokers in New York City, where he was ordained by Cardinal Francis Spellman in 1958, then served as secretary to Cardinal Terence Cooke in the 1970s—both Church leaders with national and international profiles. (The New York archdiocese and its respective cardinals have been players in US international activities for decades: before, during, and after the Cold War.) McCarrick was laicized in 2018 for child sexual abuse, the highest Church figure to be so punished, but in 2014 he was still an *éminence grise* to US foreign policy makers.[35]

As Rhodes described him, "McCarrick was eighty-three and retired from his official duties, but he was still something of a troubleshooter around the world for the Vatican."[36] While Rhodes may have considered him a "troubleshooter for the Vatican," he was not. In fact, in Rome he was considered "an albatross," in the words of a well-connected American bishop who added that McCarrick tried to "insert himself" into any international gambit. But he was a useful agent for the US government, who used his titles and religious garb to accomplish tasks that aligned with Washington's interests.[37]

McDonough and Rhodes met with McCarrick in the White House mess. They asked him how he thought the Holy See would operationalize its involvement. McCarrick explained that the pope would engage Cardinal Ortega because, first, he was the Church's main interlocutor with the Castro brothers and, second, Francis's governance style puts a strong accent on consulting with brother bishops.

Indeed, McCarrick anticipated Francis's next move: the pope summoned Ortega to Rome and gave the prelate two letters, one addressed to President

Castro, the other to President Obama, urging them to "resolve humanitarian questions . . . including the situation of certain prisoners." He also offered to facilitate meetings.

McCarrick flew to Havana to pick up the letter addressed to Obama, but Ortega insisted on hand delivering it. The Cuban cardinal said the pope asked him to complete the task personally. For Francis, Ortega was a pivotal player because Raúl Castro knows that Ortega and Francis are close; the Cuban cardinal can stand for the Argentinian pontiff, while McCarrick was associated with American power. In sum, McCarrick tried to insert himself into the Vatican's scenario, and Ortega's refusal to give him a role was not an accident. McCarrick did contribute one element: he organized an event at Georgetown University to serve as cover for Ortega's trip to Washington.

To avoid being listed on the White House visitors log, on August 18, Ortega was brought through a side entrance to a patio next to the chief of staff's office. Then President Obama joined Rhodes, Zúñiga, and McDonough to hear Ortega read Francis's letter out loud "with a sense of ceremony."[38] As well, the Cuban told Obama that Raúl Castro considered him an honest man who inherited a bad policy. "I appreciate that," said the US president, according to Ortega.[39] Pope Francis also called each leader several times to encourage them on the road to reconciliation.

Sources at the beautiful villa where the archdiocese of Havana is based confirm that Alejandro Castro was in constant contact with his father regarding the progress of negotiations with the Americans. Although Raúl is hardly a practicing Catholic, Pope Francis has gut-level influence on him. A rosary-reciting Catholic mother baptized and raised Raúl and Fidel. They attended high school at the Jesuit-run Belen College, although Raúl didn't finish. The brothers regularly, if hypocritically, paid respect to the Catholic Church.[40]

BREAKTHROUGH

After Ortega delivered the pope's intercessions addressed to each leader, two things happened quickly: First, the Cuban delegation notified the White House that it would be willing to release Sarraff—a Cuban intelligence double agent, jailed in 1995 for working with the CIA and sentenced to twenty-five years—in exchange for Hernández of the Cuban Five. Sarraff had worked as a cryptologist in Cuba's Directorate of Intelligence; he gave the CIA massive amounts of intel.[41] As *New Yorker* journalist Jon Lee Anderson observed, "The Cubans had evidently been uncertain whether to proceed, and the Vatican diplomacy helped them decide."[42]

Second, Obama became directly involved. "Suddenly," writes Rhodes, "it felt as if the pieces were aligning. Ricardo and I asked for a meeting with Obama to see if we could get guidance on the final package we should pursue. Up to this point, he hadn't been in the weeds. . . . Now with the deal imminent and the Vatican involved, Obama got serious."[43] The president sought to maximize concessions related to the release of political prisoners, better access to the internet, and restoration of diplomatic relations.

The US team flew to Toronto to meet Castro's side for some final hard bargaining. Another month, they changed it up and met on a Caribbean island. Fundamentally, although the two delegations had become personally friendly, they could not overcome the deep distrust the countries had maintained since 1959. That's why they needed a neutral third party to assure accountability that both sides would honor their agreements. Because Francis is a Latin pope, who even wrote a book on dialogue between John Paul II and Fidel Castro, the Cubans trusted him like no pope before.[44] For the Americans, their engagement with the Holy See was political, not cultural: Francis was useful because his involvement might mollify Catholics in Congress, plus the Cubans trusted him.

The two sides decided on a process for using the Vatican as a guarantor: Each country would memorialize its understanding of the agreement and give those statements to the Holy See. Once accepted by Rome, neither side could change the terms or back away from the agreement. The diplomats would also write up what subjects continued to divide the two countries and deposit those summaries with the Vatican as well.[45] For example, Cuba still objected to the trade embargo—an instrument of pressure that had to be nullified by Congress, not the president—and the US naval base at Guantanamo. The United States opposed the lack of freedom and limits on human rights. The process took on some aspects of family counseling once priests were engaged.

On October 28, 2014, Zúñiga and Rhodes met with their Cuban interlocutors and Parolin in the Apostolic Palace near Parolin's office in a room filled with tapestries and papal portraits. Having jump-started the process, the pope did not involve himself in the details of the day. Francis's absence was intended to underscore his full faith in his diplomatic team and to allow participants to maintain focus on the negotiation process.

Parolin recommended a standard format for the daylong session. He wanted to meet with each delegation separately before bringing everyone together. It is a technique familiar in both pastoral work and psychiatry: the mediator creates the opportunity for the parties to express their private fears or hopes. Parolin could probe for weaknesses or blind spots in the respective assumptions. Both sides agreed to the counseling format. One question Parolin asked the Americans was, "Does [Secretary of State] John Kerry know about this?"[46] They assured the cardinal that Kerry was briefed and supportive. The stickiest elements of the spy exchange were concluded in Rome, which allowed the widest reconfiguration of the relationship to emerge.

What was announced by Barack Obama and Raúl Castro on December 17 (known as "17D" in Cuba) was a breathtaking agreement including a spy exchange, renewed diplomatic recognition, and normalized relations (including removing Cuba from the US terrorism list). Washington agreed to make it easier for tourists to travel to the island, for Cuban-Americans to send more money back home, and for businesses to expand commercial sales.[47] On its side, Havana agreed to free fifty-three political prisoners, allow citizens greater access to the internet, and let the Red Cross and UN set up local offices.[48]

VALUE ADDED

What we see in the engagement of the Holy See in Cuba-US negotiations is the value of a moral authority, proven to be impartial and sensitive to the needs and perceptions of both sides. Why couldn't Canada, for example, have served this role instead of just defending the perimeter of the neutral meeting location? What about the United Nations or the International Court of Justice? For one thing, it would be impossible to keep negotiations quiet in order to protect them in almost any multilateral forum imaginable.

The affirmation of the Holy See's unique value is directly tied to its sanctification as a spiritual authority, because the US and Cuba were basically deferring to Cardinal Parolin as a man with higher power. The two sides had largely decided what each was willing to do. What they sought at the Vatican was a blessing on the arrangement and a referee with the authority to call out either side if it reneged.

Ben Rhodes confirms the idea that the Holy See brought a religious dimension to the proceedings. He told the *New Yorker*,

> There was something pretty powerful about it being in a religious venue, because they blessed this process literally and spiritually. We'd had this laborious, tedious series of discussions for a year and a half, then you have people of spiritual stature speaking in very soaring words about what this would mean to people around the world, and how it would be a hopeful sign in the darkness.[49]

In Cuba, although active worship has decreased, over 60 percent of the population self-identifies as Catholic, and even the syncretistic folk religions include strong elements of Catholic ritual.[50] When the nation's patron saint, Our Lady of Charity, a small Marian figure, was transported from one end of Cuba to the other in 2001, some five million people came out to see her.[51] What a blessing from the Holy See represented was an endorsement superior to the support any other country or multilateral entity could offer.

HEALTHY CHURCH IN AN UNHEALTHY SOCIETY

The Catholic Church experienced a marked resurrection in Cuba, especially after John Paul II's pilgrimage in 1998. The number of priests and nuns doubled between 2008 and 2018, most coming from abroad. A new seminary opened in November 2010, the first church construction since 1959. Raúl Castro attended the dedication, together with a large American delegation led by Archbishop Thomas Wenski of Miami and Carl Anderson, supreme knight of the Knights of Columbus. The Knights of Columbus, the world's largest Catholic lay organization with over 1.9 million members, provided $4 million in construction costs of the $5 million total.[52] As of 2020, the seminary had approximately fifty students.

Most important, over the last three decades the state has accepted the Church's provision of social welfare and charitable contributions outside the specifically religious scope of celebrating Mass. The Church now runs day-care centers and helps the elderly. It quietly teaches religion and computer skills and screens foreign films for teen groups. The rule is that activities must occur on church property. So, for example, pro-life posters can be found in church foyers, but the same poster would be illegal outside, since the state advocates unrestricted and free abortion.[53]

There is active debate on all kinds of issues within church boundaries, a kind of civil society inside the church. However, the regime, together with Ortega, persisted in muzzling anti-Castro opposition—that's what his critics assert. For example, when *Vitral*, a respected anti-Communist Catholic publication, became too outspoken, it suddenly had no funds to publish. Yet there are also examples of how Ortega quietly helped those who got crossways with the Cuban government, including the *Damas de Blanco* (Ladies in White), a daring group of women who protest political incarceration.

COMPROMISING CATHOLICISM?

At four key moments in the last thirty-five years, the Castro brothers have turned to Catholic leadership to help them escape the implications of dictatorship—and thus to preserve their political longevity. From the mid-1980s, hoping to undermine the American embargo, the Castros initiated a relationship with leaders of the US Catholic hierarchy, a relationship initially managed by Boston's Cardinal Bernard Law. In 1996, in the midst of an economic meltdown and desperate for new external allies and trade, Fidel Castro invited John Paul II to visit Cuba, which he did two years later. In 2010, Raúl Castro relied on Cardinal Ortega to defuse tension with political prisoners by negotiating a controversial release that exiled many regime critics to Spain—a solution that cast a shadow on Pope Benedict's 2012 pilgrimage.[54] And in 2014, Francis and his small, savvy team served as guarantors of the US-Cuba agreement to normalize diplomatic relations, with no conditions related to human rights.

Has the Catholic Church allowed itself to be used by the survivalist Castros, thereby legitimizing a morally corrupt regime? Or will the Vatican's knack for maintaining the long view on political situations while keeping its eye on the needs of the local faithful—together with her theology of history, seeing God working through these events—ultimately protect the Church? Time will tell.

In mid-September 2015, before visiting the United States, Pope Francis spent four days on the island,[55] which has over the last fifty-plus years absorbed a disproportionate amount of time and attention from the Holy See. Although feeble and homebound, Fidel Castro insisted on the same homage from Francis that he got from the pope's two predecessors: following a Mass offered before thousands in Havana's Revolution Square (exactly where John Paul II and Benedict XVI had said Mass in prior visits), Francis visited the unrepentant guerrilla at his home with his wife and an assortment of children and grandchildren. Dressed in a blue-and-white Adidas tracksuit, the old revolutionary looked extremely frail. Yet he and his brother had dictated the terms of the pope's visit.

Like Benedict and John Paul II, Francis failed to meet with regime opponents, most of them Catholics, many convicted in bravery by Christ's example of fealty to the truth.[56] This was not a surprising decision. The Holy See avoids politics and insists the Catholic Church should not be reduced to the role of opposition party or insurgency.

In fact, Pope Francis's ability to broker the US-Cuban agreement was premised on the long working relationship between the Cuban Catholic Church and Fidel and Raúl Castro. That's one reason why Ortega's engagement was mission critical: the Castros knew him, worked with him, and trusted him. Since 1981, Ortega has explained the Castros to Rome and Rome to the Castros. Francis benefited from decades of accommodation made by the Catholic Church to the dictatorial ruling power: diligently avoiding political confrontation with the power in order to maintain Church autonomy, on the one hand, while collaborating with the state to defuse significant social conflicts, oppose the US embargo, and support incremental economic reform, on the other.

It's an awkward balance between risk avoidance and courting controversy, vigorously criticized by some, especially Cubans in the exile community. But the Catholic Church often eschews political cost-benefit calculations, taking a longer view.

CUBA'S VERSION OF OSTPOLITIK

To see how far the Church in Cuba has come, we need to glance at the revolution's early years. The Church was not initially a regime target. In fact, many priests and bishops preached against the corrupt government of Fulgencio Batista, overthrown by Fidel on New Year's Eve 1958. Many religious sided with Castro when he took power, forswearing a radical agenda.[57]

But after the April 1961 Bay of Pigs invasion, Fidel Castro turned on the Church with a vengeance, a strategy that coincided with increased Soviet involvement on the island.[58] All told, some 3,500 priests and nuns were jailed, killed, or pressured to leave the island—most foreign born, but many Cubans too. Seminaries, schools, and all other Catholic properties were confiscated. Cardinal Manuel Arteaga y Betancourt, archbishop of Havana (1941–1963), took refuge in the Argentinian embassy, where he died. However, Fidel Castro never severed diplomatic relations with the Holy See the way Communist parties in Eastern Europe and China did. And he kept an ambassador to the Holy See posted in Rome.

A diplomat sent to serve as secretary to the nuncio in 1961, Msgr. Cesare Zacchi, became chargé d'affaires two years later when the nuncio departed. Since Fidel accused the local Church of being a foreign operation, he preferred dealing with Rome's representative, Zacchi (a graduate of the *Accademia*), while native Cuban priests, such as Fr. Jaime Ortega, did time in a labor camp (1966–1967)—in fact, Zacchi's intervention reportedly curtailed Fidel's plan to send all remaining priests to camps.[59] The Italian priest described his role: "Here, my principal task is to reduce the distrust between the Cuban clergy and the government."[60]

Zacchi was clever. He produced ten thousand copies of Pope John XXIII's *Pacem in Terris* (1963) on a state-controlled printing press for distribution with Fidel Castro's permission.[61] Most important, he made a point of getting along with Fidel. He reported to Rome that his most successful method for getting an issue in front of the dictator was to drop a little note in his pocket. Zacchi said that never failed to get Castro's attention, and it often got good results, typically on behalf of individuals. Fidel even attended a party celebrating the diplomat's elevation to the rank of bishop in 1967. Although Cuban clergy complained that Zacchi "capitulated" to Fidel, the diplomat was executing his guidance from Rome to protect dialogue, which he did.[62]

For nearly fifteen years, the entire church-state relationship rested on Zacchi. His next assignment was back in Rome. Fittingly, in 1975 he became president of the Pontifical Ecclesiastical Academy. With Zacchi gone, Archbishop Francisco Ricardo Oves Fernández of Havana was under a brighter light, and Fidel didn't like him much. So Rome began looking for a better candidate. Because bishops are vested with God's power as direct descendants of the apostles, they are not mere "employees" of the Holy See; it is very rare for an under-seventy-five-year-old prelate to be evicted from his diocese while still alive.

Yet in 1980 Oves got sick, suffering "nerves," and in a highly unusual move, he was sent to Rome and replaced by an apostolic administrator. In 1981, Pope John Paul II, with Fidel's accord, appointed a new archbishop for Havana: Bishop Jaime Lucas Ortega y Alamino of Pinar del Rio. Ortega held the position until his retirement thirty-five years later—through three popes and two Castros and as an interlocutor to five US administrations.[63] What happened to poor Archbishop Oves? He was given a parish in El Paso, Texas, where he served until a heart attack killed him—ten years after his airlift from Cuba. Ortega flew in to preside at his predecessor's Requiem Mass in Miami. The fate of Oves resembles that of Hungarian Cardinal József Mindszenty and Czech Cardinal Josef Beran: all were sacrificed to the Vatican's efforts to placate Communist regimes.

So, Jaime Ortega was the joint choice of Rome and the Cuban regime for the pivotal role he played for decades, first as archbishop, then in 1994 as cardinal: managing Church relations with the Castros, shadowed by a series of competent but low-key nuncios over the years. The Vatican strategy, especially under a dictatorial regime, is to maintain a presence and resist being swallowed. The group of core faithful might remain small, but the Church itself will not become something else. Some twenty-five years after the revolution, the local Church gained new support from abroad, mainly from Western episcopal conferences.

QUID PRO QUO

In the class of bishops rising when John Paul II's papacy was young, Bernard Law stood out for his academic pedigree (a BA in medieval history from Harvard University), patrician good looks, and international upbringing. The son of a US Army Air Corps colonel, Law was born in Mexico, where he learned to speak flawless Spanish. While serving as bishop in southern Missouri, he visited Cuba for the first time as a churchman. He met Fidel. He met Jaime Ortega. And he was disturbed by the stark isolation of the Church and its people.

Soon thereafter, Law was named archbishop of Boston, then given a red hat in 1985. Cuba remained with him, but his hands were full in Beantown. In 1987, Msgr. William Murphy returned to Boston after thirteen years of service as staff theologian, then undersecretary, at the Pontifical Council for Justice and Peace, a busy locus of activity under Pope John Paul II. Murphy brought a world of contacts and knowledge back with him to Boston, and Law soon deployed his assistant to Cuba to cultivate new ties.[64]

The relationship that developed between the Boston archdiocese and Fidel Castro's Cuba demonstrates how decentralized units of the Catholic Church take on diplomatic initiatives only loosely coordinated by Rome. A similar pattern unfolded between Cardinal John O'Connor, archbishop of New York, and the official Church in China as we will see in chapter 11.

Murphy flew to Cuba via Panama. He remembers, "The first time I met Jaime Ortega was in his car with the motor running, outside the Havana airport. We spoke French."[65] Havana's top churchman was necessarily cautious. The American stayed at the *Casa Sacerdotal* for visiting priests, which Ortega had renovated with funds donated to him in 1983 by Law—money he received as congratulatory gifts for his new post in Boston. Ortega used it to buy back an old convent from the government and turned it into a guesthouse for visitors. Thus began a long relationship of assistance from Boston to Cuba, which strengthened the island Church, especially its charitable dimension.

Murphy went to Cuba about twice a year, sometimes with Law. When the cardinal was on board, Fidel was sure to arrange a "short meeting of four to five hours." The bearded Marxist was soft spoken and deferential to the cardinal, Murphy remembers: "'Si, si, Eminencia,' he would coo, even after Law read a list of political prisoners he wanted freed, something he did on each trip." More often, Murphy traveled with his peer, Auxiliary Bishop Roberto González, OFM, now archbishop of San Juan, Puerto Rico.

The Soviet collapse had a crushing impact on Cuba; the former Soviet Union subsidized the island economy to the tune of $4–5 billion a year.[66] As hardship began to unfold, Murphy and González were in Havana, meeting with José Carneada Rodríguez, Communist Party overseer of religious affairs. In 1991, one request they made, for example, was that the Cuban official control vigilantes—young Communist groups trained to disrupt Mass in parish churches. According to Murphy, that year Carneada said, "We're in bad shape because we can't get medicines." The priests took the request to Law who quietly launched regular shipments.

Murphy found a place, "somewhere in Virginia," where ten cents could buy a dollar's worth of medicine. So a $50,000 purchase became a half-million-dollar donation. He personally flew with the cargo via National Jets, piloted by Tom Boy, from Ft. Lauderdale to Havana or to a city at the other end of the island, Santiago de Cuba. Treasury and State Department contacts secured the required exemptions from the embargo. Such undertakings were facilitated by Law's close friend, George H. W. Bush, who was vice president and then president—not to mention a former CIA director. Bottom line: these were special missions only possible with the highest level of US government engagement.

Although the Cuban government would have been happy to cut out the local Church, instead, Cardinal Law insisted on three conditions: no medicines could go to the military, no medicines could go to the Cuban hospitals reserved for non-Cuban foreigners, and the Church in Cuba would receive the medicines as the Cuban recipient. This led to setting up a Church agency, Caritas, the Cuban branch of the Church's international network of charitable agencies, which the Church operated to distribute goods to clinics and hospitals. Over time, Caritas grew, eventually establishing offices in every diocese—eleven today.

A report about the medical donations from Boston to Cuba from another source of Catholic lay support, Pax Christi Netherlands, includes a more ominous quote from Fidel: "In February 1991, Cardinal Law of Boston brought in a private airplane filled with medicine. On that occasion, Fidel assured the episcopate, 'There will be no changes here. Do not let yourself be taken by the propaganda of the international press. We prefer a holocaust to a change of direction here.'"[67]

Boston sent more than medicine. The archbishop of Santiago asked Murphy if he could find shoes for poor children. Law found a wealthy benefactor in Boston who offered five thousand pairs of sneakers. When the donor learned there were seven bishops on the island—and each needed a shoe delivery—the donor threw in another two thousand. The delivery followed the same route as the pharmaceuticals, a straight flight from Florida to Cuba.

Reflecting on the experience, Bishop Murphy told me, "I'm very much with Pope Francis on this, namely, dialogue always helps, even if you are not solving big problems. Big problems are easier to handle if you are willing to talk with one another, even if it is about small things." An idea in sync with the diplomatic principles of Cardinal Richelieu![68]

The relationships built through that decade of assistance helped change the Castros' attitude toward the Church. In 1992, Havana amended its constitution, removing a definition of the state as Marxist-Leninist, thus atheist, and adding an article banning religious discrimination. The quiet work also laid the ground for Pope John Paul II's historic visit in 1998, when he declared upon arrival, "May Cuba, with all its magnificent potential, open itself up to the world, and may the world open itself up to Cuba." Streets were filled with posters with the message "John Paul II, ¡Bendícenos! [Bless us!]," which of course he did.

Millions of Cubans participated in the pope's five-day pilgrimage, including Fidel, who sat in the front row of most events, including Mass, wearing a suit and tie rather than his standard combat fatigues. Not since 1960 had an alternative vision of life and love been presented, publicly, on the island. Most who participated were convinced change was coming, much as the pope's journey to Poland in 1979 was the first step in unwinding that dictatorship. And there were some immediate signs of a new day: Fidel declared Christmas a national holiday six weeks before John Paul II's touchdown.

A HOLY MAN: OSWALDO PAYÁ

John Paul II inspired many, including Oswaldo Payá Sardiñas, a brave, brilliant, and almost mystically devout medical equipment engineer who founded the *Movimiento Cristiano Liberacion* (Christian Liberation Movement, MCL) in 1987 with friends from his small parish in Havana. Payá was the leader of the most daring grassroots democracy effort since 1959, known as the Varela Project, a nationwide signature campaign that unfolded between 1998 and 2003 demanding a referendum on fundamental freedoms. It was premised on an article in the Cuban constitution that said the National Assembly had to consider any initiative supported by at least ten thousand citizens. The project was named after a nineteenth-century priest, Fr. Felix Varela, who confronted Spanish colonial power, demanding freedom for Cubans.

Not since Fidel Castro took power in 1959 had Cubans had a chance like this, to democratically petition their government. Payá and MCL, together with other activists, presented a first round of more than eleven thousand signatures to the Cuban National Assembly in 2002. A year later, some seventy-five Varela Project leaders were jailed in a crackdown known as the "Black Spring." Payá was one of the few activists not arrested. Many believe international publicity—and his visit to Rome, where he met personally with Pope John Paul II in 2002—helped protect him.

Payá explained to me the Varela Project's importance in moving—and explicitly Christian—terms: "It challenged Cubans to have faith and be inspired. There is something you can do. You can act with the freedom God gave you, that no one can take away from you. Demand your rights and the rights of all Cubans. This is liberation." Although he was sorry to tell me that Church leadership was staunchly distant from MCL and his efforts, he enjoyed friendship and support from many religious in Havana and across the island: "When we finally free ourselves from this dictatorship, Cardinal Ortega will be happy MCL worked so hard!" he laughed.[69]

He described the group's origin in a national Catholic encounter of lay and religious leaders held in 1986. The *Encuentro Nacional Eclesial Cubano* (ENEC) was considered a turning point in the history of the Catholic Church in Cuba after the revolution. Why? Payá explained:

> ENEC had a tremendous impact on the Church's orientation toward power. I was always against the submission of the Catholic Church to Communism. We believed that the Church must be free, and the Church should never serve as an instrument of Communism. Most people identified with what we felt. But there were some elements, even in the Church, who felt that in order for our faith to lead, not just survive, we would have to enter government circles and influence the power from inside.
>
> This strategy was ultimately rejected as a result of the ENEC discussions and dialogue. Instead, our plan had two main points. First, the Church had to go out and meet the Cuban people with the Gospel, and second, no matter how difficult the conditions, the Church had to stay on Christ's tasks. For the laity, this meant staying in your work and testifying wherever you found yourself. So, for example, I am an engineer fixing medical equipment. It's what I've done for a long time. From this place, as a humble Cuban citizen, I am a witness for Christ, and I am trying to create the conditions for permanent change.

This was the wisdom of a true Christian.

When I met Payá, tension was high all over Cuba as a result of the February 28, 2010, death of Orlando Zapada Tamayo, a tenacious political prisoner who endured an eighty-five-day hunger strike protesting mistreatment of the dissidents. Arrested during the Black Spring crackdown, Zapada's death galvanized the Ladies in White, women who had marched every Sunday after Mass at Santa Rita Church in Havana since 2003 to protest prison conditions and unjust detention. They were relatives of men arrested for their affiliation with the Varela Project. Dressed in white and carrying gladiolas, the women are a vivid symbol of peaceful association. But after Zapada's death, they increasingly attracted thuggish mobs shoving and spitting on them. Projected around the world, the images suggested a Cuba on the verge of violent change. The ladies often used Payá's house to gather and share information.

Sitting in his small living room under a giant portrait of the Sacred Heart of Jesus, Payá told me that while individual priests and nuns on the island came to his house and helped support MCL's political prisoners, the Cuban Church hierarchy had always been cold. With his wife Ofelia and daughter Rosa Maria sitting nearby, Oswaldo calmly told me why the Church was wrong to give democracy activists the cold shoulder. "John Paul II prohibited the Polish Church from negotiating with the Communist regime. This is why Solidarity won and the Catholic Church remained unscathed. Here, the Church sees its role as engaged in dialogue with the Castros."

"From my perspective, dialogue requires respect for all parties, and as long as they jail us for advocating freedom, Christ himself would refuse to speak," Payá told me, without an ounce of resentment in his voice.

A CHURCH THAT TURNED ITS BACK

One Lenten evening in March 2010, I slipped into a side chapel of Old Havana's ancient cathedral, the eighteenth-century Cathedral of the Virgin Mary of the Immaculate Conception, an otherworldly Baroque composition of coral blocks cut from the ocean floor with marine fossils embedded in the stone. Cardinal Ortega was giving a *lectio divino* to a rapt audience of some fifty faithful of all ages. He spoke for over an hour, quietly, passionately, about Christ and selfless love. After the homey session, he and I sat for an impromptu chat. No assistant hovered nearby. Ortega spoke quite frankly of challenges, including the ire he inspired, specifically among Americans of Cuban descent in Florida.

"They think I sell out for trying to work with the Castros," he said. "It's suffering I am used to, being a pariah to my countrymen in the USA. It's my cross, and they will never understand." I was sympathetic to the cardinal, yet also harbored a puzzle. Why had the Cuban Catholic Church not supported the Varela Project, especially in 2002–2003?

"What do you think of Oswaldo Payá?" I asked Cardinal Ortega. "Why didn't the Church support this great movement, MCL?" He paused. "Oswaldo Payá is certainly a good Catholic man," he said quietly. "But we can't get involved in politics. We can't oppose the government," he added. "If the Church is just another political party, we become opponents, with no possibility of bringing the Word to the people. We can't do that."

I mentioned that John Paul II received Payá and blessed his work. The cardinal then replied, "Payá is a good man, but he does not have a program for the future." He suggested I look up a socialist anthropologist, Manuel Cuesta Morúa, "who has a program." Cuesta Morúa became Washington's Cuban favorite. He got financial support through National Endowment for Democracy. He was even seated next to President Obama during his 2016 visit to Cuba.[70]

In this exchange, I sensed for the first time in a very personal way how morally fraught the effort to cope with an amoral political protagonist really is. Cardinal Ortega did not think the Church was capable of providing even marginal spiritual guidance and succor to Catholics fighting for freedom, a natural and God-given right, in a profoundly unfree society.[71] I reassured myself that at least religious men and women in the city were quietly helping the Payá family.

THE CARDINAL FACILITATES FORCED EXILE

A few months after I met him, Jaime Ortega was in the news announcing a plan devised with Raúl Castro to release scores of political prisoners. Over the next six months, more than one hundred political prisoners were released. Ortega had accomplished something no one anticipated, but backlash against the cardinal's role as mediator was swift among both prisoners and observers who pray for regime collapse. Why? Because Ortega personally lobbied families and prisoners, by phone, to accept the regime's conditions for release: one-way tickets to Spain with their families—even if they preferred to stay home.

"I was called by the guards to the phone, and it was Cardinal Ortega," former political prisoner Ariel Sigler recounted. "He told me I would be released to fly to Spain with my family. I told him, 'I won't go to Spain,' and he said, 'Then you won't leave jail!'"[72] With relatives living in Miami, Sigler managed to get released to the United States for treatment; the former boxer, and Varela Project activist, had become paralyzed while incarcerated. (When I met him in Florida, he was on his way to walking again.)

The deal did not lead to true freedom but forced exile, according to critics, including Rep. Ileana Ros-Lehtinen, then chair of the House Foreign Affairs Committee, who accused Ortega of being a Communist collaborator. What Ortega did, they say, was take pressure off the Castro regime, just when it was building, internally and internationally.

According to Ortega, his involvement with the prisoners flowed from his attempt to negotiate on behalf of the Ladies in White, at their request. In spring 2010, just days after the cardinal helped negotiate their right to gather unmolested on Sundays, party leaders contacted him to discuss their husbands' and sons' fates—and how to defuse the overall situation. So Ortega was at the center of a prisoner release scheme, which he felt was in the best interests of each family, and the country.

Soon after the prisoner release announcement, Ortega was on his way to Washington to receive a $100,000 prize from the Knights of Columbus. In his acceptance speech he astounded Cuba watchers by calling the jailed democracy activists "convicts—so-called political prisoners," embarrassing evidence that he was sucking up to the regime.

The next day, he briefed General James Jones, White House national security adviser, and Arturo Valenzuela, assistant secretary of state for Western Hemisphere affairs. The prelate even spent over an hour in a secret meeting with former Speaker of the House of Representatives Newt Gingrich and his wife Callista, US ambassador to the Holy See under the Trump administration. Ortega's pitch in these meetings was to encourage the US government and Congress to interpret the prisoner release as evidence of the regime's good faith—and to reward that good behavior.

Specifically, Ortega argued that the prisoner release should pave the way for closer US-Cuba relations, including lifting the trade embargo. Within six months, the White House did lift restrictions on travel for academic, religious, and cultural groups. From the Church's perspective, Ortega's role was not to speak for the Cuban government but to pursue reconciliation, the idea that opposing groups must find a way to understand each other as the basis for mutual settlements. The approach posits the Church as mediator: present, persistent, but politically nonpartisan. Ortega foreshadowed the very role Pope Francis would play on a larger scale four years later.[73]

TO DUST WE SHALL RETURN

The last time I talked to Oswaldo Payá by phone was while Pope Benedict XVI was visiting Cuba at Easter time in 2012; he was frustrated that the pope seemed unwilling to meet with any of the Ladies in White or MCL members, including him. When he and Ofelia left their small house to attend the pope's open-air Mass, security police surrounded them. They went anyway. By then, American officials at the US Interest Section in Havana, and American bishops who used to visit and pray with him, were no longer calling. Oswaldo Payá and his movement felt abandoned.

Four months after Pope Benedict's visit to Cuba, Cardinal Ortega presided over Oswaldo Payá's funeral. The democracy leader and his assistant, Harold Cepero, were killed on a beautiful summer day, on a straight country highway, when an unmarked police car ran them off the road and rammed their car from behind. The two Cuban men were sitting together in the back, traveling to an MCL meeting.[74] Two foreign visitors in the front seats, from Sweden and Spain, were not harmed, although the driver, a young Spanish Christian activist, was hospitalized, drugged, jailed, and hustled out of the country five months later to complete his sentence in his homeland.[75] The driver convincingly reports that Payá was murdered.[76]

Ofelia told me she was not allowed to kiss her husband's face when his body was delivered in a casket. The ladies who prepared his corpse said there were no wounds on his body, but his head was badly damaged. The government refused to provide an autopsy to the family or to allow an independent investigation. It's as though the Catholic Church's mission to protect the institutional Church includes the obligation to stand aside, making room for those who follow Christ all the way to crucifixion.

Pope Francis met in Rome with Oswaldo's wife, two sons, and only daughter, who has boldly taken up her father's cause. Ofelia and Rosa Maria told me the pope was very quiet, yet kind and prayerful.[77] Within the Church, there are diplomats, and there are martyrs: "there are different forms of service but the same Lord."[78]

When Jaime Ortega died of cancer in July 2019, the Cuban regime did him no favors either.[79] Prominent Catholics, including priests, were denied entry to his Requiem Mass while secular politicians sat in the front pews. His burial was unusually fast, less than forty-eight hours after his death. Colleagues say it was part of a clampdown on public assembly, including a ban on religious processions.

Francis has continued the Catholic Church's long-standing dialogue with the monstrous Castro regime, which remains in place despite Raul's retirement. As the timeworn cliché reminds us, love the sinner, hate the sin.

8

Diminishing Division
Kenya

> Unless you dialogue and listen to one another, there will always be tribalism eating away at society like woodworms. Let us stand up and take each other's hand as a sign of opposition to tribalism. We are all one nation! Let us all be one nation! That is the way we should feel, where our heart should be.
>
> —Pope Francis, Meeting with Young People, Nairobi, Kenya, November 27, 2015[1]

Preparing for a visit with all Kenya's bishops in April 2015, Pope Francis discerned worrisome trends despite a local Church bursting with healthy, substantial growth. The archdiocese covering the capital city of Nairobi had seven times as many Catholics in 2013 as in 1980. Nationwide, Catholics comprised about 27 percent of the nation's fifty-one million citizens.[2] The Catholic Church ran 31 percent of the nation's schools.[3] President Uhuru Kenyatta, son of the country's founding father, was a practicing member of the faith. But three things worried the pope: terrorism, ethnic rivalry, and tension among the bishops themselves—the shepherds were not united.

The story of how Francis, between 2015 and 2018, helped form the bishops of Kenya into a more united, positive force, then encouraged them to spread reconciliation to the political elite through constant, concrete interventions—with help from an array of Catholic institutions shy about taking credit—is subtle and little known. The upshot was very public: President Kenyatta and his perennial rival Raila Odinga shook hands on March 9, 2018, and pledged to work together following a very tense election. As one former US State Department official wrote at the time, "It is not quite clear how to account for the reconciliation now."⁴ It was a stark contrast with postelection violence that had killed thousands of Kenyans ten years before.

This is an account of how Catholic diplomatic influence made a difference in Kenya. Because many interview sources are unwilling to be named, I provide a path of breadcrumbs from public sources to confirm the claims of anonymous informants.

TERRORISM AND ETHNIC DIVISION

When an Islamist group, Al-Shabab (Arabic for "the youth"), shot its way past security guards at Garissa University College, gunmen then methodically slayed people who said they were Christian—on the Thursday before Easter in 2015. Most of the 148 people murdered were students; it was the second-deadliest terror attack in the country's history.⁵ The public university is located in Eastern Kenya, a few hours from the border with Somalia, where the extremists have a militant base. Facing this disturbing attack, the Church worshipped harder: three days later, the nearby cathedral was full despite security concerns; a bishop baptized twenty-eight children.⁶

Terrorism was driving down tourism, a major element in Kenya's economy. It was radicalizing youth, who faced 26 percent national unemployment.⁷ Many feared it would cause Christians to turn on the Muslim minority in response to these abhorrent tactics: When Shabab killers invaded an upscale shopping mall in Nairobi in 2013, one way they identified Christians was by quizzing shoppers on Muslim facts, like, "What is the name of Prophet Muhammad's first wife?" (answer: Khadījah). Ignorance could lead to death.⁸

Older than terrorism, another phenomenon that has caused grief is ethnic violence. Kenya has forty-seven ethnic groups, and a fractious spirit emerged after the Kenyan parliament legalized multipartism in 1991, repealing a section of the constitution making it a one-party state.⁹ Too often, political patronage, including land, was distributed on an unfair ethnic basis; postelection frustration led to conflict along divisive ethnic lines.

National elections on December 30, 2007, led to traumatizing violence. Rampaging gangs contested results by setting fire to homes and businesses. People were burned alive. Over twelve hundred people died and six hundred thousand were displaced. Witnesses described people being dragged out of their homes and clubbed to death based on ethnic loyalties.¹⁰ Unspeakably, twelve people were burned in a church where they were taking cover.¹¹ The frequent engagement of young people in the brutality was particularly disturbing, as was the participation of many Christians.

The incumbent, President Mwai Kibaki, was a member of the nation's largest ethnic group, the Kikuyu, traditionally based in the central highlands. The challenger, Raila Odinga (son of independent Kenya's first vice president), was a Luo, traditionally fisherfolk living near Lake Victoria in the West,[12] who were promoted as teachers by British colonial rulers. Odinga had been an early democracy activist, jailed several times in the 1980s and early 1990s; Kibaki and Odinga had once been allies.

What halted the postelectoral carnage in 2008 was a power-sharing pact between Kibaki and Odinga negotiated by former UN secretary general Kofi Annan, who grew up in Ghana. He appealed directly to the two men. Odinga, who controlled the largest party in parliament, became prime minister. He told Kenyans to "destroy the monster that is ethnicity."[13] Ministry portfolios were divided between the incumbent government and opposition.

Five years later, elections in 2013 echoed the ethnic face-off of the 2007–2008 catastrophe. This time Odinga ran against businessman Uhuru Kenyatta, son of Jomo Kenyatta, postcolonial Kenya's first president (1964–1978), and his fourth wife, a devout Catholic. When the political scion won with 50.07 percent of the vote, the country avoided a runoff. Only a handful of people died as a result of the Kikuyu-Luo clashes, but that was mainly due to heavy police presence and protest bans, not the absence of tension.[14]

CONTENTION WITHIN THE EPISCOPATE

What disturbed Pope Francis while reviewing a dossier in preparation for his first visit with Kenya's twenty-six bishops was evidence that ethnic tension could be found among the bishops themselves. Two of the most powerful—Cardinal John Njue, archbishop of Nairobi, and Zacchaeus Okoth, president of the Catholic Justice and Peace Commission (CJPC) and archbishop of Kisumu, the country's westernmost archdiocese—had a history of subtle jabs at each other.

Kenya's only cardinal, Archbishop Njue, was elevated to the College of Cardinals just a month before the frenzy of violence in 2007–2008. A member of the Embu ethnic group (which lives alongside the Kikuyus), Njue was considered close to the president based on their sympathetic community backgrounds. Njue had been known to take political positions favored by the ruling elite—stands opposed by Okoth, a Luo who had a longtime personal relationship with Raila Odinga.

For example, Njue opposed the devolution of power to the local level, as did President Kibaki. Bishop Okoth favored decentralization as a way to increase political participation—as Odinga and other Luo kinsmen did. After the electoral cataclysm, this reform gained support and is now embedded in a new constitution, approved in 2010.[15] Clergy at the Congregation for Divine Worship remember Nigeria's Cardinal Francis Arinze, who served as prefect at the time, flying from Rome to Nairobi to reconcile Njue and Okoth with each other in 2008.

In the years since, the Kenyan Conference of Catholic Bishops (KCCB), especially through the CJPC, has done serious work to prevent political violence. Academic-quality baseline field research in seven counties was conducted to determine factors contributing to disunity.[16] Among the conclusions of the three-year study, "A Walk toward Sustainable Peace," was that competition over resources was often more significant than ethnic rivalry in triggering violence.[17] Training catechists, engaging in more Bible study, and deepening the youth ministry were other, pastoral approaches KCCB used to ameliorate the causes of social tension.

From reports penned by Kenya's nuncio Archbishop Charles Daniel Balvo (a 1987 *Accademia* graduate from Brooklyn, New York), Pope Francis drew examples of KCCB's activism for the good of all: defending the rights of poor children to secondary education by challenging the Ministry of Education's criteria for selecting applicants, and testing a tetanus vaccine intended for nationwide use based on evidence that it harmed people in the Philippines and Mexico—and finding tainted vials the Health Ministry assumed to be safe.

Nevertheless, Francis was concerned. He saw some troubling hints of Church shepherds becoming contentious (Njue) and possibly, dangerously worldly (Okoth). For example, on a 2013 trip to Africa, in Senegal, President Barack Obama said homosexuals across the continent ought to be treated equally under the law, although each nation on its own needs to decide the legality of same-sex marriage.[18] Kenya's political leadership slapped back; Deputy President William Ruto declared his country a "God-fearing nation," with no intention of revoking a law that homosexuality is illegal.[19]

Speaking at the Consolata Shrine in Nairobi, Cardinal Njue was even more emphatic: "Let him [Obama] forget, forget and forget. I don't think God was making a mistake when he created Adam and Eve and told them what to do. . . . We must be proud of who we are. Those who have already ruined their society cannot come here to teach us what we should do."[20]

Three days later, a headline in the *Star*, a daily Nairobi-based newspaper, announced that the American nuncio had sided against the local cardinal: "Pope's Envoy Champions Gays and Lesbian Rights." But the American nuncio said he was misquoted and had only repeated the Catholic catechism, which counsels respect for the human dignity of all people.[21] The misunderstanding, or tiff, signified something the pope fears: hot-button issues, like gay rights, quickly become polarizing. Harping on negativity is no basis for building social unity, a more pressing requirement in most places and for most people.

More problematic, a TV-news exposé alleged that Archbishop Okoth collected money from Rome for church structures—a chapel, a convent building, a seminary dorm—never actually built. Journalists confronted local priests in Kisumu diocese with original documents from offices in Rome authorizing funds, which locals were baffled to see, since the buildings didn't exist. The nuncio went on camera to say that if the funds were not properly used, the guilty party could lose his job. The episode infuriated Okoth, who gave an extended rebuttal at a press conference, claiming the documents revealed by the press were stolen from the nuncio's mail, in violation of international law. He said the story was a smear against the Church, since journalists did not seek the truth.

Unacceptable to Francis was a state of disharmony within the Church community that put all at odds with each other: nuncio against bishops, priests against the shepherd, secular journalists against the Church. Questions on funds could be sorted out—and would be. The long-term implications of internal strife, rivalry, and suspicion were far more complex and damaging.

FRANCIS REDIRECTS BISHOPS

Kenya's bishops had a great model of holy practice in their own memory: Cardinal Maurice Otunga, son of a Bukusu chief with seventy wives, became a priest rather than a tribal leader. He was ordained bishop under Pope Pius XII, then served for decades as archbishop of Nairobi (1971–1997) and was given a red hat by Pope Paul VI in 1973. The cardinal possessed legendary humility and generosity, rushing to take the place of an imprisoned priest jailed for an antigovernment speech, as detailed in a 2015 *Kenya Today* article titled "Pope Francis: Here Is Why Kenyans Don't Like Cardinal Njue."[22]

Otunga's main focus was education: establishing schools and advancing the imperative of educating girls. When he had a stroke in 1997, he preferred living in a modest elderly home run by the Little Sisters of the Poor, when he could have retired to Rome. His funeral was held in the National Stadium, so many people loved him. Otunga's cause for sainthood is underway.[23]

At the 2015 *ad limina* meeting in Rome, Francis went back to basics. Unity is central in Christian theology: the unity of God and man in Christ, the unity of Christ and his Church, the unity between bishops, clergy, and flock—these are all sacred. As long as the Church actively cultivates these bonds, the Church has the credibility to promote wider social reconciliation. "The Church's mission, though multifaceted, is one: much more will be accomplished for the praise and glory of God's name when our actions are in harmony," he told the bishops.[24]

He also urged them to improve relationships with other faiths in order to combat violence like the horror of Garissa: "May you strengthen your commitment to working with Christian and non-Christian leaders alike, in promoting peace and justice in your country through dialogue, fraternity and friendship."

"He is giving us big, big lessons of how to be Christian," said Archbishop Anthony Muheria, talking about Francis's message to the assembled bishops. Muheria, a rising talent and the first Opus Dei archbishop in Africa, described the pope as humorous and human. Warm. Concerned with the well-being of the bishops themselves. "He reminded us Christian life is about holding hands, lifting, reaching out."[25]

The bishops begged Francis to come to Kenya as the best way to model the Church mission, especially since the country's president had already invited him. The pope tentatively agreed, if logistically possible, as long as the bishops stepped up peace-building work. Then the Secretariat of State checked in with other Kenyan sources to weigh possible themes. One organization consulted was the Catholic Members of Parliament Spiritual Support Initiative (CAMPSSI), which provided some of the most insightful material according to experts in the curia.

Pope Francis's guidance had a decisive impact on the bishops, especially his request that they go out of their way to find concrete ways to embody faith. The bishops' conference already had programs for young people in place—celebrating the twenty-fifth anniversary of the Nairobi youth center *Mji wa Furaha* ("City of Joy" in Swahili), seven thousand children from all twenty-six dioceses participated.[26] After returning from Rome, KCCB structured activities involving the young, for example, deepening interreligious ties and protecting the environment, themes linked to the pope's visit.[27]

Gestures of unity were given more credence: Archbishop Okoth brought President Kenyatta and Raila Odinga together to a Church event in Kisumu where they shared cake. According to local reports, elderly women were moved to tears.[28] A gift to President Kenyatta of a huge replica of the Arc of the Covenant, to be installed at a Catholic shrine, was offered by a delegation from Israel in another unusual event leading up to the pope's arrival in Kenya on November 25, 2015—his first stop in Africa.[29]

FRANCIS DESCENDS ON NAIROBI

The pope's three days in Kenya included many of his standard moments: a meeting with state officials and diplomats, an ecumenical and interreligious meeting including representatives of traditional religion, and a visit to a slum on the city's periphery.[30] Torrential rain turned the park used for Mass into mud, but two hundred thousand people came anyway. With joyful singing and dancing, prayers in Swahili and other languages, and President Kenyatta and his wife actively swaying and praying, the Mass felt like a national celebration. Pope Francis "encouraged us as families, as a nation and as different tribes and religions to work together and build our foundation on the rock which is God," said one local businessman in the crowd.[31]

The high point was probably the pope's meeting with seventy thousand young people in a national stadium. Youth from across the country converged. Some brought saplings to be blessed, then planted them back home to promote environmental awareness. From the coastal city of Mombasa, where violence was on an upswing, the youth ministry organized an interfaith peace caravan to come see the pope together. A month's worth of rosaries was prayed, tallied, and given to the pope as a spiritual gift.[32] The atmosphere was electric.[33]

The pope tossed his script and preached in Spanish, asking the stadium to join hands as he explained, "Unless you dialogue and listen to one another, there will always be tribalism eating away at society like woodworms. Let us stand up and take each other's hand as a sign of opposition to tribalism. We are all one nation! Let us all be one nation! That is the way we should feel, where our heart should be."[34] It was a moment of evangelization, which showed Francis modeling the exuberance and conviction he expects from all the faithful.

The arrival of a pope galvanizes the Catholics of any nation and is used as a point to organize toward and draw inspiration from. As he came to understand Kenya's reality, Francis urged even greater dedication to two KCCB projects in the works that satisfied his preference for achieving concrete "deliverables," encouraging the peripheries and promoting social justice. One was a network of radio stations serving remote areas, including pastoral communities on arid lands in the north.[35]

Another was a land project putting three thousand acres of idle Church land into productive use to yield food, employment, and economic development. The land-use pilot was implemented in Kenya, and the practice has since expanded to six other African countries.[36] As Francis said during his visit with the poor, everyone has a "sacred right to the 'three Ls': Land, Lodging, Labor. This is not a question of philanthropy; rather it is a moral duty incumbent upon all of us."[37] He had also used the "three Ls" slogan while in Ecuador, and it became a rhetorical staple. Of course, securing the three Ls invariably involves the faithful in politics, which the pope encourages as a way to achieve the common good.

To the bishops, he challenged them to prioritize reconciliation in order to more successfully promote national unity and political peace. It was not a difficult assignment because the very process of organizing and realizing the pope's visit brought greater cohesion to Kenya's Catholic community, especially the hierarchy.

2017 ELECTIONS: ANY PAPAL IMPACT?

Was the pope's visit just a few days of temporary good feeling? The test would come in the 2017 general elections, pitting President Kenyatta against opposition stalwart Raila Odinga once again. A full year before, Cardinal Njue began echoing the pope about renouncing ethnic identity as the basis for voting, using the same key words as Francis: peace, unity, and dialogue.[38]

The bishops' conference designed an Easter season campaign around the theme "Peaceful and Credible Elections for Leaders of Integrity," reinforcing the message during the forty days of Lent. KCCB opened the period of reflection at the University of Nairobi with the president's participation.[39] All told, the presidential campaign was relatively calm. In the run-up to Election Day on August 8, the bishops initiated a novena for peace and issued a pastoral letter reinforcing the Eastertide injunction, reiterating the call for a "unified nation."[40]

A foreboding preelection murder, though, was a macabre sign: ten days before the election, a senior IT manager for the Independent Electoral and Boundaries Commission (IEBC) who was a member of the Luo community was found dead, his body dumped in a forest. Odinga's coalition, the National Super Alliance (NASA), suspected it was evidence of tampering with the electronic voting system.[41] By Election Day, the contest was considered too close to call.[42]

President Kenyatta won in the first round with 54 percent to Odinga's 45 percent, a difference of over one million votes. No international observers detected illegalities in the process. Former secretary of state John Kerry, heading the Carter Center's delegation, said the process was a testimony to Kenya's democratic credentials, with only a few minor flaws. "Don't let anyone besmirch that," he said.[43]

But Odinga immediately called the results "fictitious," blaming computer hacking. At age seventy-two, running for the fourth and last time due to an age restriction for presidential contenders, the perennial candidate was in no mood to lose. Even before the big day, his optimism was tinged with a threat: "We are more than confident we will get a very decisive victory, and any attempt to cheat Kenyans of their future will not be tolerated," he told

Al Jazeera.[44] Odinga's declaration that the election was rigged triggered violence. Within days, sixteen people were dead.

Kenyatta's inauguration was postponed in exchange for NASA's agreement to let the judicial system examine charges of voting irregularities. The compromise stanched the clashes everyone feared. Unexpectedly, the Supreme Court nullified Kenyatta's victory on September 1 on procedural grounds and mismanagement. The court ordered a rematch in sixty days. The president declared it a "coup" and a "monstrous injustice,"[45] while NASA supporters danced in the streets. Suddenly Kenya was split in half by ethnicity again.

Religious figures from across the country convened in Nairobi, announcing an effort to use their influence to bring NASA and Kenyatta's Jubilee Party together for talks.[46] They agreed to relentlessly preach peace but could not persuade the rivals to meet. Cardinal Njue convincingly spoke as one favoring neither candidate, continuously calling both to dialogue.[47] His challenge to Kenyatta and Odinga about cooling their rhetoric was echoed by the media. Behind the scenes, his power of persuasion was more successful. He helped convince the president to accept repeat elections while NASA was talking about a boycott because Odinga did not trust the government's ability—or willingness—to fix election administration. Nuncio Balvo submitted almost daily reports to Pope Francis, who found discretionary funds for the KCCB to increase election engagement.

Njue went into high gear, mobilizing the whole Church to help assure a clean second election. Over 1,500 observers were trained as volunteer poll monitors, with women religious serving as voter educators too.[48] A central Church-run center was set up for observers to submit problems and tallies.

With constant prodding, NASA and Jubilee leaders worked to contain edgy followers, but members of the Supreme Court and IBEC officials received death threats. Political pressure on the election bureau was so intense that a commissioner fled to the United States requesting asylum a few weeks before the October 28 redo of the presidential contest, which NASA boycotted while continuing to hold massive demonstrations, and Kenyatta warned that security forces had been "enhanced."[49]

Kenyatta won the one-sided election with 98 percent of the vote. Considering the low participation, the result risked prolonging the political crisis. Some rioting occurred, and around a hundred people were killed, but significant police mobilization limited the chaos. Kenyatta assured reporters he would reach out to his opponent (although he'd said the same thing in August), while NASA accused the process of being a "sham."[50] The opposition quickly filed petitions challenging the election in court.

Four days after the election, a well-respected prelate from the western part of the country died. Bishop Cornelius Korir was instrumental in soothing ethnic divisions in a region called the North Rift. After the 2008 election violence, he housed some ten thousand people in the Eldoret cathedral compound to protect them from rampaging mobs. The priest used development goals to build consensus: specifically, he helped organize the construction of two dams shared by clashing ethnic groups, and he attracted investment for milk-cooling facilities, which increased milk production. With prosperity, the conflict dramatically diminished.[51] Korir wrote a book on his experience, *Amani Mashinani* (Peace at the Grassroots). He was at work with local representatives of NASA and Jubilee just before he died, counseling constructive ways to moderate demands.

His funeral was attended by thousands, including the president, supporters of both factions, tribal elders, and Protestant clerics. It became an occasion for many to reflect on the bishop's example. President Kenyatta said, "Let us all do everything we can to emulate him. Let us emulate his respect for human dignity, his respect for people regardless of their color or ethnicity and his deep desire to see a peaceful and united Kenya." The vice president called the bishop a crusader for unity.

Cardinal Njue and Balvo offered a Requiem Mass for the beloved bishop. Both talked about bridge building and peace building as national priorities.[52] The next day, following another Mass for Korir, Kenya's bishops launched an initiative reviewed and blessed by Pope Francis: the National Dialogue Forum. To explain their rationale, three bishops read a "State of the Nation" report—a heartfelt review of the country's situation.[53]

Addressed to "Dear people of God, fellow Kenyans," the report thanked the country for the hope and restraint exhibited during the trying electoral process. It cataloged the many efforts made by the bishops to highlight problems such as elections, security, poverty, corruption, radicalization, hate speech, youth unemployment, ethnic polarization, and political intolerance, often with other civil society actors. Despite hoping the elections could become an opportunity for unity, greater division was the result. So the bishops prophetically interrogated the sources of conflict that seemed to emerge every election:

> Anybody who loves this country can see the inequality in the distribution of the resources we have, the lack of political will to economically pull up those regions of our country bedeviled by extreme poverty; the looting of public resources meant for the poor and for development of the country; the manipulation of the population by some politicians and the radicalization of politics. All these underlying issues and more are taking our country into dangerous waters of intolerance and anger that could destroy us all. This situation, if unchecked, leads to more hatred and mistrust, which could easily lead to anarchy and breakdown of social order.[54]

And in a departure from the past, the nation's bishops indicted politicians, all of them, for fanning the flames of disunity, demanding specific steps to avoid the abyss:

> Our leaders!:
> - Stop calling others names; stop the politics of division and ethnic profiling.
> - Stop the agitation for secession, because all is not lost.
> - Stop the corruption that is killing our country.
> - Stop the killings and police brutality.
> - Stop taking sides along tribal and party lines.
> - Stop selfish hard-line positions that are only leading our country to civil strife.
> - Stop the senseless chest thumping and meaningless political competitions, and for once think of the good of the nation.

The report proposed constructive dialogue as a way out of the crisis:

> Favoring dialogue, in any form whatsoever, is a fundamental responsibility of politics. Sadly, all too often we see how politics is becoming instead a forum for clashes between opposing forces. . . . Dialogue is replaced either by a futile antagonism that can even threaten civil coexistence, or by the domination of a single political power that constrains and obstructs a true experience of democracy. In the one, bridges are burned; in the other, walls are erected.[55]

The document became the Catholic Church's "position paper" for the next four months, guiding a diplomatic strategy to pressure all politicians to do the right thing. Meanwhile, the National Dialogue Forum institutionalized communication beyond the Church while the Church helped assure the forum's neutrality. On November 28, after the courts confirmed a legitimate election, Kenyatta was sworn in as president.

GETTING TO YES

As in Colombia, Church officials began focusing on the primary victims of insecurity and unrest—the citizens themselves—in order to challenge political rivals to focus on the common good.

For Bishop Okoth, Christmas was an exceptional occasion to reinforce the message that dialogue was the best path for Kenya. He observed, "Politicians must cease from preaching hate and animosity that will further divide Kenyans along political lines," a patently true observation, but significant in a region that was accustomed to defending Odinga as the wronged party. He added that politicians are responsible for the suffering and death of innocent people who get caught in the illogic of electoral antagonism, so these officials must confess and reconcile with the victims of violence, harmed by their attitude.[56] It was a marked shift in focus for the senior churchman.

Okoth and Odinga were bound together not just by ethnic ties, but they shared a profound experience of risk from democracy's fledgling days. Odinga was an activist who had challenged the authoritarian Moi government. In 1991, the US embassy shared intelligence with the opposition that Odinga was about to be arrested, so he entered an underground safe-house network after the US embassy refused to give him sanctuary. It was Bishop Okoth who arranged to take the opposition leader out of Kenya to Uganda.

Odinga was disguised as a Catholic priest and driven in the backseat of a car, between an American nun and a Kenyan priest. The group made it past police roadblocks to Lake Victoria, where the fictitious "Fr. Augustine" was transported by boat to Uganda, and from there to Norway—dressed as a Muslim heading to Mecca on pilgrimage.[57] It was a shared experience that created loyalty for life.

By late 2017, the Catholic bishops felt confident they had convinced Kenyatta and Odinga to collaborate formally. The president had already been using the language of peace and reconciliation for months. Close aides say he was authentically moved by the example of Bishop Korir and felt that his untimely death was a message from God that we have limited time to do the right thing. Kenyatta had just one more term.

However, some in Odinga's inner circle convinced him to hold an inauguration ceremony, and the impetuous septuagenarian was sworn in on January 30 as the "people's president" in Nairobi's Uhuru Park before thousands of supporters. The government jammed media feeds to limit coverage, but Odinga was undeterred: his Twitter profile was changed to "President of Kenya" after the ceremony.

Once again, Kenya's political class took the country to the brink. The attorney general announced plans to charge Odinga with "high treason" because his oath was illegal, but in the end only a few high-level advisers were arrested. Although President Kenyatta contemplated arresting his nemesis, he decided against that course because he realized it would spark riots. Cardinal Njue was one of the voices counseling restraint. Instead, Kenyatta began talking to Odinga by phone to find a face-saving solution.

What Okoth counseled Odinga was this: The lifelong activist could accomplish far more by working with Kenyatta than by limiting himself to mass rallies in Nairobi and Western Kenya. The dire need for his energy, ideas, and popular following argued for negotiating a pact with the president, advised Okoth. Meanwhile, Cardinal Njue was continuously in touch with Kenyatta, who was already convinced in November that a contentious course was the losing one.

The two Catholic prelates had developed long-term relationships with men who emerged as the nation's most important protagonists, men who held in their hands Kenya's stability. The bishops used those relationships in parallel to help move them toward negotiating the terms of a power-sharing relationship. When it came to settling the details of the agreement, Okoth and Njue stepped aside, since the issues pertained to office space, pension, and the division of portfolios.[58]

On March 9, President Kenyatta and Raila Odinga surprised the world by appearing together on TV to shake hands as "brothers" and publicly commit themselves to collaboration. The president said, "We have come to a common understanding, an understanding that this country of Kenya is bigger than any one individual,"[59] while Odinga emphasized the importance of focusing on the next generation and its needs.

International media was skeptical, pointing to a visit by US Secretary of State Rex Tillerson later that day as motivating the truce.[60] Whether or not the heavyweight's arrival put positive pressure on the announcement, it was a gift to the nation. The *Star* newspaper extolled, "As the country was hurtling into the abyss of division and darkness, the famous handshake brought immediate relief countrywide."

While the bishops saw "the hand of God" in the breakthrough,[61] the political agreement itself gives a hint of its pedigree: Building Bridges to a New Kenyan Nation is a concept straight out of Rome's lexicon, one of Francis's guiding principles of diplomacy. The Catholic parliamentarians, coordinated by CAMPSSI, had ghostwritten significant parts of the plan.

Building Bridges acknowledges that "[e]thnic antagonism and divisive political competition have become a way of life," and people are "crying out for leadership that shows the path to dignity, prosperity and security." From that admission of shortcomings, the men pledged to work for a "united nation for all Kenyans." The document listed nine priority issues as the focus of intensive national dialogue: ethnic antagonism and competition, lack of a national ethos, inclusivity, devolution [of power to local government], divisive elections, safety and security, corruption, shared prosperity, and rights and responsibilities, a list that closely matches the bishops' priorities.

To implement a systematic review of Kenyatta and Odinga's "shared objectives," the leaders committed to establishing an office with advisers from both parties.[62] Known as the Bridge Program, Bishop Okoth was named one of the thirteen adviser members, together with an Anglican bishop and Methodist priest. KCCB issued a statement of support for the new collaboration, "A Call to Healing and Reconciliation," reiterating the need for it to be based on an "inclusive participatory process from the grassroots to the national level."[63] Having worked hard to get the two men on the same page, the Church was not going to let them monopolize the process.

Pope Francis spontaneously initiated a collective handshake with seventy thousand people in the National Stadium in November 2015, a handshake that symbolized and prefigured national reconciliation. And the gesture was passed on: While attending a local official's funeral, Odinga saw two rival politicians, a governor and former minister. Odinga called them up to the stage as the crowd enthused, "Go! Go! It's time for a handshake!" The national leader convinced one to drop an election-related lawsuit against the other and solidified both their standing by asking Jubilee not to run a candidate in that district.[64] It is a small local example of Pope Francis's conviction that once people have the habits of dialogue and diplomacy, they become go-to tools for problem solving.

Francis and the Secretariat of State seek input from multiple sources. The pope has relationships with all the elements of foreign policy: nuncios, cardinals, bishops, specialist priests, missionaries, and lay organizations with ongoing relationships with the nation. In Kenya, the nuncio conveyed information up and down the chain, but he was not the pivotal player in a strategy that saw individual bishops acting as discreet advisers pushing gently toward a common goal: peace. It was Francis who pressed the KCCB to work more closely together in order to project the reconciliation onto the wider political picture. The plan worked, but it is a story never publicly acknowledged and is bound to flow, forgotten, into the wide river of things the Church accomplishes in a hidden way.

Participating in the 2018 Youth Synod in Rome, Archbishop Muheria confirmed that the biggest challenge in Kenya has been ethnic violence. He recounted that during the pope's 2015 visit, Francis "made us make a covenant with God. He asked us to be one, fight corruption, fight ethnic violence, and we've repeated it over and over again,"[65] confirming the value of a simple, powerful mantra on an entire society.

9

Letting War's Victims Lead
Colombia

> We have to break the chain that is presented as inescapable, and doing that is only possible with forgiveness and concrete reconciliation. Colombia: Open your heart as God's people and let yourself be reconciled.
>
> —Pope Francis, Villavicencio, Colombia, September 9, 2017[1]

From his first weeks in office until yesterday (if Francis is now sitting on St. Peter's throne), he is working on the Rubik's Cube of peace in a country that has suffered the longest-running civil war in the Western Hemisphere. In Colombia, Pope Francis has discreetly orchestrated papal diplomacy using a range of Church assets, although the Holy See would never claim credit for the negotiations that kicked off in 2012 or the agreement secured four years later. Many, many players have been involved, from the European Union to Notre Dame University, from Pax Christi International to the government of Japan. Francis mainly used his office to beseech, coax, encourage, persuade, and request reconciliation—both personally and through the Catholic Church's multifaceted network.

The Church's efforts under Francis comprised a sort of diplomatic herding toward the goal of achieving a concrete agreement, then supporting its implementation. Especially because Church engagement has been quiet, behind the scenes, and many sided, it is worthwhile to point out its sinews. What's especially enthralling in this case study is that even when the Vatican provided little direct support for diplomatic efforts to end the war, especially under Pope John Paul II, the Church of the people on the ground provided the nation's earliest models for building peace through local community action and negotiating with violent protagonists.

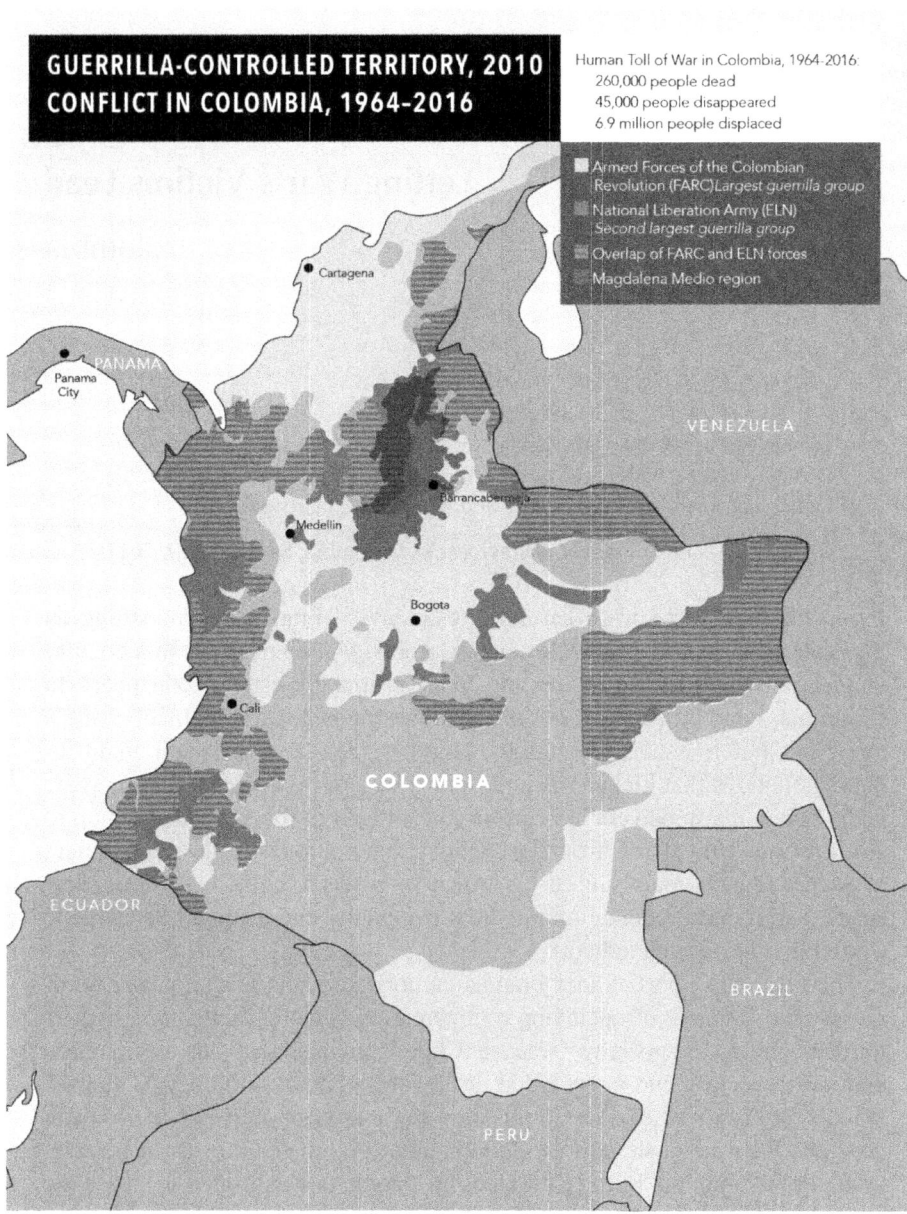

I take the formal signing on November 24, 2016, as the end point in this diplomatic drama and use the past tense to describe the conflict. However, not all guerrillas put down their weapons, and violent skirmishes continue, although the number of conflict-related kidnappings, for example, fell dramatically, from a high of 3,572 in 2000 to 174 in 2018.[2] Sustaining peace, especially in the context of Colombia's vast illegal drug economy, is an enduring challenge.

WHAT CHANGED WITH FRANCIS

Approximately 82 percent of the country's population is Catholic, so Church members were found in every quarter of the conflict.[3] Catholics were among the victims—kidnapped pawns, injured bystanders, and murdered campesinos, rural peasants trying to survive—living in conditions of terror. They were among the combatants—revolutionaries, private paramilitary groups, and military forces, a heavily armed triad of death, aiming guns, bombs, and machetes at each other—who killed over 262,000 people (1958–2016), 80 percent of them innocent civilians.[4] And of course the faithful were prominent among the citizens, journalists, and academics debating how to arrest war and its related pathologies: narco-trafficking and corruption.

Catholics were also on both sides of the debate among the political elite regarding the treatment of combatants. Former president Juan Manuel Santos (2010–2018), who led breakthrough negotiations and received the Nobel Peace Prize, is Catholic. So is the most vocal opponent of the deal, former president Álvaro Uribe Vélez (2002–2010). He was credited with aggressively confronting the Armed Forces of the Colombian Revolution (FARC) and shrinking its ranks, causing it to come to the bargaining table. A Marxist guerrilla movement, FARC emerged in the mid-1960s out of clashes between the military and rural farmers.[5]

Because FARC had Marxist origins—and many of its leaders were indeed trained in the Soviet Union, East Germany, or Cuba—the battle against it was framed in Cold War terms during the first part of John Paul II's papacy, when the Holy See generally sided with the state and conservative bishops were appointed. After the Cold War was over, key members of the curia from Colombia maintained old-school assumptions.[6] Although Pope Benedict expressed personal anxiety about the human costs of endless war and encouraged bishops to engage in humanitarian efforts, including negotiations to free hostages, his diplomatic apparatus failed to prioritize conflict resolution. What changed in March 2013 when Pope Francis took office was the ascent of empirical reality: the pope's personal familiarity with Colombia's tortuous history, his admiration for some of the innovative practices spearheaded by the Church on the ground, and his desire to support peace building. As always, to set the stage for Francis, we must look at the legacies of his predecessors.

JOHN PAUL II'S VIEW OF COLOMBIA FRAMED BY COLD WAR POLITICS

Pope John Paul II's first trip abroad was a pilgrimage to Mexico, including a stop in Puebla, where he opened the third general conference of the *Consejo Episcopal Latinoamericano* (Latin American Episcopal Conference, CELAM), created in 1955 with the blessing of Pope Pius XII. CELAM was the Church's first continent-wide organization. It has helped unify Catholicism across borders in South America, Central America, and Mexico—a unity rooted in popular piety and practice regardless of the religion's arrival via colonial power. CELAM was the crucible in which liberation theology was forged—a new commitment to social activism by the Church on behalf of the poor, and against injustice, which flowed from the Second Vatican Council.[7]

By the time Pope John Paul II arrived in Puebla just three months into his pontificate, a more conservative influence had been exerted on CELAM through the work of Alfonso López Trujillo, a Colombian bishop who became general secretary in 1972. López Trujillo feared that "liberation theology was a Trojan horse in which Communism would enter the church," according to one Brazilian theologian.[8] He aggressively rejected the commonsense attitude that new interpretations of Catholic social doctrine on behalf of the poor and of those literally under the gun were appropriate, even necessary, for the Church to fulfill its mission.

In Pope John Paul II's address to the assembled bishops at Puebla, he explained the core mistake he perceived in liberation theology, without ever naming it:

> This idea of Christ as a political figure, a revolutionary, as the subversive man from Nazareth, does not tally with the Church's catechesis. . . . [Jesus] does not accept the position of those who mixed the things of God with merely political attitudes (cf. Mt 22:21, Mk 12:17, Jn 18:36). He unequivocally rejects recourse to violence. He opens his message of conversion to everybody, without excluding the very Publicans. The perspective of his mission is much deeper. It consists in complete salvation through a transforming, peacemaking, pardoning and reconciling love.[9]

John Paul II's active hostility toward left-wing politics made him wary of involving the Church in Colombia's revolutionary conflict. This attitude was reinforced by López Trujillo, by now archbishop of Medellín, the country's drug capital (where narco-trafficker Pablo Escobar was pulling in about $25 billion per year). In 1983, at the unusual age of forty-seven, the pope made him the youngest cardinal; he assumed responsibilities in the curia, which gave him outsized influence regarding the Church in Latin American.[10]

POPE PLUNGES INTO THE COLOMBIAN CONFLICT

Pope John Paul II spent a week in Colombia in 1986, visiting twelve cities, including places victimized by war. Before the trip, FARC and another guerrilla group, M-19, asked him to mediate an end to the conflict. In fact, an M-19 leader came to Rome to make the request. The pope explained his response to reporters: "I am going to a country that has its sovereignty, its institutions, its authorities, and these are the first people who are responsible for resolving these problems."[11] It is never the Church's role to displace political responsibility; yet in the case of Latin America, Pope John Paul II categorized guerrilla movements, aligned with Communist powers, as the enemy, and he put trust in national governments to hold the line against them.

President Belisario Betancur Cuartas was in his last months in office when the pope arrived. A member of the Conservative Party, he tried to get peace negotiations started, but those attempts literally blew up in November 1985 when members of M-19 machine-gunned their way into the Palace of Justice in Bogotá, killing security guards and taking three hundred people hostage, including forty-four judges.[12] The military quickly counterattacked, without serious negotiations. In the end, some one hundred people died, including almost half the Supreme Court. The building itself was destroyed. The siege was just a sample of the ruthlessness that had made its way even to the capital city.

Revolutionaries and police played cat and mouse in the lead-up to John Paul II's arrival. Guerrillas from the National Liberation Army (ELN), the second-largest radical group after the FARC, planted dynamite in López Trujillo's office. Police defused it. Rebels also broke into the prelate's residence, although he wasn't home, and vandalized seminaries.[13] It was a near miracle that a cease-fire held throughout the pontiff's journey, something few thought possible, except the pope himself.

John Paul II recognized conflict as having roots in political and economic grievances, but, he explained, ideology, foreign intervention, and moral collapse further harm society.[14] He begged a stadium of seventy thousand young people to reject war. Unfortunately, following the pope's visit, the violence continued unabated, with a 15 percent increase in homicides in 1987 over 1986. Political revolution fused with drug trafficking. By the late 1980s, Colombia's illegal drug trade earned more than its principal legal export, coffee.[15]

Guerrillas extorted drug farmers and smugglers to finance the armed struggle. Meanwhile, narco-traffickers, ranchers, private industry, and US corporations began training mercenary groups to counter the guerrillas. One of the first was called MAS, an acronym for Death to Kidnappers. Predictably, the violence metastasized with the expansion of paramilitary organizations; the brutality increasingly victimized people and entire villages merely caught in the middle of clashes between right-wing mercenaries and left-wing revolutionaries.[16]

BRUTALITY, UNABATED

The 1990s saw several unsavory trends. Two major guerrilla armies continued to gain strength. FARC (fifteen thousand fighters) controlled much of the country's jungle in the south and the eastern border with Venezuela. FARC was big and rich, bringing in $200–$300 million annually, at least half from drugs, the rest from extortion.[17] As FARC recruited members, it used the country's vast jungles as virtually impenetrable cover for bases, training camps, and weapons depots, its growth fueled by drug trafficking to foreign markets.

A smaller guerrilla group, inspired by the Cuban revolution, the National Liberation Army (Ejército de Liberación Nacional, ELN), was based in the north. Several early leaders were former priests, motivated by liberation theology.[18] To raise funds, ELN avoided drug trafficking as a capitalist tactic but used extortion to great effect.[19] It was especially destructive and cruel in its (intentionally high-profile) attacks. With special mastery in explosives, it blew up oil pipelines in 1992 outside Barrancabermeja, Colombia's oil capital, polluting streams that served as drinking water for the poorest citizens. Five years later it shot a helicopter out of the air that was carrying engineers in to repair yet another pipeline ELN had destroyed. All twenty-four people on board died. In 1999, ELN committed an utterly bizarre terrorist act: Audacious operatives (one wearing a Roman collar, hopefully an impostor) hijacked an Avianca domestic flight, then took hostages from the plane on canoes into the jungle.[20] Some elderly and children were released, but thirty-five people, including a congressman and a mayor, were held hostage for over a year.[21] The next month, ELN descended on La Maria Catholic Church in a wealthy neighborhood during Mass, loaded some hundred hostages, including children and the parish priest, into trucks, and made off with them.[22]

Another brutal trend was the systematic murder of civilians by paramilitary groups based on suspicion, vengeance, or bounty hunting. In February 2000, three hundred mercenaries surrounded a small village, El Salado, and set up an improvised killing floor on an outdoor basketball court. They spent three days torturing, raping, and murdering local residents while partying to the radio. Colombian armed forces set up checkpoints to prevent help from reaching the town, so the military was complicit in the carnage. When *New York Times* reporters went to interview survivors six months later in nearby towns, they were being protected by Catholic Church representatives and human rights activists.[23]

A gruesome practice among mercenaries was to kill peasants and then dress them—or merely designate them—as guerrillas. By turning in the dead bodies of people called rebels, they were paid about $1,800 per body.[24]

Even bishops considered "traditional" were compelled to demand justice. Bishop Darío Castrillón Hoyos, for example, took unusual steps to confront protagonists. He publicly challenged mayors, police, and the presidency when he realized the poorest members of his community were being murdered—by the state or private militias, who could know? The bishop even dressed as a milkman to get close to the drug lord Pablo Escobar. Appealing to his Catholic faith, Castrillón asked Escobar to dismantle his violent network. He heard the criminal's confession. But for Castrillón, justice was a personal assignment, not a mission for the Church qua Church.[25] Under John Paul II, even after the Soviet Union's collapse, Rome failed to align the institutional Church with brave people and movements unfolding locally.[26]

PAX CHRISTI BLAZES NEW PATH

Alongside the chaos and barbarity of this complex war grew a daring mobilization for peace in the late 1980s and 1990s. One of the first transnational Catholic lay organizations active in Colombia was Pax Christi Netherlands, a national branch of Pax Christi International (PCI). PCI was founded in postwar France by a Catholic bishop who had been interned in a Nazi transit camp and a lay Catholic woman who had helped hide Jewish families. The two were dedicated to reconciliation between the French and German people. Today, PCI is a worldwide network active in sixty countries.

Responding to local requests for international monitoring, Pax Christi Netherlands (PCN) visited Colombia in 1988 with an international human rights delegation and was horrified at the range of human rights abuses people were suffering, isolated from world attention. Focusing on the victims, Liduine Zumpolle, coordinator of PCN's Latin American department, and Jan ter Laak, a Catholic priest and PCN's general secretary, organized the first human rights investigation, documenting the crimes in a report, "Impunity in Colombia," which they presented to the first European conference on the human rights situation in Colombia and to the UN Human Rights Council in Geneva. Although the chapter in the report on the role of the Church hierarchy was written, as Zumpolle says, with "soft hands, very polite," it criticized local Catholic bishops for not playing a more active role, thus provoking the ire of Archbishop López Trujillo.

"López Trujillo traveled to Rome several times and tried to suppress publication of the report, asking the pope to declare an official disconnection with Pax Christi, but the Vatican would not do that," recalled Zumpolle. "He then went to Holland to persuade Cardinal Adrianus Simonis not to publish it. They spoke [to each other] in Latin! López Trujillo ultimately sent four bishops to Geneva to protest it. He was a real criminal because he got money from the drug mafia and Pablo Escobar in Medellín. He would send very active priests involved in social work to dangerous areas of the country to be killed or to be disappeared. It was well known among the clergy. Luckily, the Vatican decided to get López Trujillo out of Colombia. His behavior caused a scandal. They called him to Rome, and he never came back."[27] López Trujillo was appointed president of the Pontifical Council for the Family in 1990.[28] With the obsessed cardinal out of the way, Zumpolle and others agree that more Colombian bishops became active at the regional level.

FIRST NEGOTIATED DEMOBILIZATION

Zumpolle and Ter Laak again played an unusual role when PCN was asked by *Corriente de Renovación Socialista* (CRS), a dissident group of eight hundred guerrillas, to help save peace negotiations between CRS and the government. It was CRS that first went to the government seeking a path to democratic political engagement. But just a month after sitting down together, two CRS negotiators were murdered by the army—while returning from the negotiation table! The army claimed miscommunication, and the guerillas called off bargaining and looked for help abroad, in this case from Pax Christi Netherlands.

According to observers, what PCN contributed was establishing trust with the guerrillas and adding accountability to the process, especially by engaging international actors. "The guerrillas didn't trust the government, so they knocked on my door because they knew me from my previous activities. We then contacted the Dutch government and began a year and a half of talks and negotiations. I took two of them [CRS ex-combatants] to the European Commission, European governments, the academic world, media, and Church leaders in about four countries. With so much international support, the Colombian government also came along. Some eight hundred CRS guerrillas and urban militias accepted to disarm," explained Zumpolle.[29] It was the first time international engagement had successfully led to demobilization. The reintegration plan also gave limited support to families through monthly allowances, education loans, health care, and psychosocial assistance.

"We signed the peace agreement in 1994 in a little village in the region of Montes de Maria, with nine ambassadors present. The Dutch government agreed to monitor the deal for ten years to ensure that the Colombian government would comply. In turn, Pax, as an NGO, would try to guarantee that the paramilitary would not kill the ex-guerrillas after laying down their arms. We, Pax, were trusted by all parties—the guerrillas, the paramilitary, and the government—because we didn't have political or economic interests and we kept our word."[30] The Dutch embassy followed up with monthly meetings with Colombia's diplomats to make sure the process was on course.

As one academic study of the agreement concluded, "Pax Christi fulfilled a role as trust builder, and the trust between the CRS and Pax Christi made the former a more stable and influential negotiating partner. Also, by raising attention for the process, Pax Christi contributed to the status of the CRS. Accordingly, Pax Christi contributed to the balancing of the asymmetry between the CRS and the government."[31] The lay organization also helped gain access to European decision makers and the UN to educate them on the conflict. "Time after time, we go to places at war to discover good people are living with determination, creativity, and energy even in the middle of madness," explained Pax Christi copresident Marie Dennis. "Pax Christi's conviction is that the international community should support the good work of local people."[32]

CATHOLIC MEDIATION AND REGIONAL STRATEGIES

With López Trujillo out of the picture, the Church came into its own, especially through regional problem solving. It stepped into new roles, for example, mediating between gangs in Bogotá, Cali, and Medellín, while advancing specifically Catholic responses, such as communal Stations of the Cross. The Catholic Church's contributions to peace building are organized into four categories by the US Institute of Peace: (1) it fostered the creation of mechanisms promoting peace and social justice at all levels; (2) it educated the faithful on Christian values and solidarity; (3) it worked across boundaries to collaborate with other church groups—a new practice; and (4) it supported local experiments in reconciliation.[33]

What was especially prescient in shaping the nation's way forward was the creation of an organizational infrastructure for reconciliation. From peace communities to department-level[34] working groups, the Church actively experimented with ways to build sustained consensus for peace, from the ground up, through persistent engagement, which included entering into dialogue with armed protagonists in some of the most dangerous areas. Local mediation by priests was often required to move communities caught in the death trap of war.

A particularly dangerous, chronically poor area in north central Colombia surrounded the city of Barrancabermeja, on the banks of the Magdalena River, nicknamed the oil capital because it had the country's largest refinery. Despite this big employer, an active union, and rich natural resources, the region experienced 70 percent poverty, well over the national average. Unequal land distribution was one major problem, which contributed to the birth of ELN in the region and then the emergence of a counterterrorist national umbrella organization, the Self-Defense Units of Colombia (*Autodefensas Unidas de Colombia*, AUC).

Weak state administration led to substandard schools, health care, law enforcement, and public services. In this vacuum, armed combatants battled for control. First, guerrillas clashed with state security forces; then paramilitary units entered the fray. Regular people were caught in the middle.

As the conflict unfolded, Fr. Francisco "Pacho" de Roux, SJ, emerged in the 1980s as one of the country's most important proponents of peace. Working with others, in 1993 he founded the *Programa de Desarrollo y Paz del Magdalena Medio* (Program for Development and Peace in Magdalena Medio, PDPMM), covering an area about the size of Belgium, including Barrancabermeja. Since then, he has devoted his life to working with all sides, praying and burying, negotiating hostage releases and cease-fires. De Roux became a leading actor and thinker on how to puncture cycles of violence based on a daring social experiment in the Magdalena Medio, but not without stunning loss: twenty-seven of his collaborators were murdered, twenty-four by paramilitary groups and three by guerrilla fighters.

Sorrowfully, it's essential to know just how brutal the war was in order to appreciate the authentic heroism of those who persisted with peace. It took seven days for de Roux to negotiate with ELN for the release of his kidnapped colleague Alma Rosa Jaramillo, a lawyer working on land reform. Soon thereafter, paramilitary mercenaries took their turn and murdered her. They hacked her arms and legs off her body with a chainsaw, a ghastly sacrilege meant to terrify her Christian associates.[35] Yet a woman volunteered to continue Alma's work by keeping open the office she ran. That's the irrational power of people motivated by faith.

The PDPMM began by surveying the population on very basic real-life questions: Why are people so poor? What causes random killing? Over 1,500 people participated in the inquiry, often in open settings that brought long-time opponents together. "We proposed dialogue with all the people involved in the internal conflict," explained de Roux. "We invite people to focus on human dignity. Dignity is what everyone has—an absolute value based on being a human being, not granted by society, or law, or government, or the military."[36]

As a Catholic priest, de Roux never hesitated to explain that his view of human dignity flows from the Christian viewpoint: we are all sacred and made in the image of God. He believes Jesus awakens us to the significance of our dignity, which is the basis for the value of every life. In phase two of PDPMM, known as "The Beginning" (1996–1998), core groups were formed in towns and villages across the region. Each nucleus of citizens (*nucleos de pobladores*) was trained in a participatory process for identifying a specific project it would like to adopt to advance development in order to achieve peace.

The PDPMM's program was accepted for funding by the World Bank in 1998, and then the European Union and several bilateral development agencies came along.[37] Colombia's national oil company contributed over $1 million. Having this high-level financial support did not make it less dangerous, especially when paramilitary activity intensified as the program got off the ground.[38]

Fr. de Roux focused unwaveringly on the centrality of the victim as a focal point for Colombians working toward peace. In a way, this strategy is counterintuitive. Superficially, you might assume, getting beyond national trauma requires letting go of the past and focusing on the future. De Roux says no, the only way to authentically overcome past brutality is to acknowledge the harm, find ways to restore those who suffered, seek forgiveness through acts of restoration, and make justice the path to peace—not amnesia. And de Roux did not mean something akin to therapy for individual victims, but victims united with their community, coming to terms with the past as a function of collective strength, in imitation of Christ's suffering—a Christian approach to transitional justice.

PDPMM's largest external donor, the World Bank, distributed a five-page description of the Medio Magdalena program in 2001 without using either the word *Catholic* or the word *Church* in describing its origin, innovation, achievement, or national value.[39] Core concepts such as human dignity were not reflected in the write-up. Yet other analysts considered PDPMM's Catholic identity to be critical to its success. Miquel Barreto Henriques, an international relations professor at Portugal's University of Coimbra, wrote,

In all Laboratories, and particularly in Magdelena Medio, a social actor is vital—the Church.... Without the Church there would probably be no Peace Laboratory.... The Church has a high capacity of summons in territories where the conflict is very intense and where there is a total polarization. All armed actors respect the Church, its social work, and its role in peace negotiations, albeit sometimes even the Church is in danger and under threat. Its status and credibility has allowed the Laboratory to enter very difficult and violent zones and carry out projects in them. It has been functioning as a kind of umbrella for the process and the civil society. Moreover, even if the Peace Laboratory and the PDPMM are not religious proposals, there is a certain philosophical Christian influence in them, namely by the Social Doctrine of the Church and the Liberation Theory concepts and views.[40]

De Roux's work was supported and amplified by his confreres in the Society of Jesus. In 1972, the Jesuits founded the Center for Research and Popular Education (*Centro de Investigación y Educación Popular*, CINEP), and in 1987 the *Programa por la Paz* (Program for Peace, PPP) was added. As an example of the kind of solidarity the Jesuits showed early on with the plight of people caught between the military and insurgents, PPP advocated against federal programs (strongly supported by the US government) to eradicate illegal crops because the tactics poisoned the land and water, causing immediate loss of income to poor farmers, and violated citizens' rights to consultation.[41] The Latin American Federation of the Society of Jesus is based in Bogotá; it compensated for the lack of support from the Vatican through its regional and international Jesuit network.[42]

PDPMM was not a one-of-a-kind effort. In the late 1990s, Pax Christi Netherlands supported the diocese of Apartadó by creating and securing two peace communities in the Urabá region, bordering Panama. Some seventeen thousand refugees who fled violence perpetrated by guerrillas *and* paramilitary units were desperate for ways to get home. With advice from local priests and under the supervision of the diocese, PCN helped establish conditions for return (while negotiating with the belligerents): returnees publicly declared neutrality, committed to remaining unarmed, refused to provide intel to combatants, and banned combatants from participating in village problem solving. It was a tall order and hard to police. Yet three years after the risky strategy, villagers were home, and some had land titles for the first time.[43] However, long term, the Church and international monitors could not prevent regional guerrilla forces from regaining sociopolitical and economic influence there.

By 1995, the bishops' conference was finally coming along with its own solutions. Bogotá Archbishop Pedro Sáenz founded the National Reconciliation Commission, an independent group of leaders from diverse backgrounds—journalists, trade unionists, academics—who took on constructive roles, defending human rights and finding ways to facilitate trust between insurgents and the government.[44]

BENEDICT'S VOICE IN THE JUNGLE

While campaigning for the presidency in 2002, Senator Íngrid Betancourt Pulecio, a popular Bogotá-born daughter of a diplomat, drove into a FARC demilitarized zone after the government denied her use of a military helicopter. At a FARC checkpoint in Amazonian territory, she was kidnapped and brought into the jungle. Six years later, she and fifteen other hostages were rescued in an audacious military operation involving state security agents dressed as FARC rebels pretending to take the hostages to a meeting with international observers. Colombia's defense minister Juan Manuel Santos oversaw the daring extraction.[45]

Two months after the rescue, Betancourt went to Italy to meet Pope Benedict to thank him. She said it was her Catholic faith that helped her survive torture and the primitive living conditions—and the knowledge that Benedict was praying for her. She once turned on the radio, exhausted, and heard Pope Benedict speaking about her plight. "It's hard to explain the psychological effect this has on a prisoner, what it meant to know we hadn't been forgotten at a time when we thought we didn't exist. The voice of the Holy Father was like a light."[46] To pray, she made a rosary out of jungle vines, which she wore to her meeting with the pope.[47]

To Benedict, accompanying the victims of Colombia's internal wars was a critical Christian activity, preserving the Church's political neutrality. Victims included economic and political hostages, families of the disappeared and murdered, the wounded, and even those traumatized by the fear of being harmed. Benedict remained personally involved, following cases, making appeals, and meeting with former hostages.[48] He met with six Colombian police and military personnel who were hostages longer than any others, held for twelve to fourteen years in remote jungles, secured with heavy chains that attracted lightning. All told brutal stories of suffering—and uplifting ones of faith.[49] Benedict said he could hardly imagine the difficulty of their lives in those years.[50] Pope Benedict encouraged the Church in Colombia to focus on humanitarian intervention.

Thus, the *Conferencia Episcopal Colombiana* (Episcopal Conference of Colombia, CEC) took more leadership in local mediation efforts, making repeated humanitarian appeals to return all hostages within the framework of international agreements. Around the country, building on a foundation laid quietly for years, bishops met with FARC and ELN commanders and consulted with the government's high commissioner for peace to untie specific cases. They even traveled, quietly, to European capitals to gain support—insisting that the Church was simply a facilitator of humanitarian solutions, not a negotiator substituting for the government.[51]

The range of global Catholic engagement in the Colombian tragedy was signified at one event in particular: the Catholic Peacebuilding Network gathered hundreds of experts from Chile, East Timor, Haiti, Kenya, Mozambique, Nigeria, the Philippines, Rwanda, and South Africa together in Bogotá to share strategies for a week in June 2007.[52] The theme, "Building a Climate for Reconciliation: Opening Space for Truth, Justice, and Reparation," produced talks and connections used as references for many years.

The month before, the pope was in Aparecida, Brazil, where he met with bishops from across the continent at the CELAM gathering, which he opened.[53] Benedict specifically encouraged the bishops from Colombia—a country he visited twice as cardinal—to emphasize faith as the antidote to violence. On the flight to Brazil, he told reporters, "I am not an expert, but I am convinced that it is here, at least in part—and a fundamental part—that the future of the Catholic Church is being decided. This has always been evident to me."[54] Benedict was prophetic: at Aparecida, Cardinal Jorge Bergoglio, archbishop of Buenos Aires, penned a final report that would serve as the blueprint for his pontificate just six years later.[55]

FEDERAL SHIFT TOWARD PEACE TALKS

President Juan Manuel Santos, elected in 2010 with the support of Uribe (blocked by term limits from running again), increasingly moved in the direction of negotiating a political settlement with the rebels—with strong support from his friends among the Catholic bishops—while Uribe opposed talks, calling FARC's concessions "trickery." In 2012, Santos announced in Havana that Colombia would open negotiations with FARC in Oslo, Norway, the first serious negotiations in a decade.[56] Benedict was among the world leaders who saluted the announcement.[57]

Meanwhile, some eighty-nine Colombian bishops traveled to Italy to meet the pontiff at his summer residence in Castel Gandolfo for an *ad limina* visit. He urged them to be "more and more seekers of reconciliation," a goal some had already dedicated half their lives to achieving—men like Bogotá's archbishop Rubén Salazar Gómez, president of the episcopal conference. Salazar was ordained in 1967 and helped establish a social ministry network. His first appointment as bishop, in 1992, was in Cúcuta, on the country's northeast border with Venezuela, where he was exposed to extensive brutality. His perseverance and humility gained great respect among all parties. His conviction? That war would only end through dialogue and consensus.[58]

Pope Benedict made Salazar a cardinal in November 2012, the pontiff's last consistory. The Colombian signified the ascent of a new corps of more activist bishops and clergy, determined to center "just peace" as the Catholic Church's raison d'être (rather than the far more famous concept of just war).[59] Meanwhile, the risk of being a priest in Colombia was too real: in the first five weeks of 2013, three priests were murdered.[60]

ALL IN: FRANCIS'S COMMITMENT TO COLOMBIA

Virginia Bouvier (known as Ginny de la Paz to friends in Colombia) was an expert adviser to the peace process known for bringing more women into the endeavor, including women religious. A Catholic working at the US Institute of Peace, Bouvier dedicated much of her adult life to Colombia. Immediately after Pope Francis took over, she saw a difference in the willingness of bishops to openly engage in the national peace process.

"The Church was absent from national-level negotiations in 2012, when President Santos and FARC finally sat down, first in Oslo, then in Havana," she told me. "Very busy, very constructive on the local and regional level, but hesitant to be vocal nationally. Pope Francis changed that immediately. By late spring 2013, we saw a new Church, openly advocating the same points made for decades at the grassroots."[61] The fact that clergy were immediately prepared to step up to the task proved that good seeds were sown under the pontificates of John Paul II and Benedict XVI, seeds that flowered under Francis's watering can.

The pope had a chance to meet President Santos in Rome just two months into his papacy, at the canonization of Colombia's first saint, Sr. Laura Montoya, "Madre Laura," a teacher and spiritual mother to the indigenous community. The next day, the pope spoke to Santos in his private library, focusing on the prospects for peace. "The Holy Father told me, 'Only the brave insist that these type of goals be accomplished,'" recalled the president after the meeting.[62] Santos said the pope's encouragement filled him with "emotion, optimism, and energy."[63] The pope and president agreed to keep in touch regularly.

Before establishing a personal relationship with President Santos, the pope had already activated two other diplomatic instruments to advance peace efforts: he gave instructions to the country's new nuncio, Archbishop Ettore Balestrero, and to the bishops' conference that peace must be the top priority.[64]

Pope Francis shared with his new envoy his impressions of Colombia and his philosophy of dialogue. The pope wanted the nuncio to be highly supportive of Santos's efforts. He wanted to see strong bridges built with the bishops' conference as well as with the many international organizations engaged on the ground. He also suggested coordinating with Archbishop Parolin, stationed in Venezuela.[65] Son of an American mother and Italian father, Balestrero speaks fluent English and has uncommon insight into the US perspective, a benefit because the US government plays a major, controversial role on the ground in Colombia. By introducing massive money and military machinery in a $10 billion, fifteen-year counterinsurgency effort, with little interest in human rights, the United States was accused by many stakeholders of inflaming the war before contributing to its end.[66]

The second diplomatic asset Pope Francis empowered to play a stronger role was the CEC led by Cardinal Salazar. In April 2013, its peace commission released "*La Paz es Obra de la Justicia*" (Peace is the Work of Justice), a declaration that concisely summarized wisdom born of decades of work at the grassroots.[67] Its principles had been developed, refined, tested, and implemented through blood, sweat, tears, and death. Until Francis, though, Rome did not welcome a proclamation of these insights. In fact, it was Francis who asked Salazar, in Rome for the conclave, to issue such a public statement.

"Peace Is the Work of Justice" presented the bishops' outlook on the peace talks that had gone on already for a year. It confirmed the Church's well-established position that dialogue, without a time limit, was the best path. However, the bishops warned that the final agreement should not treat criminal acts with impunity or people would not support it. The bishops offered a framework for a "just peace"—one that would last because it simultaneously recognized the causes of war.

They urged negotiators to hear from the victims of conflict, whose rights to truth, justice, and reparations were central to lasting peace: "The bishops are convinced that peace necessarily involves the recognition of the dignity of the victims of violence and the effective protection of their rights to truth, justice, and reparation."[68] The bishops called on insurgents to stop attacking civilians, and they offered to facilitate dialogue with ELN, not yet included in official negotiations. CEC reminded officials that reintegrating former combatants into Colombian society represented a major challenge.

Explicitly Catholic liturgical elements accompanied the idea of centering victims as a way to overcome the past. For example, in December 2013, for the first time, Bogotá mayor Gustavo Petro Urrego participated in a memorial for the victims of war, held at a church where Fr. Dario Echeverri, secretary general of the National Reconciliation Commission, was pastor. Petro had been a revolutionary, a member of M-19 in the 1980s, which was dismantled in 1990 following negotiations that awarded amnesty to all its members, including the mayor. The meeting of victims and former perpetrators of violence was a way of facilitating communal forgiveness.

"It is us, the priests and bishops, who are in touch with the pain of the Colombians," explained Echeverri. "And we are the ones who can influence everyone else, from the sons of the guerrillas to the sons of the foremen and the landowners."[69]

Between 2009 and 2012, the Church had initiated broad consultation on essential features of a peace agreement. Encouraged by the Vatican, CEC released its conclusions, *Minimal Proposals for Reconciliation and Peace in Colombia*, in November 2013, a ninety-page book that calls for economic development and equitable land distribution, besides ending war.[70] The risks the Church assumed by putting itself out as an assertive proponent of change could be seen in just one data point: nineteen priests, one woman religious, and two lay employees suffered violent deaths in Colombia in 2013.[71]

With a green light from the Holy See for the Church to play a more active role in the Havana peace talks, Fr. Echeverri and the CEC president began taking groups of victims to testify about the impact of war on their lives beginning in August 2014.[72] "Their stories produced tears from everyone: the guerrilla leaders, the army chiefs, the state negotiators," recalled Echeverri. "As a result . . . everyone at the table started to realize that the agreement had to put the victims at the center; otherwise, it made no sense. Any conflict dehumanizes the human person, and only forgiveness provides a way out."

Five groups of victims, each group comprised of twelve people, ultimately participated in the peace talks under the wing of the Catholic Church. Cardinal Salazar offered a theological explanation for the priority given to victims. At the Third World Apostolic Conference on Mercy held in 2014, he explained:

> To address the topic of mercy from the victims' perspective, we must look at Christ as victim. Because if Christ is not seen as victim, then what the role of the victim is cannot be understood. What was Christ's role as victim? It was to accept pain. The Lord did not refuse when faced with pain. He did not try to escape from pain, to avoid it. No, the Lord accepted the pain, looked face-forward at the pain, and upon making it His own, permitted that His heart be filled with love towards those who were causing that pain.[73]

The audience gave his talk a standing ovation.

But the Church insisted on its neutrality regarding what unfolded at the bargaining table in Havana. These were political details, part of the realm of "low politics"[74] in Pope Francis's view, so the CEC stayed out. Even as talks made slow, steady progress—by early spring 2015, FARC had agreed to a unilateral cease-fire, pledged not to recruit children under age seventeen, and agreed to destroy land mines—random attacks risked undermining negotiations. In November, an army general was kidnapped, and the government suspended talks for two weeks until he was released.[75] In April, ten soldiers were killed. Santos ordered guerrilla encampments bombed (resulting in heavy FARC casualties), but he did not cancel the Havana meetings.[76] Former president Uribe, always sniping from the sideline, called the ongoing negotiations a risk to the nation.[77] Thus, even as the two sides made steady progress, the overall endeavor was on shaky ground.

To maintain pressure on the process, neighboring parishes organized silent marches. Even in remote locations such as Tumaco, on the Pacific Ocean, inhabited mainly by indigenous people, the Church was able to gather over five thousand people to march for peace.[78] Meanwhile, at the national level, twenty-six religious leaders from every tradition signed a letter to the government and insurgents titled "Weapons Are the Failure of the Word."[79] Across the country, local jurisdictions celebrated a Week of Peace using a theme from Pope Francis, "I Greet Others," since a greeting is a sign of peace.[80]

HAVANA ACCORDS: COMPREHENSIVE? CONTROVERSIAL!

On August 24, the two adversaries signed an agreement in Havana without fanfare.[81] The president addressed the nation to summarize the deal, which would begin with the demobilization of some seven thousand troops. The plan called for FARC to (1) leave the jungles to live in twenty-three safe zones, and (2) turn their weapons over to the UN over the course of six months. Lower-level fighters would get amnesty if contrite; higher-ranking rebels would receive reduced sentences if they confessed and asked for forgiveness—unless they were guilty of specific crimes, including sexual violence. Some former rebels would gain positions in Congress to continue work on the transition. Eventually FARC would become a political party.

The Secretariat of State released a statement for Pope Francis, saying he "reiterates his support for the goal of attaining the peace and reconciliation of the entire Colombian people, in light of human rights and Christian values, which are at the heart of Latin American culture."[82] Maintaining a certain distance from the specifics, the pope demurred when asked to appoint a representative to the committee selecting judges for a Special Jurisdiction for Peace to rule on the culpability of FARC members.

The text was not immediately released, but an October 2 plebiscite was set to provide popular affirmation—or rejection. The CEC did not publicly urge Colombians to vote yes on the agreement but urged them to examine their consciences and participate.[83] One priest in Cartagena told a Spanish reporter that he thought the very idea of a yes/no vote divided the unity essential for the country to build peace.[84] The Church took seriously its role of educating voters about the process envisioned by the Havana Accords. The fact was Catholics were leading both "Yes" and "No" campaigns.

The text of the "Agreement to End the Armed Conflict and Build a Stable and Lasting Peace" included topics the Catholic Church had been talking about for decades. Five of the six substantive sections had been highlighted by the Church in prenegotiation recommendations: agrarian reform, a cease-fire, the centrality of victims and their needs, full political participation, and confronting the negative role of illegal drugs in perpetuating conflict (the final section is mainly logistical). The longest chapter concerns victims, the Church's central focus.

Yet the document's stilted, rhetoric-filled language gave an immense role to government and new "mechanisms" for delivering peace. Even supporters admitted the final document was written with minimal input from Colombian citizens.[85] It purported to be a "comprehensive system for truth, justice, reparations, and non-reoccurrence," but it sounded like an overengineered machine promising to deliver a better world. Human beings were scarce: "The comprehensive nature of the System also contributes to the elucidation of the truth about the conflict and to construction of historical memory."[86] The word "system" was oddly capitalized. Twice, the document mentioned CEC's future role in facilitating communal reconciliation events, but it got the group's name wrong—a small but revealing mistake.

Besides awkward language, two main problems struck many about the Havana Accords. First, there was widespread skepticism about rewarding criminals with amnesty or short prison sentences, along with five automatic seats in both chambers of Congress. Violence had convulsed the country for decades, yet the perpetrators seemed to be getting off rather easy.

The second issue that upset many Christians (meaning the majority of adults) was that although God was absent from the document, the terms "gender based" and "LGBTI" occurred over one hundred times. As one insider account of the talks recounted, "Experts agree that the continuous presence of . . . LGBTI experts and advocacy groups in Havana during the process had a significant impact on the members of both delegations." Whether this was a core problem for the war-torn society is debatable. It *is* a priority concern for several UN entities that had representatives participating in the peace talks.[87] It's also a major preoccupation of Raúl Castro's daughter, Mariela, director of Cuba's National Center for Sex Education, and the subject of an HBO documentary, *Mariela's March: Cuba's LGBT Revolution.*[88]

The opposition, led by former president Uribe, Santos's predecessor and nemesis, seized this "gender-focused" thread and pulled hard. The country was already sensitive to the claim that the government was trying to force gender ideology on schools through an eventually aborted plan to update school textbooks, and here the issue was again, "coming in the backdoor" as an unexpected feature in the peace treaty. Uribe opened an aggressive campaign to vote no, while saying he, of course, favored peace. According to people on the ground, Evangelical and Pentecostal Church communities were among the treaty's strongest opponents.

A PATRON SAINT'S BLESSING WAS NOT ENOUGH

Santos needed a very big show of support for the treaty, so he invited a global audience to a signing ceremony on September 26, the eve of the feast day of Colombia's patron, St. Peter Claver, SJ. The celebration unfolded in Cartagena in front of a church named after the saint. For forty years (1614–1654), this Spanish Jesuit priest ministered to slaves arriving at the port in Cartagena from Africa. He met slave ships and cared for the sick in the hold, rescued thousands, and visited and served captives on plantations, refusing to stay in the homes of owners.[89] Santos called Peter Claver "a great champion of human rights" as he explicitly linked the signing event to the saint's legacy.[90]

The president's language on the challenges facing Colombia was strongly informed by Christian concepts, especially the central role of forgiveness: "Making peace is much more difficult than making war because you need to change sentiments of people, people who have suffered, to try to persuade them to forgive," he explained.

On the festive signing day at noon, before a sea of 2,500 people dressed in white—including fifteen presidents, three former presidents, and twenty-seven foreign ministers—Cardinal Pietro Parolin offered Mass at the altar where St. Peter Claver's body is entombed. Speaking Spanish, the Holy See's secretary of state continued the focus on victims that characterized the Church's mantra during negotiations: "Colombia should begin to ease the pain of so many of its people by working to build a better future and by rebuilding the dignity of those who have suffered," he said.[91]

Parolin assured the assembly that Francis followed "the search for harmony and reconciliation" closely; the Holy Father "encouraged these efforts without taking part in the concrete solutions," he explained, because ultimately the decisions rest with Colombians. President Santos offered a prayer during Mass as well: "Oh God, Father and Lord of Colombia, we grant to always be in your hands and fight together to make us one family, in which no one feels alone and excluded."[92]

With the entire nation following events on live TV, the Mass for peace served to spiritually ground the day's proceedings in the will of God. Later on the plaza, the assembly witnessed the president and FARC's Marxist leader Rodrigo Londoño (aka Timochenko) sign the accord with a pen made from a bullet inscribed, "Bullets wrote our past. Education, our future." Londoño gave an emotional speech apologizing for the pain FARC had caused.[93] King Juan Carlos of Spain, UN leader Ban Ki-Moon, and US secretary of state John Kerry were among the witnesses.

The day was such a national high, everyone expected the popular vote, held six days later, to continue the positive momentum. As the *New York Times* reported, "Polls indicate [the referendum] will coast to victory by a wide double-digit margin."[94]

But it failed. With anemic participation below 40 percent of eligible voters, "No" received 50.22 percent and "Yes" received 49.78 percent. The Uribe-led campaign against the treaty capitalized on both the fear that insurgents were getting off too easy and the suspicion that the treaty itself was a Trojan horse for gender ideology.[95] The results demonstrated how polarized Colombia was. Further, it suggested that Santos, who was not even legally required to submit the question to the public, had lost touch with the people.[96] The results left Colombia in a state of confusion.

When, four days later, the Nobel Prize Committee announced Santos as the 2016 Nobel Peace Prize recipient, it acknowledged Colombia's precarious situation: The no vote "has created great uncertainty as to the future of Colombia. There is a real danger that the peace process will come to a halt and that civil war will flare up again."[97]

ON THE BRINK OF FAILURE, SANTOS TURNS TO FRANCIS

Pope Francis immediately delivered a message to the president, the nuncio, and Cardinal Salazar: don't give up. In the Holy Father's view, Colombia's voters were understandably fearful. Insufficient time had been spent educating them about the implementation process, and they did not share the government's faith in FARC because they had not experienced the Havana talks where a relationship developed between former adversaries.

Government representatives went back to the drawing board to study the treaty's text. They invited consultation with civil socicty groups, including religious leaders. On behalf of CEC, its secretary general, Cali Archbishop Dario Monsalve, focused on three concerns: the family and women should be more prominent as protagonists of peace, but the language evoking gender theory should be minimized.[98] Santos's side offered the Church a chance to review the final proposal and take a more prominent role in helping to reintegrate FARC's former soldiers into society.[99]

By early November, Santos's team presented over five hundred revisions to FARC in Havana. Some were significant, such as making FARC liquidate all assets to pay for victim restitution, eliminating foreign magistrates from special judicial tribunals, and allowing the agreement to be amended in the future, but core provisions such as amnesty and congressional seats remained.[100] FARC accepted most revisions as the only path forward.

Santos decided to present the new Final Agreement to Congress because his governing coalition controlled both chambers. On November 29–30, 2016, the Senate and House approved the proposal unanimously—because Uribe and his allies walked out instead of voting. Congress still had to consider legislation to implement demobilization, so Uribe's obstinacy was a major problem.[101]

President Santos turned to the only person who might influence Uribe to collaborate with him: Pope Francis.

The pope's diplomatic appeals are often most successful with Catholic leaders because they see the pontiff through the eyes of faith: Jesus Christ's earthly representative is summoning. The Holy See had already scheduled Santos for a visit with Francis on the president's return trip to Bogotá from Oslo, where he would receive the peace prize on December 10. The pope decided to request Uribe's presence too. It was like marriage counseling to the relational pontiff.

At 10:30 a.m. on Friday, December 16, Pope Francis met in his private study with President Santos, who then went to talk to Parolin and Gallagher. At noon, the pope met with Senator Uribe in the same room. At 12:35 p.m., Santos joined the two men. The three met privately for twenty-five minutes. The Vatican bulletin on the meeting predictably highlighted the pope's message on the "culture of encounter," the importance of dialogue, and the local Church's commitment to provide "education in forgiveness and harmony."[102] He also asked the two men to maintain civility and calm as they sought a way forward.

Although major media reported that the meeting was inconclusive, it did at least three things: it modeled the very encounter Francis thinks is key for the nation's future, demonstrating that nothing is so anxiety ridden that it can't be discussed; it allowed a spiritual father to show personal concern for two believers at the heart of a national crisis; and it opened a three-way relationship that led directly to Pope Francis's pastoral voyage to Colombia nine months later.

FRANCIS'S PASTORAL VISIT

Pope Francis had already agreed to visit the country "when everything is airtight," as he said on a flight home from Azerbaijan as the referendum was taking place.[103] Leaving the pope's study, Santos handed him an "official" invitation. Francis answered on the spot, "When everything is settled, I will go." But the Holy See's team in the field—the nuncio and CEC—soon began lobbying for a commitment that would serve as an incentive for all of the stakeholders to make measurable progress.

The local Church was neck deep in the implementation effort, as Santos himself requested. Most of the action—moving seven thousand FARC soldiers from jungle outposts to twenty-six transition zones—occurred in remote areas of the country where the government had little presence, but there was always a Catholic parish. The Church was also propelling peace talks with ELN, the smaller guerrilla group that had still not renounced war. A public phase of negotiations between ELN and the government opened after the failed referendum vote, with five bishops accompanying the process.[104]

It was President Santos who made the announcement in March that Francis would visit September 6–11: "His Holiness gave us courage, he gave us momentum, he encouraged all Colombians to persevere in the search for peace and now he will come to Colombia during a unique moment for our country," declared the president.[105]

The demobilization was real. Although the Colombian government ran behind schedule in building livable transition areas for FARC, and the UN took longer than expected to collect weapons and certify soldiers who gave them up, overall the process in 2017 was smooth—and FARC soldiers were remarkably patient. On June 27, Santos, Timochenko, and UN inspectors held a ceremony marking the final count: over seven thousand weapons sealed in containers to be shipped abroad.[106]

The Catholic Church stepped up most dramatically in the next phase: reintegrating former rebels into society. Priests offered sacraments and pastoral care in the transition zones. Church social workers helped find the relatives of former soldiers using technology, public records, and parish networks. Educators explained the terms of peace to ex-combatants, peasants, victims, and puzzled citizens. Job training was arranged and provided. Opportunities for encounter were created.

The pope's imminent arrival helped achieve benchmarks not directly related to the Church but precisely tied to keeping peace on course. ELN, in the middle of peace talks with the government in Ecuador, proposed a three-month bilateral cease-fire in honor of the pope's arrival;[107] FARC held its first post-military congress, launching its new political party, the Common Alternative Revolutionary Force, with the same acronym, FARC.

The pope called the trip "a bit special" because it was more mission oriented than other pastoral visits.[108] The explicit goal was to inspire unity, to harness the pope's spiritual and moral authority to catapult Colombians toward a new culture of forgiveness and reconciliation. As he arrived, children mobbed the pope, including a young boy born in the jungle to Íngrid Betancourt's campaign assistant. Then Francis met with injured veterans of land mines and artillery, while the Bogotá Philharmonic Orchestra played.[109] Both moving encounters occurred before the pontiff even left the airport on day one.

From his base in Bogotá, Francis traveled on daily missions to meet the nation.[110] A high point came in Villavicencio, a former war zone. Over six hundred thousand people attended a Mass during which Francis beatified a bishop murdered in 1989 and a priest chopped into pieces in 1948. Later he hosted an Encounter of Reconciliation, bringing together ex-combatants (both rebels and paramilitary fighters) and victims to give testimony of their experiences. People offered heart-wrenching accounts of the war's mad depravity and uplifting stories of how they opened their hearts to forgiveness. As the mayor explained, "It's a city of 500,000 people, and 146,000 are registered with the victims' office."[111] Although the *New York Times* called his visit a "victory," there could be little joy in meeting, for example, a woman who lost her father, husband, and two children during the conflict.[112] Yet with God's help, she discovered the power to "name the unnamable and forgive the unforgiveable."[113]

FARC'S MARXIST LEADER BEGS FORGIVENESS

Of the perpetrators, one of the most famous, FARC lead negotiator—and Soviet-trained guerrilla commander—Timochenko was inspired by the pope's presence to seek his forgiveness via letter. "Your frequent reminders about the infinite mercy of God move me to beg for your forgiveness for any tear or pain we've caused Colombian society or any of its individuals," wrote the former Marxist commander, under medical care in Cuba following a stroke.[114]

Senator Uribe, who didn't participate as an official in any formal meetings, released a letter to the pope publicly, defiantly expanding on why the standing agreement was unjust: amnesty for lower-level troops was acceptable but not for insurgent leadership; illegal assets would now be used to bankroll political campaigns; the deal did little to promote private enterprise.[115] And then he showed up in the crowd with his family for a papal Mass in Medellín (which one million people attended), and his subsequent tweet reflected a humbled attitude: "Holiness, many thanks for the impressions left in my soul, I will strive to improve my weaknesses."[116]

Pope Francis strived to embrace the whole nation with eloquent, prophetic addresses. He preached courage, forgiveness, reconciliation, truth and justice, and encounter. At his final Mass, offered in Cartagena, he explained why mechanisms like those outlined in the Havana Accords could never be sufficient for true peace:

> Nothing can replace that healing encounter; no collective process excuses us from the challenge of meeting, clarifying, forgiving. Deep historic wounds necessarily require moments where justice is done, where victims are given the opportunity to know the truth, where damage is adequately repaired and clear commitments are made to avoid repeating those crimes. But that is only the beginning of the Christian response. We Christians are required to generate "from below," to generate a change in culture: to respond to the culture of death and violence with the culture of life and encounter. . . . In short, the demand is to build peace, "speaking not with the tongue but with hands and works" (Saint Peter Claver), and to lift up our eyes to heaven together. The Lord is able to untangle that which seems impossible to us; he has promised to accompany us to the end of time and will not allow our efforts to come to nothing.[117]

This was diplomacy on the order of Moses: channeling God's Word to rescue a nation from itself.

Francis could rely on some magnificent brothers and sisters to carry out the Church's vision—and work. Significantly, Fr. de Roux was selected to lead the eleven-person Commission for Truth, Coexistence, and Non-Recurrence. The peace agreement created the commission—modeled on South Africa's Truth and Reconciliation Commission led by Archbishop Desmond Tutu. In Colombia, the objective of the group is to understand the conflict, especially by centering the experience of over eight million people who suffered as a result.[118] As the Jesuit who brought the practice of encounter and dialogue to Colombia's conflict resolution task more than twenty years before, one could hardly imagine a better man for the job. The clearest evidence that peace was catching hold could be seen in the homicide data: 11,901 victims were killed in 2012, when negotiations with FARC opened; as of November 1, 2017, 343 people had been killed that year, according to statistics kept by the government's unit of victims.[119]

In August 2018, Juan Manuel Santos left the presidency, having served two terms. He gave a final address to the nation on TV, calling the peace agreement with FARC his greatest achievement. He described the generosity of victims who came forward as witnesses to the terror, the nation's "greatest teachers." He finished by recalling Pope Francis's words during his visit: "Let us listen to him! Do not let yourselves be robbed of peace," he said, summoning his adviser once more.

Liduine Zumpolle, the Dutch Catholic peace builder, has been in Colombia for decades trying to help its people find higher ground. She still has hope, but implementation of the 2016 agreement has not been smooth. I give her the last word: "Now I'm monitoring the government's compliance with the peace agreement. I report to the European Union. The ex-FARC combatants asked for that, for international monitoring. Of course, the government does not comply with everything, but the other side doesn't comply either. They [the government] do not even recognize the suffering they caused among the population, let alone compensate the victims as the Havana agreement stipulated. The guerrillas have not all been compensated economically as was agreed. The lack of security is what hampers a successful reintegration [of guerrillas]. For instance, in South Africa, after the end of Apartheid, the government had weekly TV programs about reconciliation, extensively presenting the victims' stories, etc. It's hard to understand how much people suffered in this country, and they're not recognized. They did far more in South Africa psychologically and morally for the victims, which is not happening here, and that is a new reason to resume resentment and violence."

10

Piecing Together the Middle East
Lebanon, Syria, Iran, and Saudi Arabia

> When all the world is as it is today, at war—piecemeal though that war may be—a little here, a little there and everywhere, there is no justification. And God weeps. Jesus weeps.
>
> —Pope Francis, Homily, Casa Santa Marta, November 17, 2015[1]

> Lebanon's strength and stability will be safeguarded by its neutrality.
>
> —Cardinal Béchara Boutros Raï, patriarch of Antioch and all the East, August 17, 2020[2]

The Catholic Church might be built like a monarchy, but it is not autocratic. A source of its dynamism, especially under Pope Francis, is its capacity for deference to local reality, especially in places such as the Middle East, where there are bishops with the title "patriarch" who carry the prestige of age-old sees. Unlike the case of Ukraine and Russia reviewed in chapter 6, where the pope asserted his diplomatic priorities over the preferences of a local Byzantine-rite Church, in the Middle East the head of the Lebanon-based Maronite Church is one of the most active religious leaders in the region and often the face of Catholic diplomacy.

The existential threat to Christians across the region has compelled Cardinal Béchara Boutros Raï, Maronite Patriarch of Antioch and all the East, to build bridges in every direction, with encouragement from the Holy See.[3] In a high-stakes crisis in 2017 that saw the abrupt resignation of Lebanon's Sunni Muslim prime minister Saad Hariri—inexplicably, while he was in Saudi Arabia—it was Raï who landed in Riyadh, verified the prime minister's safety, and assured the world that he would return home. Francis blessed the trip. The only outward signs of papal engagement were tell-tale flight

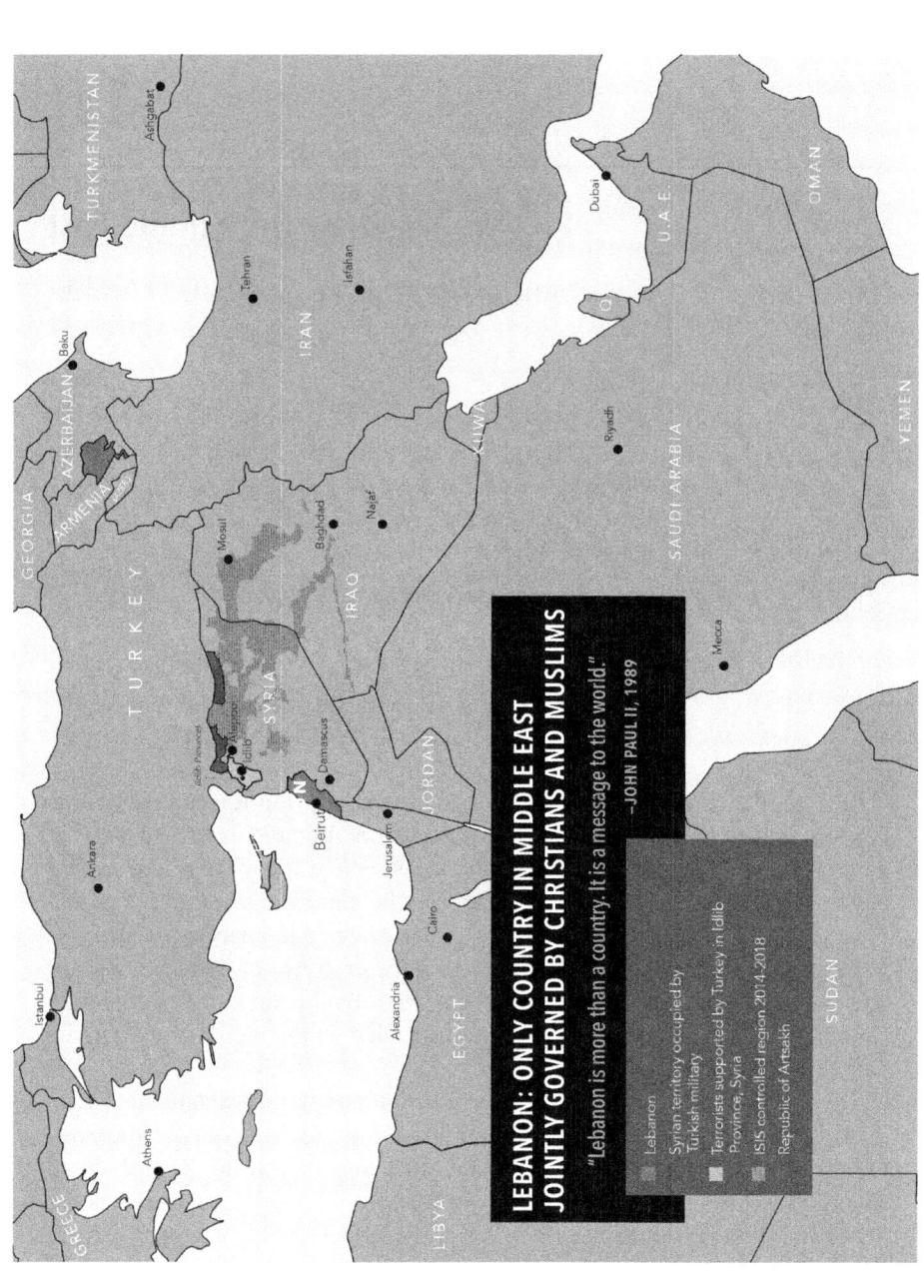

patterns: protagonists appeared in Rome soon after to brief Francis (Raï) and to thank him (Saudi officials). By reviewing Raï's bold moves in the context of the pope's approach to the Middle East, we see how levels of Church governance reinforce and amplify each other, even when taking different tacks.

The axis around which this story unfolds is Lebanon, a small country of 6.8 million people (including some 1.5 million Syrian and Palestinian refugees), where the largest Christian community is the Maronite Church, one of twenty-three Eastern Catholic branches in full communion with Rome.[4] Founded in 685, it takes its name from a fourth-century hermit monk, St. Maron. The patriarch is based in Bkerké, Lebanon, just north of Beirut, with sizable faith communities beyond Lebanon primarily in Syria, Cyprus, and Israel—as well as an active global diaspora. The Maronites served a key role in founding the Lebanese Republic, when the country formally ended its status as a French protectorate (1923–1943). The constitution assures a central role for Maronites: the nation's presidency.

To focus on Lebanon, we must first widen the lens to see Rome's perspective.

FALLOUT FROM REGENSBURG

It's not far from Rome's mind that much of the mess in the Middle East was anticipated by the Holy See. On the eve of the US invasion of Iraq, John Paul II sent an envoy directly to President George W. Bush. Cardinal Pio Laghi warned the White House that three things would follow from its aggression: regional instability, including murder and mayhem unleashed on Christian communities; radicalization of Islamic groups that would launch jihad against the West; and an assertive Iran, with extensive influence over Iraq, its neighbor and former enemy. "All that happened," confirms Rep. Francis Rooney, former US ambassador to the Holy See under George W. Bush.[5]

Pope Francis frequently references John Paul II when talking about Islam, undoubtedly because the Polish pope was far more popular in the Muslim world than Benedict XVI. John Paul II was intensely dedicated to deepening relations with Muslims; he was the first pope to pray in a mosque, where his discourse touched on mutual forgiveness.[6] In contrast, the overall relationship between the Holy See and Islam under Benedict was problematic. In fact, much of the Benedict pontificate amounted to playing defense with regard to Muslims outside Iran, where reasonable relations were maintained with Shia clerical leaders.[7]

Specifically, the Vatican diplomatic apparatus spent significant time recovering from global blowback against Benedict's infamous 2006 lecture at the University of Regensburg in Germany. Discussing a favorite theme, reason and faith, the pope quoted from an obscure text by a fourteenth-century Byzantine emperor who said Prophet Muhammad's innovations amounted to using violence to spread his faith: "Show me just what Muhammad brought that was new, and there you will find things only evil and inhuman, such as his command to spread by the sword the faith he preached."[8]

Although the pope did not quote the emperor to affirm him, Sunni communities, especially, took great umbrage, mounting protests, rioting, and even killing an Italian nun and her driver in Somalia. An Iraqi priest's brutal murder is also suspected of being related to Regensburg revenge. By repeating a condescending remark, albeit a 615-year-old aside, Benedict provoked epic anger because many Muslims heard only the slur against Islam, and perception is reality, especially on the global stage. The pope's intention, to inspire an intellectual debate, didn't matter, nor the fact that it was given at his old university before academics, theologians, and students. In retrospect, it was naive, and his timing could not have been worse, considering the war in Iraq, already provoking radical jihadists, as well as internal weakness in the Secretariat of State.[9] To bolster Catholic-Muslim relations following the unforced error, Benedict appointed Cardinal Jean-Louis Tauran president of the Pontifical Council for Interreligious Dialogue, a "quintessential diplomat" according to the US government.[10]

Francis thus began his papacy at a time of relatively strained relations between the Church and the Muslim world, a status quo he was well prepared to ameliorate given his background. As archbishop of Buenos Aires, Jorge Bergoglio was the first Catholic prelate to visit Argentina's Islamic Center in May 2004. From then on, he maintained regular, close relations with the center's leadership and helped establish an interfaith dialogue institute, which led Tauran to refer to "an Argentine model of interreligious dialogue, unique in the world."[11] By consistently cultivating exchange with the Muslim community locally, the Catholic-Muslim relationship in Argentina was insulated from the Regensburg fallout. Tauran liked to tell the story of how Bergoglio contacted him asking for the best basic Arab-language program to give to his priests. As well, Pope Francis's Latin American identity gives him additional credibility because Muslim leaders see him as independent of a perceived European bias that tarred Benedict.

Although the Regensburg incident hobbled Benedict's effectiveness in the Middle East, it had no lasting impact. Pope Francis has managed to substantially overcome suspicions, especially in the Sunni community, through his relentless dedication to building personal relationships while activating the Holy See's diplomatic assets to solve problems step by step.

NEUTRALITY

The most important thing Francis did for relations with the Middle East was establishing the Holy See's neutrality vis-à-vis Western powers, which he did within the first six months of his pontificate—a fact that laid the ground for many accomplishments.

Francis was quickly pulled into the geopolitical aspect of the Syrian crisis when President Bashar al-Assad was accused of using chemical weapons against his own citizens on August 21, 2013. As tensions escalated, the pontiff met with the Holy See's closest Sunni Muslim collaborator, King Abdullah II of Jordan. It was the first meeting between the two men; they affirmed dialogue as the only acceptable path in Syria.[12]

Francis appealed for a nonmilitary solution and scheduled a September 7 worldwide prayer vigil for peace in Syria. Meanwhile, the Holy See summoned seventy ambassadors to brief them on the potential devastation that would result from a military response. Both the briefing and the prayer vigil echoed Pope John Paul II's strategy when he urged President George W. Bush not to invade Iraq in 2003—although JPII's petition was famously unsuccessful.

Then, on the eve of a G20 meeting of the world's most powerful political leaders held in St. Petersburg, Russia, Pope Francis sent President Vladimir Putin a letter concerning the "dramatic situation of the beloved Syrian people," imploring the leaders to find a nonmilitary solution.[13] Putin himself maintained an aggressive public campaign against the US bombing threat, even publishing a "plea for caution" in the *New York Times* on September 11. Russian Orthodox patriarch Kirill wrote a letter to President Obama marking the 9/11 anniversary by telling him that Middle East Christian leadership unanimously opposed armed intervention.[14]

Soon after, US secretary of state John Kerry and Russian foreign minister Sergei Lavrov announced a plan to transfer Syria's chemical weapons to international control—thus diverting the United States from military retaliation. Whether the pope's engagement influenced the US decision not to bomb Syria matters less than the credit Francis got from several important quarters for sticking his neck out, especially in Syria, Lebanon, and Iran.[15] With the United States having backed down, the Holy See looked like a lion slayer and emerged as staunchly independent of the bellicose West. A Syrian state minister delivered a letter of thanks to the Holy See from Assad in late 2013 for the pope's positions against outside interference in the war-torn country.[16]

When Pope Francis and President Putin met for the first time in person, Syria was at the top of their agenda.[17] Putin explained that because the Orthodox faith is an intrinsic element of Russian identity, he prioritized the protection of Christians across the Middle East—a point of commonality with Francis, for whom this crisis has been a constant concern. Before Francis arrived on the scene, Russia was already working to fortify Orthodox faith communities in the Middle East, using its embassy in Beirut as a strategic center.[18]

Russia's sense of responsibility toward Middle Eastern Christians has a long history. Following the Ottoman triumph over the Byzantine Empire in 1453, the Russian Church was the world's strongest Orthodox power and perceived itself as the successor to Constantinople. Russian leadership evokes the historical relationship with Middle Eastern Christians as an important rationale for its military engagement in the Syrian war, and the Russian Orthodox Church salutes Putin's military support for the Syrian regime.[19]

LOCAL CHURCHMEN CONFRONT CRISIS IN SYRIA

Even before Francis appeared on the world stage, Cardinal Raï realized the quickly metastasizing violence in Syria required a unified front of Catholic and Orthodox leadership across the Lebanon-Syria border, despite long-standing tension between the two countries. Historically, the Maronite Church has been hostile to the Syrian government, which occupied Lebanon between 1976 and 2005. The Syrian army literally bombed a Maronite prime minister, General Michel Aoun, out of the Lebanese presidential palace in October 1990—one day after an eighteen-year-old Shiite Muslim tried to assassinate him.[20]

Aoun fled the palace for the French embassy, where he was sheltered for ten months until retreating to Paris. He returned to Lebanon in 2005 as soon as Syria pulled troops out of Lebanon following the assassination of former prime minister Rafic Hariri. Yes, politics is dangerous business in Lebanon.

To reassure his neighbors of his closeness and solidarity, in February 2013 Cardinal Raï became the first Maronite patriarch in seventy years to travel to Damascus. He attended the enthronement of a new patriarch of the Greek Orthodox Church of Antioch, John X, which turned into a demonstration of unity between Orthodox and Catholic leaders.[21] More commonly known as the Antiochian Church, before the Syrian war it had about one million members, the biggest Christian community in the country.[22]

Raï made clear he was on a pastoral visit—some forty-six thousand Maronite Catholics lived in Syria before the war,[23] while overall about 10 percent of Syria was Christian—and he celebrated the Feast of St. Maron at St. Anthony's Maronite Cathedral in the capital city. His most powerful presentation came during a Sunday service broadcast live on Syrian state TV, where he compared the long, destructive war in Lebanon to Syria's experience, prophetically describing the conflict as "futile."[24]

The patriarch declared, "Everything that is said and demanded in the name of what is called reform and human rights and democracy is not worth the spilt blood of an innocent person." Addressing the Greek Orthodox leader directly, and speaking on behalf of the other leaders, Raï pledged, "We came today to stress the bonds of unity, love and affection among us, and we came also to assure Your Beatitude of our solidarity with you and with the suffering people."[25] It was a moving demonstration of Raï's standing in the region that he was given this role.

No shortage of horrifying incidents in 2013 proved that extremists were ascendant. In April, two Orthodox bishops were kidnapped in Syria. They were driving back to Aleppo from a mission to negotiate the release of two kidnapped priests when their driver, a deacon, was shot dead. Syriac Orthodox Archbishop Yohanna Ibrahim and Antiochian Orthodox Metropolitan Paul Yazigi (brother of Patriarch John X) were taken at gunpoint. They were never seen or heard from again.

When jihadists plundered and burned a Franciscan convent in northern Syria near the Turkish border, they shot a Syrian priest who had taken sanctuary there. The Convent of St. Anthony is part of the Custody of the Holy Lands, protected by the Franciscans. (St. Francis of Assisi created a province for the region in 1217.) These religious men, unarmed, continue to manage many holy sites in the region, risking their lives to stay on. The elected leader of the Holy Land Franciscans openly expressed his frustration at the siege, calling Syria a "battleground, and not just between Syrian forces, but also for other Arab countries and the international community. The ones paying the price are the poor, the small, and the least, including the Christians."[26]

Other Catholic churchmen were increasingly vocal as they witnessed the acceleration and widening of the Syrian conflict. They openly resented that the United States was arming rebels opposed to Assad.[27] Syriac Catholic Patriarch Youssef III Younan blamed the hypocrisy of Western politicians, whose misapplication of democracy theory to Syria was provoking disaster: "In Syria, the situation was much more complex than in Tunisia or Egypt or Libya," he told me, adding that the media turned a war "inflicted on Syria" into an "Arab Spring" fantasy.

"Even Catholic leaders [in the United States and Western Europe], lured by the media and your hypocritical politicians, would tell us [Christian leaders in the Middle East], 'The Syrian regime has to go,' assuming it was a matter of months," which was inappropriate because "you have no right to interfere in an independent country that is still recognized by the UN," said the Syrian-born patriarch.[28]

"Western politicians said, 'We have to export democracy,' but what kind of democracy do you export to a country that has never known the separation of religion and state? If you don't have that separation, you will have no democracy, and you will end up denying the rights of non-Muslims. What kind of democracy is that?" Younan asked rhetorically.

"American, French, English, European Union politicians—they knew that, and now they harvest what they have sowed," added the imposing man, who reminds me of an Old Testament prophet.[29] He was based in Newark, New Jersey, for fourteen years leading the Syriac Catholic Church in the United States before being elected patriarch in 2009. The Syriac Catholic headquarters is in Lebanon. Worldwide, it has some two hundred thousand members.

BROTHER BISHOPS AND THE FRANCIS TOOLBOX IN THE MIDDLE EAST

From his entry on the balcony overlooking St. Peter's Square on March 13, 2013, when he repeatedly referred to himself as bishop of Rome, Pope Francis modeled his intent to consider brother bishops as fellow governors of the Church. Far more than his two immediate predecessors, Francis has listened and even deferred to the insight of local Church leadership.

In the Middle East, bishops watched—and their communities suffered—as reform movements in Libya, Egypt, and Syria played into the hands of deadly extremist factions of political Islam. With Francis's ascension, there was no doubt which side Catholic clerical elite were on: local Christian consensus decided that their security was assured by the Syrian government, despite the fact that many had bitterly protested excesses and abuses committed by Assad as well as his father, who ruled from 1970 to 2000. Francis heard this analysis, understood it, and embraced it.

Francis met with all the patriarchs of the Eastern-rite churches eight months after his election and pledged to defend them: "We must not resign ourselves to thinking of a Middle East without Christians."[30] It was a thought straight from Pope Benedict XVI's last apostolic exhortation, *Ecclesia in Medio Oriente* (Church in the Middle East, 2012), signed in Lebanon on Benedict's last trip abroad: "A Middle East without Christians, or with only a few Christians, would no longer be the Middle East." So many principles found in that document are consistent with what Francis upholds, such as that both Muslims and Christians oppose violence and must lock arms against fundamentalism because it manipulates religion to take power, hurting everyone.[31]

What Benedict did *not* have was instrumentality for these ideas. Of course, the Holy See's diplomatic apparatus was available in theory, but these were not tools he had ever used himself, as he was never a diplomat, not even a pastor; his work as one of the twentieth century's greatest theologians required none of the parry and thrust of building secular solutions to earthly puzzles. Besides that, Benedict's secretary of state, Tarcisio Bertone, had no diplomatic experience either!

For Francis, however, lofty thoughts must *land*—in expressive gestures and acts of solidarity; in the practice of talking, walking, eating, and *being* with others; in joint agreements rather than proclamations. That's what we see from him, step by step, in his stabilization of relationships in the Middle East.

FRANCIS'S HOLY LANDS TRIP: CONTROVERSY BEFORE, RELIEF AFTER

In May 2014, Francis visited the Holy Lands of Jordan, Palestine, and Israel to mark the fiftieth anniversary of the historic meeting in Jerusalem of Pope Paul VI and Orthodox Ecumenical Patriarch Athenagoras, which symbolically ended the rupture between Western and Eastern Christianity. Similar pilgrimages were made in 2000 by John Paul II and in 2009 by Benedict XVI.

Because Francis tries to model the "culture of encounter" on a personal level, not just as a political or ecumenical program, he invited two friends from Argentina to accompany him, a rabbi and an Islamic studies professor.[32] The Holy See also encouraged key Church leaders from the region to join, including Cardinal Raï. Maronites live in the places the pope was visiting, including some ten thousand Maronite faithful in Israel.

But the prospect of stepping foot in Israel caused immediate grief for the patriarch. One Beirut-based daily newspaper billed the trip as a "historic sin."[33] It's illegal for Lebanese citizens to go to Israel, interact with its people, or buy its products.[34] The boycott law dates back to 1955. But as recently as 2006, a brief, intense war at the Israel-Lebanon border led to 1,400 Lebanese and 159 Israeli deaths and thousands of injuries on both sides—plus billions of dollars in infrastructure damage.[35] Thus the tension has recent, not just historic, roots. Raï sought to minimize controversy by assuring fellow Lebanese that he would not meet with Israeli officials or serve as an official member of the pope's delegation, visiting Maronite parishes instead.[36] The controversy demonstrated how difficult Christian attempts to build bridges in the region really are.

But Cardinal Raï made it abundantly clear that no one, not even a pope, *made* him come to Israel. As patriarch, his authority flows back to the apostles and across the region, regardless of national boundaries. In Jordan, where the papal pilgrimage started, Raï sat down for a live interview with France

24 TV. Asked why he was going to Israel, the cardinal explained in fluent French, "I am the patriarch and make my own decisions." When the reporter persisted, repeating criticism from Muslim sources that Raï's decision was a "suicidal step," Raï gave up. He took off the mic and left the studio as cameras rolled.[37] As one sign of the prelate's sensitivity to the criticism, he traveled in the region on a Vatican diplomatic passport.

Not surprising, every detail of a papal outing is planned with great care, with special attention to nonverbal communication—Catholicism's forte. Subtle differences distinguish the 2014 itinerary from the visits of Francis's predecessors. Both John Paul II and Benedict started in Jordan, friendly ground. From Amman they flew to Israel, then entered Palestine under Israeli guard via military checkpoints. For Francis's route, all care was taken to avoid the Israeli military. The pope took a helicopter from Jordan to Palestine, where he referred to the "State of Palestine" (a place-name neither John Paul II nor Benedict XVI used) in prepared remarks. The pope then offered Mass on Manger Square in Bethlehem—in front of a giant mural of Baby Jesus wrapped in a Palestinian kaffiyeh.[38]

Instead of driving ten minutes through a checkpoint in the huge wall separating Bethlehem from Jerusalem, the pope entered Israel airspace via helicopter from Bethlehem, landing at an international airport in Tel Aviv, where the nunciature is located. (Although Israel declared Jerusalem its capital city in 1980, the Church, together with the UN and the majority of sovereign states, believe Jerusalem should have unique international status, as it is holy to three world religions: Christianity, Islam, and Judaism.[39]) The elaborate plan was designed to undercut the impression that Israel has power over Palestinian territory.[40]

While regional experts, no doubt, picked up signals seeking to boost the status of Palestine embedded in the pope's itinerary, the most dramatic gesture of Francis's sympathy for this cause came in real time—with an impact on the entire Muslim world, not just specialists.

As the popemobile approached Manger Square, the soaring sounds of an excited crowd already audible, Francis signaled for his driver to stop. With a sober face, the pope, in white, climbed down from the little white cart and limped toward the twenty-seven-foot high wall separating Palestine from Israel. His security detail shooed onlookers away to clear his unexpected path. The wall, built in 2003, is described as a security essential by Jewish officials but symbolizes Israeli occupation and intransigence in the view of Christians and Muslims who live there.[41]

At the point where Francis chose to stop, red graffiti declared "Free Palestine" near "Apartheid Wall" in black. The pope put his right hand flat on the wall. He briefly touched his forehead to it too. A little girl holding a Palestinian flag looked on, a foot away from the prayerful man, who remained there in silence for several minutes. He kissed the wall. Then he turned back to his vehicle, without a word, and was on his way. If there was any doubt about the meaning of the gesture, his spokesman filled in the blanks later: "It was a very significant way to demonstrate his participation in suffering. . . . It was a profound spiritual moment in front of a symbol of division."[42]

The dramatic, spontaneous image projected worldwide of the pope leaning into the wall, head down, as though beseeching God to help him melt it away, was read, rightly, as his sympathy for those locked out, and his specific concern for the Palestinian people.

The pope offered other moving gestures on the trip. For example, he kissed the hands of six Holocaust survivors at Yad Vashem, Israel's memorial to the best-known genocide of the twentieth century. Nothing captured his empathy like the prayer at the wall, however.[43] When the Holy See signed its first bilateral agreement with the State of Palestine a year later, recognition was already fact.[44] The affirmation Francis gave to a core concern of the Muslim world—namely, the status of Palestine—negated sniping against Cardinal Raï and strengthened Rome's standing, especially with Sunni Islam.

LEBANON'S CONFESSIONAL STATE

While Pope Francis was in Israel, Lebanon's Maronite president completed a six-year term and left office—with no replacement selected by a fractious parliament.[45] It wasn't good timing for a power vacuum. Just a month later, the Syrian war spilled across Lebanon's eastern border when extremists associated with Daesh (known as ISIS or ISIL in the United States) briefly captured the town of Arsal.[46] This was bad news for Rome. Every pope has prioritized peace in Lebanon since Pope Paul VI went out of his way to visit in 1964, albeit for a few hours at the airport on his way to India. Lebanon's very constitution is premised on the idea that Muslims and Christians can flourish together, a conviction central to Catholic thought, reinforced explicitly at the Second Vatican Council. A famous observation by John Paul II in a 1989 letter to all bishops is still evoked regularly: "Lebanon is more than a country. It is a message of freedom and an example of pluralism for East and West."[47]

Political reality in Lebanon is the product of a complex interplay between external actors exerting substantial pressure and the country's numerous confessional communities—Shia Muslims protected by Hezbollah, a political party and military force allied with Iran; Sunni Muslims allied in recent decades with Saudi Arabia; Christians, including the Orthodox Church and five autonomous Eastern Catholic churches in communion with Rome, the Maronites (the most important political players) and the Greek Melkite, Armenian, Syriac, and Chaldean Catholics allied with the West, especially France, the United States, and the Vatican; and the Druze, a monotheistic faith combining Islamic elements with Greek philosophy and Gnosticism. Finding political balance entails constant, dizzying adjustment between these many actors.

Despite waves of crisis, including a civil war that lasted fifteen years (1975–1990), Lebanon has survived with its constitutional commitment to Muslim-Christian collaboration intact.[48] Francis intended to bring his contribution to the persistent challenge, relying heavily on local leaders.

CHARITY, COMMUNION, AND SOLIDARITY IN BEIRUT

In trips to Lebanon in 2015 and 2016, I witnessed Church engagement dramatic on the humanitarian plane, subtle in politics, and innovative in public relations.

One of the pope's favorite metaphors for the Church is that it should function as a field hospital. Across the Middle East, the Church literally *is* a field hospital for the wounded and displaced. Nowhere is this more the case than in Lebanon, where humanitarian services delivered through local churches and Catholic relief groups serve over five hundred thousand people a year, mainly refugees from Syria hoping to go home someday.[49] In fall 2015, over 1.2 million refugees were sheltering in Lebanon, one in five people in the country, a mindboggling number that required extensive private, especially faith-based, support.[50]

To care for refugees who fled the war in Syria into neighboring Lebanon, the UN set up camps, but hundreds of thousands settled on their own in Beirut hoping to work, especially Christians who say they are not safe in Muslim-majority UN-sponsored facilities. Across the sprawling capital city, tucked down innumerable meandering alleys, in office high-rises, on university campuses, and in church basements, refugees from the nearby war were accommodated seemingly everywhere.

At a job training center sponsored by Caritas, I met eighteen displaced Syrian women learning seamstress and cosmetology skills.[51] They were Muslims and Christians, mostly from Aleppo, Syria. One said, "Before we came here [to Lebanon], we were friendly, the Muslim and Christian families, but now we are even more united." The sentiment surprised me, but all the women nodded in agreement. Not one woman wanted to move to Europe; all hoped to return to Syria as soon as the war ended.

As I left the center, a Caritas staffer mentioned Archbishop Gabriele Caccia, apostolic nuncio to Lebanon (an *Accademia* graduate), who had recently visited. "In the last two years, the nuncio has supported Caritas a lot. He is very interested and helpful. He must have come with Pope Francis," she guessed. But no, Pope Benedict XVI posted the nuncio to Lebanon in 2009. Briefing visitors from the West, the archbishop was known to openly bemoan the fact that the Christian community was divided (several Christian factions vied for power), but he continued to describe the country as a model for Christian-Muslim coexistence, explaining, "There are no majorities or minorities here, but each one is part of the whole."[52]

Exploring just two gestures of solidarity made by Caccia that I witnessed—outreach to the Shia in southern Beirut and to the Armenian Catholics in Beirut and Iran—one begins to see the local networking Pope Francis and the Secretariat of State encourage. Small, concrete signs of compassion designed to bind the periphery with the center.

COMBATING EXTREMISM

On November 12, 2015, two suicide bombers detonated explosives in the busy Shia neighborhood of Bourj el-Barajneh in southern Beirut, killing at least forty-six people and wounding more than two hundred at rush hour. It was the worst attack on civilians since the end of the civil war. Daesh claimed credit. The attack was read as revenge for Hezbollah's active support for Syrian president Assad and his army.[53] Hezbollah was founded in response to the 1982 invasion of southern Lebanon and siege of Beirut by Israel. It was funded mainly by Iran, and the Iranian Revolutionary Guard trained its first recruits. To this day, Israel, the United States, some European Union countries, and the Arab League categorize Hezbollah as a terrorist organization, but it is a fixture in Lebanese politics. It's also allied with the biggest Christian political party, the Free Patriotic Movement (FPM).[54]

The Church responded to the 2015 Beirut bombings with an unusually public sign of solidarity. Archbishop Caccia visited wounded Muslim victims at Bahman and Rasoul al-Azam Hospitals. Accompanying the nuncio was a Shia cleric, a Maronite archbishop, and members of a local religious order, *Mission de Vie* (Mission of Life). During the visits, Caccia said, "God loves tolerance, and He is bigger than any desire for vengeance. Lebanon's message of diversity should be preserved . . . despite all crises."[55] From a Western perspective, it was an edgy gesture. For one thing, it meant close, *public* interaction with a controversial political actor: Hezbollah reportedly controls Rasoul al-Azam (Mighty Prophet) Hospital where the wounded were located.

(Vatican diplomats have been willing to engage privately with groups labeled "terrorist" by Western governments for decades, as Parolin explained to US officials in 2006.[56])

However, this attention-getting event underscored a message important to Pope Francis: terrorists are equally the enemy of Christians and Muslims. By visiting victims of a Daesh bombing together with Shiite clerics, Caccia demonstrated that the Church stands with the injured against perpetrators of evil. The nuncio's message underscored the idea that all authentic believers must stand together against all extremism. It's the way Francis conceptualizes the path forward in the Middle East, with strong affirmation from Parolin and Tauran, president of the Pontifical Council for Interreligious Dialogue from June 2007 until his death in July 2018.

As the pope said during a mid-flight press conference on his way back from an ecumenical conference in Switzerland, "If you say that there are religions of peace, I ask myself, where are the religions of war?"[57] Francis opposes the notion of a clash of civilizations in which rival religious and cultural identities propel conflict, an idea popularized by Harvard University professor Samuel Huntington in 1993.[58]

Pope Francis sees extremists such as Daesh exploiting religion to advance nihilism, hatred, and political and financial interests; he rejects the inference that violence is an inherent aspect of Islam. A week after Archbishop Caccia's visit to the wounded in Beirut, Pope Francis was in the Central African Republic holding an "encounter with the Muslim community." It was not his first official foray into a mosque—that was in Turkey the year before—but it was the first time he addressed a Muslim audience on the nature of sectarian violence. At the central mosque in Koudoukou, Bangui, located in an active war zone, the pope took off his shoes, bowed toward Mecca, then offered his vision of authentic, God-fearing believers on one side against pretenders:

> Those who claim to believe in God must also be men and women of peace. Christians, Muslims, and members of the traditional religions have lived together in peace for many years. They ought, therefore, to remain united in working for an end to every act which, from whatever side, disfigures the face of God and whose ultimate aim is to defend particular interests by any and all means, to the detriment of the common good. Together, we must say no to hatred, no to revenge and no to violence, particularly that violence which is perpetrated in the name of a religion or of God Himself. God is peace, God *salam*.[59]

A man representing Muslims living in the mosque as a result of sectarian conflict told the *Guardian*, "We are very proud to welcome him. The pope is not only for the Christians, he is a servant of God for all Central Africans."[60]

SUPPORTING CHRISTIAN COMMUNITIES, NO MATTER HOW SMALL

Four days before his atypical hospital visits to console wounded bomb victims, Caccia participated in a festive consecration of two new bishops for the Armenian Catholic Church, headquartered in Lebanon.[61] Its main place of worship, St. Elie and St. Gregory the Illuminator Armenian Catholic Cathedral, is in downtown Beirut. The new bishops were assigned, respectively, to Beirut and the diocese of Isfahan, Iran, which covers the entire country.[62]

With a total of twenty living bishops worldwide, the event represented 10 percent of the Armenian Catholic Church's episcopal leadership. Hundreds of well-coifed women, distinguished men, and polite youngsters gathered for the twilight ceremony, greeted by a uniformed drum and bugle corps of teenage scouts with wooden rosary decades looped in blue epaulets. Local clergy assembled with bishops from abroad, all in sumptuous vestments of red and gold or white brocade accompanied by young men shaking golden disks on tall staffs, making a pleasant racket. Guests came from both Catholic and Orthodox communities.

Catholicos-Patriarch Gregory Peter XX Ghabroyan, capped with an exquisite miter and with a bejeweled engolpion of Jesus Christ on his chest, solemnly processed up the main aisle flanked by a Lebanese soldier. The patriarch, who was born in Aleppo, Syria, was elected in July 2015, brought out of retirement at age eighty to take the helm after serving as bishop in Paris for thirty-six years.[63] The patriarch's selection was evidence that the Middle East's indigenous churches are not going down without a fight; they are putting their best and brightest in key posts. Ghabroyan has extensive connections in the West, which translate into fund-raising and (some) geopolitical muscle. France, in particular, remains closely involved in Lebanese politics as the power that shaped the country after it escaped Ottoman control.

As the Holy See's representative, Archbishop Caccia was treated as a special guest. Sitting to one side, at the end of the Divine Liturgy he read a letter in French from Cardinal Leonardo Sandri, prefect of the Congregation for the Oriental Churches, acknowledging the current suffering of Christians in the region. Pope Francis has a special fondness for the Armenian Church, which has a strong presence in Buenos Aires. Earlier in the year, he celebrated Mass in St. Peter's Basilica with both Armenian Catholic and Orthodox clergy to commemorate the one hundredth anniversary of the "century's first genocide," in the pope's words.[64]

Why was this event important? No resident Armenian Catholic bishop had lived in Tehran since 2005. Yet Armenian Catholics are the largest Catholic community in Iran, with some twenty thousand souls. The Church is local in

Iran through this small, but hardy community, which is engaged in endless encounters with the dominant culture. Pope Francis wanted to fill this post as a sign of the importance of maintaining bridges to Iran. The Holy See established diplomatic relations with the country in 1954, and the link has never been interrupted. I asked Bishop Sarkis Davidian what his mission in Iran is, and he had a quick response: "cooperate for peace."[65] Against stereotypes of an insular nation, Davidian's assignment took him to a country where Muslims and Catholics have been engaged in dialogue for centuries.

As I mingled among these cheerful believers, who had nobly maintained faith through one hundred years of difficulty, several things became clear: Francis's strategy of small concrete gestures and steps has a real impact on people; the existential threat of radical fundamentalism has forged intense, close bonds between Orthodox and Catholics; and the Holy See is listening—and taking cues—from the local Church.[66]

Not only is this small Catholic community valued, but Iran is an important partner to the Holy See. Two months later, Pope Francis met Iranian president Hassan Rouhani in the Apostolic Palace—more evidence of the importance of a relationship cultivated by his two predecessors. The Catholic appreciation for Shia Islam provides insight into how the Holy See's perspective on the Middle East differs sharply from US foreign policy.

DURABLE HOLY SEE–IRANIAN RELATIONSHIP BUILT ON RELIGIOUS RESPECT

The two theocracies, the Holy See and the Islamic Republic of Iran, have spent decades developing and refining a relationship based on mutual respect. The doctrinal foundation for an openhearted Catholic attitude toward Islam flows from the Second Vatican Council. The 1965 encyclical *Nostra Aetate* virtually ordered the faithful to turn from past prejudice and see Islam in a new, positive way because Christians and Muslims worship a merciful God, who judges humans and rewards the just.[67] Between Sunni and Shia practice, though, Shia Islam is closer in key ways to Catholicism, in practice not dogma.

In Iran, religious authority is far more centralized than in Sunni-majority countries. The supreme leader is elected from the Assembly of Experts comprised of some eighty ayatollahs. The system is analogous to the Orthodox and Catholic systems of selecting patriarchs and popes. Shia imams are considered divine instruments of God, giving them the power to intercede between the faithful and heaven, like priests. As well, many Christians share with Shia Muslims devotion to a central mother figure. Mary, mother of

Jesus, plays a similar role to Fatima (known as al-Zahra, the Shining One), daughter of Muhammad, wife of Imam Ali, and mother of Imam Hussein.[68]

What made strengthening the relationship between the Holy See and Iran most urgent in 2014–2015 was the need to protect Christian communities in Syria and Iraq against Daesh and related extremist insurgents. Iran and its Lebanese ally, Hezbollah, were key to that objective as both were heavily involved in the Syrian war, on President Assad's side. Because Assad is a member of the minority Alawite community, a sect of Shia Islam, Syria and Iran are religious allies.[69]

The Holy See shares with Iran an attitude toward Daesh—which also targeted Shia Muslims—as *kaffir*, Arabic for disbelievers. These extremist combatants have abandoned faith for barbarity. Especially during those darkest days in 2014–2015, there was talk in Rome of a "Shia option" with regard to Syria—a strategy of quietly aligning with Iran to protect Christian communities.[70] The brutality was largely caused by extremist ideologies adopted by Sunni factions, including Wahhabism, financed by Saudi Arabia, and the Muslim Brotherhood, financed by Qatar and Turkey. (However, as a savvy Maronite bishop cautioned me, the Shia aim in Syria is not so much to protect Christians as to protect their own interests.)

In the context of war in Syria, the relationship was put to a pragmatic test. As Archbishop Silvano Maria Tomasi, permanent observer of the Holy See to the UN in Geneva, said, "Iran is an integral part of the dialogue and negotiation that can lead to peace or, at least, the immediate cessation of violence in the Middle East and, in particular with regard to Syria, to find a common, coordinated and reasonable response by the international community to the elusive Islamic State, which only brings evil and negative consequences not only in the region but also in other parts of the world."[71] Francis underscored this conviction in his January 2016 meeting with Rouhani; the two men spent much of their visit discussing how to achieve peace in Syria.[72]

As well, the Iranian president thanked Francis for the Church's positive interventions on behalf of the US-Iran nuclear disarmament agreement. The US Conference of Catholic Bishops, encouraged by the Holy See, was especially supportive of the breakthrough, even sending a delegation to Iran to meet with Shia clerics and sign a joint statement against nuclear weapons while the bilateral document was still being negotiated. The joint declaration stated, "Shia Islam opposes and forbids the production, stockpiling, use, and threat to use weapons of mass destruction. Catholicism is also working for a world without weapons of mass destruction and calls on all nations to rid themselves of these indiscriminate weapons."[73] What most influenced the American prelates was the fact that two supreme leaders had issued fatwas, religious bans with the power of an obligation, against the use of nuclear and chemical weapons. The joint statement confirmed that the antinuke fatwa was still in force and established the Catholic Church as an enthusiastic cheerleader for the US-Iran nuclear agreement achieved fifteen months later.[74] It was an excellent example of two of Francis's priorities: a concrete diplomatic achievement and evidence that religious leaders, across theological divides, can model reconciliation for secular counterparts.

When Pope Francis lauded the US-Iran agreement at the United Nations, he honored the spirit of "sincerity, patience, and constancy" that led to its achievement.[75] In the speech's next paragraph, the pope returned to a necessary obsession: the impossible choice between flight or enslavement facing Christian religious communities in the Middle East. The physical security experienced by Catholic and Orthodox Christians in stable Shia-majority nations went a long way in garnering goodwill. "Find a time when Shia targeted us en masse with death," challenged one Arab Catholic priest at a Catholic university in Beirut.

In Lebanon, leadership of the 1.6 million Shia community has maintained ongoing rapport with the Catholic Church. Imam Mohammad Mehdi Chamseddine, a lifelong proponent of interreligious dialogue, once declared, "There is no Lebanon without its Christians and no Lebanon without its Muslims."[76] His son, Ibrahim, told me the spiritual leader considered Pope John Paul II a valued friend; the two met in person and shared similar opinions on world affairs.[77]

CREATING STABILITY IN LEBANON

Pope Francis directed his diplomatic representatives in Lebanon to help achieve greater unity, not only between Christians and Muslims but also among Christian factions, in order to bring domestic political stability. One reason the presidency—reserved for a Maronite Catholic, remember—remained vacant beginning in May 2014 was rivalry between several Maronite-led political parties, especially General Michel Aoun's Free Patriotic Movement, allied with Hezbollah, and an anti-Hezbollah party led by Samir Geagea.[78]

Francis pressed all levers to gain consensus, through direct engagement by the Holy See and local efforts through his nuncio. In January 2016, Geagea endorsed Aoun, and nine months later Aoun was elected president by parliament. Aoun had maintained a ten-year alliance with Hezbollah—a written understanding was signed in the Mar Mikhaël Maronite Church a few blocks from Hezbollah's headquarters in southern Beirut in 2006. Although many Catholics in Lebanon (including religious women at a free medical clinic for refugees) told me they respected Hezbollah for defending Lebanon's border with Syria and, in the recent past, for defending Lebanon against Israel, there was also a nagging fear that Hezbollah's power was increasingly linked to corruption.[79]

Aoun's first move was to name a new prime minister, Sunni businessman Saad Hariri, who had served as premier between 2009 and 2011. (It was the assassination of Hariri's father, Rafic, that led to the withdrawal of Syrian troops from the country in response to mass protests, sometimes called the Cedar Revolution, in 2005.) In March 2017, Aoun made his first official trip to Europe, starting with a visit not to Paris, Lebanon's traditional European ally, which harbored Aoun for years, but to Pope Francis in Rome. The president told reporters at the airport, "On behalf of the Lebanese I bring to the Pope a message of love that Lebanon has recovered and is on the road to unity."[80] Not only had Lebanon healed the split among rival groups of Christians, but it had managed to avoid the widening fault line between Shia and Sunni Muslims across the region by forming a new government that balanced these interests.

SECTARIAN PRESSURE ON LEBANON INCREASES

In downtown Beirut, abutting the Maronite St. George Cathedral, is the Hariri Mosque, a huge blue-domed structure with four towering minarets. (Rafic Hariri financed the mosque and made many of its design decisions.) It is the largest mosque in the country, dwarfing everything around it, including the cathedral. All of its stone was brought from Saudi Arabia. Hariri, who made his fortune in Saudi Arabia, is buried next to the mosque, which was officially opened in 2008 by his son and political heir, Saad.[81]

Through the Hariri family, the Saudi Kingdom (which naturally considers itself the Sunni control center since Mecca and Medina are located there) has pressed its interests. Through Hezbollah, Iran (the self-appointed Shia control center) has a hand in Lebanese politics. As a multireligious, multicultural nation, Lebanon has long been vulnerable to scenarios in which local communities become proxies for bigger powers.[82] Heightened Sunni-Shia rivalry fomented by the clash between Saudi Arabia and Iran was exacerbated by the US invasion of Iraq.[83]

By early 2017, Daesh was done. In the view of many, the Assad regime survived because Hezbollah fighters, with Iranian backing, came to its aid with support from Russian airpower, plus Russian military police who trained Assad's Syrian Arab Armed Forces. Wins by this coalition persuaded the diverse array of countries provisioning insurgents—from Turkey and Saudi

Arabia to the UK and US—to back off. It was no secret in Lebanon that those associated with the Catholic Church were relieved by Moscow's decision to engage. A priest from Aleppo assigned to minister to displaced Christians living in Beirut told me, "Everyone is exhausted. The Church in Syria is on its knees. The Russians are our last hope. At the end of the day, we [Christians] have no army." Almost as soon as Russia joined the war, the Syrian army was on the offensive against a complex array of opponents, including the vicious extremists who comprise Daesh.

As Melkite Archbishop Jean-Clément Jeanbart of Aleppo told a Swiss TV station, "Putin is solving a problem" that "serves the Christian cause."[84] Even the Catholic press in the West saluted Russia's role. A September 30, 2015, headline in the London-based *Catholic Herald* read, "Will Russia's Holy War Save Syria's Christians? America and Britain Have Helped Endanger Minorities in the Middle East." It's an understanding that diverges dramatically from anything you will hear reported in Western capitals, demonstrating that although it is located in Italy, the Holy See under Pope Francis no longer has a Western European outlook.

Hezbollah and Iran gained muscle as a result of successfully defending Assad in Syria. Saudi leadership was not happy about this outcome and, among its responses, decided to lean on proxies in Lebanon to diminish Shia authority. The way this played out in late 2017 threw Lebanon into a bizarre political crisis, which Cardinal Raï played an integral role in mediating.

RAÏ STABILIZES LEBANON BY CROSSING ANOTHER BOUNDARY: SAUDI ARABIA

On November 4, 2017, Saad Hariri resigned from his position as prime minister of Lebanon, making the announcement on television—from Riyadh, Saudi Arabia. His family keeps a house in the kingdom, and Saad maintains Saudi citizenship, but his own advisers were astonished since he told no one of this plan. They pointed out that the language Hariri used in his resignation was not his typical speech. He accused Hezbollah of threatening to assassinate him and warned of Iran's designs on the country. Many in Lebanon, including President Aoun and Hezbollah leader Hassan Nasrallah, asserted that Hariri had been pressured into resigning and was under house arrest.[85]

Aoun and the Lebanese government refused to accept Hariri's resignation, asserting that he had to submit it in person. Meanwhile, the Saudi government ordered its citizens to leave Lebanon immediately, causing panic that Saudi Arabia was planning war.[86] Around the world, many suspected a power play by Crown Prince Mohammed bin Salman (MBS, as he is known), who was fomenting anti-Shia conflict across the region. The Saudi-Iran rivalry was squeezing little Lebanon. US Secretary of State Rex Tillerson cautioned Riyadh against manipulating Lebanon "as a venue for proxy conflicts."[87]

Incredibly, it was Patriarch Raï who stepped in to calm the high-stakes political drama. He was the first Lebanese leader to travel to Riyadh to visit Hariri, who had met with Pope Francis at the Vatican just three weeks before his sudden resignation. In Rome, the prime minister had vowed to preserve stability.[88] At the time, absolutely nothing suggested he was about to jump ship. Although the cardinal and his bishops demurred that the Saudi visit had been in the works for months and was not pegged to the Hariri crisis, several smart regional analysts saw it as an example of the unique Christian ability to mediate between competing Muslim factions irrationally bent on destruction.

In Riyadh, Raï was a guest of Saudi royalty and stayed at one of the king's palaces. He met with aging King Salman bin Abdulaziz Al Saud and the ambitious yet ham-handed MBS. With the Saudi leadership, the cardinal's two main topics were Lebanon's status as a nonaligned country and the value of interreligious dialogue—somewhat ironic considering that Saudi Arabia bans all religions but Islam. The cardinal, accompanied by two Maronite bishops, appeared calm and relaxed in footage of the historic visit. It was the first time a Catholic cardinal stepped foot in the Saudi Kingdom.[89]

Separately, the cardinal met Hariri at the Lebanese embassy. Raï publicly professed sympathy for Hariri's explanation for why he resigned, adding that the prime minister would soon return to Lebanon: "Hariri is ready to carry on serving this nation."[90] He cast blame in no direction; he portrayed Saudi officials as fond of Lebanon, defusing the antagonism growing back home. At a press conference before his departure, Raï said, "Nothing can affect the Lebanese-Saudi relations, and this is what we heard today from the Saudi king, crown prince, and Prince Bandar. They all maintain their love and support for Lebanon."

Raï had skillfully stepped into the role of mediator and bridge builder, which he is personally disposed to fulfill, a function Francis always counsels. Sources say President Aoun considered the patriarch to be the nation's best representative, and the Holy See blessed Raï's involvement. From Riyadh, the cardinal flew straight to Rome to bring Francis and Parolin up to speed. Then he returned to Beirut to brief President Aoun.[91]

Prime Minister Hariri returned to Beirut on November 22 after visiting President Emmanuel Macron in Paris, President Abdel Fattah el-Sisi in Cairo, and President Nicos Anastasiades in Larnaca, Cyprus. This wide range of advisers counseled Hariri to go home and take up his position. Landing in Beirut on the country's Independence Day, he postponed his resignation at the president's request.

On the same day, Pope Francis received at the Vatican, at the Saudis' request, Abdullah bin Fahad Al Eidan, the country's minister counselor for Muslim affairs, who brought a fifteen-person entourage. The Saudis offered a gift honoring the pope as "the promoter of peace and coexistence in the world."[92] Sources in Rome say the meeting acknowledged the pope's endorsement of the cardinal's constructive role in the Hariri affair.

Prime Minister Hariri formally revoked his resignation following a cabinet meeting at which the government reaffirmed its commitment to disengage from "Arab affairs." Aoun pledged to make sure Hezbollah retreated from Iraq and Syria as soon as Daesh was destroyed.[93] Commentators read the bizarre incident as evidence that Lebanon is resisting the efforts of outside forces to foment conflict—opting for unity over division. The saga also showed Christians in a role they would like to play more often: acting as mediators and partners counseling love over hate.

SAUDI ARABIA

Cardinal Raï's November 2017 trip to Riyadh contributed a "concrete step" for the Church in its goal to multiply Christian-Muslim collaboration against extremism. Another step soon followed: Cardinal Tauran was invited to meet MBS in person. On April 14, Tauran became the second high-level Catholic official—after Raï—to arrive in the Saudi Kingdom as a guest of its royal family.[94]

Saudi Arabia is one of the few countries with no diplomatic relations with the Holy See. Pope Benedict XVI met with King Abdullah in 2007, inspiring discussion of opening a Catholic Church in Saudi Arabia,[95] but nothing came of it. The Holy See's main issues with Saudi Arabia center on Saudi limits on Christian religious expression, international export of intolerance, and its ravaging war against Yemen.

While in Riyadh, Tauran, bent over and tremoring as a result of advanced Parkinson's disease, gave a memorable and passionate account of what threatens the world. He said, "I think, practically, we have two enemies: terrorism and ignorance. I don't believe in the clash of civilizations, but I believe in the clash of ignorances because many times people react because they don't know who they are and who you are."[96] He also used some tough love and told his hosts that Christians should not be considered second-class citizens, especially thinking of the millions of guest workers in the kingdom, many Catholic, with limited ability to worship.[97]

Tauran signed a cooperation agreement with Muslim World League Secretary General Mohammed bin Abdul Karim al-Issa, who met with Tauran and Francis in 2017. The agreement created a coordinating committee to meet annually in order to plan wider, biannual occasions for dialogue and to strengthen religious and spiritual ties.[98] The format was hardly an innovative device, yet these regular exchanges are proven methods of building and maintaining contact spanning governments, papacies, and the lives of the individuals who start the process.

Three months after his breakthrough in Saudi Arabia, Cardinal Tauran died of the disease that claimed Pope John Paul II. As cardinals celebrating Tauran's Requiem Mass processed to the altar in St. Peter's Basilica, a mournful pope was already sitting near the casket, an unusual gesture and evidence of Francis's esteem for the long-serving French churchman.[99] To so many who worked with him, Tauran was one of the greatest diplomats of his generation.[100]

Archbishop Joseph Marino, president of the *Accademia*, was ordained in Birmingham, Alabama, by Tauran, his mentor, and recalls this unsung hero's special character:

> Tauran was extremely intelligent, a true man of the Church, who worked tirelessly for peace in line with the Holy See's position which was captured so well by Pope John Paul II, "war is an adventure of no return," [a phrase] probably formulated by Tauran. He was extremely kind and friendly, yet in his official role he was always serious, expressing himself with clarity and conviction. He was a true diplomat in the long line of the great ones in the Church. He was Secretary of Relations with States during the war in Kosovo and the war in Iraq. Pope John Paul II had total trust in him—and so did Pope Francis.[101]

Tauran's second diplomatic post was in Lebanon, where he served for four years during the civil war (1979–1983). For God's diplomats, the longevity of their calling contributes to being effective.

SAFEGUARDING NEUTRALITY

Unclassified and publicly available documents pertaining to Lebanon's conflict-filled history demonstrate that the Maronite Church is often doing its thing in the domestic arena, while the Vatican functions in the geostrategic zone, consulting with sovereign peers especially in France, Jordan, and the United States. However, all Catholic actors agree on the fundamental importance of guarding Lebanon's political cohesion. The consistent position has been to protect Lebanon's pluralism, territorial integrity, and national independence. A moderate country where Christians and Muslims coexist is considered an essential model for the region.

Historically, it's no surprise that sometimes Rome and Bkerké (the Maronite HQ) diverge. With the start of civil war in 1975, US and Vatican diplomats consulted frequently on Lebanon, beginning with a meeting between President Gerald Ford and Pope Paul VI—despite the lack of diplomatic relations with the United States at the time. Chargé d'affaires Peter Sarros recalls convincing Archbishop Agostino Casaroli, secretary of the Sacred Congregation for Extraordinary Ecclesiastical Affairs (comparable to foreign minister at the time), that, incredibly, "Syria's presence [in Lebanon] was a factor working for reconciliation" because, the United States argued, Syria could enforce a cease-fire giving all sides time to negotiate. But Pope Paul VI refused to make any public statements because the Vatican remained leery about Syria's designs on Lebanon's sovereignty.[102] This nuanced position was not held by the Maronite patriarch, as the local Church opposed external Muslim influence in any guise.[103] (During that period, the Vatican began getting intel from the US government because Casaroli concluded information from his nuncio in Beirut was "inadequate."[104]) More often, Rome and Bkerké have been in sync against foreign intervention.

Fast-forward thirty years. An August 2006 US State Department cable reports that multiple Vatican diplomats have "contacted us frequently to express alarm over the bloodshed, and a desire that the US press Israel for an immediate halt to violence. Qana took this conflict to another level for the Vatican."[105] Qana was a village in southern Lebanon that Israeli Defense Forces (IDF) bombed, killing twenty-eight people, sixteen of them children, in retaliation for Hezbollah's forays against the IDF in northern Israel.

Pietro Parolin, acting foreign minister at the time, was particularly distraught at the prospect of Lebanon being engulfed by violence yet again. He reported to his American peers that the Holy See's campaign to curb violence included outreach to the Israeli ambassador, the apostolic delegate in Jerusalem, the nuncio in Beirut, and the International Committee of the Red Cross, for starters.

A few months later, another State Department cable on Lebanon notes, "Parolin is passionate about the country," and reveals his fear that Hezbollah's increasing strength could destabilize the government.[106] Then in December, Parolin is consulting with the Americans again, this time sharing his concern that division among lay Christian leaders was undermining the country and that Michel Aoun, former prime minister (1988–1990) and leader of the Free Patriotic Movement, was "manipulated by Hizballah [*sic*]."[107]

The more things change, the more they stay the same.

At his first general audience in over six months, in September 2020, Pope Francis saw a priest holding Lebanon's red-and-white flag with a green cedar tree in its center. The pope prayed over the flag, then invited the priest to come sit by him, with flag unfurled, as the pontiff prayed for the people of Lebanon and their country.[108] He also convened a day of fasting for Lebanon on September 4 and sent Cardinal Parolin to Beirut on his behalf.

In Lebanon, the county he has worried about for some fifteen years, Parolin surveyed damage from the August chemical explosion (which killed 190 people, injured thousands, and left over 300,000 homeless), met with President Aoun, spoke at the Maronite cathedral to an interreligious gathering of leaders from every faith community as well as humanitarian groups, and then visited the Hariri Mosque next door. At the end of the day, Parolin retreated to Bkerké overlooking the Mediterranean, met with all the Catholic patriarchs including Raï, and offered Mass outdoors, under a statue of Mother Mary.[109]

Since there is no time to relax in a place perennially under siege, the men discussed a position paper Raï issued publicly on August 17, 2020, calling for "active neutrality," a plan to make Lebanon a sort of Switzerland of the Middle East, especially to benefit economic development and political stability.[110] Earlier in the summer, Raï used two homilies to criticize Hezbollah (although not by name) for undermining the country's future, hijacking its autonomy, and preventing the country from getting much-needed foreign investment.[111] It was another instance of the cardinal's risk taking—this time crossing into highly charged political territory that even appeared to indict the country's octogenarian president—expressing a sentiment Parolin shared privately fifteen years earlier. Without a doubt, Lebanon will remain on the secretariat's docket for the rest of Francis's papacy and beyond.

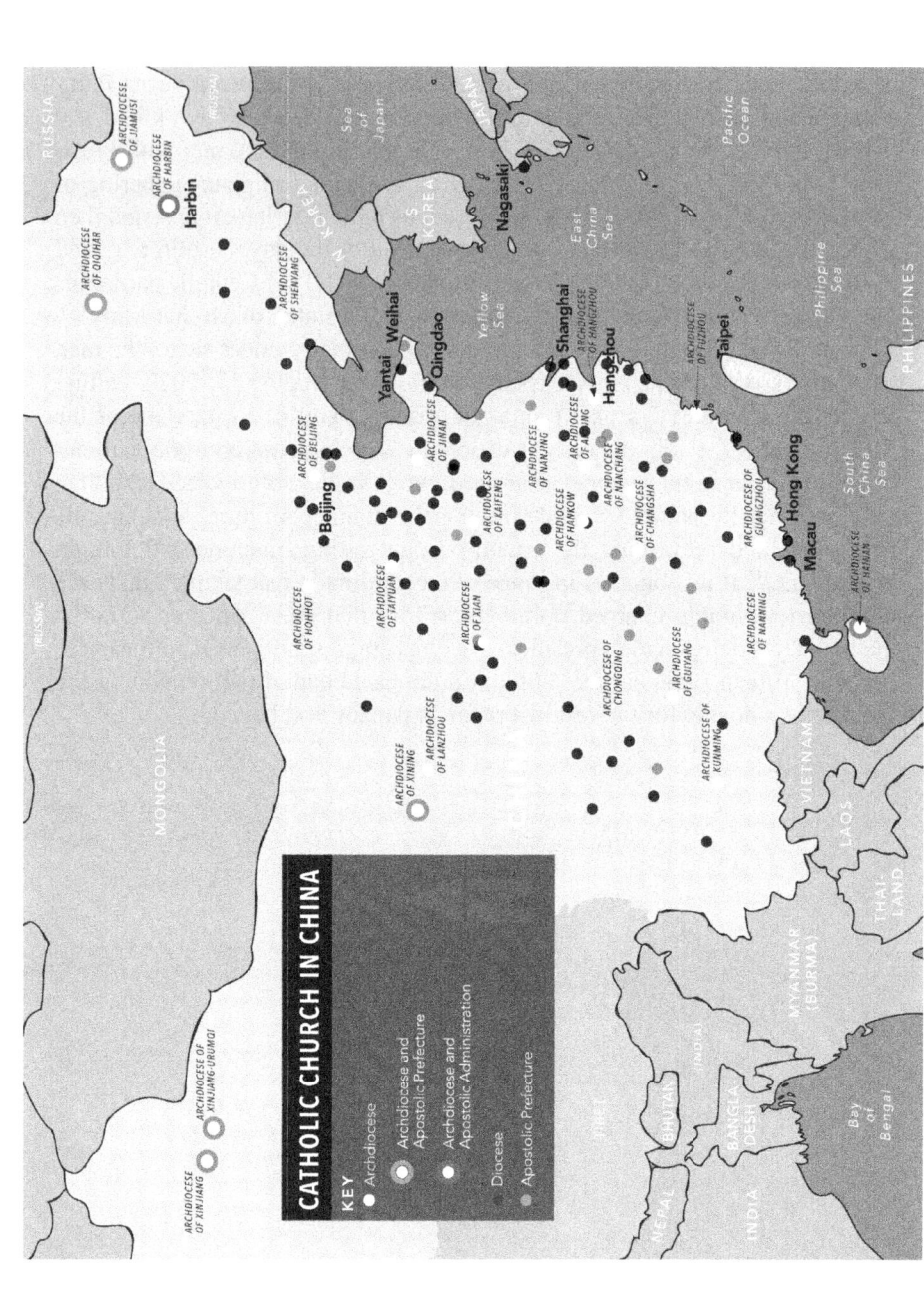

11

Unifying the "Religion of the Lord of Heaven"
China

> The approach is a combination of idealism and pragmatism. Idealism means the objective is broad and spiritual and ambitious. It doesn't mean you are unrealistic, but you have aspirations for something better than the current situation. Pragmatism means a willingness to develop concrete arrangements for advance, as long as they don't violate principles.
>
> From what I know about the secret compromise, neither the pope nor China have given up authority. They are trying to find a way to cooperate. That's very good. It's worth a try. If it fails, I don't think the Church has lost anything.
>
> —Ambassador Charles W. Freeman Jr., April 16, 2019[1]

Compared in terms of state territory, economic power, or nuclear throw weight, no two places differ more than China and Vatican City, the world's most populous nation and the country with the fewest residents.[2] But measured as two empires with indelible historical presence, communal identity, and cultural wealth, China and the Holy See share a lot—including a sense of time in which years are a standard planning unit rather than weeks or months. They also have close to the same number of citizens: 1.4 billion Chinese compared to 1.2 billion Catholics.

If there is one country that similarly preoccupied John Paul II, perplexed Benedict XVI, and then engrossed Francis, it is China. Clarity and consistency in his diplomatic approach brought Francis the farthest in defining a modus operandi with Beijing. The fact that it required negotiating with a regime some consider an enemy has delivered plenty of daggers as a result.

The pope's lifelong fondness for China is linked to a Jesuit hero he read about as a young man. Matteo Ricci was an Italian Jesuit who arrived in Macau in 1582, learned classical Chinese fluently, and, in 1601, became the first Westerner invited to enter the Forbidden City to advise the Imperial Court.[3] He believed traditional Chinese values were fully consistent with Christian theology. The missionary, who wore traditional Chinese garb and a long beard, encouraged biblical interpretation through a distinctly Eastern lens, incorporating into Catholic liturgy an unusual term for God, the Lord of Heaven, drawn from both Confucian and Christian thought. (Catholicism is still known as the Religion of the Lord of Heaven in China.) He wrote a summary of Catholic doctrine in the form of a dialogue between a Chinese and a Christian scholar, using Confucian concepts to explain his faith—because he found the two belief systems highly compatible.[4]

In part due to very different histories of arrival and evangelization, Catholicism and Protestantism are categorized by the Chinese government as two different religions—of the five considered legal. And although the 1982 Constitution assures freedom of religious belief, it also warns, "Religious bodies and religious affairs are not subject to any foreign domination"—a provision that succinctly summarizes ambivalence toward Rome and its insistence that apostolic succession and unity of the faithful require papal approval of all bishops.[5] This was the claim at the core of the power struggle between Beijing and Rome for close to forty years, until Pope Francis untied the knot.

A question related to the specific matter of bishops is a broader one: Can a Chinese Catholic be a good citizen *and* a member of a religion that defers to the bishop of Rome? With the founding of the People's Republic of China (PRC) by Mao Zedong, the answer was a resounding no, as the Communist Party imposed a revolutionary purge of external influences, from foreign corporations to foreign missionaries. During the Cultural Revolution (1966–1976), when churches were shuttered and priests jailed or sent to labor camps, it was not even clear Catholic worship would survive.

The opening of China under Deng Xiaoping coincided with the start of Pope John Paul II's reign, bringing welcome news that Catholic believers were alive and well.[6] The Polish pope and his diplomatic advisers knew the drill: gather intel on the state of the awakening Church, encourage the faithful overtly and covertly, and try to normalize relations with Beijing enough to gain essential breathing room. Rome dealt with a gallery of similar problems with other Communist regimes at the time.

ONE CHURCH, TWO WAYS OF COPING WITH THE STATE

Belgian missionary Jeroom Heyndrickx is a man who projects the solidity of a plowman while speaking with the logical precision of a barrister. He's a member of the Congregation of the Immaculate Heart of Mary (*Congregatio Immaculati Cordis Mariae* in Latin, CICM), an order founded in 1862 by a Brussels-based priest dedicated to the evangelization of China. By the time Fr. Heyndrickx finished seminary, Mao was in power, and foreign priests couldn't get in. So he went to Taiwan instead. He learned to speak fluent Mandarin, served the people, and joined a veritable legion of Catholic priests and nuns, brothers and bishops, sent packing from the mainland by the Communist Party, together with Chiang Kai-shek.[7]

With the advent of Deng's reforms, Heyndrickx immediately established an academic link between Leuven University, a Catholic institution, and Chinese universities. He made his first trip in 1982. Between his language skill and his jovial personality, the priest was welcomed in many quarters. The person most interested in what he learned was Pope John Paul II.

"The pope wanted to know what was going on. The Holy See knew a lot about the underground, but they knew nothing about the official Church. I met with both, and this was what the pope was most anxious to understand," remembered Fr. Heyndrickx some thirty-five years later, sitting in a café within sight of the Apostolic Palace. "What I told the Holy Father was, Catholics are all standing behind the pope and the universal Church, but they have different visions about how to relate to the Communists—that is where the difference lies."

"Pope John Paul . . . yes, he is connected with destroying the Iron Curtain, but when it came to China, he was always very low key and very open to dialogue. He told me, 'We must do whatever is possible to establish dialogue with the Chinese government. Set up all the necessary structures,' and he did that. Even after Tiananmen Square. He reacted in a very low-key way. Even when five illegal bishops were appointed by the government, he never shut the door to dialogue. I spoke with him and met with him many times," the priest told me. "Basically, he was very strongly anti-Communist, but he did whatever possible to keep the dialogue open with China."[8]

The Holy See always works through many sources. Another missionary priest, this one from the United States, told me a similar story about the unshakable loyalty of Catholic clergy to Rome as they restored the Chinese Church following the Cultural Revolution—and the pope's passion for the subject. Maryknoller priest Lawrence T. Murphy, who spent ten years in Washington, DC, assigned to the US Conference of Catholic Bishops and US State Department, received an invitation to a Kennedy Center gala organized for Deng Xiaoping in January 1978, on the Chinese leader's first trip to the United States. The two countries had established full diplomatic relations the month before, and Deng's trip to DC, Georgia, Texas, and Washington State demonstrated that the United States intended to help integrate China into the global order—and encouraged the Holy See to do the same.[9]

As president of Seton Hall University, a Catholic university in northern New Jersey, Murphy was keen to start exchanges between his school and China, a pitch the diminutive leader eagerly accepted because higher education in the sciences was a priority. Within months, two Chinese mathematicians and two chemists were at Seton Hall, and four American graduate students in Asian studies went to China. Many more exchanges followed. In June 1980, Murphy led a delegation, including New Jersey's governor, to Beijing.

On that trip, at an official dinner, government handlers introduced Murphy to Bishop Dong Guangqing from Wuhan. He was notorious as the first bishop appointed by the Chinese Catholic Patriotic Association (CCPA) with no input from Rome—against Catholic canon law. Soon after Mao took power, following the Marxist-Leninist blueprint, the regime set up local associations to control Church finance, governance, and outreach—designed to block external influence. The apostolic nuncio complained and was expelled in 1951.[10] Pope Pius XII issued an encyclical threatening excommunication for any believer who participated in state-imposed schismatic structures. Most priests and nuns resisted; they were punished and imprisoned as a result. But the party forged ahead and established the national-level CCPA in 1957. Among its functions was registering churches (following clergy reeducation to impose state loyalty) and selecting compliant bishops. Dong was the first, ordained in 1958; by 1962, the CCPA had created forty-two illicit bishops.[11]

Murphy retired to his hotel room after the banquet and soon heard a quiet knock at the door. It was Bishop Dong in civilian clothes—not even wearing his episcopal ring. Once in the room, Dong turned on the TV and faucets to create noise so no one could hear him. He told the Mandarin-speaking American he wanted a message conveyed straight to the pope because he was old (age sixty-two), and the Holy Father needed the truth: "We've always been completely faithful and never allowed anything in the diocese that the Vatican would not approve," the conflicted prelate explained. Dong agreed to Murphy's request for a handwritten letter to the pope with this message, on one challenging condition: that the American carry it on his person until he could personally hand it to John Paul II.

Honoring the unusual commitment, Murphy, a graduate of the US Naval Academy, traveled straightaway to the Vatican and located the pope's lead man on China, Msgr. Claudio Celli, an *Accademia* graduate. Celli arranged for Murphy to concelebrate Mass with John Paul II, then brief the pontiff over breakfast—when he handed over Dong's letter. "The Holy Father was fascinated by what I had seen. His commitment to supporting the Church and God's people there was overwhelming," remembers Murphy, who was given assignments by Celli and the pope's China team for the next fifteen years. The American, another missionary functioning as a diplomat, estimates he made thirty-five trips to China and North Korea for the Holy See. He was even in Beijing the night of the Tiananmen massacre.[12]

ONE CHURCH, TWO WAYS OF COPING WITH THE STATE

Over time and based on a multiplication of briefings, Pope John Paul II concluded there was *one* Church in China, united in its devotion to the vicar of Christ but divided when it came to accommodating invasive state demands. Church leadership, especially, pursued divergent strategies for coping with the Communist Party and its controlling worldview. One community registered with the state. Its priests received regular salaries as well as help with church upkeep. This official Church ran seminaries, where many foreign priests were invited to teach; its clergy had more chances to travel and study abroad. The unregistered, or underground, Church, often in rural areas, ignored official structures. The downside to independence was often weak seminary training and catechism. Without doubt, many bishops and clergy in the defiant community were heroic in standing for religious freedom.

Then there were bishops who publicly made concessions to officialdom but quietly communicated with the Holy See and even gained secret approval for their ordination.

Perhaps the most famous case was a talented and devout Shanghai Jesuit who agreed to take leading roles in the official Church after suffering decades of persecution in jail cells and labor camps. Punished for being a Rome-educated priest who resisted party authority, Aloysius Jin Luxian agreed to direct Shanghai's seminary when the government reopened it in 1982. Jin simply decided, he told people over the years, it was more important to preserve the Church and serve its people than to wage a hopeless battle against the regime through the unofficial, underground network. Asked to become a state-sanctioned bishop in 1985, he unsuccessfully sought Vatican approval—and went ahead as a patriotic bishop in the face of ostensible papal silence.[13]

Under Jin's leadership, the Shanghai diocese revived scores of churches, trained hundreds of priests, started a Catholic publishing company, founded a retreat center, and attracted new faithful. Jin rose to national prominence in both the Patriotic Association and the Catholic bishops' conference. He even gained approval for parishioners to pray for the pope during Mass. He shaped the Chinese-language liturgy that is now standard throughout the country. (Mass was typically said in Latin in the 1980s because Second Vatican Council reforms were not incorporated until 1989.)

By 2005, it was revealed that the Vatican had quietly blessed Bishop Jin's episcopal ordination, although he was formally described in paperwork as an auxiliary bishop, ranked below Shanghai's underground bishop, a faithful priest but an ineffective administrator, considering he lived under house arrest.[14] (By canon law, a diocese can have only one chief bishop at a time.) When Jin died in 2013, he was widely eulogized as an exceptional Catholic leader—by the Holy See.[15]

As time passed, differences blurred between the two communities, official and unofficial. Between priests in the respective communities, friendly relations were increasingly the rule.[16] What caused confusion for the faithful and trouble at ordinations was the role of illicit bishops. They wreaked havoc every time they showed up on an altar because their presence could putrefy a legitimate ordination, not to mention that the faithful were dubious about the purity of their sacraments.[17]

CALLING MOTHER TERESA

The Polish pope was creative and persistent, but his success against Soviet Communists made Beijing suspicious of his motives: perhaps Catholicism was a Trojan Horse for anti-regime agitation, party officials muttered. So John Paul II turned to one of his closest collaborators, hoping she could break into the Middle Kingdom in his stead. Mother Teresa of Calcutta visited Beijing in 1985, the guest of Supreme Leader Deng's oldest son, Deng Pufang, who was starting a national association for the disabled. As a paraplegic confined to a wheelchair—injured when Mao-inspired Red Guards threw him from a Beijing University third-story window in 1968—the leader's son wanted to develop China's nascent charitable sector for the disabled.

The younger Deng wrote to Mother Teresa (having won the Nobel Peace Prize in 1979, she was famous) and invited her to Beijing. According to an American priest who advised the Albanian missionary and her order, Fr. John Worthley, "Mother thought this was an invitation to open a house" for the Missionaries of Charity.[18] During her four-day sojourn, Teresa attended Mass and visited a home for the elderly and a factory employing the disabled. She met with Anthony Liu Bainian, CCPA secretary general since 1980, the country's most powerful lay Catholic.[19] Heyndrickx says many in Rome considered Liu Bainian "the devil," but the Belgian priest maintained cordial relations with him. So did New York's Cardinal John O'Connor.

Much like the bonds forged between Boston's Cardinal Bernard Law and the Church in Cuba during the 1980s and 1990s (see chapter 7), O'Connor interacted with the highest echelons of patriotic Catholicism. Introduced by Fr. Murphy, the prelate found financial resources to support Liu Bainian's projects as well as Bishop Jin's diocese. O'Connor facilitated education in New York for scores of Chinese clergy and sent Americans to teach in mainland seminaries and universities.[20] In 1985, O'Connor invited ten government-approved bishops to New York where they dined at his residence.

At this time in Washington, the pope's nuncio, Archbishop Pio Laghi (1980–1990), became close to Vice President George H. W. Bush, his neighbor on Massachusetts Avenue. Bush was passionate about China, where he served as the top US diplomat in the mid-1970s.

The US-China relationship was an emerging priority under the Reagan administration. For example, in 1986 American warships sailed into Qingdao harbor on a friendly "port call," the first since 1949, and the government announced a $550 million equipment sale to the People's Liberation Army Air Force, worth $1.3 billion today.[21] The Catholic Church's interest in China coincided with American interests. Laghi had a special bond with John O'Connor as he did with Bernard Law: he facilitated their appointment to two of the most important Catholic cities in the United States, New York and Boston, and endorsed their far-reaching missions in China and Cuba, respectively.

Liu Bainian grew up in a community dominated by German Catholics in Qingdao. He served as an altar boy at the St. Michael Cathedral in Qingdao. He remembers being on the altar with a visiting European bishop and looking into the congregation where he saw mostly foreign faces. The Chinese official told Worthley this experience shaped his deep commitment to build an indigenous Catholic Church. Stories such as these reveal that even leaders of China's official Church were practicing Catholics with complex attitudes toward the nation but few doubts about belief.[22]

With forty-one-year-old Deng Pufang, Mother Teresa gently sparred over God and atheism, later saying she was happy to see God's name published in Chinese newspapers as a result of her official exchanges.[23] When she expressed her wish to bring her sisters to China, Deng said she would need government approval. Later, he cautioned; the time was not right. Teresa flew to Rome to brief the pontiff on her experience.

Twice more, Mother Teresa tried to find a path in China to "plant tabernacles." She tried in 1993 in Shanghai, declaring in advance, "I have to go to China; the Holy Father wants me to go."[24] Her plan was to visit Bishop Jin, speak to his seminarians, then travel north to Beijing. When no officials were at the airport to greet her and the missionary sisters, they knew they had a problem. Later it emerged that regime hard-liners claimed she had broken protocol by starting her trip in Shanghai, so the prospect of an ongoing presence was blocked. Similar disappointment scotched a project to care for orphaned and disabled children in Hainan Province the following year.[25] At Teresa's 2016 canonization in Rome, the priest charged with guiding her cause through the demanding sainthood process told me her "last and only unfulfilled wish" was to bring her work to China.[26]

Despite disappointment, Mother Teresa's efforts (on behalf of her beloved pope) bore real fruit. The first Catholic nonprofit organization providing humanitarian service was founded by a Catholic priest inspired to create a center in her honor. Fr. John Baptist Zhang Shijiang founded the Beifang Jinde Catholic Social Service Center in Hebei Province in 1997. It is recognized by the registered and the unofficial Church alike. With the motto "Practicing Charity, Witnessing the Faith," the group branded its donations with a cross and grew through the Catholic infrastructure of parishes. As it branched into hospitals, clinics, homes for the elderly and disabled, and HIV prevention, women religious emerged as key actors in what became a registered foundation, Jinde Charities, in 2011.

Although Jinde nuns periodically have been forced by state officials to take classes on socialist ideology, state and provincial officials regularly turn to the group for assistance in providing services to the poor, elderly, disabled, and sick. It is a living witness to Mother Teresa's legacy and represents Catholicism in Chinese characters.

Another local manifestation of the saint's influence is the Mother Teresa China Charity, founded in 2004 by a successful businesswoman, Li Baofu, who was inspired by Mother Teresa's beatification. The group grew through parishes, one at a time, centered in the historically Catholic province of Hebei, where many families trace their religious roots back to Jesuits who came to China hundreds of years ago. Today, the movement has spread to five provinces and has about twenty thousand members.

Beautifully attired in a blue-and-white silk headscarf reminiscent of Missionaries of Charity sisters' blue-and-white saris, Li Baofu attended Mother Teresa's 2016 canonization in Rome, part of a delegation of twelve laypeople and two priests from Hebei: "We came to Rome to pray for the Church and China, but also for the whole world, which needs Jesus Christ," she told me. "What is most important is imitating Mother Teresa's devotion and service."[27]

FATAL LACK OF CONSULTATION

A Chinese Church achievement in the first two decades of the country's opening was the surge of ordinations. Both patriotic and underground seminaries were full in the 1980s–1990s. But the millennial year was not auspicious. First, the Holy See and China went toe-to-toe, each ordaining new batches of bishops unilaterally on Epiphany, January 6, 2000. John Paul II ordained twelve in St. Peter's Basilica, while Beijing named seven.[28]

Then the two sides clashed over the canonization of the first Chinese saints. It was no surprise that Pope John Paul II was keen to canonize Chinese martyrs: there were no Chinese saints, and sainthood was one of his favorite evangelizing tools. On October 1, 2000, in St. Peter's Square, the pope declared that 120 martyrs who died for the faith in China between 1648 and 1930 were saints. Of these, eighty-seven were ethnic Chinese and thirty-three were European missionaries.[29]

Although careful not to declare a saint among those killed during the Communist rampage against religious people, the Vatican nevertheless incurred the regime's ire because the ceremony was held on China's National Day, fifty-one years after the founding of the People's Republic. The Church's response? It's the feast day of St. Theresa of Lisieux, patron saint of missions! The Chinese response? A harsh media campaign focusing on the sins of foreign missionaries, using terminology reminiscent of Mao's Cultural Revolution.[30]

In sum, a major obstacle to progress under Pope John Paul II's pontificate was the Holy See's propensity to forget to give China a "heads-up" on decisions or events pertaining to the Middle Kingdom—let alone consult with government officials on those decisions. In the last years of John Paul's pontificate, there was no illusion that the two sovereigns were close to restoring diplomatic relations, although the Vatican had already decided it was willing to abandon diplomatic recognition of Taiwan in favor of Beijing if that would facilitate reconciliation.[31] (The Holy See is still the only European country where Taiwan sends an ambassador and has an embassy.) The task of finding a way to work with China passed to Benedict XVI.

WEAK DIPLOMACY YIELDS TO IDEOLOGY

Pope Benedict XVI did not signal immediate changes in Vatican diplomatic strategy, retaining his predecessor's secretary of state for over a year. Archbishop Pietro Parolin, an *Accademia* graduate and effectively deputy foreign minister, immediately took the lead on China. He established direct dialogue with Beijing and suggested novel gestures, such as inviting bishops aligned with the patriotic Church to a prestigious world synod of bishops in Rome. Three of the four invitations went to official bishops while one went to an underground leader. Despite the government blocking all four from the synod in the end, the offer helped thaw relations. Parolin confirmed to US diplomats in August 2005 that "informal, unofficial dialogue" with China was underway, while cautioning that specific breakthroughs would take time.[32]

What did not change was Beijing's propensity for tit-for-tat reactions to perceived threats. In April and May 2006, the CCPA authorized the ordination of three bishops without Rome's blessing, in response to the elevation of Hong Kong Bishop Joseph Zen Ze-kiun to the College of Cardinals without prior warning to Beijing.[33] Zen was born in Shanghai in 1932 and moved to Hong Kong in 1949. He was invited to the mainland to teach in official seminaries in Shanghai, Wuhan, Xian, Beijing, and Shijiazhuang from 1989 (soon after the Tiananmen massacre) until 1996, for six months every year. In his own words, he was "very, very warmly received by authorities." It was a time of "building bridges," and Zen was part of it. He planned to retire in 2007 and return to Shanghai to teach. Instead, in 2006 he was given an international platform when he was elevated to the College of Cardinals;[34] he has used it to undermine evolving Vatican-Chinese relations ever since.

Liu Bainian was reportedly "incensed" that after spending years cultivating stronger ties with Rome (and trusting Zen during his eight years teaching at sanctioned seminaries, when they became friends), the official Church community was broadsided with a high-level appointment that reintroduced "Cold War" rhetoric. A source who knows both Zen and Liu told me that each considers himself betrayed by the other. Their personal antagonism and public pronouncements are amplified by extremists on both sides and, unfortunately, divide the Church. Fr. Heyndrickx told me he warned the Secretariat of State in 2006: "I told Claudio Celli, 'You think you want a strong cardinal in Hong Kong but from now on, you will have two Holy Sees regarding China: one in Hong Kong and one in Rome.' I was so right!"[35]

Despite the setback, in June 2006, a mission by Msgr. Gianfranco Rota Graziosi, a China specialist who graduated from the *Accademia*, and Archbishop Celli, another *Accademia* graduate who served as undersecretary for relations with states (1990–1995), embarked to Beijing for mid-level talks, attracting international media attention because it was the first public evidence in about five years that the Vatican and Beijing were still negotiating.[36] Yet it was a tentative move, mainly just to open a channel. Meanwhile, the government barreled ahead, sponsoring Church infrastructure by opening the nation's largest seminary under the Patriotic Association's control—designed by Liu Bainian.[37]

To widen the number of stakeholders thinking creatively about the way forward, Parolin suggested an internal summit, bringing top Catholic China hands, from cardinals down to missionaries, to Rome. At the January 2007 assembly, participants were each given a binder with a draft letter from Benedict to Chinese Catholics—a document begun under the Polish pope. As the meeting ended, the binders were collected before anyone could leave.

The Holy See publicly released the "Letter of Pope Benedict XVI, to the Bishops, Priests, Consecrated Persons, and Lay Faithful of the Catholic Church in the People's Republic of China" on the Feast of Pentecost, fifty days after Easter. The letter described the goal for all Chinese believers as growing in unity. Yet it did not back down from the central disagreement with secular authorities: the unity of a universal Church is assured through the lineage of bishops "in visible and concrete communion with the Pope." Rather than being received as a gauntlet thrown, the Chinese government accelerated discussions, and for the next two years, all episcopal ordinations were jointly managed.

The letter was the most important gesture toward China of Benedict XVI's papacy, with both diplomatic and spiritual weight. It was a charitable, theologically grounded presentation of the problem of having two communities of faithful coexisting, cooperating in some places and at each other's throats in others. It is a sophisticated document, conceptualized from a vista of sympathy and wisdom, written with great clarity, and animated by generosity, yet bluntly repudiating the patriotic association (named in a footnote as the target of the punch) as "incompatible with Catholic doctrine."[38]

Despite the fact that the great majority of bishops and priests were by then in communion with Rome, division on the ground persisted.[39] The letter reminded the faithful that to be part of the body of Christ requires communion and dedication to unity. It reassured the government that Church teaching "invites the faithful to be good citizens," with no "mission to change the structure or the administration of the State," while asserting the expectation that religious freedom will be respected. It articulated some of the specific problems attached to having two communities within one faith—even clarifying that sacraments offered by illegitimate bishops are valid—and formally revoked the special faculties that allowed underground bishops to select new bishops outside Rome's normal command and control structure.

Mainly, Benedict's letter called all Catholics to employ charity, love, and forgiveness to end division. On the diplomatic front, the letter repeated the Holy See's offer to normalize relations through negotiation. It also conceded a role for the official Church, not religious but administrative.

A sign of goodwill on the regime's side came a few months after the letter's release. Beijing Archbishop Fu Tieshan, chairman of the CCPA since 1998 and vice president of the People's National Assembly, died at an elite party hospital. His powerful establishment status was demonstrated when President Hu Jintao visited the bishop in his final days; Fu received a state burial—attended by few Catholics.

Instead of promoting another party stalwart to fill the high-profile post, the CCPA, via its purportedly democratic process of selecting candidates with input from priests and laypeople, named a parish priest with prior approval from Rome, Fr. Joseph Li Shan.[40] A Beijing native from a longtime Catholic family, Li had never traveled abroad and was popular among the faithful for challenging the patriotic Church on occasion.[41]

For the next two years, Beijing and Rome were quietly engaged in diplomatic talks led by Parolin. Operating behind the scenes, the most explicit evidence that things were going well was the arrival in Rome, in May 2008, of the Chinese Philharmonic Orchestra together with the Shanghai Opera House Chorus appearing for the first time at the Vatican.[42] They performed Mozart's Requiem—a bit of cultural diplomacy especially appealing to Pope Benedict, a devoted classical pianist.

A year later, Archbishop Parolin flew to Beijing with a draft agreement including the names of ten new bishops, endorsed by the Chinese and approved by the Vatican, as well as the outline of a process for their future selection in his briefcase. A Chinese analyst close to political power, Ren Yanli, explained to the Italian magazine *30 Days* that it was the very fact of stubborn faith and the rejection of patriotic bishops—few Catholics would even accept sacraments from them—that caused the government to shift its policy, accepting the inevitability of papal engagement:

> [I]f in the past someone might have been tempted to make a career in an independent Church, the faith of the people helped everyone to make the design ineffectual. And that also helped the government to redirect its policy. If the government wants bishops to be pastors respected and followed by the faithful, and not be seen as isolated officials imposed from outside, now it has understood that appointment by the Pope, and full communion with him, are indispensable elements that cannot be done without. This means that the idea of imposing independence on the Church that separates it from Rome and the universal Church has been set aside in fact.[43]

While the government might have shifted its attitude, the moment for a formal commitment was still not ripe, and neither side signed the proposal Parolin carried. He wasn't given any more time to negotiate either, because in August 2009 he was sent as apostolic nuncio to Venezuela to cope with socialist ruler Hugo Chávez, who was opposed by most of the nation's bishops. Certainly, the country required a capable diplomat as tensions rose, especially after "Chavistas" invaded the chancery of the Caracas archdiocese and attacked the nunciature with a bomb.[44]

But several priests who worked in the curia confirmed a common understanding that Cardinal Tarcisio Bertone, secretary of state, sent Parolin far away as a direct result of dissatisfaction that the younger man favored a conciliatory approach to Beijing. Claudio Celli, considered one of the secretariat's leading China hands, had already been banished from diplomacy to serve as president of the Pontifical Council for Social Communications—an odd assignment since he had no experience in the field.

One cardinal in particular was gunning for a more hard-line approach: Cardinal Zen of Hong Kong. He privately criticized the Holy See's policy as bordering "on appeasement, sending the wrong message to the Government of China and undermining the underground church," when he briefed US diplomats in Rome in early 2008.[45] He mentioned Parolin by name as the driver of China policy, adding that neither Bertone nor Cardinal Ivan Dias, prefect of the Congregation for the Evangelization of Peoples, had sufficient expertise to manage the relationship.

The fact is, Zen had outsized weight in influencing Sino-Vatican policy. He and Bertone are members of the Salesians of Don Bosco religious order, founded by a nineteenth-century Italian priest, dedicated to educating poor children. Having not attended the *Accademia*, Bertone was less committed to the cadre of Vatican diplomats, and he deferred to Salesian confreres, especially Zen and Savio Hon Tai-fai, elevated to the key position of secretary of the Congregation for the Evangelization of Peoples in late 2010. Hon, a Hong Kong Salesian close to Benedict and mentored by Zen, was the native Chinese with the highest position in the curia under Benedict—and fiercely opposed reconciliation with Beijing.[46] Thus, under a weak cardinal secretary of state, a coterie of ideologically driven missionaries captured and redirected China policy, killing diplomatic momentum.[47] The task of finding a way to dialogue with Beijing passed to Francis.

NEW, CONSISTENT APPROACH OF RESPECT AND QUIET CONSULTATION

On Francis's first day in office, he noted a sign that marked China for special attention: Beijing selected a new leader just one day after the pope got his new job.[48] Thus, the reign of Francis and Xi Jinping began together. One of Francis's first official acts was writing a personal letter to the Chinese president. This congratulatory letter came from Francis's heart.

From the time Jorge Bergoglio was a boy, using a globe to trace his grandparents' route to Argentina from Italy in steerage class on a passenger ship, he turned the axis to find China. When Bergoglio finished philosophy studies at seminary in 1963, advancing another step toward priesthood, he wrote to the Jesuit superior general in Rome requesting an assignment to the mission in

Japan, since China was closed to foreign priests. But the aspiring missionary was blocked because his superiors considered him physically fragile: surgery removing half his lung at age twenty-one left him with physical limits, such as no heavy lifting. Now God had put China in his orbit, and Pope Francis discerned a pontifical priority when Xi replied, contrary to Vatican staff expectations. In revealing this exchange to Italy's *Corriere della Sera*, the pope said, "We are close to China. . . . The relationships are there. They are a great people whom I love."[49] The "relationships" the pope referred to were those between diplomats.

For the incoming pope, the secretary of state post was the most important position to fill. Presented with a short list of candidates and thick binders of supporting documentation, Pope Francis decided quickly and picked up the phone to call a man he knew in Caracas. "Pietro. Do you want to help me?" he asked playfully. With no hesitation, Pietro Parolin said yes. One of the attributes that singled him out in Francis's view was his deep knowledge of the Middle Kingdom. The pope wanted an experienced China hand by his side, former US ambassador to the Holy See Francis Rooney told me.[50]

Based on briefings in 2013, the pope made three decisions that would guide diplomatic engagement with China as Rome pursued dialogue. First, he streamlined the channels of information informing policy in order to control who had authority to speak for the Vatican. "He made himself the principal voice speaking to the Chinese people, to the Church in China, to the government—really, personalizing the relationship—while a small cadre of diplomats led by Parolin function invisibly behind the scenes," explained a well-informed member of the curia.

Second, the diplomatic team's focus was tightened in terms of topics and interlocutors. The primary goal became finding consensus on the issue of episcopal appointments because it was an urgent pastoral issue that brought to bear the core tension over Rome's role vis-à-vis the local Church. Many bishoprics were empty, and where sees were filled, many prelates were elderly, leaving weak leadership nationwide. To settle that issue, God's diplomats would engage with national-level decision makers, including deciders at the Ministry of Foreign Affairs, the State Administration for Religious Affairs (SARA), and the CCPA. Communication with the PRC's embassy in Rome protected the secret engagement with Beijing.

Third, the Holy See shifted its understanding of the patriotic association, seeing it as an instrument of civil control with no rival religious authority, mainly because priests loyal to Rome were thoroughly represented in the organization by 2013. Under this reading, the association did not qualify as an enemy but as a network and organization of social control with which the Catholic Church had to cope—and could probably co-opt.

The reconstituted diplomatic core team of Parolin, Celli, and Rota Graziosi began planning a strategy centering on Pope Francis's faith in dialogue as a technique for creating trust. In fact, the pope's mantra is embedded in diplomatic theory as taught at the *Accademia*: patience is a virtue fostering stronger agreements, produced over time.

Yet in late 2013 there was precious little trust between Rome and Beijing. There was also disturbing evidence that Xi's presidency had ushered in a new era of anti-Christian activism. In one of the best-known Christian enclaves, in Zhejiang Province, church crosses—some huge, requiring heavy equipment to get them down, others modest rooftop symbols—were systematically ripped down by local officials. Mostly Protestant but some Catholic churches were hit too, provoking numerous physical standoffs between believers and police.[51] It was a bad sign that zealous Xi supporters considered overt religious persecution acceptable.[52]

REENGAGING

An official team from the PRC flew to Rome in June 2014 for secret talks with the Holy See. Parolin was quietly hoping he could pick up where he left off in 2009, but the intervening five years had depleted not only trust but a basic understanding of Catholic ecclesiology. Little progress was made. One friendly gesture encouraged the pope, though: two months later, the Chinese government permitted Francis to use its airspace for his trip to South Korea, the first pope ever given this privilege.[53] As is the custom, he sent a telegram to President Xi while overflying the country, invoking "divine blessings of peace and wellbeing" on China, a bit of protocol, which nevertheless made the pope "very emotional, something that does not usually happen to me."[54]

Francis and Parolin's enthusiasm for dialogue had a positive impact on the perennial question of appointing bishops. Breakthroughs in the summer of 2015 confirmed that the parties were on a new road. A look at two cases makes clear their significance, piecemeal though the problem solving went. Bishop Joseph Martin Wu Qinjing studied in the United States between 2000 and 2005 and was by many accounts a rising star. Pope Benedict appointed Wu to be ordained bishop clandestinely in Shaanxi Province at age thirty-seven.[55]

Two years later, he publicly told his flock he was a bishop, which perturbed local officials. They detained him and kept him in a seminary in Shaanxi, although the faithful were allowed to visit. For eight years, his status remained in limbo. But in July 2015, Wu was appointed bishop of Zhouzhi. He concelebrated with seventy-three priests in a cathedral Mass. To Rome, official acceptance came better late than never.[56]

Then in August, the first jointly approved episcopal consecration in three years was held.[57] Fr. Joseph Zhang Yinlin, forty-four, was made the coadjutor bishop of the Weihui diocese in Henan Province, where the sitting bishop was ninety years old. Before a congregation of twelve hundred people, seventy-five priests concelebrated. An American sociologist and China expert called it "the most important news from a Catholic perspective to come out of China in years" because it meant Chinese authorities under Xi accepted the Holy See's essential role in the all-important task of selecting bishops.[58]

PROVIDENTIAL SCHEDULING: XI WITNESSES PAPAL POWER

Case-by-case resolution of the standing of individual bishops occurred far below the level of China's central power. A trip to the United States put Francis on President Xi Jinping's personal radar, though. In late September 2015, the two leaders were both in the United States for the seventieth anniversary of the UN; they even had White House meetings just forty-eight hours apart—the first time in American history two state visits occurred in the same week.[59] As the Chinese president finished a photo op in Seattle with tech industry titans (where he spoke a little Mandarin with Facebook's Mark Zuckerberg), Xi's handlers postponed takeoff for Washington, DC, because Francis was still there. The capital city's papal lovefest was still in full swing following Francis's congressional address, which had the Speaker of the House of Representatives in tears.[60] (The Chinese embassy had asked if Xi could speak to Congress but was flatly told no.)

The Chinese took note of how Xi was received compared to the pope. Francis was met at the airport by President and Mrs. Obama, for example, while Xi was greeted by Vice President Joseph Biden and his wife.[61] Reporting on Xi's appearance in the White House Rose Garden with President Obama, Reuters described it as a "sideshow" compared to the pontiff, who "firmly overshadowed" the Chinese leader in terms of public enthusiasm and media coverage.[62]

In fact, while Chinese state media played every minute of the president's seventh visit to the United States (his first was in 1985 as an animal-feed official visiting Iowa), television news mentioned Francis twenty-five times more frequently than Xi.[63] The Chinese delegation noticed this recognition differential. "Xi himself saw the real power of the pope. For the first time, the Holy See's soft power was tangible, and astonishing to national political leaders who had given little thought to the Catholic Church," reports Fr. Worthley, who got to know many officials as a public administration professor in China before before being ordained a Catholic priest.[64]

Worthley was also on an unusual—and unofficial—diplomatic assignment during the pope's visit. He accompanied three high-level Beijing-approved bishops "on a holy pilgrimage to seek reconciliation," in the priest's words. Their tour dates, September 15–25, coincided with the pope's visit. Bishop Joseph Ma Yinglin, president of the Chinese Catholic Bishops' Conference (a group unrecognized by the Vatican), was ordained without Rome's permission in April 2006. His two vice presidents (one illicit, the other approved by both the Vatican and the Chinese in 2011) spent ten days making connections—at Yale Divinity School, Seton Hall University, the University of Notre Dame, and Loyola University in Chicago. They even stopped in Hawaii and met with a priest who served as Mother Teresa's chaplain for many years.[65]

The three bishops wrote an inscription to the pope in a Bible, "We love you, we pray for you, we wait for you in China," which was given to Boston's Cardinal Sean O'Malley to pass to the pope himself. The sentiment was yet more evidence that the Communist scheme to create an independent Catholic Church, launched in 1957, had failed.

With the direct exposure of Chinese political and religious officials to Francis in action, the Catholic Church leaped way up on the list of worthwhile interlocutors for the regime. Until then, Rome was considered close to irrelevant, an occasional nuisance, by Beijing's top decision makers. God's diplomats felt their new prestige immediately.

MAJOR CHANGE IN ATTITUDE

Less than a month after the experience of "parallel play" in the United States, the Chinese government offered to host a new round of stealth meetings with Vatican diplomats in Beijing. The Holy See sent a six-person delegation from the Secretariat of State and the Congregation for the Evangelization of Peoples, including the long-serving second section China expert, Msgr. Rota Graziosi. The group met with Bishop Ma, who was rector of Beijing's national seminary besides heading the bishops' conference. Close observers agreed that such a visit was only possible because negotiations were closing in on agreement.

One incident that occurred during the visit demonstrated how progress advances via personal gestures: Archbishop Celli asked to meet with the handful of Beijing-approved bishops, ordained without clearance from Rome. The government set up a meeting in a neutral space—a hotel. As the get-together was ending, Celli suggested they reverence each other's episcopal rings, which they did. As a priest who accompanied the group reported, "Archbishop Celli said, 'We are all brothers,' and he kissed Bishop Ma's ring, and Bishop Ma kissed Celli's ring in return. It was a totally informal, but nonetheless terribly significant, gesture."

Over the next twenty-six months, the Sino-Vatican working group met six times—in January, April, and November 2016 and in March, June, and December 2017—alternating locations between Beijing and Rome.[66]

For Chinese New Year in 2016, Pope Francis sent greetings to President Xi and the Chinese people via an unusual interview with the Asia Times, intended for Western audiences, too.[67] Noting China's "great richness of culture and wisdom," the pope expressed his respect for its people and sympathized with the sacrifices they have made. He counseled the world not to fear China's fast development but to meet the Middle Kingdom in dialogue, his mantra.

> Encounter is achieved through dialogue. The true balance of peace is realized through dialogue. Dialogue does not mean that we end up with a compromise, half the cake for you and the other half for me. This is what happened in Yalta and we saw the results. No, dialogue means: look, we have got to this point, I may or may not agree, but let us walk together; this is what it means to build. And the cake stays whole, walking together.

Hong Kong Cardinal John Tong Hon (Zen's successor, who was part of the quiet bridge building for decades) served as an important supporter of the Vatican's initiatives at this juncture. Writing in an online diocese publication in July 2016, the cardinal offered keys to understanding the nature of shuttle diplomacy between Rome and Beijing. Its religious goal was to restore unity between the universal and the local Church; its pastoral goal was gaining legal protection—and religious freedom—for the clandestine Church; its diplomatic goal was a "mutually acceptable plan" to overcome past discord.[68] In Tong's narrative, discord is the product of misunderstanding. The Chinese government saw Rome's insistence on a role in selecting bishops as invasive and potentially destabilizing, while the Church considers the appointment of bishops a nonpolitical, internal, religious matter.

A GIFT FROM XI

Evidence that the pope and President Xi had gotten much further than any modern pontiff in "walking together" came in October 2016, when Xi sent a gift to Francis through a delegation from the China Biodiversity Conservation and Green Development Foundation attending a Vatican conference on environmental issues. A friend of Xi, who is also the son of a former Communist Party leader, led the delegation, which presented the pope with a nine-foot-long silk drape printed with the image of the Nestorian, or Xi'an, stele, a vertical history of early Christianity in Northwestern China.

Xi'an was located at the start of the Silk Road, and Eastern Christianity spread from the Middle East to this juncture of civilizations. The limestone monument was installed in 781. In Chinese and Syriac language, it tells the 150-year story of Christians living in the area, including references to key theological concepts such as baptism, the Trinity, and the incarnation.

What's most important about the gift is what it says about Xi's perception of Christianity as being part of traditional China with a history that predates modern missionaries—foreign missionaries being a negative and exploitative force in the eyes of the Communist Party.[69] For Xi, whose watchword is the term "Sinicization" (filtering all influences, especially religion, through Chinese dogma), the stele was welcome evidence that he sees Christianity as having an indisputable historic place in China's domestic culture. Even Buddhism, for that matter, originally came to China from India.

Certainly, the archaeological replica was a green light from Xi to the pope to proceed with the painstaking negotiations over formalizing a role for Rome in the process of selecting bishops for the Church in China. Both men have hard-liners in their decision-making circles, discouraging reconciliation, but the path has been, in the main, toward agreement since 2014.

SMALL STEPS . . . AND MORE JOINT BISHOPS

Three months later, in Beijing, the Ninth National Assembly of Chinese Catholic Representatives met, the first gathering of the organization since 2010. Instead of telling bishops not to attend, as the Vatican did under Benedict XVI, the Holy See let the bishops handle the situation on their own.[70] The reality by then was that both the Vatican and the regime had jointly approved the vast majority of bishops: of approximately 110 bishops in China, about 70 were jointly approved by Rome and Beijing, some 30 were solely endorsed by the Holy See, and the rest were state-appointed bishops, unapproved by Rome.

The assembly reaffirmed Bishop Ma as president of the bishops' conference —illicit, but as we have seen, almost openly devoted to Rome. This was a surprise because Ma expected to be replaced. To lead the CCPA, Bishop Johan Fang Xinyao of Linyi (Shandong Province) was reelected; he was ordained in 1997 with papal approval. So, the status quo was maintained with the patriotic bureaucrats.[71]

Just before the assembly, three jointly approved episcopal ordinations were held—two on November 30, in Chengdu diocese (Sichuan Province) and Ankang diocese (Shaanxi Province); the other in Xichang diocese (Sichuan Province) on December 2. The Chengdu celebration was marred by the presence of an illicit bishop, Paul Lei Shiyin, but, interestingly, he did not concelebrate, perhaps because congregants tried to prevent his participation, holding up banners in front of the church warning of his excommunication.[72] He also showed up in Xichang, where the last bishop had died—seventeen years before! This diocese exemplified the problem of leaving prelate posts vacant: with thirty-five thousand Catholics, eleven churches, six active chapels, ten priests, twenty-five nuns, and a leper colony, Xichang really needed a bishop.[73] Cardinal Parolin's negotiating team finally got one.

TRIAL BALLOONS, BACKLASH, AND REGIONAL REALITY, 2017 AND 2018

By late January 2017, the Holy See was confident enough about progress that it gave Cardinal Tong another text, walking through the logic of a Sino-Vatican agreement. It was written to explain Rome's perspective, while serving as a trial balloon, invariably attracting darts, that would show Beijing the parameters even a monarch must abide by.

On January 25, the Feast of the Conversion of St. Paul the Apostle, Tong announced in the *Hong Kong Sunday Examiner*, a weekly English-language publication, that Beijing and Rome had "already reached consensus" on episcopal appointments.[74] In length, style, and rhetorical subtlety, the text is so different from Tong's typically direct approach that most of his colleagues assume Vatican diplomats penned it. According to Tong, Chinese bishops would recommend episcopal candidates, and the pope would have a "right of veto."

International media coverage magnified Tong's little online essay. The *South China Morning Post* headline declared, "Vatican and Beijing Near Deal on Bishops, Hong Kong Bishop Says." But Cardinal Zen, Tong's predecessor as bishop of Hong Kong, had gotten the jump on Tong's argument and already issued a scathing opposing view through the *Wall Street Journal*. In an interview titled "The Vatican's Illusions about Chinese Communism,"[75] Zen accused Pope Francis of being naive about Beijing, a criminal regime in the cardinal's eyes.

Yet in China empirical reality kept demonstrating how critical it was to get the ecclesial house in order. CNN circulated a story about persecution of the underground Church featuring Paul Dong, an excommunicated priest who self-ordained himself bishop.[76] CNN portrayed him sympathetically, posing him as a counterpoint to an open-church priest who in fact was approved by both church and state. What upset the curia most was something clear in the film: scores of faithful kneeling in prayer in Dong's yard. The biggest sin of the general confusion in China is that it risks misleading believers themselves.

CASE BY CASE: DIPLOMATIC ENDGAME

Having agreed in principle on a consultative process for selecting bishops, which, importantly, gave the Holy See veto power if the pope felt the candidate was unfit to lead, negotiations in late 2017 pivoted to a new phase: working through solutions for eight individual cases—illicit bishops who had written to the pope requesting pardon and approval. The stickiest cases were two dioceses where an official Church bishop and an underground bishop coexisted.

In the diocese of Shantou (Guangdong Province), the Holy See was prepared to recognize patriotic bishop Joseph Huang Bingzhang, a member of the National People's Congress, excommunicated in 2011 for being ordained without papal approval. So Rome sent a letter to underground Bishop Peter Zhuang Jianjian asking him to retire, since, at age eighty-eight, he was thirteen years past the age at which bishops are required under canon law to submit their resignations.[77] Zhuang, ordained secretly in 2006, refused to step down—a highly irregular and canonically verboten decision. At the next round of negotiations in December, Archbishop Celli summoned Bishop Zhuang to Beijing to explain the rules and request his resignation in person.[78]

A trickier situation faced the Church in the diocese of Mindong (Fujian Province), where the underground Church community, with some fifty priests, two hundred women religious, and scores of lay catechists, is more powerful and far more historically rooted than the official one. The faith was introduced in Mindong in the late sixteenth century. Bishop Guo Xijin was coadjutor bishop for eight years, credited with helping to build a particularly dynamic community.[79] He took over as full bishop when his predecessor died in 2016. Guo was regularly harassed by officials. Just before Easter 2017, he was arrested and forced into twenty days of reeducation, then released to a relieved congregation. He also logged jail time in 1990–1992, 1993–1994, and 1996.[80]

In the same diocese, patriotic Bishop Vincent Zhan Silu, age fifty-seven, was illicitly ordained in 2006.[81] Despite having a flock about one-tenth the size of the unregistered Church, Zhan Silu gained local permission to build a new cathedral facing the sea. In December 2017, Archbishop Celli asked

Guo to accept a demotion to serve as auxiliary bishop under Zhan Silu, who would become the jointly approved bishop of the diocese under a new agreement being finalized. Told the request came from the pope himself on behalf of the universal Church (but also told these were not orders or instructions), Guo agreed.[82]

Meanwhile, the two mainstays of the official Church community, the patriotic association and bishops' conference, were convinced that rapprochement between Rome and Beijing was supported at the highest level. During the October Communist Party Congress, when President Xi was awarded a second five-year term, he very publicly walked up to bishops' conference president Joseph Ma Yinglin, dressed in full clerical garb, and shook his hand. Ma read that as a sign of approval for the reconciliation effort. "It was not a random gesture. When it happened, Ma felt that the agreement was set, and he was delighted that after so many years, he would be approved," said his friend, Fr. Worthley.

When word of Rome's requests to Zhuang and Guo—strong evidence of an endgame—began circulating in the Catholic press in January 2018, a backlash quickly developed, led by the stalwart enemy of negotiations with Beijing, Cardinal Zen. He obtained a letter from the "old, distressed" Bishop Zhuang and flew to Rome to hand deliver it to Francis. The pope accepted it at a standard Wednesday general meeting (not in a private audience) and told the Hong Konger, in a private meeting two days later, that he does not want to create another "Mindszenty case."[83]

Cardinal Parolin defended the Holy See in *La Stampa*. Explaining the Church's objectives as consistent for over thirty years, he said the overarching goal is unity for all Chinese Catholics so they can practice the faith peacefully and evangelize the world.

He reproved those who interpret the Church's actions politically, cautioning that words such as "surrender" and "sabotage" are not appropriate when the pastoral reality aligns with "forgiveness" and "mercy." Parolin said the Church proceeds through "trust in the Lord who guides history," not faith in negotiations per se, and believes Chinese Catholics "will know how to recognize that the action of the Holy See is animated by this trust, which does not respond to worldly logic."[84]

Pope Francis addressed Zen's accusations head on with the understanding of a friend. He told Reuters,

> Cardinal Zen taught theology in patriotic seminaries. I think he's a little scared. Perhaps age might have some influence. He is a good man. He came to talk to me. I received him, but he's a bit scared. Dialogue is a risk, but I prefer the risk to the sure defeat of not talking. With respect to time, someone mentioned Chinese time. I think it is God's time, forward, calm.[85]

Historically, in every country where the Holy See has felt compelled to compromise with authoritarian regimes, there have also been local leaders who refuse to stand down from the truth of oppression. Hungarian Cardinal József Mindszenty, Ukrainian Major Archbishop Josyf Slipyj, Czech Cardinal Josef Beran, and Cuban Archbishop Oves Fernández are among those who heroically embodied and cried out on behalf of persecuted believers. The Holy See did not suppress their views. Cardinal Zen is in this line of prophetic voices, whose job is not diplomacy.

I met Cardinal Zen in the sanctuary of St. Jude's Church in Hong Kong after he gave a second-year memorial Mass for a Chinese priest found mysteriously drowned in 2015. That popular forty-year-old priest was on his way to a catechetical meeting by train when he disappeared. When officials notified his family that his body was found in the Fen River, they claimed the priest killed himself. But no one in the Catholic community believed that priest would commit suicide.[86]

"You . . . can . . . not . . . trust . . . them!" Zen hissed quietly in my ear, drawing out the words. Would the octogenarian follow the Holy See if it signed an agreement? "Of course. I'm a priest," he said quickly, adding, "and I won't ask the underground to disobey the pope or criticize an agreement, if there is one."[87] Yet Zen is the most outspoken enemy of reconciliation in the hierarchy.[88]

In blunt contradiction to Cardinal Zen stand his two successors as Hong Kong bishop. Cardinal Tong, seven years Zen's junior, was a discreet and trusted envoy to China and North Korea on behalf of three popes. Tong's successor, Bishop Michael Yeung Ming-cheung, told me that Hong Kong, and its five hundred thousand Catholics, are "a bridge between Chinese authorities and the Holy See."[89] When Yeung died of liver failure in 2019, Francis asked Tong to leave retirement and serve as Hong Kong's apostolic administrator, a decision that shocked even Tong because it appeared to block the appointment of an auxiliary bishop critical of the Chinese government.[90]

SO CLOSE AND YET SO FAR . . .

In February 2018, the Holy See and the Chinese Foreign Affairs Ministry agreed to sign a provisional agreement laying out a process for selecting Chinese bishops that enshrined a consultative process. In exchange, the Holy See accepted seven illicit bishops as legitimate, with sole responsibility for governing their episcopal jurisdictions, and welcomed a bishop back into the fold retroactively, because when he died, during the negotiations, he "expressed the desire to be reconciled with the Apostolic See," the Vatican said.[91]

The deal opened a door for ongoing negotiations to continue untying other knots. The document was set for signatures the first week of April, the week following Easter, at the Urbaniana, the Pontifical Urban University under the authority of the Congregation for the Evangelization of Peoples. Rome was the next location in the rotation of meeting places because the working group had met in Beijing in December.

Confirmation of an imminent agreement came mainly from Chinese officials. Bishop Guo Jincai, secretary general of the bishops' conference, told the *Global Times* the deal was in its "final stages."[92] Bishop Peter Fang Jianping, a member of the National People's Congress, made an unusual statement on Chinese TV endorsing the relationship between Beijing and Rome. *Sing Tao Daily* reported Bishop Vincent Zhan Silu saying there were "no obstacles," especially if the focus was on peace.[93]

Then Mindong diocese provided a tripwire just three days before Easter: Bishop Guo celebrated an early-morning Chrism Mass on Holy Thursday, a special liturgy with ancient roots. Three holy oils used throughout the year are blessed by the bishop and priests in a Mass that signifies the unity that joins priests with their bishop in every diocese. Local officials were angry that Guo did not celebrate the Mass with Bishop Zhan Silu, but in Guo's view, the agreement was not yet signed when Holy Thursday arrived, so his obligation was to bless the oils.[94]

Cold feet in Rome also undercut the signing ceremony. Local officials in several provinces said they would begin enforcing a ban on church attendance for children that stemmed from the separation between religion and education.[95] Priests in Hebei Province were told to post signs prohibiting minors from entering.[96] The Vatican was displeased with such an offensive development. Both sides hesitated, and the signing ceremony was canceled. Pope Francis respected the assessment of his collaborators, but he asked them to press on, to keep meeting, and to find ways to maintain dialogue. In this spirit, Bishops Guo and Silo had dinner together to iron out misunderstandings.[97]

RIPE FRUIT

A Chinese diplomat, an éminence grise, said Pope Francis is the most "Zen" Western leader. "Time does not hurry him," said the astute observer of the bilateral relationship. What has gotten Rome and Beijing so close is patience, respect, discretion, and mature judgment. "John Paul II was never trusted because he was the anti-Communist who helped destroy the Soviet Empire, although we consider he saved the Castros. Pope Benedict's team became dominated by ideologues. Under Pope Francis, we see real diplomacy," said the admirer.

In diplomatic theory there is an idea of "ripeness," which means what it says: "Substantive answers are fruitless until the moment is ripe," writes I. William Zartman, a renowned theorist of negotiation.[98] Between 2016 and 2018, the relationship between the Holy See and China fit Zartman's definitional requirements for a conflict approaching ripeness. The two parties first perceive themselves as suffering and, second, perceive the possibility of a bargain. Suffering for the Chinese government related to its inability to control the Catholic community unless it acknowledged a role for the pope. For the Holy See, suffering was tied to its inability to govern the vast community of Chinese Catholics unless the pope tolerated the intervention of civil administrative units in Church life.

And suddenly, the fruit was ripe. After numerous false starts and disappointments, on September 22, 2018, Msgr. Antoine Camilleri, fifty-three, undersecretary for relations with states (an *Accademia* graduate from Malta), and Deputy Foreign Minister Wang Chao, fifty-eight,[99] born in Hebei Province,[100] sat at a standard wooden conference table on a warm day in Beijing's swank Chaoyang District and signed a provisional agreement. It structured the collaborative selection of Catholic bishops, lifted the excommunication of seven sitting bishops, and created a new diocese in China, the first step in updating the Church's territorial organization.[101]

Geopolitical circumstances can flip fast, and they do. Regarding Beijing, in late March 2018, grown men in the curia were apoplectic, fearing that the long-sought deal would slip away once again. Pope Francis never doubted his discernment that God wills harmony between Beijing and Rome, nor did he doubt the capability of God's diplomats, some having worked on this puzzle since the 1980s.

The *New York Times* recognized the provisional agreement as "a historic breakthrough after 70 years of icy relations," although it was anticlimactic considering how many times it had been anticipated.[102] What can't be underestimated is this: the agreement meant the Chinese government recognized that the Catholic Church's true spiritual and administrative center is the Holy See; that authentic Catholic bishops are joined to Jesus Christ in an apostolic succession guaranteed by the pope; and that without his blessing, there *is* no bishop with the authority required by the faithful and the universal Church. Mao Zedong's version of Catholicism was sidestepped. For the first time in postwar history, all Chinese bishops were united with the Holy See.

Jesuit missionaries in 1692 convinced the Chinese emperor that Catholic teaching was "compatible with other teachings that sustained imperial rule."[103] The first Jesuit pope has done the same—convinced a twenty-first-century emperor that Catholicism is compatible with his vision of empire restored. Whether the legion of provincial officials will let the Catholic Church thrive is a different question.

On the papal flight from Estonia to Rome, Francis was asked how he responded to Cardinal Zen's perennial accusation that the Vatican "sold out" the underground Church to the Chinese government. Without mentioning Zen or breaking down the logistics, the pope assured the captive audience how aware he is of the great suffering of so many Chinese Catholics. At the same time, he alluded to communication with Chinese Catholics: "They have great faith and they write, they send messages, affirming that what the Holy See says, what Peter says, is what Jesus says," meaning Catholics in China trust the pope even if some of his own cardinals do not.

He also assured journalists that with regard to the selection of bishops, he has primacy: "[I]t is a dialogue about potential candidates. The matter is carried out through dialogue. But the appointment is by Rome; the appointment is by the Pope. This is clear." The pontiff singled out for thanks three diplomats: Archbishop Celli, Msgr. Rota Graziosi, and Cardinal Parolin.[104] As in classic diplomatic practice, patience, humility, and deep knowledge won the day.

For the pope, passing through one door yields the prospect of new passages. He immediately invited two Chinese bishops to attend the Synod of Bishops on Youth—the first prelates from the PRC ever to participate in a Holy See synod. "Pope Francis, who knows very well the situation of the Catholic Church in China, did not want to leave us, did not want to separate us from the Universal Church," observed Bishop John Baptist Yang, one of the Chinese participants. "In the love of Christ, in the love of God, we are always one family; the universal Church is always like a family. Even if we live in different countries and even if there is diversity between our cultures, liturgies and other things, our faith in the Lord is always one."[105]

On the plane of spiritual unity, the picture in China is a net gain. But the picture on the ground remains muddy as overzealous local authorities try to intimidate some underground priests into signing a registration document many still find compromising because it refers to an "independent" Church. It is as though, having found resolution to the status of bishops in 2018, the church-state tension that emerged in 2019 concerned the status of hundreds of priests.

The Holy See issued "pastoral guidelines" for Chinese bishops and clergy in June 2019. Although the Vatican clearly outlined reasons priests should feel comfortable registering—the Chinese constitution provides religious liberty; the government now recognizes Rome's essential role; "independence" can be read politically, not ecclesiastically; and everywhere in the world, civil authorities are concerned about the political independence of local organizations—it also explicitly states that "the Holy See does not intend to force anyone's conscience."[106]

The guidance offered a course of action for priests who feel their faith is "disrespected" by the process: they should write a short statement confirming that the signer remains faithful to Catholic doctrine. If a written statement is not possible, a verbal statement with a witness present can be made.[107] Meanwhile, the Vatican promised to keep negotiating for a registration format that balances the pursuit of social order with freedom of conscience. Regarding bishops, the yield has been a bit disappointing: a handful of new bishops were ordained following the breakthrough pact, despite about one-third of China's ninety-eight dioceses requiring appointments.[108]

In October 2020, the Vatican-China agreement was renewed. Francis is looking to expand the relationship in order to further normalize it and create more channels for the resolution of friction. Sources in the curia say his objective is full diplomatic relations with China, one of the few countries with which the Vatican does not have formal ties. Steps toward that goal were taken publicly when, for the first time, Chinese foreign minister Wang Yi and Archbishop Gallagher met on the sidelines of the Munich Security Conference in February 2020.[109]

Reuters described the meeting as "rare," which is true. So is this astonishingly simple fact stated in the short article: "Both sides now recognize the pope as the supreme leader of the Catholic Church." Pope Francis certainly deserves credit for *that* epic breakthrough.

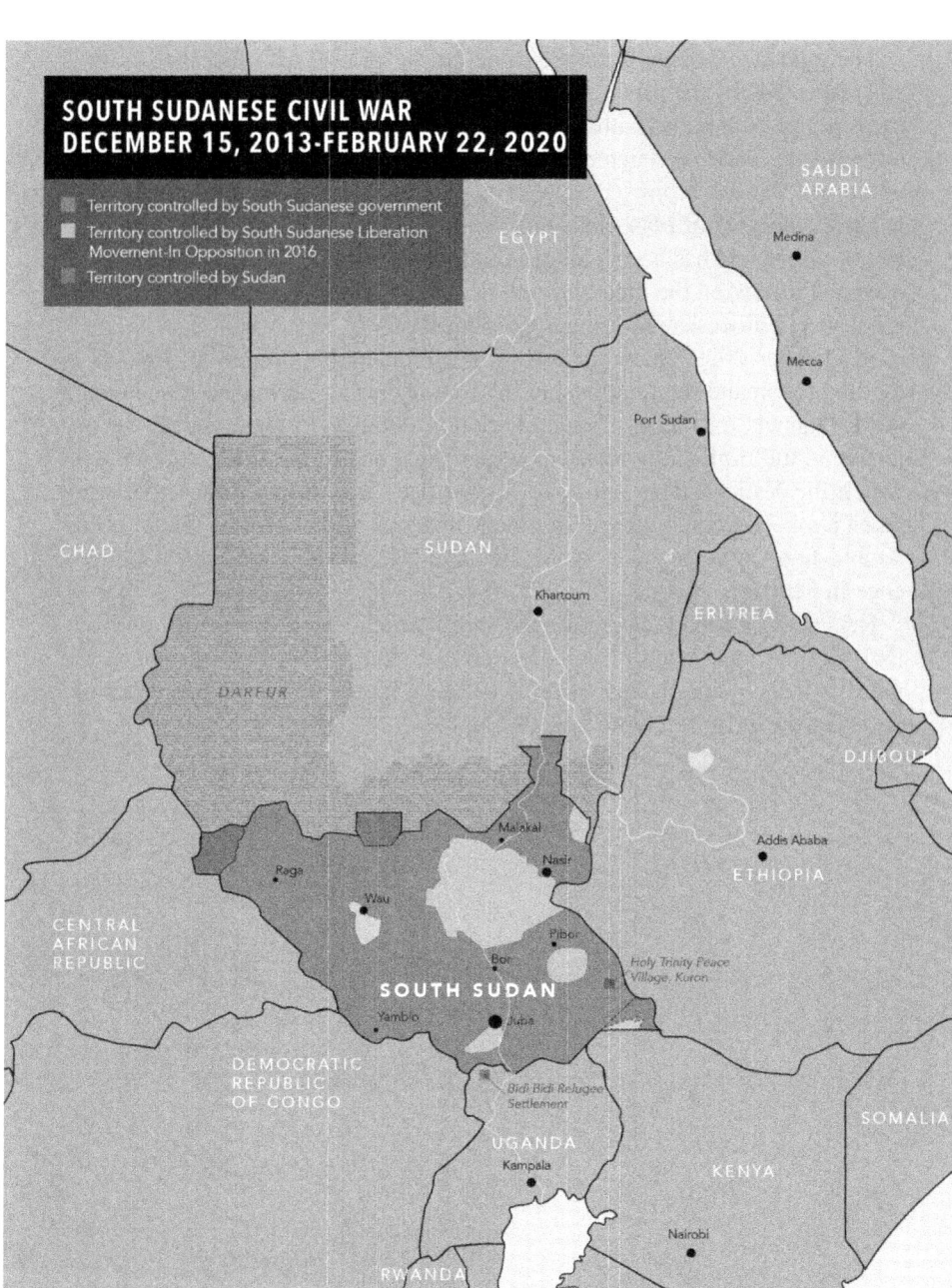

12

Piercing Gestures
South Sudan

> The whole world was shocked when His Holiness knell [*sic*] down to kiss our feet. I was personally shocked and deeply touched and of course I trembled. We thank his Holiness for what was truly a piercing experience to the soul, the mind, and the heart.
>
> —Salva Kiir Mayardit, President of South Sudan,
> Easter Statement to the Nation, April 21, 2019[1]

It takes optimism beyond measure—or faith in God—to imagine that South Sudan could achieve peace under its exasperating leaders. Just two years after independence, the newest country on earth descended into brutal civil war in December 2013. The two men who formed the country's first government . . . torched it. They reconciled, then reneged. A former US official called South Sudan's two main political protagonists, President Salva Kiir and First Vice President Riek Machar, "irredeemably compromised."[2] Kiir is a Dinka, the country's largest ethnic group, while Machar is from the second-largest community, the Nuer. Their personal rivalry mutated into ethnic-based violence that spread destruction across the perilously poor country between 2013 and 2018. Despite a cease-fire, the country teetered on a churning miasma of irrational hatred, contained by hundreds of UN troops and humanitarians of many sorts, including Catholic religious.

Yet there was Kiir, suited up for an official visit at the Holy See on March 16, 2019—which amounted to a consult with his spiritual leader, since the Big Man is a churchgoing Catholic.[3] Francis first met the former army commander for a fifteen-minute meeting in Kampala, arranged by the president of Uganda during Francis's 2015 maiden pilgrimage to the continent. Soon after that exchange, the pope started talking about adding South Sudan to his next African itinerary. He was disappointed that papal security specialists kept knocking the idea off the table as too dangerous.

During his trip to Rome, Kiir appealed to the Vatican for help, a request deemed sincere. One bit of evidence was that he came hatless to the Apostolic Palace, despite rarely appearing in public without a black Stetson on his head.[4] In fact, the pope had been following South Sudan's trajectory closely since taking office. When Kiir admitted that a peace process facilitated by the Intergovernmental Authority on Development (IGAD), an East African regional group, was stuck, Francis seized the moment. A practitioner of "strike while the iron is hot," Francis sent his number-two diplomatic adviser to South Sudan to follow up less than a week later.

Archbishop Paul Gallagher, secretary for relations with states, was sent to Juba, the young nation's capital city, with a five-day pass. His task was to canvass the country's active Catholic community, meet key ecumenical allies, and touch base with the UN's sizable peacekeeping force. Roving Vatican diplomats have a two-part job: first, assess what is happening in a country and, second, help the pope decide on the best response, one coherent with Catholic teachings, a direction that advances the common good—meaning for all people, not just believers.[5] Gallagher also had a secret mission component: to weigh the value of a spiritual retreat for the country's top leadership to take place in Rome a month later, just before Easter.

Arriving in Juba, Gallagher was reminded of his longest assignment as a papal nuncio: six years in Burundi, which, like South Sudan, is a Christian-majority country in East Africa where Catholics comprise the largest faith group. In both places, the Church is close to the people and is thus frustrated with the lack of progress and the lack of priority given by the government to people's basic needs. The diplomat knew he would hear complaints from his brother bishops about the time it was taking for the regime to get its act together.

South Sudan's bishops had recently written an open letter expressing concern about the government's competence to implement the peace plan it signed in 2018: "Politics alone will not resolve the conflicts in South Sudan. While many ordinary people long for peace, there is no will or commitment for peace amongst many of our leaders, hate speech and propaganda abound, and there is a thirst for revenge amongst many of our communities. What is needed is conversion, a change of heart, amongst individuals and communities. . . . Only then will the political efforts bear fruit."[6] For Christians, "change of heart" is not just a figure of speech but a moment of dramatic transformation in the lives the Church most admires. Moses had a change of heart, inspired by a burning bush. St. Paul's change of heart came on the road to Damascus. St. Ignatius of Loyola had one while recovering from a cannonball wound. Trust in the possibility of conversion is at the heart of Pope Francis's diplomacy in South Sudan.

SERVING THE POOR, THAT IS, MOST OF THE NATION

Evidence of government failure was as clear to a discerning visitor as evidence of a persevering Church.[7] The civil war propelled an already poor country to the very bottom of global wellness: one in seven women died in childbirth, 73 percent of adults could not read or write, and 80 percent lived on less than one dollar a day.[8] Hardly a drop of the nation's oil wealth trickled down to its citizens. Having fought for decades to free the South from the North's grip, the new government failed to pivot to institution building and service delivery. International organizations and faith-based organizations picked up the slack.

Although there are not as many today as in the mid-twentieth century, Catholic missionaries are active in key fields, especially education, health care, and agricultural development. Facing the vast range of needs, men and women religious from some thirty congregations invented a new way to serve in South Sudan. They collaborate across religious orders and concentrate their most intensive programs on training teachers, health care workers, and midwives. Ten years ago, Solidarity with South Sudan opened a teacher training college in Yambio and the Catholic Health Training Institute in Wau, far from the capital.[9] A few years earlier, Catholic priests founded the Catholic University of South Sudan at the request of the Sudanese bishops' conference. The university has over 1,800 students enrolled.[10] Throughout the war, it was the only university that stayed open for graduate students, according to its Washington, DC–based patron, the South Sudan Relief Fund.[11]

A special focus of Catholic efforts is the status of women and girls. An encouraging example is a school educating children from kindergarten through high school, ages five through twenty, run by the Irish Sisters of Loreto, the order that first sent Mother Teresa to India. Founded in 2006, the Loreto Rumbeck School has over 250 girls enrolled in secondary school. It integrates girls from different ethnic groups and from across the country to undermine the conflict that has torn South Sudan apart. (The Irish principal, Sister Orla Treacy, speaks Dinka.) What might seem unremarkable in the West is pathbreaking in a country where over 50 percent of girls are married by age eighteen. Parents must sign an agreement not to remove high schoolers from school for marriage proposals. The school recently grew to include a primary school serving six hundred youngsters and a medical clinic. Local leaders requested both resources.[12]

Another focal point for women and men religious are displaced people at refugee centers known as Protection of Civilians (POC) camps, guarded by UN peacekeepers. Two million South Sudanese fled violence and landed in neighboring countries, while another two million found relative safety in-country. Most are still afraid to return home, where whole villages were set on fire in frenzied mayhem during the war. The majority of refugees are women and children; two-thirds are under age eighteen. A variety of Church funding streams support these efforts, including Caritas Internationalis, Aid to the Church in Need (a papal charity), Jesuit Relief Services, and country-specific groups such as the Baltimore-based Catholic Relief Services (CRS). Since it started in 1983, for example, CRS estimated it had helped 1.4 million people in South Sudan by 2019.[13]

Although Francis prioritizes diplomacy, he expects bishops to remain close to the ground, oriented toward the people. For example, the pope met with all the bishops of Sudan and South Sudan in September 2018 for an *ad limina* visit. Politics was on the agenda, but Francis's main message was to stay focused on the flock, especially the most marginalized. He even recommended a field trip, suggesting that the bishops visit a refugee camp for a few days. So they did. A month after their return from Rome, the bishops traveled to the Bidi Bidi Refugee Settlement in Uganda, on South Sudan's border. A quarter million displaced Sudanese have created a city where, just five years ago, barren grassland grew. The bishops remained for six days and "wiped many tears" from their eyes, according to Bishop Edward Hiiboro Kussala, president of the conference.[14]

SHARED SACRIFICE

Religious leaders suffered alongside the people, from the first weeks of civil war. In the city of Malakal, civilians fled rampaging rebels, taking refuge in the biggest structures, churches. The Catholic cathedral harbored 6,500 people until uniformed goons pulled guns on the clergy, causing all to flee.[15] The entire city, once the country's second largest, has been decimated as authority changed hands twelve times across the course of the conflict. As the gateway to oil fields discovered in 1978, Malakal was a symbol of power. By late 2015, the BBC described it as "the city that vanished in South Sudan."[16]

Random destruction of entire communities was routine. Rebels who controlled the town of Leer starting looting and burning it as government troops moved in. Town residents, including Comboni missionaries, fled to the bush, where they spent several weeks avoiding mercenaries. Together with civilians, the priests hid in swamps populated by crocodiles and hippos. When the ashes settled, most of the mission compound of buildings, residences, and schools had been looted or destroyed. Vehicles were stolen or burned, although the chapel was undamaged. After suspending operations for six months, the religious men rebuilt, only to be attacked again a year later.

Asked why they remained as the region descended into violence, one of the priests explained, "We thought that our presence around Leer would somehow inhibit atrocities and harm towards innocent civilians."[17] Founded in 1867 by Italian Daniele Comboni, the first Catholic bishop of Central Africa, the Comboni Missionaries and an order for women, Comboni Missionary Sisters, did much to spread Christianity in Sudan based on the founder's vision of "Africans saving Africa," typically through indigenous education.[18]

Anglican Archbishop Justin Welby of Canterbury visited Bor, South Sudan, in January 2014, just weeks after a massacre there. He recalled with distress:

> At the cathedral, we found bodies of clergy, lay leaders, and others who had fled there. . . . We stood with the bodies at our feet and the smell of death around us and we prayed. The shock of so much destruction. 6,000 dead, maybe more, half of them buried. . . . All the women raped, the most atrocious sexual violence, was very overwhelming, very desperate. Shocking not just for us coming from . . . places where we didn't see that kind of stuff very often, but even for the South Sudanese, who have seen much suffering. We must be battering at the gates of Heaven in prayer. Remorseless, unceasing prayer . . . against human evil.[19]

What mitigated despair for the British primate was witnessing the faithful springing to action, helping people abandoned by the state. He described the centrality of the Episcopalian Church in building bridges and leading reconciliation. What he said applied to all Christians: "Churches are mobilizing against despair and violence."[20]

LEGITIMACY AND INFLUENCE

Shared sacrifice helps explain the respect for religious leaders demonstrated in a 2019 report sponsored by the US Institute of Peace. "The Religious Landscape in South Sudan: Challenges and Opportunities for Engagement" explores South Sudanese perceptions of religion in light of the country's major problems. It investigates how to break out of the brutal stalemate that quieted the guns in 2018 but failed to bring necessary stability after. Based on extensive polling of Christians and nonbelievers in four locations, the assessment found that 72 percent of participants considered politics and corruption the drivers of conflict, while 21 percent blamed ethnicity. In a slightly different question, a whopping 88 percent said political actors caused the war, and only 17 percent saw "a certain ethnic group" behind national strife.[21]

The poll's most spellbinding results pertain to legitimacy and influence. Regarding who respondents turn to for guidance besides family and friends, 82 percent said religious leaders, while the next highest category was elders (10 percent). On a scale of importance to the peace process, religious actors and institutions were described as very important (83 percent) or important (16 percent)—near-unanimous affirmation.[22] Regarding specific institutions, the Catholic and Episcopal Churches were singled out in each location, with the Catholic Church attracting the most votes because participants mentioned the greatest number of its bishops by name: Juba Archbishop Paulino Lokudu Loro, who held the post for thirty-six long years (1983–2019); Bishop Emeritus Paride Taban, founder of the ecumenical New Sudan Council of Churches in 1990; and the youngest prelate mentioned by name, Bishop Hiiboro Kussala.

Regarding various Christian leaders, participants had specific examples of what gave them legitimacy, based on actions during the long conflict: efforts to mediate peace among combatants, risks taken to travel in dangerous territory, long presence with the people, delivering food, and willingness to challenge corruption and indifference among political leadership. As the report concluded, the legitimacy of religious actors is tied to their advocacy for peace.

Archbishop Lokudu was credited with continued presence among the people, negotiating the release of prisoners, participating in a national dialogue, and because "He always preaches a message of love, unity, and reconciliation."[23] Bishop Paride Taban shuttled between rebels and the government for about a year in order to negotiate a cease-fire in 2014 and was awarded a peace prize from the UN for "unique contributions" in 2013.[24] In 2019, Bishop Hiiboro Kussala was still engaged in the dangerous business of negotiating for the release of child soldiers, with assistance from the Catholic Medical Mission Board and multilateral organizations.[25]

What constrains the more effective participation of religious actors, concluded the author, is the risk of negative attention—detention, retribution—from unsympathetic local hoodlums, as well as a sense among clergy that to be politically engaged could mean losing influence among believers because the political sphere is so thoroughly discredited.

EXTERNAL INFLUENCE

Politics is inscrutable in part because local politicians are thoroughly enmeshed in intrigue sponsored by regional and international actors. In 2019, celebrity activist George Clooney released "The Taking of South Sudan," an analysis of corrupt business interests behind the country's destruction. The report described a "kleptocracy" governing the country, enabled by foreign businesses. One example involved Salva Kiir's twenty-year-old daughter Winnie, who obtained mining licenses with three Chinese investors. Six weeks later, thousands of innocent residents were brutally cleared from the permitted land through violence, including mass rape.[26] Clooney and his Africa-focused investigative group, the Sentry, called on Western governments and banks to use financial pressure against implicated businesses, describing the strategy as "a much more effective tool than trying to shame a warlord."[27]

Israeli lawyer Eitay Mack offers a chilling account of the origins of the civil war sparked in Juba in December 2013. He explained to me that Christian rebels based in the south, fighting for greater autonomy from Arab-controlled Khartoum, received support from Israeli intelligence, the Mossad, beginning in the 1960s.[28] Mack is an Israeli human rights activist who filed a series of petitions with the Israeli Supreme Court to prevent its military and intelligence services from committing "crimes against humanity."[29]

With the United States, Israel promoted independence for South Sudan, which it gained in 2011. But as Mack points out, "the people who established the government were never united. They had their own conflicts from the beginning." These rivalries intensified, and in late 2013, Israel "transferred a huge amount of automatic rifles to the private farm of Salva Kiir." The president's loyalists were trained with weapons that they turned on Riek Machar's allies soon after.[30]

Surveillance equipment for the country's lawless National Security Service[31] was also transferred to South Sudan through routes arranged by Mossad, says Mack. What motivated Israel to get so deeply involved in this dirt-poor county's misfortunes? "Because Bashir's Islamic government [in Sudan][32] was so anti-Israel," replied Mack. Later, Israel used Ugandan troops ordered into South Sudan to help Salva Kiir as a cover for ongoing arms transfers, according to the activist.

The upshot is this: From the start, South Sudan's shocking slaughter was cast as being fueled by ethnic conflict. Certainly, massacres that spread across the country were often acted out by one ethnic group against another. However, the country's civil war was also a case of geopolitics and regional power struggles contrived as tribal warfare, according to close observers. As Missionary of Africa Fr. Jim Greene, executive director of Solidarity with South Sudan, says, "A lot of the story is about oil and the control of it." The Irish missionary also summarized the importance of the regional power struggle:

"Sudan and Uganda are the two big regional players, and if they are interested in having peace, there will be peace."[33]

Or as the conference of Catholic bishops' incisive adviser, John Ashworth, explained, "South Sudan became a pawn" regarding the issues that Uganda, Ethiopia, Kenya, Sudan, and major powers beyond "have with each other."[34]

BACK TO GALLAGHER

On his exploratory mission to Juba, Archbishop Gallagher performed some standard ceremonies with the faithful, such as laying a foundation stone for a new Institute for Justice and Peace Studies at the Catholic University of South Sudan, accompanied by the Nairobi-based nuncio to Kenya and South Sudan.[35] But the Church had no illusions about going it alone. Gallagher had to visit Juba in person because so many actors are required to orchestrate reconciliation. As we saw in chapter 9 on Colombia, international NGOs and UN peacekeepers are as much stakeholders in the efforts' success as dysfunctional government ministries. So are faith leaders of every stripe.

What Francis believes strongly—and strategically—is that local religious groups are critical accountability partners when it comes to war and peace. They can help government do the right thing while holding political leaders accountable. The pope prioritizes interfaith and ecumenical relationships in every diplomatic effort. His vision of what steps to take in South Sudan were no exception.

In stark contrast to politicians, South Sudanese faith leaders are unusually united. So collaborative are Christians across formal structures, Bishop Hiiboro is said to coordinate schedules with his Episcopalian colleague in the same region so they are not both out of the country at the same time.[36] The South Sudan Council of Churches (SSCC) brings together seven faith groups, including Catholics, Episcopalians, Pentecostals, and Presbyterians.[37] It is organized down to the regional level; a major role for it has been serving as a guide and adviser to international relief organizations trying to figure out how to deliver help.[38]

Early in 2016, Pope Francis wanted to invite President Kiir and Vice President Machar to facilitate progress toward peace. But the year shaped up to be a giant failure for reconciliation when Machar returned to Juba to join a new unity government but fled the country months later. It seems the Vatican could not find the former rebel leader in order to give him an invitation to Rome.[39] Instead the Holy See invited a delegation from the SSCC to brief the pontiff. They arrived in late October 2016 and pressed Francis to help broker peace between Kiir and Machar. According to *La Stampa*, Episcopalian

Archbishop Daniel Deng Bul Yak said a joint visit by the pope and Deng's spiritual leader, British Archbishop Welby, would advance the peace process significantly.[40] Underscoring the precarious tensions back home, that same week, the UN High Commissioner for Human Rights publicly announced his fear that escalating hate speech targeting specific ethnic groups had the power to "result in mass atrocities if not reined in by community and political leaders at the highest levels."[41]

PREACHING TO THE BIG MAN

While his main goal was to size up the potential impact of a Vatican-sponsored VIP retreat by consulting with the many actors who would be part of an unfolding peace strategy, Gallagher also wanted to see President Kiir in his home element.

A tactic sometimes employed by God's diplomats when dealing with Catholic interlocutors is, naturally, to use religious language to activate a deeper level of engagement—and possibly more meaningful commitment. Sunday, March 24, 2019, found Gallagher preaching a homily at St. Theresa's Cathedral in Juba.[42] It can be read as a message for Kiir, who sits on a sofa in the front row of the cathedral, which he attends most Sundays.[43]

The priest acknowledged that when we experience misery or tribulation, we all wonder why God has abandoned us, but he assured listeners that God knows our suffering. He explained that God asks to be welcomed. He wants to save, yet salvation is a matter of personal consent and conversion. He reminded congregants that Moses killed someone but eventually renounced his pride. King David, too, converted and changed course.

> This is the project God has imagined for all of us. We are invited to follow the right path to the very end. We must not get discouraged and not stop. Don't stop at the halfway point. Moses guides his flock through the desert! He leads his people to the land of milk and honey! . . . The mercy of God urges us to sincere compassion for our neighbor, not remaining indifferent to the pain and suffering of the other. God calls us to choose life, purify and transform our hearts, to forgive and favor dialogue.[44]

When Gallagher points to Moses, you can surely hear him aiming for the president. In making a targeted appeal for peace in the guise of a religious meditation, Gallagher foreshadowed Francis's own use of Christian symbolism to break through to a Christian political class resisting the core biblical concept of servant leadership focused on a nation's collective good.

Two weeks after Gallaher departed Juba, Vatican News announced a spiritual retreat for South Sudan's "highest civil and ecclesiastical authorities," to be led by the archbishop of Canterbury and held—the next day. Former moderator of the Church of Scotland, Rev. John Chalmers, was on board too.[45] President Kiir, several designated vice presidents, including Riek Machar, plus eight clergy from the SSCC leadership would attend.[46] One of the politicians on the new team was Rebecca Nyandeng Garang, widow of the national leader, Dr. John Garang, whose 2005 death in a plane crash propelled Kiir into the presidency. Described as "ecumenical and diplomatic at the same time," the unusual two-day event would unfold in the former convent where Francis lives, the Domus Sanctae Marthae in Vatican City.[47]

JOINT APPEARANCES AND THE WELBY CONNECTION

Much as the pope invited former Israeli president Shimon Peres and Palestinian president Mahmoud Abbas to Rome in 2014, with the participation of Orthodox Ecumenical Patriarch Bartholomew, Francis's objective was to facilitate dialogue in a neutral setting and to broaden religious representation in order to reduce the appearance of the Catholic Church making some institutional power play.[48] The value of hosting in Rome is fairly straightforward: By taking people away from their daily pressures, it becomes easier for them to see and experience the humanity of the other. Sponsorship by the Holy See is intended to add a spiritual dimension—at least, a dimension disinterested in worldly concerns—and it's not irrelevant that Rome is a beautiful city that makes most visitors happy.

In the case of South Sudan, the neutral location had practical benefits. First, since instability undermined the pope's chance to meet South Sudan's leaders on their home turf, why not bring them to him? And second, because a key actor in South Sudan's fatal drama, Riek Machar, said he was chased out of the country and trusted neither the president's willingness nor his ability to protect him in Juba, meeting in Rome was a way to assure the rebel leader's participation.[49] Most of all, bringing together Catholic, Episcopalian, and Presbyterian Church leaders meant aggregating the only organizations representing the beleaguered Sudanese people—some seven million of the eleven million population belong to these three faiths.[50]

The Vatican credits Justin Welby, leader of the Church of England and "first among equals" of the global Anglican Communion, as having the idea of bringing South Sudan's political leadership together under an ecumenical umbrella. The British prelate was enthroned in April 2013, a few days after Francis took office. The men met at the Vatican less than two months later and maintain an easy rapport. Welby and Gallagher, both British, first met in Burundi, and both appreciate each other as well.

At a joint vespers service to celebrate the fiftieth anniversary of a historic meeting between Pope Paul VI and Anglican Archbishop Michael Ramsey in Rome in 1966 (the first such meeting since the Reformation, it marked the start of theological dialogue between the two faith traditions), the camaraderie between Francis and Welby was evident.[51] In his address, the pope emphasized what the two communities share, a common mission and commitment to service, regardless of variance on questions such as women priests:

> We acknowledge one another as brothers and sisters with different traditions but inspired by the same Gospel to undertake the same mission to the world. It would always be good, before beginning a particular activity to ask ourselves the following questions. Can we not do this together with our Anglican brothers and sisters? Can we not witness to Jesus by working together with our Catholic brothers and sisters?[52]

At the end of the service, the two leaders blessed nineteen pairs of Catholic and Anglican bishops from around the world to initiative joint activities in home communities.[53] Among the teams were pairs from Central Africa and Ghana; it's in Africa where both the Catholic Church and Anglican Communion are experiencing the fastest membership growth.

The occasion came just eight months after the meeting between Francis and Russian patriarch Kirill, at which, similarly, unity in mission and service was the glue that overcame far more tangled doctrinal questions. In 2016, Francis's intention to portray the pontiff as an equal partner with other global religious leaders emerged prominently. Importantly, these relationships were purposeful: to address specific urgencies of war, famine, and extermination and to promote mercy and peace.

SEEKING CONVERSION OF HEARTS

As dawn broke on game day, Riek Machar had still not arrived. He could not leave his home in Khartoum without permission from the Intergovernmental Authority on Development—an odd factor that proved just how complicated the country's fate had become.[54] When the Nuer leader's arrival at Leonardo da Vinci International Airport at 11 a.m. Roman time was posted on Twitter, relief spread through the Secretariat of State, charged with organizing the event.[55]

In the convent's quiet, Cardinal Secretary of State Pietro Parolin opened the meeting. He described the encounter as an opportunity for reconciliation for those with a special mission on behalf of the people of South Sudan. Speaking to the assembled guests beneath the country's flag of black, red, green, blue, and yellow, he explained that a retreat is also a chance to prayerfully speak to God, to seek His counsel regarding the tasks ahead.

A Catholic retreat is led by a spiritual director who gives a talk, proposes subjects for meditation, and leads participants in making resolutions, deepening faith, and growing in love for Christ. Francis named two priests to lead: Nigerian Fr. Agbonkhianmeghe Orobator, president of the Jesuit Conference of Africa and Madagascar, and Ugandan Archbishop John Baptist Odama of Gulu.

Orobator described a retreat as a time "for God to meet us" and asked guests to speak honestly so the peace agreement would be "signed in our hearts." He went on to give a challenging reflection on the country's national anthem, which opens and closes with references to God. Contrasting the joy of independence with the misery abounding eight years later, he urged politicians to "choose life," which requires national reconciliation.[56]

Odama helped mediate peace talks in Sudan and Uganda. He was convinced his own country had played a negative role in fomenting conflict in South Sudan. His meditation concentrated on the role of forgiveness in leaving behind the habits of war. Both priests designed their spiritual direction to address the lack of trust between the leaders.

By the time Pope Francis joined the others on Thursday afternoon, there was a sense that the encounter had exceeded expectations. National leaders had spoken to each other with unusual candor. They had renounced revenge and committed themselves to national unity. The painting dominating the room, depicting Mary untying a knotted ribbon with the help of angels, symbolized their efforts.[57] What was left was a benediction from the Holy Father, then on to a celebratory meal.

"ALLOW ME"

Sitting at a table next to Archbishop Welby who was wearing purple, with Scottish Presbyterian Reverend Chalmers in red nearby, the white-cassocked pope read his message in Italian, while the Sudanese followed an English translation printed in booklets. He observed that all must meet "the gaze of the Lord . . . who is able to see the truth in us and to lead us fully to that truth" and asked them to focus on the suffering citizens of South Sudan: "Seek what unites you, beginning with belonging to the same people, and overcome all that divides you. People are tired and exhausted by now from past wars." The pontiff lauded the politicians for validating dialogue and praised the clergy for working ceaselessly for reconciliation while caring for the impoverished. He concluded with a prayer: "May the whole-hearted search for peace resolve disputes, may love conquer hatred, and may revenge be disarmed by forgiveness."[58] Then he veered off script.

Francis stood and begged the leaders to "stay in peace. I'm asking you with my heart." Suddenly emotional with an intensity not apparent while he read, the pope assured the Sudanese that by remaining united they will "become fathers of the nation." Turning to his young translator, he murmured, "Come with me," conveyed to the audience via the pope's small white lapel mic.

Francis crossed the sitting room and approached Kiir, who looked apprehensive. Grabbing his aide's arm for balance, the pope dropped to his knees, leaned over, and audibly kissed the president's feet. (Kneeling is difficult for Francis because he has sciatica, back pain caused by the sciatic nerve.) He then struggled to stand up with support from Kiir and the translator and quickly moved to Machar, whispering, "Allow me." Breathing heavily, he sunk down once more, kissing the man's feet as his white zucchetto tumbled off his head. A third time, with effort, wheezing by now, the pontiff kissed the feet of Vice President Taban Deng Gai, Francis's black shoes unceremoniously aloft.

Finally, the octogenarian crossed the room, briefly gripping the hands of Machar and Kiir as he passed, and stood before the vibrantly robed Rebecca Garang, who covered her face with her hands in astonishment. The pope dropped down a fourth time, steadied by his translator and the woman, who wept. Some twenty people watched the pope's three-minute supplication in astonished silence.

INTERPRETING THE KISS

What did it mean? What was the pope trying to say with this stunning, almost surreal expression of humility? A supplication is a petition or form of prayer, a humble request that something be granted. Add to this, in the Bible, a kiss is usually a sign of love and respect. Francis nearly prostrated himself before these secular leaders to express his profound request that they unite and overcome political differences to focus on the good of the nation. Francis was not unaware that his action was being photographed, filmed, and recorded. The picture conveyed to millions across the world, but especially to the people of Sudan, many of whom are illiterate: with respect, the pope is begging your leaders to use their offices beneficially.

The pope's complex form of nonverbal communication also evoked Jesus's gesture when he washed the feet of his disciples a week before being crucified. As described in the Gospel of John, Christ and his twelve disciples were eating dinner when the Son of God unexpectedly got up and began washing the feet of the apostles, who hardly understood what was happening. Once finished, back at table, Jesus explained, "You call me 'teacher' and 'master' and rightly so, for indeed I am. If I, therefore, the master and teacher, have washed your feet, you ought to wash one another's feet. I have given you a model to follow, so that as I have done for you, you should also do."[59]

Thus Jesus told his followers that an attitude of humility and mutual respect would bring success in their mission: spreading the word of God and achieving salvation. Similarly, Francis was telling the Sudanese, by humbly helping and respecting each other as equals, you will successfully build peace.

Finally, with the kiss, Francis anointed his guests and sent them into the world with an assignment. In Catholic theology, the pope has the authority Christ gave to Peter: "Whatever you bind on earth shall be bound in Heaven."[60] The pope's kiss was thus a request *and* a task. The four people Francis singled out are Christian, but only one, Kiir, is Catholic. Of the others, Machar and Deng are Presbyterians, and Garang is an Episcopalian. Might they be offended to be enveloped in a gesture rooted in Catholic theology? It seems a fair question, although, by their participation, the guests obviously signaled a willingness to enter reflection in a Catholic context.

"African people love Francis. There would be no need for him to distinguish Catholics from Protestants; it just wouldn't be relevant," an East African Comboni missionary explained to me. "Personally, I think Africans sense that the pope cares about the continent far beyond what powerful white Westerners ever do." The missionary's insight is supported by the South Sudan Pentecostal Church general overseer, Bishop Dr. Isaiah Dau, who was at the retreat. He described the pope's gesture as a message from God:

> I was there when the pope went down on his knees and kissed the feet of our leaders.... We all cried in that room, an 83-year-old man with one lung kneeling down and breathing heavily and kissing the feet of leaders of this republic. That kiss can mean a blessing if we do what he told us, but if it's not done be careful, it's going to be a curse and it's going to be personal before it's national. Let us change, South Sudan is loved by God. There is no country in the world where the pope ever did that, not even in his own country. It's because God loves this country, and God would like to bless this country. Let our political leaders put their act together.[61]

Ecumenism was restored in the form of a parting gift for retreat participants. Each received a Bible signed by Chalmers, Francis, and Welby, with the message, "Seek that which unites. Overcome that which divides."

"PIERCING EXPERIENCE"

Across the country, people celebrated the pope's gesture as giving valuable impetus to the peace process. The SSCC summarized the act as the essence of Easter: "His Holiness . . . kissing the feet of our leaders, as if to say, I serve you, now serve your people."[62] Kiir himself issued an Easter letter in which he wrote, "The whole world was shocked when His Holiness knell [sic] down to kiss our feet. I was personally shocked and deeply touched and of course I trembled. We thank his Holiness for what was truly a piercing experience to the soul, the mind, and the heart."[63]

Meanwhile, priests around the country used the event to preach homilies on humility, peace, and God's message for South Sudan.[64] Sr. Orla Treacy talked about the value for her girl students of seeing a "Big Man" bowing low before other men as a function of Christian values of forgiveness and love. She explained, "What he did that day spoke more words than I could say in a year."[65]

But what *actions* demonstrate a greater than rhetorical impact on Kiir and Machar's behavior? The change of heart took real shape in January and February 2020, first through an expanded peace agreement with recalcitrant opposition groups, and then with the formation of a unity government based on concessions made by both men.

Vatican diplomacy is never riding just one track; the retreat was a very public initiative, but quieter initiatives were underway too. When Salva Kiir visited Rome in March 2019, the Secretariat of State arranged his visit to the headquarters of Sant'Egidio, a lay movement well known in Africa for brokering a peace settlement in Mozambique that succeeded, as described in chapter 1.[66] Sant'Egidio had been working in Sudan since 1986, and in the Vatican's view, it was time to deploy its diplomatic prowess. Following the retreat, Machar and Garang joined Sant'Egidio for a prayer service and discussion of the road ahead.[67] Over the next nine months, Sant'Egidio worked with the South Sudan Conference of Churches, government representatives, and rebel groups that had never signed the peace agreement (mainly assembled as the South Sudan Opposition Movements Alliance, SSOMA) to define a more inclusive vision of peace. On January 13, the parties signed a ten-point agreement committing to a cease-fire, continued dialogue, and humanitarian access to the dispossessed.[68]

Of greatest concern to God's diplomats was the status of the much-promised, several-times-postponed unity government that would formally join Kiir and Machar together. Scheduled for May 2019, then postponed to November, the second time this initiative was pushed off (for ninety days), the pope felt prompted to act. What was left in his quiver?

The prospect the South Sudanese leadership seemed most keen for the Vatican to fructify was a papal visit. So Francis threw it out once more. On November 13, 2019, the Vatican announced that Francis and Archbishop Welby would visit South Sudan if the country's leadership formed a unity government in the next three months.[69] The two men had said as much in the past but were happy to repeat it in the hope that it could somehow incentivize the commitment Kiir and Machar had repeatedly made, even in Francis's own home. The United States, however, felt played by the second postponement, so it responded by withdrawing its ambassador from South Sudan and imposing sanctions on government officials.

A major sticking point was a dispute over the country's number of states. Machar wanted Kiir to reduce the number from thirty-two to ten. The opposition leader asserted that gerrymandering had created an unacceptable patchwork of fiefdoms and that a return to South Sudan's original number of states was most fair. When the president finally made this concession, the road was open for a new government.[70] In turn, Machar accepted that his security be provided by the president's existing team.

I HAVE FORGIVEN AND ASK FOR FORGIVENESS

At a February 22, 2020, State House ceremony in Juba to install a Transitional Government of National Unity, the spiritual language of reconciliation was woven through each address. President Kiir announced, "My brother Dr. Machar and I are now partners in the peace agreement. I have forgiven my brother and I also ask for his forgiveness. I invite all the people of South Sudan to forgive each other, especially the Nuer and Dinka communities." Machar sought to reassure citizens that they would be the government's central focus, promising, "We will work collectively to end your long suffering."[71]

The Vatican's role in getting to that day was mentioned by all the speakers, and as the ceremony opened, the political principals were presented with photographs of the pope's dramatic gesture beseeching them to unite.[72] "We are proud to report to him that we are reconciled," intoned President Kiir to applause.

Machar thanked by name the three religious leaders who led the retreat, as well as the African church leaders for their prayers and spiritual guidance, and Sant'Egidio for leading ongoing negotiations. Regarding Francis, he said, "We are greatly humbled and challenged by the pope kissing our feet of which one is not worthy." Most lyrical, Garang said she witnessed "how God loved the people of South Sudan when he led the leaders of the country to the altar and allowed us to pray together." She then addressed Francis directly:

"Your Holiness, God has answered your prayers and peace has come to South Sudan—through a spirit of love."[73]

What the diplomacy of Pope Francis gave these leaders was a spiritual interlude to meet each other, recognize each other's humanity, pledge diligence toward peace, and commit to a shared goal, with no sacrifice to personal honor or identity—which catalyzed a change of heart. It was a priceless gift and a diplomatic coup.

Contrast that with the US stance. Asked at the Vatican retreat's conclusion what he expected its impact would be, a UN expert on South Sudan (and former US foreign service officer) told the *Washington Post*, it was "one of those moments where it leaves me without words. It would literally take a miracle from God for Riek and Salva to ever be part of the solution here."[74] Ten months later, foreign diplomats were still keeping a distance; few, besides Sudan, Uganda, and South Africa, sent officials to attend the swearing-in ceremony. Not only wasn't a representative from the US embassy at the ceremony, but the US Treasury Department sanctioned Vice President Deng in January 2020 for engaging in "serious human rights abuses."[75]

Can we conclude that the Holy See's approach to foreign affairs is idealistic? Yes, it believes all sinners are capable of conversion—profound changes of heart. Yet, in South Sudan as everywhere else, the Church rarely has one approach. Its idealism is equally balanced by pragmatism, as reflected by God's diplomats on the ground.

Talking to an Italian priest who is often in the region and knows the South Sudan case well, one hears an eminently realistic viewpoint: "The issue of South Sudan is complicated. The country has been at war forever. And before the civil war, it was in a constant social tension against the North and against the British colonialists," the priest told me.

"In no way could South Sudan move forward under the leadership of foreigners. South Sudanese are divided, filled with negative ethnicity, often unprepared for the modern world, yet they will not accept someone from the outside," he continued.

"Of course there are foreigners who are respected and even sought. Yet the public face of any decision and implementation must be local. It is true that Salva Kiir and Riek Machar are not the best solution for South Sudan. However, there are no other leaders who could easily replace them. So we work with them, and the dialogue is very sincere."

Like the bishops, their adviser John Ashworth is unconvinced that the country's leadership has sufficient political will to implement the comprehensive peace treaty they signed in 2018, but he confirms there's no alternative: "It's a flawed peace process, but it is the only peace process we have," he told me.

The Church's long horizon gives its analysts a more sanguine attitude toward social change. A missionary who taught in South Sudan explains: "I often said that South Sudan needs a few decades of instability before finding its place in Africa. I still believe this assessment. One cannot change a tribal, village-based life into a modern state overnight. It needs time." He continued, "Consider also that South Sudan is an artificial country. Each ethnic group believes itself to be a nation on its own, and some, like the Dinka, believe they have a natural duty to be the leaders. It will take time to go from this to democracy."

Even on this fundamental point, regarding the problem of interethnic conflict in South Sudan, the Church simultaneously acknowledges and challenges it. One of the most innovative social experiments in the country is the Kuron Peace Village, also known as the Holy Trinity Peace Village. It is an "intentional community" founded by Bishop Taban in 2000, where people from a variety of ethnic groups live together. Located in Kuron near the border with Ethiopia and Kenya, the village is engaged in sustainable agriculture. It has a school, a health center, and a peace academy, where it brings leaders from around the country. The idea came to the bishop when he visited Neve Shalom, a town in Israel where Palestinian and Jewish citizens live together. He explained, "This is one of the safest areas in South Sudan. It is a safe haven. Peace is rooted in communities, not in agreements or rules. You do not fight against someone you know, your neighbor."[76]

Meanwhile, the Church will work to train teachers and health care professionals, reconcile neighbors, minister to refugees, and lift up talented students. The Church's hands and feet at the grassroots are not waiting for South Sudan's presidency 2.0 to deliver salvation. Catholic humanitarians aren't even waiting for the Vatican's miracles to work: "The Vatican is important, but they're not *that* powerful," a priest on the ground observed.

In South Sudan, the long-term diplomatic mission runs through the people. "The Church is bringing out the voice of the people, at the grassroots and at the top. It has no interests. It's completely impartial," summarized Ashworth. And that, quite sadly but also profoundly, is a radical program.

Acknowledgments

This book's journey began in Romania's Carpathian Mountains in a small Catholic Church dedicated to St. Anthony of Padua. Bombed by the allies during World War II, shuttered by Communists (brought and installed by Soviet troops), priestless for close to 20 years, the work of a small group of dedicated Vatican diplomats in the 1960s and 1970s gave little St. Anthony's new life and drew me in. A dedicated, powerful cantor's voice was tolerated, and the beautiful sound of an organ was allowed. Yet, they were enough and so liberating for the soul and the mind of a child to plunge into a dream: Dare, take off, make it to St. Anthony of Padua—in Italy! The cantor's voice encouraged me.

When I met some of the priests behind Ostpolitik decades later—Cardinals Giovanni Cheli, Luigi Poggi, and Achille Silvestrini, as well as Archbishop John Bukovsky of the Divine Word—their great humility and wisdom made me want to understand the world as they saw it: sinful and corrupt yet ever capable of renewal and hope. Conversations with these greats were my first peek over the wall. As a result, I've spent some part of the past 15 years researching the story of the Holy See's diplomatic practice while writing for Catholic News Service, *National Catholic Register*, *Foreign Affairs*, and *America* magazine.

During an unforgettable evening car tour of Vatican City in 2019 with Cardinal Francesco Monterisi behind the wheel, following a free-wheeling conversation about his assignments in Bosnia-Herzegovina, Korea, and a short mission to Transylvania, I finally felt the indwelling of Spirit sufficient to complete *God's Diplomats*. . . .

This text benefitted from close review by two extraordinary editors who I count as friends: Barb Fraze, international news editor at Catholic News Service (one of my first, most encouraging editors), and dexterous Nathaniel Brown, who read the manuscript and made crucial suggestions. Even earlier, Dylan Colligan at Javelin, helped me conceptualize the book and Ruth Olsen set the first style guidelines.

For many years, Jeanette DeMello, editor-in-chief of the *National Catholic Register* stood by me, together with Tom Wehner and Tom McFeely. The *Register* allowed me to cover the work of the Church in over twenty countries, especially during periods of peril. I'm also grateful to brilliant and thorough *Foreign Affairs* editors: Sigrid Von Wendel, Katherine Allawala, Nathaniel Brown, Park MacDougald, Laura Secor, and Kanishk Tharoor. Each taught me how to make a sharper, more provocative, evidence-driven argument.

At key moments, valued peers encouraged the project. Thanks go to John Burger, Austen Ivereigh, Christopher Lamb, Robert Mickens, and Francesco Sisci in particular. Having people I admire affirm this effort has touched me deeply. Prominent among them are Carlos Eire, Professor of History and Religious Studies at Yale University and Nicolai Petro, Professor of Political Science at the University of Rhode Island. Fr. James McCann, S.J., a Russia expert, and Catholic chaplain at Georgetown Law School, has been a peerless adviser. Helpful too has been Fr. Jack Hurley, my parish priest at St. Matthews Cathedral who started his career as a foreign service officer with the US State Department! Among incisive diplomats I consulted, Edward Stafford proved especially trenchant about working with Vatican counterparts.

Insight—and the gift of time—flowed from an invaluable elite: presidents past and present of the Pontifical Ecclesiastical Academy, the storied *Accademia*. Cardinal Justin Francis Rigali invited me to Tennessee. Archbishop Giampiero Gloder sat with me in Rome. Archbishop Joseph Marino's generosity arrived via email.

Ambassador James Creagan provided precious first-hand information regarding US-Vatican exchanges during moments of crisis between the two sovereigns. Ambassador Francis Rooney (author of *Global Vatican*, which I admire) shared insight and encouragement despite immense congressional duties. Ambassador Charles Freeman, President Richard Nixon's lead China translator shared indispensable tenets of diplomacy #101, ominously no longer followed by the United States.

For each case study chapter in Part II, I am happy to acknowledge key people. The Ukrainian-Russian conflict can't be fathomed without tackling the religious dispute and talking to *all* parties. I am especially thankful to the following experts who provided me with thoughtful presentations of their views: Cardinal Kurt Koch; Bishop Brian Farrell; Archbishop Thomas Gullickson, nuncio to Ukraine; Archbishop Mechislav Mokshinsky of the Latin Catholic Church in Ukraine (former secretary to John Paul II and Benedict XVI); Fr. Hyacinthe Destivelle, OP; Ukrainian Greek Catholic Church (UGCC) Major Archbishop Sviatoslav Shevchuk; Cardinal Lubomyr Husar, who preceded Shevchuk as UGCC leader; and Archbishop Borys Gudziak. Romanian Archbishop Ion Robu and Bishop Petru Gherghel shared important insights into this conflict too.

From the Orthodox Church, controversial Ukrainian Orthodox Metropolitan Filaret has played an unmatched role and it was interesting to meet him in person. More constructive have been leaders I learned from such as Archimandrite Elpidophoros of America (former chief secretary of the Patriarchate of Constantinople) and Metropolitan Nifon of Tirgoviste. I also benefited from frank comments provided by French and German diplomats following the Ukrainian-Russia conflict closely.

A highpoint of my life was getting to know the late Oswaldo Payá, his wife Ofelia and daughter Rosa Maria in Havana in 2010. The murder of Oswaldo and his assistant Harold Cepero two years later was a monstrous act of evil. While in Cuba, I met with brave women marching as Ladies in White, and with dedicated lay Catholics and priests, who asked not to be named in order to protect their charitable work with the elderly, disabled, and sick—programs the state was fully aware of but pretended didn't exist.

A remarkable source for the Cuba chapter has been Bishop William Murphy, who was Cardinal Bernard Law's point man for Cuba in the 1980s and 1990s. He shared with me events from his trips to Cuba and conversations with Fidel Castro, Cardinal Jaime Ortega, as well as a range of high-ranking US and Cuban officials involved in the US-Vatican-Cuba game. Alberto de la Cruz, founder of BabaluBlog.com, has provided useful insight otherwise not available, as did Germán Miret, an astute Cuba watcher.

Most sources regarding Kenya insisted on anonymity. However, my wonderful friend, Fr. Barthelemy Bazemo, a leading light among the Missionaries of Africa, helped me identify good people to verify and affirm the chapter.

Regarding peace building in Colombia, I'm indebted to Fr. Adrian Marina Salcedo, SJ and Liduine Zumpolle for reading, correcting, commenting, and offering additional sources. Sincere thanks to Ben Schenik of Pax Christi Netherlands for trusting me with original, never-before-published documents related to meetings with Fidel Castro and other work in Cuba and Colombia.

For the Middle East chapter, I'm eternally grateful to Syriac Catholic Patriarch Ignatius Joseph III Younan of Antioch who invited me to spend time at the Harissa Monastery on the outskirts of Beirut in 2017 where I met and interviewed Iraqi and Syrian bishops, priests, and nuns who escaped the slaughter of Daesh (better known as ISIS in the United States). I also benefited from the perspective of Ignatius Aphreim II, Patriarch of the Syriac Orthodox Church of Antioch and All the East. Three leaders of the Maronite Church were particularly helpful dissecting the complex interconnections in Lebanon: Bishop Gregory Mansour, Bishop Elias Zaidan, and Archbishop Paul Sayah.

Other valued advisers or sources include: Bishop Sarkis Davidian, leading the Armenian Catholic Church in Iran (who I interviewed in Beirut days before he undertook his assignment in Tehran); Melkite Archbishop Jean-Clément Jeanbart of Aleppo, Syria; Archbishop Khajag Barsamian, the Armenian's Church Legate to the Holy See; Fr. Salim Daccache SJ, rector of St. Joseph University in Beirut; and Ibrahim Chamseddine, an erudite Shia scholar and advocate of inter-faith dialogue.

Wisdom has come to me from Abbas Kadhim, the Atlantic Council's Iraq Initiative director and resident senior fellow for Middle East programs, who helped me navigate the labyrinthian Middle East events. Wisdom, too, from Bishop John Bryce Chane, who shared a stunning account of Rumsfeld-Wolfowitz's attempt to co-opt religious leaders on the "need" to attack Iraq, months before the misguided US invasion was launched.

In Korea, so many Catholics opened their hearts to me. The Catholic Church in Korea is a great inspiration. Former Ambassador to the Holy See Thomas Hong-Soon Han has been a guide on many fronts. His expert comments and corrections have been so beneficial.

Cardinal Andrew Yeom Soo-jung and Archbishop Hyginus Kim Hee-joon were generous too. In Seoul, I had a memorable dinner with Fr. Paul Yoo, a priest close to President Moon Jae-in. While there, I witnessed the excellent work of Msgr. Marco Sprizzi (who moved on to serve in Timor-Leste and Malaysia). At the height of the most bellicose rhetoric between US and North Korea, an assembly of Catholic leaders and diplomats believed that Armageddon could be avoided by switching from threats (coupled with an arms race and military exercises in each other's face), to the classical rules of diplomacy. Then, for a while hope was high, by the surprising dialog and encounter between the most implacable enemies, President Trump and North Korea's Kim Jong-un.

From Fr. Larry Murphy, I learned stories about North Korea straight out of a spy novel, all of which were confirmed by Seton Hall University professor Yeomin Yoo, a discreet insider in the Washington-Seoul-Beijing-Pyongyang diplomatic dance that unfolded in the 1980s and 1990s. It was such a gift to hear their experiences.

Asia is a frontier that Pope Francis has concentrated on, so much more than his predecessor. Time spent in the region helped me understand why. In Hong Kong, Fr. Peter Barry and Yat Ming Fung were exceptionally helpful and it was a delight to spend time with Bishop Michael Yeung Ming-cheung and scholars at the Holy Spirit Research Center. In Taiwan, Fu Jen Catholic University Vice President Michael Lee; Fr. Otfried Chan; Fr. Al Doyle, MM; Fr. Willy Ollevier, CICM; Sr. Emma Lee, DC, executive director of Caritas Taiwan; and Fr. Joyalito Tajonera, MM shared hospitality and guidance despite relentless obligations.

For the China chapter, I'm especially indebted to two priests who have dedicated their lives to the country and the health of the Catholic Church there: Fr. Jeroom Heyndricks, CICM and Fr. John Worthley. Both men spent decades in China, talking to all parties, working with all: Chinese officials, the registered and unregistered churches, Vatican representatives, and officials from the US and Europe. Other fascinating people who contributed to the chapter are Sister Nirmala Joshi, MC, Fr. Bernardo Cervellera, Claretian Father Francisco Carin, and Mother Teresa China Charity founder Li Baofu.

Two extraordinarily knowledgeable priests dedicated to South Sudan clarified key aspects of the chapter: Fr. Jim Greene, MAfr, executive director of the Catholic charity Solidarity with South Sudan and John Ashworth, advisor to the South Sudan Council of Churches.

I've relied on the prayers of priests on earth and saints in Heaven. Considering limits of space, I'll single out just three, Msgr. Gabriel Quicke, president of Holy Spirit College and Leo XIII Seminary in Leuven, Belgium; Fr. Julien Cormier, a Missionary of Africa with a tremendous heart for encouraging his neighbor; and Fr. Gerard Hammond, a Maryknoller in Seoul, Korea whose welcome was a key to opening Asia for me.

My Rowman & Littlefield editor, Jon Sisk, his assistant Benjamin Knepp, and R&L's patient senior production editor, Elaine McGarraugh, kept me on task throughout the pandemic. Thank you, Jon, for trusting the value of this subject. *Mille grazie* to the artists who actualized *God's Diplomats*: sophisticated book designer Chloe Batch; Mauro Pallotta, whose street tag is, "Maupal," maker of the marvelous cover art, "Pope Savior;" and talented map designer Nelly Ambrose who captured key cartographic elements for five cases.

Sincere gratitude to unknown hands who have organized and preserved documents in the Vatican Secret Archives, the US National Archives and Records Administration, collections of Eastern European intelligence services, and smaller libraries maintained by missionary orders—which I was allowed to use. Everything depends on history's preservation, the most relevant context for diplomacy, which unfolds in time. Special thanks to those who shared insights but preferred not to be quoted, especially men and women religious and clergy, whose self-sacrifice is beautiful—and profoundly countercultural.

Above all and through all, homage to my wife, Eleanor, and our five children, who encourage me continuously.

Notes

EPIGRAPH

i. Pope Francis, "Christmas Greetings to the Roman Curia" (address, Clementine Hall, Rome, December 21, 2019), http://www.vatican.va/content/francesco/en/speeches/2019/december/documents/papa-francesco_20191221_curia-romana.html#_ftn14.

PREFACE

1. Elise Ann Allen, "Vatican China Deal to be Renewed, with No Changes to Terms," Crux, October 20, 2022.

INTRODUCTION

1. The relationship is brilliantly explored in Massimo Franco's *Parallel Empires: The United States and the Vatican—Two Centuries of Alliance and Conflict*, trans. Roland Flamini (New York: Doubleday, 2008). Regarding the Philippines, the United States and Spain signed the Treaty of Paris on December 10, 1898, to conclude the Spanish-American War: Spain relinquished sovereignty over Cuba and ceded the Philippines, Puerto Rico, and Guam outright to the United States for $20 million (over $627 billion in 2019 dollars). The war and subsequent US occupation imperiled the Church by destroying property and institutions, dismembering parishes, and jailing, murdering, or driving away Spanish priests. In 1898, Pope Leo XIII (the first pope of the modern era, as we will see in chapter 4) appointed Archbishop Placide Chapelle of New Orleans to serve as apostolic delegate to Cuba and Puerto Rico and extraordinary envoy to the Philippines. Chapelle perceived US strategy as hostile to the Church. For

Pope Leo XIII, the American aggression was itself a violation of Catholic principles. Five years later, a new papal envoy arrived in Manila armed with a constitution for the Filipino Church, *Quai Mari Sinico* (1902). To this day, the Vatican maintains an apostolic delegate to Puerto Rico, who also serves as nuncio to the Dominican Republic. See Scott Wright, "The 'Northwestern Chronicle' and the Spanish-American War: American Catholic Attitudes Regarding the 'Splendid Little War,'" *American Catholic Studies* 116, no. 4 (2005): 55–68; Daniel Franklin Pilario, CM, and Gerardo Vibar, CM, eds., *Philippine Local Churches after the Spanish Regime: Quae Mari Sinico and Beyond* (Manila: Adamson University, 2015), 1–89.

2. Fr. Paul Glynn and Shusako Endo, *A Song for Nagasaki: The Story of Takashi Nagai: Scientist, Convert, and Survivor of the Atomic Bomb* (San Francisco: Ignatius Press, 2009). A fascinating account of the second US atomic bombing, based on declassified documents, is in Alex Wellerstein, "Nagasaki: The Last Bomb," *New Yorker*, August 7, 2015.

3. Andrea Tornielli, "The War that 'God Wants': When Pius XII Did Not Engage with USA," *La Stampa*, July 24, 2017, https://www.lastampa.it/vatican-insider/en/2017/07/24/news/the-war-that-god-wants-when-pius-xii-did-not-engage-with-usa-1.34457082.

4. Gordon Thomas, *Gideon's Spies: The Secret History of the Mossad* (New York: Thomas Dunne, 2012), 215–16.

5. Cardinal Loris Capovilla, interview with the author, Sotto il Monte Giovanni XXIII, Italy, June 22, 2014. Pope Francis made Capovilla a cardinal in February 2014 to honor his loyalty to Pope John XXIII.

6. Wilton Wynn, *Keepers of the Keys: John XXIII, Paul VI and John Paul II; Three Who Changed the Church* (New York: Random House, 1988), 196. Paul VI was not spared criticism, especially for his policy of diplomatic engagement with Communist regimes in order to preserve the Catholic Church, a policy known as Ostpolitik. Also see Fr. Pablo Migone, "Pope Paul VI and President Lyndon Johnson during the Vietnam War," Patheos, https://www.patheos.com/blogs/labmind/2010/07/pope-paul-vi-and-president-lyndon-johnson-during-the-vietnam-war.html.

7. Gerard O'Connell, "When Bush Put John Paul II's Letter on the Side Table without Opening It," *La Stampa*, December 23, 2011, http://www.lastampa.it/2011/09/17/vaticaninsider/eng/world-news/when-bush-put-john-paul-iis-letter-on-the-side-table-without-opening-it-HV7tYBqmgNTokCOj7OUr9H/pagina.html.

8. Laghi came to the United States as an apostolic delegate and left as an apostolic nuncio because he negotiated full diplomatic relations between the Holy See and the United States. The historic agreement was signed on January 10, 1984.

9. Franco, *Parallel Empires*, 141. Franco's account of this meeting and Laghi's recollection of it are detailed and fascinating.

10. Archbishop Joseph Marino, personal communication with the author, August 13, 2020. Interestingly, Archbishop Montalvo also served as *Accademia* president from 1993 to 1998.

11. Andrea Tornielli, "Wojtyla, the Islamist Invasion and Those Words Spoken to Bush Jr.," *La Stampa*, https://www.lastampa.it/2017/11/21/vaticaninsider/wojtyla-the-islamist-invasion-and-those-words-spoken-to-bush-jr-msqsrMHMto5ubPbS0yOkIO/pagina.html.

12. Malcolm Moore, "Pope: Nothing Positive Happening in Iraq," *Telegraph*, April 9, 2007, https://www.telegraph.co.uk/news/uknews/1548020/Pope-Nothing-positive-happening-in-Iraq.html.

13. The WikiLeaks cables include several examples of Vatican officials challenging Americans regarding the efficacy of war, as well as democracy promotion, as foreign policy tactics.

14. Victor Gaetan, "The Church Undivided: Benedict's Quest to Bring Christians Back Together," *Foreign Affairs*, May/June 2013, https://www.foreignaffairs.com/articles/2013-04-03/church-undivided.

15. Tension along the lines of NATO expansion emerged at the April 2008 NATO summit in Bucharest, Romania. See "Timeline of US-Russia Relations (1983–2020)," Harvard Kennedy School of Government, Russia Matters, https://www.russiamatters.org/facts/timeline-us-russia-relations-1983-february-2020. The Holy See and Russia established diplomatic relations in 2009.

16. Eric Lyman, "Report Says US Tapped Cardinals' Phones ahead of Conclave," Religious News Service, October 30, 2013, https://www.washingtonpost.com/national/on-faith/report-says-us-tapped-cardinals-phones-ahead-of-conclave/2013/10/30/9293708a-419f-11e3-b028-de922d7a3f47_story.html; Nick Squires, "US 'Spied on Future Pope Francis during Conclave,'" *Telegraph*, October 30, 2013, https://www.telegraph.co.uk/news/worldnews/europe/vaticancityandholysee/10415228/US-spied-on-future-Pope-Francis-during-Vatican-conclave.html. Bergoglio was first mentioned as *papabili* (potential pope material) in a State Department cable in 2003, when American diplomats began speculating about who might replace an increasingly frail John Paul II. "A Latin American Pope? Cardinal Rodriguez Deemed Papabile, Speculation May Aid His Anti-Corruption Campaign," WikiLeaks, cable 03TEGUCIGALPA1642_a, dated July 11, 2003, https://wikileaks.org/plusd/cables/03TEGUCIGALPA1642_a.html. It was a well-informed list: two years later, Bergoglio was runner-up to Joseph Ratzinger, who became Benedict XVI. In each of the four rounds of voting it took for Ratzinger to get the seventy-seven votes he needed to win, Bergoglio came in second: 47–10, 65–35, 72–40, and 84–26. Gerard O'Connell, *The Election of Pope Francis: An Inside Account of the Conclave That Changed History* (Maryknoll, NY: Orbis, 2019), 19.

17. "NSA Spied on Future Pope before and during Vatican Conclave: Report," National Post, October 13, 2013, https://nationalpost.com/news/nsa-spied-on-the-future-pope-francis-before-and-during-vatican-conclave-report.

18. The best book-length treatment on the opposition to Francis is Christopher Lamb, *The Outsider: Pope Francis and His Battle to Reform the Church* (Maryknoll, NY: Orbis, 2020). Lamb includes a "timeline of opposition" that documents criticism of Francis since he took office in 2013. Yet an acceleration of attacks occurred between 2017 and 2019. It also shows the persistent barrage of criticism on all sorts of topics, from Francis's supposed lax attitude toward divorced and remarried Catholics receiving the Eucharist, to his purported nonchalance facing pagan ritual in the Vatican garden, to his imagined indifference to Chinese Catholics suffering persecution—the criticism is a fusillade, much of it simplistic exaggeration. What Lamb does not do is suggest there could be a hidden hand behind the "death by a thousand cuts" nature of this campaign to undermine papal authority.

19. Caitlin McFall, "Vatican Denies Pompeo Audience with Pope, Accuses Him of Playing Politics," Fox News, September 30, 2020, https://www.foxnews.com/world/vatican-denies-pompeo-audience-with-pope-accuses-him-of-playing-politics.

20. Dwight D. Eisenhower, "The Chance for Peace," Washington, DC, April 16, 1953, http://www.edchange.org/multicultural/speeches/ike_chance_for_peace.html. For excellent data on the relationship between war and business in contemporary America, see Julian Vigo, "The Blurred Line between War and Business," Truthdig, May 6, 2018, https://www.truthdig.com/articles/conflicts-of-interest-drive-wars-from-iraq-to-syria.

21. President Dwight David Eisenhower, "President Dwight Eisenhower Farewell Address," c-span.org, January 17, 1961, 16:00, https://www.c-span.org/video/?15026-1/president-dwight-eisenhower-farewell-address.

22. "Pope Francis Prays at Bethlehem Wall, Calls for Middle East Peace," *Chicago Tribune*, May 25, 2014, https://www.chicagotribune.com/news/chi-pope-middle-east-20140525-story.html.

23. "Pope Joins Global Condemnation of Trump's Endorsement of Jerusalem's Annexation," Middle East Monitor, December 6, 2017, https://www.middleeastmonitor.com/20171206-pope-joins-global-condemnation-of-trumps-endorsement-of-jerusalems-annexation; "Russia, UN and Vatican Condemn Unilateral Israeli Annexation Plan," *Times of Israel*, May 20, 2020, https://www.timesofisrael.com/russia-un-and-vatican-condemn-unilateral-israeli-annexation-plan.

24. Edward Pentin, "Steve Bannon: Crisis in the Church Will Worsen, Laity Needs to Act," Edward Pentin blog, June 16, 2019, https://edwardpentin.co.uk/steve-bannon-predicts-crisis-in-the-church-will-worsen-laity-needs-to-act.

25. Elisa Harris and John Allen, "Challenging Pope on Multiple Fronts, Bannon Wants to Train Gladiators," Crux, April 1, 2019, https://cruxnow.com/interviews/2019/04/challenging-pope-on-multiple-fronts-bannon-wants-to-train-gladiators.

26. Silvia Sciorilli Borrelli, "Cardinal Objects to Bannon's Far-Right Academy Plan," Politico, May 6, 2019, https://www.politico.eu/article/steve-bannon-italy-trisulti-charterhouse-callepardo-cardinal-renato-maria-martino-objects-to-far-right-academy-plan; Chico Harlan, "With Support from Steve Bannon, a Medieval Monastery Could Become a Populist Training Ground," *Washington Post*, December 25, 2018, https://www.washingtonpost.com/world/europe/with-support-from-steve-bannon-a-medieval-monastery-could-become-a-populist-training-ground/2018/12/25/86dac38a-d3c4-11e8-a4db-184311d27129_story.html.

27. Carol Glatz, "Italian Ministry Revokes Permit for Catholic-Inspired Institute," Crux, June 4, 2019, https://cruxnow.com/church-in-europe/2019/06/italian-ministry-revokes-permit-for-catholic-inspired-institute.

28. "Citing Alignment with Steve Bannon, Cardinal Burke Cuts Ties with Dignitatis Humanae," *America* (magazine), June 25, 2019, https://www.americamagazine.org/faith/2019/06/25/citing-alignment-steve-bannon-cardinal-burke-cuts-ties-dignitatis-humanae. The Latin term "dignitatis humanae" was appropriated from the Second Vatican Council's declaration on religious freedom.

29. Elizabeth Zerofsky, "Steve Bannon's Roman Holiday," *New Yorker*, April 11, 2019, https://www.newyorker.com/news/dispatch/steve-bannons-roman-holiday;

Maia de Baume and Silvia Borrelli, "Steve Bannon's Stuttering European Adventure," Politico, March 5, 2019, https://www.politico.eu/article/steve-bannon-european-parliament-the-movement-stuttering-european-adventure.

30. Geoff Earle, "Stephen Bannon Arrested, Indicted for Multimillion Wall Fraud," *Daily Mail*, August 20, 2020, https://www.dailymail.co.uk/news/article-8647401/Steven-Bannon-arrested-INDICTED-multi-million-wall-fraud.html; Joshua Green, "The End of Steve Bannon—and Maybe Trump, Too," Bloomberg, August 21, 2020, https://www.msn.com/en-us/news/politics/the-end-of-steve-bannon—and-maybe-trump-too/ar-BB18e4l2.

31. Patrick J. Gallo, "Beyond *The Deputy*: Origins of the New Revisionism," in *Pius XII, the Holocaust and the Revisionists: Essays* (Jefferson, NC: McFarland, 2006).

32. "Italy/File: An Italian Investigative Commission Has Said Former Soviet Union Leaders Ordered the Shooting of Pope John Paul II in 1981," Reuters, March 4, 2006, https://reuters.screenocean.com/record/335554.

33. My translation. The book has not been published in English. See Horacio Verbitsky, *El silencio. De Paulo VI a Bergoglio. Las relaciones secretas de la Iglesia con la ESMA* (Bogota: Sudamericana, 2005).

34. The AP article reporting on the lawsuit mentioned Verbitsky but not the woman who filed it nor her political affiliation: "Argentine Archbishop Named in Kidnap Lawsuit," Associated Press, April 17, 2005, https://www.latimes.com/archives/la-xpm-2005-apr-17-fg-cardinal17-story.html. On Bergman's politics, see Wikipedia, s.v. "Myriam Bergman," last modified December 3, 2020, https://en.wikipedia.org/wiki/Myriam_Bregman.

Verbitsky went on to publish *four* more books attacking the Church between 2005 and 2010, all while he was writing as a journalist, serving as president of the Centro de Estudios Legales y Sociales (Center for Legal and Social Studies, CELS), and advising various politicians, including Néstor Carlos Kirchner Jr. (president, 2003–2007) and his wife, Christina (President, 2007–2015).

35. Center for Legal and Social Studies, SourceWatch, https://www.sourcewatch.org/index.php?title=Center_of_Legal_and_Social_Studies.

36. NED's cofounder, Allen Weinstein, remarked, "A lot of what we do today was done covertly 25 years ago by the CIA." David Ignatius, "Innocence Abroad: The New World of Spyless Coups," *Washington Post*, September 22, 1991, https://www.washingtonpost.com/archive/opinions/1991/09/22/innocence-abroad-the-new-world-of-spyless-coups/92bb989a-de6e-4bb8-99b9-462c76b59a16. See also Brendan Koerner, "Bush Aims to Raise Whose Budget? The Skinny on the National Endowment for Democracy," Slate, January 22, 2004, https://slate.com/news-and-politics/2004/01/what-s-the-national-endowment-for-democracy.html. As Koerner observes, "The most common complaint is that the NED's money only goes to support movements and politicians that fit into the United States' foreign-policy objectives, regardless of whether those who receive the money engage in undemocratic campaigns." Regarding the role of the Ford Foundation as a front for intelligence goals, see Frances Stonor Saunders, *The Cultural Cold War: The CIA and the World of Arts and Letters* (New York: New Press, 1999), 113, 116.

37. Victor Gaetan, "Anatomy of a Lie: The Assault on Pope Francis' Reputation," *National Catholic Register*, March 30, 2013, https://www.ncregister.com/daily-news/anatomy-of-a-lie-the-assault-on-pope-francis-reputation.

38. General William Odom, interview with the author, Washington, DC, March 25, 2003.

39. Evan Lehmann, "Retired General: Iraq Invasion Was a 'Strategic Disaster,'" *Lowell Sun*, September 29, 2005, https://www.lowellsun.com/2005/09/29/retired-general-iraq-invasion-was-strategic-disaster-2.

40. Gabriel Levinas, *Doble Agente: La Biografía Inesperada de Horacio Verbitsky* [Double agent: The unexpected biography of Horacio Verbitsky] (Buenos Aires: Editorial Sudamericana, 2015). Unfortunately, it has not yet been translated into English.

41. President Arturo Illia was democratically elected in 1963 and overthrown in 1966. He quickly issued a number of protectionist decrees, which negatively affected foreign business interests in the oil, pharmaceutical, and mining industries, including Standard Oil of New Jersey (presently, Exxon) and Shell. Illia also refused to support the United States' 1965 military intervention in the Dominican Republic.

42. Personal communication with the author, May 25, 2020.

43. Frances Stonor Saunders, "Modern Art Was CIA 'Weapon,'" *Independent*, October 22, 1995, https://www.independent.co.uk/news/world/modern-art-was-cia-weapon-1578808.html.

44. Saunders, *Cultural Cold War*, 212–34.

45. Another relevant example from Saunders's remarkable study: The "godfather of neoconservatism," Irving Kristol, founded a literary magazine, *Encounter*, in 1953, which was financed covertly by the CIA and British intelligence, MI6, until 1991. Multiple channels of support were used, including the Congress for Cultural Freedom, the Fairfield Foundation, the British Society of Cultural Freedom, the Ford Foundation, the Rockefeller Foundation, and the *Partisan Review*. Saunders, *Cultural Cold War*, 138–58.

46. Saunders, *Cultural Cold War*, 212. Saunders observed that Truman, like most Americans, viewed abstract art as cultural subversion.

47. Peter Finn and Petra Couvée, "CIA Turned 'Zhivago' into Cold Warrior," *Washington Post*, April 6, 2014, https://www.washingtonpost.com/world/national-security/during-cold-war-cia-used-doctor-zhivago-as-a-tool-to-undermine-soviet-union/2014/04/05/2ef3d9c6-b9ee-11e3-9a05-c739f29ccb08_story.html.

48. Henry Kissinger, *Diplomacy* (New York: Simon & Schuster, 1994).

49. Maureen Dowd, "Jimmy Carter Lusts for a Trump Posting," *New York Times*, October 21, 2017, https://www.nytimes.com/2017/10/21/opinion/sunday/jimmy-carter-lusts-trump-posting.html.

50. "Commemorative Remembrance of Hiroshima and Nagasaki: 75thAnniversary," Voices for a World Free of Nuclear Weapons," August 6, 2020, 1:01:58, https://www.youtube.com/watch?v=yTigpUvzB78.

51. See for example an exceptional discussion sponsored by the Simone Weil Center for Political Philosophy, especially the remarks of Professor Nicolai Petro, University of Rhode Island: "Theo-Politics, Tragedy, and Memory," December 16, 2020, 1:49:07, https://www.youtube.com/watch?v=l2q9cZy96p0.

52. Pope Benedict XVI, "Declaratio," Vatican, February 10, 2013, http://w2.vatican.va/content/benedict-xvi/en/speeches/2013/february/documents/hf_ben-xvi_spe_20130211_declaratio.html.

53. "Pope Decided to Resign after Cuba Trip, Vatican Advisor Says," Catholic News Agency, February 13, 2013, https://www.catholicnewsagency.com/news/pope-decided-to-resign-after-cuba-trip-vatican-advisor-says. Scandal involving his personal butler, who passed confidential documents to a journalist, as well as the revelation that corrupt vested interests were at war within the curia combined to further exhaust the introverted pontiff.

54. Pope Francis, "Chrism Mass Homily," Vatican, March 28, 2013, http://www.vatican.va/content/francesco/en/homilies/2013/documents/papa-francesco_20130328_messa-crismale.html.

CHAPTER 1

1. Anne O'Hare McCormick, "Italy and Popes and Parliaments," *New York Times*, July 24, 1921, S3, 8–9. At the time, the Catholic Church and Italian government were at odds over the Holy See's legal status, so the Vatican had no independent, physical footprint. Despite this limbo, as the journalist observed, the Vatican functioned as a hive of global outreach and awareness.

2. To rationalize the invasion, the US government argued that it was an act of self-defense and that it was necessary because Panama was abrogating elements of the Panama Canal Treaty. See Thomas Quigley, "The Legality of the US Invasion of Panama," *Yale Journal of International Law* 15 (1990): 276–315, https://digitalcommons.law.yale.edu/cgi/viewcontent.cgi?article=1561&context=yjil.

3. Larry Rohter, "The Noriega Case: Panama City; Papal Envoy Asserts Psychology, Not Ultimatum, Swayed Noriega," *New York Times*, January 6, 1990, https://www.nytimes.com/1990/01/06/world/noriega-case-panama-city-papal-envoy-asserts-psychology-not-ultimatum-swayed.html; Richard Boudreaux, "The Surrender of Noriega: Secluded Existence at Embassy Was Anything but Good Life for General: Refuge: Noriega Apparently Remained as Stubborn and Secretive as He Was in Power, Clerics and Visitors Say," *Los Angeles Times*, January 4, 1990, http://articles.latimes.com/1990-01-04/news/mn-336_1_noriega/2.

4. James Creagan, "Christmas at the Vatican," *Foreign Service Journal* 95, no. 1 (January/February 2018): 42, http://www.afsa.org/sites/default/files/januaryfebruary2018fsj.pdf.

5. Tauran was an important adviser to Pope Francis and to his two predecessors. He held a string of important positions from undersecretary to secretary for relations with states (1990–2003), effectively the Holy See's foreign minister. Pope John Paul II appointed Tauran to the College of Cardinals in 2003. He served as president of the Pontifical Council for Interreligious Dialogue (2007–2018). It was Tauran who announced to the world, from a balcony overlooking St. Peter's Square, Jorge Bergoglio's selection as pope. Tauran was a close adviser to Pope Francis until his death

while undergoing treatment for Parkinson's disease in 2018, just a few months after traveling to Saudi Arabia in a diplomatic breakthrough encouraged by the pope.

6. A diplomat from the Secretariat of State's second section, Msgr. Giacinto Berloco, was sent with verbal instructions to help the nuncio manage the situation. Soon after the crisis in Panama, he was ordained archbishop and sent to serve Zimbabwe and Mozambique as nuncio.

7. Personal communication with Ambassador Jim Creagan, July 9, 2020.

8. Ambassador Jim Creagan.

9. Rohter, "The Noriega Case."

10. Ed Magnuson, "A Guest Who Wore Out His Welcome," *Time*, January 15, 1990.

11. Carrie Kahn, "Former Panamanian Dictator and CIA Informant Manuel Noriega Dies," National Public Radio (NPR), May 30, 2017, https://www.npr.org/2017/05/30/530799394/former-panamanian-dictator-and-cia-informant-manuel-noriega-dies; "The U.S. Invades Panama," History, February 9, 2010, https://www.history.com/this-day-in-history/the-u-s-invades-panama.

12. At the height of US-Vatican tension over Noriega as a "refugee" in the nunciature, Jean-Louis Tauran told Chargé d'Affaires Creagan that Laboa "was clearly not of the *Accademia*." Tauran, an *Accademia* graduate, said if Laboa had attended the Vatican's school for diplomats he would have "barred" the door. The Holy See does not formally recognize "diplomatic asylum." According to Creagan, Tauran remarked more than once that Laboa had asked the United States to watch the nunciature property in Panama as other political leaders in crisis had sought protection in Holy See residences—especially in Latin America. Instead, the United States focused on watching the Cuban and Nicaraguan embassies.

13. Romans 2:5–6.

14. John Allen, *All the Pope's Men: The Inside Story of How the Vatican Really Thinks* (New York: Doubleday, 2004), 74.

15. Cardinal Archbishop James Harvey, interview with the author, Basilica of St. Paul Outside the Walls, Rome, September 2, 2017.

16. Gordon Thomas, *Gideon's Spies: The Secret History of the Mossad* (New York: Thomas Dunne, 2012), 213, emphasis added.

17. "Vienna Convention on Diplomatic Relations," opened for signature April 18, 1961, *United Nations Treaty Series* 500, no. 7310 (1964): 95, http://legal.un.org/ilc/texts/instruments/english/conventions/9_1_1961.pdf.

18. Pope Gelasius I (492–496) elaborated a theory regarding the relationship between temporal and ecclesial power, which depicted priestly authority as superior to royal authority because the priest must answer to God for the behavior of the temporal ruler. Known as the "two swords theory," it was deployed in later centuries to rationalize papal supremacy.

19. The IAEA referral came in 2005 but rumors about US military action against Iran were very much alive in 2006. See for example, Seymour Hersh, "The Iran Plans: Would President Bush Go to War?" *New Yorker*, April 9, 2006.

20. "Vatican: Iran Should Respect Nuclear Obligations," WikiLeaks, cable 06VATICAN29_a, dated February 22, 2006, https://wikileaks.org/plusd/cables/06VATICAN29_a.html.

21. "Holy See Concerned by US-India Nuclear Cooperation, Iran," WikiLeaks, cable 06VATICAN51_a, dated March 27, 2006, https://wikileaks.org/plusd/cables/06VATICAN51_a.html.

22. Janne Matlary, "The Diplomacy of Universal Values," in *Terzo Centenario (1701–2001)* (Rome: Tipografia Vaticana, 2003), 140.

23. "The Global Influence of the Holy See's Network," Jesuits in Britain, March 18, 2014, https://www.jesuit.org.uk/global-influence-holy-sees-network.

24. As an Arab speaker who studied Islam his whole career, and as a member of the Society of the Missionaries of Africa, Fitzgerald was an excellent choice to serve in Egypt, where Christians comprise about 10 percent of its ninety million people. According to his missionary confreres, though, the archbishop believed he was evicted from Rome because some in Benedict's circle wanted to decrease attention to interreligious dialogue. Pope Francis made Fitzgerald a cardinal in 2019. The 2006 transition of secretaries of state involved a rather hostile handoff from Cardinal Angelo Sodano, secretary of state from 1991 to 2006, to Cardinal Tarcisio Bertone, a confident of Benedict's with minimal diplomatic experience.

25. "Archbishop Martin Krebs Appointed New Apostolic Nuncio," CathNews New Zealand, May 10, 2013, https://cathnews.co.nz/2013/05/10/archbishop-martin-krebs-appointed-apostolic-nuncio.

26. Haidee Eugenio, "Nun: We Didn't Want to Lie for Apuron," Pacific Daily News, November 15, 2016, http://www.guampdn.com/story/news/2016/11/14/2m-donor-broker-we-did-not-want-lie-apuron-sammut-over-yona-property/93844028.

27. Wikipedia, s.v. "Pedro López Quintana," last modified April 9, 2020, https://en.wikipedia.org/wiki/Pedro_L%C3%B3pez_Quintana.

28. The International Atomic Energy Agency (IAEA), the UN High Commissioner for Refugees, the UN Office for Disarmament Affairs, and the International Organization for Migration (IOM) are examples of UN agencies based in Vienna with which the Vatican often engages. Another organization in Vienna that the Holy See collaborates with is the King Abdullah bin Abdulaziz International Centre for Interreligious and Intercultural Dialogue, inaugurated in 2012.

29. "The United Nations in Vienna," United Nations Information Service Vienna, last modified January 16, 2020, http://www.unis.unvienna.org/unis/en/unvienna.html.

30. "New Nuncio to Kuwait, Qatar Affirms Pope's Commitment to Interreligious Dialogue," *Vatican News*, January 8, 2021, https://www.vaticannews.va/en/vatican-city/news/2021-01/nuncio-speaks-about-service-in-haiti-and-now-to-kuwait-and-qatar.html.

31. Peter Wells, "Archbishop Peter Wells 2017," Archdiocese of Oklahoma City, April 3, 2017, YouTube video, 29:04, https://www.youtube.com/watch?v=3wDoMOQ9FVg.

32. Wells, "Archbishop Peter Wells 2017."

33. "Pope Appoints New Vatican Ambassador to Israel," *Times of Israel*, September 13, 2017, https://www.timesofisrael.com/pope-appoints-new-vatican-ambassador-to-israel.

34. "Tension between Turkey and Cyprus over Gas Search," EuroNews, February 11, 2018, http://www.euronews.com/2018/02/11/tension-between-turkey-and-cyprus-over-gas-search.

35. David Alvarez, "The Professionalization of the Papal Diplomatic Service, 1909–1967," *Catholic Historical Review* 75, no. 2 (April 1989): 247–48. The school was renamed May 26, 1939, a few months after Pius XII took office.

36. Bernardito Auza, "Pope Francis' Diplomacy" (lecture, School of Diplomacy and International Relations, South Orange, NJ, March 1, 2017), https://holyseemission.org/contents/statements/58ba0b742bc1b.php.

37. Archbishop Bernardito C. Auza, "Lecture on Papal Diplomacy," Seton Hall University School of Diplomacy and International Relations, South Orange, NJ, YouTube video, 1:04:38, https://www.youtube.com/watch?v=WRtaEfBDGX8.

38. Justine Jablonska, "Independent Poland's Baptism by Fire: The Battle of Warsaw, 1919–1920," *Cosmopolitan Review* 2, no. 3 (October 2010), http://cosmopolitanreview.com/battle-of-warsaw-1919-1920; Paul Suski, "The Miracle on Assumption Day," Catholic Insight, November 23, 2017.

39. This is Pius XI, who negotiated the landmark Lateran Accords—a monumental treaty signed with Italian prime minister Benito Mussolini that preserved the Catholic Church's independence while formalizing its sovereignty. For a superb account of Ratti's sojourn in Poland, see Neal Pease, *Rome's Most Faithful Daughter: The Catholic Church and Independent Poland, 1914–1939* (Athens: Ohio University Press, 2009).

40. Jason Horowitz, "Vatican Official Is Killed by Gunmen in Burundi," *New York Times*, December 30, 2003, https://www.nytimes.com/2003/12/30/world/vatican-official-is-killed-by-gunmen-in-burundi.html.

41. Paddy Agnew, "Vatican Diplomat Who Acts as Pope's Eyes on the World," *Irish Independent*, August 5, 2018, https://www.independent.ie/world-news/europe/vatican-diplomat-who-acts-as-popes-eyes-on-the-world-37185383.html.

42. "A Private Man Whose View Was Formed by Awareness of Suffering," *Irish Times*, January 3, 2004, https://www.irishtimes.com/news/a-private-man-whose-view-was-formed-by-awareness-of-suffering-1.1128778.

43. Mark Dew, "Archbishop Paul Gallagher: The Gregarious Diplomat," *Catholic Herald*, November 13, 2014, https://catholicherald.co.uk/archbishop-paul-gallagher-the-gregarious-diplomat.

44. Elise Harris and Andrea Gagliarducci, "'Beloved' Syria's New Cardinal a Sign of the Pope's Closeness," Catholic News Agency, November 15, 2016, https://www.catholicnewsagency.com/news/beloved-syrias-new-cardinal-a-sign-of-the-popes-closeness-46297.

45. Elise Harris, "Pope Makes Appeal for 'Beloved and Martyred Syria, Where the War Has Exploded Again,'" *National Catholic Register*, February 26, 2018, http://www.ncregister.com/daily-news/pope-makes-appeal-for-beloved-and-martyred-syria-where-the-war-has-exploded.

46. "25th Annual Path to Peace Gala Spotlights Syria in Honoring Cardinal Zenari," Permanent Observer of the Holy See to the United Nations, last modified April 10, 2020, https://holyseemission.org/contents/events/592c52ef186c4.php.

47. In 1870, the First Vatican Council declared the pope "infallible," a power move to counteract his imminent loss of temporal clout, as we will explore in chapter 4. (The First Vatican Council convened in December 1869, and its last votes were taken in July 1870. The council intended to reconvene. However, on September 20, 1870, Italian troops marched on Rome, took possession of the city, and declared it the Kingdom of Italy's capital. In October, Pius IX issued a papal bull suspending the council indefinitely.) To invoke infallibility, the pope is required to formally declare that a new doctrine must be believed. The authority is rarely used and was last invoked in 1950 by Pope Pius XII regarding Mary's assumption into heaven. The Second Vatican Council promoted a revised vision of Church infallibility as emerging from the agreement between pope and bishops regarding a definitive teaching. So, although the doctrine of infallibility stands, it is perceived as a historically situated decree with limited contemporary value.

48. Matthew 16:18: "And so I say to you, you are Peter, and upon this rock I will build my church, and the gates of the netherworld shall not prevail against it."

49. Joseph Ratzinger, *Church, Ecumenism, and Politics: New Endeavors in Ecclesiology* (San Francisco: Ignatius, 2008).

50. The Papal States were about the size of Switzerland. Switzerland: 41,285 km^2 (15,940 sq. mi.) vs. Papal States: 44,030 km^2 (17,000 sq. mi.).

51. Pope Pius VI's successor, Pope Pius VII (1800–1823), tried to reconcile with Napoleon; he even agreed to crown him emperor at Notre Dame Cathedral in 1804. But Pius VII, too, was eventually kidnapped by the French, hustled out of Rome, and exiled. For some five years, the pope, a Benedictine monk, survived in modest quarters, which seemed to bother him little, according to his peerless secretary of state, Cardinal Ercole Consalvi, who was ordered to Paris with the rest of the College of Cardinals. Napoleon abdicated in 1814 soon after being trounced by the Prussians, then the Russians. The emperor's defeat freed Pope Pius VII and his entourage to ride back to Rome in triumph. Consalvi masterfully managed to regain the Papal States at the 1815 Congress of Vienna. Such an extreme battle of wills between state and church is what Vatican diplomacy seeks to ameliorate. As we will see in chapter 4, the loss of landed interests drastically changed the nature of church-state rivalry.

52. Thomas J. Reese, *Inside the Vatican: The Politics and Organization of the Catholic Church* (Cambridge, MA: Harvard University Press, 1996), 175.

53. The *Annuario Pontificio* lists the Holy See's employees and a host of other information. It is a gesture of real transparency that the information is released each year on December 31. In 2020, the secretariat's first section (general affairs) employed 132 people, while the second section (relations with states) had 55. A new third section (diplomatic staff), created by Francis for the professional needs of the diplomatic corps, had 3 employees. Francis has not increased the size of the SOS staff. Most employees are priests, but I counted about twenty women religious in 2020 as well as some lay experts, including a few laywomen.

54. Francis Rooney, interview with the author, Washington, DC, August 16, 2017. The secretary of state has been the most important official adviser to the pope since 1692 when Pope Innocent XI permanently eliminated the nepotistic office of cardinal nephew, a top administrative position typically given to a pope's nephew, relative,

or close friend. One of the first cardinal nephews with a portfolio combining administration of the Papal States, high-level Church matters, and diplomatic relationships across Europe—and the title secretary of state—was St. Charles Borromeo. At age twenty-two, his uncle Pope Pius IV brought him to Rome to serve this elevated function. Three years later, he became a priest. See Joseph Murphy, "The Pontifical Diplomatic Service," *Ecclesiastical Review* 11, no 1 (July 1909), 2–3.

55. Each title has an interesting history, typically going back centuries.

56. The 1988 apostolic constitution *Pastor Bonus* regulates the structure and responsibilities of these offices until Pope Francis releases a new apostolic constitution, *Praedicate Evangelium*. This reorganization effort got underway in 2013. See http://w2.vatican.va/content/romancuria/en.html for current list.

57. On the roles and responsibilities of dicasteries (a term used as a synonym for all these offices) as well as overlapping functions, see Reese, *Inside the Vatican*, 115–36. Another confusing fact in Vaticanese is the use of different titles for the cardinals who head up curial offices: those in charge of a congregation are called "prefects," while those who head a council are called "presidents." Varied nomenclature flows from the history of each office. The term *dicastery* is used as a synonym for each office in the curia, in addition to being, it seems, Pope Francis's preferred term for new, consolidated entities.

58. Francis's first prominent organizational reform was to combine four councils to create a new dicastery: pontifical councils for justice and peace, charity (Cor Unum), migrants and itinerant peoples, and health care workers became the Dicastery for Promoting Integral Human Development headed by Cardinal Peter Turkson from Ghana, former president of the Pontifical Council for Justice and Peace (PCJP). The new dicastery began work on January 1, 2017. The PCJP, founded by Pope Paul VI, was a particularly high-profile player, albeit with little real power. Francis's rationale for folding it into a bigger structure is not entirely clear. Within that new dicastery is a section dedicated to migrants and refugees, reporting directly to the supreme pontiff according to the statutes released on August 17, 2016: https://w2.vatican.va/content/francesco/en/motu_proprio/documents/papa-francesco_20160817_statuto-dicastero-servizio-sviluppo-umano-integrale.html.

59. The last major reorganization was implemented by Pope John Paul II and outlined in his apostolic constitution *Pastor Bonus* (Good Shepherd, 1988). On the vision embodied by Francis's anticipated reforms in *Praedicate Evangelium*, see Richard Gaillardetz, "Francis' Draft of Curial Reform Fundamentally Reimagines Vatican's Role," *National Catholic Reporter*, June 5, 2019, https://www.ncronline.org/news/opinion/francis-draft-curial-reform-fundamentally-reimagines-vaticans-role.

60. "Christmas Greetings to the Roman Curia, Address of His Holiness Pope Francis, Clementine Hall" (address, Holy See, December 21, 2019), http://www.vatican.va/content/francesco/en/speeches/2019/december/documents/papa-francesco_20191221_curia-romana.html#_ftn14.

61. Known for centuries as the Congregation for the Propagation of the Faith, *Propaganda Fide Sacra Congregatio de Propaganda Fide* in Latin, one still hears references to *Propaganda Fide* or just *Propaganda* in Rome. Pope John Paul II changed its name in 1982 but did not change its mission.

62. "Christmas Greetings," December 21, 2019.

63. "Pope Francis: Future Holy See Diplomats Will Spend a Year on Mission," Vatican News, February 17, 2020, https://www.vaticannews.va/en/pope/news/2020-02/pope-francis-letter-vatican-diplomats-spend-year-on-mission.html.

64. For a brief history of the Congregation for Oriental Churches, see http://www.vatican.va/roman_curia/congregations/orientchurch/profilo/rc_con_corient_pro_20030320_profile.html.

65. Victor Gaetan, "The Church Undivided: Benedict's Quest to Bring Christians Back Together," *Foreign Affairs*, May/June 2013, https://www.foreignaffairs.com/articles/2013-04-03/church-undivided.

66. Cardinal Kurt Koch, interview with the author, Kolymvari, Greece, June 21, 2016.

67. In 1059, Pope Nicolas II gave cardinals this authority in the papal bull *In Nomine Domini*.

68. *Ingravescentem Aetatem* (age limit set for functions by cardinals) Motu Proprio, November 21, 1970, https://www.ewtn.com/catholicism/library/age-limit-set-for-functions-by-cardinals-8998. Another significant reform introduced by Pope Paul VI says 120 should be the maximum number of cardinal electors, although Pope John Paul II and Pope Francis both surpassed this upper limit at various points: Apostolic constitution *Regimini Ecclesiae Universae* of August 15, 1967.

69. Reese, *Inside the Vatican*, 69.

70. Pope Francis, "Chirograph by Which a Council of Cardinals Is Established to Assist the Holy Father in the Governance of the Universal Church and to Study Possible Revisions of the Apostolic Constitution 'Pastor Bonus' on the Roman Curia," Holy See, September 28, 2013, http://w2.vatican.va/content/francesco/en/letters/2013/documents/papa-francesco_20130928_chirografo-consiglio-cardinali.html.

71. The last cardinal who was not a priest was canon lawyer and curial judge Teodolfo Mertel, who died in 1899. In 1962, Pope John XXIII ruled that all cardinals must be consecrated bishops in the moto proprio *Cum Gravissima*. A few priests have been given dispensation from that requirement, especially those made cardinal when they are over age of eighty. For example, Pope Benedict XVI named Jesuit biblical scholar Albert Vanhoye, SJ, cardinal in 2006, when he was eighty-two years old, thus beyond the age for participating in a papal conclave.

72. Only cardinals can head up the prestigious offices known as congregations (and most pontifical councils are led by cardinals, although a few are led by bishops). It was Pope Sixtus V (1585–1590) who first distributed significant administrative functions between "congregations" of cardinals, fifteen in all, in the 1588 apostolic constitution *Immensa Aeterni Dei*. Several were dedicated to managing papal territory, including the Congregation for Equipping the Fleet and Maintaining It for the Defense of the Church. The Holy See had a navy from about the ninth century until Pope Leo XIII decommissioned the last boat, a small warship, the *Immaculate Conception*.

73. Statistics are updated often: http://press.vatican.va/content/salastampa/en/documentation/cardinali---statistiche/composizione-per-area.html.

74. An article that reflects the esteem in which the archbishop was held in Mexico is by Jorge E. Traslosheros, "Why the U.S. Won the Lottery with New Papal Envoy,"

Crux, May 17, 2016, https://cruxnow.com/church/2016/05/why-the-u-s-won-the-lottery-with-new-papal-envoy.

75. Gerard O'Connell, "Pope Francis Appoints New Nuncio to the United States," *America* (magazine), April 12, 2016, https://www.americamagazine.org/issue/pope-appoints-french-born-archbishop-christophe-pierre-new-nuncio-united-states.

76. Archbishop Christophe Pierre, interview with the author, Washington, DC, September 13, 2017. When I interviewed Archbishop Pierre, rather than discuss his accomplishments, he turned most questions back to his childhood, extolling the beauty of his village in Brittany, France, and the Christian values impressed on him in the "domestic Church," his family.

77. Exceptions are not uncommon. Pope Paul VI appointed Archbishop Luigi Poggi nuncio-at-large for Eastern Europe in 1973, a function passed to another archbishop in 1986. See Hansjakob Stehle, "Papal Eastern Diplomacy and the Vatican Apparatus," in *Catholicism and Politics in Communist Societies*, ed. Pedro Ramet (Durham, NC: Duke University Press, 1990), 344.

78. Zsolt Aradi, James I. Tucek, and James C. O'Neill, *Pope John XXIII: An Authoritative Biography* (New York: Farrar, Straus & Cudahy, 1959), 146–47.

79. Reese, *Inside the Vatican*, 24.

80. Pope Paul IV, "Dogmatic Constitution on the Church, *Lumen Gentium*, Solemnly Promulgated by His Holiness Pope Paul VI," Holy See, November 21, 1964, http://www.vatican.va/archive/hist_councils/ii_vatican_council/documents/vat-ii_const_19641121_lumen-gentium_en.html. One of the earliest forms of Church governance was the gathering of bishops in councils or synods, dating back to the second century in Asia Minor (Turkey today). But as recently as the 1917 Code of Canon Law, heroically assembled under Pope Pius X and completed by Pope Benedict XV's staff, provincial councils were only required every twenty years, they needed approval from Rome, and they had restricted authority—decentralization was obviously not in vogue.

81. "Synodality: Walking Together," The Dialogue, August 27, 2018, http://thedialog.org/catechetical-corner/synodality-walking-together.

82. As Thomas Reese, SJ, explains, "The Second Vatican Council (1962–65) made episcopal conferences not only possible but absolutely necessary" (Reese, *Inside the Vatican*, 32). The only way to manage reform such as changing the language of the liturgy into local vernacular languages was to manage translations from Latin through an authoritative local coordinating mechanism. That task fell to the national bishops' conferences. Reese makes clear, though, that power is not "given" to these conferences but derives from the fact that a bishop has inherent authority to govern his jurisdiction. Of course, balanced against papal primacy, the Holy See can ultimately regulate—or, in extreme cases, curtail—a bishop's local authority.

83. John L. Allen Jr., "Ex-Vatican Spokesmen Challenge Papal Accuser over Davis Meeting," Crux, September 3, 2015, https://cruxnow.com/vatican/2018/09/03/ex-vatican-spokesmen-challenge-papal-accuser-over-davis-meeting; Jay Levine, "Vatican Source: Pope Blindsided by Meeting with Controversial Kentucky Clerk," CBS Chicago (website), October 1, 2015, https://chicago.cbslocal.com/2015/10/01/vatican-source-pope-blindsided-by-meeting-with-controversial-kentucky-clerk.

84. The account reported by Michael Sean Winters at the *National Catholic Reporter* gives insight into Vatican decision making. Winters reports that the night before the private "meet and greet" event, Viganò asked Pope Francis, who was staying overnight at the nunciature, if he would agree to see a woman Viganò described as a "conscientious objector." Francis told the nuncio to run it by Cardinal Parolin, who was already at a local hotel. Viganò went to find the secretary of state but he was asleep, so he spoke to the *sostituto*, Archbishop Angelo Becciu, and the secretary for relations with states, Archbishop Gallagher. Neither man was familiar with the Davis case and, based on the nuncio's description of her cause as a matter of religious freedom, OK'd the inclusion of Davis and her husband. Meanwhile, the couple was on standby, waiting for Viganò's green light. The nuncio failed to tell the Vatican officials that local bishops had already weighed in on the idea with a negative assessment. Michael Sean Winters, "Viganò's Latest Statement Part of Concerted Campaign to Attack Papacy," *National Catholic Reporter*, September 2, 2018, https://www.ncronline.org/news/opinion/distinctly-catholic/vigan-s-latest-statement-part-concerted-campaign-attack-papacy.

85. According to some sources, Viganò's anger at being sent into retirement over this offense fueled so much resentment of Francis that he unleashed one of the least characteristic acts of any nuncio in the last one hundred years: a public attack on the pontiff, in the form of a letter, calling for Francis's resignation. Jason Horowitz, "The Man Who Took on the Pope: The Story behind the Viganò Letter," *New York Times*, August 28, 2018, https://www.nytimes.com/2018/08/28/world/europe/archbishop-carlo-maria-vigano-pope-francis.html.

86. Rep. Francis Rooney, interview with the author, Washington, DC, August 16, 2017.

87. The Vatican, "Catholic Church Statistics 2020," Agenzia Fides, October 16, 2020, http://www.fides.org/en/stats/68840-VATICAN_CATHOLIC_CHURCH_STATISTICS_2020

88. Niall Ferguson, *The Square and the Tower: Networks and Power, from the Freemasons to Facebook* (New York: Penguin, 2018). Similar ideas are presented in Ferguson's "The False Prophesy of Hyperconnectivity," *Foreign Affairs*, September/October 2017, 68–79.

89. A node could be an individual believer, a single church, a parish, a Catholic school, or a Catholic charity, all with relationships and interactions involving the faith. Betweenness centrality measures whether a node lies on a path between other nodes. The nuncio and the bishop have very high betweenness centrality. Removal of these nodes from the system disrupts its functionality because they serve as important switching points for information.

90. The Society of Jesus was also founded to educate, teach, and serve the pope, but missionary work was part of its original raison d'être. See John W. O'Malley, *The Jesuits: A History from Ignatius to the Present* (London: Rowman & Littlefield, 2014).

91. Victor Gaetan, "From Texas to Siberia to Kyrgyzstan," *National Catholic Register*, March 11, 2019, https://www.ncregister.com/interview/from-texas-to-siberia-to-kyrgyzstan-one-priest-s-missionary-journey.

92. Maria-Pia Negro Chin, "Mission of Love in Korea," Maryknoll, January 1, 2017, https://maryknollmagazine.org/2017/01/mission-love-korea; Victor Gaetan, "North Korea: Another Option," *National Catholic Register*, April 28, 2017, http://www.ncregister.com/daily-news/north-korea-another-option; Victor Gaetan, "South Korea's Hidden Treasure: A Vibrant Catholic Church," *National Catholic Register*, November 28, 2017, http://www.ncregister.com/daily-news/south-koreas-hidden-treasure-a-vibrant-catholic-church.

93. Fr. Gerard Hammond, MM (Ham Je Do), interview with the author, Seoul, South Korea, November 3, 2017.

94. Lydia O'Kane, "Pope Honors Italian Missionary Nun at General Audience," Vatican News, March 27, 2019, https://www.vaticannews.va/en/pope/news/2019-03/pope-honours-italian-missionary-nun-at-general-audience.html.

95. Ferguson, "The False Prophecy," 73.

96. GianPaolo Salvini, SJ, "Church Numbers in the World," *La Civiltà Cattolica*, June 29, 2020, https://www.laciviltacattolica.com/church-numbers-in-the-world.

97. Massimo Faggioli, *Sorting Out Catholicism: A Brief History of the New Ecclesial Movements* (Collegeville, MN: Michael Glazer, 2014).

98. John L. Allen Jr., "On Giussani Milestone, Communion and Liberation Still Going Strong," Crux, February 22, 2017, https://cruxnow.com/analysis/2017/02/21/giussani-milestone-communion-liberation-still-going-strong.

99. Thomas M. Landy, "Italian Lay Organization Sant'Egidio Focuses on Prayer, Service, Friendship," Catholics & Cultures, updated July 31, 2018, https://www.catholicsandcultures.org/italy/lay-organizations/santegidio.

100. John L. Allen Jr., "Memo to a Divided Church: Meet the Focolare," *All Things Catholic* (blog), *National Catholic Reporter*, March 10, 2011, https://www.ncronline.org/blogs/all-things-catholic/memo-divided-church-meet-focolare.

101. William Collinge, *Historical Dictionary of Catholicism* (Metuchen, NJ: Scarecrow Press, 2012), 299.

102. "Who We Are," Caritas, last updated April 9, 2020, https://www.caritas.org/who-we-are.

103. Cesar A. Chelala, "Mozambique Can Be Brought Back from the Brink," *Christian Science Monitor*, June 9, 1992, https://www.csmonitor.com/1992/0609/09192.html.

104. Eric Morier-Genoud and Pierre Anouilh, "Revolution, War and Democracy: The Catholic Church in Mozambique," in *Religion and Politics in a Global Society: Comparative Perspectives from the Portuguese-Speaking World*, ed. Paul C. Manuel, Alynna Lyon, and Clyde Wilcox (Lanham, MD: Lexington Books, 2013), 185–203.

105. "Dom Jaime Gonçalves' Funeral to Be Held on Saturday in Beira, Mozambique," Club of Mozambique, April 6, 2016, http://clubofmozambique.com/news/dom-jaime-goncalves-funeral-to-be-held-on-saturday-in-beira-mozambique.

106. Cameron Hume, *Ending Mozambique's War: The Role of Mediation and Good Offices* (Washington, DC: US Institute for Peace, 1994), 32.

107. "War, Mother of All Poverty: Mozambique," Community of Sant'Egidio website, http://www.santegidio.org/en/pace/pace3.htm.

108. Hume, *Ending Mozambique's War*.

109. "General Peace Agreement for Mozambique," *Peace Accords Matrix*, University of Notre Dame website, Croc Institute for International Peace Studies, updated April 9, 2020, https://peaceaccords.nd.edu/accord/general-peace-agreement-mozambique.

110. David Smock, "Divine Intervention: Regional Reconciliation through Faith," *Harvard International Review* 25, no. 4 (Winter 2004): 3, http://hir.harvard.edu/article/?a=1190.

111. Antonio M. D. Nucifora and Luiz A. Pereira da Silva, "Rapid Growth and Economic Transformation in Mozambique, 1993–2009," in *Yes Africa Can: Success Stories from a Dynamic Continent*, ed. Punam Chuhan-Pole and Manka Angwafo (Washington, DC: World Bank, 2011), 65, https://issuu.com/world.bank.publications/docs/9780821387450.

112. John L. Allen Jr., "Interview with Sant'Egidio Founder Andrea Riccardi," *National Catholic Reporter*, July 23, 2004, http://www.natcath.org/mainpage/specialdocuments/riccardi.htm.

113. "The Community," Community of Sant'Egidio website, updated April 9, 2020, https://www.santegidio.org/pageID/30008/langID/en/THE-COMMUNITY.html.

114. Morier-Genoud and Anouilh, "Revolution, War and Democracy."

CHAPTER 2

1. Pope Pius XI, "Speech to the Students of Mondragone College" (May 14, 1929), in Robert A. Graham, SJ, *Vatican Diplomacy: Study of Church and State on the International Plane* (Princeton, NJ: Princeton University Press, 1959), 351. According to Graham, the pope was indirectly referencing a dispute with Prime Minister Benito Mussolini over education; the Holy See and Mussolini had signed the Lateran Treaty, establishing Vatican City, just three months before. Mondragone College was a Jesuit-run high school for young men (1865–1953) located just outside Rome.

2. Pope Francis, "Address of His Holiness Pope Francis to the Community of the Pontifical Ecclesiastical Academy" (address, Consistory Hall of the Vatican Apostolic Palace, Vatican City, June 25, 2015), http://w2.vatican.va/content/francesco/en/speeches/2015/june/documents/papa-francesco_20150625_pontificia-*Accademia*-ecclesiastica.html.

3. A contemporary example is the Holy See's September 2018 agreement with the Chinese government, which I explore in chapter 11.

4. "Remembering Pearl Harbor: A Pearl Harbor Fact Sheet," United States Census Bureau, last modified November 7, 2016, https://www.census.gov/history/pdf/pearl-harbor-fact-sheet-1.pdf. The USS *Arizona* had a crew of 1,177 men, including twenty-three sets of brothers; Barbara Maranzani, "5 Facts about Pearl Harbor and USS *Arizona*," History, updated December 7, 2018, https://www.history.com/news/5-facts-about-pearl-harbor-and-the-uss-arizona.

5. Pierre Blet, *Pius XII and the Second World War: According to the Archives of the Vatican* (Mahwah, NJ: Paulist Press, 1999), 127. The message was first conveyed

to the secretary of state, Cardinal Maglione, by Francesco Babuscio, counselor at the Italian embassy to the Holy See. Luigi Maglione said the Holy Father would approve the request, but it should come from the Vatican's own representative in Tokyo, an apostolic delegate in-post. Within two weeks, the apostolic delegate met with Japan's foreign minister, received the request formally, and cabled it to Rome. Blet's summary is based on documents he reviewed in the Vatican archives. What's clear is that the decision was not controversial in the eyes of the pope or the Secretariat of State's office.

6. Gerard O'Connell, "Pope Francis Highlights Friendly Relations between Japan and the Holy See," *America* (magazine), May 20, 2016, https://www.americamagazine.org/content/dispatches/japan-and-holy-see.

7. Harold Tittmann Jr., *Inside the Vatican of Pius XII* (New York: Doubleday, 2004), 103–4.

8. Blet, *Pius XII*, 129–30.

9. Tittmann, *Inside the Vatican*, 104.

10. Tittmann, *Inside the Vatican*, 102.

11. Tittmann, *Inside the Vatican*, 103.

12. Tittmann, *Inside the Vatican*, 106.

13. Tittmann, *Inside the Vatican*, 109.

14. Pope Pius XI, "Speech to the Students of Mondragone College."

15. The Vienna Convention on Diplomatic Relations of 1961 provides the framework for relations between independent states. It defines the privileges and immunities of accredited diplomatic agents. Article 14 recognizes "ambassadors or nuncios accredited to heads of state" as comprising the first class of diplomatic agent. https://treaties.un.org/doc/Treaties/1964/06/19640624%2002-10%20AM/Ch_III_3p.pdf.

16. Jesus advised the Pharisees, "Then repay to Caesar what belongs to Caesar and to God what belongs to God," when asked if they should pay a census tax. Matthew 22:21.

17. The Great Commission is described in the last passage of the Gospel of Matthew. Matthew 28:19.

18. Raymond Cohen and Raymond Westbrook, eds., *Amarna Diplomacy: The Beginnings of International Relations* (Baltimore, MD: Johns Hopkins University Press, 2002). As a side note, the first non-Egyptian to describe a key piece of evidence regarding the Amarna era under the rule of Pharaoh Akhenaten was a Jesuit priest, Claude Sicard, SJ, who in 1717 recognized the importance of a boundary stele and copied down its inscriptions.

19. Garrett Mattingly, "The First Resident Embassies: Mediaeval Italian Origins of Modern Diplomacy," *Speculum: A Journal of Mediaeval Studies* 12, no. 4 (October 1937): 434–35. The importance of permanent embassies is that with their widespread acceptance we see the institutionalization of foreign policy conducted through accredited agents; Graham, *Vatican Diplomacy*, 100–03. Even Catholic accounts of papal diplomacy typically credit Venice as being the first sovereign to deploy a system of permanent, resident ambassadors. This was a significant innovation, but more fundamental is the concept of a sovereign's envoy granted special privileges by another power *because* he stands as a living representative of the sending sovereign. That

system of mission-specific diplomats was established by the Holy See in the classical era, as described.

20. The earliest record of the bishop of Rome being called "pope" is in the late third century, when the appellation was used for Pope Marcellinus (294–306).

21. Bruce Shelley, "325 the First Council of Nicaea," *Christianity Today*, October 1, 1990, https://www.christianitytoday.com/history/issues/issue-28/325-first-council-of-nicea.html.

22. *The Catholic Encyclopedia*, vol. 9 (1910), s.v. "Legate," New Advent, https://www.newadvent.org/cathen/09118a.htm.

23. *The Catholic Encyclopedia*, vol. 1 (1907), s.v. "Apocrisiarius," New Advent, https://www.newadvent.org/cathen/01599a.htm.

24. Graham, *Vatican Diplomacy*, 114–16.

25. John Tracy Ellis, "The Catholic Church and Peace Efforts," *Notre Dame Law Review* 9, no. 2 (1934): 173–214, https://scholarship.law.nd.edu/ndlr/vol9/iss2/2.

26. The conflict is also known as the Albigensian Crusade.

27. Graham, *Vatican Diplomacy*, 118–19.

28. The term *embassies* can refer to entourages, led by an ambassador, with diplomatic purpose.

29. Mattingly, "The First Resident Embassies," 434–36

30. Mattingly, "The First Resident Embassies," 435.

31. Ellis, "The Catholic Church and Peace Efforts," 177; *The Catholic Encyclopedia*, vol. 8 (1910), s.v. "Innocent I," New Advent, https://www.newadvent.org/cathen/08011a.htm.

32. N. S. Gill, "Attila the Hun Portraits," ThoughtCo., updated March 8, 2017, https://www.thoughtco.com/attila-the-hun-portraits-4122675; Hartman Grisar, SJ, *History of Rome and the Popes in the Middle Ages* (London: Kegan Paul, Trench, Trübner & Co., 1911).

33. *The Catholic Encyclopedia*, vol. 9 (1912), s.v. "Vandals," New Advent, http://www.newadvent.org/cathen/15268b.htm: "It is said that on 2 June, 455 . . ."

34. Ellis, "The Catholic Church and Peace Efforts," 177–78.

35. Maximus defeated Emperor Gratian, who was killed while trying to flee.

36. Trier, on the banks of the Moselle River (a tributary of the Rhine), was the key city of the Roman northern territories. It is considered Germany's oldest city and is the burial place of St. Matthias, the apostle selected to replace Judas.

37. Kevin Kaatz, *Early Controversies and the Growth of Christianity* (Westport, CT: Praeger, 2012), 121–23.

38. Edward Gibbon, *History of the Decline and Fall of the Roman Empire*, vol. 5 (London: W. Strahan, 1783; Ann Arbor, MI: Text Creation Partnership, 2011), chap. 27, 65–72, https://quod.lib.umich.edu/e/ecco/004848826.0001.005?rgn=main;view=fulltext; Lorenzo Cappelletti, "Ambrose and Theodosius: From Emotion to Penance to Respect of Public Authorities," *30 Days*, January 2010, http://www.30giorni.it/articoli_id_22194_l3.htm.

39. Matthew 22:21.

40. "How John Paul II Helped Chile and Argentina Avoid Going to War," Rome Reports, November 30, 2009, YouTube video, 2:52, https://www.youtube.com/watch?v=6D6zXEk2SKs.

41. Thomas Princen, *Intermediaries in International Conflict* (Princeton, NJ: Princeton University Press, 1992), is the most detailed source on Vatican engagement in the conflict from start to finish. In 1971, the two governments had agreed to binding arbitration, using the process for resolving boundary matters established in a 1902 treaty between the countries. But when Queen Elizabeth II affirmed the findings of the International Court at The Hague in favor of awarding three islands to Chile, Argentina balked. Its government simply rejected the ruling and started using economic and military pressure on Chile to reopen negotiations. When Chile refused to relent (because it considered that international law had already found in its favor) in late 1978, the situation careened toward war. In Argentina's view, by conceding three islands at the mouth of the Beagle Channel to Chile, Argentina was offering to "share" the Atlantic—which it saw as contrary to national security *and* sovereignty.

42. For the US perspective on the crisis, see P. Peter Sarros's excellent book based on his role as an American diplomat working in Rome at the Presidential Mission at the Vatican: P. Peter Sarros, "Beagle Channel Mediation: Diplomacy and War Prevention," in *U.S.-Vatican Relations, 1975–1980: A Diplomatic Study* (Notre Dame, IN: University of Notre Dame Press, 2020), 37–52.

43. Samorè was accompanied by two native Spanish speakers from the curia, one from Colombia and another from Spain.

44. Quoted in Thomas Princen, "Beagle Channel Negotiations," *Pew Case Studies in International Affairs*, Institute for the Study of Diplomacy (1985): 18, https://muse.jhu.edu/chapter/1295848.

45. Princen, "Beagle Channel Negotiations," 14. It should be noted that the Holy See also benefited from a constant stream of intelligence from the United States. Neither country trusted the Carter administration, but information gathered by US embassies in the region was transmitted to Carter's personal representative in Rome, who shared it with the Secretariat of State.

46. As opposed to a two-hundred-mile exclusive zone granted by the Hague tribunal.

47. Martin Andersen, "Chile, Argentina Sign Protocol on Beagle," *Washington Post*, October 19, 1984, https://www.washingtonpost.com/archive/politics/1984/10/19/chile-argentina-sign-protocol-on-beagle/f8e5a9db-f01c-4a5a-9691-f91861c095eb.

48. Princen, *Intermediaries*, 161. Although possession of the three islands might seem to be the major prize, the Argentinian obsession was a "bi-oceanic principle" that left Argentina in control of the Atlantic Ocean since Chile controlled access to the Pacific. The treaty's elaborate ocean demarcation allowed Argentina to declare victory with regard to control of the Atlantic Ocean.

49. Princen, *Intermediaries*, 172.

50. One of these, Archbishop Pio Laghi, nuncio to Argentina (1974–1980), was next posted to the United States (1980–1990) where he became friendly with then Vice President George H. W. Bush. In 2003, Pope John Paul II sent Cardinal Laghi on

a mission from Rome to Washington, DC, to personally appeal to President George W. Bush against the imminent invasion of Iraq.

51. "Cardenal Antonio Samorè Pass, an Andean Border Road," Dangerous Roads, last modified April 16, 2020, https://www.dangerousroads.org/south-america/chile/4319-paso-cardenal-antonio-samor. In November 2009, the presidents of Argentina and Chile joined Pope Benedict XVI to celebrate the twenty-fifth anniversary of the treaty. The pope highlighted the patience required and the "will for peace against the barbarism and unreason of violence and war"; "Anniversary of Peace Treaty between Argentina and Chile," Vatican Information Service, November 30, 2009, https://visnews-en.blogspot.com/2009/11/anniversary-of-peace-treaty-between.html.

52. P. W. Brown, "Pactum Calixtinum: An Innovation in Papal Diplomacy," *Catholic Historical Review* 8, no. 2 (1922): 180–90. Brown argues that this agreement should not be called a concordat but rather a *Pactum Calixtinum* because the term *concordat* did not gain currency until Nicholas de Cusa wrote *De Concordantia Catholica* in 1435.

53. Napoleon never stopped persecuting the universal Church. Despite the agreement, Napoleon and Pope Pius VII were in continuous conflict; the emperor invaded and annexed the Papal States in 1808, arrested the pope, and confined him in the Château de Fontainebleau, south of Paris.

54. Agostino Casaroli, *The Martyrdom of Patience: The Holy See and the Communist Countries (1963–89)* (Toronto: Ave Maria Centre of Peace, 2007), xvi l, 49–60.

55. Jan de Weydenthal, "East: Casaroli Remembered at Vatican as Consummate Diplomat," Radio Free Europe/Radio Liberty, June 9, 1998, https://www.rferl.org/a/1088859.html.

56. Alessandra Stanley, "Agostino Cardinal Casaroli, 83, Dies; Led Vatican to Détente," *New York Times*, June 10, 1998, http://www.nytimes.com/1998/06/10/world/agostino-cardinal-casaroli-83-dies-led-vatican-to-detente.html.

57. One of the best books on this subject is Andras Fejerdy, ed., *The Vatican "Ostpolitik" 1958–1978: Responsibility and Witness during John XXIII and Paul VI* (Rome: Viella Libreria Editrice, 2014). In excellent chapters, two authors in the volume, Pal Hatos and Roberto Morozzo della Rocca, conclude that the policy should be seen in continuity with contemporary cultural and intellectual processes in Western Europe.

58. Pope Francis has frequently used the term to refer to the practice of Western governments and multilateral organizations to pressure developing countries to adopt liberal norms regarding traditional family issues, especially support for same-sex marriage, abortion, and gender theory. In 2019, Secretary of State Parolin presented these concerns to the UN's General Assembly. See "Cardinal Parolin Warns against Ideological Colonization at UN," Catholic News Service, September 26, 2019, https://angelusnews.com/news/world/cardinal-parolin-warns-against-ideological-colonization-at-un.

59. John 14:6.

60. MacDonald Dzirutwe, "Zimbabwe's Mugabe Sacks VP Seen as Top Succession Candidate," Reuters, November 6, 2017, https://www.reuters.com/article/us

-zimbabwe-politics/zimbabwes-mugabe-sacks-vp-seen-as-top-succession-candidate-idUSKBN1D61WU.

61. Farai Mutsaka, "5 Things to Know about Zimbabwe's 1st Lady, Likely Successor," Associated Press, November 8, 2017, https://www.apnews.com/a0eb1389c13a4f11b2660b77c220ce78.

62. Desmond Kumbuka, Godfrey Marawanyika, and Brian Latham, "Zimbabwe's Ousted Vice President Flees after Death Threats," Bloomberg, November 8, 2017, https://www.bloomberg.com/news/articles/2017-11-08/mugabe-guts-zimbabwe-security-state-with-deputy-s-dismissal.

63. "Zimbabwe's Mugabe 'Under House Arrest' after Army Takeover," BBC, November 15, 2017, https://www.bbc.com/news/world-africa-41997982.

64. Russell Pollitt, "An Interview with the Zimbabwean Jesuit Who Mediated Mugabe's Fall from Power," *America* (magazine), December 14, 2017, https://www.americamagazine.org/politics-society/2017/12/14/interview-zimbabwean-jesuit-who-mediated-mugabes-fall-power.

65. Harry Farley, "Zimbabwe: Who Is the Catholic Priest behind Robert Mugabe?," *Christianity Today*, November 16, 2017, https://www.christiantoday.com/article/zimbabwe-who-is-the-catholic-priest-behind-robert-mugabe/118823.htm.

66. Stuart Doran, "New Documents Claim to Prove Mugabe Ordered Gukurahundi Killings," *The Guardian*, May 19, 2015, https://www.theguardian.com/world/2015/may/19/mugabe-zimbabwe-gukurahundi-massacre-matabeleland.

67. Ofeibea Quist-Arcton, "How a Priest Convinced Robert Mugabe to Step Down," NPR, December 17, 2017, https://www.npr.org/2017/12/17/571443627/how-a-priest-convinced-robert-mugabe-to-step-down.

68. Tanks rolled into Harare on Wednesday, November 14, and he resigned on Tuesday, November 21.

69. Pollitt, "Interview with the Zimbabwean."

70. Fidelis Mukonori, SJ, *Man in the Middle: A Memoir* (Harare, Zimbabwe: House of Books, 2017).

71. Heidi Holland, *Dinner with Mugabe: The Untold Story of a Freedom Fighter Who Became a Tyrant* (New York: Penguin, 2009).

72. Pollitt, "Interview with the Zimbabwean."

73. Quist-Arcton, "How a Priest Convinced Robert Mugabe"; Emelia Sithole-Matarise, "Zimbabwe's Mugabe 'Glowed' with Relief after He Quit: Priest," Reuters, November 26, 2017, https://www.reuters.com/article/us-zimbabwe-politics/zimbabwes-mugabe-glowed-with-relief-after-he-quit-priest-idUSKBN1DQ0BB; "The Impact of Religion on Robert Mugabe," *Economist*, November 20, 2017, https://www.economist.com/blogs/erasmus/2017/11/piety-and-president; Eliza Mackintosh, "Zimbabwe's Military Takeover Was the World's Strangest Coup," CNN, November 21, 2017, https://www.cnn.com/2017/11/20/africa/zimbabwe-military-takeover-strangest-coup/index.html.

74. Devin Watkins, "Zimbabwe Nuncio: 'Historic Moment for Change, Rebirth' as Interim President Sworn In," Vatican News, November 24, 2017, https://www.vaticannews.va/en/world/news/2017-11/zimbabwe-nuncio---historic-moment-for-change--rebirth-.html.

75. Festo Mkenda, "Review—Man in the Middle: A Memoir," *Spotlight Africa*, January 2, 2018, https://spotlight.africa/2018/01/02/man-in-the-middle-a-memoir.
76. Pollitt, "Interview with the Zimbabwean."
77. Psalms 23:1–3.
78. Bishop Robert Barron, "How to Build a Better Priest," interview by *U.S. Catholic*, December, 1997, http://www.uscatholic.org/church/2010/05/how-build-better-priest.
79. St. John Chrysostom, *Treatise on the Priesthood*, book 4, chap. 3, EWTN, last modified April 19, 2020, https://www.ewtn.com/catholicism/library/treatise-on-the-priesthood-9110.
80. Pope Paul VI, "Address of His Holiness Pope Paul VI to the Community of the Pontifical Ecclesiastic Academy" (address, Pontifical Ecclesiastical Academy, February 22, 1971), http://w2.vatican.va/content/paul-vi/en/speeches/1971/february/documents/hf_p-vi_spe_19710222_pont-*Accademia*.html.
81. Filip Mazurczak, "Cardinal Sapieha: Foe of Nazis and Communists, Shepherd of a Young John Paul II," *National Catholic Register*, May 14, 2017, http://www.ncregister.com/blog/mazurczak/cardinal-sapieha-foe-of-nazis-and-communists-shepherd-of-john-paul-ii.
82. Pope John Paul II, "Address of John Paul II to the Community of the Pontifical Ecclesiastical Academy" (address, Pontifical Ecclesiastical Academy, Rome, Italy, April 26, 2001), http://w2.vatican.va/content/john-paul-ii/en/speeches/2001/april/documents/hf_jp-ii_spe_20010426_*Accademia*-ecclesiastica.html.
83. Pope Benedict XVI, "Address of His Holiness Benedict XVI to the Priests of the Pontifical Ecclesiastical Academy" (address, Pontifical Ecclesiastical Academy, May 20, 2005), http://w2.vatican.va/content/benedict-xvi/en/speeches/2005/may/documents/hf_ben-xvi_spe_20050520_ecclesiastical-academy.html.
84. Pope Francis, "Address of His Holiness Pope Francis to the Community of the Pontifical Ecclesiastical Academy" (address, Consistory Hall of the Vatican Apostolic Palace, Vatican City, June 25, 2015), http://w2.vatican.va/content/francesco/en/speeches/2015/june/documents/papa-francesco_20150625_pontificia-*Accademia*-ecclesiastica.html.
85. Zsolt Aradi, *Pope John XXIII, an Authoritative Biography* (New York: Farrar, Straus & Cudahy, 1959), 88–89.
86. Assigned to the titular see of Areopoli, in modern Jordan.
87. Aradi, *Pope John XXIII*, 162–69.
88. Designated "Righteous among Nations," he helped save almost 120,000 Jews out of the 150,000 population in Budapest in March 1944.
89. Peter Hebblethwaite, *Pope John XXIII: Shepherd of the Modern World—The Definitive Biography of Angelo Roncalli* (New York: Doubleday, 1985), 95.
90. Aradi, *Pope John XXIII*, 121.
91. Rinaldo Marmara, *John XXIII: Friend of the Turks* (Istanbul: Culture Ministry of the Republic of Turkey, 2000), 69–70.
92. Marmara, *John XXIII*, 69.
93. Baruch Tenembaum, "Angelo Roncalli (Pope John XXIII) Rescuer of Victims of the Holocaust," International Raoul Wallenberg Foundation, last modi-

fied June 25, 2013, http://www.raoulwallenberg.net/especial/roncalliyadvashem/ron calli02.html.

94. Tenembaum, "Angelo Roncalli."

95. Kenneth Woodward, *Making Saints: How the Catholic Church Determines Who Becomes a Saint, Who Doesn't, and Why?* (New York: Touchstone Books, 1990), 303. During the Nuremburg trials, Roncalli wrote an unsolicited letter on behalf of von Papen confirming, "He gave me the chance to save the lives of 24,000 Jews"; Hebblethwaite, *Pope John XXIII*, 95: Roncalli's biographer, Peter Hebblethwaite, speculates that the letter saved von Papen's life.

96. Pope John XXIII, *Journal of a Soul: The Autobiography of Pope John XXIII* (New York: Doubleday, 1980), 268. Fr. James Martin, SJ, observes that what is most remarkable about the posthumously published text is how *little* the man's spiritual dedication changed, despite his increased power. "Blessed Angelo Roncalli; Blessed John XXIII," *America* (magazine), October 11, 2010, https://www.americamagazine.org/content/all-things/blessed-angelo-roncalli-blessed-john-xxiii.

97. Aradi, *Pope John XXIII*, 194.

98. Aradi, *Pope John XXIII*, 232.

99. Pope Francis, "To Participants in the Papal Representatives Days" (address, Clementine Hall, Rome, June 21, 2013), http://www.vatican.va/content/francesco/en/speeches/2013/june/documents/papa-francesco_20130621_rappresentanti-pontifici.html.

100. Pope Francis, "To the Community of the Pontifical Ecclesiastical Community" (address, Clementine Hall, Rome, June 6, 2013), http://www.vatican.va/content/francesco/en/speeches/2013/june/documents/papa-francesco_20130606_pontificia-*Accademia*-ecclesiastica.html.

101. In July 2013, Francis approved a decision to canonize Pope John XXIII despite the lack of a second miracle attributed to his intercession. It was the pope's preference to canonize both John XXIII and John Paul II at the same time, on April 27, 2014.

102. The idea of a servant Church was also drawn from the writings of French theologian Yves Congar, described by papal biographer Austin Ivereigh as a central influence on Jorge Bergoglio. See Austin Ivereigh, *The Great Reformer: Francis and the Making of a Radical Pope* (New York: Henry Holt, 2015), xv. In a speech Roncalli gave in Istanbul on May 28, 1944, you hear the spiritual rudiments that motivated his life: "Jesus has come to pull down these barriers. He died to proclaim universal brotherhood. Charity is the main point of his teaching. Love is what unites him to all human beings." Marmara, *John XXIII*, xv.

CHAPTER 3

1. Pope John Paul II, "Address of John Paul II to the Community of the Pontifical Ecclesiastical Academy" (address, Pontifical Ecclesiastical Academy, Rome, Italy, April 26, 2001), http://w2.vatican.va/content/john-paul-ii/en/speeches/2001/april/documents/hf_jp-ii_spe_20010426_*Accademia*-ecclesiastica.html.

2. Jason Daley, "Researchers Catalogue the Grisly Deaths of Soldiers in the Thirty Years' War," *Smithsonian Magazine*, June 6, 2017, https://www.smithsonian mag.com/smart-news/researchers-catalogue-grisly-deaths-soldiers-thirty-years-war-180963531; "Thirty Years' War," History, updated August 21, 2018, https://www.history.com/topics/reformation/thirty-years-war.

3. Lutheranism was already legal since 1555 with the conclusion of the Treaty of Augsburg signed between Emperor Charles V and the Schmalkaldic League, a military alliance of Lutheran princes. The treaty enshrined the idea of *Cuius regio, eius religio*, Latin for "whose realm, his religion," giving civil leaders within the Holy Roman Empire the authority to decide the religion for his jurisdiction.

4. E. A. Ryan, "Catholics and the Peace of Westphalia," *Theological Studies* 9, no. 4 (1948): 597.

5. King Louis XIV was only four when his father, King Louis XIII, died of gangrene at age forty-one in 1643. The child's mother, Queen Anne of Austria, was regent while her deceased husband's chief minister, Cardinal Mazarin, advised the royal family on all aspects of foreign affairs until his death in 1661.

6. As his name suggests, Albani was the descendant of Christians in northern Albania, near the ancient city of Shkodër, who fought on the side of the Republic of Venice in the fifteenth-century Albanian-Venetian War. A gifted child, he was sent to Rome at age eleven to study at the Roman College (*Collegio Romana*), a school founded by St. Ignatius of Loyola in 1551 to educate Catholic boys from primary school through university. The *Collegio* was a dynamic center of scholarship and culture that embraced the Jesuit passion for science. By the mid-seventeenth century, it had over two thousand students taught by renowned intellectuals. Albani took degrees in both civil and canon law and gained a lifelong fascination with archeology, manuscripts, and Christianity's global mission.

7. Few memoirs by Vatican diplomats have been written. A rare exemplar is *My Years in Vatican Service* by Cardinal Edward Iris Cassidy, a 1955 *Accademia* graduate and the first ever from Australia. He devotes just a page to his two years at the school.

8. On the Vatican website and in published lists of alumni, the *Accademia* lists the year a student enters, not when he graduates, as confirmed by Archbishop Joseph Marino, president of the Pontifical Ecclesiastical Academy since October 2019. Personal communication with the author, August 5, 2020. http://www.vatican.va/roman_curia/pontifical_academies/acdeccles/documents/1850-1899.htm.

9. Cardinal Justin Rigali, interview with the author, Knoxville, TN, September 18, 2017.

10. Francis MacNutt, *A Papal Chamberlain: The Personal Chronicle of Francis Augustus MacNutt* (London: Longmans, Green, 1936). The American did not break his special ties to Rome for long. MacNutt returned to Rome with a wife in tow to serve as Pope Leo's chamberlain, one of four, who assisted in state visits, receptions, and ceremonial functions. MacNutt explained, "Pope Leo was inclined to accentuate the international, the universal character of his court and was pleased to see representative Catholics from abroad around him" (218). MacNutt served as a liaison especially to visitors from the United States, including Governor William Howard Taft,

governor general of the Philippines and Cuba, who came to Rome in 1902 to discuss the status of the Church in the US-controlled territories, especially the Philippines. As is true today, Catholic professionals often contribute service to the Church, and the Holy See's formal diplomatic network relies on informal partners.

MacNutt continued in service with the 1903 election of Pope Pius X, who named Msgr. Merry del Val as his secretary of state, at age thirty-eight, one of the youngest in Vatican history —and a former colleague of MacNutt's at the *Accademia*. In his autobiography, MacNutt expressed admiration and sympathy for the diplomatic life he had rejected: "[E]ndless patience and the capacity for taking endless pains they must possess. Their material compensation is insignificant, but the Holy Spirit rewards these devoted servants of the Church with high dignities. They exercise power, and they rightly enjoy consideration, but no body of men under the sun leads a drearier existence" (148–49). Acknowledging his life of service, the American is listed as attending the *Accademia* in 1887 from "Westminister," the UK diocese whose bishop recommended him, although in his autobiography he described himself as a quitter.

11. Archbishop Joseph Marino, president, Pontifical Ecclesiastical Academy, personal communication with the author, August 7, 2020.

12. Gabriella Geraso, "Archbishop Marino on Value of Missionary Year for Vatican Diplomats," Vatican News, February 17, 2020, https://www.vaticannews.va/en/vatican-city/news/2020-02/archbishop-marino-missionary-year-vatican-diplomats.html.

13. See Archbishop Celestinio Migliore's account in "The Pontifical Ecclesiastical Academy and the Roman Curia," *Scottish Catholic Observant* (blog), January 24, 2012, http://hughie-scottishcatholicobservant.blogspot.com/2012/01/pontifical-ecclesiastical-academy-and.html; Thomas Reese, *Inside the Vatican* (Cambridge, MA: Harvard University Press, 1996), 151–52; author's personal communication with graduates.

14. Cardinal Rigali, interview.

15. See Monica-Elena Herghelegiu, *Reservatio Papalis: A Study on the Application of a Legal Prescription according to the 1983 Code of Canon Law*, Tübinger Kirchenrechtliche Studien 8 (Berlin, Germany: LIT Verlag, 2008).

16. Cardinal Orlando B. Quevedo, OMI, interview with the author, St. Louis, MO, August 3, 2015.

17. Thomas Pereira was a Portuguese missionary who arrived in China in 1672. Jean-François Gerbillon led a group of French Jesuits to China, arriving in 1685. Both were invited to advise the emperor, map the country on trips with him, and help Chinese astronomers in the imperial observatory.

18. G. Patrick Marsh, *Eastern Destiny: Russia in Asia and the North Pacific* (Westport, CT: Praeger, 1996), 52–53.

19. Henry Brock, "Jean-François Gerbillon," *The Catholic Encyclopedia* (New York: Robert Appleton, 1909), http://www.newadvent.org/cathen/06471a.htm.

20. John Martin Robinson, *Cardinal Consalvi, 1757–1824* (London: Bodley Head, 1987), 101. One ally of Austria, strangely enough, was Napoleon Bonaparte's brother-in-law, Marshal Joachuim Murat, who was appointed King of Naples in 1808

and was hanging on to power as the Vienna Congress unfolded. Austria's powerful foreign minister Prince Klemens von Metternich had promised the Legations, a papal territory, to Murat or to Napoleon's second wife, Archduchess Marie-Louise, an Austrian. Consalvi was aware of this intrigue.

21. George Augustus Frederick was the prince regent who effectively ruled from 1811 to 1820 while his father, King George III, was ill and mentally unstable. When George III died in 1820, King George IV was crowned. He is the British royal whom Consalvi met and befriended.

22. Robinson, *Cardinal Consalvi*, 104–7.

23. Robinson, *Cardinal Consalvi*, 118–23.

24. France also retained possession of a small papal territory in southern France known as the Comtat Venaissin located in the Provence-Alpes-Côte d'Azur region.

25. Another achievement with long-term consequences must be mentioned. Not only did Consalvi regain all the Holy See's territory—thereby restoring economic security—but he also helped to solve a sticky diplomatic issue that had complicated interstate relations for centuries: the matter of precedence. The Vienna agreement replaced a list ordering world powers devised by Pope Julius II in 1501 with a straightforward rule listing diplomats by seniority based on when they formally presented their credentials to a host government. The secretary of state artfully protected the Holy See's historical status as dean of the diplomatic corps in places where that tradition was practiced, a special status incorporated into the Vienna Convention on Diplomatic Relations of 1961.

26. Robinson, *Cardinal Consalvi*, 115–16.

27. Henry A. Kissinger, *Diplomacy* (New York: Simon & Schuster, 1994), 615–16. In this contemporary classic, Henry Kissinger points to the quintessential European diplomatic strategy with the most long-lasting positive impact: balancing power while leaving room for national interest. He says this was achieved in Vienna in 1814–1815. Europeans have no illusion of underlying harmony in national goals. Kissinger thinks the United States assumes too often that nations have common objectives in interstate relations.

28. The Italian government, dominated by anti-Catholic freemasons, inserted Article 15 into the secret treaty, known as the Treaty of London. Wikisource, s.v. "Treaty of London (1915)," last modified October 24, 2016, https://en.wikisource.org/wiki/Treaty_of_London_(1915).

29. Writing in 1939, Cardinal Celso Costantini wrote, "22 years have passed and Europe is still without peace. Why? Because Versailles established a peace that was not Christian but instead was inspired by egotism and the interests of the victors." Celso Costantini, *The Secrets of a Vatican Cardinal: Celso Costantini's Wartime Diaries, 1938–1947*, ed. Bruno Fabio Pighin, trans. Laurence B. Mussio (Montreal: McGill-Queens University Press, 2014), 23.

30. Costantini, *Secrets of a Vatican Cardinal*, 144.

31. "Inflation Calculator," Dollar Times, accessed March 1, 2021, https://www.dollartimes.com/inflation/inflation.php?amount=1&year=1919.

32. John F. Pollard, *The Unknown Pope: Benedict XV and the Pursuit of Peace* (London: Geoffrey Chapman, 1999), 145; Kissinger has a cogent summary of the

risky ways Europe was divided: "At the end of this process [remaking the map], which was conducted in the name of self-determination, nearly as many people lived under foreign rule as during the days of the Austro-Hungarian Empire, except that now they were distributed across many more, much weaker, nation states which, to undermine stability even further, were in conflict with each other." *Diplomacy*, 241.

33. Pollard, *The Unknown Pope*, 133–34.

34. Pope Benedict XV, *Pacem Dei Munus Pulcherrimum* (Peace, On Christian Reconciliation, 1920), Papal Encyclicals, http://www.papalencyclicals.net/ben15/b15pulch.htm.

35. Michael Neiberg, *The Treaty of Versailles: A Concise History* (London: Oxford University Press, 2017); Margaret MacMillan, *Paris 1919: Six Months That Changed the World* (New York: Random House, 2003); Elazar Barkan, *The Guilt of Nations: Restitution and Negotiating Historical Injustices* (New York: Norton, 2000); Kissinger, *Diplomacy*.

36. Created in 1967 under the rubric of the United Nations Development Programme (UNDP), since 1971 the entity has reported directly to the UN's General Assembly. Its name was changed in 1987 to the United Nations Population Fund, although it is still referred to by the old acronym, UNFPA. Since it is based in New York, the Permanent Observer Mission of the Holy See to the United Nations monitors UNFPA activities, which had a budget of $1.30 billion in 2019. The largest program is Integrated Sexual and Reproductive Health Services, which got close to $560 million of the overall 2019 budget. https://www.unfpa.org/sites/default/files/board-documents/main-document/Statistical_and_Financial_Review_-_2019_FB-formatted.pdf.

37. As explained by Cardinal Renato Martino, the Holy See's permanent observer to the UN (1986–2002) who served as Rome's delegation leader to the ICPD, the ground for legitimizing abortion was already laid in 1968 when birth control was introduced as a human right in the UN's Declaration of Tehran. Cardinal Renato Raffaele Martino, "The Witness of Truth and Political-Diplomatic Dialogue: The Holy See and the United Nations," *Bulletin of the Social Doctrine of the Church*, 32014, http://www.vanthuanobservatory.org/eng/everything-began-in-cairo-cardinal-martino-speaks-out. With support from President Ronald Reagan, the Vatican managed to include language in a 1984 Mexico City ICPD document that "abortion should never be promoted as a means of birth control," but because the Clinton administration was elected with a pro-abortion agenda in 1992, the United States was no longer an ally going into the high-profile Cairo conference.

38. Genesis 1:26–28.

39. Catholic Church, "The family is the *original cell of social life*," para. 2207, in the *Catechism of the Catholic Church*, 2nd ed. (Washington, DC: United States Conference of Catholic Bishops, 2019), 533.

40. Martino, "The Witness of Truth."

41. Drew Christiansen, SJ, "The Church Does Diplomacy," review of *A Living Tradition*, by A. Alexander Stummvoll, *America* (magazine), August 24, 2018, https://www.americamagazine.org/arts-culture/2018/08/24/review-church-does-diplomacy: "Clinton then sent Vice President Al Gore to head the US delegation with

instructions to work with the Vatican. A few months later, the tough-minded Bishop Jim McHugh, a member of the Holy See delegation and a hawk on pro-life issues, told me excitedly, 'Al Gore is a friend. Tim Wirth [State Department undersecretary] is not, but Al Gore is a friend.'"

42. Alan Cowell, "Vatican Attacks Population Stand Supported by the U.S.," *New York Times*, August 9, 1994, https://www.nytimes.com/1994/08/09/world/vatican-attacks-population-stand-supported-by-us.html.

43. John Tagliabue, "Vatican Seeks Islamic Allies in UN Population Dispute," *New York Times*, August 18, 1994, https://www.nytimes.com/1994/08/18/world/vatican-seeks-islamic-allies-in-un-population-dispute.html. Besides extensive negative press, the high-profile nature of this contest also provoked a flurry of articles in academic journals challenging the Holy See's status as a permanent observer.

44. According to the UNFPA, 179 governments and almost 11,000 registered participants attended.

45. For example, as Martino noted in his final speech, the Church opposed general recognition of abortion as a "dimension of population policy, and indeed, of primary health care." Application of terms such as "reproductive rights" and "sexual rights" to nonmarried couples including adolescents led the Holy See to clearly state that it construed the entire frontier of "reproductive health" as relevant to married couples only.

46. An excellent source on Vatican strategy regarding the 1994 Cairo ICPD is Alexander Stummvoll's book *Living Tradition* (Eugene, OR: Cascade Books, 2018). He explores divergence in perspectives between the Holy See and Muslim-majority countries.

47. Christiansen, "The Church Does Diplomacy."
48. Matthew 28:19–20.
49. Acts 2:1–11.
50. Matthew 25:31–46.
51. In an insightful reading of this exchange, University of Notre Dame professor Fred Dallmayr makes the important point that Christ does not describe his kingdom as in competition with the regime nor bent on its destruction. Dallmayr writes, "[H]is ministry was designed not to trump the world (by establishing a worldly superpower) or to destroy or eradicate this world (along millenarian lines) but to salvage and redeem the world through truth and divine grace. In political terms, Jesus' ministry inaugurated neither a superpolitics nor an antipolitics but an 'other' kind of politics— what might be called a politics of sacred or redemptive nonsovereignty. The notion of an 'other' kind of politics seems to collide with a widespread (liberal) view that faith is entirely a private matter." Fred Dallmayr, "Sacred Nonsovereignty," in *The Sacred and the Sovereign: Religion and International Politics*, ed. John Carlson and Erik Owens (Washington, DC: Georgetown University Press, 2003), 260–61.

52. Matthew 8:23–26.
53. Matthew 7:4–5.
54. John 8:1–11.
55. Romans 2:14–15.
56. Romans 13:1.

57. Thomas Aquinas, *De Regimine Principum*, "On the Government of Rulers," in *The Political Ideas of St. Thomas Aquinas*, ed. Dino Bigongiari (New York: Hafner Press, 1953), chap. 1, no. 8, p. 176.

58. If the king seeks his private interest instead of the common good, virtue will be suppressed. Aquinas suggests ways to prevent a wicked tyrant from emerging and contemplates scenarios in which private people seek "to proceed against the cruelty of tyrants." Thomas Aquinas, "*De Regno ad Regem Cypri* (On Kingship to the King of Cyprus)," trans. Gerald B. Phelan, rev. I. Th. Eschmann, O.P. (Toronto: Pontifical Institute of Mediaeval Studies, 1949), no. 48, https://isidore.co/aquinas/DeRegno.htm. But he suggests that the outcome of rebellion is often worse than the original problem and counsels appeals to God and patience, for "[i]t can . . . scarcely come to pass that the government of a tyrant will endure for a long time," Aquinas, *De regno*, no. 80.

59. Pope Francis, "Greetings of His Holiness Pope Francis to Participants of the Fortune-Time Global Forum" (address, Fortune-Time Global Forum, Vatican City, December 3, 2016), https://w2.vatican.va/content/francesco/en/speeches/2016/december/documents/papa-francesco_20161203_imprenditori.html.

60. Pope John XXIII, "Opening Speech for Council of Vatican II" (speech, Second Ecumenical Council of the Vatican, Vatican City, October 11, 1962), https://www.ourladyswarriors.org/teach/v2open.htm.

61. Pope Paul VI, "Dogmatic Constitution on the Church, Lumen Gentium," Holy See, http://www.vatican.va/archive/hist_councils/ii_vatican_council/documents/vat-ii_const_19641121_lumen-gentium_en.html.

62. As part of his extensive organizational reforms of the Roman Curia following the Second Vatican Council, Pope Paul VI issued *Sollicitudo Omnium Ecclesiarum* on June 24, 1969, a *motu proprio* that echoes *Gaudium et Spes* in describing a broad role for papal diplomats: they will help "achieve the implementation of great human hopes, peace between nations, the domestic tranquility and progress of each country." http://w2.vatican.va/content/paul-vi/it/motu_proprio/documents/hf_p-vi_motu-proprio_19690624_sollicitudo-omnium-ecclesiarum.html.

63. Ian Linden, *Global Catholicism: Diversity and Change since Vatican II* (London: C. Hurst, 2009), 67–90, is especially good on the Second Vatican Council's "new vision."

64. Pope John XXIII's successor, Giovanni Battista Montini (Pope Paul VI), was a graduate of the Pontifical Ecclesiastical Academy and a thirty-year veteran of the Secretariat of State. It was Pope Paul who was the true midwife of the Second Vatican Council.

65. Quoted in Francis Rooney, *The Global Vatican: An Inside Look at the Catholic Church, World Politics, and the Extraordinary Relationship between the United States and the Holy See* (Lanham, MD: Rowman & Littlefield, 2013), 123.

66. Peter Hebblethwaite, *Pope John XXIII: Shepherd of the Modern World* (Garden City, NY: Doubleday, 1985), 445–46.

67. Norman Cousins, *The Improbable Triumvirate: John F. Kennedy, Pope John, Nikita Khrushchev* (New York: Norton, 1972), 17.

68. Cousins, *Improbable Triumvirate*, 446–47.

69. Cousins, *Improbable Triumvirate*, 45. It was on that December 1962 trip to Moscow that Cousins shared with Chairman Khrushchev the Vatican's hope that the Soviet Union could facilitate the release of Archbishop Josyf Slipyj, a Ukrainian prelate who had been jailed for eighteen years. As a former Ukrainian party official, the chairman knew exactly who Slipyj was. Less than two months later, Slipyj was freed.

70. Hebblethwaite, *Pope John XXIII*, 447; Cardinal Loris Capovilla, interview with the author, Monte del Sotto Giovanni XXIII, June 15, 2014.

71. Cousins, *Improbable Triumvirate*, 80–92.

72. Pope Paul VI, "*Dignitatis Humanae*: On the Right of the Person and of Communities to Social and Civil Freedom in matters Religious," Holy See, December 7, 1965, http://www.vatican.va/archive/hist_councils/ii_vatican_council/documents/vat-ii_decl_19651207_dignitatis-humanae_en.html.

73. Gordon Thomas, *Gideon's Spies: The Secret History of the Mossad* (New York: St. Martin's, 2012), 216.

74. Thomas, *Gideon's Spies*, 216.

75. Interview with the author, June 15, 2014, Sotto il Monte Giovanni XXIII, Italy.

76. For example, Fargo, North Dakota, Bishop Aloisius Muench, an ethnic German fluent in the language, was named apostolic visitor to the American Zone of Occupation (1946–1949), then nuncio to the newly created German Federal Republic (1951–1959). He was considered one of the most powerful Catholics in postwar Germany as he moved between the US government and American Zone of Occupation, the German government and German Catholic communities, and the Vatican. An excellent biography shows the US attitude and evolution of the priest's perspective: Colman J. Barry, OSB, *American Nuncio: Cardinal Aloisius Muench* (Collegeville, MN: Saint John University Press, 1969). Dwight Eisenhower's chief of staff, Beetle Smith, told Muench, "[T]he chief of the mission can only be an American" (58), but Muench was shocked by the degree of destruction he witnessed: "The misery and overcrowding in the makeshift refugee camps on the outskirts of the destroyed cities, separated families, less than subsistence food and scraps of clothing, but especially the pall of despair and the hopeless eyes of women, children and old people" (64). In time, Muench joined the German bishops in opposing the secular education system imposed by the United States and the concept of collective guilt (82). Together they worked tirelessly to preserve the 1933 concordat (written by Eugenio Pacelli, the future Pius XII), which preserved German Church unity. Muench and Roncalli (future Pope John XXIII), then nuncio to Paris, organized transportation corridors to get food, medicine, and clothing from France for the dispossessed in the American sector. Pope John XXIII made the American a cardinal in 1959. He never returned to the United States.

Bishop Joseph Hurley from St. Augustine, Florida, was the first American appointed apostolic nuncio when he was sent to represent the Holy See in Yugoslavia in 1945. Hurley was angered by the experience of witnessing a brutal regime's tyranny, while the US government, in an effort to lure Tito from the Soviet camp, changed Yugoslavia's designation from foe to ally and granted it millions of dollars in loans—despite Hurley's reports, sent directly to President Truman, of increased mass ethnic and religious repression. See Charles R. Gallagher, SJ, *Vatican Secret Diplomacy: Joseph P. Hurley and Pope Pius XII* (New Haven, CT: Yale University Press, 2008).

The bishop of Savannah, Georgia, Gerard O'Hara, was sent to Bucharest, Romania, where he served as nuncio from 1947 to 1950, when he was expelled, accused of being a spy for Western interests. During O'Hara's tenure, Romania passed from being a constitutional monarchy to a Communist republic. The American witnessed helplessly as Communists obliterated the Greek-Catholic Church, closed and confiscated all Roman Catholic properties, and imprisoned Church leadership—most tortured to death. His reports to Washington and Rome elicited no remedies.

None of these three men were *Accademia* trained.

77. Matthew 22:21.

78. Aquinas, *De regno*, no. 17.

79. Catholic Church, "The citizen is obliged in conscience," para. 2242, in *Catechism of the Catholic Church*, 541; Catholic Church, "Armed resistance to oppression by political authority is not legitimate," para. 2243, *Catechism of the Catholic Church*, 542.

80. Pope Pius XI, "Quadragesimo Anno," Holy See, https://w2.vatican.va/content/pius-xi/en/encyclicals/documents/hf_p-xi_enc_19310515_quadragesimo-anno.html.

81. Quoted in James V. Schall, *The Church, the State, and Society in the Thought of John Paul II* (Chicago: Franciscan Herald Press, 1982), 71.

82. Joseph Ratzinger, *Introduction to Christianity* (1968; San Francisco: Ignatius Books, 2004), 27.

83. The exact source of this oft-referenced quote seems lost to the sands of time. Or, he said versions of it so often that no one source exists.

84. Pope Paul VI, *Dignitatis Humanae*.

85. Pope Paul VI, "Declaration on the Relation of the Church to Non-Christian Religions, *Nostra Aetate*," Holy See, para. 3, http://www.vatican.va/archive/hist_councils/ii_vatican_council/documents/vat-ii_decl_19651028_nostra-aetate_en.html.

86. "The Pope in Israel," *New York Times*, January 6, 1964, https://www.nytimes.com/1964/01/06/the-pope-in-israel.html.

87. "Joint Catholic-Orthodox Declaration of His Holiness Pope Paul VI and the Ecumenical Patriarch Athenagoras I," Holy See, https://w2.vatican.va/content/paul-vi/en/speeches/1965/documents/hf_p-vi_spe_19651207_common-declaration.html.

88. Yet even some of his own diplomats felt he should have taken stronger action to publicly decry Nazi invasions of sovereign countries and persecution campaigns, including Msgr. Joseph P. Hurley, who was appointed in 1934 (and sent home in 1940) as the first American to serve in the Secretariat of State. See Gallagher, *Vatican Secret Diplomacy*, 89–105.

89. "Address of the Holy Father to the United Nations Organization," Holy See, October 4, 1965, http://www.vatican.va/content/paul-vi/en/speeches/1965/documents/hf_p-vi_spe_19651004_united-nations.html.

90. See Pope Paul VI, "*Populorum Progressio*: Encyclical on the Development of Peoples," Holy See, March 26, 1967, http://w2.vatican.va/content/paul-vi/en/encyclicals/documents/hf_p-vi_enc_26031967_populorum.html. One of Pope Francis's fa-

vorite papal documents is Pope Paul VI's *Evangelii Nuntiandi* (Evangelization in the Modern World, 1975), which proposes the task of evangelization for every believer. The document was the product of a synod on evangelization at which Cardinal Karol Wojtyła, archbishop of Kraków, served as the general rapporteur and helped draft the text. Pope Paul VI, "*Evangelii Nuntiandi*: Apostolic Exhortation," Holy See, December 8, 1975, http://www.vatican.va/content/paul-vi/en/apost_exhortations/documents/hf_p-vi_exh_19751208_evangelii-nuntiandi.html.

91. The role of dialogue and finding common ground in diplomacy is obviously an old, better *classic*, concept. The Holy See has demonstrated that it is willing to talk even after being radically insulted. Think of this: Cardinal Consalvi signed a landmark concordat with France in 1801, just three years after the French government stormed Rome and kidnapped Pius VI.

92. John XXIII even agreed to meet with Khrushchev's daughter, Rada, and son-in-law, Alexei Adjubei, director of the newspaper *Izvestia*, for over half an hour at the Vatican in March 1963, about six weeks before he died; Agostino Casaroli, *Il martirio della pazienza: La Santa Sede e i paesi comunisti, 1963–1989* (Turin, Italy: Einaudi, 2000), 25–26.

CHAPTER 4

1. Jacques Maritain, *The Things That Are Not Caesar's* (New York: Scribner, 1931), 42.

2. Cars driving the pope bear the license plate "SCV," for *Status Civitatis Vaticanae* in Latin, or *Stato della Città del Vaticano* in Italian.

3. Master list: Wikipedia, s.v. "Category: Treaties of the Holy See," last modified August 4, 2019, https://en.wikipedia.org/wiki/Category:Treaties_of_the_Holy_See.

4. "U.N. General Assembly Resolution A/58/314 Participation of the Holy See in the Work of the United Nations Fifty-Eighth Session Agenda item 59 16 July 2004: Note from the Secretary General," Permanent Observer Mission of the Holy See to the United Nations, https://holyseemission.org/contents//mission/mission-55e373817eecc8.37288214.php.

5. Of the UN's fifteen specialized agencies, the Holy See is a member or observer of nine, while the Vatican City State (VCS) belongs to two: the International Telecommunication Union and the Universal Postal Union. The four entities that neither belong to are the International Civil Aviation Organization, the World Bank Group, the International Monetary Fund, and the International Maritime Organization. Since VCS has no airport, economic development needs, or body of water, it's self-evident why the Holy See does not formally engage with them.

6. Quoted in Robert John Araujo, "The International Personality and Sovereignty of the Holy See," *Catholic University Law Review* 50, no. 2 (Winter 2001): 343.

7. Note: I use *Catholic Church* as synonymous with *Holy See* here because, for practical purposes and common understanding, the two are intrinsically related, and, of course, the pope heads both. However, under canon law (the legal code guiding the Catholic Church), the two are distinct juridical persons (see Araujo, "International

Personality and Sovereignty," 291–360, especially footnote 9). The Holy See is defined in Canon Law No. 361 as the supreme pontiff, the Secretariat of State, and the dicasteries that help the pope govern the Church. The dogmatic constitution of the Church, *Lumen Gentium* (Light of the Nations, 1964), explores multiple images of the Catholic Church as the Body of Christ, the bride of Christ, and the communion of the faithful, but it does not mention the Holy See by name.

8. The definition of a state was most decisively outlined in the 1933 Montevideo Convention on the Rights and Duties of States by the International Conference of American States and signed by nineteen countries. Article 1 lists the following as constituent elements of a state: permanent population, defined territory, a political authority, and the ability to enter into relations with other states. A state automatically has what is known in international law as "international personality," meaning the rights and responsibilities of an actor covered by international law. Although the Montevideo definition has been criticized, it remains a standard reference in discussions of sovereignty. Regarding Vatican City State (VCS), the well-respected scholar Jorri Duursma, for example, argues that VCS has a weak claim to statehood for two reasons: it does not have permanent citizenship, and its existence is dependent on the Holy See. Duursma assigns international personality to the Holy See alone: Jorri Carolina Duursma, *Fragmentation and the International Relations of Micro-States: Self-Determination and Statehood* (Cambridge: Cambridge University Press, 1996), 110–32, 410–19. In another authoritative view, even as he complimented Duursma's analysis as "the best modern study of the issue," James Crawford, an Australian jurist and former judge at the International Court of Justice, asserted, "[I]t is clear that the Vatican City is a State in international law, despite its size and special circumstances." He saw the existence of two legal persons, the Holy See and VCS, both with international personality. James Crawford, *The Creation of States in International Law*, 2nd ed. (Oxford: Clarendon Press, 2006), 221–33. Demonstrating variance among the most prestigious analysts of international law on this issue, consider the position of German scholar L. F. L. Oppenheim, widely considered the father of international law. He concluded that together the Holy See and VCS, as a composite, possess international personality, which, he wrote, the Holy See lost during the period 1870–1929 and regained with the Lateran Treaty, although he did not think VCS alone possesses sovereignty. Robert Jennings and Arthur Watts, eds., *Peace*, vol. 1 of *Oppenheim's International Law*, 9th ed. (Oxford: Oxford University Press, 1992), 328. What is most important is that based on very different logic, all three consider the Holy See, as the governing body of the Catholic Church, to be a sovereign actor under international law.

9. Robert Jackson, *Sovereignty: Evolution of an Idea* (Cambridge: Polity Press, 2007), xi.

10. Catherine Fletcher, *Divorce of Henry VIII: The Untold Story from Inside the Vatican* (London: Palgrave Macmillan, 2012).

11. Francisco Suárez, "A Defense of the Catholic and Apostolic Faith," 1613, available online from Liberty Fund Inc. Suárez writes, "[T]here exists within the Church no one supreme temporal prince over that whole body, that is to say, over all the kingdoms of the Church; but that, on the contrary, there are as many princes as there are kingdoms, or sovereign states . . . the Roman Pontiffs themselves have never

assumed power of the sort in question" (book 5, nos. 7–9), https://oll.libertyfund.org/titles/selections-from-three-works.

12. Graham, *Vatican Diplomacy*, 41–43.

13. As papal historian Robert Graham writes, "Diplomacy is not dependent on international law. On the contrary, historically it has developed according to its own laws." *Vatican Diplomacy*, 185.

14. Graham, *Vatican Diplomacy*, 48–49. While Humboldt was in Rome, French troops swarmed the Italian Peninsula, seizing the pope's temporal holdings. Humboldt's government classified the pope as a "secular prince" in order to ignore his religious identity. Thus, the French invasion could have been interpreted as toppling the ruler (especially since Napoleon ordered him evicted from Rome, to boot), thereby ending the ambassador's assignment. But Humboldt argued he should stay since "he was accredited to the Pope not as sovereign of the Papal States but as the head of the Catholic Church," according to Humboldt's biographer, quoted in Graham, *Vatican Diplomacy*, 52–53. Prussia agreed with Humboldt and let him remain in Rome until 1808.

15. It is interesting to note that the General Treaty of the Final Act of the Congress of Vienna (signed June 9, 1815) includes the header, "In the name of the Most Holy and Undivided Trinity," which are the opening words of the Westphalian Treaty of 1648. Wikisource, s.v. "Final Act of the Congress of Vienna/General Treaty," last modified November 6, 2018: https://en.wikisource.org/wiki/Final_Act_of_the_Congress_of_Vienna/General_Treaty.

16. Araujo, "International Personality and Sovereignty," 294.

17. Also see Gaetano Arangio-Ruiz, "On the Nature of the International Personality of the Holy See," *Revue Belge de Droit International* 29 (1996), http://uniset.ca/microstates2/va_intl-personality.pdf.

18. Frank J. Coppa, "Realpolitik and Conviction in the Conflict between Piedmont and the Papacy during the Risorgimento," *Catholic Historical Review* 54, no. 4 (1969): 579–612.

19. John Gilmary Shea, *Life of Pope Pius IX and the Great Events in the History of the Church during His Pontificate* (New York: Thomas Kelly, 1877), 111, https://books.google.com/books?id=_e1gAAAAMAAJ&pg=PA114&dq=cardinal+Antonelli+pius+IX&hl=en&sa=X&ved=0ahUKEwjlzPuEl9LaAhXxmuAKHcwJDVUQ6AEIOzAD#v=onepage&q=cardinal%20Antonelli%20pius%20IX&f=true.

20. *The Catholic Encyclopedia*, vol. 13 (1912), s.v. "Pellegrino Rossi," New Advent, http://www.newadvent.org/cathen/13204a.htm.

21. Shea, *Life of Pope Pius IX*, 127.

22. Shea, *Life of Pope Pius IX*, 125–44. Gaeta was part of the Kingdom of Naples at the time, also protected by the French.

23. Elected in 1848 to serve a four-year term, he declared himself emperor when he was constitutionally barred from standing for reelection—and held power until 1870.

24. The pope's experience in exile made him hugely distrustful of the very democratic experiments he initially supported. On the other side, Piedmont strategists had concluded that the Holy See was the major institutional roadblock standing in the way

of Italian unification, so liberals systematically portrayed the Church as an obstinate irredentist and backed the Holy See into a corner by proposing increasingly extreme anticlerical measures. See Coppa, "Realpolitik and Conviction," 579–612.

25. William C. Mills, "Unity Deferred: The Roman Question in Italian History, 1861–1882," *Past Imperfect* 4 (1995): 33.

26. Mills, "Unity Deferred," 40.

27. R. De Cesare, *The Last Days of Papal Rome* (New York: Houghton Mifflin, 1909), 454.

28. De Cesare, *The Last Days of Papal Rome*, 454–55. An assault on the Porta San Giovanni could also be heard.

29. "The King of Italy Guarantees Independence to the Pope," *Trove*, https://trove.nla.gov.au/newspaper/article/30581235; Samuel William Halperin, *Italy and the Vatican at War* (Chicago: University of Chicago Press, 1939), 109. Halperin points out that in the cabinet's edict issued in October announcing incorporation of Rome into the kingdom, Article 2 states, "The supreme pontiff retains the dignity, the inviolability and all the personal prerogatives of a sovereign." Scrutinized by radical anticlerical elements around the king who were loath to allow any suggestion that the pope might regain temporal sovereignty, the Italian legal formulation places sovereignty in the person of the pope.

30. The Law of Guarantees also gave extraterritorial status to Vatican buildings, granted independent postal and telegraph offices, gave the Church the right to run its schools and seminaries "without any interference," promised to treat Church couriers as though they worked for a "foreign government," and offered significant financial compensation for the captured territory. Halperin, *Italy and the Vatican at War*, 104–35; Sidney Ehler and John Morrall, *Church and State through the Centuries: A Collection of Historic Documents with Commentaries* (London: Burns and Oates, 1954), 285–91.

31. Graham, *Vatican Diplomacy*, 25.

32. John Allen, *All the Pope's Men: The Inside Story of How the Vatican Really Thinks* (New York: Doubleday, 2004), 24.

33. L. F. L. Oppenheim, *Peace*, vol. 1 of *International Law: A Treatise*, ed. H. Lauterpacht, 8th ed. (London/New York: Longmans, Green, 1955), 125. However, Oppenheim did not give the Holy See's international personality a ringing endorsement, describing the Church as having a "quasi international position," as quoted in Crawford, *The Creation of States*, 222. An updated version of this theory is found in the work of Georg Schwarzenberger, *A Manual of International Law*, 6th ed. (London: Stevens & Sons, 1976), 56.

34. Oddly, with regard to the Holy See, Oppenheim was not convinced it retained sovereignty during the 1870–1929 interregnum, but others have used his ideas to argue that diplomatic recognition is a key element in the Holy See's possession of international personality. See P. Ciprotti, "The Holy See: Its Function, Form and Status in International Law," *Concilium* 8 (1970): 63–73.

35. Jozef Batora and Nik Hynek, *Fringe Players and the Diplomatic Order* (London: Palgrave Macmillan, 2014).

36. "The Italian Occupation of Rome," *New York Tribune*, September 22, 1870, https://search-proquest-com.proxygw.wrlc.org/docview/572444591/9F506C0D94C1 4288PQ/1?accountid=11243.

37. De Cesare, *The Last Days of Papal Rome*, 423. Jesuits writing in *La Civiltà Cattolica*, the journal vetted by the Secretariat of State, had already explored the idea that the doctrine of papal infallibility might suitably replace the dogma of temporal sovereignty. This strategy was not favored by everyone, though. Some prominent Church figures, especially from Germany and England, including Catholic luminary Lord John Acton, disagreed with the wisdom of the initiative. See Roland Hill, *Lord Acton* (New Haven, CT: Yale University Press, 2000).

38. "Infallibility: Scenes in the Council at Rome: Efforts of the Minority Bishops," *New York Times*, August 8, 1870. There were only two "no" votes, which came from an American and a Sicilian bishop.

39. De Cesare, *The Last Days of Papal Rome*, 429. To the Italians bent on national unification, that would have amounted to a declaration of war against the Risorgimento, which had already captured the Papal States beyond Rome.

40. Pope Pius IX revived the collection through the encyclical letter *Saepe Venerabilis*, issued on August 5, 1871. Also see Francis Pollard, *Money and the Rise of the Modern Papacy: Financing the Vatican, 1850–1950* (Cambridge: Cambridge University Press, 2009).

41. Vincent Viaene, "A Pope's Dilemma: Temporal Power and Moral Authority in the History of the Modern Vatican," in *World Views and Worldly Wisdom*, ed. Jan de Maeyer and Vincent Viaene (Leuven: Leuven University Press, 2016), 248.

42. John Julius Norwich, *Absolute Monarchs: A History of the Papacy* (New York: Random House, 2011), 421.

43. Norwich, *Absolute Monarchs*, 418–19.

44. John Tracy Ellis, "The Catholic Church and Peace Efforts," *Notre Dame Law Review* 9, no. 2 (1934): 206–7, https://scholarship.law.nd.edu/ndlr/vol9/iss2/2. Utilizing his diplomatic talents—while acting out an ancient papal role that underscores its transcendent status—Pope Leo offered the Holy See as a channel for mediation in his encyclical *Diuturnum Illud* (1881). That same year, Leo assigned Secretary of State Cardinal Mariano Rampolla to settle a disagreement between Great Britain and Portugal over navigation on an East African river. Meanwhile, Leo handled a problem Belgium's King Leopold II brought to him regarding the Congo Free State, a colony of Portugal. Four years later, Haiti and Santo Domingo agreed to respect arbitration from the pope on their borders.

45. Norwich, *Absolute Monarchs*, 420.

46. Quoted in Graham, *Vatican Diplomacy*, 87.

47. Ellis, "The Catholic Church and Peace Efforts," 207–8.

48. Summarized roughly, Aquinas knows God to be a lawgiver and he sees God's eternal laws in nature. Through reason and observation, we can discern the truth of reality. God's laws are also written on every human heart. The human capacity, through reason and free will, to discern what is good or bad—morality—is a manifestation of natural law. Human law is most effective and beneficial when it codifies rules for a political community that help people conform to natural law.

49. Wikipedia, s.v. "List of Encyclicals of Pope Leo XIII," last modified March 15, 2020, https://en.wikipedia.org/wiki/List_of_encyclicals_of_Pope_Leo_XIII. In contrast, Pope St. John Paul II issued fourteen in a pontificate that lasted slightly longer: twenty-six years.

50. Pope Leo XIII, "*Rerum Novarum*: Encyclical of Pope Leo XIII on Capital and Labor," May 15, 1891, Holy See, http://w2.vatican.va/content/leo-xiii/en/encyclicals/documents/hf_l-xiii_enc_15051891_rerum-novarum.html.

51. Joseph Koterski, SJ, "The Philosophical Underpinnings of Catholic Social Teaching: The Role of Nature and Natural Law" (St. Thomas Day Lecture, Fordham University, Bronx, NY, March 7, 2017), https://thomasaquinas.edu/news/st-thomas-day-lecture-rev-joseph-koterski-sj.

52. Graham, *Vatican Diplomacy*, 33. Vienna was the exception.

53. Many expected Leo's secretary of state and alter ego, Rampolla, to succeed him in 1903, but Austrian emperor Franz Joseph used a veto (known as the *jus exclusivae*) to block the favorite, hoping to get a pope less sympathetic to France and less likely to continue Leo's social justice ministry.

54. Pollard, *Money and the Rise of the Modern Papacy*, 21: "Cardinal Rampolla and his assistant della Chiesa worked to avoid the rupture, but their style of diplomacy was not welcome and they soon moved to other positions."

55. For the text of Wilson's response to the pontiff, see Walter H. Peters, *The Life of Benedict XV* (Milwaukee, WI: Bruce Publishing Company, 1959), 149–51.

56. Pope Benedict XV, "*Ad Beatissimi Apostolorum*: Encyclical of Pope Benedict XV Appealing for Peace," Holy See, January 11, 1914, 2020, http://w2.vatican.va/content/benedict-xv/en/encyclicals/documents/hf_ben-xv_enc_01111914_ad-beatissimi-apostolorum.html.

57. If the Holy See betrayed any bias, it was against Russia, which they feared might expand, possibly taking over Constantinople—and this was before the Bolshevik Revolution.

58. Quoted in Francis Rooney, *The Global Vatican* (Lanham, MD: Rowman & Littlefield, 2013), 74.

59. On the eve of Christmas Eve, 1914, having tried to engineer a twenty-four-hour cease-fire for the holiday, the Holy See published a decree offering "spiritual and material assistance to prisoners." Pollard, *Money and the Rise of the Modern Papacy*, 113.

60. Pollard, *Money and the Rise of the Modern Papacy*, 113–14.

61. John F. Pollard, *The Unknown Pope: Benedict XV and the Pursuit of Peace* (London: Geoffrey Chapman, 1999), 116; see also Stewart A. Stehlin, "The Emergence of a New Vatican Diplomacy during the Great War and Its Aftermath, 1914–1929," in *Papal Diplomacy in the Modern Age*, ed. Peter C. Kent and John F. Pollard (Westport, CT: Praeger, 1994).

62. Benedict did not just provide for the needy in Western Europe. The Bolshevik Revolution and subsequent civil war led to widespread famine, so the Holy See led relief efforts, raising money around the world for food aid to the Orthodox population. See Peters, *The Life of Benedict XV*, 179–86.

63. Valentine Iheanacho, "Benedict XV and the Rethinking of Catholic Missionary Strategy," Holy Spirit Study Center, *Tripod* 36, no. 183 (Winter 2016), http://www.hsstudyc.org.hk/en/tripod_en/en_tripod_183_05.html.

64. Benedict XV, "Apostolic Letter *Maximum Illud* of the Supreme Pontiff Benedict XV to the Patriarchs, Primates, Archbishops and Bishops of the Catholic World on the Propagation of the Faith throughout the World," Holy See, http://www.vatican.va/content/benedict-xv/en/apost_letters/documents/hf_ben-xv_apl_19191130_maximum-illud.html. The encyclical is an anticolonial statement, the most important Vatican document on the subject until Paul VI's exhortation *Evangelii Nuntiandi*, a favorite of Pope Francis's.

65. In the nineteenth century, missions were too often an extension of colonial policy for the Great Powers. One positive result of the postwar settlement was this: with a bevy of new countries created by the peace, the pope had the cheerful task of, for example, naming ten new bishops for newly independent Poland. The country's first nuncio had served as apostolic delegate: Msgr. Achille Ratti, who would be elected the next pope, Pius XI.

66. Anne O'Hare McCormick, "The Old Pope and Papal Prestige," *New York Times*, February 12, 1922, https://www.nytimes.com/1922/02/12/archives/the-old-pope-and-papal-prestige.html.

67. In international law, the standard definition of "international personality" turns on an entity's being "capable of possessing international rights and having the capacity to maintain its rights by bringing an international claim." Tiyanjana Maluwa, "The Holy See and the Concept of International Legal Personality: Some Reflections," *Comparative and International Law Journal of Southern Africa* 19, no. 1 (March 1986): 1–26, https://www.jstor.org/stable/23905611.

68. Maluwa, "The Holy See," 12.

69. Maluwa, "The Holy See," 12.

70. McCormick, "The Old Pope."

71. Published in a newspaper founded by Mussolini, *Il Popolo d'Italia*, November 18, 1919, as quoted in Pollard, *Money and the Rise of the Modern Papacy*, 22.

72. As pointed out by historian Robert Kertzer, Mussolini's father, a blacksmith, named his son after a Mexican Indian who became president and thoroughly despised the Catholic Church: Benito Juárez. Robert Kertzer, *The Pope and Mussolini: The Secret History of Pius XI and the Rise of Fascism in Europe* (New York: Penguin Random House, 2014), 19.

73. Kertzer, *The Pope and Mussolini*, 58–59.

74. Gyles Isham, "Empire and Papacy—A Modern Problem," *Blackfriars* 79, no. 2 (October 1926), 612–17.

75. Francis Pollard, *The Vatican and Italian Fascism, 1929–1932* (Cambridge: Cambridge University Press, 1985), 15.

76. In fact, under Pope Benedict XV, Mussolini met surreptitiously with Cardinal Secretary Gasparri in 1922 to ascertain the Holy See's bottom line regarding a settlement. The meeting was arranged in a private home under conditions of strict secrecy. See Peters, *The Life of Benedict XV*, 194.

77. Elisa Carrillo, "Alcide de Gasperi and the Lateran Pacts," *Catholic Historical Review* 49, no. 4 (1964): 533; Pollard, *The Vatican and Italian Fascism*, 42.

78. Pollard, *The Vatican and Italian Fascism*, 42.

79. Sticking points centered on the Holy See's intention to keep excommunicated priests out of public office, to restore recognition of religious marriage, and to protect the independence of lay organizations such as Catholic Action and youth groups—movements close to Pius XI's heart but obstacles to the Fascist desire to control the youth field. To defend his position, the pope had to shut down negotiations at one point. He prevailed, winning juridical recognition for Catholic Action and its offshoots.

80. For one reason, because his trusted envoy, Domenico Barone, died unexpectedly.

81. Kertzer, *The Pope and Mussolini*, 105–12.

82. As quoted in Carrillo, "Alcide de Gasperi," 534.

83. Pope Pius XI, "*Non Abbiamo Bisogno*: Encyclical of Pope Pius XI on Catholic Action in Italy," June 29, 1931, Holy See, http://w2.vatican.va/content/pius-xi/en/encyclicals/documents/hf_p-xi_enc_29061931_non-abbiamo-bisogno.html.

84. Two documents comprise the Lateran Accords (named after the basilica where they were signed, the Papal Archbasilica of St. John [in] Lateran): the treaty creating Vatican City State, with an annex describing a financial settlement awarding the Holy See compensation for the properties lost to the Kingdom of Italy, and a concordat outlining the relationship between the Catholic Church and Italy.

85. "Lateran Pacts of 1929," art. 2, http://www.aloha.net/~mikesch/treaty.htm.

86. This usage, "microstate," is standard among academics and particularly appropriate with regard to Vatican City State.

87. Lateran Treaty, art. 3.

88. Actually, the Pentagon is slightly larger than Vatican City.

89. Lateran Treaty, Preamble, para. 2.

90. Timothy A. Byrnes, "Sovereignty, Supranationalism, and Soft Power: The Holy See in International Relations," *Review of Faith & International Affairs* 15, no. 4 (2017): 6–20.

91. Dan Kurzman, *A Special Mission: Hitler's Secret Plot to Seize the Vatican and Kidnap Pope Pius XII* (Boston: Da Capo, 2007), 79.

92. Kurzman, *A Special Mission*, 133–34.

93. "Lateran Pacts of 1929," Bible Light, http://www.aloha.net/~mikesch/treaty.htm.

94. As Edwin Ryan points out, "Concordats came into being to remedy or regularize abnormal situations." The modern genesis of the Holy See's use of concordats was to settle tensions or to resolve confusion and to protect the sacraments, the security of bishops, and the Church's essential functionality. He considers concordats to be a form of peace treaty, although legally he compares them to contracts. Edwin Ryan, "Papal Concordats in Modern Times," *Catholic Historical Review* 16, no. 3 (1930): 304.

95. The king died January 9, 1878. Pope Pius IX died less than a month later on February 7. The Pantheon was a Catholic Church that started life as a pagan temple in the center of Rome.

96. The modification can be found in the encyclical *Il Fermo Proposito* (June 11, 1905).

97. A spellbinding diversity of opinion exists regarding the status of Vatican City State. On one side is Jorri Duursma, a major expert on microstates, who concludes that VCS is not really a state because: (1) it is dependent on the Holy See, as openly stated in the Lateran Treaty, and (2) because it fails the test of having "permanent citizenship," a criterion included in the Montevideo definition of a state. However, she locates the VCS's legal personality in the Holy See. Conversely, Tiyanjana Maluwa asserts that VCS is most certainly a state, but it is the Holy See's sovereignty that requires a stronger basis (and he proposes a social need theory to serve as that basis.) An excellent, nuanced discussion can be found in James Crawford's landmark *The Creation of States in International Law*. Crawford observes, "It cannot be denied that the position of the Vatican City is peculiar. . . . However, peculiarity is not of itself a ground for denying statehood where other factors point to the opposite conclusion. . . . The international status of the Holy See itself contributed to the acknowledgement of the statehood of the Vatican." He concludes, "Vatican City is a State in international law despite its size and special circumstances" (225).

98. Joseph Nye, *Bound to Lead: The Changing Nature of American Power* (New York: Basic Books, 1990).

99. Eric O. Hanson, *The Catholic Church in World Politics* (Princeton, NJ: Princeton University Press), 3–5, 361–62. Hanson credits another academic, Ivan Vallier, with applying the concept of instrumental versus expressive power to the Holy See in "The Roman Catholic Church: A Transnational Actor?," in *Transnational Relations and World Politics*, ed. Robert O. Keohane and Joseph F. Nye (Cambridge, MA: Harvard University Press, 1972), 145.

100. Although it would be wrong to use numerology excessively, certain numbers such as three and twelve reoccur with such frequency in the Bible, as well as in Catholic architecture and design, that their symbolic significance can't be ignored. "Numbers, Religious," Catholic Culture, https://www.catholicculture.org/culture/library/dictionary/index.cfm?id=35179; "Use of Numbers in the Church," *The Catholic Encyclopedia*, vol. 11 (1911), s.v. "Cathen," New Advent, http://wwwnewadvent.org/cathen/11151a.htm.

101. D. D. Emmons, "How the Lateran Treaty Created Vatican City," Our Sunday Visitor, July 2, 2019, https://www.osvnews.com/2019/07/02/how-the-lateran-treaty-created-vatican-city. Emmons writes that the amount was equivalent to $92 million at the time, an amount equivalent to $1.4 billion today: https://www.in2013dollars.com/us/inflation/1929.

102. Article 6 of the treaty stipulates that Italy will "provide for direct connection with other States by means of telegraph, telephone, wireless, broadcasting, and postal services in the Vatican City." It also makes Italy responsible for providing VCS's water supply.

103. "Pope Becomes Ruler of a State Again," *New York Times*, June 7, 1929, https://learning.blogs.nytimes.com/on-this-day/june-7. On June 7, 1929, the pope also promulgated a governing document, the Fundamental Law of Vatican City (Law n. I). Its first law (of seven) described the supreme pontiff as possessing full execu-

tive, legislative, and judicial power. In 2000, Pope John Paul II replaced the 1929 law with a new twenty-article Fundamental Law. Article 2 describes the Secretariat of State as representing the VCS in relations with foreign nations on behalf of the pope.

104. Vatican City joined the International Telegraph Union (now known as the International Telecommunication Union) on May 31, 1929, and the Universal Postal Union on June 1, 1929. These memberships became especially valuable after the creation of the United Nations, when both organizations became special UN agencies, thus bringing the Holy See into the UN community.

105. Pope John Paul II's speech to the UN in 1995 is a magnificent summary of the Catholic Church's view of the obligations each state has to its citizens. Pope John Paul II, "Address of His Holiness John Paul II" (address, Fiftieth Session of the United Nations General Assembly, New York, NY, October 5, 1995), https://w2.vatican.va/content/john-paul-ii/en/speeches/1995/october/documents/hf_jp-ii_spe_05101995_address-to-uno.html.

106. Quoted in Crawford, *The Creation of States*, 224. Pope Pius XII and his circle were dissatisfied with a specific aspect of UN organization: by creating a Security Council comprised of the war's victors, the UN enshrined the new dominant powers, in contradiction to Catholic practice of avoiding the creation of winners and losers in settlements, as we will see in chapter 5.

107. Dorothy V. Jones, "Sober Expectations: The United Nations and a 'Sensible Machinery' for Peace," in *The Dumbarton Oaks Conversations and the United Nations, 1944–1994*, ed. Ernest May and Angeliki Laiou (Washington, DC: Dumbarton Oaks Research Library and Collection, 1998).

108. H. E. Cardinale, *The Holy See and the International Order* (Toronto: Macmillan Company of Canada, 1976), 229–32.

109. Specifically, the United Nations Education, Scientific and Cultural Organization (UNESCO) created the Committee on the Theoretical Bases of Human Rights, of which Maritain was a member. Mary Ann Glendon, "Knowing the Universal Declaration of Human Rights," *Notre Dame Law Review* 73, no. 5 (1998), http://scholarship.law.nd.edu/ndlr/vol73/iss5/18.

110. The UPU joined on July 1, 1948. As papal historian and diplomat Hyginus Eugene Cardinale confirmed, "[i]n reality, the Holy See ultimately owes its connection with the United Nations and the Specialized Agencies to the State of the Vatican City. It was thanks to the latter's membership in the U.P.U. and the I.T.U. that the former established its first official contact with the United Nations." Cardinale, *The Holy See and the International Order*.

111. Roman A. Melnyk, *Vatican Diplomacy at the United Nations: A History of Catholic Global Engagement* (Lewiston, NY: Mellen, 2010), 29–34. Born in Quebec City, Canada, the FAO moved to Rome in 1951.

112. Melnyk, *Vatican Diplomacy*, 41–46.

113. Cardinale, *The Holy See and the International Order*, 256, footnote; Dag Hammarskjöld met Pope Pius XII at the Vatican on April 30, 1957.

114. Ramses Nassif, *U Thant in New York, 1961–1971: A Portrait of the Third UN Secretary-General* (London: C. Hurst, 1977), 16–20; Peter Hebblethwaite, *Paul VI: The First Modern Pope* (New York: Paulist Press, 1993), 316; U Thant House

(@uthanthouse), "52 Years Ago: U Thant Welcomes Pope Paul to the United Nations," photograph, Facebook, November 27, 2017.

115. Walter Dorn and Robert Pauk, "Unsung Mediator: U Thant and the Cuban Missile Crisis," *Diplomatic History* 33, no. 2 (2009): 261–92. Regarding impartiality, U Thant told a moderator during a television discussion, "Whoever occupies the office of the Secretary-General of the UN must be impartial but not necessarily neutral. . . . In regard to moral issues, he could not and should not remain neutral or passive." Nassif, *U Thant in New York*, 8.

116. Hebblethwaite, *Paul VI,* 316.

117. Pope Paul VI, "Address of Pope Paul VI to the Secretary General of the United Nations Organization" (address, Rome, Italy, July 11, 1963), https://w2.vatican.va/content/paul-vi/en/speeches/1963/documents/hf_p-vi_spe_19630711_u-thant.html.

118. Nassif, *U Thant in New York*, 49.

119. U Thant even served as a go-between for the Holy See with North Vietnam's Ho Chi Minh as Paul VI tried to organize a trip to both North and South Vietnam in 1968. Nassif, *U Thant in New York*, 55–71.

120. Melnyk, *Vatican Diplomacy*, 111–12, letter dated March 21, 1964.

121. Melnyk, *Vatican Diplomacy*, 112, letter dated April 6, 1964. Strangely, Vatican sources list March 21, 1964, as the appointment date for Archbishop Alberto Giovannetti, the first envoy to serve as permanent observer.

122. Monaco, South Korea, South Vietnam, Switzerland, and West Germany. South Vietnam merged with Vietnam in 1976. The other four eventually became full members.

123. Evan Luard, *The Age of Decolonization, 1955–1965*, vol. 2 of *A History of the United Nations* (New York: St. Martin's, 1982), 211–12.

124. Xavier Rynne, "Letter from Vatican City," *New Yorker*, December 18, 1965, https://www.newyorker.com/magazine/1965/12/25/letter-from-vatican-city-10.

125. Nassif, *U Thant in New York*, 71.

126. Hebblethwaite, *Paul VI,* 437.

127. Pope Paul VI, "Address of the Holy Father Paul VI to the United Nations Organization" (address, Twentieth Session of the United Nations General Assembly, New York, NY, October 4, 1965), https://w2.vatican.va/content/paul-vi/en/speeches/1965/documents/hf_p-vi_spe_19651004_united-nations.html.

128. Colman McCarthy, "Pope Paul VI—Sought Christian Unity," *Washington Post*, August 7, 1978, https://www.washingtonpost.com/archive/politics/1978/08/07/pope-paul-vi-sought-christian-unity/75495ccd-7ca7-4c82-90f7-0384d1fef69b/?utm_term=.faa86658a3bb.

129. The coincidence of Pope Paul's visit to the UN while the council completed work on *Gaudium et Spes* is an event Catholics read as laden with the presence of the Holy Spirit. It was Vatican II that fully affirmed multilateral diplomacy by prioritizing interfaith and ecumenical dialogue while underscoring the Church's strong moral footing in natural law.

130. UNEP was founded in 1972, and UN-HABITAT was created in 1978.

131. "Pope Appoints Woman Undersecretary in Vatican Secretariat of State," Vatican News, January 15, 2020, https://www.vaticannews.va/en/vatican-city/news/2020-01/pope-appoints-woman-undersecretary-in-secretariat-of-state.html.

132. In 1945, the Swiss government concluded that UN membership and neutrality were incompatible. In 1986, Swiss voters defeated a referendum on membership. In 2002, they approved it.

133. Rooney, *The Global Vatican*, 206–7.

134. In a meditation on the pope's nearing death, Paul Ellie memorably observed, "John Paul has made his entire pontificate a pilgrimage—one full of implications for the pilgrimage of the ordinary believer. Through his trips he has made clear that the whole world—not just a certain 108 acres within Rome—is pilgrim territory." "In Search of a Pope," *Atlantic*, September 2004, https://www.theatlantic.com/magazine/archive/2004/09/in-search-of-a-pope/303410.

135. UN General Assembly Resolution A/RES/58/314, "Participation of the Holy See in the Work of the United Nations," Holy See, July 16, 2004, http://www.vatican.va/roman_curia/secretariat_state/pdf-diplomazia/2004-july1-Resolution%20ONU%20Holy%20See.pdf.

136. "Vatican's Role at UN Unanimously Endorsed by General Assembly," July 9, 2004, Friday Fax, Catholic Family and Human Rights Institute, https://web.archive.org/web/20120330160103/http://www.c-fam.org/fridayfax/volume-7/vaticans-role-at-un-unanimously-endorsed-by-general-assembly.html.

137. Catholics for a Free Choice was one of the most vociferous, launching a campaign, "See Change," in 1999 challenging the Holy See's legitimacy and sovereignty: Jon O'Brien, "How Catholics for a Free Choice Saved Civilization," *Conscience*, Spring 2007, Catholics for Choice, http://www.catholicsforchoice.org/issues_publications/how-catholics-for-a-free-choice-saved-civilization; "The Vatican's Obstructionism on Women's Rights and Reproductive Rights at the UN Forced a Response from International NGOs," Catholics for Choice, January 8, 2014, http://www.catholicsforchoice.org/campaign/global-interfaith-secular-alliance/the-vaticans-obstructionism-on-womens-rights-and-reproductive-rights-at-the-un-forced-a-response-from-international-ngos.

138. Cardinal Pietro Parolin, "The Holy See's Diplomatic Mission in Today's World," in Archbishop Silvano M. Tomasi, *The Vatican in the Family of Nations: Diplomatic Actions of the Holy See at the UN and Other International Organizations in Geneva* (Cambridge: Cambridge University Press, 2015), xii.

139. Tomasi, *The Vatican in the Family of Nations*, 830.

CHAPTER 5

1. Among the excellent books with moving accounts of Catholicism in China, persecution under Mao, and the gradual renaissance of the Church after paramount leader Deng Xiaoping introduced wide-ranging reforms in 1978: Anthony S. K. Lam, *The Catholic Church in Present-Day China* (Hong Kong: Ferdinand Verbiest Foundation and Holy Spirit Study Centre, 1997); Richard Madsen, *China's Catholics:*

Tragedy and Hope in an Emerging Civil Society (Berkeley: University of California Press, 1998); Henrietta Harrison, *The Missionary's Curse and Other Tales from a Chinese Catholic Village* (Berkeley: University of California Press, 2013); and Gerolamo Fazzini, ed., and Charlotte Fassi, trans., *Diaries of the Chinese Martyrs: Stories of Heroic Catholics Living in Mao's China* (Manchester, NH: Sophia Institute Press, 2016). For an excellent synopsis, see Eric O. Hanson, "The Catholic Church in China," in *Catholicism and Politics in Communist Societies*, ed. Pedro Ramet (Durham, NC: Duke University Press, 1990).

2. The two prelates were well known to Rome and Beijing; they were at the heart of careful attempts to create unity out of division. In December 2018, underground Bishop Vincent Guo Xijin agreed to Rome's request that he accept a "downgrade" and become auxiliary bishop under government-approved Bishop Vincenzo Zhan Silu, one of the seven illicit bishops accepted by Rome in September 2018. This diocese was one of only two with such a "head-to-head" conflict: an underground and official bishop presiding in the same jurisdiction. In the second case, in Shantou diocese located in Guangdong Province, an eighty-eight-year-old underground bishop retired to make way for a newly approved official bishop. It is against canon law for two bishops to lead the same diocese. "Mindong: Msgr. Guo Xijin, Underground Bishop, Gives Way to Formerly Excommunicated Msgr. Zhan Silu," AsiaNews, December 13, 2018, http://www.asianews.it/news-en/Mindong:-Msgr.-Guo-Xijin,-underground-bishop,-gives-way-to-formerly-excommunicated-Msgr.-Zhan-Silu-45738.html; "Second Chinese Underground Catholic Bishop Steps Aside to Be Succeeded by Party Approved Clergyman," Agence France-Presse, December 18, 2018, https://www.scmp.com/news/china/politics/article/2178717/second-chinese-underground-catholic-bishop-steps-aside-be.

3. "For where two or three are gathered together in my name, there am I in the midst of them." Matthew 18:20.

4. "Wang Chao, Former Vice-Minister of the Ministry of Foreign Affairs," China Vitae, last modified July 2, 2019, http://www.chinavitae.com/biography/Wang_Chao.

5. "Wang Chao, Vice Minister of Foreign Affairs," Ministry of Foreign Affairs of the People's Republic of China, https://www.fmprc.gov.cn/mfa_eng/wjb_663304/zygy_663314/gyjl_663316/wc_666656.

6. The text was not released when the Vatican renewed the agreement on October 22, 2020, either. Nicole Winfield, "Vatican, China Extend Bishop Agreement over US Opposition," Associated Press, October 22, 2020, https://apnews.com/article/beijing-china-pope-francis-europe-vatican-city-5c5f822b98317f1bb5002887e383473f; Jason Horowitz, "Vatican Extends Deal with China over Appointment of Bishops," *New York Times*, October 22, 2020, https://www.nytimes.com/2020/10/22/world/europe/vatican-china-bishops.html.

7. Ruohan Li, "Vatican to Send Delegation to China before Possible Bishops Deal: Sources," *Global Times*, September 18, 2019, http://www.globaltimes.cn/content/1120054.shtml.

8. Armand du Plessis, *The Political Testament of Cardinal Richelieu*, trans. Paul Sonnino (Lanham, MD: Rowman & Littlefield, 2020), 146–49.

9. du Plessis, *The Political Testament*, 146.

10. See the excellent assessment of the cardinal's contributions to the field of diplomacy, G. R. Berridge, "Richelieu," in *Diplomatic Theory from Machiavelli to Kissinger*, ed. G. R. Berridge, H. M. A. Keens-Soper, and T. G. Otte (London: Palgrave, 2001).

11. It should be noted that Machiavelli supported continuous negotiation and permanent diplomatic representation even before Richelieu, although the Florentine's reasoning was cynical: you never know if today's friends might become tomorrow's enemies, so the fickle nature of *fortuna* requires diplomats to be constantly engaged.

12. Harold Nicolson, *The Evolution of Diplomatic Method: Being the Chichele Lectures Delivered at the University of Oxford in November 1953* (New York: Macmillan, 1954), 62.

13. François de Callières, *On the Manner of Negotiating with Princes*, trans. A. F. Whyte (Boston: Houghton Mifflin, 2000), 3, 40.

14. de Callières, *On the Manner of Negotiating*, 107.

15. de Callières, *On the Manner of Negotiating*, 86.

16. de Callières, *On the Manner of Negotiating*, 21.

17. de Callières, *On the Manner of Negotiating*, 69, 97.

18. de Callières, *On the Manner of Negotiating*, 82.

19. Sefania Falasca, "What I Would Have Said at the Consistory: An Interview with Cardinal Jorge Mario Bergoglio, Archbishop of Buenos Aires," *30 Days*, November 2007, http://www.30giorni.it/articoli_id_16457_l3.htm.

20. For example, in *Evangelii Gaudium*, the pope writes, "The message of peace is not about a negotiated settlement but rather the conviction that the unity brought by the Spirit can harmonize every diversity." Pope Francis, "Apostolic Exhortation *Evangelii Gaudium*," Holy See, November 24, 2013, no. 230, https://w2.vatican.va/content/francesco/en/apost_exhortations/documents/papa-francesco_esortazione-ap_20131124_evangelii-gaudium.html.

21. Pope Francis, "United Is a Reconciled Diversity," *L'Osservatore Romano*, English ed., June 9, 2017, 6.

22. de Callières, *On the Manner of Negotiating*, 91.

23. de Callières, *On the Manner of Negotiating*, 92.

24. Nicolson, *Evolution of Diplomatic Method*. Nicolson points out that it was especially the assumption that diplomacy should be conducted in secret that was challenged after World War I by citizens in democracies who felt deceived by what secret deals and alliances had wrought. Nicolson's book, together with his 1939 monograph *Diplomacy*, are contemporary classics. The former British diplomat (1909–1929) turned Labor Party parliamentarian offers an eloquent account of diplomacy, defined as "the management of international relations by negotiation" (4). He believed practitioners should be truthful, precise, calm, loyal, and modest—and should never "go native" in their assigned posts. His memorable description of Italian diplomacy is reminiscent of the Holy See: "Italy's foreign policy . . . is the antithesis of the German system, since instead of basing diplomacy on power, she bases power on diplomacy" (82). Nicolson's description of Germany's "warrior" diplomacy could apply to the United States today.

25. Quoted in John F. Pollard, *The Unknown Pope: Benedict XV and the Pursuit of Peace* (London: Geoffrey Chapman, 1999), 144.

26. Founding member Chiang Kai-shek was defeated by Mao and fled with his followers to the island of Taiwan where the defeated Chinese created the Republic of China, which was ousted unceremoniously from the Security Council in 1971 in order to bring Mao's People's Republic of China into the inner circle.

27. At the 1815 Congress of Vienna, Pope Pius VII already saw a distinct advantage in positioning the Holy See as an impartial actor. It was the best way to assure a small state's security among the power players who divided Europe in order to balance each other's interests. Plus, neutrality was in the air: Switzerland's "perpetual neutrality" was declared as a result of the congress.

28. Lateran Treaty, art. 24.

29. Twice, Pacelli met secretly with Georgy Chicherin, Lenin's pro-German minster of foreign affairs.

30. David G. Dalin and Joseph Bottum, *The Pius War: Responses to the Critics of Pius XII* (Lanham, MD: Lexington Books, 2004), 17. Dalin analyzed speeches Eugene Pacelli gave as a papal nuncio between 1917 and 1929 and concluded that forty of the forty-four speeches "denounced some aspect of the emerging Nazi ideology."

31. Alessandra Stanley, "Pope, in Damascus, Goes to a Mosque in Move for Unity," *New York Times*, May 7, 2001, https://www.nytimes.com/2001/05/07/world/pope-in-damascus-goes-to-a-mosque-in-move-for-unity.html. Demonstrating respect for Islam is one face of political neutrality, which established the basis for better relations between the Holy See and the Muslim world, certainly under the papacies of John Paul II and Francis.

32. "Mgr Alfred Xuereb Ordained Bishop; Pope Says: No Politicking, No High Society," *Malta Independent*, March 20, 2018, http://www.independent.com.mt/articles/2018-03-20/local-news/Mgr-Alfred-Xuereb-appointed-bishop-Pope-says-no-politicking-no-high-society-6736186521.

33. Carol Glatz, "Catholics Must Be Active in Politics, No Matter How 'Dirty,'" Pope Says," *National Catholic Reporter*, May 1, 2015, https://www.ncronline.org/blogs/francis-chronicles/catholics-must-be-active-politics-no-matter-how-dirty-pope-says. Of course, Catholic clergy can be found on many sides of political contests: nuns were arrested in the US Capitol rotunda in the summer of 2019 protesting the detention of migrants at the southern border, priests in Hong Kong were in the streets with students challenging the city's chief executive over new extradition rules, Congolese bishops challenged the legitimacy of a presidential election in early 2020 based on data Catholic observers collected across the country. In each national context, political engagement takes many and varied forms.

34. Joseph Ratzinger (Pope Benedict XVI), *A Turning Point for Europe?* (San Francisco: Ignatius Press, 1991), 62–63.

35. "Vietnamese Seminary Marks 25 Years," Union of Catholic Asian News, February 27, 2017, https://www.ucanews.com/news/vietnamese-seminary-marks-25-years/78495.

36. "Cardinal Roger Etchegaray Represents Pope at Cardinal Can's Funeral," Union of Catholic Asian News, May 22, 1990, https://www.ucanews.com/story-archive

/?post_name=/1990/05/22/cardinal-roger-etchegaray-represents-pope-at-cardinal-cans-funeral&post_id=30581.

37. "Vietnamese Clinic Wins Praise for 25 Years of Service," Union of Catholic Asian News, January 3, 2018, https://www.ucanews.com/news/vietnam-clinic-wins-praise-for-25-years-of-service/81152.

38. "Diocese of Xuân Lộc," Catholic-Hierarchy, last modified April 6, 2020, http://www.catholic-hierarchy.org/diocese/dxuan.html.

39. Embassy Vatican, "Vatican Delegation Sees Progress in Vietnam," WikiLeaks, cable 04VATICAN1988_a, dated May 21, 2004, https://185.165.168.41/plusd/cables/04VATICAN1988_a.html.

40. Embassy Vatican, "Ambassador Meets with New Catholic Archbishop," WikiLeaks, cable 05HANOI989_a, dated April 28, 2005, https://wikileaks.org/plusd/cables/05HANOI989_a.html. Before that, the seminary was allowed to matriculate students every six years.

41. "2nd Meeting of VN-Holy See Joint Working Group Takes Place in Vatican," Vietnam Plus, June 26, 2010, https://en.vietnamplus.vn/2nd-meeting-of-vnholy-see-joint-working-group-takes-place-in-vatican/20349.vnp. Pope Francis named a new representative in 2018. Polish-born, *Accademia*-trained Archbishop Marek Zalewski keeps an eye on Vietnam while serving as apostolic nuncio to Singapore. He also represents the Holy See to the Association of Southeast Asian Nations (ASEAN). "New Vatican Envoy Named to Vietnam and Singapore," Union of Catholic Asian News, May 22, 2018, https://www.ucanews.com/news/new-vatican-envoy-named-to-vietnam-and-singapore/82373.

42. Michael Sainsbury, "Vietnam Deal Points Way for Vatican-China Progress," Union of Catholic Asian News, October 11, 2018, https://www.ucanews.com/news/vietnam-deal-points-way-for-china-vatican-progress/83550. The agreement between Hanoi and Rome was largely negotiated by Parolin, although it was announced in 2011 after he had already moved to Caracas to serve as nuncio. Despite some periods when it seemed Hanoi was moving too slowly, evidence that the relationship has been productive came in October 2019, for example, when the Holy See announced the appointment of a new archbishop for the country's largest archdiocese, Ho Chi Minh City: "Vietnam Names New Archbishop in Vietnam," Union of Catholic Asian News, October 21, 2019, https://www.ucanews.com/news/vatican-names-new-archbishop-in-vietnam/86369.

43. "Catholic Vietnam: Growing despite Communist Oppression," Catholic World Report, December 5, 2016, https://www.catholicworldreport.com/2016/12/05/catholic-vietnam-growing-despite-communist-oppression.

44. "Vietnamese Minorities to End Long Wait for Church," Union of Catholic Asian News, May 8, 2018, https://www.ucanews.com/news/vietnamese-minorities-to-end-long-wait-for-church/82242.

45. "Vietnam's Catholics, Buddhists Strengthen Ties," Union of Catholic Asian News, May 15, 2017, https://www.ucanews.com/news/vietnams-catholics-buddhists-strengthen-ties/79210.

46. Cardinal Joseph Zen, as witnessed by the author, Washington, DC, September 28, 2019.

47. "Meeting with the Muslim Leaders, Omayyad Great Mosque, Address of the Holy Father" (address, May 6, 2001), https://w2.vatican.va/content/john-paul-ii/en/speeches/2001/may/documents/hf_jp-ii_spe_20010506_omayyadi.html.

48. "Pope Urges Peace in Golan Heights," CNN, May 7, 2001, http://www.cnn.com/2001/WORLD/meast/05/07/pope.syria.

49. Embassy Vatican, "CODEL Shays Engages Vatican on Middle East, Sudan," WikiLeaks, cable 06VATICAN179_a, dated August 29, 2006, https://wikileaks.org/plusd/cables/06VATICAN179_a.html.

50. "Foreign Terrorist Organizations," US Department of State, accessed March 3, 2021, https://www.state.gov/j/ct/rls/other/des/123085.htm.

51. Embassy Vatican, "Vatican on Haiti: Church Losses and Responses," WikiLeaks, cable 10VATICAN11_a, dated January 20, 2010, https://wikileaks.org/plusd/cables/10VATICAN11_a.html.

52. Embassy Vatican, "How Vatican Charities Work with Unfriendly Regimes in China, North Korea, and Burma," WikiLeaks, cable 09VATICAN128_a, dated December 7, 2009, https://wikileaks.org/plusd/cables/09VATICAN128_a.html.

53. Embassy Vatican, "How Vatican Charities Work."

54. Pope Francis, "Apostolic Exhortation *Evangelii Gaudium* of the Holy Father Francis to the Bishops, Clergy, Consecrated Persons and the Lay Faithful on the Proclamation of the Gospel in Today's World," Holy See, November 24, 2013, no. 24, https://w2.vatican.va/content/francesco/en/apost_exhortations/documents/papa-francesco_esortazione-ap_20131124_evangelii-gaudium.html.

55. The term was coined by Professor Joseph Nye in 1990 to describe the ability to persuade another country using culture, values, or policies rather than military might.

56. Pope Francis, *Evangelii Gaudium*, nos. 222–25. As papal biographer Austin Ivereigh explains, Jorge Bergoglio developed the ideas as a result of his interest in "politics and institutional change" based on his study of German theologian Fr. Romano Guardini (1885–1968). See Austin Ivereigh, *The Great Reformer: Francis and the Making of a Radical Pope* (New York: Henry Holt, 2015), 197–98. The best analysis of the relationship between Bergoglio and Guardini is Massimo Borghesi, *The Mind of Pope Francis: Jorge Mario Bergoglio's Intellectual Journey*, trans. Barry Hudock (Collegeville, MN: Liturgical Press Academic, 2018), chap. 3, Kindle. For an interesting analysis of these principles in light of ecumenism, see Joseph Xavier, SJ, "Culture of Encounter and Reconciled Diversity: Pope Francis' Vision of Ecumenism," *Asia Horizons* 11, no. 2 (June 2017): 357–72.

57. Pope Francis, "Apostolic Exhortation *Evangelii Gaudium*," no. 221.

58. Pope Francis, "Apostolic Exhortation *Evangelii Gaudium*," no. 220.

59. Ivereigh, *The Great Reformer*, 320.

60. Fr. Antonio Spadaro, "Interview with Pope Francis," Holy See, September 21, 2013, http://www.vatican.va/content/francesco/en/speeches/2013/september/documents/papa-francesco_20130921_intervista-spadaro.html.

61. Luke 10:29–37.

62. Archbishop Bernardito C. Auza, "Lecture on Papal Diplomacy," Seton Hall University School of Diplomacy and International Relations, South Orange, NJ, YouTube video, 1:04:38, https://www.youtube.com/watch?v=WRtaEfBDGX8.

63. "'Rebel' Pope Urges Youth 'Make a Mess' in Dioceses," Associated Press, July 27, 2013, https://newsinfo.inquirer.net/453569/rebel-pope-urges-youth-to-make-a-mess-in-dioceses.

64. Pope Francis, "Apostolic Exhortation *Evangelii Gaudium*," no. 227.

65. "Nicaraguan Bishops Say They Have Not Been Invited to Political Dialogue," Catholic News Service, March 4, 2019, https://www.catholicregister.org/home/international/item/29103-nicaraguan-bishops-say-they-have-not-been-invited-to-political-dialogue.

66. "Nicaragua Bishop Rejects That Chapel Fire Was Accidental," Associated Press, August 5, 2020, https://apnews.com/8fdd4323390dbb4465ede2991c7869a5#:~:text=MANAGUA%2C%20Nicaragua%20(AP)%20%E2%80%94,reported%20by%20the%20National%20Police; Ivette Munguia, "Nicaraguan Cardinal Brenes Denounces 'a Terrorist Act,'" Havana Times, August 3, 2020, https://havanatimes.org/features/nicaraguan-cardinal-brenes-denounces-a-terrorist-act.

67. Pope Francis, "Apostolic Journey to Rio de Janeiro on the Occasion of the XXVIII World Youth Day: Meeting with Young People from Argentina" (address, Rio de Janeiro, Brazil, July 25, 2013), http://www.vatican.va/content/francesco/en/speeches/2013/july/documents/papa-francesco_20130725_gmg-argentini-rio.html.

68. Gerard O'Connell, "Myanmar and Holy See Establish Diplomatic Relations," *America* (magazine), May 4, 2017, https://www.americamagazine.org/faith/2017/05/04/myanmar-and-holy-see-establish-diplomatic-relations.

69. Jason Horowitz, "In Myanmar, Pope Calls for Peace without Saying Rohingya," *New York Times*, November 28, 2017, https://www.nytimes.com/2017/11/28/world/asia/pope-francis-myanmar-rohingya.html.

70. "Pope Francis Uses Term Rohingya in Bangladesh Meeting," BBC, December 1, 2017, https://www.bbc.com/news/world-asia-42193813.

71. Romano Guardini, *The End of the Modern World* (Wilmington, DE: Intercollegiate Studies Institute, 1998), 140–47.

72. "Myanmar Catholics Welcome Pope Francis' Appointment of Country's First Cardinal," Associated Press, January 5, 2017, https://www.foxnews.com/world/myanmar-catholics-welcome-pope-francis-appointment-of-countrys-first-cardinal.

73. Paula Cocozza, "What Happened to the 12 Syrian Refugees Rescued by the Pope?," *The Guardian*, May 25, 2016, https://www.theguardian.com/world/2016/may/25/what-happened-pope-francis-syrian-refugees-rescued-lesbos-vatican-rome.

74. Derek Gatopoulos, Nicole Winfield, and Elena Becatoros, "Pope Brings 12 Syrian Refugees Back with Him on Plane to Italy," Associated Press, April 16, 2016, https://www.theglobeandmail.com/news/world/pope-brings-12-syrian-refugees-to-italy-as-lesson-for-europe/article29653363.

75. "Violence Cannot Be Committed in Name of God: Pope Francis," Egyptian Streets.com, April 28, 2017, https://egyptianstreets.com/2017/04/28/violence-cannot-be-committed-in-name-of-god-pope-francis.

76. Interesting, too, that the reason we know about the call is because al-Tayeb made it public. "Pope Francis Greets Grand Imam of al Azhar on Advent of Holy Ramadan," Egypt Today, April 24, 2020, https://www.egypttoday.com/Article/1/85061/Pope-Francis-greets-Grand-Imam-of-Al-Azhar-on-advent.

77. "Cardinal Urges Catholics to Join Struggle for Racial Justice: This Is the Christian Message," *National Catholic Register*, June 30, 2020, https://www.ncregister.com/daily-news/cardinal-urges-catholics-to-join-struggle-for-racial-justice-this-is-the-ch.

78. Thomas Meany, "The Machiavelli of Maryland," *Guardian*, December 9, 2015, https://www.theguardian.com/world/2015/dec/09/edward-luttwak-machiavelli-of-maryland. Massimo Franco gives Edward Luttwak several pages in his classic *Parallel Empires: The Vatican and the United States—Two Centuries of Alliance and Conflict*, trans. Roland Flamini (New York: Doubleday, 2008), 193–95.

79. "Press Conference on the Return Flight from Abu Dhabi to Rome," Vatican.va, February 5, 2019, http://www.vatican.va/content/francesco/en/speeches/2019/february/documents/papa-francesco_20190205_emiratiarabi-voloritorno.html.

80. Meghan Keneally, "From 'Fire and Fury' to 'Rocket Man,' the Various Barbs Traded by Trump and Kim Jong Un," ABC News, June 12, 2018, https://abcnews.go.com/International/fire-fury-rocket-man-barbs-traded-trump-kim/story?id=53634996. However, the relationship improved enough between President Trump and the leader of North Korea that they held three summits.

81. Joe Slama, "El Salvador's First Cardinal a Friend of Blessed Oscar Romero," Catholic News Agency, June 21, 2017, https://www.catholicnewsagency.com/news/el-salvadors-first-cardinal-a-friend-of-blessed-oscar-romero-29328.

82. Tom Gibb, "The Killing of Archbishop Oscar Romero Was One of the Most Notorious of the Crimes of the Cold War. Was the CIA to Blame?," *The Guardian*, March 23, 2000, https://www.theguardian.com/theguardian/2000/mar/23/features11.g21.

83. Harriet Sherwood, "Murdered Salvadoran Priest Óscar Romero to Be Made a Saint," *The Guardian*, March 7, 2018, https://www.theguardian.com/world/2018/mar/07/oscar-romero-el-salvador-priest-to-be-made-a-saint-pope-francis.

84. Slama, "El Salvador's First Cardinal."

85. Junno Arocho Esteves, "Salvadoran Cardinal: Pope Sending Him to Korea to Work for Peace," Crux, July 11, 2017, https://cruxnow.com/global-church/2017/07/11/salvadoran-cardinal-pope-sending-korea-work-peace.

86. Effective January 1, 2017, out of four existing councils, Francis created the Dicastery for Promoting Integral Human Development, a rather blasé academic term for efforts central to the pope's program. It implements and oversees work in charity, justice, peace, and migration. The four councils absorbed were created in response to Vatican II: Cor Unum, Justice and Peace, Pastoral Assistance to Health Care Workers, and Pastoral Care for Migrants and Itinerant People.

87. Beth Griffin, "During LI Visit, Salvadoran Cardinal Urges Prayer, Time for Family," Long Island Catholic, August 2017, http://licatholic.org/during-li-visit-salvadoran-cardinal-urges-prayer-time-for-family.

88. The pope drew from the Aparecida document's wisdom to frame each of his major documents: *Evangelii Gaudium* (On the Proclamation of the Gospel in Today's World, 2013), *Laudato Si* (On Care for Our Common Home, 2015), *Amoris Laetitia* (On Love in the Family, 2016), and *Fratelli Tutti* (On Fraternity and Social Friendship, 2020).

89. Victor Gaetan, "North Korea: Another Option," *National Catholic Register*, April 28, 2017, http://www.ncregister.com/daily-news/north-korea-another-option.

90. Kirsteen Kim, "Are Koreans the World's Most Dynamic Catholics?," Herald Malaysia, November 10, 2010, http://www.heraldmalaysia.com/news/are-koreans-the-worlds-most-dynamic-catholics/33029/2.

91. Adam Taylor, "South Korea Will Not Develop or Possess Nuclear Weapons, President Says," *Washington Post*, October 31, 2017, https://www.washingtonpost.com/world/south-korea-will-not-develop-or-possess-nuclear-weapons-president-says/2017/10/31/e440b2da-beaa-11e7-af84-d3e2ee4b2af1_story.html?utm_term=.cf0c741c4fe7.

92. Ray Cavanaugh, "When North Korea's Capital Had So Many Christians It Was Called the 'Jerusalem of the East,'" *Christianity Today*, April 19, 2017, https://www.christiantoday.com/article/when.north.koreas.capital.had.so.many.christians.it.was.called.the.jerusalem.of.the.east/107588.htm.

93. An extremely transparent bishops' conference publishes extensive data on its website: "Statistics of the Catholic Church in Korea, 2019," Catholic Bishops' Conference of Korea, August 12, 2020, https://cbck.or.kr/en/News/20200821.

94. Victor Gaetan, "Has Mon Jai-in's Catholicism Influenced His Diplomacy?," *Foreign Affairs*, September 22, 2017, https://www.foreignaffairs.com/articles/asia/2017-09-22/has-moon-jae-ins-catholicism-influenced-his-diplomacy.

95. Victor Gaetan, "Vatican Asked to Step into Korean Cauldron for 'Authentic Peace Talks,'" *National Catholic Register*, August 21, 2017, http://www.ncregister.com/daily-news/vatican-asked-to-step-into-korean-cauldron-for-authentic-peace-talks.

96. Archbishop Hyginus Kim Hee-jong, interview with the author, Seoul, Korea, November 1, 2017.

97. Victor Gaetan, "Prelude to a 'Miracle': Korean Peace," *National Catholic Register*, May 4, 2018, http://www.ncregister.com/daily-news/prelude-to-a-miracle-korean-peace.

98. Choe Sang-Hun, "$8 Million to Aid Poor North Koreans? South Korea and Japan Disagree," *New York Times*, September 15, 2017, https://www.nytimes.com/2017/09/15/world/asia/north-korea-humanitarian-aid.html.

99. Gaetan, "Has Moon Jae-in's Catholicism Influenced His Diplomacy?

100. "Catholicism Most Trusted Religion for Koreans," AsiaNews, October 29, 2015, http://www.asianews.it/news-en/Catholicism-most-trusted-religion-for-Koreans-35726.html.

101. Ambassador Thomas Hong-soon Han, personal communication with the author, May 3, 2018.

102. Pope Francis, "Homily, Holy Mass for Peace and Reconciliation" (homily, Seoul, South Korea, August 18, 2014), Holy See, https://w2.vatican.va/content/francesco/en/homilies/2014/documents/papa-francesco_20140818_corea-omelia-pace-riconciliazione.html.

103. "Mgr Alfred Xuereb Ordained Bishop; Pope Says: No Politicking, No High Society," *Malta Independent*, March 20, 2018, http://www.independent.com.mt

/articles/2018-03-20/local-news/Mgr-Alfred-Xuereb-appointed-bishop-Pope-says-no-politicking-no-high-society-673618652.

104. Ko Dung-hwan, "Kim: I Will Visit Seoul Soon," *Korea Times*, September 19, 2018, http://www.koreatimes.co.kr/www/nation/2018/09/103_255797.html.

105. "South Korea President Unveils 'Peace Gift' Puppies," BBC, November 25, 2018, https://www.bbc.com/news/world-asia-46336353.

106. Kim Yoo-chul, "Moon to Ask Europe to Ease Sanctions on NK," *Korea Times*, October 17, 2018, http://www.koreatimes.co.kr/www/nation/2018/10/103_257179.html; Victor Gaetan, "Church in Korea's Pivotal Role in Trump-Kim Meeting Could Lead to Papal Visit," *National Catholic Register*, July 9, 2019, https://www.ncregister.com/daily-news/church-in-koreas-pivotal-role-in-trump-kim-meeting-could-lead-to-papal-visi.

PART II INTRODUCTION

1. Sefania Falasca, "What I Would Have Said at the Consistory," *30 Days*, November 2007, http://www.30giorni.it/articoli_id_16457_l3.htm.

2. "Why Bergoglio Travels So Little," *La Stampa*, March 29, 2014, https://www.lastampa.it/vatican-insider/en/2014/03/29/news/why-bergoglio-travels-so-little-1.35783447.

3. This is the convincing thesis Italian journalist and Vatican expert Marco Politi laid out. He writes, "Compulsory resignation en masse would strip the Bertone clan and the other curial factions of their influence. . . . It was a gesture at once noble, humble, courageous—and revolutionary." Marco Politi, *Pope Francis among the Wolves: The Inside Story of a Revolution*, trans. William McCuaig (New York: Columbia University Press, 2015), 27–33. One of the weakest links in the Benedict pontificate was his secretary of state, Cardinal Tarcisio Bertone, who was inexperienced in diplomacy. Many were unhappy with his performance and urged Benedict to replace him, but Benedict was loyal to a fault toward a man who had served as his assistant at the Congregation for the Doctrine of the Faith. Politi explains, "Bertone had shown himself incapable of establishing a productive working relationship with the Roman Curia. Its members accused him of being a centralizer, of not knowing the inner workings of the bureaucracy and lacking diplomatic experience and being too much of an improviser." *Among the Wolves*, 27. Vaticanista Robert Mickens called Bertone "arguably the worst of his [Benedict's] many bad appointments." "Cardinal Tarcisio Bertone: A Lightning Rod for Controversy," UCANews, April 7, 2016, https://www.ucanews.com/news/cardinal-tarcisio-bertone-a-lightning-rod-for-controversy/75685#.

4. Gerald O'Connell, *The Election of Pope Francis: An Inside Account of the Conclave That Changed History* (Maryknoll, NY: Orbis, 2019); Frederic Martel, *In the Closet of the Vatican: Power, Homosexuality, Hypocrisy*, trans. Shaun Whiteside (London: Bloomsbury Continuum, 2019); Robert Mickens, "Twilight Time for the Vatican's Godfather: Chile's Sex Abuse Scandal and the Man Who Once Ruled

the Roman Curia," *La Croix International*, February 23, 2018, https://international.la-croix.com/news/twilight-time-for-the-vatican-s-godfather/7013; Paul Vallely, *Pope Francis: Untying the Knots* (London: Bloomsbury, 2013); Politi, *Among the Wolves*.

5. O'Connell, *Election of Pope Francis*, 211. He also has determination. Christopher Lamb reports that when Francis felt staff were moving too slowly to organize his first trip outside Rome to the island of Lampedusa, where migrants from Africa seeking entry to Europe languished, he called Alitalia himself and booked a commercial airline ticket using his birth name. When an Alitalia official called the Vatican to report that someone was impersonating the pope, his staff quickly arranged the visit, which occurred on July 8, 2013. Christopher Lamb, *The Outsider: Pope Francis and His Battle to Reform the Church* (Maryknoll, NY: Orbis, 2020), 48.

6. The most authoritative account of Jesuit politics in Argentina and Bergoglio's early priestly life is a superb biography to which I am indebted: Austen Ivereigh, *The Great Reformer: Francis and the Making of a Radical Pope* (New York: Henry Holt, 2015).

7. To this day, Francis often rails against ideology. In a homily on January 17, 2019, he declared, "And how much harm do ideologues do to the people of God, how much harm! Because they close the way to the work of the Holy Spirit." "Word of God Is Not Ideology, It Is Life That Makes Us Grow," Vatican News, January 17, 2019, https://www.vaticannews.va/en/pope-francis/mass-casa-santa-marta/2019-01/word-of-god-is-not-ideology-it-is-life-that-makes-us-grow.html.

8. "During the dirty war, some 20 priests and members of religious orders were killed, 84 disappeared, and 77 exiled and many hundreds of lay activists shared their fate." Ivereigh, *The Great Reformer*, 135–36. As well, three bishops were killed in suspicious car accidents, two carrying files on the "disappeared." The files were never recovered from the crime scene.

9. Ivereigh, *The Great Reformer*, 148.

10. Ivereigh, *The Great Reformer*, 118.

11. According to Ivereigh, Bergoglio's ideas in this regard also draw from the French Dominican theologian Yves Congar, especially his book *True and False Reform in the Church*, trans. Paul Philibert (Collegeville, MN: Liturgical Press, 1950). Congar had a strong influence on the Second Vatican Council's documents. Massimo Borghesi credits Argentine philosopher Amelia Podetti with inspiring Bergoglio's ideas about periphery in his book *The Mind of Pope Francis: Jorge Mario Bergoglio's Intellectual Journey*, trans. Barry Huddock (Collegeville, MN: Liturgical Press Academic, 2018), Kindle.

12. He was appointed to participate in offices dedicated to the liturgy, clergy, consecrated life, family, and Latin America.

13. "The Global Catholic Population," Pew Research Center, February 13, 2013, https://www.pewforum.org/2013/02/13/the-global-catholic-population.

14. Francis Rocca, "Jesuit Argentine Elected Pope, Takes Name Francis," Catholic News Service, March 13, 2013, https://web.archive.org/web/20130316025854/http://www.jesuit.org/2013/03/13/jesuit-argentine-cardinal-jesuit-bergoglio-elected-pope-takes-name-francis-i.

15. Haley Cohen, "Slum Priests: Pope Francis' Early Years," *The Atlantic*, March 20, 2013, https://www.theatlantic.com/international/archive/2013/03/slum-priests-pope-franciss-early-years/274201.

16. John Allen Jr., "Former Aide Says Francis May Close Vatican Bank," *National Catholic Reporter*, April 4, 2013, https://www.ncronline.org/blogs/ncr-today/former-aide-says-francis-may-close-vatican-bank; John Allen Jr., "Facing Scandal and Debt, Francis Shifts into High Gear for Financial Reform," Crux, July 1, 2020, https://cruxnow.com/news-analysis/2020/07/facing-scandal-and-debt-pope-shifts-into-high-gear-on-financial-reform.

17. Allen, "Facing Scandal and Debt."

18. Nicole Winfield, "Vatican Office Struggles to Keep Up with Clergy Abuse Cases," Associated Press, December 20, 2019, https://apnews.com/6e99b1ddf64d5fd7ff85fe065d699e7b.

19. Numerous prestigious commentators have used the idea of Aparecida as a "blueprint," including Jim Yardley, "A Humble Pope Challenging the World," *New York Times*, September 18, 2015, https://www.nytimes.com/2015/09/19/world/europe/pope-francis.html.

20. Antonio Spadaro, SJ, "Interview with Pope Francis," Holy See, August 19, 2013, https://w2.vatican.va/content/francesco/en/speeches/2013/september/documents/papa-francesco_20130921_intervista-spadaro.html.

21. Incredibly, the first cardinal from modern Africa, Laurean Rugambwa, who came from Tanzania, was chosen by Pope John XXIII in 1960.

22. Jorge Bergoglio encountered the concept of the periphery in the work of Argentine philosopher Amelia Podetti, who died at age fifty-one in 1979. She taught at a Catholic university in Buenos Aires and had an important impact on his thinking: Massimo Borghesi, "La Mujer que Inspiró a Bergoglio," Tierras de América, November 21, 2017, http://www.tierrasdeamerica.com/2017/11/21/la-mujer-que-inspiro-bergoglio-francisco-de-ella-amalia-podetti-tome-la-intuicion-de-las-periferias.

23. Paolo Fossati, "Backed by Pope Francis, an International Conference on the Rohingya Coming Soon, Says Card Bo," AsiaNews, May 11, 2018, http://www.asianews.it/news-en/Backed-by-Pope-Francis,-an-international-conference-on-the-Rohingya-coming-soon,-says-Card-Bo-43856.html.

24. "Pope Says Mass at U.S.-Mexico Border, Honors Migrants Who've Died Crossing," Fox News, https://www.foxnews.com/world/pope-says-mass-at-u-s-mexico-border-honors-migrants-whove-died-crossing.

25. I met Fr. Simoni in 2007, standing out in front of a cathedral (converted into an atheism museum under Communism) in Shkoder, Albania. He was cheerfully greeting passersby and urging them into the church for confession. See Victor Gaetan, "Cardinal-Elect Simoni's Appointment Elevating Albania's Martyrs," *National Catholic Register*, November 16, 2016, https://www.ncregister.com/daily-news/cardinal-elect-simonis-appointment-elevating-albanias-martyrs.

26. "Simoni Card. Ernest," Holy See, November 19, 2016, https://press.vatican.va/content/salastampa/en/documentation/cardinali_biografie/cardinali_bio_simoni_e.html.

27. Borghesi, *The Mind of Pope Francis*.

28. Victor Gaetan, "The Political Pope," *Foreign Affairs*, September 25, 2015, https://www.foreignaffairs.com/articles/2015-09-25/political-pope.

29. Nina Easton, "How CEOs Can Be Partners with God," *Fortune*, December 2, 2016, https://fortune.com/2016/12/02/ceo-partner-god-global-forum.

30. Andrew Nusca, "Pope Francis: We Must Listen to the Voices of the Poor," *Fortune*, December 3, 2016, https://time.com/collection-post/4589651/pope-francis-global-forum.

31. Pope Francis, "Greetings to Participants of the Fortune-Time Global Forum, Clementine Hall," Holy See, December 3, 2016, http://w2.vatican.va/content/francesco/en/speeches/2016/december/documents/papa-francesco_20161203_imprenditori.html.

32. Nancy Gibbs, "The 21st Century Challenge: Forging a New Social Compact," *Time*, December 3, 3016, https://time.com/collection-post/4589745/fortune-time-global-forum-report.

33. Borghesi, *The Mind of Pope Francis*, chap. 3; Edward Pentin, "Author: Pope Francis Is a 'Mystic' Trying to Solve Left-Right Dichotomy in the Church," *National Catholic Register*, April 21, 2018, http://www.ncregister.com/daily-news/author-pope-francis-is-a-mystic-trying-to-solve-left-right-dichotomy.

34. Pope Francis, "Mass for the Progress of Peoples: Homily of His Holiness Pope Francis" (homily, Apostolic Journey of Pope Francis to Chile and Peru, Temuco, Chile, January 17, 2018), https://w2.vatican.va/content/francesco/en/homilies/2018/documents/papa-francesco_20180117_omelia-cile-temuco.html.

35. *Evangelii Gaudium*, para. 223.

36. Quoted in Ivereigh, *The Great Reformer*, 179.

37. From interview with *Corriere della Sera* on January 2016, quoted by Sylvia Pogiolli, "How Pope Francis Became a Foreign Policy Player," NPR, April 14, 2016, https://www.npr.org/sections/parallels/2016/04/14/474130428/how-pope-francis-became-a-foreign-policy-player.

38. Br. Anthony Josemaria, "The Catholic Holocaust of Nagasaki—'Why, Lord?'" Homiletic & Pastoral Review, August 1, 2010, https://www.hprweb.com/2010/08/the-catholic-holocaust-of-nagasaki-why-lord.

CHAPTER 6

1. Jim Yardley, "Pope and Russian Orthodox Leader Meet in Historic Step," *New York Times*, February 12, 2016, https://www.nytimes.com/2016/02/13/world/americas/pope-arrives-in-cuba-for-historic-meeting-with-russian-orthodox-leader.html.

2. Pope Francis with Dominique Wolton, *A Future of Faith: The Path of Change in Politics and Society* (New York: St. Martin's Essentials, 2018), 104.

3. Pope Francis, *Evangelii Gaudium*, para. 221.

4. Victor Gaetan, "Pope Francis' Holy Diplomacy in Ukraine," *Foreign Affairs*, September 5, 2019, https://www.foreignaffairs.com/articles/ukraine/2019-09-05/pope-francis-holy-diplomacy-ukraine.

5. Note: AP and the *New York Times* have used *Kyiv* since 2019. See "Why Kiev Is Now Kyiv," https://www.cjr.org/language_corner/Kyiv-kyiv.php.

6. Serhii Plokhii, personal communication with the author, December 21, 2013.

7. Plokhii, personal communication.

8. Gabriel Gatehouse, "The Untold Story of the Maidan Massacre," BBC, February 12, 2015, https://www.bbc.com/news/magazine-31359021.

9. Andrew Higgins and Peter Baker, "Russia Claims US Is Meddling over Ukraine," *New York Times*, February 6, 2014, https://www.nytimes.com/2014/02/07/world/europe/ukraine.html.

10. Leonid Bershidsky, "The West Backed the Wrong Man in Ukraine," Bloomberg, December 5, 2017, https://www.bloomberg.com/opinion/articles/2017-12-05/the-west-backed-the-wrong-man-in-ukraine.

11. Svetlana Savranskaya and Tom Blanton, "NATO Expansion: What Gorbachev Heard," National Security Archive, December 12, 2017, https://nsarchive.gwu.edu/briefing-book/russia-programs/2017-12-12/nato-expansion-what-gorbachev-heard-western-leaders-early. See also Jack F. Matlock Jr., "Speech at National Press Club (February 22, 2015)" in "Historian Matlock Lambasts US Policy toward Russia" (press release, Pressenza International Press Agency, February 24, 2015); Madeline Roache, "Breaking Down the Complicated Relationship between Russia and NATO," *Time*, April 4, 2019, https://time.com/5564207/russia-nato-relationship.

12. David Rohde and Arshad Mohammed, "Special Report: How the US Made Its Putin Problem Worse," Reuters, April 14, 2014, https://www.reuters.com/article/us-ukraine-putin-diplomacy-special-repor/special-report-how-the-u-s-made-its-putin-problem-worse-idUSBREA3H0OQ20140418.

13. The history of Crimea includes a tragic period of "ethnic cleansing" when dictator Joseph Stalin ordered the deportation of the indigenous Crimean Tartar community, a Turkic, traditionally Muslim community that had lived there for centuries. See Gus Lubin, "How Russians Became Crimea's Ethnic Majority in One Haunting Chart," *Business Insider*, March 14, 2014, https://www.businessinsider.com/crimea-demographics-chart-2014-3. In 2013, approximately 13 percent of people living in Crimea considered themselves Tartars.

14. Numerous explanations for the Khrushchev "gift" have been suggested. This technical and pragmatic reason is provided by Sergey Khrushchev, son of Nikita Khrushchev: "Sergey Khrushchev on Crimea [Excerpt]," Wilson Center Digital Archive, 2010, from *Nikita Khrushchev: Reformator* (Moscow: Vremya, 2010), trans. Anna Melyakova for the National Security Archive, http://digitalarchive.wilsoncenter.org/document/119639; also Sergey Khrushchev, interview with the author, Cranston, RI, November 17, 2018. Another explanation is more sentimental: Khrushchev spent most of World War II in Ukraine and served as Ukraine's first secretary of the Communist Party after. The gift was a "symbolic gesture toward his favorite republic," according to his granddaughter, Nina Khrushcheva, an international affairs professor at the New School in New York City. See Krishnadev Calamuc, "Crimea: A Gift to Ukraine Becomes a Political Flash Point," NPR, February 27, 2014, https://www.npr.org/sections/parallels/2014/02/27/283481587/crimea-a-gift-to-ukraine-becomes-a-political-flash-point.

15. This interpretation is convincingly argued by an American analyst with direct access to Moscow's thinking. See Daniel Treisman, "Why Putin Took Crimea: The Gambler in the Kremlin," *Foreign Affairs*, May/June 2016, https://www.foreignaffairs.com/articles/ukraine/2016-04-18/why-russian-president-putin-took-crimea-from-ukraine.

16. Ukraine also has much smaller Latin and Ruthenian Catholic communities—a legacy of Western Ukraine's history as Polish and Austro-Hungarian territory.

17. Victor Gaetan, "Ukraine at the Breaking Point but Spirit Undefeated," *National Catholic Register*, February 19, 2014, https://www.ncregister.com/daily-news/ukraine-at-the-breaking-point-26-dead-but-spirit-undefeated; Archbishop Borys Gudziak, personal communication with the author, February 14, 2014.

18. Shevchuk was posted in Argentina from 2009 to 2011. He left when he was elected to the UGCC's highest office, major archbishop, by the Synod of Ukrainian Catholic Bishops at just forty years of age. Pope Benedict XVI then confirmed the selection. Since Paul VI, the Holy See has insisted the office's title be major archbishop, although many Church leaders would like their leader to be called "patriarch." On this issue, see Andrea Gagliarducci, "Analysis: Why Greek Catholics of Ukraine Seek Recognition as a Patriarchate," Catholic News Agency, March 4, 2018, https://www.catholicnewsagency.com/news/analysis-why-greek-catholics-of-ukraine-seek-recognition-as-a-patriarchate-20202.

19. Gaetan, "Ukraine at the Breaking Point."

20. At the time, the Orthodox Church was divided into three groups: the Ukrainian Orthodox Church–Moscow Patriarchate, the country's largest faith community, is a self-governed church within the canonical jurisdiction of the Russian Orthodox Church; the Ukrainian Orthodox Church–Kyiv Patriarchate asserted its independence from Moscow in 1992; and the small Ukrainian Autocephalous Orthodox Church was founded in 1921 when the country was briefly independent. On December 15, 2018, the second two groups dissolved to create a new autocephalous formation, the Orthodox Church of Ukraine, by the authority of Ecumenical Patriarch Bartholomew. The Russian Orthodox Church protested the canonical legality of this new autocephalous church and broke communion with the Orthodox Church of Constantinople over the issue. Pope Francis instructed Ukrainian Catholics to stay out of the dispute. See Victor Gaetan, "New Cold War by Proxy? Religious Conflict on Ukrainian Territory," *National Catholic Register*, November 5, 2018, https://www.ncregister.com/daily-news/new-cold-war-by-proxy-religious-conflict-on-ukrainian-territory.

21. Nataliya Trach et al., "From Kyiv Post Archives: Heroes of Euro-Maidan," *Kyiv Post*, February 20, 2016, http://www.Kyivpost.com/content/ukraine/heroes-of-euromaidan-334031.html.

22. "Nine Hours Straight Protesters Are Keeping Defense at Independence Square. Many Priests There," Religious Information Service of Ukraine, December 11, 2013, http://risu.org.ua/en/index/all_news/state/national_religious_question/54578.

23. When he was at the Maidan protest, he served as a bishop, or "eparch," of France, Benelux, and Switzerland. Since June 2019, he has governed the UGCC in the United States with the title archeparch (comparable to archbishop) of the Ukrainian Catholic Archeparchy of Philadelphia.

24. "Euromaidan Rally Begins with Ecumenical Prayer," Religious Information Service of Ukraine, December 15, 2013, http://risu.org.ua/en/index/all_news/state/national_religious_question/54637.

25. Archbishop Stefan Soroka, personal communication with the author, December 19, 2013. *Duch* or *duc*, meaning "spirit" as well as "breath," is a powerful word in Bulgarian, Czech, Polish, Romanian, Russian, Ukrainian, Serbo-Croatian, Slovak, and Slovenian, with a strong divine connotation. There is nothing comparable in English.

26. Tim Williams, "Head of Ukrainian Greek Catholic Church, Major Archbishop Sviatoslav Shevchuk, Visits Adelaide and Blames Bloodshed on Russia," *Advertiser*, September 23, 2014, https://www.adelaidenow.com.au/news/south-australia/head-of-ukrainian-greek-catholic-church-major-archbishop-sviatoslav-shevchuk-visits-adelaide-and-blames-bloodshed-on-russia/news-story/8d3feebaa55d0a0664079cec80da2397.

27. Archbishop Thomas Gullickson, interview with the author, Kyiv, Ukraine, October 20, 2014. The meeting was arranged by the UGCC as part of a one-week media study tour.

28. Gullickson, personal communication with the author, January 18, 2015. See chapter 7 footnote 32 for more on Becciu.

29. Archbishop Gullickson recalled that Pope Benedict XVI gave him one task when he sent the American to Ukraine in 2011: to make peace between Greek and Latin Catholics, divided by issues related to property and respective proximity to political power. He laughingly told a journalist, "I failed" at the task. See "Archbishop Thomas Gullickson: The Nuncio Should Do Everything to Promote Peace in Ukraine," Religious Information Service of Ukraine, October 12, 2015, https://risu.org.ua/en/index/expert_thought/interview/61366. Latin Catholics in Ukraine are led by a superstar in his own right: Polish-born Archbishop Mieczysław Mokrzycki of the Latins is a former personal secretary to both John Paul II (1996–2005) and Benedict XVI (2005–2008). I met the soft-spoken archbishop in St. Louis, Missouri, where he attended a Knights of Columbus convention. Through a translator he told me most Catholics across Ukraine oppose war, most men do not want to mobilize, and efforts to get weapons from the United States are contrary to the nation's interests.

He minimized problems with the UGCC, blaming the harsh experience of Communism on the complexity of the current situation, although he expressed frustration that the division of physical assets returned by the state was proving "far too difficult between brothers." Successive Ukrainian governments have played the two communities off each other when returning property expropriated by the Communists. If a once Catholic property is to be returned, the government will typically insist that the Latins and Greeks work out among themselves which group should hold title to the restored property. This has led to unfortunate "religious wars" that are often fought in public. Various Ukrainian governments have capitalized on this weakness for their own political purposes.

30. "Pope Francis' Address to Ukrainian Bishops on Their Ad Limina Visit," Zenit, February 20, 2015, http://www.zenit.org/en/articles/pope-francis-address-to-ukrainian-bishops-on-their-ad-limina-visit.

31. At that time, the conflict had already displaced approximately two million people in less than a year and killed over ten thousand people, mostly civilians. Nowhere did Francis mention Russia or speculate on the scope or nature of the war. He appealed for all parties to observe the mid-February cease-fire, known as Minsk II, and to implement the conditions required for it to hold.

32. "'Pope for Ukraine' Project," Dicastery for Promoting Integral Human Development, November 18, 2018, http://www.humandevelopment.va/en/progetti/il-papa-per-l-ucraina.html.

33. Robert Moynihan, "Letter #18, 2019: Vatican Nuncio to Ukraine: Interview," *Inside the Vatican*, April 24, 2019, https://insidethevatican.com/news/newsflash/letter-18-2019-vatican-nuncio-to-ukraine-interview. Francis brought Gugerotti from Belarus to Ukraine in 2015. An expert on Byzantine-rite theology as well as the Armenian language, he worked in the curia at the Congregation for Eastern Churches (1985–2001), then was appointed nuncio to Georgia, Armenia, and Azerbaijan despite never attending the *Accademia*.

34. Victor Gaetan, "A Former Ambassador Finds Much to Like in Pope Francis' Diplomatic Instincts," *America* (magazine), April 16, 2019, https://www.americamagazine.org/politics-society/2019/04/16/former-ambassador-finds-much-pope-francis-diplomatic-instincts.

35. Ambassador Charles W. Freeman Jr., interview with the author, Washington, DC, March 19, 2019.

36. "Patriarch Kirill Grateful to Pope for Considered Stance on Ukraine, Condemns Uniates," Interfax, May 5, 2015, http://www.interfax-religion.com/?act=news&div=12012.

37. "Decree on Ecumenism, *Unitatis Redintegratio*," Holy See, November 21, 1964, http://www.vatican.va/archive/hist_councils/ii_vatican_council/documents/vat-ii_decree_19641121_unitatis-redintegratio_en.html.

38. In 1054 in Rome, Pope Leo IX excommunicated the Patriarch of Constantinople, Michael I Cerularius, who countered with an excommunication of the pope, rupturing the Church into East and West. However, the issues that drove the two branches of Christianity apart had festered for centuries and were theological, political, cultural, and even economic. An excellent short summary can be found in a classic brief history by Orthodox Bishop Kallistos of Diokleia, writing under his birth name: Timothy Ware, *The Orthodox Church: New Edition* (London: Penguin, 1997), 43–73. A longer treatment by a Dominican scholar is Aidan Nichols, OP, *Rome and the Eastern Churches: A Study in Schism*, 2nd ed. (San Francisco: Ignatius Press, 2010).

39. Pope John Paul II, "Ioannes Paulus PP. II, Ut Unum Sint: On Commitment to Ecumenism," Holy See, May 25, 1995, http://www.vatican.va/holy_father/john_paul_ii/encyclicals/documents/hf_jp-ii_enc_25051995_ut-unum-sint_en.html.

40. In the Orthodox hierarchy, patriarchs have tremendous authority over believers; for most, territorial authority covers an entire country. No one patriarch is superior to another—that's a key difference with Catholicism, and the main stumbling block to reunification—although the "first among equals" is the patriarch of Constan-

tinople, based in Istanbul, considered the spiritual leader of all Orthodox believers. The powerhouse church in terms of believers and political clout is the Russian Orthodox Church, led by the patriarch of Moscow and all Russia. With approximately 101 million members, the Russian Orthodox Church comprises the largest national constituent of the 260 million Eastern Orthodox believers around the world. "Orthodox Christianity in the 21st Century," Pew Research Center, November 8, 2017, https://www.pewforum.org/2017/11/08/orthodox-christianity-in-the-21st-century.

41. The pope's Romanian tutor was Msgr. Anton Lucaci, a native Romanian who worked in the Roman Curia. Lucaci told me John Paul II studied the Romance language for seven weeks before his visit, spending five days a week, three to five hours per day, on his lessons. The pope also had daily briefings each day for three hours after lunch because he considered the trip so sensitive: "The Holy Father wanted deep knowledge of the country's essence," he explained. Interview with the author, Rome, Italy, July 21, 2018.

42. "Priests Are Targeted as Churches Clash," *The Guardian*, April 25, 2002, http://www.guardian.co.uk/world/2002/apr/25/worlddispatch.

43. Victor Gaetan, "Seeking an End to the Scandalous Disunity of East and West," *National Catholic Register*, January 29, 2015, https://www.ncregister.com/daily-news/seeking-an-end-to-the-scandalous-disunity-between-east-and-west.5.

44. Robert Moynihan, interview with the author, Washington, DC, January 7, 2015.

45. "Icon Revered by Pope Returned to Russian Orthodox Church," AP Archive, July 21, 2015, YouTube video, 2:45, https://www.youtube.com/watch?v=klVLYmmHrOE.

46. David Holley, "In Gesture to Russian Church, Vatican Returns Icon," *Los Angeles Times*, August 29, 2004, http://articles.latimes.com/2004/aug/29/world/fg-icon29.

47. Ian Fisher, "In a Gesture of Conciliation, the Pope Returns Orthodox Relics," *New York Times*, November 28, 2004, https://www.nytimes.com/2004/11/28/world/europe/in-a-gesture-of-conciliation-the-pope-returns-orthodox-relics.html.

48. "Ecumenical Celebration on the Occasion of the Transferral from Rome to Constantinople of the Relics of STS Gregory of Nazianzen and John Chrysostom," Holy See, November 27, 2004, http://w2.vatican.va/content/john-paul-ii/en/letters/2004/documents/hf_jp-ii_let_20041127_consegna-reliquie.html.

49. Pope Benedict XVI, "Missa Pro Ecclesia: First Message of His Holiness Benedict XVI, at the End of the Eucharistic Concelebration with the Members of the College of Cardinals in the Sistine Chapel," Holy See, April 20, 2005, http://www.vatican.va/holy_father/benedict_xvi/messages/pont-messages/2005/documents/hf_ben-xvi_mes_20050420_missa-pro-ecclesia_en.html.

50. Pope Benedict XVI, "Apostolic Journey to Cologne on the Occasion of the XX World Youth Day, Ecumenical Meeting, Address of His Holiness Pope Benedict XVI" (address, Cologne, Germany, August 19, 2005), http://www.vatican.va/holy_father/benedict_xvi/speeches/2005/august/documents/hf_ben-xvi_spe_20050819_ecumenical-meeting_en.html.

51. "Synod for Africa Ponders How to Tackle Polygamy, Meddling by Foreign Interests," Catholic News Agency, October 9, 2009, http://www.catholicnewsagency.com/news/synod_for_africa_ponders_how_to_tackle_polygamy_meddling_by_foreign_interests.

52. Psalms 133:1.

53. Victor Gaetan, "Turkey: Secularist Siege against Orthodox Church," *National Catholic Register*, July 8, 2014, https://www.ncregister.com/blog/turkey-secularist-siege-against-orthodox-church.

54. Cardinal Kurt Koch, interview with the author, Kolymvari, Greece, June 22, 2016.

55. Sophia Kishkovsky, "Relations Warm between Russian Orthodox Church and Vatican," *New York Times*, May 22, 2009, http://www.nytimes.com/2009/05/22/world/europe/22iht-orthodox.html.

56. He won 508 votes from the 702 eligible electors, considered a decisive victory. "Metropolitan Kirill Elected Patriarch of Moscow and All Russia," Interfax, January 27, 2009, http://www.interfax-religion.com/?act=news&div=5635.

57. "The Father of Patriarch Kirill Was Imprisoned for Writing the *God* with a Capital Letter," Interfax, November 25, 2009, http://www.interfax-religion.com/?act=news&div=6672.

58. Alan Cooperman et al., "Religious Belief and National Belonging in Central and Eastern Europe," Pew Research Center, May 10, 2017, http://assets.pewresearch.org/wp-content/uploads/sites/11/2017/05/15120244/CEUP-FULL-REPORT.pdf.

59. Nicolai N. Petro, "The Russian Orthodox Church," in *The Routledge Handbook of Russian Foreign Policy*, ed. Andrei Tsygankov (London: Routledge, 2018), 219; Serge Schmemann, "Soul of Russia," *National Geographic*, April 2009, https://www.nationalgeographic.com/magazine/2009/04/orthodox: "In 1987 there were only three monasteries in Russia; today [2009] there are 478. Then there were just two seminaries; now there are 25. Most striking is the explosion of churches. . . . The Russian Orthodox Church has grown into a sprawling institution, with dozens of publishing houses and hundreds of thriving journals, newspapers, and websites."

60. George Soroka, "Putin's Patriarch: Does the Kremlin Control the Church?," *Foreign Affairs*, February 11, 2016, https://www.foreignaffairs.com/articles/russian-federation/2016-02-11/putins-patriarch.

61. Petro, "The Russian Orthodox Church," 219.

62. "His Holiness Patriarch Kirill Meets with Mr. Xi Jinping, President of the People's Republic of China," Russian Orthodox Church, Department for External Church Relations, May 8, 2015, https://mospat.ru/en/2015/05/08/news118852.

63. Embassy Vatican, "Holy See: Putin's Meetings at the Vatican," WikiLeaks, cable 07VATICAN65_a, dated March 23, 2007, https://wikileaks.org/plusd/cables/07VATICAN65_a.html.

64. Pope Benedict XVI, "Address of His Holiness Benedict XVI" (address, Days of Russian Culture and Spirituality in the Vatican, Vatican City, May 10, 2010), https://w2.vatican.va/content/benedict-xvi/en/speeches/2010/may/documents/hf_ben-xvi_spe_20100520_concerto-kirill.html.

65. "Orthodox Patriarch to Attend Pope Francis' Investiture," *USA Today*, March 18, 2013, https://www.usatoday.com/story/news/world/2013/03/18/orthodox-patriarch-pope-francis-investiture/1997319.

66. George Demacopoulos, "The Extraordinary Historical Significance of Ecumenical Patriarch Bartholomew's Presence at Pope Francis' Installation as Bishop of Rome," Greek Orthodox Archdiocese of America, March 19, 2013, https://www.goarch.org/-/the-extraordinary-historical-significance-of-ecumenical-patriarch-bartholomew-s-presence-at-pope-francis-installation-as-bishop-of-rome.

67. Edward Pentin, "Greek Patriarch to Attend Papal Inaugural Mass for First Time since 1054," *National Catholic Register*, March 18, 2013, http://www.ncregister.com/daily-news/greek-patriarch-to-attend-papal-inaugural-mass-for-first-time-since-1054.

68. Josephine McKenna, "Pope Francis and Patriarch Bartholomew: A Budding Bromance?," *Washington Post*, June 6, 2014, https://www.washingtonpost.com/national/religion/pope-francis-and-patriarch-bartholomew-a-budding-bromance/2014/06/06/17c11824-edb8-11e3-8a8a-e17c08f80871_story.html.

69. Dominique Wolton and Pope Francis, *A Future of Faith: The Path of Change in Politics and Society* (New York: St. Martin's, 2018), 104.

70. See Marek Inglot, SJ, *How the Jesuits Survived Their Suppression: The Society of Jesus in the Russian Empire (1773–1814)* (Philadelphia: St. Joseph's University Press, 2015).

71. Victor Gaetan, "The Pontiff and the Pariah: What Putin and Pope Francis Discussed in the Vatican," *Foreign Affairs*, June 16, 2015, https://www.foreignaffairs.com/articles/russian-federation/2015-06-16/pontiff-and-pariah.

72. The Minsk Protocol, signed on September 5, 2014, called for a cease-fire. Persistent fighting led to renewed negotiation between France, Germany, Russia, and Ukraine, which resulted in a new set of terms, known as Minsk II. It was signed on February 12, 2015. Together, they comprise the Minsk agreements, named for the capitol of Belarus, where the parties met.

73. Victor Gaetan, "Pope Francis Comes to Bosnia Armed with the Gospel," *National Catholic Register*, June 5, 2015, https://www.ncregister.com/daily-news/pope-francis-comes-to-bosnia-armed-with-the-gospel.

74. Jim Yardley, "Pope Urges Putin to Make a 'Great Effort' to Resolve the Crisis in Ukraine," *New York Times*, June 10, 2015, https://www.nytimes.com/2015/06/11/world/europe/vladimir-putin-on-visit-to-italy-criticizes-ukraine-sanctions.html.

75. "Joint Press Release of the Holy See and of the Patriarchate of Moscow," Russian Orthodox Church, Department for External Church Relations, May 2, 2016, https://mospat.ru/en/2016/02/05/news127862.

76. "Patriarch Kirill Goes on Tour of Latin America," Interfax, February 5, 2016, http://www.interfax-religion.com/?act=news&div=12717.

77. "Meeting of His Holiness Pope Francis with His Holiness Kirill, Patriarch of Moscow and All Russia—Signing of the Joint Declaration," Holy See, February 12, 2016, http://w2.vatican.va/content/francesco/en/speeches/2016/february/documents/papa-francesco_20160212_dichiarazione-comune-kirill.pdf.

78. Mark Pattison, "Head of Ukrainian Catholic Church Skeptical of Papal-Orthodox Declaration," Catholic News Service, February 18, 2016, http://thedialog.org/international-news/head-of-ukrainian-catholic-church-skeptical-of-papal-orthodox-declaration; Jonathan Luxmoore, "Pope's Russian Outreach Stirs Anxieties," *National Catholic Reporter*, March 8, 2016, https://www.ncronline.org/news/vatican/popes-russian-outreach-stirs-anxieties.

79. "Common Declaration of Pope Benedict XVI and the Ecumenical Patriarch Bartholomew I," Holy See, NoveNber 30, 2006, http://w2.vatican.va/content/benedict-xvi/en/speeches/2006/november/documents/hf_ben-xvi_spe_20061130_dichiarazione-comune.html.

80. Victor Gaetan, "Five Insights about Pope Francis–Patriarch Kirill's Meeting," *National Catholic Register*, February 12, 2016, https://www.ncregister.com/daily-news/five-insights-about-todays-pope-francis-patriarch-kirill-meeting.

81. "Pope: Divisions among Christians 'Scandal to the World,'" Breaking News, November 30, 2006, http://www.breakingnews.ie/world/pope-divisions-among-christians-scandal-to-the-world-287287.html.

82. Vouthon, "Pope John XXIII on Orthodox Church (1926)," Catholic Answers Forums, March 7, 2012, https://forums.catholic.com/t/pope-john-xxiii-on-orthodox-church-1926/276390.

83. Peter Hebblethwaite, *Pope John XXIII: Shepherd of the Modern World—The Definitive Biography of Angelo Roncalli* (New York: Doubleday, 1985), 321–22.

84. "St. John XXIII, Patron Saint of Christian Unity?," *La Stampa*, March 24, 2014, http://www.lastampa.it/2014/03/24/vaticaninsider/eng/reviews/st-john-xxiii-patron-saint-of-christian-unity-HjCVo7kDlcH4Qh6LZRA1aJ/pagina.html.

85. James McCann, SJ, interview with the author, Washington, DC, February 10, 2016.

86. Gerard O'Connell, "Transcript of Part of Pope's Press Conference on Plane," *America* (magazine), November 30, 2014, https://www.americamagazine.org/content/dispatches/transcript-part-popes-press-conference-plane.

87. Marta Allevato, "Syria, the Pope, China: A Conversation with Orthodox Metropolitan Hilarion," AsiaNews, August 30, 2013, http://www.asianews.it/news-en/Syria,-the-Pope,-China:-A-Conversation-with-Orthodox-Metropolitan-Hilarion-28880.html.

88. O'Connell, "Pope's Press Conference on Plane."

89. Victor Gaetan, "Ukraine: Latest Ceasefire Holds for Now," *National Catholic Register*, March 11, 2015, https://www.ncregister.com/daily-news/ukraine-latest-ceasefire-holds-for-now.

CHAPTER 7

1. Barack Obama, "Statement by the President on Cuba Policy Changes" (press statement, Office of the Press Secretary, White House, December 17, 2014), https://obamawhitehouse.archives.gov/the-press-office/2014/12/17/statement-president-cuba-policy-changes.

2. Pope Francis, "Welcoming Ceremony: Address of His Holiness Pope Francis" (address, Apostolic Journey of His Holiness Pope Francis to Cuba, to the United States of America, and to Visit the United Nations Headquarters, Havana, Cuba, September 19, 2015), https://w2.vatican.va/content/francesco/en/speeches/2015/september/documents/papa-francesco_20150919_cuba-benvenuto.html.

3. Agostino Casaroli, *The Martyrdom of Patience: The Holy See and the Communist Countries (1963–89)* (Toronto: Ave Maria Centre of Peace, 2007).

4. Barack Obama, "Remarks to the Cuban American National Foundation in Miami, Florida, May 23, 2008," The Presidency Project, University of California at Santa Barbara, http://www.presidency.ucsb.edu/ws/index.php?pid=77357.

5. Jeff Zeleny, "Obama, in Miami, Calls for Engaging with Cuba," *New York Times*, May 24, 2018, https://www.nytimes.com/2008/05/24/us/politics/24campaign.html.

6. Victor Gaetan, "Change Coming to Cuba? Founder of Island's Christian Liberation Movement Discusses Release of Political Prisoners," *National Catholic Register*, July 13, 2010, https://www.ncregister.com/daily-news/sensing_change_in_cuba.

7. "US Secretly Created 'Cuban Twitter' to Stir Unrest and Undermine Government," *Guardian*, April 3, 2014, http://www.theguardian.com/world/2014/apr/03/us-cuban-twitter-zunzuneo-stir-unrest.

8. David Adams, "US to Pay $3.2 Million to Contractor Freed from Cuban Jail," Reuters, December 24, 2014, https://www.reuters.com/article/us-cuba-usa-gross/u-s-to-pay-3-2-million-to-contractor-freed-from-cuba-prison-idUSKBN0K11TL20141224.

9. Stanley Cohen, "An Overview of Jewish History in Cuba," B'nai B'rith International, http://www.bnaibrith.org/cuba-history.html.

10. "Synagogues and Congregations," The Jews of Cuba, last modified February 24, 2019, http://jewishcuba.org/synagogues.html.

11. The Associated Press did a deep dive into the contractor's trip reports to his employer, Development Alternatives Inc.: Desmond Butler, "AP Impact: USAID Contractor Work in Cuba Detailed," Associated Press, February 12, 2012, https://www.sandiegouniontribune.com/sdut-ap-impact-usaid-contractor-work-in-cuba-detailed-2012feb12-story.html.

12. Jeffrey Goldberg, "Our Man in Havana, or, the Strange Case of Alan Gross," *The Atlantic*, February 13, 2012, http://www.theatlantic.com/international/archive/2012/02/our-man-in-havana-or-the-strange-case-of-alan-gross/253025.

13. "Cuba to End Exit Permits for Foreign Travel," BBC, October 16, 2017, https://www.bbc.com/news/world-latin-america-19958577.

14. Lisa Paravisini-Gebert, "Raúl Castro Lights Hanukkah Menorah at Havana Synagogue," *Repeating Islands* (blog), December 7, 2010, http://repeatingislands.com/2010/12/07/raul-castro-lights-hanukkah-menorah-at-havana-synagogue.

15. Frances Robles and Julie Hirschfeld Davis, "US Frees Last of the Cuban Five: Part of a 1990s Spy Ring," *New York Times*, December 18, 2014, https://www.nytimes.com/2014/12/18/world/americas/us-frees-last-of-the-cuban-five-part-of-a-1990s-spy-ring-.html. Julia Sweig makes the point that it was the Obama administration that "quite cynically drew the American Jewish community to campaign

for Gross's release." Julia Sweig, *Cuba: What Everyone Needs to Know*, 3rd ed. (New York: Oxford University Press, 2016), 279.

16. William M. LeoGrande and Peter Kornbluh, *Back Channel to Cuba: The Hidden History of Negotiations between Washington and Havana* (Chapel Hill: University of North Carolina Press, 2015), 421–24.

17. For an excellent short explanation of the significance of the "Cuban Five," five intelligence officers arrested in 1998 and prosecuted for conspiracy, see Sweig, *Cuba: What Everyone Needs to Know*, 183–85.

18. Hillary Clinton, *Hard Choices* (New York: Simon & Schuster, 2014), 265.

19. Sibylla Brodzinsky, "Drug Policy and Cuba Headline Summit of the Americas," *Christian Science Monitor*, April 16, 2012, https://www.csmonitor.com/World/Americas/2012/0416/Drug-policy-and-Cuba-headline-Summit-of-the-Americas.

20. "Pope Benedict Helped Free Alan Gross from Cuba," *Haaretz*, December 18, 2014, https://www.haaretz.com/pope-benedict-helped-free-alan-gross-from-cuba-1.5349173.

21. Darren Sands, "Democratic Public Relations Firm SKDK Helped American Freed by Cuba," BuzzFeed News, December 17, 2014, http://www.buzzfeed.com/darrensands/democratic-public-relations-firm-skdk-helped-freed-cuban-det#.deWoBOaNj. A website with the domain name bringalanhome.org had numerous documents and letters posted, but it is no longer available.

22. Victor Gaetan, "The Cuban Knot: The Vatican's Strategy in Havana," *Foreign Affairs*, December 30, 2014, https://www.foreignaffairs.com/articles/cuba/2014-12-30/cuban-knot.

23. "Ricardo Zúñiga, el Hondureño que Negoció en Secreto Acuerdo EEUU-Cuba [Ricardo Zúñiga, the Honduran who negotiated an agreement in secret]," *El País*, December 18, 2014, https://www.elpais.cr/2014/12/19/ricardo-zuniga-el-hondureno-que-negocio-en-secreto-acuerdo-eeuu-cuba; "Human Rights Study Project Students Interview Dissident Leaders, Study Free Speech in Cuba," *UVA Lawyer*, Summer 2003, http://www.law.virginia.edu/html/alumni/uvalawyer/sum03/hrsp.htm.

24. Daniel Trotta, "A Castro Son Rises in Cuba," Reuters, June 17, 2015, https://www.reuters.com/article/us-cuba-castro/a-castro-son-rises-in-cuba-idUSKBN0OX1SU20150617.

25. Ben Rhodes, *The World as It Is: A Memoir of the Obama White House* (New York: Random House, 2018), 213–17.

26. Rhodes, *The World as It Is*, 216.

27. Austen Ivereigh, *The Great Reformer: Francis and the Making of a Radical Pope* (New York: Henry Holt, 2015), 198, 247; Massimo Borghesi, *The Mind of Pope Francis: Jorge Mario Bergoglio's Intellectual Journey*, trans. Barry Hudock (Collegeville, MN: Liturgical Press Academic, 2018), chap. 3, Kindle.

28. Pope Francis, *Evangelii Gaudium*, para. 88.

29. LeoGrande and Kornbluh, *Back Channel to Cuba*.

30. William Donohue, "The Confusion over Kerry's Annulment," Catholic League for Religious and Civil Rights, May 22, 2004, https://www.catholicleague.org/the-confusion-over-kerrys-annulment.

31. "Shuttle Diplomacy: Kerry and Vatican's Parolin: In Whirlwind Conference, They Discuss Syria, Mideast, US Health Mandate," *America* (magazine), January 14, 2014, http://www.americamagazine.org/issue/shuttle-diplomacy-kerry-and-vaticans-parolin; Warren Strobel, "Kerry Asks Vatican to Help Win Release of American Jailed in Cuba," Reuters, January 14, 2014, https://www.reuters.com/article/us-kerry-vatican/kerry-asks-vatican-to-help-win-release-of-american-jailed-in-cuba-idUSBREA0D14220140114.

32. Becciu was nuncio to Cuba (2009–2011). Rumors in Havana that he received special permission from the Cuban government to hire his Italian brother's firm to install fixtures at the nunciature proved true. From Cuba he was elevated to *sostituto* in 2011 by Cardinal Bertone, Benedict XVI's secretary of state, and continued in the position under Pope Francis. Francis gave Becciu a red hat—named him to the College of Cardinals—in 2018 but took the office's privileges away when he sacked Becciu for financial corruption, including schemes that benefited his family. The Vatican put him under investigation.

33. Rhodes, *The World as It Is*, 284.

34. Rhodes, *The World as It Is*.

35. American Catholics continue to ask how it was possible for McCarrick to climb so high in the Church hierarchy when rumors of perverse behavior were known long before victims registered specific accusations. His lifelong talent for ingratiating himself with officeholders, proudly boasting of those connections, and a related prowess in fund-raising as intense as any American politician, appears to have inoculated him from the scrutiny he deserved.

36. Rhodes, *The World as It Is*, 285.

37. Even before he was ordained archbishop of Washington, DC, in January 2001, McCarrick was wearing the mantle of US government officialdom: he was appointed to the US Commission on International Religious Freedom (USCIRF) under President Bill Clinton in 1999, a year after Congress established the commission. McCarrick served on the board of directors and board of trustees of Catholic Relief Services (CRS) for eighteen years, which meant numerous opportunities for international travel, especially to poor, remote places. He regularly checked in with US embassies abroad and State Department offices at home to share his impressions. I interviewed McCarrick for over four hours in two sessions (October 20 and November 1, 2015) to learn more about his diplomatic endeavors. Our interviews took place at the seminary where he lived, Redemptoris Mater, the archdiocesan missionary seminary. As he reminded me, he was eighty-five years old. His stories ranged the globe, from the Balkans to Japan and from China to Cuba. He was particularly preoccupied with Christian-Muslim relations. One "adventure" was the source of extra pride: he worked with Episcopalian Bishop John Bryson Chane to secure the release of two Americans accused of espionage by the Iranian government and jailed for two years (see Thomas Erdbrink and Ian Shapiro, "Iran Frees American Hikers after Two Years," *Washington Post*, September 21, 2011, https://www.washingtonpost.com/world/middle-east/iran-frees-american-hikers-after-two-years/2011/09/21/gIQAFZYAmK_story.html). McCarrick told me the State Department turned to the clerics when they had run out of diplomatic options.

When I asked him what gave him hope about the potential for peace in the world, his response was centered on American politics: "I think the work John Kerry did was good for us [Americans], good for them [Iranians], and good for the world." He gleefully recounted a recent trip: A few months before our meetings, on his way to China, McCarrick had visited Japanese prime minister Shinzo Abe at his summer residence on Lake Kawaguchi. The exotic adventure came as a result of getting to know Japanese officials at their Washington embassy. From Tokyo, he flew to Istanbul, as a guest of the Norwegian government, to discuss ways to defeat ISIS. What was his main takeaway? That the US government should stop arming the Iraqi militia, and "I told them [American officials] when I came home to support the Kurdish Peshmerga instead." It's clear that McCarrick was useful to, and used by, the American foreign policy establishment—a role he invited and savored—under the Clinton, Bush, and Obama administrations.

He relished the mystique of operating in ways that blurred the lines between church and state authority. None of his accounts to me referenced the Vatican's foreign policy apparatus. When I probed, he said he did not need "permission" from Rome when he traveled to China, for example, because he was merely visiting "old friends." I established that the origin of his activity in China was, again, American connections, not assignments from Rome. As bishop of Metuchen, New Jersey (1981–1986), then archbishop of Newark (1986–2000), McCarrick was involved with Seton Hall University's early exchange programs with China. See chapter 11.

38. Rhodes, *The World as It Is*, 286.

39. Ruadhan Mac Cormaic, "Cardinal's Secret US Visit Paved Way for Obama-Castro Détente," *Irish Times*, March 16, 2017, https://www.irishtimes.com/news/world/cardinal-s-secret-us-visit-paved-way-for-obama-castro-d%C3%A9tente-1.3011667.

40. Victor Gaetan, "The Castros' Ambiguous Relationship with the Catholic Church," *National Catholic Register*, August 3, 2010, http://www.ncregister.com/daily-news/cuba-the-castros-ambiguous-relationship-with-the-catholic-church.

41. In Julia Sweig's account, Sarraff wrote to Ortega proposing himself as part of the spy swap, but it is hard to imagine how Sarraff, in jail at the time, would be so up to date on secret negotiations unless the Cuban government wanted him to send that message, to become part of the deal. Sweig, *Cuba: What Everyone Needs to Know*, 292.

42. Jon Lee Anderson, "A New Cuba," *New Yorker*, September 26, 2016, https://www.newyorker.com/magazine/2016/10/03/a-new-cuba.

43. Rhodes, *The World as It Is*, 287.

44. Bishop Jorge Bergoglio was in Pope John Paul II's entourage for the pope's January 1998 pilgrimage to Cuba. A month later, he was installed archbishop of Buenos Aires, and later that year he published *Diologos entre Juan Pablo II y Fidel Castro* (Dialogues between John Paul II and Fidel Castro) criticizing the regime for restricting freedom and destroying popular culture while criticizing "neoliberalism" for elevating money over human dignity.

45. Rhodes, *The World as It Is*, 289.

46. Rhodes, *The World as It Is*, 301.

47. "Fact Sheet: Charting a New Course in Cuba," Office of the Press Secretary, White House, December 17, 2014, https://obamawhitehouse.archives.gov/the-press-office/2014/12/17/fact-sheet-charting-new-course-cuba. Exemplifying how startling the deal was even to well-informed experts is Julia Sweig's response. As she listened to the December 17 announcement, "the scope of the until-then secret deal quickly exceeded the expectations of what most Cuba watchers thought possible." She credited Pope Francis with providing "a crucial, personal push." Sweig, *Cuba: What Everyone Needs to Know*, 289, 291.

48. Peter Baker, "US to Restore Full Relations with Cuba, Erasing a Last Trace of Cold War Hostility," *New York Times*, December 17, 2014, https://www.nytimes.com/2014/12/18/world/americas/us-cuba-relations.html. The prisoner release element was a tip of the hat to the Catholic Church, which centered this request at every opportunity. As a sign of goodwill before his arrival in Cuba in 2015, for example, the Cuban government released over 3,500 prisoners from Cuban jails. Some of the American concessions relating to travel and trade were rolled back by President Donald J. Trump in late 2017.

49. Anderson, "A New Cuba."

50. "Statistics of the Catholic Church in Cuba and the United States of America," Vatican Information Service, September 15, 2015, http://visnews-en.blogspot.com/2015/09/statistics-of-catholic-church-in-cuba.html.

51. Lisa Paravisini-Gebert, "Virgin de la Caridad del Cobre: Cuban Relic Ends Pilgrimage at Huge Open-Air Mass," *Repeating Islands* (blog), December 31, 2011, http://repeatingislands.com/2011/12/31/virgen-de-la-caridad-del-cobre-cuban-relic-ends-pilgrimage-at-huge-open-air-mass.

52. Victor Gaetan, "A New Seminary in Cuba," *National Catholic Register*, November 4, 2010, http://www.ncregister.com/daily-news/a-new-seminary-in-cuba. The Knights of Columbus is an excellent example of a transnational Catholic lay organization that has played a variety of supportive roles in international relations on behalf of the Church. In 2018, it donated over $185 million and contributed over seventy-six million hours of service. It is active in about fifteen countries and US territories.

53. Victor Gaetan, "The Catholic Church in Cuba: Beyond the Headlines," *National Catholic Register*, August 2, 2010, https://www.ncregister.com/daily-news/the-catholic-church-in-cuba.

54. Victor Gaetan, "How the Catholic Church Is Preparing for a Post-Castro Cuba," *Foreign Affairs*, February 27, 2012, https://www.foreignaffairs.com/articles/americas/2012-02-27/how-catholic-church-preparing-post-castro-cuba.

55. "Apostolic Journey of His Holiness Pope Francis to Cuba, the United States of America and Visit to the United Nations Organization Headquarters on the Occasion of His Participation at the Eighth World Meeting of Families in Philadelphia," Holy See, September 19–28, 2015, http://w2.vatican.va/content/francesco/en/travels/2015/outside/documents/papa-francesco-cuba-usa-onu-2015.html.

56. Victor Gaetan, "Pope Francis to Step into the Cuban Caldron," *National Catholic Register*, September 15, 2015, https://www.ncregister.com/site/article/cuban-cauldron-awaits-pope.

57. Victor Gaetan, "The Death of a Dictator: Fidel Castro (1926–2016)," *National Catholic Register*, December 2, 2016, https://www.ncregister.com/daily-news/the-death-of-a-dictator-fidel-castro-1926-2016.

58. Thomas Quigley, who served as Latin America adviser to the US Conference of Catholic Bishops in the 1970s, debunks standard explanations for why Fidel Castro turned on the Church, including assumptions that it was elitist, urban, or dominated by anti-Communist priests from Spain. Thomas Quigley, "The Catholic Church in Cuba," in *Catholicism and Politics in Communist Societies*, ed. Pedro Ramet (Durham, NC: Duke University Press, 1990). Some armchair analysts point to the presence of two Catholic chaplains among the Bay of Pigs forces as triggering Fidel's angry response. But based on experience in China, Eastern Europe, North Korea, Russia, and Vietnam, the Left eventually turns on the Church as it consolidates power because believers—and a rival structure of authority—threaten its full control. As well, documents found in archives of the former Soviet Union demonstrate that Fidel's attitudes against the Catholic Church had hardened by 1961. He considered the Church "counterrevolutionary" and decided to come down hard on its people and assets. See compiled original documents in James Hershberg, "New Russian Evidence on Soviet-Cuban Relations, 1960–61: When Nikita Met Fidel, the Bay of Pigs, and Assassination Plotting," Working Paper No. 90, Cold War International History Project, Wilson Center, February 2019, https://www.wilsoncenter.org/sites/default/files/media/documents/publication/cwihp_working_paper_90_new_russian_evidence_on_soviet-cuban_relations_1960-61.pdf.

59. Quigley, "The Catholic Church," 306.

60. Mateo Jover Marimon, "The Church," in *Revolutionary Change in Cuba*, ed. Carmelo Mesa-Lago (Pittsburgh, PA: University of Pittsburgh Press, 1971), 405.

61. Arthur Jones, "The Early Stages of the Cuban Revolution: A Retrospective," *National Catholic Reporter*, January 13, 2015, https://www.ncronline.org/news/world/early-stages-cuban-revolution-retrospective.

62. Quigley, "The Catholic Church," 306.

63. Victor Gaetan, "Havana's Cardinal Ortega: Stepping Down and Staying Put," *National Catholic Register*, May 20, 2016, http://www.ncregister.com/daily-news/havanas-cardinal-ortega-stepping-down-and-staying-put; Victor Gaetan, "Cardinal Jaime Ortega: A Product of Two Castros, Three Popes, One Discreet US Hand," *National Catholic Register*, August 21, 2019, https://www.ncregister.com/daily-news/cardinal-jaime-ortega-a-product-of-two-castros-three-popes-one-discreet-us-.

64. The international role played by the Boston cardinal was passed to his successor, Cardinal Seán O'Malley, much as successive New York cardinals played various postwar international roles.

65. Bishop William Murphy, interview with the author, Rockville Center, NY, January 27, 2020.

66. Clyde Farnsworth, "Soviet Said to Reduce Support for Cuban Economy," *New York Times*, March 16, 1988, https://www.nytimes.com/1988/03/16/world/soviet-said-to-reduce-support-for-cuban-economy.html.

67. "Interview before Departure with Latin American Scientists Who Know Cuba Thoroughly," Pax Christi International, typed report, August 20, 1991, 12. Unpublished document in the possession of the author.

68. See chapter 5 on the contribution of Cardinal Armand Jean du Plessis, Duke of Richelieu, to the Holy See's diplomatic practice.

69. Oswaldo Payá Sardiñas, interview with the author, Havana, Cuba, March 22, 2010.

70. Cardinal Jaime Ortega, interview with the author, Havana, Cuba, March 20, 2010; Manuel Cuesta Morúa, "Can Communist Regimes Reform? The Case of Cuba; Road to Reform?," Geneva Summit for Human Rights and Democracy, February 25, 2015, YouTube video, 14:25, https://www.youtube.com/watch?v=3A9hZtQPPxs. The US taxpayer supported National Endowment for Democracy (NED) programming in Cuba moved away from the Catholic leader, Payá, to promote a variety of secular activists such as Cuesta Morúa and blogger Yoani Sanchez.See Ivan Garcia, "What Do Cuban Dissidents Think of Diaz-Canel?," Translating Cuba, May 15, 2018, http://translatingcuba.com/category/authors/manuel-cuesta.

71. Gaetan, "Cardinal Jaime Ortega."

72. Ariel Sigler, interview with the author, Miami, Florida, April 10, 2012.

73. In one of the last international interviews he gave, speaking to the *Irish Times* in 2017, Ortega emphasized that Francis saw his engagement in human terms: Sending letters carried personally by a close envoy "was a way of putting them in contact. That was the desire of the Holy Father. People must communicate. He was not a mediator between two nations or between two governments, but he wanted to put the two presidents in contact." Mac Cormaic, "Cardinal's Secret."

74. Victor Gaetan, "US Calls for Investigation of Cuban Catholic Opposition Leader's Death," *National Catholic Register*, April 9, 2013, https://www.ncregister.com/daily-news/US-calls-for-investigation-of-cuban-catholic-opposition-leaders-death.

75. Juan Tamayo, "Carromero Says Cuban Officer Forced Him to Change Crash Story," *Miami Herald*, August 13, 2013, http://www.miamiherald.com/news/nation-world/world/americas/article1954098.html; Nora Gámez Torres, "Spaniard Convicted in Death of Cuban Activist Payá Recounts Ordeal in Visit to Miami," *Miami Herald*, October 11, 2014, http://www.miamiherald.com/news/nation-world/world/americas/cuba/article2674868.html.

76. Belén Marty, "Evidence Mounts That Oswaldo Payá Was Assassinated by the Castros," *PanAm Post*, July 23, 2015, https://panampost.com/belen-marty/2015/07/23/evidence-mounts-that-oswaldo-Payá-was-assassinated-by-the-castros; Gaetan, "US Calls for Investigation."

77. Ofelia Acevedo (widow of Oswaldo), interview with the author, Washington, DC, June 8, 2018.

78. 1 Corinthians 12:5.

79. Gaetan, "Cardinal Jaime Ortega."

CHAPTER 8

1. Pope Francis, "Meeting with the Young People: Address of His Holiness Pope Francis" (address, Apostolic Journey of His Holiness Pope Francis to Kenya, Uganda, and the Central African Republic, Nairobi, Kenya, November 27, 2015), https://w2.vatican.va/content/francesco/en/speeches/2015/november/documents/papa-francesco_20151127_kenya-giovani.html.

2. David Cheney, "Archdiocese of Nairobi," Catholic-Hierarchy, last modified April 3, 2020, http://www.catholic-hierarchy.org/diocese/dnair.html; as a percentage of total population in the Nairobi archdiocese, Church statistics show that Catholics comprised 27 percent in 1980 and 62 percent in 2013. Fredrick Nzwili, "Pope Francis' Trip to Africa Draws Excitement, Trepidation in Kenya," Religion News Service, November 2, 2015, https://religionnews.com/2015/11/02/pope-francis-trip-africa-draws-excitement-trepidation-kenya.

3. "Catholic Church Plays Great Role in Education," *The Standard*, November 26, 2015, https://www.standardmedia.co.ke/article/2000183626/catholic-church-plays-great-role-in-education.

4. John Campbell, "Kenyatta and Odinga Call for Reconciliation in Kenya," Council on Foreign Relations, March 9, 2018, https://www.cfr.org/blog/kenyatta-and-odinga-call-reconciliation-kenya.

5. "Garissa University College Attack in Kenya: What Happened?," BBC, June 19, 2019, https://www.bbc.com/news/world-africa-48621924.

6. Edward Pentin, "Kenyan Bishop on the Holy Thursday Massacre: 'We Could Hear Every Gunshot,'" *National Catholic Register*, April 22, 2015, http://www.ncregister.com/daily-news/kenyan-bishop-on-the-holy-thursday-massacre-we-could-hear-every-gunshot.

7. H. Plecher, "Kenya: Youth Unemployment Rate from 1999 to 2019," Statista, February 12, 2020, https://www.statista.com/statistics/812147/youth-unemployment-rate-in-kenya.

8. Jeffrey Gettleman, Isma'il Kushkush, and Rukmini Callimachi, "Somali Militants Kill 147 at Kenyan University," *New York Times*, April 2, 2015, https://www.nytimes.com/2015/04/03/world/africa/garissa-university-college-shooting-in-kenya.html.

9. Fred Olouch, "Agitation That Shaped Today's Politics," *Daily Nation*, October 7, 2013, https://www.nation.co.ke/lifestyle/dn2/Kenya-Multiparty-politics/957860-2020838-14ea6gp/index.html; Pat Nyhan and Helen Epstein, "Kenya's Unfinished Democracy: A Human Rights Agenda for the New Government," *Human Rights Watch* 14, no. 10 (December 2002), https://www.hrw.org/reports/2002/kenya2/Kenya1202-01.htm.

10. Jeffrey Gettleman, "Disputed Vote Plunges Kenya into Bloodshed," *New York Times*, December 31, 2007, https://www.nytimes.com/2007/12/31/world/africa/31kenya.html.

11. Stephanie McCrummen, "Kenyan Rivals Sign Power-Sharing Agreement," *Washington Post*, February 29, 2008, http://www.washingtonpost.com/wp-dyn/content/article/2008/02/28/AR2008022801040.html?noredirect=on.

12. "Kenya Tribes," Kenya Information Guide, http://www.kenya-information-guide.com/kenya-tribes.html.

13. Jeffrey Gettleman, "Kenya Rivals Reach Peace Agreement," *New York Times*, February 29, 2008, https://www.nytimes.com/2008/02/29/world/africa/29kenya.html.

14. Jeffrey Gettleman, "Spurts of Violence Punctuate Calm after Kenyan Vote Is Upheld," *New York Times*, March 31, 2013, https://www.nytimes.com/2013/04/01/world/africa/kenya-sees-some-violence-after-vote-is-upheld.html.

15. Jeffrey Gettleman, "Kenyans Approve New Constitution," *New York Times*, August 5, 2010, https://www.nytimes.com/2010/08/06/world/africa/06kenya.html.

16. A Swedish NGO, Diakonia, helped with this research.

17. Kenya Conference of Catholic Bishops, *Baseline Report on the Challenges and Prospects of Devolution with Respect to Violence* (Nairobi: Kenya Catholic Justice and Peace Commission, 2015), http://www.kccb.or.ke/home/wp-content/uploads/2015/03/cjpc_baseline_report.pdf.

18. Tamba Jean-Matthew III, "Obama Wants Equal Rights for Gays," *Daily Nation*, June 27, 2013, https://www.nation.co.ke/news/1056-1896906-1203oa5z/index.html.

19. Emily Stanton, "Kenyan Leaders Slam President Obama's Gay Rights Comments," *U.S. News and World Report*, July 1, 2013, https://www.usnews.com/news/blogs/washington-whispers/2013/07/01/kenyan-leaders-slam-president-obamas-gay-rights-comments.

20. Aggrey Mutambo, "Cardinal Njue Criticizes Obama's Gay Stance," *Daily Nation*, June 28, 2013, https://www.nation.co.ke/news/Cardinal-Njue-criticises-Obama-gay-stance/1056-1897702-bcc3d4/index.html.

21. Reuben Githinji, "Kenya: Pope's Envoy Champions Gays and Lesbians Rights," *The Star*, July 1, 2013, https://www.the-star.co.ke/news/2013-06-30-popes-envoy-champions-gays-and-lebians-rights2. Although the nuncio said he was misquoted, the cardinal was nevertheless furious.

22. "Dear Pope Francis, Here Is Why Kenyans Don't Like Cardinal John Njue," *Kenya Today*, November 25, 2015, https://www.kenya-today.com/opinion/dear-pope-francis-kenyans-dont-like-cardinal-john-njue.

23. "Inquiry into Beatification of Cardinal Otunga Begins in Nairobi," Catholic News Agency, September 13, 2009, https://www.catholicnewsagency.com/news/inquiry_into_beatification_of_cardinal_otunga_begins_in_nairobi.

24. Pope Francis, "Address of His Holiness Pope Francis to the Bishops of the Episcopal Conference on Their 'ad Limina' Visit" (address, Vatican City, April 16, 2015), https://w2.vatican.va/content/francesco/en/speeches/2015/april/documents/papa-francesco_20150416_ad-limina-kenya.html.

25. "Rt. Rev. Anthony Muheria mp4," YouTube, November 4, 2015, video, 6:18, https://www.youtube.com/watch?v=0Amblc2BO50. Muheria was elevated as archbishop of Nyeri in 2017. In 2015 he was bishop of Kitui.

26. Rose Achiego, "Mji Wa Furah Celebrates Silver Jubilee," Kenya Conference of Catholic Bishops, March 11, 2015, https://www.kccb.or.ke/home/news-2/mji-wa-furah-celebrates-silver-jubilee.

27. Rose Achiego, "Catholic Youth Pray Rosary for the Intention of the Pope's Visit to Kenya," Kenya Conference of Catholic Bishops, October 22, 2015, https://www.kccb.or.ke/home/news-2/catholic-youth-pray-rosary-for-the-intention-of-the-popes-visit-to-kenya.

28. Emeka-Mayaka Gekara and Anita Chepkoech, "Paradigm Shift as Uhuru Kenyatta and Raila Odinga Share the Podium in Nyanza Event," *Daily Nation*, July 4, 2015, https://www.nation.co.ke/news/politics/Uhuru-Kenyatta-Raila-Odinga-Kisumu-Event/1064-2775472-pc1ugk/index.html.

29. "Apostolic Journey of His Holiness Pope Francis to Kenya, Uganda, and the Central African Republic," Holy See, https://w2.vatican.va/content/francesco/en/travels/2015/outside/documents/papa-francesco-africa-2015.html.

30. For the Mass celebrated in Nairobi, Francis wore an outer garment decorated with beading in ethnic Maasai patterns, made for him by tailors who lived in Kangemi, the well-known slum he visited.

31. "Huge Crowds as Pope Francis Celebrates First Mass in Africa," *Jordan Times*, November 26, 2015, http://www.jordantimes.com/news/world/huge-crowds-pope-francis-celebrates-first-mass-africa.

32. Achiego, "Catholic Youth Pray."

33. Allen Ottaro, "A Young Catholic from Kenya Reflects on the Pope's African Visit," Catholic World Report, December 28, 2015, https://www.catholicworldreport.com/2015/12/28/a-young-catholic-from-kenya-reflects-on-the-popes-african-visit.

34. Pope Francis, "Meeting with the Young People."

35. "Eleven Catholic Radio Stations Launched in Kenya," Paulines Africa, September 16, 2016, http://paulinesafrica.org/eleventh-catholic-radio-station-launched-kenya.

36. Rose Achiego, "Kenya: Outgoing PMS National Director Appointed Regional Coordinator for Agriculture Initiative Program in Africa," Amecea News Blog, February 2, 2018, https://amecea.blogspot.com/2018/02/kenya-outgoing-pms-national-director.html; Fredrick Nzwili, "Kenya's Catholic Church to Fight Hunger by Farming Its Vast Land Reserves," *EarthBeat* (blog), *National Catholic Reporter*, March 12, 2015, https://www.ncronline.org/blogs/eco-catholic/kenya-s-catholic-church-fight-hunger-farming-its-vast-land-reserves; Rose Achiego, "Church to Use Its Idle Land in Africa for Agriculture," Vatican Radio, April 7, 2016, http://www.archivioradiovaticana.va/storico/2016/04/07/church_to_use_its_idle_land_in_africa_for_agriculture/en-1220871.

37. Pope Francis, "Visit to Kangemi Slum: Address of His Holiness Pope Francis" (address, Apostolic Journey of His Holiness Pope Francis to Kenya, Uganda, and the Central African Republic, Nairobi, Kenya, November 27, 2015), https://w2.vatican.va/content/francesco/en/speeches/2015/november/documents/papa-francesco_20151127_kenya-kangemi.html.

38. John Njue, "Cardinal John Njue Urges Kenya to Shun Tribalism," Daily Nation, October 31, 2016, YouTube, video, 2:01, https://www.youtube.com/watch?v=WDl02qHK0Q4.

39. William Mwangi, "Catholic Bishops Urge Warring Communities to Embrace Peace, Drop Weapons," *The Star*, February 25, 2017, https://www.the-star.co.ke

/news/2017-02-25-catholic-bishops-urge-warring-communities-to-embrace-peace-drop-weapons.

40. Martha Calderon, "Vote Wisely, Seek Peace, Bishops Say ahead of Kenya's Elections," Catholic News Agency, November 26, 2015, https://www.catholicnewsagency.com/news/vote-wisely-seek-peace-bishops-say-ahead-of-kenyas-elections-72508.

41. Kimiko de Freytas-Tamura, "Kenyan Election Official Is Killed on Eve of Vote," *New York Times*, July 31, 2017, https://www.nytimes.com/2017/07/31/world/africa/chris-musando-kenya-election-official-dead.html. According to a well-placed source, "The officer in question had been compromised by giving the passwords of the electoral commission servers to the opposition. Police think he was killed because he had given away this precious information that the opposition wanted to use to alter the results. So, who did electoral tampering? The simple answer is that everyone wanted to tamper with the results."

42. "Country on a Knife Edge ahead of High-Stakes Elections," *Daily Nation*, August 6, 2017, https://www.nation.co.ke/news/politics/Two-days-until-polls-open/1064-4046872-irqhamz/index.html.

43. David Lewis, "International Observers Say Kenyan Election Was Fair and Free from Hackers," *Christian Science Monitor*, August 10, 2017, https://www.csmonitor.com/World/Africa/2017/0810/International-observers-say-Kenyan-election-was-fair-and-free-from-hackers.

44. "Protests over Election Fraud Claim Turn Deadly in Kenya," Al Jazeera, August 9, 2017, https://www.aljazeera.com/news/2017/08/kenya-police-protesters-clash-poll-fraud-claim-170809081850902.html.

45. George Obulutsa and John Ndiso, "Kenyan President Says Supreme Court Election Ruling was 'Coup,'" Reuters, September 21, 2017, https://www.reuters.com/article/us-kenya-election/kenyan-president-says-supreme-court-election-ruling-was-coup-idUSKCN1BW1DC.

46. Ibrahim Oruko, "Religious Leaders Attempt to Solve Election Issue," *Daily Nation*, September 25, 2017, https://www.nation.co.ke/news/Religious-leaders-attempt-to-solve-election-issue/1056-4111884-93ogwq/index.html.

47. Fredrick Nzwili, "Kenyan Cardinal Appeals to Politicians to Use Dialogue to Calm the Country ahead of Election Re-Run," *The Tablet*, September 25, 2017, https://www.thetablet.co.uk/news/7812/kenyan-cardinal-appeals-to-politicians-to-use-dialogue-to-calm-the-country-ahead-of-election-re-run.

48. Lilian Muendo, "Sisters on Front Lines as Kenya Prepares for Historic Repeat Election," *National Catholic Reporter*, October 26, 2017, https://www.ncronline.org/preview/sisters-front-lines-kenya-prepares-historic-repeat-election.

49. Robyn Dixon, "Kenyan Election Official Flees to U.S. in Fear for Her Life, Saying New Election Will Not Be Fair," *Los Angeles Times*, October 18, 2017, http://www.latimes.com/world/africa/la-fg-kenya-election-threats-20171018-story.html; Duncan Miriri and Maggie Fick, "Eyes on Odinga as Kenya Election Board CEO Takes Leave before Vote," Reuters, October 20, 2017, https://www.reuters.com/article/us-kenya-election/eyes-on-odinga-as-kenya-election-board-ceo-takes-leave-before-vote-idUSKBN1CP0FP.

50. "Uhuru Hopes for United Post-Vote Kenya," *Daily Nation*, October 27, 2017, https://www.nation.co.ke/news/Presidential-candidates-condemn-Raila-Odinga/1056-4158026-syu0um/index.html.

51. Wycliff Kipsang, "Fare Thee Well Bishop Cornelius Korir, the Eternal Optimist," *Daily Nation*, November 11, 2017, https://www.nation.co.ke/news/Fare-thee-well-Bishop-Korir/1056-4182194-bjbdmqz/index.html.

52. Jeremiah Wakaya, "President Kenyatta Stressed Need for Peace to Enhance Development," Capital News, November 11, 2017, https://www.capitalfm.co.ke/news/2017/11/president-kenyatta-stresses-need-peace-enhance-development.

53. Philip Anyolo, "A New Heart and a New Spirit" (address, Nakuru, Kenya, November 9, 2017), http://amecea.blogspot.com/2017/11/kenya-catholic-bishops-address-to.html.

54. Anyolo, "A New Heart."

55. Anyolo, "A New Heart."

56. Mactilda Mbenywe, "Kenya Should Not Experience More Deaths Due to Elections, Says Cleric," *The Standard*, December 26, 2017, Kenya, https://www.standardmedia.co.ke/article/2001264165/kenya-should-not-experience-more-deaths-due-to-elections-says-cleric.

57. Sera Bi Ali, "How Raila Tricked Moi, Escaped Death to Norway," Hivisasa, https://hivisasa.com/posts/how-raila-tricked-moi-escaped-death-to-norway.

58. Justus Wanga, "Intrigues in Surprise Uhuru-Raila Harambee House Meeting," Daily Nation, March 11, 2018, https://www.nation.co.ke/news/Intrigues-in-surprise-Uhuru-Raila-meeting/1056-4336744-l1x6elz/index.html.

59. Fredrick Nzwili, "Kenyan Bishops See 'Hand of God' in Government Opponents' Gesture," *National Catholic Reporter*, March 15, 2018, https://www.ncronline.org/news/world/kenyan-bishops-see-hand-god-government-opponents-gesture.

60. "Kenyatta and Odinga Vow to Work Out Differences," Al Jazeera, March 10, 2018, https://www.aljazeera.com/news/2018/03/kenyatta-odinga-amends-tillerson-visit-180309172042412.html.

61. Nzwili, "Kenyan Bishops."

62. "Joint Statement by President Kenyatta, Raila on Their Partnership," Capital News, March 9, 2018, https://www.capitalfm.co.ke/news/2018/03/joint-statement-president-kenyatta-raila-partnership.

63. Paul Samasumo, "Kenyan Bishops Urge President and Opposition Leader to Go beyond Handshake," Vatican News, April 18, 2018, https://www.vaticannews.va/en/africa/news/2018-04/kenyan-bishops-urge-president-and-opposition-leader-to-go-beyond.html; Philip Anyolo, "A Call to Healing and Reconciliation" (press statement, Kenyan Conference of Catholic Bishops, Nairobi, Kenya, March 14, 2018), https://www.kccb.or.ke/home/com/press-statement-a-call-to-healing-and-reconciliation.

64. Kepher Otieno and Caleb Kingwara, "Drama as Raila Reconciles Ayacko and Obado," *The Standard*, July 11, 2018, https://www.standardmedia.co.ke/article/2001287554/drama-as-raila-reconciles-ayacko-and-obado.

65. Inés San Martín, "Kenyan Prelate to Fellow Bishops: 'Waste Time with Young People,'" Crux, October 16, 2018, https://cruxnow.com/synod-of-bishops-on-youth/2018/10/16/kenyan-prelate-to-fellow-bishops-waste-time-with-young-people.

CHAPTER 9

1. "Pope Pleads from Villavicencio: Colombia, Let Yourself be Reconciled," Rome Reports, September 9, 2017, https://www.romereports.com/en/2017/09/09/pope-pleads-from-villavicencio-colombia-let-yourself-be-reconciled.
2. "Kidnapping and Extortion," Colombia Reports, July 20, 2019, https://colombiareports.com/colombia-kidnapping-and-extortion-statistics. Disturbing evidence of ongoing conflict since the 2016 peace deal is the systematic murder of human rights monitors and social leaders working to implement terms of the agreement. Over three hundred were killed between November 2016 and December 2019. See "Colombia Peace: Important Numbers," Washington Office on Latin America, May 13, 2020, https://colombiapeace.org/numbers.
3. "Religions in Colombia," Pew-Templeton Global Religious Futures Project, http://www.globalreligiousfutures.org/countries/colombia#/?affiliations_religion_id=26&affiliations_year=2010&region_name=All%20Countries&restrictions_year=2016.
4. Adriaan Alsema, "Guerrillas Responsible for 17% of Civilian Deaths in Colombia's Armed Conflict," Colombia Reports, August 3, 2018, https://colombiareports.com/guerrillas-responsible-for-17-of-civilian-deaths-in-colombias-armed-conflict. Note that private paramilitary groups, often allied with state military, killed almost three times as many people as the guerillas, 46 percent of the deaths versus 17 percent.
5. For a good introduction to Colombia's political history, see "Colombia," in Lawrence Clayton, Michael Conniff, and Susan Gauss, *A New History of Modern Latin America*, 3rd ed. (Oakland: University of California Press, 2017), 472–94.
6. Especially Cardinal Alfonso López Trujillo, secretary general of the Latin American Episcopal Council (CELEM, 1972–1984) and president of the Pontifical Council on the Family (1990–2008). However, a highly capable nuncio, an *Accademia* graduate, represented the Holy See in Bogotá at the height of the war: Archbishop Benjamin Stella (1999–2007).
7. See Christian Smith, *The Emergence of Liberation Theology: Radical Religion and Social Movement Theory* (Chicago: University of Chicago Press, 1991).
8. Jim Yardley and Simon Romero, "Pope's Focus on Poor Revives Scorned Theology," *New York Times*, May 23, 2015, https://www.nytimes.com/2015/05/24/world/europe/popes-focus-on-poor-revives-scorned-theology.html. Trujillo was secretary general of CELAM for twelve years and worked to limit the organization's commitment to social justice. Sources in Colombia, including a Benedictine monk who worked for him, accuse Trujillo of taking money from local drug cartels, being involved with paramilitary units, and providing information to them against left-leaning priests, some of whom wound up dead. See Frédéric Martel, *In the Closet of the Vatican: Power, Homosexuality, Hypocrisy* (London: Bloomsbury Continuum,

2019), 279–96. Martel, who visited Colombia four times for this research, also provides convincing evidence that the cardinal was an active homosexual and sexual predator who used his ill-gained fortune to buy influence.

9. Pope John Paul II, "Address of His Holiness John Paul II" (address, Third General Conference of the Latin American Episcopate, Puebla, Mexico), Holy See, January 28, 1979, https://w2.vatican.va/cotent/john-paul-ii/en/speeches/1979/january/documents/hf_jp-ii_spe_19790128_messico-puebla-episc-latam.html.

10. As López Trujillo's obituary in the *Guardian* confirms, he was "a workaholic with an acute understanding of church politics. He was therefore able, first at CELAM and later at the Pontifical Council for the Family, to ensure that his favoured candidates were appointed to vacant sees in Latin America." Peter Stanford, "Cardinal Alfonso López Trujillo: Hardline Roman Catholic Opposed to Abortion and Condoms," *The Guardian*, April 21, 2008, https://www.theguardian.com/world/2008/apr/22/catholicism.colombia.

11. Eugene Dionne, "Pope, in Colombia, Attacks Economic Inequality," *New York Times*, July 2, 1986, https://www.nytimes.com/1986/07/02/world/pope-in-colombia-attacks-economic-inequality.html.

12. M-19 was founded in 1970 and purported to have a nationalistic ideology. By the late 1980s, its leadership renounced violence and gave up its weapons in exchange for pardons.

13. Bradley Graham, "Pope Starts Visit to Colombia," *Washington Post*, July 2, 1986, https://www.washingtonpost.com/archive/politics/1986/07/02/pope-starts-visit-to-colombia/eecb1577-48ab-4ab1-abc6-2cd96ce94db1/?noredirect=on&utm_term=.ddc93cc03544.

14. Dionne, "Pope, in Colombia, Attacks Economic Inequality."

15. Bruce Bagley, "Colombia and the War on Drugs," *Foreign Affairs*, Fall 1988, https://www.foreignaffairs.com/articles/bolivia/1988-09-01/colombia-and-war-drugs.

16. William Avilés, "Paramilitarism and Colombia's Low-Intensity Democracy," *Journal of Latin American Studies* 38, no. 2 (May 2006): 392–93.

17. Stephanie Hanson, "FARC, ELN: Colombia's Left-Wing Guerrillas," *Washington Post*, March 12, 2008, http://www.washingtonpost.com/wp-dyn/content/article/2008/03/12/AR2008031202036.html.

18. Among ELN's early, highly visible supporters were left-wing priests such as Fr. Camilo Torres Restrepo, gunned down by the military while taking a gun from a dead soldier. His motto was "Revolution is the aim of Christianity." Jeremy McDermott, "Colombia's Rebel Kidnappers," BBC, January 7, 2002, http://news.bbc.co.uk/2/hi/americas/1746914.stm; Gerald Theisen, "The Case of Camilo Perres Restrepo," *Journal of Church and State* 16, no. 2 (Spring 1974): 301–15, https://www.jstor.org/stable/23914573. A former Spanish priest, Manuel Pérez Martínez, helped reinvigorate the group, using kidnapping schemes and blackmail against the oil industry to raise money in the 1980s. Daniel García-Peña, "The National Liberation Army (ELN) Creates a Different Peace Process," NACLA, September 25, 2007, https://nacla.org/article/national-liberation-army-eln-creates-different-peace-proces; Richard Emblin, "Walter Broderick and the Story of ELN Leader Camilo Torres,"

The City Paper (Bogotá), May 22, 2016, https://thecitypaperbogota.com/features/walter-broderick-story-eln-camilo-torres/12923.

19. ELN members pledged to avoid drug trafficking in 1989, but by 2005 some units were using it to fund activities. Unlike FARC, which was structured hierarchically and included many full-time soldiers living in the jungle, ELN is more decentralized, with part-time members integrated in communities especially in certain counties. It continues to use extortion as a major fund-raiser. For example, sabotaging infrastructure allows ELN to get kickbacks from public contracts for repairs. See "The ELN," Colombia Peace: Monitoring Progress in Peace Dialogues, April 12, 2020, https://colombiapeace.org/the-eln.

20. "Terror on Flight 9463," *The Guardian*, April 27, 1999, https://www.theguardian.com/theguardian/1999/apr/28/features11.g23.

21. Brett Borkan, "Avianca Plane Hijacker Gets 40 Years Jail," Colombia Reports, June 24, 2010, https://colombiareports.com/eln-hijacker-of-avianca-flight-gets-40-years-in-jail.

22. Timothy Pratt, "Colombian Rebels Seize 99 Hostages at Church," *Washington Post*, May 31, 1999, https://www.washingtonpost.com/archive/politics/1999/05/31/colombian-rebels-seize-99-hostages-at-church/8e838b5f-e8a8-4fe1-ab97-4316431b9282. It seems ELN was desperate for attention because the president had awarded FARC with a temporary demilitarized zone the size of Switzerland in the south, representing about one-third of the country's territory. It was the price for opening peace negotiations, which continued on and off for Andrés Pastrana's tenure. The president cut ELN off from talks after the Avianca and Cali hostage offenses.

23. Larry Rohter, "Colombians Tell of Massacre, as Army Stood By," *New York Times*, July 14, 2000, https://www.nytimes.com/2000/07/14/world/colombians-tell-of-massacre-as-army-stood-by.html. In 2017, people painted a giant peace sign on the basketball court: Mary Bowerman, "Artist Works alongside Community to Paint over Spot of Massacre in Colombia," *USA Today*, October 20, 2017, https://www.usatoday.com/story/news/nation-now/2017/10/20/artist-works-alongside-community-paint-over-spot-massacre-colombia/779164001.

24. Mike Power, "The Devastation of Colombia's Civil War," *The Guardian*, April 22, 2011, https://www.theguardian.com/lifeandstyle/2011/apr/23/colombia-farc-killed-mothers-justice.

25. The bishop took a position in Rome in 1996 as prefect of the Congregation of the Clergy and was named cardinal two years later. Colombian Nobel Prize winner Gabriel Garcia Márquez visited the cardinal in Rome and wrote admiringly of the churchman's love for country and his attitude toward the priesthood as a "crusade for social justice." "Cardinal Who Humbled a Drugs Baron," *The Guardian*, April 23, 1999, https://www.theguardian.com/books/1999/apr/24/books.guardianreview13.

26. Chris Kraul and Henry Chu, "Latin American Catholics Problem with Pope JPII," *Seattle Times*, April 11, 2005, https://www.seattletimes.com/nation-world/latin-american-catholics-problem-with-pope-john-paul-ii.

27. Liduine Zumpolle, personal communication with the author, September 1, 2020.

28. Trujillo never returned to Colombia after he left. According to journalist and author Gerard O'Connell, Trujillo began quietly lobbying for Joseph Ratzinger to

succeed John Paul II in 2002. He hosted "as many as" one hundred lunches and dinners in his apartment for fellow cardinals to advance Ratzinger. Gerard O'Connell, *The Election of Pope Francis: An Inside Account of the Conclave That Changed History* (Maryknoll, NY: Orbis, 2019), 16. When he died, he was buried in Rome, but Pope Francis had his body repatriated in 2017, almost ten years after his death. Martel suggests the pope was wary of a scandal emerging around the man's double life. Martel, *In the Closet*, 296.

29. Liduine Zumpolle, personal communication with the author, September 14, 2020.

30. Liduine Zumpolle, personal communication with the author, September 1, 2020.

31. Annely Koudstaal, "Parallel Motion: National and International Dimensions of Peace Processes in Colombia," University of Amsterdam, July 2008. PDF in possession of the author.

32. Marie Dennis, interview with the author, Washington, DC, September 13, 2019.

33. Virginia Bouvier, *Colombia: Building Peace in a Time of War* (Washington, DC: US Institute of Peace, 2009).

34. In Colombia, "departments" are subnational jurisdictions like provinces or states.

35. Francisco de Roux, SJ, "Tensions between Peace and Violence," Thinking Faith, June 28, 2016, https://www.thinkingfaith.org/articles/tensions-between-peace-and-violence.

36. Francisco de Roux, "Francisco de Roux at Regis University #2," Institute on the Common Good, July 1, 2008, YouTube video, 10:00, https://www.youtube.com/watch?v=EBU6_Q8HTEA.

37. "Colombia: Development and Peace in the Magdalena Medio Region," *En Breve*, no. 5 (July 2002), World Bank, https://openknowledge.worldbank.org/bitstream/handle/10986/10406/267140English01o1050Magdalena1Medio.pdf.

38. "The Curse of the Vigilantes," *Economist*, April 21, 2001, https://www.economist.com/special-report/2001/04/19/the-curse-of-the-vigilantes.

39. "Colombia: Development."

40. Miguel Barreto Henriques, "Peace Laboratory of Magdalena Medio: 'A Peace Laboratory?'" (working paper, no. 6, CERAC—Centro de Recursos para el Análisis de Conflictos, December 2007), http://cerac.org.co/assets/pdf/Other%20publications/CERAC_WP_6.pdf. Did the ideas animating PDPMM, so eloquently presented by Fr. Pacho, constitute liberation theology? No and yes. It was emphatically nonviolent and dedicated to participatory democracy and the equality of all people, thus not radical. Yet the effort affirmed some of liberation theory's key insights: the Church should accompany the poor, poverty stems from structural social problems, and working for socioeconomic justice is an appropriate pursuit for the Catholic Church—these ideas were at work in the PDPMM and similar projects.

41. Horacio Arango, SJ, "Respect for Life and Personal Integrity Should Prevail in Zones of Conflict," Programa por la Paz, August 22, 1996, https://colombiasupport.net/archive/199608/arango.html.

42. Fr. Jorge Enrique Salcedo Martínez, SJ, a professor at the Pontifical Xavierian University and a historian of the Society of Jesus in Colombia, points out that many diocesan priests across the country eagerly participated in CINEP activities and programs sponsored by the Jesuits. For example, Way of the Cross processions organized annually became opportunities to protest the killing while mourning. Peace-building efforts led by Jesuits found ready participation at the parish level. Personal communication with the author, June 4, 2020.

43. "*Comunidades de Paz*; A Local Peace Initiative in Colombia: Evaluation of an Experiment," Pax Christi Netherlands, September 2000. Unpublished document in possession of author. Thanks to Ben Schennink, Center for International Conflict Analysis and Management, Radboud University, and a principal analyst for Pax Christi Netherlands for providing me with remarkable unpublished documents on PCN's work in Colombia.

44. Alvaro Campos, "The National Reconciliation Commission, A Hope for Peace," *Harvard Review of Latin America*, Spring 2003, https://revista.drclas.harvard.edu/book/national-conciliation-commission.

45. Ed Vulliamy, "Interview: Ingrid Betancourt," *The Guardian*, November 29, 2008, https://www.theguardian.com/world/2008/nov/30/ingrid-betancourt-columbia-freedom-interview. She was abducted in San Vicente del Caguán in Caquetá Department.

46. "Ingrid Betancourt Meets with Pope Benedict," *New York Times*, September 1, 2008, https://www.nytimes.com/2008/09/01/world/europe/01iht-ingrid.4.15802775.html.

47. Vulliamy, "Interview: Ingrid Betancourt."

48. Arturo Wallace, "Colombian Girl's Kidnap Highlights Children's Plight," BBC, October 12, 2011, https://www.bbc.com/news/world-latin-america-15270976.

49. H. Sergio Mora, "Former Colombian Prisoners Recount Torments," Zenit, June 8, 2012, https://zenit.org/articles/former-colombian-prisoners-recount-torments; Toby Muse, "Colombian Farc Rebels Release Hostages after Decade of Jungle Captivity," *The Guardian*, April 3, 2012, https://www.theguardian.com/world/2012/apr/03/colombian-farc-releases-hostages-jungle.

50. Luca Caruso, "'Peace Is to Be Reached through Justice and Truth, Respecting the Victims': Interview to César Mauricio Velásquez," Fondazione Ratzinger, http://www.fondazioneratzinger.va/content/fondazioneratzinger/en/news/notizie/rimandi-news/_la-pace-va-cercata-con-giustizia-e-verita--rispettando-le-vitti.html.

51. In January 2012, FARC announced it would no longer use kidnapping for ransom as a weapon of war. At its height in the late 1990s, FARC took three thousand hostages per year, jailing them in remote jungle locations. President Uribe's military offensive caused the guerilla army to shrink from twenty thousand to eight thousand fighters. Assassination of several top commanders further weakened the organization. They were forced to the bargaining table, conceding, "For our part, we believe that there are no more excuses for not starting talks." See Toby Muse, "Colombia's FARC Rebels to Free All Captives," *The Guardian*, February 27, 2012, https://www.theguardian.com/world/2012/feb/27/colombia-farc-rebels-free-captives.

52. "Creating a Climate of Reconciliation: Opening Space for Truth, Justice and Reparation," Fourth Annual Catholic Peacebuilding Network Conference, Bogotá, Colombia, June 24–29, 2007, University of Notre Dame website, https://cpn.nd.edu/news-events/past-events/colombia-2007.

53. "Interview of His Holiness Benedict XVI during the Flight to Brazil," Holy See, May 9, 2007, http://w2.vatican.va/content/benedict-xvi/en/speeches/2007/may/documents/hf_ben-xvi_spe_20070509_interview-brazil.html.

54. "Interview of His Holiness." Benedict's conviction that Latin America held the Church's future is one reason he approved Archbishop Stella's promotion from nuncio to president of the Pontifical Ecclesiastical Academy—the *Accademia*—in 2007. Despite Benedict's timidity toward politics, he believed the Holy See's diplomatic corps should be instructed in exactly the kind of sacrifice, fortitude, and discretion defending the Church required—skills Stella demonstrated in Colombia.

55. Austin Ivereigh, *The Great Reformer: Francis and the Making of a Radical Pope* (New York: Henry Holt, 2015), 295–301.

56. Bishops participated in four rounds of preliminary peace talks with ELN in Havana in 2006, but FARC was always the biggest guerrilla force and no peace efforts gained traction under Uribe. According to Liduine Zumpolle, Santos already began exploring national-level peace efforts while he was minister of defense.

57. Joey O'Gorman, "Colombia Peace Talks Receive Broad International Support," Colombia Reports, September 5, 2012, https://colombiareports.com/colombia-peace-talks-receive-international-support.

58. Ezra Fieser, "New Colombian Cardinal Has Worked to Help End Country's Civil War," *National Catholic Reporter*, October 25, 2012, https://www.ncronline.org/news/vatican/new-colombian-cardinal-has-worked-help-end-countrys-civil-war.

59. The concept of "just war" was evoked by St. Augustine in *The City of God*, published in 426. St. Thomas Aquinas elaborated on the idea, defining three conditions when war was allowed, in the second part of the *Summa Theologica*.

60. "Diocese Threatened by Armed Group," Agenzia Fides, April 13, 2013, http://www.fides.org/en/news/33505-AMERICA_COLOMBIA_Diocese_threatened_by_armed_group.

61. Virginia Bouvier, interview with the author, Washington, DC, March 6, 2016.

62. "Pope Meets with Colombia's President, Juan Manuel Santos," Rome Reports, May 13, 2013, YouTube video, 3:01, or https://www.youtube.com/watch?v=AlqMKbqY3_w.

63. Ginny (Virginia) Bouvier, "The Pope and the Bishops Speak of Peace in Colombia," *Colombia Calls* (blog), May 19, 2013, https://vbouvier.wordpress.com/2013/05/19/the-pope-and-the-bishops-speak-of-peace-in-colombia.

64. Balestrero served as undersecretary for relations with states (2009–2013), successor to Cardinal Parolin. His appointment to Colombia was announced after Pope Benedict's resignation yet before a new pope was selected, meaning he was promoted by Cardinal Secretary of State Bertone, who created a clannish set of diplomatic players, involved in questionable financial intrigues that Francis continued to unravel in 2021. Balestrero was accused by the Italian government of money laundering in the

1990s when he was a young diplomat in South Korea. He paid over $8 million in a plea bargain in 2021, justifying it as a family business transfer. The story is not over.

65. The government of Venezuela was intimately involved in the Colombian peace talks, advising FARC and attending proceedings in Havana.

66. Deborah Sontag, "The Secret History of Colombia's Paramilitary and the US War on Drugs," *New York Times*, September 10, 2016, https://www.nytimes.com/2016/09/11/world/americas/colombia-cocaine-human-rights.html.

67. Rubén Salazar Gómez, "Comunicado Sobre el Desarrollo de los Diálogos de Paz" [Statement on the development of the peace dialogues], May 27, 2013, Episcopal Conference of Colombia, https://www.cec.org.co/sites/default/files/WEB_CEC/Documentos/Presidencia/2013/pdf/2013%20Desarrollo%20de%20los%20dia%CC%81logos%20de%20paz.pdf.

68. "Obispos Colombianos Recuerdan que 'la Paz es Obra de la Justicia' [Colombian bishops recall that "peace is the work of justice"], ACI Prensa, April 26, 2013, https://www.aciprensa.com/noticias/obispos-colombianos-recuerdan-que-la-paz-es-obra-de-la-justicia-88809.

69. "The Peacemakers of Colombia," Deutsche Welle, December 16, 2013, YouTube video, 5:37, https://www.dw.com/en/the-peacemakers-of-colombia/av-17298739.

70. "A Second Agreement Has Been Reached, the Church Proposes 'a Policy of Reconciliation for Definitive Peace,'" Agenzia Fides, November 8, 2013, http://www.fides.org/en/news/34647-AMERICA_COLOMBIA_A_second_agreement_has_been_reached_the_Church_proposes_a_policy_of_reconciliation_for_definitive_peace.

71. "Pastoral Care Workers Killed in 2013," Agenzia Fides, December 30, 2013, http://www.fides.org/en/news/34966-VATICAN_PASTORAL_CARE_WORKERS_KILLED_IN_2013.

72. "The First 12 Members of the Delegation of the Victims Will Participate in Peace Talks Which Take Place in Cuba," Agenzia Fides, August 18, 2014, http://www.fides.org/en/news/36215-AMERICA_COLOMBIA_The_first_12_members_of_the_delegation_of_the_victims_will_participate_in_Peace_Talks_which_take_place_in_Cuba.

73. Rubén Salazar Gómez, "Our Suffering Has Not Been Useless" (address, Third World Congress on Mercy, Bogotá, Colombia, August 16, 2014), https://www.thedivinemercy.org/news/story.php?NID=6189&PLID=71.

74. Pope Francis with Dominique Wolton, *A Future of Faith: The Path of Change in Politics and Society* (New York: St. Martin's Essentials, 2018), 101.

75. "Colombian General Alzate Freed by Farc Rebels," BBC, December 1, 2014, https://www.bbc.com/news/world-latin-america-30268694.

76. "Colombian Farc: The Norwegian Who Helped Broker Peace," BBC, August 28, 2016, https://www.bbc.com/news/world-latin-america-37206714.

77. William Neuman, "Killing of 10 Soldiers Deals a Setback to Colombian Peace Talks with FARC Rebels," *New York Times*, April 15, 2015, https://www.nytimes.com/2015/04/16/world/americas/colombia-attack-attributed-to-farc-threatens-peace-talks.html.

78. "Silent March in Tumaco: After 60 Years of Violence It Is Now Time to Form 'a Truly Civilized Society,'" Agenzia Fides, June 17, 2015, http://www.fides.org/en/news/38009-AMERICA_COLOMBIA_Silent_march_in_Tumaco_after_60_years_of_violence_it_is_now_time_to_form_a_truly_civilized_society.

79. "'The Peace Process Is Alive,' Said Mgr. Castro Quiroga; Letter of the Religious Leaders," Agenzia Fides, July 9, 2015, http://www.fides.org/en/news/38155-AMERICA_COLOMBIA_The_peace_process_is_alive_said_Mgr_Castro_Quiroga_letter_of_the_religious_leaders.

80. "Week of Peace: Colombians Want a Date for Talks with the ELN," Agenzia Fides, September 11, 2015, http://www.fides.org/en/news/38448-AMERICA_COLOMBIA_Week_of_Peace_Colombians_want_a_date_for_talks_with_the_ELN.

81. The last major hurdle was cleared in June when the two sides agreed on a ceasefire. For that announcement, six Latin American presidents and UN general secretary Ban Ki-moon traveled to celebrate with Santos and the negotiators. Nick Miroff, "Colombia Announces Cease-Fire Deal to End 52-Year Conflict with Rebels," *Washington Post*, June 23, 2016, https://www.washingtonpost.com/world/the_americas/colombia-announces-cease-fire-deal-to-end-52-year-conflict-with-farc/2016/06/23/3b85e53a-37ff-11e6-af02-1df55f0c77ff_story.html?utm_term=.b01135769eb6.

82. Hannah Brockhaus, "Francis Welcomes Peace Deal in Colombia," Catholic News Agency, August 31, 2016, https://www.catholicnewsagency.com/news/francis-welcomes-peace-deal-between-colombias-government-rebels-11050.

83. "The Bishops Invite All Colombians to Commit Themselves to Building Peace," Agenzia Fides, June 27, 2016, http://www.fides.org/en/news/60331-AMERICA_COLOMBIA_The_Bishops_invite_all_Colombians_to_commit_themselves_to_building_peace.

84. "San Pedro Claver, Defender of Slaves and Model for a Colombia at Peace," *San Diego Union-Tribune*, September 11, 2016, http://www.sandiegouniontribune.com/hoy-san-diego/sdhoy-san-pedro-claver-defender-of-slaves-and-model-for-2016sep11-story.html.

85. Renata Segura and Delphine Mechoulan, "Made in Havana: How Colombia and the FARC Decided to End the War," International Peace Institute, February 2017, https://www.ipinst.org/wp-content/uploads/2017/02/IPI-Rpt-Made-in-Havana.pdf. An informative report, sympathetic to what the peace talks in Havana accomplished, admits, "The Colombian government was more successful at raising international support for the peace process than in convincing its own people about the importance of the agreement with FARC" (34).

86. "Full Agreement on Victims," FARC-EP International, Section 5.1, http://www.farc-epeace.org/peace-process/agreements/agreements/item/939-agreement-victims. "System" is capitalized in the text.

87. Segura and Mechoulan, "Made in Havana."

88. Segura and Mechoulan, "Made in Havana." The reason "gender" cropped up so frequently in the text seems to be the heavy involvement of UN organizations in Havana, at a time when promoting gender equality was a high priority for the UN. For example, "Gender" was one of three standing subcommissions informing the negotiations, together with "Legal" and "End of Conflict." The gender subcommis-

sion was created in September 2014. The New York–based UN Women brought five delegations of women and LGBT representatives to speak to negotiators. Their recommendations were then continuously pressed on the process by the subcommission. This all occurred apart from, and away from, Colombia itself.

89. See "St. Peter Claver, SJ (1580–1654)," in *The Cambridge Encyclopedia of the Jesuits*, ed. Thomas Worcester, SJ (Cambridge: Cambridge University Press, 2017).

90. "Colombia Celebrates Peace and a Jesuit 'Champion of Human Rights,'" Jesuits in Britain, September 29, 2016, https://www.jesuit.org.uk/colombia-celebrates-peace-and-jesuit-%E2%80%98champion-human-rights%E2%80%99. In 1537, Pope Paul III (1534–1549) issued *Sublimus Dei*, declaring that native peoples should not be enslaved.

91. Catholic News Service, "Colombian Peace Agreement Is Start of Change, Says Vatican Official," Northwest Catholic, September 27, 2016, http://www.nwcatholic.org/news/international-news/farc-peace-agreement-new-beginning-says-vatican.html.

92. "'La justicia abraza a la paz': Misa en iglesia San Pedro Claver" ['Justice embraces peace': Mass at the Church of St. Peter Claver], El Universal, http://www.eluniversal.com.co/colombia/bogota/la-justicia-abraza-la-paz-misa-en-iglesia-san-pedro-claver-236436.

93. "'Justice Embraces Peace': The Signing of the Peace Agreements at the Tomb of St. Peter Claver," Agenzia Fides, September 27, 2016, http://www.fides.org/en/news/60840-AMERICA_COLOMBIA_Justice_embraces_peace_the_signing_of_the_peace_agreements_at_the_tomb_of_St_Peter_Claver.

94. Nicholas Casey, "Colombia Signs Peace Agreement with FARC after 5 Decades of War," *New York Times*, September 27, 2016, https://www.nytimes.com/2016/09/27/world/americas/colombia-farc-peace-agreement.html.

95. Nicholas Casey, "Colombian Opposition to Peace Deal Feeds off Gay Rights Backlash," *New York Times*, October 9, 2016, https://www.nytimes.com/2016/10/09/world/americas/colombian-opposition-to-peace-deal-feeds-off-gay-rights-backlash.html.

96. Javier Lafuente, "Shock as Voters in Colombia Reject FARC Peace Deal," *El Pais*, October 3, 2016, https://elpais.com/elpais/2016/10/03/inenglish/1475483785_893407.html.

97. "The Nobel Peace Prize for 2016" (press release, Norwegian Nobel Committee, October 7, 2016), https://www.nobelprize.org/prizes/peace/2016/press-release.

98. "The Church May Participate in the Final Phase of the Peace Agreements," Agenzia Fides, November 3, 2016, http://www.fides.org/en/news/61094-AMERICA_COLOMBIA_The_Church_may_participate_in_the_final_phase_of_the_peace_agreements.

99. "The Church May Participate."

100. "Colombia and the FARC Strike a New Peace Agreement," *Economist*, November 13, 2016, https://www.economist.com/the-americas/2016/11/13/colombia-and-the-farc-strike-a-new-peace-agreement.

101. Helen Murphy, "Colombian Peace Deal Passed by Congress, Ending 52-Year War," Reuters, November 30, 2016, https://www.reuters.com/article/us-colombia-peace/colombian-peace-deal-passed-by-congress-ending-52-year-war-idUSKBN13P1D2.

102. "The Pope Receives the President of Colombia, Juan Manuel Santos Calderón, and Former President, Senator Álvaro Uribe Vélez" (summary of Bulletin, Holy See Press Office, December 16, 2016), https://press.vatican.va/content/salastampa/en/bollettino/pubblico/2016/12/16/161216b.html.

103. Pope Francis, "Apostolic Journey of His Holiness Pope Francis to Georgia and Azerbaijan (30 September–2 October 2016)" (in-flight press conference of His Holiness Pope Francis from Azerbaijan to Rome, Holy See, October 2, 2016), http://w2.vatican.va/content/francesco/en/speeches/2016/october/documents/papa-francesco_20161002_georgia-azerbaijan-conferenza-stampa.html.

104. "Five Bishops Will Participate in the Public Phase of the Talks between Government and ELN," Agenzia Fides, October 12, 2016, http://www.fides.org/en/news/60956-AMERICA_COLOMBIA_Five_Bishops_will_participate_in_the_public_phase_of_the_talks_between_government_and_ELN.

105. Reuters, "Pope to Make Four-Day Visit to Colombia in September," March 10, 2017, https://af.reuters.com/article/worldNews/idAFKBN16H20A.

106. Nicholas Casey and Joe Parkin Daniels, "'Goodbye, Weapons!' FARC Disarmament in Colombia Signals New Era," New York Times, June 27, 2017, https://www.nytimes.com/2017/06/27/world/americas/colombia-farc-rebels-disarmament.html.

107. Stephen Gill, "Colombia's ELN Rebels Propose Ceasefire ahead of Pope's Visit," Colombia Reports, June 6, 2017, https://colombiareports.com/colombias-eln-rebels-propose-ceasefire-ahead-popes-visit.

108. Joshua J. McElwee, "On Papal Flight, Francis Says Colombia Trip a Push to 'Go Forward on Path to Peace,'" National Catholic Reporter, September 6, 2017, https://www.ncronline.org/news/vatican/papal-flight-francis-says-colombia-trip-push-go-forward-path-peace.

109. Chris Kraul, "Pope Francis Arrives for Colombia's First Papal Visit since 1986," Los Angeles Times, September 6, 2017, http://www.latimes.com/world/mexico-americas/la-fg-colombia-pope-20170906-story.html.

110. "Apostolic Journey of His Holiness Pope Francis to Colombia 6–11 September 2017," Holy See, http://w2.vatican.va/content/francesco/en/travels/2017/outside/documents/papa-francesco-colombia_2017.html.

111. Katy Watson, "Victims and Perpetrators Gather for Pope's Colombia Visit," BBC News, September 9, 2017, https://www.bbc.com/news/world-latin-america-41211025.

112. Nicholas Casey and Susan Abad, "Pope Francis Visits Colombia Where Even Peace Is Polarizing," New York Times, September 6, 2017, https://www.nytimes.com/2017/09/06/world/americas/pope-francis-visits-colombia-where-even-peace-is-polarizing.html.

113. Philip Pullella, "Nelson Bocanegra, Pope Urges Skeptical Colombians to Accept Peace with Guerrillas," Reuters, September 8, 2017, https://www.reuters.

com/article/us-pope-colombia/colombias-farc-leader-asks-popes-forgiveness-for-war-pain-idUSKCN1BJ1TQ.

114. Rodrigo Londoño Echeverri adopted the nom de guerre Timochenko after a Soviet general he admired. He studied medicine in the Soviet Union and Cuba and got military training in Yugoslavia. After leading negotiations for FARC in Havana, he took charge as president of the new political party Common Alternative Revolutionary Force—known as FARC—and took a seat in the Colombian parliament.

115. Andrea Tornielli, "Uribe to the Pope, 'We Do Not Oppose Peace, but Total Impunity for Those Responsible for Atrocious Crimes,'" *La Stampa*, last modified July 5, 2019, https://www.lastampa.it/vatican-insider/en/2017/09/08/news/uribe-to-the-pope-we-do-not-oppose-peace-but-total-impunity-for-those-responsible-for-atrocious-crimes-1.34416238.

116. Andrea Tornielli, "Opposition Leader Uribe among the Pilgrims at Pope's Mass," *La Stampa*, last modified July 5, 2019, http://www.lastampa.it/2017/09/10/vaticaninsider/opposition-leader-uribe-among-the-pilgrims-at-popes-mass-K7Jt8TsszQx3Rf41K5lqdK/pagina.html.

117. Pope Francis, "The Dignity of the Person and Human Rights" (address, Holy Mass Homily of His Holiness Pope Francis to Colombia, Port of Contecar, Colombia, September 10, 2017), Holy See, https://w2.vatican.va/content/francesco/en/homilies/2017/documents/papa-francesco_20170910_omelia-viaggioapostolico-colombiacartagena.html.

118. Beth Griffin, "Church Helps People in Colombia Move from 'Vengeance' to Reconciliation," *National Catholic Reporter*, February 6, 2018, https://www.ncronline.org/news/world/church-helps-people-colombia-move-vengeance-reconciliation.

119. "Víctimas Conflicto Armad" [Victims of the armed conflict], Gov.co, last updated February 10, 2020, https://www.unidadvictimas.gov.co/es/registro-unico-de-victimas-ruv/37394.

CHAPTER 10

1. "Pope's Morning Mass: Jesus Weeps Today Too, Because We've Chosen the Way of War," Zenit, November 19, 2015, https://zenit.org/articles/pope-s-morning-mass-jesus-weeps-today-too-because-we-ve-chosen-the-way-of-war.

2. Cardinal Béchara Raï, "Memorandum on Active Neutrality," Syriac Press, August 17, 2020, https://syriacpress.com/blog/2020/08/18/memorandum-on-lebanon-and-active-neutrality-syriac-maronite-patriarch-bechara-boutros-rai.

3. Raï was selected patriarch in 2011 when his predecessor, Cardinal Nasrallah Boutros Sfeir, age ninety-one, stepped aside due to declining health. All patriarchs take the name Boutros, "Peter" in Arabic, after the traditional first bishop of Antioch, St. Peter, who then moved to Rome. Raï was named cardinal in Pope Benedict's last consistory, held in November 2012. Benedict's last trip abroad was to Lebanon in September 2011.

4. "Eastern Catholic Churches," Catholic-Hierarchy, http://www.catholic-hierarchy.org/rite.

5. Rep. Francis Rooney, interview with the author, Washington, DC, August 16, 2017. See "Vatican Strongly Opposes War," Associated Press, March 12, 2003, http://www.foxnews.com/story/2003/03/12/vatican-strongly-opposes-iraq-war.html; Alex Kingsbury, "A Rift over Iraq between President and Pope: The Vatican and the White House Have Disagreed over the War," *U.S. News & World Report*, April 16, 2008, https://www.usnews.com/news/national/articles/2008/04/16/a-rift-over-iraq-between-president-and-pope.

6. As he entered the Umayyad Mosque—also the site of St. John the Baptist's tomb—John Paul II kissed a Quran as a sign of respect for Islam and its people, a theme captured in his address when he used a family metaphor to describe relations between the two faith groups. See Pope John Paul II, "Address of the Holy Father" (address, Meeting with Muslim Leaders at Omayyad Great Mosque, Damascus, Syria, May 6, 2001), https://w2.vatican.va/content/john-paul-ii/en/speeches/2001/may/documents/hf_jp-ii_spe_20010506_omayyadi.html.

7. A December 28, 2006, US State Department cable reveals that Iranian president Mahmoud Ahmadinejad sent a letter to Pope Benedict via the Iranian foreign minister reaffirming positive bilateral relations between the two sovereigns, a backchannel message underscoring Ahmadinejad's "measured statements" following the Regensburg speech. See, Embassy Vatican, "Pope Meets Iranian FM; Remains Firm on Nukes," WikiLeaks, cable 06VATICAN270_a, dated December 28, 2006, https://wikileaks.org/plusd/cables/06VATICAN270_a.html. The Sunni-Shiite split dates back to the seventh century, 632 to be exact, and turns on the question of the Prophet Muhammad's successor. In recent centuries, relations between the two groups were relatively calm, but Iran's Islamic Revolution in 1979, the Iran-Iraq war in 1980, and the US-led invasion of Iraq in 2003 all served to heighten sectarian rivalry, with a geopolitical face: Iran is the Shia powerhouse, and Saudi Arabia is the mother ship of Sunni Islam. The Shia branch of Islam represents 10–15 percent of the 1.6 billion Muslims worldwide. Most Shiites live in four countries: Iran, Pakistan, India, and Iraq. There are also significant communities in Lebanon and Syria, specifically the Alawites, the faith tradition to which President Bashar al-Assad belongs. "The Sunni-Shia Divide," Council on Foreign Relations, November 6, 2017, https://www.cfr.org/interactives/sunni-shia-divide#!/sunni-shia-divide; Mike Shuster, "The Origins of the Sunni-Shiite Split," NPR, February 12, 2007, http://www.npr.org/sections/parallels/2007/02/12/7332087/the-origins-of-the-shiite-sunni-split; "The Future of the Global Muslim Population," Pew Research Center, Religion and Public Life, January 27, 2011, https://www.pewforum.org/2011/01/27/the-future-of-the-global-muslim-population.

8. Pope Benedict XVI, "Faith, Reason and the University: Memories and Reflections" (lecture, University of Regensburg, Regensburg, Bavaria, September 12, 2007), http://www.vatican.va/content/benedict-xvi/en/speeches/2006/september/documents/hf_ben-xvi_spe_20060912_university-regensburg.html.

9. See chapter 1, and note 23, for a longer discussion of weaknesses in the Vatican's Secretariat of State and the curia's coverage of the Muslim world during 2006.

10. Embassy Vatican, "Former Foreign Minister to Be Islam Czar," WikiLeaks, cable 07VATICAN102_a, dated June 28, 2007, https://wikileaks.org/plusd/cables/07VATICAN102_a.html.

11. Austin Ivereigh, *The Great Reformer: Francis and the Making of a Radical Pope* (New York: Henry Holt, 2015), 321.

12. Alessandro Speciale, "Pope Francis, Jordan King Say Dialogue Is 'Only Option' in Syria Conflict," *Washington Post*, August 29, 2013, https://www.washingtonpost.com/national/on-faith/pope-francis-jordan-king-say-dialogue-is-only-option-in-syria-conflict/2013/08/29/70882542-10eb-11e3-a2b3-5e107edf9897_story.html.

13. Pope Francis, "Letter to President Vladimir Putin on the Occasion of the G20 Summit in St. Petersburg," Holy See, September 4, 2013, http://www.vatican.va/content/francesco/en/letters/2013/documents/papa-francesco_20130904_putin-g20.html.

14. "Russia's Protectorate over Middle Eastern Christians," *La Stampa*, last modified December 30, 2019, http://www.lastampa.it/2013/10/24/vaticaninsider/russias-protectorate-over-middle-eastern-christians-7VuzVaS3bHfgxa3SvKGpEL/pagina.html.

15. White House adviser Ben Rhodes says it was a domestic political calculation that led President Obama to pull back from the bombing. He documents how Congress moved away from the harsh option over the course of several weeks, while Francis was lobbying his followers against aggression. One can't discount the possibility that members of Congress were influenced by the pope's effort. Ben Rhodes, *The World as It Is: A Memoir of the Obama White House* (New York: Random House, 2018), 228–40.

16. "Assad Addresses Thankful Letter to Pope Francis for His Positions," National News Agency (Lebanon), December 28, 2013, http://www.nna-leb.gov.lb/en/show-news/18817/nna-leb.gov.lb/en.

17. Victor Gaetan, "The Pontiff and the Pariah," *Foreign Affairs*, June 16, 2015, https://www.foreignaffairs.com/articles/russian-federation/2015-06-16/pontiff-and-pariah.

18. Nasser Chararah, "In Lebanon, Russia Supports Political Christian Orthodoxy," Al-Monitor, December 24, 2012, https://www.al-monitor.com/pulse/originals/2012/al-monitor/russia-orthodoxy-lebanon.html.

19. Amie Ferris-Rotman, "During Easter Season, Some Russians Look to Strengthen Bonds with Syria's Embattled Christians: The Kremlin Has Cast Itself as a Guardian of Syria's Ancient Christian Communities," *Washington Post*, April 20, 2019, https://www.washingtonpost.com/world/2019/04/20/during-easter-season-some-russians-look-strengthen-bonds-with-syrias-embattled-christians.

20. "Lebanese Christian General Flees Compound under Syrian Bombing," Associated Press, October 13, 1990, https://www.nytimes.com/1990/10/13/world/lebanese-christian-general-flees-compound-under-syrian-bombing.html.

21. Nasser Chararah, "Fear of Islamic Extremism Brings Eastern Churches Closer," al-Monitor, March 7, 2013, http://www.al-monitor.com/pulse/originals/2013/03/eastern-churches-islamism-threat.html#.

22. "Syria's Beleaguered Christians," BBC, February 25, 2015, https://www.bbc.com/news/world-middle-east-22270455. The Antiochian Church is known for recit-

ing the Divine Liturgy in Aramaic, Christ's tongue. Some Maronite prayers are also in Aramaic.

23. "Syria, Statistics by Diocese," Catholic-Hierarchy, http://www.catholic-hierarchy.org/country/scsy1.html.

24. Khaled Yacoub Oweis, "Patriarch Beshara al-Rai Warns against Syrian Uprising, Likens It to Lebanon Civil War," Reuters, February 10, 2013, http://www.huffingtonpost.com/2013/02/10/patriarch-warns-syrians-o_n_2658046.html.

25. Chararah, "Fear of Islamic Extremism."

26. Cindy Wooden, "Syrian Priest Killed during Rebel Attack on Franciscan Convent," Catholic News Service, June 25, 2013, https://catholicphilly.com/2013/06/news/world-news/syrian-priest-killed-during-rebel-attack-on-franciscan-convent. The Franciscan quoted, Fr. Pierbattista Pizzaballa, was promoted to serve as apostolic administrator of Jerusalem representing the Holy See soon after.

27. Peter Jesserer Smith, "Catholic Leaders Decry US Arms to Syrian Rebels," *National Catholic Register*, July 1, 2013, http://www.ncregister.com/daily-news/catholic-leaders-decry-US-arms-to-syrian-rebels.

28. His Beatitude Youssef III Younan, patriarch of the Syriac Catholic Church of Antioch, interview with the author, Rome, July 5, 2016; St. Louis, MO, August 1, 2017; Beirut, Lebanon, August 25–29, 2017.

29. Victor Gaetan, "Syriac Catholic Patriarch Warns: Western Politicians and Media Misled World on Middle East," *National Catholic Register*, July 21, 2016, https://www.ncregister.com/daily-news/syriac-catholic-patriarch-warns-western-politicians-and-media-mislead-world.

30. Pope Francis, "Address of Pope Francis" (address, Plenary Assembly for the Oriental Churches, Vatican City, November 21, 2013), http://www.vatican.va/content/francesco/en/speeches/2013/november/documents/papa-francesco_20131121_plenaria-congreg-chiese-orientali.html.

31. Pope Benedict XVI, "Post-synodal Apostolic Exhortation, *Ecclesia in Medio Oriente* on the Church in the Middle East: Communion and Witness," Holy See, September 14, 2012, http://www.vatican.va/content/benedict-xvi/en/apost_exhortations/documents/hf_ben-xvi_exh_20120914_ecclesia-in-medio-oriente.html. The document was based on a synod dedicated to the Church in the Middle East convened in October 2010 by Pope Benedict. It was the first synod dedicated to a region. The fact that it took two years to produce, a period that saw the start of the devastating war in Syria, suggests that despite the urgency expressed by the patriarchs who came to Rome and the sympathy expressed by Pope Benedict, there was no tactical plan attached to the exhortation.

32. Jorge Rouillon, "Pope Francis' Holy Land Partners in Faith: Argentinian Journalist Jorge Rouillon Profiles the Pope's Relationship with the Jewish Rabbi and the Muslim Layman who Will Accompany the Holy Father on This Week's Papal Pilgrimage," *National Catholic Register*, May 23, 2014, https://www.ncregister.com/daily-news/pope-francis-holy-land-partners-in-faith.

33. "Report: Maronite Patriarch Jerusalem Visit a 'Historic Sin,'" Agence France-Presse, May 3, 2014, https://english.alarabiya.net/en/News/middle-east/2014/05/03/Report-Maronite-patriach-Jerusalem-visit-a-historic-sin-.html.

34. "Facing the Enemy: We Talked to Lebanese Who Met Israelis Abroad," Step Feed, September 15, 2017, https://stepfeed.com/facing-the-enemy-we-talked-to-lebanese-who-met-israelis-abroad-1781.

35. "Background: Facts and Figures about the 2006 Israel-Hezbollah War," ReliefWeb, July 12, 2007, https://reliefweb.int/report/lebanon/background-facts-and-figures-about-2006-israel-hezbollah-war.

36. Doreen Abi Raad, "Maronite Official: Patriarch Won't Legitimize Israel's Political Claims," Catholic News Service, May 20, 2014, https://www.catholicnews.com/services/englishnews/2014/maronite-official-patriarch-won-t-legitimize-israel-s-political-claims.cfm. Complicating things, Raï's argument that he was obligated to meet his spiritual leader, Pope Francis, was undercut by his own predecessor, Cardinal Nasrallah Boutros Sfeir (1986–2011), who refused to meet John Paul II when he visited Jerusalem and, later, when the pope was in Damascus. Sfeir did meet Benedict in Jordan in 2009 but refused the onward journey to Israel.

37. "Rai Tells France 24: 'I Am the Patriarch and I Make My Own Decisions,'" Ya Libnan, May 23, 2014, https://yalibnan.com/2014/05/23/rai-tells-france-24-patriarch-make-decisions.

38. Pope John Paul II's 2000 itinerary referred to the "Autonomous Palestinian Territories": "Jubilee Pilgrimage to the Holy Land (March 20–26, 2000)," Holy See, http://www.vatican.va/content/john-paul-ii/en/travels/2000/travels/documents/trav_holyland-2000.html. While in Palestine, Pope Benedict said, "[T]he Holy See supports the right of your people to a sovereign Palestinian homeland": "Address of His Holiness Benedict XVI" (address, Pilgrimage to the Holy Land Welcoming Ceremony, Bethlehem, Palestine, May 13, 2009), http://www.vatican.va/content/benedict-xvi/en/speeches/2009/may/documents/hf_ben-xvi_spe_20090513_welcome-betlemme.html. The kaffiyeh is a national symbol: Majdi Habash, "The History of Keffiyeh: A Traditional Scarf from Palestine," *Handmade Palestine* (blog), September 24, 2018, https://handmadepalestine.com/blogs/news/history-of-keffiyeh-the-traditional-palestinian-headdress.

39. Sergio Centofanti, "Jerusalem: A City for All," Vatican News, March 30, 2019, https://www.vaticannews.va/en/vatican-city/news/2019-03/holy-see-status-of-jerusalem-city-for-all.html.

40. President Donald J. Trump announced December 6, 2017, that the United States recognized Jerusalem as the capital of Israel. The United Nations, the European Union, and the Holy See criticized the move. The United States relocated its embassy from Tel Aviv to Jerusalem five months later. See Jason Horowitz, "UN, European Union, and Pope Criticize Trump's Jerusalem Announcement," *New York Times*, December 6, 2017, https://www.nytimes.com/2017/12/06/world/europe/trump-jerusalem-pope.html.

41. Netta Ahituv, "15 Years of Separation: The Palestinians Cut Off from Jerusalem by the Wall," Haaretz, March 10, 2018, https://www.haaretz.com/israel-news/.premium.MAGAZINE-15-years-of-separation-palestinians-cut-off-from-jerusalem-by-a-wall-1.5888001.

42. "Pope Francis Offers Prayers at Israeli Separation Wall in Bethlehem," *The Guardian*, May 25, 2014, https://www.theguardian.com/world/2014/may/25/pope-francis-israeli-separation-wall-bethlehem.

43. Jay Perini, "Why Did Pope Francis Pray at the Wall?," CNN, May 27, 2014, https://www.cnn.com/2014/05/27/opinion/parini-pope-francis-prayer-at-wall/index.html.

44. The Holy See confirmed support for Palestinian statehood in late 2012 when it affirmed a UN resolution approved by the General Assembly that awarded Palestine "nonmember observer status" on November 22, 2012. See Yair Rosenberg, "Actually, the Vatican Recognized Palestine in 2012—Not Today," *The Tablet*, May 13, 2015, https://www.tabletmag.com/sections/news/articles/no-the-vatican-didnt-just-recognize-palestine.

45. Nicholas Blanford, "Lebanese President's Term Ends, with No One to Take His Place," *Christian Science Monitor*, May 25, 2014, https://www.csmonitor.com/World/Middle-East/2014/0525/Lebanese-president-s-term-ends-with-no-one-to-take-his-place.

46. *Daesh* is the Arabic acronym used most often in the Middle East to refer to the Islamic State of Iraq and Syria (ISIS) or the Islamic State of Iraq and the Levant (ISIL). It is preferred because it distinguishes the group from Islam, rather than making it part of Islam as the names ISIS and ISIL suggest. The word in Arabic includes the derogatory connotation of "lacking dignity."

47. Pope John Paul II, "Message to All the Bishops of the Catholic Church on the Situation in Lebanon," Holy See, September 7, 1989, https://www.vatican.va/content/john-paul-ii/fr/messages/pont_messages/1989/documents/hf_jp-ii_mes_19890907_situazione-libano.html. Lebanon was the last foreign country that Pope Benedict XVI visited, in September 2012: "Three Glorious Days Adorn Lebanon as Pope Benedict XVI Visits the Country," National News Agency, December 27, 2012, http://nna-leb.gov.lb/en/show-report/213/nna-leb.gov.lb/en. While Benedict was in Beirut, riots were underway in a city further north, Tripoli. It showed how the Syrian war had bled into Lebanon, as fighting was between Sunni Muslims and Alawites, a branch of Shia Islam, of which Syria's president is a member.

48. Based on a 1943 agreement, the prime minister is a Sunni, the speaker of the parliament is a Shia, and the president is a Maronite. Statistics are elusive, but the US State Department considered the most reliable recent demographic data to reflect an even population split between Sunnis and Shia, each with 27 percent of the country, while Christians comprised 36 percent, divided mainly between Maronites (21 percent), Orthodox (8 percent), and other Eastern-rite Catholics (5 percent). The Druze comprise 5.6 percent. The Lebanese constitution mandates that seats in parliament be divided fifty-fifty between Christians and Muslims, and the parliament elects the president for a six-year term. Since the agreement that ended the civil war, the 1989 Taif Accord, eighteen religious sects are recognized, and all have seats in parliament.

49. "How Caritas Helps in Syria," Caritas International, September 13, 2018, https://www.caritas.org/2018/09/how-caritas-helps-in-syria.

50. "Syria's Refugee Crisis in Numbers," Amnesty International, September 4, 2015, https://www.amnesty.org/en/latest/news/2015/09/syrias-refugee-crisis-in-numbers.

51. The program had support as well from the UN High Commissioner for Refugees (UNHCR) and the US Agency for International Development (USAID).

52. Kevin Jones, "The Lebanese Model: A Multireligious Solution for Syria and Iraq?," Catholic News Agency, November 13, 2014, https://www.catholicnewsagency.com/news/the-lebanese-model-a-multi-religious-solution-for-syria-and-iraq-50377. Caccia was posted in Lebanon for eight years (2009–2017) then moved to the Philippines (2017–2019), where he served the biggest Catholic-majority country in Asia, with the third-largest Catholic population in the world (following Brazil and Mexico). In November 2019, Francis appointed him to one of the Vatican's most prestigious diplomatic assignments: permanent observer to the United Nations in New York.

53. Anne Barnard and Hwaida Saad, "ISIS Claims Responsibility for Blasts That Killed Dozens in Beirut," *New York Times*, November 12, 2015, https://www.nytimes.com/2015/11/13/world/middleeast/lebanon-explosions-southern-beirut-hezbollah.html.

54. Reuters calls Hezbollah "the most powerful group in Lebanon": "Factbox: Lebanon's Main Political Players," Reuters, May 3, 2018, https://www.reuters.com/article/us-lebanon-election-parties-factbox/factbox-lebanons-main-political-players-idUSKBN1I41ZV.

55. Doreen Abi Raad, "Lebanon's Nuncio Visits Muslim Bomb Victims, Stresses Nation's Diversity," Catholic News Service, November 25, 2015, https://www.catholicnews.com/services/englishnews/2015/lebanons-nuncio-visits-muslim-bomb-victims-stresses-nations-diversity.cfm.

56. Embassy Vatican, "CODEL Shays Engages Vatican on Middle East, Sudan," WikiLeaks, cable 06VATICAN179_a, dated August 29, 2006, https://wikileaks.org/plusd/cables/06VATICAN179_a.html. Parolin told the congressional delegation concerned that Vatican diplomats would negotiate with groups the US government called terrorists: "We will not seek contact, but neither will we refuse it if approached," he said.

57. "Full Text of Pope Francis' In-Flight Press Conference from Geneva," Catholic News Agency, June 21, 2018, https://www.catholicnewsagency.com/news/full-text-of-pope-francis-in-flight-press-conference-from-geneva-20080.

58. Samuel Huntington, "The Clash of Civilizations?," *Foreign Affairs*, Summer 1993, 22–49, https://www.foreignaffairs.com/articles/united-states/1993-06-01/clash-civilizations.

59. Pope Francis, "Address of His Holiness Pope Francis" (address, Meeting with the Muslim Community in Bangui, Bangui, Central African Republic, November 30, 2015), https://w2.vatican.va/content/francesco/en/speeches/2015/november/documents/papa-francesco_20151130_repubblica-centrafricana-musulmani.pdf.

60. Harlet Sherwood, "Pope Francis Visits Besieged Mosque in Central African Republic," *The Guardian*, November 30, 2015, https://www.theguardian.com/world/2015/nov/30/pope-francis-mosque-central-african-republic; Francis's moving visit

with Muslims at the end of his trip to the Central African Republic came just fourteen years after Pope St. John Paul II visited the Umayyad Mosque in Damascus while retracing the path of St. Paul: Alessandra Stanley, "Pope, in Damascus, Goes to a Mosque in Move for Unity," *New York Times*, May 7, 2001, https://www.nytimes.com/2001/05/07/world/pope-in-damascus-goes-to-a-mosque-in-move-for-unity.html.

61. Fr. Kévork Assadourian, born in Qamishli, Syria, was ordained as auxiliary bishop in Beirut, and Msgr. Sarkis Davidian, born in Aleppo, Syria, was selected as bishop of Isfahan, Iran.

62. Isfahan was the capital of Persia in the sixteenth and seventeenth centuries, and still today you'll find Our Lady of the Rosary Cathedral there, built by Dominicans in 1681. The bishop resides in Tehran, a ten-minute walk from the Holy See's nunciature, where Francis sent a new representative, Archbishop Leo Boccardi (an *Accademia* graduate), the same month Bishop Davidian was consecrated. When the nuncio presented his credentials to the Iranian foreign minister, the two discussed the disaster in Syria. "Pope Francis Seeks Closer Iran Ties: Vatican Envoy," *The Iran Project* (blog), November 4, 2013, https://theiranproject.com/blog/2013/11/04/pope-francis-seeks-closer-iran-ties-vatican-envoy.

63. Elise Harris, "New Armenian Catholic Patriarch Pulled from Retirement to Take the Reins," Catholic News Agency, August 1, 2015, https://www.catholicnewsagency.com/news/new-armenian-catholic-patriarch-pulled-from-retirement-to-take-the-reins-65435.

64. Victor Gaetan, "Remembering the Armenian Genocide," *National Catholic Register*, April 14, 2015, https://www.ncregister.com/daily-news/remembering-the-armenian-genocide.

65. Bishop Sarkis Davidian, interview with the author, Beirut, Lebanon, November 21, 2015. More recently, he observed that based on his experience in Iran, the Church has full religious and political freedom. "Bishop Davidian: Armenians Enjoy Full Religious Freedom in Iran," *Tehran Times*, September 3, 2018, https://www.tehrantimes.com/news/427126/Bishop-Davidian-Armenians-enjoy-full-religious-freedom-in-Iran. As a testament to this freedom, Armenians have two reserved seats in the country's parliament, and at Christmas, Armenian communities celebrate publicly.

66. As the first pope to speak publicly about the Armenian genocide, Francis is especially beloved in this community, as participants were quick to tell me.

67. Pope Paul VI, *Nostra Aetate*.

68. Anthony O'Mahony, Wulstan Peterburs, and Mohammad Ali Shomal, eds., *A Catholic-Shi'a Engagement: Faith and Reason in Theory and Practice* (London: Melisende Publishing, 2006), http://biblicalstudies.org.uk/pdf/anvil/23-2_omahony.pdf. Imam Hussein, Muhammad's grandson (and son of Imam Ali, who Shia faithful believe was the Prophet's rightful successor, the core historical disagreement with Sunnis), was brutally martyred at the Battle of Karbala in 680 AD. Every year, Shia commemorate Hussein's sacrifice on the holy day of Asura. In Iran (as well as in Lebanon and other places where Shia live), some flagellate themselves to suffer as Hussein did. Hussein's death and Asura echo Jesus Christ's sacrifice and crucifixion.

69. Victor Gaetan, "The Vatican's Middle East Politics," *Foreign Affairs*, December 9, 2015, https://www.foreignaffairs.com/articles/syria/2015-12-09/vaticans-middle-east-politics.

70. Carlo Marroni, "Rouhani Visits Rome to Reassert Historic Links between Tehran and the Holy See," *Il Sole 24 Ore*, November 13, 2015, http://www.italy24.ilsole24ore.com/art/panorama/2015-11-12/rouhani-visit-to-rome-to-reassert-historic-links-between-tehran-and-the-holy-see-130334.php?uuid=ACJOfSYB.

71. Carlo Marroni, "Iran Nuclear Agreement Welcomed by Vatican as a 'Major Achievement,'" *Il Sole 24 Ore*, July 21, 2015, http://www.italy24.ilsole24ore.com/art/panorama/2015-07-15/agreement-on-the-iranian-nuclear-issue-214448.php?uuid=ACukHJS. On September 25, 2020, Pope Francis unexpectedly announced that Tomasi would be raised to the College of Cardinals, acknowledging his dedication as a diplomat and the value of this ministry to the pope.

72. The meeting was originally scheduled for November 2015 but was postponed due to terrorist attacks in Paris. It should be noted that much of the pope's conversation with Russian President Vladimir Putin included a significant exchange on the embattled country.

73. "U.S. Bishops, Iran Religious Leaders Jointly Declare Opposition to Violations of Human Life and Dignity, Including Weapons of Mass Destruction," United States Conference of Catholic Bishops, June 17, 2014, https://www.usccb.org/news/2014/us-bishops-iran-religious-leaders-jointly-declare-opposition-violations-human-life-and.

74. Stephen Colecchi, director, Office of International Justice and Peace, USCCB, interview with the author, Washington, DC, February 11, 2016; Bishop Denis Madden, interview with the author, Baltimore, MD, November 4, 2015; Theodore McCarrick, interview with the author, Hyattsville, MD, October 20, 2015.

75. Pope Francis, "Address of the Holy Father" (address, Seventieth Session of the United Nations General Assembly, New York, NY, September 25, 2015), http://w2.vatican.va/content/francesco/en/speeches/2015/september/documents/papa-francesco_20150925_onu-visita.html.

76. "Lebanon Buries Highest Shia Cleric," BBC, January 12, 2001, http://news.bbc.co.uk/2/hi/middle_east/1114154.stm.

77. Ibrahim Chamseddine, interview with the author, Beirut, Lebanon, November 24, 2015; Victor Gaetan, "Conflict in the Middle East: Will the Work of Three Popes Inspire World Leadership?," *National Catholic Register*, January 18, 2016, http://www.ncregister.com/daily-news/conflict-in-the-middle-east-will-the-work-of-three-popes-inspire-world-lead.

78. Two other Maronite political parties in the mix were the Phalange Party led by Samy Gemayel and the Marada Movement led by Suleiman Franjieh. See "Factbox: Lebanon's Main Political Player," Reuters, May 3, 2018, https://www.reuters.com/article/us-lebanon-election-parties-factbox/factbox-lebanons-main-political-players-idUSKBN1I41ZV.

79. Halim Shebaya, "Where Do Lebanon's Christians Stand on Hezbollah?," Al Jazeera, November 30, 2017, https://www.aljazeera.com/indepth/opinion/lebanon-christians-stand-hezbollah-171128102446572.html. It was widely known that

Hezbollah, functioning as both a political party and a militia, passed goods across the border with Syria, ignoring customs rules. So, while the militia (aka terrorists) successfully prevented the sprawling Syrian conflict from overwhelming the small country, it also used that prowess to benefit itself, undermining the fragile balance between constituent elements inside Lebanon.

80. "Aoun in Rome to Meet Pope Francis," Naharnet, March 15, 2017, http://www.naharnet.com/stories/en/226965.

81. When I visited the mosque in 2015, the lead imam told me he was trained in Egypt, where some of the world's most talented Sunni preachers are educated.

82. A classic text on the country's complex politics, *The Tragedy of Lebanon: Christian Warlords, Israeli Adventurers, and American Bunglers*, documents how Maronite hard-liners were allied with Israel in the first phase of a disastrous civil war that started in 1975, targeting Palestinian refugees living in southern Lebanon. That bellicose effort failed and led to the birth of Hezbollah in 1982, which arose to defend Lebanon from Israel. Jonathan Randal, *The Tragedy of Lebanon: Christian Warlords, Israeli Adventurers, and American Bunglers* (Charlotteville, VA: Just World Books, 2012), 33–92.

83. See, for example, Heba Salah, "Sunni and Shia: Explaining the Divide," *Financial Times*, January 6, 2016, https://www.ft.com/content/413ea2ea-b3df-11e5-8358-9a82b43f6b2f; Jonathan Marcus, "Why Saudi Arabia and Iran Are Bitter Rivals," BBC, September 16, 2019, https://www.bbc.com/news/world-middle-east-42008809; Mike Shuster, "Iraq War Deepens Sunni-Shia Divide," NPR, February 15, 2007, https://www.npr.org/2007/02/15/7411762/iraq-war-deepens-sunni-shia-divide.

84. Simon Caldwell, "Aleppo Archbishop Calls Russian Bombing 'a Source of Hope' for Syria," Catholic News Service, October 9, 2015, https://www.americamagazine.org/issue/syrian-bishops-express-support-russian-strikes.

85. "Michel Aoun: Nothing Justifies Saad Hariri's Detention," Al Jazeera, November 15, 2017, https://www.aljazeera.com/news/2017/11/michel-aoun-justifies-saad-hariri-detention-171115150827644.html.

86. Anne Barnard, "Saudi Arabia Orders Its Citizens Out of Lebanon, Raising Fears of War," *New York Times*, November 9, 2017, https://www.nytimes.com/2017/11/09/world/middleeast/saudi-arabia-lebanon-war.html.

87. Kylie Atwood, "Rex Tillerson Warns against Using Lebanon as Venue for Proxy Contests," CBS News, November 10, 2017, https://www.cbsnews.com/news/tillerson-warns-against-using-lebanon-as-venue-for-proxy-conflicts.

88. "Vowing Stability in Lebanon, Hariri Meets Pope Francis in Rome," Al Bawaba, October 14, 2017, https://www.albawaba.com/news/vowing-stability-lebanon-hariri-meets-pope-francis-rome-1033652.

89. "Cardinal Rai Wraps Historic Visit to Saudi Arabia, Meets Lebanese P.M.," Catholic Philly, November 14, 2017, http://catholicphilly.com/2017/11/news/world-news/lebanese-cardinal-concludes-historic-visit-to-saudi-arabia-meets-hariri. A Maronite bishop and adviser to the cardinal confirmed to me that he was treated "basically, like a head of state" by Saudi royalty.

90. "Cardinal Rai Wraps Historic Visit."

91. "Rai Briefs Aoun on Visit to Saudi Arabia, Rome," *Daily Star*, November 28, 2017, http://www.dailystar.com.lb/News/Lebanon-News/2017/Nov-28/428184-rai-briefs-aoun-on-visit-to-saudi-arabia-rome.ashx.

92. "Pope Francis Meets with Saudi Arabian Representative in the Vatican," Rome Reports, November 22, 2017, YouTube video, 1:43, https://www.youtube.com/watch?v=3_aVhy-v0BE.

93. "Saad Hariri Withdraws Resignation after Cabinet Meeting," Al Jazeera, November 5, 2017, https://www.aljazeera.com/news/2017/12/saad-hariri-withdraws-resignation-cabinet-meeting-171205142228292.html.

94. As Vaticanista Andrea Gagliarducci pointed out, the ground for Tauran's visit was first established in 2012 with the creation of the Vienna-based International Centre for Interreligious and Intercultural Dialogue (KAICIID), financed by Saudi King Abdullah bin Abdulaziz. The Holy See is a founding observer. Tauran oversaw the development of this relationship as president of the Pontifical Council for Interreligious Dialogue. Andrea Gagliarducci, "Remembering Cardinal Jean-Louis Tauran," MondayVatican, July 16, 2018, http://www.mondayvatican.com/vatican/remembering-cardinal-jean-louis-tauran.

95. John Hooper, "Vatican in Saudi Talks on Building Churches," *The Guardian*, March 17, 2008, https://www.theguardian.com/world/2008/mar/18/religion.saudiarabia.

96. "A Delegation from the Vatican Is Visiting Etidal (Global Center for Combatting Extremist Ideology, Riyadh, Saudi Arabia)," YouTube, video, 1:08, https://www.youtube.com/watch?v=-4pXJbbBFkU.

97. Philip Pullella, "Christians Should Not Be Second Class Citizens, Cardinal Tells Saudi Arabia," Reuters, April 26, 2018, https://www.reuters.com/article/us-saudi-vatican-cardinal/christians-should-not-be-second-class-citizens-cardinal-tells-saudi-arabia-idUSKBN1HX19D. In June 2019 there were over six million guest workers in Saudi Arabia. See "Nearly 2 Million Foreign Workers Flee Saudi Arabia," AsiaNews.it, http://www.asianews.it/news-en/Nearly-2-million-foreign-workers-flee-Saudi-Arabia-48056.html. Some 1.5 million of the guest workers are thought to be Christian. "Will It Finally Be Possible to Build a Church in Saudi Arabia?," Abouna.org, April 21, 2018, https://abouna.org/english/en/content/will-it-finally-be-possible-build-church-saudi-arabia.

98. Muhammed Al-Sulami, "Muslim World League, Vatican Boost Religious Ties," Arab News, April 22, 2018, http://www.arabnews.com/node/1289131/saudi-arabia.

99. "Pope Pays Rare Tribute to French Cardinal, Attends Full Mass," Associated Press, July 12, 2018, https://apnews.com/3bdf543b732d45f399c23691ad34ff91/Pope-pays-rare-tribute-to-French-cardinal,-attends-full-Mass.

100. US ambassador James Creagan, who negotiated for ten days in Rome with Tauran (who was undersecretary for relations with states at the time) to settle the 1989–1990 Panama crisis (see chapter 1), called him "a great diplomat and friend, who Pope John Paul II respected very much." Personal communication with the author, March 5, 2019.

101. Personal communication with the author, August 14, 2020. Among the unheralded peace efforts Tauran embarked on was a trip to Serbia while NATO was bombing the county in 1999 (perhaps in an effort to halt the ongoing bombardment of Belgrade, even on Orthodox Easter Sunday). Marino was Tauran's assistant at the time, covering the Balkans for the Secretariat of State. He confirms that the two met with Serbian president Slobodan Milošević—more evidence that God's diplomats leave no stone unturned.

102. P. Peter Sarros, *U.S.-Vatican Relations, 1975–1980* (Notre Dame, IN: University of Notre Dame, 2020), 158–70.

103. Randal, *The Tragedy of Lebanon*.

104. Sarros, *U.S.-Vatican Relations*, 169.

105. Embassy Vatican, "Holy See Asks USG to Prevent Infrastructure Destruction in Lebanon," WikiLeaks, cable 06VATICAN162_a, dated August 3, 2006, https://wikileaks.org/plusd/cables/06VATICAN162_a.html.

106. Embassy Vatican, "NEA DAS Grey's November 15 Meeting with Deputy FM Parolin," WikiLeaks, cable 06VATICAN_239_a, dated November 21, 2006, https://search.wikileaks.org/plusd/cables/06VATICAN239_a.html.

107. Embassy Vatican, "Lebanon Crisis: Request for High Level Call to Holy See," WikiLeaks, cable 06VATICAN253_a, dated December 6, 2006, https://search.wikileaks.org/plusd/cables/06VATICAN253_a.html.

108. Giada Zampano, "Pope Prays for Lebanon in 1st Public Audience in Months," Associated Press, September 2, 2020, https://www.startribune.com/pope-prays-for-lebanon-during-1st-public-audience-in-months/572293242.

109. Doreen Abi Raad, "Visiting Lebanon, Cardinal Parolin Emphasizes 'You Are Not Alone,'" Catholic News Service, September 4, 2020, https://angelusnews.com/news/world/visiting-lebanon-cardinal-parolin-emphasizes-you-are-not-alone.

110. Raï, "Memorandum on Active Neutrality."

111. "Lebanese Maronite Patriarch Reiterates Criticism of Hezbollah, Confirms Shift," Arab Weekly, July 12, 2020, https://thearabweekly.com/lebanese-maronite-patriarch-reiterates-criticism-hezbollah-confirms-shift.

CHAPTER 11

1. Interview with the author, Washington, DC, March 19, 2019. See Victor Gaetan, "A Former Ambassador Finds Much to Like in Pope Francis' Diplomatic Instincts," *America* (magazine), April 16, 2019, https://www.americamagazine.org/politics-society/2019/04/16/former-ambassador-finds-much-pope-francis-diplomatic-instincts. Ambassador Freeman was the principal translator for President Richard Nixon during his historic 1972 meetings with Mao Zedong in Beijing, which opened diplomatic relations between the two countries. As part of a long career under both Republican and Democrat administrations, he served in many posts, including ambassador to Saudi Arabia (1989–1993) as well as assistant secretary of defense at the Department of Defense (1993–1994). He is not a Catholic.

2. According to the most recent data posted by the Vatican City State (dated February 1, 2019), the number of citizens is 618, but only 246 live within the state limits because most are on diplomatic assignment. The page notes an average birth rate of one person per year and an average death rate of five per year. The statistical summary acknowledges just one pet—a lonely dog, which just cannot be right. There's a cat in Vatican City someplace. "Population," Vatican City State, February 1, 2019, https://www.vaticanstate.va/it/stato-governo/note-generali/popolazione.html. On Vatican City as a country, see Christopher Klein, "Ten Things You May Not Know about the Vatican," History, October 28, 2018, http://www.history.com/news/10-things-you-may-not-know-about-the-vatican.

3. In an interview timed to coincide with Lunar New Year in 2016, Francis told a China-based media outlet, "For me, as a boy, whenever I read anything about China, it had the capacity to inspire my admiration. I have admiration for China. Later I looked into Matteo Ricci's life and I saw how this man felt the same thing in the exact way I did, admiration, and how he was able to enter into dialogue with this great culture, and with this age-old wisdom. He was able to 'encounter' it." Francesco Sisci, "Pope Francis Urges World Not to Fear China's Rise," AsiaTimes, February 2, 2016, https://asiatimes.com/2016/02/at-exclusive-pope-francis-urges-world-not-to-fear-chinas-rise. Francis has also advanced the process by which Ricci could be made a saint of the Church.

4. Jonathan D. Spence, *The Memory Palace of Matteo Ricci* (New York: Viking Penguin, 1984), 151–61.

5. "Constitution of the Chinese People's Republic of China," adopted on December 4, 1982, Article 36, http://en.people.cn/constitution/constitution.html.

6. In December 1978, two months after John Paul II's election, Supreme Leader Deng Xiaoping laid out a new policy of reform and economic opening at the Central Committee of the Communist Party's Third Plenary Session.

7. Heyndrickx is exactly the sort of priest who has maintained an intense commitment to the Middle Kingdom, a spiritual romance that captivated thousands of Catholic clergy for centuries. At age sixteen, Jeroom heard a Sunday-evening talk given by the elderly CICM bishop of Xiwanzi, China, located in Inner Mongolia. His mission was destroyed by Communists on December 9, 1946: two hundred Catholics killed, a huge cathedral destroyed, and over one hundred dragged from a seminary in the snow, who never returned. But Bishop Leo De Smedt, who was from Heyndrickx's hometown, explained that, still, he would return to Xiwanzi—which he did, and died there as prisoner of the Communists in 1951. The young man vowed that same Sunday night, at age sixteen, to join CICM.

8. Fr. Jeroom Heyndrickx, personal communication with the author, February 28, 2016, and January 20, 2017. Fr. Heyndrickx's path in China was not always easy. For three years in the 1980s, he was considered persona non grata and barred from entry; twice he was detained and interrogated. Five times his visa entry was refused. In spite of all this, he managed to obtain permission from civil authorities to teach theology in major official Chinese seminaries beginning in 1985 as the first foreigner to teach in Shanghai's Sheshan Seminary. Through the 1990s and until 2010, he taught at the Beijing National Seminary. He visited the country more than eighty times after 1982,

always speaking to members of both the registered and unregistered Church, to civil authorities in China, and to authorities in Rome. Fr. Heyndrickx is a missionary who has been a diplomat without portfolio vis-à-vis China for almost forty years.

9. Jimmy Carter's national security adviser, Zbigniew Brzezinski, is rightly given credit for the strategy of elevating China into the international order both to counter Soviet power and to manage the emergence of new actors on the world scene. See Frederico Pachetti, "Going Global: Zbigniew Brzezinski and China's Rise," Wilson Center, October 10, 2017, https://www.wilsoncenter.org/blog-post/going-global-zbigniew-brzezinski-and-chinas-rise. As a Polish American Catholic, Brzezinski had close relations to the Vatican.

In October 1979, when Pope John Paul II visited the United States, one meeting that was not on the agenda was the pope's multi-hour sit-down with Brzezinski at the Vatican embassy in Washington reviewing multiple global hot spots. One can assume this survey included China. George Weigel, *Witness to Hope: The Biography of Pope John Paul II* (New York: Harper, 2005), 352.

Brzezinski's strategy was to flank the Soviet Union on its 5,068-mile border with China. Less than three months after Deng's inaugural voyage to Washington, the White House hosted Romania's husband-wife dictators, Nicolae and Elena Ceaușescu, with honors that surpassed Deng's, including a grand banquet at the National Gallery of Art and lodging at Blair House. A similar strategy was at work: Romania's 804-mile border with the Soviets was not as long as China's, but President Ceaușescu was heralded as an anti-Soviet maverick, according to President Reagan's national security adviser Frank Carlucci. In Carlucci's words, Brzezinski's strategy was to open two fronts on the Soviet Union's borders: on its southern border with China and on its western border with Romania. Interview with the author, Washington, DC, August 5, 2009.

10. Archbishop Antonio Riberi from Monaco, a graduate of the *Accademia*, served in Beijing from 1946 to 1951. Bilateral relations between the Holy See and Beijing had only been established in 1944 based on a new attitude toward the country implemented by Pope Pius XII. (Relations between the Church and China were interrupted in the seventeenth and eighteenth centuries due to the "Chinese Rites" dispute over forms of ancestor reverence and the status of philosopher Confucius.) Within weeks of becoming pontiff in 1939, Pius XII ordered changes to standing papal policy on Chinese traditions. His instruction in *Plane Compertum est* (It Is Entirely, 1939) was accepted by the Chinese government and facilitated rapid development of bilateral relations. The decree permitted Catholics to be present at ceremonies in honor of Confucius in Confucian temples or in schools, to hang an image of Confucius or a tablet with his name in Catholic schools, to attend public ceremonies honoring ancestors or Confucius even if some superstitions seemed apparent, and to bow their heads and show other forms of civil observance before the deceased or their images. In 1946, Thomas Tien Ken-sin, the apostolic vicar of Qingdao, became the first Chinese national named cardinal.

11. On Dong, see "First 'Patriotic' Bishop Named by Communist Government in China Dies," Catholic News Agency, May 15, 2007, https://www.catholicnewsagency.com/news/first_patriotic_bishop_named_by_communist_government

_in_china_dies. On the origins of the CCPA, see Richard Madsen, *China's Catholics: Tragedy and Hope in an Emerging Civil Society* (Berkeley: University of California Press, 1998), 34–39; John Tong, "The Church from 1949–1990," in *The Catholic Church in Modern China*, ed. Edmund Tang and Jean-Pierre Wiest (Maryknoll, NY: Orbis, 1993). Cardinal Tong is bishop emeritus of Hong Kong.

12. Interview with the author, Maryknoll Society Center, Ossining, NY, January 12, 2017; Victor Gaetan, "North Korea: Another Option," *National Catholic Register*, April 28, 2017. See also Kevin Coyne, "The Asia Connection," *Seton Hall Magazine*, January 20, 2017, https://blogs.shu.edu/magazine/2017/01/the-asia-connection. Murphy told me he also went to North Korea five times and was received by the third-ranking North Korean official, Hwang Jang-yop, who spoke on behalf of Kim Il-sung, the country's founder. Together with Korean-American professor Yeomin Yoo, Murphy flew between Beijing, Pyongyang, and Beijing on Chinese carriers, and Beijing gave permission for him to rest at a central Beijing hotel. One thing remained consistent, the priest told me: from his first to his last encounter with Hwang, the official was eager to develop ties with the United States similar to those China established with the United States—educational, cultural, scientific, and athletic exchanges with American universities and other institutions. After each visit Murphy delivered messages to the State Department and to the Holy See. "On my last trip, in 1995, Kim Il-sung's son, Kim Jong-il, had taken power," Murphy said. "The last night I was there, Hwang Jang-yop invited me to dinner at his home, which was very unusual. He told me it was very important for him to develop ties with Americans—political and religious figures. I told him I would help, but Washington, as in previous years, balked." The next time Murphy saw the Korean top dog, he was in Washington, DC, having defected from his homeland in 1997.

13. In fact, John Paul II sent at least one friendly witness to the ordination as a sign of mercy: he asked Fr. John Tong Hon to attend. Tong later served as bishop of Hong Kong (2009–2017) and was named cardinal in 2012 by Pope Benedict XVI.

14. Paul Mariani, "The Four Catholic Bishops of Shanghai: Underground and 'Patriotic' Church Competition and Sino-Vatican Relations in Reform-Era China," *Journal of Church and State*, August 19, 2014, https://academic.oup.com/jcs/article-abstract/58/1/38/2459003/The-Four-Catholic-Bishops-of-Shanghai-Underground?redirectedFrom=fulltext.

15. "China: Secretary of State Note on Death of Bishop Jin Luxian," *Clerical Whispers* (Blog), April 30, 2013.

16. There are even unregistered communities that use official churches for Mass without animosity from either side. Often, internal migration served to erase the divisions. Catholics were historically based predominantly in rural areas where churches were typically unregistered. When Catholics migrated to the cities—and China has experienced massive population mobility since the 1980s—many began attending Mass in official churches for convenience, not as a political preference. Another problem emerged as some underground communities grew dependent on outside funding that helped sustain many for decades. So, the antiauthoritarian identity in those places became more economic than political or spiritual, and Rome had no interest in maintaining disunity that was mainly a function of external income streams.

17. Counterintuitively, sacraments given by illicit bishops and priests ordained by them are considered legitimate or "valid" by the Holy See. So, for example, a Catholic who was dying could seek the sacrament of the anointing of the sick from an illicit bishop or priest, and the sacrament would be valid, although in normal circumstances believers are not supposed to seek them out.

18. Personal communication with the author, March 22, 2016. Worthley, who grew up on Long Island in New York, first visited China in 1983 to teach public administration. He met many local and provincial officials in that capacity. Called to the priesthood, he was ordained in 1990 for the diocese of Rockville Centre, New York. As he continued to visit China every year, teaching, writing, and networking on public finance, service delivery, and management, he came to know the country from an unusual insider's viewpoint. As his students rose through officialdom, they continued to consult him. Mother Teresa asked Worthley to help her gain permission to bring the Missionaries of Charity to China. After her death, the priest continued to advance her legacy in the Middle Kingdom, advising lay organizations dedicated to her. Worthley's perspective has been especially valued by Pope Francis and his diplomats.

19. Barb Fraze, "China's 'Black Pope:' Catholic Layman Wields Enormous Influence within Church," Catholic News Service, April 5, 2007, http://www.catholicnews.com/data/stories/cns/0701905.htm. It is said that Liu Bainian was baptized by missionaries with the Society of the Divine Word, the Catholic Church's largest missionary congregation. In 2020, it had 6,023 priests and religious brothers working in more than seventy countries.

20. Although considered a hard-line social conservative, O'Connor had spent twenty-seven years in the US navy as a chaplain (including four years as chief of all chaplains), retiring as a rear admiral. He was savvy about geopolitics and unabashed in criticizing the United States for excessive militarization. On China, O'Connor was profoundly openhearted, much like Pope John Paul II.

21. Julian Baum, "Washington's Patience Pays Off: US Ships Call at Chinese Port. It's US's First China Shore Leave since USS Dixie Called in 1949," *Christian Science Monitor*, November 5, 1986, https://www.csmonitor.com/1986/1105/osail.html; Edward Gargan, "After a 37-Year Absence, U.S. Vessels Hit China," *New York Times*, November 6, 1986, http://www.navsource.org/archives/07/0746a.htm.

22. See also John A. Worthley, "The Risks for the Catholic Church in China Are Real—But the Church is Ready to Face Them," *America* (magazine), March 21, 2019, https://www.americamagazine.org/faith/2019/03/21/risks-catholic-church-china-are-real-church-ready-face-them.

23. Ron Redmond, "Mother Teresa Meets Deng's Son," United Press International, January 22, 1985, http://www.upi.com/Archives/1985/01/22/Mother-Teresa-meets-Dengs-son/3890475218000.

24. "Mother Teresa Begins 'Momentous' Visit to China, Hopes to Open a House," UCA News, October 19, 1993, https://www.ucanews.com/story-archive/?post_name=/1993/10/19/mother-teresa-begins-momentous-visit-to-china-hopes-to-open-a-house&post_id=44153.

25. Victor Gaetan, "Mother Teresa's Secret Missions in China: Full Disclosure," *National Catholic Register*, September 6, 2016, https://www.ncregister.com/daily-news/mother-teresas-secret-missions-in-china-full-disclosure.

26. Fr. Brian Kolodiejchuk, interview with the author, Rome, Italy, September 2, 2016.

27. Li Baofu, interview with the author, Rome, Italy, September 2, 2016. Translation provided by Fr. Bernardo Cervellera, editor of AsiaNews.it. See also Gaetan, "Mother Teresa's Secret Missions."

28. According to AsiaNews.it, the number of patriot bishops ordained in China was seven, not twelve, because some dropped out when they learned the ordination was not approved by the Holy See: Bernardo Cervellera, "Fu Tieshan, 'Tragic' Figure of the Chinese Patriotic Church, Dies," AsiaNews, April 20, 2007, http://www.asianews.it/news-en/Fu-Tieshan,-tragic-figure-of-the-Chinese-Patriotic-Church,-dies-9060.html.

29. Many of the foreign missionaries were killed during the Boxer Rebellion, and Beijing considers them imperialist interlopers, so the canonization also fueled a clash in perceptions of Chinese history. On October 1, 2020, the pope also elevated four others to sainthood, including American Katherine Drexel (1858–1955) and Sudanese-Italian religious sister Josephine Bakhita (1869–1947).

30. Jeroom Heyndrickx, "Listen to Chinese Bishops," Union of Catholic Asian News, April 1, 2011, https://www.ucanews.com/news/listen-to-chinese-bishops/10695.

31. Cardinal Secretary of State Angelo Sodano told Beijing the Holy See was willing to make the switch "tonight not tomorrow" at least twice, according to the secretariat's China desk officer, Gianfranco Rota Graziosi, in 2002. The diplomat (an *Academia* graduate) also told US officials it would "take years, if not decades," for Beijing to accept religious freedom because influencing Chinese resistance is "like drops of water sculpting the stone." Embassy Vatican, "Vatican-China: Holy See Welcomes U.S. Push on Dialogue, but Expects Little Movement Prior to Party Congress," WikiLeaks, cable 02VATICAN3962_a, dated August 13, 2002, https://wikileaks.org/plusd/cables/02VATICAN3962_a.html.

32. Embassy Vatican, "Optimism on China from Deputy FM Parolin," WikiLeaks, cable 05VATICAN512_a, dated August 16, 2005, https://wikileaks.org/plusd/cables/05VATICAN512_a.html.

33. "Pope Displeased by Illicit Ordinations in China," Zenit, May 4, 2006, https://zenit.org/articles/pope-displeased-by-illicit-ordinations-in-china; Gianni Valente, "The Long Road and 'Accidents along the Way,'" *30 Days*, January 2007, http://www.30giorni.it/articoli_id_12905_13.htm.

34. Paul Mariani, "Cardinal Joseph Zen of Hong Kong: Fighter, Teacher, Risk-Taker," Catholic World Report, April 12, 2019, https://www.catholicworldreport.com/2019/04/12/cardinal-joseph-zen-of-hong-kong-fighter-teacher-risk-taker.

35. Fr. Jeroom Heyndrickx, personal communication with the author, December 29, 2016.

36. Elisabeth Rosenthal, "Delegation of 2 Is Vatican's First to China in Years," *New York Times*, June 29, 2006, https://www.nytimes.com/2006/06/29/world/asia/29vatican.html.

37. "China Opens Largest Seminary of Catholic Church (09/28/06)," Embassy of the People's Republic of China in the United States of America, September 28, 2006, http://www.china-embassy.org/eng/zt/zgrq/t274147.htm. In the 1990s, Liu Bainian designed Beijing's new national seminary—for which the government invested over $9 million. The design includes a sophisticated set of symbolic references to the Holy See, St. Peter's Basilica, and Chinese culture. The main building is round, referring to Chinese conceptions of heaven as round and to temple structures where sacrifices to heaven are traditionally offered. It has three tiers, symbolizing the Holy Trinity. The roof rests on twelve columns, referring to the twelve apostles. See Gregor Weimar, SVD, "The 'Sinicized' National Seminary of Beijing: Liu Bainian's Ideas for a Chinese Catholic Church," China Zentrum [China Center], http://www.china-zentrum.de/fileadmin/downloads/rctc/2018-4/RCTC_2018-4.31-51_Weimar__The_Sinicized_National_Seminary_of_Beijing.pdf.

38. Parolin was called a major drafter by some who disliked the letter. See Atila Sinke Guimarães, "Why Was Parolin Chosen?," Tradition in Action, September 30, 2013, https://www.traditioninaction.org/bev/159bev09_30_2013.htm; Pope Benedict XVI, "Letter to the Bishops, Priests, Consecrated Persons and Lay Faithful of the Catholic Church in the People's Republic of China," Holy See, May 27, 2007, footnote 36, http://w2.vatican.va/content/benedict-xvi/en/letters/2007/documents/hf_ben-xvi_let_20070527_china.html. Several sources confirm that Benedict XVI's 2007 letter was drafted under Pope John Paul II and substantially completed by 2004. Those who reviewed it included Cardinal Joseph Ratzinger and at least one prominent underground Chinese bishop. Both endorsed the text.

39. Valente, "The Long Road."

40. Peter Moody, "The Catholic Church in China Today: The Limitations of Autonomy and Enculturation," *Journal of Church and State* 55, no. 3 (September 2013): 403–31.

41. "The New Bishop of Beijing Is Elected," AsiaNews, July 18, 2007, http://www.asianews.it/news-en/The-new-Bishop-of-Beijing-is-elected-9856.html.

42. "China Philharmonic to Play at Vatican," *New York Times*, May 5, 2008, https://www.nytimes.com/2008/05/05/world/asia/05iht-vatican.1.12570243.html; "China Philharmonic to Play Mozart's 'Requiem' in Vatican Visit," Catholic News Agency, April 30, 2008, https://www.catholicnewsagency.com/news/china_philharmonic_to_play_mozarts_requiem_in_vatican_visit.

43. Gianni Valente, "Between Rome and Beijing the *Sensus Fidei* Unties the Knots," *30 Days*, December 2009, http://www.30giorni.it/articoli_id_22023_l3.htm.

44. "Chavez Supporters Invade Chancery, Expel Employees and Bishop," Catholic News Agency, February 27, 2008, https://www.catholicnewsagency.com/news/chavez_supporters_invade_chancery_expel_employees_and_bishop; "Apostolic Nunciature in Venezuela Target of Bomb Attack," Cirkev, February 19, 2008, https://www.cirkev.cz/archiv/080219-apostolic-nunciature-in-venezuela-target-of-bomb-attack.

45. Embassy Vatican, "China: Cardinal Zen on Holy See's China Diplomacy," WikiLeaks, cable 08VATICAN18_a, dated January 31, 2008, https://search.wikileaks.org/plusd/cables/08VATICAN18_a.html.

46. Parolin sent Hon to Guam in 2016 to study a disturbing case of clerical abuse, then posted him as nuncio to Greece the following year. Dedicated to his cause, in December 2019, Hon popped up on a San Francisco Bay–area speaking tour and fund-raising trip regarding demonstrations in Hong Kong. See Nicholas Wolfram Smith, "Hong Kong: 'Hatred Has Broken Out' Over Protests, Prelate Says," Catholic San Francisco, December 16, 2019, https://catholic-sf.org/news/hong-kong-hatred-has-broken-out-over-protests-prelate-says.

47. Some positive events—and others, bizarre—occurred in the Sino-Vatican relationship between 2010 and 2013. For example, the CCPA recognized an underground bishop, Joseph Baoyu Zhu, in Nanyang diocese (Henan Province), as the government-recognized bishop on the Feast of St. Joseph, June 30, 2011. He had been secretly ordained sixteen years before. According to Hong Kong's Holy Spirit Research Center, the official acceptance of Baoyu Zhu was evidence that decision making in religious affairs was still largely acted out on the local level, where relations between official and underground communities were most fluid. See "Bishop Joseph Baoyu Zhu," UCANews, https://www.ucanews.com/directory/previous/bishop-joseph-baoyu-zhu/2215.

An odd event, worth at least passing note as evidence that the Holy See continued to seek unorthodox diplomatic paths, occurred during Cardinal Bertone's tenure as secretary of state, recounted by journalist Guy Dinmore in the *Financial Times*. Three Chinese army generals and two well-placed Vatican diplomats met in Burgundy, France, in early 2011 at an eighteenth-century chateau owned by a French aristocrat with close ties to the Chinese Communist Party. Msgr. Ettore Balestrero, undersecretary for relations with states (See chapter 9, footnote 64 for accusations against Balestrero); Msgr. Rota Graziosi; and the retired generals spent two days together as guests of Baron Jean-Christophe Iseux von Pfetten (known as the Red Baron), the first European appointed to hold public offices in the PRC. Pfetten and his Italian wife are Catholic. They discussed the selection of Catholic bishops. Although Vatican sources say nothing in particular was accomplished, the event did convey something the two Italian priests imbibed at the *Academia*: maximum flexibility to engage interlocutors as a sign of willingness and open hearts, even in a medieval manor festooned with the banner, "Long Live the Communist Party!" Guy Dinmore, "China and Vatican Break Ice in Burgundy," *Financial Times*, April 8, 2011, https://www.ft.com/content/32a79c4e-6210-11e0-8ee4-00144feab49a.

48. Among lay faithful, too, there was an immediate response to Jorge Bergoglio's elevation. Hours after Cardinal Tauran declared, "*Habemus Papam!*" (We have a pope!), in Rome, a crowd descended on the 6 a.m. Mass at Beijing's East Catholic Church—a cathedral built in 1655, one of the city's biggest. A Thanksgiving Mass was offered in Francis's honor. The church and its clergy are registered with the Patriotic Association, proving the hypothesis that all Chinese Catholics are pro-pope.

49. Ferruccio de Bortoli, "English Translation of Pope Francis' Corriere della Sera Interview," Zenit, March 5, 2014, https://zenit.org/articles/english-translation-of-pope-francis-corriere-della-sera-interview.

50. Ambassador Francis Rooney, who represented the United States at the Holy See from November 2005 to January 2008, said Msgr. Parolin was his main interlocutor: "He is a great guy. One of the smartest, most calm, articulate diplomats the Holy See has." Interview with the author, Washington, DC, August 16, 2017. In his book, *The Global Vatican: An Inside Look at the Catholic Church, World Politics, and the Extraordinary Relationship between the United States and the Holy See* (Lanham, MD: Rowman & Littlefield, 2013), Rooney emphasizes Parolin's professionalism and wide-ranging knowledge (189).

51. "Chinese Christians Clash with Police over Church Cross," Radio Free Asia, July 24, 2014, YouTube video, 1:20, https://www.youtube.com/watch?v=ZXS7qXiF4Yg.

52. Xi had been a local official in that province, so the connection with the presidency was easy to make.

53. Bill Chappell, "In a Shift, China Allows Pope Francis to Use Its Airspace for Asia Trip," NPR, August 13, 2014, http://www.npr.org/sections/thetwo-way/2014/08/13/340058031/in-a-shift-china-allows-pope-francis-to-use-its-airspace-for-asia-trip. Unfortunately, the regime banned Chinese pilgrims from traveling to Korea to see the pope: "Pope Sends Message to Beijing as China Bars Catholics from Attending South Korea Event," *South China Morning Post*, August 15, 2014, https://www.scmp.com/news/asia/article/1573415/pope-sends-message-beijing-chinese-catholics-barred-south-korea-event.

54. Carol Glatz, "Church Must Respect, Dialogue with China, Pope Says in New Interview," Catholic News Service, February 2, 2016, http://www.catholicnews.com/services/englishnews/2016/pope-says-church-must-respect-dialogue-with-china.cfm.

55. Born November 11, 1968; "Bishop Martin Wu of Zhouzhi Installed Today, 10 Years after His Episcopal Ordination," CBCP News, July 10, 2015, Asia News, http://www.cbcpnews.com/cbcpnews/?p=59767.

56. "Chinese Bishop Installed with Government Recognition," Union of Catholic Asian News, July 12, 2015, https://www.ucanews.com/news/chinese-bishop-installed-with-government-recognition/73921.

57. "China Consecrates First New Bishop in Three Years," Catholic News Agency, August 7, 2015, https://www.catholicnewsagency.com/news/china-consecrates-first-new-bishop-in-three-years-37903.

58. Carl Bunderson, "Why Is Christianity Growing so Quickly in Mainland China?," Catholic News Agency, August 17, 2015, https://www.catholicnewsagency.com/news/why-is-christianity-growing-so-quickly-in-mainland-china-57545.

59. David Nakamura and Juliet Eilperin, "A President and a Pope Head to Washington," *Washington Post*, September 21, 2015, https://www.washingtonpost.com/politics/a-president-and-a-pope-head-to-washington/2015/09/21/534f87a4-607b-11e5-8e9e-dce8a2a2a679_story.html?utm_term=.ed4de9ec77bb.

60. Jane Perlez, "Not Wanting to Compete with Pope Francis, Xi Jinping Lingers in Seattle," *New York Times*, September 24, 2015, https://www.nytimes.com/interactive/projects/cp/reporters-notebook/xi-jinping-visit/china-pope-francis.

61. Jessie Jau, "So Near, Yet so Far: Chinese President Xi Jinping and Pope Francis Miss Each Other on Back-To-Back Visits to US," *South China Morning Post*, September 24, 2015, https://www.scmp.com/news/china/diplomacy-defence/article/1861188/so-near-yet-so-far-chinese-president-xi-jinping-and.

62. Ben Blanchard and David Brunnstrom, "Feted in China, Xi's U.S. Profile Dims in Shadow of Pope," Reuters, September 27, 2015, https://www.reuters.com/article/us-usa-china-xi/feted-in-china-xis-u-s-profile-dims-in-shadow-of-pope-idUSKCN0RR05W20150928.

63. The ratio was four to one for print news coverage of the pope compared to Xi between September 20 and 24. "China Bishops on Universal Church 'Reconciliation Mission,'" Union of Catholic Asian News, September 24, 2015, https://www.ucanews.com/news/china-bishops-on-universal-church-reconciliation-mission-in-us/74318. From the start of Xi's presidency, he emphasized a geostrategic outlook that includes new partners.

64. John A. Worthley, personal communication with the author, October 28, 2015. Seeing that the pope was especially welcomed by American Catholics in a special way, the Chinese presidential delegation (as well as the three leaders from the Chinese bishops' conference in the United States at the same time) also made the connection between his influence and the Catholic countries in their plan for the Belt and Road Initiative. The wildly ambitious Belt and Road Initiative, announced in 2013, includes Catholic-majority countries such as the Philippines, Poland, and Italy as well as countries where Catholic communities play significant roles, like Hungary and Lebanon. This too was noted as the Chinese president's delegation observed Francis's authority. https://www.topchinatravel.com/silk-road/one-belt-one-road.htm.

65. "Three Chinese Bishops Make Brief Hawaii Stopover," *Hawaii Catholic Herald*, October 9, 2015, http://www.hawaiicatholicherald.com/2015/10/09/three-chinese-bishops-make-brief-hawaii-stopover.

66. On the Chinese side of the table, officials from the Foreign Ministry were always engaged, since negotiations with the Holy See are cast as a bilateral, state-to-state matter, but the State Administration for Religious Affairs (SARA) took the lead, first Guo Wei, director of Division Two (Christian Affairs), then Dai Chenjing after March 2017. SARA, created in 1951, oversaw religious affairs until 2018 when it was folded into the United Front Work Department (UFWD), an early party organization set up in 1942 to keep tabs on all social entities beyond the Communist elite. The working group for the Holy See included Archbishop Claudio Maria Celli, serving past retirement at the pope's request (DOB July 20, 1941); the undersecretary for relations with states, Maltese monsignor Antoine Camilleri (an *Accademia* graduate), appointed just six days before Benedict's resignation; Msgr. Tadeusz Wojda, undersecretary at *Propaganda Fide* (until he was made a bishop of Białystok, Poland, in April 2017); Wojda's successor, Polish-born Fr. Ryszard Szmydki, a member of the

Missionary Oblates of Mary Immaculate; and Friar Gianni Huang Bao-guo, a Franciscan priest with *Propaganda Fide*.

67. Sisci, "Pope Francis Urges World."

68. John Tong, "Card. Tong: Communion of the Church in China with the Universal Church," AsiaNews, August 4, 2016, http://www.asianews.it/news-en/Card.-Tong:-Communion-of-the-Church-in-China-with-the-Universal-Church-38221.html.

69. Gianni Valente, "'China's Gift' to Pope Francis," *La Stampa*, October 6, 2016, http://www.lastampa.it/2016/10/06/vaticaninsider/chinas-gift-to-pope-francis-xd1XCDBDfzNx9yDQ0cjhQP/pagina.html.

70. In a speech opening the National Assembly, Wang Zuo'an, director of the State Administration of Religious Affairs, delivered the usual rhetoric about "promoting the establishment of a Catholic Church that conforms to the requirements of contemporary China's development and progress and conforms to the fine traditional Chinese culture," yet Wang also extolled specific achievements, such as social service delivery for which the faithful raised 180 million yuan ($26.1 million) in six years. Inclusion of this priority meant the domestic Church was allowed to perform core functions of Catholicism. Wang Zuo'an, "Speech at the Opening Ceremony" (speech, Ninth National Congress of the Chinese Catholic Church, Beijing, China, December 27, 2016), http://www.chinacatholic.cn/html/report/17020730-1.htm.

71. "Government-Controlled Catholic Groups in China Elect New Leaders," Archdiocese of Baltimore, January 19, 2012, https://www.archbalt.org/government-controlled-catholic-groups-in-china-elect-new-leaders.

72. Gianni Valente, "China: Preparations Are Underway for the 9th Assembly of 'Catholic Representatives,'" *La Stampa*, December 1, 2016, https://www.lastampa.it/vatican-insider/en/2016/12/01/news/china-preparations-are-underway-for-the-9th-assembly-of-catholic-representatives-1.34748619.

73. Valente, "China."

74. Holy See documents are typically released on relevant feast days or anniversaries, so the timing of this date was meaningful, not coincidental: John Tong, "The Future of the Sino-Vatican Dialogue from an Ecclesiological Point of View," Catholic Diocese of Hong Kong, http://catholic.org.hk/v2/en/message_bishop/y2017_churchinchina.html.

75. David Feith, "The Vatican's Illusions about Chinese Communism," *Wall Street Journal*, November 10, 2016, https://www.wsj.com/articles/the-vaticans-illusions-about-chinese-communism-1478215875; Zen described the pope's drive for reconciliation as "simply ridiculous" and any agreement "totally unacceptable." He considered concessions to the Communist Party treasonous: any deal abandons the clandestine faithful who refuse to capitulate to the Chinese Patriotic Catholic Association. It proved Zen would continue a war against détente by persistently framing the questions as political ones.

76. James Griffiths and Matt Rivers, "As Atheist China Warms to the Vatican, Religious Persecution 'Intensifies,'" CNN, March 1, 2017, https://www.cnn.com/2017/02/28/asia/china-religious-persecution-christianity/index.html.

77. "The Complicated Case of China's Catholic Bishops," Catholic News Network, January 23, 2018, https://www.catholicnewsagency.com/news/the-complicated-case-of-chinas-catholic-bishops-90994.

78. John Baptist Lin, "The Vatican Asks Legitimate Bishops to Step Aside in Favour of Illegitimate Ones," AsiaNews, January 22, 2018, http://www.asianews.it/news-en/The-Vatican-asks-legitimate-bishops-to-step-aside-in-favour-of-illegitimate-ones-42896.html.

79. Michel Chambon, "Mindong Diocese Goes beyond Beijing and the Vatican," Union of Catholic Asian News, February 14, 2018, https://www.ucanews.com/news/mindong-diocese-goes-beyond-beijing-and-the-vatican/81433.

80. Wang Zhicheng, "Underground Mindong Bishop Guo Xijin Missing for Four Days," AsiaNews, April 10, 2017, http://www.asianews.it/news-en/Underground-Mindong-Bishop-Guo-Xijin-missing-for-four-days-40436.html.

81. Charles Hutzler, "China Defies Rome over Bishop's Post," *Washington Post*, May 15, 2006, http://www.washingtonpost.com/wp-dyn/content/article/2006/05/14/AR2006051400866.html.

82. Author's confidential communication with curial officials.

83. Cardinal József Mindszenty was an anti-Communist Hungarian cardinal forced to take residence in the US Legation to avoid punishment by the regime. The cardinal was eventually removed from the embassy in 1971, after fifteen years, and called to Rome by the Holy See, where he was stripped of his titles as part of a deal sought by the Communist government and the United States in the spirit of détente.

Regarding rogue cardinals, at a private meeting in Rome in 2006, the US ambassador complained to Parolin about a pro-Sandinista cardinal in Nicaragua who perturbed the US embassy in Managua. Parolin's response? "He warned that cardinals, particularly retired ones, have considerable autonomy, and it would not be easy for the Holy See to bring him around." The same was true in spades about Cardinal Zen. Embassy Vatican, "Holy See: Ambassador Delivers Strong Message on Nicaragua, Cuba," WikiLeaks, cable 06VATICAN213_a, dated October 11, 2006, https://wikileaks.org/plusd/cables/06VATICAN213_a.html.

84. Gianni Valente, "Parolin, 'Why We Are in Dialogue with China,'" *La Stampa*, February 1, 2018, http://www.lastampa.it/2018/01/31/vaticaninsider/parolin-why-we-are-in-dialogue-with-china-C8mlJsD0PDNsmsx7db6ZIJ/pagina.html.

85. "Pope Talks to Reuters about the 'Dialogue with China,'" AsiaNews, June 20, 2018, http://www.asianews.it/news-en/Pope-talks-to-Reuters-about-the-%27dialogue-with-China%27-44224.html.

86. Fr. Pedro Yu Heping had studied in Colombia and Spain. He was the first webmaster for an online Catholic site that translated Vatican news. Zen was a frequent commentator on the site, which officials shut down. Cardinal Zen told me Fr. Yu exemplified why the pope should not negotiate with Beijing. "Chinese Underground Priest Found Dead," Union of Catholic Asian News, November 16, 2015, https://www.ucanews.com/news/chinese-underground-priest-found-dead/74620.

87. Cardinal Joseph Zen, interview with the author, Hong Kong, November 9, 2017.

88. There are many theories on why Zen turned so publicly against reconciliation. Many people mention his close ties to Hong Kong billionaire Jimmy Lai. In response to my question on Lai's $2.5 million donation to Zen personally (given without approval by the Holy See, I should add, although that's supposedly not required), the cardinal told me, "First of all, it is not only for activity in China. It is for all the things a bishop may like to do, but without help, he cannot do so many. If Jimmy Lai is going to help me again that way, I would be very happy. It's a donation to me personally, but for my personal use as cardinal, so I do not have to render account to anybody. And I'm not even telling him how I'm using the money. So it's simply a relationship between me and him. But I know many people are interested. All that money, is not enough." Interview with the author, Washington, DC, January 28, 2019. See Paul Hong, "I Received Millions and Spent Them on the Church and the Poor, Cardinal Zen Says," AsiaNews, October 20, 2011, http://www.asianews.it/news-en/I-received-millions-and-spent-them-for-the-Church-and-the-poor,-Card-Zen-says-22966.html.

89. Victor Gaetan, "Hong Kong's Catholic Church in President Xi Jinping's Era," *National Catholic Register*, January 15, 2018, http://www.ncregister.com/daily-news/hong-kongs-catholic-church-in-president-xi-jinpings-era.

90. Shirley Zhao and Ng Kang-Chang, "Shock as Vatican Brings Cardinal John Tong Out of Retirement to Be Acting Head of Hong Kong Diocese after Death of Bishop—Blocking Occupy Supporter Joseph Ha Chi-shing," South China Morning Post, January 7, 2019, https://www.scmp.com/news/hong-kong/politics/article/2181079/shock-vatican-brings-cardinal-john-tong-out-retirement-serve.

91. Cindy Wooden, "Vatican Reaches Pact with China over Naming Bishops," Catholic News Service, September 27, 2018, https://catholic-sf.org/news/vatican-reaches-pact-with-china-on-naming-bishops.

92. James Roberts, "Mixed Reports on 'Imminence' of China Deal," *The Tablet*, March 29, 2018, https://www.thetablet.co.uk/news/8818/mixed-reports-on-imminence-of-china-deal.

93. "China: Bishops Break Silence to Back Vatican Deal," Eurasia Review, March 13, 2018, https://www.eurasiareview.com/13032018-china-bishops-break-silence-to-back-vatican-deal.

94. Some Hong Kongers say Cardinal Zen urged Guo to go ahead with the Chrism Mass on his own.

95. "Catholic Church Seized as China Ramps Up Henan Crackdown," Herald Malaysia Online, April 23, 2018, http://www.heraldmalaysia.com/news/catholic-church-seized-as-china-ramps-up-henan-crackdown/41982/2.

96. "Chinese Priests Ordered to Put Up Signs Banning Children from Churches," Catholic News Service, February 9, 2018, https://catholicherald.co.uk/chinese-priests-ordered-to-put-up-signs-banning-children-from-churches.

97. An excellent account of the complex reality in Mindong can be found in Michel Chambon, "Mindong Diocese Goes beyond Beijing and the Vatican," Union of Catholic Asian News, updated February 14, 2018, https://www.ucanews.com/news/mindong-diocese-goes-beyond-beijing-and-the-vatican/81433. Chambon portrays a diocese far more integrated than the caricature of two obstinate communities facing off.

98. I. William Zartman, "Ripeness: The Hurting Stalemate and Beyond," in *International Conflict Resolution after the Cold War*, ed. Paul C. Stern and Daniel Druckman (Washington, DC: National Academies Press, 2000), 229, https://www.nap.edu/read/9897/chapter/7#228. Also see Zartman, *Ripe for Resolution: Conflict and Intervention in Africa*, 2nd ed. (New York: Oxford University Press, 1989).

99. "Wang Chao," China Vitae, Carnegie Endowment for International Peace, http://www.chinavitae.com/biography/Wang_Chao.

100. "Wang Chao," Ministry of Foreign Affairs of the People's Republic of China, Biographies, https://www.fmprc.gov.cn/mfa_eng/wjb_663304/zygy_663314/gyjl_663316/wc_666656.

101. The only media outlet that anticipated the event was the *Global Times*, an online news site close to the power in Beijing, which reported on September 18 that a Vatican delegation was expected to sign an agreement later that month. The article confirms the pope's superior role in designating bishops because, it reports, he will issue letters of appointment to new bishops. Li Ruohan, "Vatican to Send Delegation to China before Possible Bishops Deal: Sources," *Global Times*, September 18, 2018, http://www.globaltimes.cn/content/1120054.shtml.

102. Jason Horowitz, "Pope Francis Asks Chinese Catholics to Trust His Deal with Government," *New York Times*, September 26, 2018, https://www.nytimes.com/2018/09/26/world/europe/china-pope-francis-catholics.html. By not releasing the document publicly, the Holy See intentionally "stepped on its own story," minimizing confusion from exaggerated or mistaken reporting. By making the announcement as the pope flew to Lithuania, the traveling Vatican press corps could not easily file major stories on the news.

103. Richard Madsen, "Church-State Relations in China: Consequences for the Catholic Church," *Religions & Christianity in Today's China* 5, nos. 3–4 (2015): 60–68, http://www.china-zentrum.de/fileadmin/downloads/rctc/2015-3-4/RCTC_2015-3-4.60-68_Church-State_Relations_in_China_-_Consequences_for_the_Catholic_Church.pdf.

104. Pope Francis, "Press Conference on the Return Flight from Tallin (Estonia) to Rome," Holy See, September 25, 2018, http://w2.vatican.va/content/francesco/en/speeches/2018/september/documents/papa-francesco_20180925_voloritorno-estonia.html. About Parolin, the pope described him as "a very devoted man and has a particular attachment to the magnifying glass: he studies every document down to the period, comma, accent mark. . . . And this gives me a great deal of certitude." Francis explained that he reviewed every bishop's personal file, and every iteration of the agreement. Francis is a decider who *enjoys* deciding. Cardinal Zen's theory that the pope is misled by staff might have been his most outlandish claim.

105. Cindy Wooden, "Chinese Bishop Says Agreement Is Sign That Universal Church Is One," *National Catholic Reporter*, October 10, 2018, https://www.ncronline.org/news/vatican/chinese-bishop-says-agreement-sign-universal-church-one.

106. "Pastoral Guidelines of the Holy See concerning the Civil Registration of Clergy in China," Holy See, June 28, 2019, https://www.vaticannews.va/en/vatican-city/news/2019-06/china-catholic-clergy-state-register-respect-conscience.html.

107. Gerard O'Connell, "Vatican Tells Clergy to Follow Their Conscience on Government Registration," *America* (magazine), June 28, 2019, https://www.americamagazine.org/faith/2019/06/28/vatican-china-clergy-conscience-government-registration.

108. Li Ruohan, "China Ordains First Bishop since Landmark Deal with Vatican," *Global Times*, August 27, 2019, http://www.globaltimes.cn/content/1162784.shtml; "China's State Church Installs Sixth Bishop," UCANews, August 19, 2020, https://www.ucanews.com/news/chinas-state-church-installs-sixth-bishop/89209#.

109. "Chinese, Vatican Foreign Ministers Hold Rare High-Level Meeting," Reuters, February 15, 2020, https://www.aljazeera.com/news/2020/02/chinese-vatican-foreign-ministers-hold-rare-high-level-meeting-200215075901121.html.

CHAPTER 12

1. David Lumu, "I Trembled When the Pope Kissed My Feet—Salva Kiir," New Vision, April 21, 2019, https://www.newvision.co.ug/new_vision/news/1498938/trembled-pope-kissed-feet-salva-kiir.

2. "Testimony of Kate Almquist Knopf before the Senate Foreign Relations Committee," September 20, 2016, https://www.foreign.senate.gov/imo/media/doc/092016_Knopf_Testimony.pdf.

3. The term "Big Man" is often used to refer to African power players such as Salva Kiir. See, for example, the book by Canadian ambassador Nicholas Coghlan, *Collapse of a Country: A Diplomat's Memoir of South Sudan* (Montreal: McGill-Queen's University Press, 2017). See also Camilla Houeland and Sean Jacobs, "The 'Big Man' Syndrome in Africa," Africa's a Country, March 11, 2016, https://africasacountry.com/2016/03/the-big-man-syndrome-in-africa.

4. Kiir's original black Stetson was a gift from President George W. Bush when he visited the White House in 2006. Kiir liked it so much he bought thirty more while still in Washington DC. At the time, Kiir served as first vice president of the Government of National Unity of Sudan and president of the government of South Sudan, an autonomous region. See Colum Lynch, "Where Did Kiir Get His Ten-Gallon Hat?," *Foreign Policy*, September 26, 2011, https://foreignpolicy.com/2011/09/26/where-did-kiir-get-his-ten-gallon-hat.

5. Gallagher describes this two-part task himself in this short interview: "Connect5: Archbishop Paul Gallagher on the Holy See's Relations with Other States," Salt and Light Media, February 17, 2016, YouTube video, 5:00, https://www.youtube.com/watch?v=PV0EWl5fXs0.

6. "Pastoral Message from the South Sudan Catholic Bishops' Meeting, Juba, 26th–28th February 2019," February 28, 2019, Solidarity Friends, https://www.solidarityfriends.org/wp-content/uploads/2016/03/bishops_message_feb2019.pdf. Sources in South Sudan say the bishops produced the pastoral message to be sure their perspective reached Rome before the president himself got there and put his spin on the status quo.

7. Jackeline Wilson, "The Religious Landscape in South Sudan: Challenges and Opportunities for Engagement," United States Institute of Peace, June 20, 2019, https://www.usip.org/publications/2019/06/religious-landscape-south-sudan-challenges-and-opportunities-engagement.

8. "South Sudan," United Nations Development Programme, https://www.ss.undp.org/content/south_sudan/en/home/countryinfo.html.

9. "Where We Are," Solidarity with South Sudan, https://www.solidarityssudan.org/where-we-are. The country's roads are gutted and frequently impassable, so international organizations and diplomats move about via small plane. See Coghlan, *Collapse of a Country*.

10. "Historical Background," Catholic University of South Sudan, https://www.cuofss.org/historicalbgcu.php; Fr. Michael Schultheis, SJ, was a founder of the Catholic University of South Sudan who died in 2017. A short summary of his life's dedication to education in Africa conveys the single-mindedness of Catholic missionaries in this field. Fr. Peter Henriot, SJ, "Requiescat in Pace, Fr. Michael Schultheis, SJ," Jesuits West, May 19, 2017, https://jesuitswest.org/news-detail?tn=news-20170518055044.

11. "Bishop Eduardo Hiiboro Kussala," Sudan Relief Fund, https://sdnrlf.com/about-sudan-relief-fund/bishop-eduardo-hiiboro-kussala.

12. Paul Jeffrey, "At Loreto School, South Sudanese Girls from Diverse Tribes Live in Peace," Catholic Philly, June 15, 2017, https://catholicphilly.com/2017/06/news/world-news/at-loreto-school-south-sudanese-girls-from-diverse-tribes-live-in-peace; "History of the School," Loreto Rumbec, Secondary School, https://www.loretorumbek.ie/secondary-school.

13. "Isn't South Sudan the Newest Country in the World? Why Are People Fleeing?," UN High Commissioner for Refugees (UNHCR), May 1, 2019, https://www.unrefugees.org/news/south-sudan-refugee-crisis-explained; Jesuit Relief Services (JRS), "South Sudan Standing with Internally Displaced Persons," August 15, 2019, https://jrs.net/en/story/south-sudan-standing-with-idps; Catholic Relief Services (CRS), "CRS in South Sudan," https://www.crs.org/our-work-overseas/where-we-work/south-sudan.

14. Luca Attanasio, "The Bishops of South Sudan in the Largest Refugee Camp in the World," *La Stampa*, last modified July 2, 2019, https://www.lastampa.it/vatican-insider/en/2018/10/15/news/the-bishops-of-south-sudan-in-the-largest-refugee-camp-in-the-world-1.34052706.

15. Fredrick Nzwili, "In South Sudan Conflict, Churches Attacked, Looted," *National Catholic Reporter*, January 29, 2014, https://www.ncronline.org/news/world/south-sudan-conflict-churches-attacked-looted.

16. Tim Franks, "Malakal: The City That Vanished in South Sudan," BBC, October 24, 2015, https://www.bbc.com/news/world-africa-34571435.

17. "Comboni Missionaries 'With the People' in Africa's Most Dangerous Zones," Southworld, April 2014, https://www.southworld.net/comboni-missionaries-with-the-people-in-africas-most-dangerous-zones.

18. The Comboni Missionary Sisters was founded in 1872 as the first Catholic order dedicated to bringing women to evangelize in Africa.

19. "Archbishop of Canterbury on the South Sudan Crisis," Episcopal News Service, May 15, 2014, YouTube video, 6:06, https://www.youtube.com/watch?time_continue=91&v=PdeGcDNMZPQ.
20. Archbishop of Canterbury, "South Sudan Crisis."
21. Wilson, "The Religious Landscape."
22. Wilson, "The Religious Landscape."
23. Wilson, "The Religious Landscape," 11.
24. Dennis Coday, "South Sudan Enters Fragile Cease Fire," *National Catholic Reporter*, May 10, 2014, https://www.ncronline.org/blogs/ncr-today/south-sudan-enters-fragile-ceasefire; "Congratulations to Bishop Emeritus Paride Taban," Comboni, February 10, 2013, https://www.comboni.org/pt/contenuti/106342. Lokudu is a Comboni Missionary, and Taban was a lifelong collaborator with the Combonis.
25. "Youngest Casualties of War: More Child Soldiers to Be Released in South Sudan," Catholic Medical Mission Board, February 11, 2019, https://cmmb.org/youngest-casualties-of-war-more-child-soldiers-to-be-released-in-south-sudan.
26. "The Taking of South Sudan: The Tycoons, Brokers, and Multinational Corporations Complicit in Hijacking the World's Newest State," The Sentry, September 2019, 24–25, https://cdn.thesentry.org/wp-content/uploads/2019/09/TakingOfSouthSudan-Sept2019-TheSentry.pdf.
27. "Clooney Calls for Global Action as He Unveils South Sudan Corruption Report," Agence France-Presse (AFP), September 19, 2019, https://www.arabnews.com/node/1556906/world.
28. Personal communication with the author, June 20, 2020. The First Sudanese Civil War (or the Anyanya Rebellion) lasted from 1955 to 1973. The conflict reignited in 1983, and although it is called the Second Sudanese Civil War, it was basically a continuation of the first. See Peter Martell, *First Raise a Flag: How South Sudan Won the Longest War but Lost the Peace* (London: Hurst Publishers, 2018).
29. See also Ben Lynfield, "Eitay Mack Wants Israel to Reveal Its Secret Arms Sales," *Christian Science Monitor*, November 19, 2015, https://www.csmonitor.com/World/Making-a-difference/2015/1119/Eitay-Mack-wants-Israel-to-reveal-its-secret-arms-sales. A UN expert panel vindicated Mack in 2016 when it issued a report on evidence of Israeli complicity in arms deals. See "Israeli Arms 'Helping to Fuel South Sudan War,' Says UN," Agence France-Presse, October 20, 2016, https://www.timesofisrael.com/israeli-arms-helping-to-fuel-south-sudan-war-says-un.
30. Machar has long been considered an ally of Khartoum. In 1991, he split from the mainline Christian insurgent movement and the Sudan People's Liberation Army, led by the charismatic John Garang. He signed a separate agreement with Khartoum in 1997 and even served as an assistant to President Omar al-Bashir. In 2002, he rejoined forces with Garang (killed in a mysterious plane crash in 2005), but the impression has long lingered that Machar has maintained relationships with Sudan behind the scenes. Thus, for example, he is not trusted by Israel. See "Profile: South Sudan Rebel Leader Riek Machar," Al Jazeera, January 4, 2014, https://www.aljazeera.com/indepth/2013/12/profile-south-sudan-riek-machar-20131230201534595392.html.
31. Edith Lederer, "UN Experts: South Sudan's Security Service Works Outside the Law," Associated Press, May 2, 2019, https://apnews.com/96ab22a71a6940a3820334bafbd2f2fb.

32. President Omar al-Bashir ruled Sudan from 1989 to 2019. He was deposed in a coup d'état on April 11, 2019, the same day South Sudan's leadership met Pope Francis in Rome.

33. Personal communication with the author, June 15, 2020. See also "Domestic Conference, Jim Greene," SoundCloud, April 2019, audio, https://soundcloud.com/user943875091/201904-domestic-conference-jim-greene.

34. Personal communication with the author, June 20, 2020.

35. "South Sudan: Vatican's Secretary for Relations with States Visits Juba," Catholic Information Service for Africa, March 22, 2019, http://cisanewsafrica.com/south-sudan-vaticans-secretary-for-relations-with-states-visits-juba.

36. "Jim Greene Interviewed by Vatican Radio," SoundCloud, April 16, 2019, audio, https://soundcloud.com/user943875091/20190416-jim-greene-interviewed-by-radio-vatican. The Province of the Episcopal Church of South Sudan is a member of the worldwide Anglican Communion led by the archbishop of Canterbury.

37. "South Sudan Council of Churches," Friends Committee on National Legislation, https://www.fcnl.org/documents/618.

38. Wilson, "The Religious Landscape," 13.

39. Ines Martin, "Top Christians in South Sudan Urge Pope to Visit to Foster Peace," Crux, October 29, 2016, https://cruxnow.com/global-church/2016/10/top-christians-south-sudan-urge-pope-visit-foster-peace. The SSCC had a valuable intercessor at the Vatican: Spanish Archbishop Miguel Ángel Ayuso Guixot is a Comboni missionary who lived for many years in Sudan. At the time, he was secretary of the Pontifical Council for Interreligious Dialogue, of which he is president today. Francis made the Islam expert a cardinal in 2019.

40. Christopher Lamb, "Francis Ready to Visit South Sudan," *La Stampa*, last modified December 30, 2019, https://www.lastampa.it/vatican-insider/en/2016/10/27/news/francis-ready-to-visit-south-sudan-1.34795247.

41. "South Sudan: Dangerous Rise in Ethnic Hate Speech Must be Reined in—Zeid," United Nations Human Rights Office of the High Commissioner, October 25, 2016, https://www.ohchr.org/EN/NewsEvents/Pages/DisplayNews.aspx?NewsID=20757&LangID=E.

42. Archbishop Paul Richard Gallagher, "Sunday Sermon at St. Theresa Cathedral Juba, 24 March 2019," audio, 17:55, https://www.mixcloud.com/marko-logel/archbishop-paul-richard-gallagher.

43. "Domestic Conference, Jim Greene"; "Kiir Resumes Attending Church Services after 9-Month Break," Sudan Tribune, October 31, 2015, https://www.sudantribune.com/spip.php?iframe&page=imprimable&id_article=48631.

44. Gallagher, "Sunday Sermon."

45. The Church of Scotland is a Presbyterian denomination. While Rev. John Chalmers was moderator of the General Assembly of the Church of Scotland, he visited South Sudan and initiated a special partnership with the Presbyterian Church of South Sudan in 2015. "Moderator" is the highest church office, held for a one-year term.

46. The designated vice presidents listed as attending the retreat were Riek Machar, Teny Dhurgon, James Wani Igga, Taban Deng Gai, and Rebecca Nyandeng De Mabior. Together with President Kiir, this team comprised "the presidency" and

was supposed to take power on May 12, 2019, under the Revitalised Agreement on the Resolution of Conflict in South Sudan signed in Addis Ababa, Ethiopia, on September 12, 2018. In the final session with Pope Francis, Wani did not appear. The purpose of the retreat was tied to a growing sense that the presidency was still not prepared to govern together. Indeed, the date for installing the new "unity government" was moved twice, ultimately accomplished on February 22, 2020. Max Bearak, "South Sudan Forges Unity Government in Bid to End Civil War That Has Killed 400,000," *Washington Post*, February 22, 2020, https://www.washingtonpost.com/world/africa/south-sudan-forges-unity-government-in-bid-to-end-civil-war-that-has-killed-400000-lives/2020/02/22/4afea024-54f2-11ea-80ce-37a8d4266c09_story.html.

47. "Anglican Primate to Lead Spiritual Retreat for South Sudan Leaders in Vatican," Vatican News, April 9, 2019, https://www.vaticannews.va/en/vatican-city/news/2019-04/south-sudan-pope-francis-justin-welby-vatican-retreat.html. Vatican City is guarded by the pope's army, the Swiss Guard. Anyone on its streets is a member of the curia or an approved guest. A tourist cannot simply wander into this world. However, visitors to St. Peter's Basilica can enter the church without showing ID, after being screened for weapons.

48. Victor Gaetan, "Peace Be with Us: Pope Francis' Prayer Summit with Mahmoud Abbas and Shimon Peres," *Foreign Affairs*, June 8, 2014, https://www.foreignaffairs.com/print/node/1071064.

49. "President Kiir Will Not Protect FVP Machar: Spokesperson," *Sudan Tribune*, July 17, 2016, https://sudantribune.com/spip.php?article59651; "Kiir: I Have Forgiven Riek, Let Him Return to Juba," Radio Tamazuj, May 7, 2018, https://radiotamazuj.org/en/news/article/kiir-i-have-forgiven-riek-let-him-return-to-juba; Emmanuel Igunza, "South Sudan War: The Handshake That May End a Recurring Nightmare," BBC, September 13, 2018, https://www.bbc.com/news/world-africa-45511352.

50. Of course, figures are approximate in light of social chaos and displacement, but Pew Research Center's Religion in Public Life research considers 60.5 percent of South Sudan's 2020 population to be Christian, 33 percent folk religion, 6.2 percent Muslim, and less than 1 percent Orthodox. This is the best source of religious demographic data: http://www.globalreligiousfutures.org/countries/south-sudan/religious_demography#/?affiliations_religion_id=0&affiliations_year=2010.

51. There's a wonderful story about the meeting in 1966: Pope Paul VI took off his episcopal ring, given to him by the people of Milan when he became bishop of that city, and put it on the finger of Ramsey, who began to cry. The green ring, overlaid by a thin gold cross and marked with four diamonds, is worn by the Anglican archbishop whenever he is in Rome. Archbishop Welby was wearing it at the 2016 commemoration: "Commemoration of the 50th Anniversary of the Meeting of Paul VI and the Archbishop of Canterbury," Vatican News, October 5, 2016, YouTube video, 1:16:38, https://www.youtube.com/watch?v=8SZBFwA1lGQ.

52. http://www.vatican.va/content/francesco/en/speeches/2016/october/documents/papa-francesco_20161005_vespri-canterbury.html; Vespers was held in the Church of Sts. Andrea and Gregorio al Celio, which holds historic significance: A Benedictine monk was sent from this community to instruct a pagan king in Britain

in the late sixth century. He was appointed the first archbishop of Canterbury in the year 597. St. Augustine of Canterbury successfully converted King Aethelberht and is considered a founder of the British Church.

53. "Anglican and Roman Catholic Bishops 'Sent Out' for United Mission," Anglican Communion News Service, October 5, 2016, https://www.anglicannews.org/news/2016/10/anglican-and-roman-catholic-bishops-sent-out-for-united-mission.aspx.

54. Sam Mednick, "South Sudan Opposition Leader Blocked from Vatican Meeting," Associated Press, April 9, 2019, https://www.seattletimes.com/nation-world/nation/south-sudan-opposition-leader-blocked-from-vatican-meeting.

55. Puok Both Baluang (@Puok_Baluang), "H.E. Dr. Riek Machar Teny-Dhurgon, the SPLM/A (IO) Chairman and Commander in Chief and His Accompanying Delegation Arrived," Twitter, April 10, 2019, 11:10 a.m., https://twitter.com/Puok_Baluang/status/1115995585918713857.

56. "Spiritual Retreat with South Sudan Leaders in Vatican: Time to Choose Life," Vatican News, April 10, 2019, https://www.vaticannews.va/en/vatican-city/news/2019-04/spiritual-retreat-south-sudan-leaders-vatican-choose-life.html.

57. The original painting of Mary Untier of Knots is in Augsburg, Germany. It is one of Francis's favorite depictions of Mary, which he first saw while studying in Germany in 1986. When he returned to Argentina, he brought prayer cards with the image, which he distributed to parishioners. A devotion to *Maria Desatanudos* grew quickly. See Austin Ivereigh, *The Great Reformer: Francis and the Making of a Radical Pope* (New York: Henry Holt, 2015), 199–200, 229–30. Also see Victor Gaetan, "The Cuban Knot: The Vatican's Strategy in Havana," *Foreign Affairs*, December 30, 2014, https://www.foreignaffairs.com/articles/cuba/2014-12-30/cuban-knot.

58. "Pope Francis: Peace, Light, and Hope Are Possible in South Sudan," Vatican News, November 4, 2019, YouTube video, 33:29, https://www.vaticannews.va/en/pope/news/2019-04/pope-francis-spiritual-retreat-leaders-south-sudan-speech0.html.

59. John 13:13–15.

60. Matthew 16:19.

61. Koang Pal, "Pope's Feet Kissing Could Be a Blessing or a Curse," EyeRadio, May 13, 2019, https://eyeradio.org/popes-feet-kissing-could-be-a-blessing-or-curse.

62. Fredrick Nzwili, "South Sudan's Christian Leaders Say Papal Kiss Is Message of Easter," Crux, April 19, 2019, https://cruxnow.com/church-in-africa/2019/04/south-sudans-christian-leaders-say-papal-kiss-is-message-of-easter.

63. Lumu, "I Trembled"; Kiir said something similar three weeks later in a speech to the parliament: "I was shocked and trembled when His Holiness the pope kissed our feet. It was a blessing and can be a curse if we play games with the lives of our people." In fact, he might have picked up the blessing/curse idea from Bishop Dau, whose account of the retreat was shared publicly at a well-publicized funeral for a famous journalist, Alban Taban.

64. "God Shows Love for South Sudan through Voice of Pope Francis," Voice of Hope Radio, April 24, 2019, http://catholicradionetwork.org/?q=node/29287.

65. Linda Bordoni, "South Sudan's 'Women of Courage,'" Vatican News, November 4, 2019, https://www.vaticannews.va/en/church/news/2019-11/south-sudan-sr-orla-traecy-woman-of-courage-school.html.

66. "A Delegation of the Sant'Egidio Meet with Salva Kiir Mayardit President of the South Sudan," Sant'Egidio, March 18, 2019, https://www.santegidio.org/pageID/30284/langID/en/itemID/29752/A-delegation-of-the-SantEgidio-meet-with-Salva-Kiir-Mayardit-President-of-the-South-Sudan.html.

67. "South Sudan, a Vigil Prayer at Santa Maria in Trastevere," Sant'Egidio, April 12, 2019, https://www.santegidio.org/pageID/30284/langID/en/itemID/30140/South-Sudan-a-Vigil-Prayer-at-Santa-Maria-in-Trastevere.html. Sant'Egidio is a movement regarded by many as an extension of the Holy See's Secretariat of State. It was founded in 1968 by a lay Catholic, Andrea Riccardi, and Msgr. Vincenzo Paglia, today an archbishop.

68. Linda Bordoni, "South Sudan Leaders Set Date for Truce, Vow to Pursue Peace," Vatican News, January 13, 2020, https://www.vaticannews.va/en/world/news/2020-01/south-sudan-st-egidio-meeting-government-oppostion-peace-process.html; Courtney Mares, "South Sudan Peace Declaration Signed in Rome," Catholic News Agency, January 14, 2020, https://www.catholicnewsagency.com/news/south-sudan-peace-declaration-signed-in-rome-55900.

69. Associated Press, "Vatican: Pope, Anglican Head Aim for Joint South Sudan Trip," AP News, November 13, 2019, https://apnews.com/ad05211b0c0e4bfcb3cc4e00fbce1981.

70. Denis Dumo, "South Sudan Cuts Number of States from 32 to 10, Unlocking Peace Process," Reuters, February 15, 2020, https://www.reuters.com/article/us-southsudan-politics/south-sudan-cuts-number-of-states-from-32-to-10-unlocking-peace-process-idUSKBN2090AM.

71. "South Sudan: Riek Machar & Three Vice Presidents Sworn In," Dolku Media, YouTube video, 53:47, https://www.youtube.com/watch?v=5a8U4PkrNB8.

72. Maura Ajak, "South Sudan's Rivals Form Unity Government Meant to End War," Associated Press, February 22, 2020, https://apnews.com/d3b929b5a687b69068e4f3ca24cccd7f.

73. "South Sudan: Riek Machar."

74. Siobhan O'Grady, "It's Exceedingly Rare for the Pope to Kiss Feet. He Just Did It for South Sudan's Warring Leaders," *Washington Post*, April 12, 2019, https://www.washingtonpost.com/world/2019/04/12/bid-peace-pope-francis-hosts-south-sudans-warring-leaders-spiritual-summit-kisses-their-feet.

75. U.S. Department of the Treasury, "Treasury Sanctions South Sudanese First Vice President for Role in Serious Human Rights Abuse" (press release, January 8, 2020), https://home.treasury.gov/news/press-releases/sm869.

76. Bishop Paride Taban, "The Holy Trinity Peace Village," Comboni Youth, October 1, 2017, https://www.comboniyouth.org/witnesses/bishop-paride-taban-the-holy-trinity-peace-village.html.

Bibliography

Acheson, Dean. *Present at the Creation: My Years in the State Department.* New York: W. W. Norton, 1987.
Albertini, Matteo, and Chris Deliso. *The Vatican's Challenge in the Balkans: Bolstering the Catholic Church in 2015 and Beyond.* Balkananalysis.com, 2015. Kindle.
Allen, John L. *All the Pope's Men: The Inside Story of How the Vatican Really Thinks.* New York: Doubleday, 2004.
Ambrogetti, Francesca, and Sergio Rubin. *Pope Francis: Conversations with Jorge Bergoglio. His Life in His Own Words.* New York: G.P. Putnam's Sons, 2010.
Aradi, Zsolt, James I. Tucek, and James C. O'Neill, *Pope John XXIII: An Authoritative Biography.* New York: Farrar, Straus & Cudahay, 1959.
Barkan, Elazar. *The Guilt of Nations: Restitution and Negotiating Historical Injustices.* New York: W. W. Norton, 2000.
Barry, Coleman, OSB. *American Nuncio: Cardinal Aloisius Muench.* Collegeville, MN: Saint John's University Press, 1969.
Bátora, Jozef, and Nik Hynek. *Fringe Players and the Diplomatic Order: The New Heteronomy?* New York: Palgrave Macmillan, 2014.
Bernstein, Carl, and Marco Politi. *His Holiness John Paul II and the History of Our Time.* New York: Penguin Group, 1996.
Berridge, G. *Counter-Revolution in Diplomacy and Other Essays.* New York: Palgrave Macmillan, 2014.
———. "Richelieu." In *Diplomatic Theory from Machiavelli to Kissinger*, edited by G. R. Berridge, H. M. A. Keens-Soper, and T. G. Otte. London: Palgrave, 2001.
Blanchard, Jean-Vincent. *Éminence: Cardinal Richelieu and the Rise of France.* New York: Walker & Company, 2013.
Blet, Pierre, S. J. *Pius XII and the Second World War: According to the Archives of the Vatican.* Mahwah, NJ: Paulist Press, 1999.
Blight, James G., Bruce Allyn, and David Welch. *Cuba on the Brink: Castro, the Missile Crisis, and the Soviet Collapse.* New York: Rowman & Littlefield, 2002.

Borghesi, Massimo. *The Mind of Pope Francis: Jorge Mario Bergoglio's Intellectual Journey*. Translated by Barry Hudock. Collegeville, MN: Liturgical Press, 2018. Kindle.

Brzezinski, Zbigniew. *Out of Control: Global Turmoil on the Eve of the 21st Century*. New York: Charles Scribner's Sons, 1993.

Byfield, Ted, ed. *Darkness Descends: AD 350–565: The Fall of the Western Roman Empire*. The Christians: Their First Two Thousand Years, vol. 4. Christian History Project, 2002.

Casaroli, Agostino. *The Martyrdom of Patience: The Holy See and the Communist Countries (1963–1989)*. Translated by Fr. Marco Bagnarol. Toronto: Ave Maria Centre of Peace, 2007.

Cardinale, H. E. *The Holy See and the International Order*. Toronto: The Macmillan Company of Canada, 1976.

Carlson, John C., and Erik C Owens, eds. *The Sacred and the Sovereign*. Washington, DC: Georgetown University Press, 2003.

Cassidy, Edward Idris. *My Years in Vatican Service*. Mahwah, NJ: Paulist Press, 2009.

Cesare, Raffaele De. *Last Days of Papal Rome, 1850–1870*. N.p.: Nabu Press, 2010.

Chamberlin, E. R. *The Bad Popes*. New York: The Dial Press, 1969.

Chaput, Charles J. *Strangers in a Strange Land: Living the Catholic Faith in a Post-Christian World*. New York: Henry Holt & Company, 2017.

Chowdhury, Arjun. *The Myth of International Order: Why Weak States Persist and Alternatives to the State Fade Away*. New York: Oxford University Press, 2018.

Clinton, Hillary Rodham. *Hard Choices*. Waterville, ME: Thorndike Press, 2014.

Coghlan, Nicholas. *Collapse of a Country: A Diplomat's Memoir of South Sudan*. Montreal: McGill-Queen's University Press, 2017.

Cohen, Raymond, and Raymond Westbrook. *Amarna Diplomacy: The Beginnings of International Relations*. Baltimore, MD: Johns Hopkins University Press, 2002.

Congar, Yves. *True and False Reform in the Church*. Translated by Paul Philibert. Collegeville, MN: Liturgical Press, 1950.

Cooper, Andrew F., Jorge Heine, and Ramesh Thakur, eds. *The Oxford Handbook of Modern Diplomacy*. Oxford, UK: Oxford University Press, 2013.

Costantini, Celso. *The Secrets of a Vatican Cardinal: Celso Costantini's Wartime Diaries, 1938–1947*. Edited by Bruno Fabio Pighin. Translated by Laurence B. Mussio. Montreal: McGill-Queens University Press, 2014.

Cousins, Norman. *The Improbable Triumvirate: John F. Kennedy, Pope John, Nikita Khrushchev*. New York: W. W. Norton, 1984.

Crawford, James. *The Creation of States in International Law*. 2nd ed. Oxford, UK: Oxford University Press, 2006.

Dalin, David G., and Joseph Bottum. *The Pius War: Responses to the Critics of Pius XII*. Lanham, MD: Lexington Books, 2004.

Dallmayr, Fred. "Sacred Nonsovereignty." In *The Sacred and the Sovereign: Religion and International Politics*, edited by John Carlson and Erik Owens. Washington, DC: Georgetown University Press, 2003.

de Callierès, François. *On the Manner of Negotiating with Princes: Classic Principles of Diplomacy and the Art of Negotiation*. Translated by A. F. Whyte. Boston: Houghton Mifflin, 2000.

Derian, James Der. *On Diplomacy: A Genealogy of Western Estrangement*. Oxford, UK: Blackwell, 1991.

Downey, John K., et al. *Facing the World: Political Theology and Mercy*. Mahwah, NJ: Paulist Press, 2018.

du Plessis, Armand. *The Political Testament of Cardinal Richelieu*. Translated by Paul Sonnino. Lanham, MD: Rowman & Littlefield, 2020.

Duursma, Jorri Carolina. *Fragmentation and the International Relations of Micro-States: Self-Determination and Statehood*. Cambridge, UK: Cambridge University Press, 1996.

Ehler, Sidney Zdeneck, and John Brimyard Morrall, eds. *Church and State through the Centuries: A Collection of Historic Documents with Commentaries*. London: Burns and Oates, 1954.

Faggioli, Massimo. *Sorting Out Catholicism: A Brief History of the New Ecclesial Movements*. Collegeville, MN: Liturgical Press, 2014.

Ferguson, Niall. *The Square and the Tower: Networks and Power, from the Freemasons to Facebook*. New York: Penguin Press, 2018.

Farrow, Ronan. *War on Peace: The End of Diplomacy and the Decline of American Influence*. New York: W. W. Norton & Company, 2018.

Fletcher, Catherine. *The Divorce of Henry VIII: The Untold Story from inside the Vatican*. New York: Palgrave Macmillan, 2012.

Franco, Massimo. *Parallel Empires: The Vatican and the United States Two Centuries of Alliance and Conflict*. Translated by Roland Flamini. New York: Doubleday, 2009.

Gallagher, Charles R. *Vatican Secret Diplomacy: Joseph P. Hurley and Pope Pius XII*. New Haven, CT: Yale University Press, 2008.

Gallo, Patrick J. "Beyond the Deputy: Origins of the New Revisionism." In *Pius XII, the Holocaust and the Revisionists: Essays*. Edited by Patrick J. Gallo. Jefferson, NC: McFarland & Company Publishers, 2006.

Graham, Robert A. *Vatican Diplomacy: A Study of Church and State on the International Plane*. Princeton, NJ: Princeton University Press, 1959.

Gratsch, Edward J. *The Holy See and the United Nations, 1945–1995*. New York: Vantage Press, 1997.

Grisar, Hartman, S J. *History of Rome and the Popes in the Middle Ages*. London: Kegan Paul, Trench, Trübner & Co, 1911.

Guardini, Romano. *The End of the Modern World*. Wilmington, DE: Intercollegiate Studies Institute, 1998.

Halperin, Samuel William. *Italy and the Vatican at War*. Chicago: University of Chicago Press, 1939.

Hanson, Eric O. "The Catholic Church in China." In *Catholicism and Politics in Communist Societies*, edited by Pedro Ramet, 253–269. Christianity under Stress, Vol. 2. Durham, NC: Duke University Press, 1990.

———. *The Catholic Church in World Politics*. Princeton, NJ: Princeton University Press, 1987.

Hare, Paul. "Who Are the Diplomats and How Do They Operate?" In *Making Diplomacy Work: Intelligent Innovation for the Modern World*. Washington, D.C.: CQ Press, 2015.

Hatos, Pál. "Eastern Policy–Western Roots: The Cultural Context of the Vatican's Ostpolitik." In *The Vatican Ostpolitik 1958-1978: Responsibility and Witness during John XXIII and Paul VI*, edited by András Fejérdy. Rome: Bibliotheca Academiae Hungariae, 2015.

Hebblethwaite, Peter. *Pope John XXIII: Shepherd of the Modern World—The Definitive Biography of Angelo Roncalli*. New York: Doubleday, 1985.

Herghelegiu, Monica-Elena. *Reservatio Papalis: A Study on the Application of a Legal Prescription According to the 1983 Code of Canon Law*. Berlin: Lit Verlag, 2008.

Holland, Heidi. *Dinner with Mugabe: The Untold Story of a Freedom Fighter who Became a Tyrant*. New York: Penguin Group, 2009.

Hoopes, Tom. *What Pope Francis Really Said: Words of Comfort and Challenge*. Welland, ON, Canada: Servant, 2016.

Hume, Cameron. *Ending Mozambique's War: The Role of Mediation and Good Offices*. Washington, DC: US Institute for Peace, 1994.

Ignatius, St., and J. F. X. O'Conner, S.J., ed. *The Autobiography of St. Ignatius*. New York: Benziger Brothers, 1900. https://archive.org/details/stignatiusautobi00ignauoft/page/n5.

Ivereigh, Austen. *The Great Reformer: Francis and the Making of a Radical Pope*. New York: Henry Holt & Company, 2015.

———. *Wounded Shepherd: Pope Francis and His Struggles to Convert the Catholic Church*. New York: Henry Holt. 2019.

Jackson, Robert. *Sovereignty Evolution of an Idea*. Cambridge, UK: Polity Press, 2007.

Jones, Dorothy V. "Sober Expectations: The United Nations and a 'Sensible Machinery' for Peace." In *The Dumbarton Oaks Conversations and the United Nations 1944–1994*, edited by Ernest May and Angeliki Laiou. Washington, DC: Dumbarton Oaks Research Library and Collection, 1998.

John XXIII. *Pope John XXIII: Journal of a Soul*. London: Geoffrey Chapman, 1965.

Kaatz, Kevin. *Early Controversies and the Growth of Christianity*. Westport, CT: Praeger, 2012.

Kadushin, Charles. *Understanding Social Networks: Theories, Concepts and Findings*. Oxford, UK: Oxford University Press, 2012.

Kertzer, Robert. *The Pope and Mussolini: The Secret History of Pius XI and the Rise of Fascism in Europe*. New York: Penguin Random House, 2014.

Kilduff, Martin, and Wenpin Tsai. *Social Networks and Organizations*. Thousand Oaks, CA: Sage, 2011.

Kissinger, Henry A. *Diplomacy*. New York: Simon & Shuster, 1994.

Kittler, Glenn D. *The White Fathers*. New York: Harper & Brothers Publishers, 1957.

Krieg, Robert A. *Romano Guardini: A Precursor of Vatican II*. South Bend, IN: University of Notre Dame Press, 1997.
Kurzman, Dan. *A Special Mission: Hitler's Secret Plot to Seize the Vatican and Kidnap Pope Pius XII*. Boston: Da Capo Press, 2007.
Lam, Anthony S. K., Fr. Peter Barry, Norman Walling, Betty Ann Maheu, and Anne Reusch. *The Catholic Church in Present-Day China: Through Darkness and Light*. Hong Kong: Holy Spirit Study Centre, 1997.
Lamb, Christopher. *The Outsider: Pope Francis and his Battle to Reform the Church*. Maryknoll, NY: Orbis Books, 2020.
Landry, Roger J. *Plan of Life: Habits to Help You Grow Closer to God*. Boston: Pauline Books & Media, 2018.
Leguey-Feilleux, Jean-Robert. *The Dynamics of Diplomacy*. Boulder, CO: Lynne Rienner Publishers, 2009.
LeoGrande, William M., and Peter Kornbluh. *Back Channel to Cuba: The Hidden History of Negotiations between Washington and Havana*. Chapel Hill: The University of North Carolina Press, 2015.
Levinas, Gabriel. *Doble agente: La biografia inesperada de Horacio Verbitsky* (Spanish Edition). Bogota: Sudamericana, 2015.
Linden, Ian. *Global Catholicism: Diversity and Change since Vatican II*. London: Hurst & Company, 2009.
Luard, Evan. *The Age of Decolonization: 1955–1965*. A History of the United Nations, Vol. 2. New York: St Martin's Press, 1982.
MacMillan, Margaret. *Paris 1919: Six Months That Changed the World*. New York: Random House, 2003.
MacNutt, Francis. *A Papal Chamberlain: The Personal Chronicle of Francis Augustus McNutt*. London: Longmans, Green, 1936.
Madsen, Richard. *China's Catholics: Tragedy and Hope in an Emerging Civil Society*. Berkeley: University of California Press, 1998.
Marimon, Mateo Jover. "The Church." In *Revolutionary Change in Cuba*, edited by Carmelo Mesa-Lago. Pittsburgh, PA: University of Pittsburgh Press, 1971.
Maritain, Jacques. *Things That Are Not Caesar's*. New York: Charles Scribner's Sons, 1931.
Marmara, Rinaldo. *John XXIII: Friend of the Turks*. Istanbul: Culture Ministry of the Republic of Turkey, 2000.
Marsh, Patrick G. *Eastern Destiny: Russia in Asia and the North Pacific*. Westport, CT: Praeger Publishers, 1996.
Marshall, Peter. *Positive Diplomacy*. New York: St. Martin's Press, 2014.
Martell, Frédéric. *In the Closet of the Vatican: Power, Homosexuality, Hypocrisy*. London: Bloomsbury Continuum, 2019.
Martell, Peter. *First Raise the Flag: How South Sudan Won the Longest War but Lost the Peace*. London: Oxford University Press, 2019.
Mattingly, Garrett. *Renaissance Diplomacy*. New York: Penguin Books, 1965.
May, Ernest R., and Angeliki E. Laiou, eds. *The Dumbarton Oaks Conversations and the United Nations, 1944-1994*. Washington, DC: Dumbarton Oaks Research Library and Collection, 1998.

McElwee, Joshua J., and Cindy Wooden, eds. *A Pope Francis Lexicon*. Collegeville, MN: Liturgical Press, 2018.

Mearsheimer, John J. *The Great Delusion Liberal Dreams and International Realities*. New Haven, CT: Yale University Press, 2018.

Melnyk, Roman A. *Vatican Diplomacy at the United Nations: A History of Catholic Global Engagement*. Lewiston, NY: Mellen, 2010.

Morello, Gustavo, SJ. *The Catholic Church and Argentina's Dirty War*. New York: Oxford University Press, 2015.

Morier-Genoud, Eric, and Pierre Anouilh. "Revolution, War and Democracy: The Catholic Church in Mozambique." In *Religion and Politics in a Global Society: Comparative Perspectives from the Portuguese-Speaking World*, edited by Paul C. Manuel, Alynna Lyon, and Clyde Wilcox. Lanham, MD: Lexington Books, 2013.

Mukonori, Fidelis, SJ. *Man in the Middle: A Memoir*. Harare, Zimbabwe: The House of Books, 2017.

Nassif, Ramses. *U Thant in New York: 1961-1971. A Portrait of the Third UN Secretary-General*. London: C. Hurst & Co, 1977.

Neiberg, Michael S. *Treaty of Versailles: A Concise History*. New York: Oxford University Press, 2017.

Neumann, Iver B. *At Home with the Diplomats: Inside a European Foreign Ministry*. Ithaca, NY: Cornell University Press, 2012.

Nichols, Aidan, OP. *Rome and the Eastern Churches: A Study in Schism,*. 2nd ed. San Francisco: Ignatius Press, 2010.

Nichols, Peter. *The Politics of the Vatican*. New York: Frederick A. Praeger Publishers, 1968.

Nicolson, Harold. *Diplomacy*, 3rd ed. New York: Oxford University Press, 1969.

———. *The Evolution of Diplomatic Method: The Chichele Lectures at University of Oxford, Nov 1953*. New York: The MacMillan Company, 1954.

Noe, Jean-Baptiste, *Geopolitique du Vatican: La Puissance de L'influence*. Paris: Presses Universitaires de France, 2015

Numelin, Ragnar Julius. *The Beginnings of Diplomacy: A Sociological Study of Intertribal and International Relations*. London: Oxford University Press, 1950.

Nucifora, Antonio M. D., and Luiz A. Pereira da Silva, "Rapid Growth and Economic Transformation in Mozambique, 1993–2009." In *Yes Africa Can: Success Stories from a Dynamic Continent*, edited by Punam Chuhan-Pole and Manka Angwafo. Washington, DC: The World Bank, 2011.

Nye, Joseph. *Bound to Lead: The Changing Nature of American Power*. New York: Basic Books, 1990.

O'Connell, Gerard. *The Election of Pope Francis: An Inside Account of the Conclave That Changed History*. Maryknoll, NY: Orbis Books, 2019.

O'Mahony, Anthony, Wulstan Peterburs, and Mohammad Ali Shomal, eds. *A Catholic–Shi'a Engagement: Faith and Reason in Theory and Practice*. London: Melisende Publishing, 2006. http://biblicalstudies.org.uk/pdf/anvil/23-2_omahony.pdf.

O'Malley, John W. *The Jesuits: A History from Ignatius to the Present*. New York: Rowman & Littlefield, 2017.

Oppenheim, L. F. L. *Peace*, Vol. 1 of *International Law: A Treatise*. Edited by H. Lauterpacht. 8th ed. London: Longmans, Green, 1955.

Osiander, A. *The States System of Europe, 1640-1990: Peacemaking and the Conditions of International Stability*. Oxford, UK: Oxford University Press, 1994.

Pease, Neal. *Rome's Most Faithful Daughter: The Catholic Church and Independent Poland, 1914–1939.* Athens: Ohio University Press, 2009.

Pelton, Robert S., ed. *Aparacide: Quo Vasis?* Scranton, PA: University of Scranton Press, 2008.

Perry, Jon. "Catholic Peace-Making: A History and Analysis with Special Emphasis on the Work of SantEgidio,'" in *Peace on Earth: The Role of Religion in Peace and Conflict Studies*, eds. Thomas Matyók, Maureen Flaherty, Hamdesa Tuso, Jessica Senehi, and Sean Byrne. Lanham, MD: Lexington Books.

Peters, Walter H. *The Life of Benedict XV.* Milwaukee, WI: The Bruce Publishing Company. 1959.

Petro, Nicolai. "The Foreign Policy of the Russian Orthodox Church." In *The Routledge Handbook of Russian Foreign Policy*, edited by Andrei Tsygankov. London: Routledge, 2018.

Plokhy, Serhii. *Yalta: The Price of Peace*. London: Penguin, 2011.

Pollard, John F. *Benedict XV: The Unknown Pope and the Pursuit of Peace*. London: Geoffrey Chapman, 1999.

———. *Money and the Rise of the Modern Papacy: Financing the Vatican, 1850–1950*. Cambridge, UK: Cambridge University Press, 2009.

———. *The Vatican and Italian Fascism, 1929-32*. Cambridge, UK: Cambridge University Press, 1985.

Pontifical Council for Justice and Peace. *Compendium of the Social Doctrine of the Church.* Washington, DC: Libreria Editrice Vaticana, 2004.

Pope Francis, and Dominique Wolton. *A Future of Faith: The Path of Change in Politics and Society*. New York: St. Martins Essentials, 2018.

Princen, Thomas. *Beagle Channel Negotiations*. Washington, DC: Institute for the Study of Diplomacy, 1995.

———. *Intermediaries in International Conflict*. Princeton, NJ: Princeton University Press, 1992.

Quigley, Thomas. "The Catholic Church in Cuba." In *Catholicism and Politics in Communist Societies*, edited by Pedro Ramet. Durham, NC: Duke University Press, 1990.

Randal, Jonathan. *The Tragedy of Lebanon: Christian Warlords, Israeli Adventurers, and American Bunglers.* Charlottesville, VA: Just World Books, 2012.

Ratzinger, Joseph (Benedict XVI). *Church, Ecumenism, and Politics: New Endeavors in Ecclesiology*. San Francisco, CA: Ignatius Press, 2008.

Reese, Thomas J. *Inside the Vatican: The Politics and Organization of the Catholic Church*. Cambridge, MA: Harvard University Press, 1996.

Robinson, John Martin. *Cardinal Consalvi: 1757–1824*. London: The Bodley Head, 1987.

Rooney, Francis. *The Global Vatican: An Inside Look at the Catholic Church, World Politics, and the Extraordinary Relationship between the United States and the Holy See*. New York: Rowman & Littlefield, 2013.

Rubin, Sergio, and Francesca Ambrogetti. *Pope Francis Conversations with Jorge Bergoglio*. G.P. New York: Putnam's Sons, 2013.

Sanders, Frances Stonor. *The Cultural Cold War: The CIA and the World of Arts and Letters*. New York: The New Press, 1999.

Sarros, P. Peter. *U.S.-Vatican Relations, 1975–1980: A Diplomatic Study*. Notre Dame, IN: University of Notre Dame, 2020.

Satow, Ernest Mason, and Neville Bland. *A Guide to Diplomatic Practice*. London: Longmans, Green, 1957.

Scavo, Nello. *Bergoglio's List: How a Young Francis Defied a Dictatorship and Saved Dozens of Lives*. Translated by Bret Thoman. Charlotte, NC: St. Benedict Press, 2014.

Schall, James V. *The Church, the State, and Society in the Thought of John Paul II*. Chicago: Franciscan Herald Press, 1982.

Schlesinger, Stephen C. *Act of Creation: The Founding of the United Nations*. Boulder, CO: Westview, 2004.

Schwarzenberger, Georg. *A Manual of International Law*. London: Stevens & Sons, 1976.

Secor, Laura. *Children of Paradise: The Struggle for the Soul of Iran*. New York: Riverhead Books, 2016.

Sharp, Paul, and Geoffrey Wiseman. *The Diplomatic Corps as an Institution of International Society*. New York: Palgrave Macmillan, 2008.

Shea, John Gilmary. *Life of Pope Pius IX and the Great Events in the History of the Church during His Pontificate*. New York: Thomas Kelly, 1877.

Smith, Christian. *The Emergence of Liberation Theology: Radical Religion and Social Movement Theory*. Chicago: University of Chicago Press, 1991.

Starkey, Brigid, Mark A. Boyer, and Jonathan Wilkenfeld. *International Negotiation in a Complex World*. 3rd ed. New York: Rowman & Littlefield, 2010.

Stocker, James. *Spheres of Intervention: US Foreign Policy and the Collapse of Lebanon, 1967–1976*. Ithaca, NY: Cornell University Press, 2016.

Stummvoll, A. Alexander. *A Living Tradition: Catholic Social Doctrine and Holy See Diplomacy*. Eugene, OR: Cascade Books, 2018.

Sturdy, David J. *Richelieu and Mazarin: A Study in Statesmanship*. New York: Palgrave MacMillan, 2004.

Sweig, Julia. *Cuba: What Everyone Needs to Know®*, 3rd edition. New York: Oxford University Press, 2016.

Tavassoli, Sasan. *Christian Encounters with Iran: Engaging Muslim Thinkers after the Revolution*. London: I.B. Tauris, 2011.

Terzo Centenario 1701–2001: Pontificia Accademia Ecclesiastica. Rome: Libreria Editrice Vaticana, 2003.

Thavis, John. *The Vatican Diaries: A Behind-the-Scenes Look at the Power, Personalities, and Politics at the Heart of the Catholic Church*. New York: Penguin Books, 2014.

Thomas, Gordon. *Gideon's Spies: The Secret History of the Mossad*. New York: Thomas Dunne Books, 2012.

Thompson, Augustine, O.P. *Francis of Assisi: A New Biography*. Ithaca, NY: Cornell University Press, 2012.

Tittmann, Harold H., Jr. *Inside the Vatican of Pius XII: The Memoir of an American Diplomat during World War II*. Edited by Harold H. Tittmann, III. New York: Doubleday, 2004.

Tomasi, Silvano M. *The Vatican in the Family of Nations: Diplomatic Actions of the Holy See at the UN and Other International Organizations in Geneva*. Cambridge, UK: Cambridge University Press, 2018.

Valente, Gianni, and Andrea Tornielli. *Il Giorno Del Giudizio: Conflitti, Guerre Di Potere, Abusi e Scandali*. Milan: Piemme, 2018.

Vallely, Paul. *Pope Francis: Untying the Knots*. London: Bloomsbury, 2013.

Viaene, Vincent. "A Pope's Dilemma: Temporal Power and Moral Authority in The History of the Modern Vatican." In *World Views and Worldly Wisdom*, edited by Jan de Maeyer and Vincent Viaene. Leuven: Leuven University Press, 2016.

Ware, Timothy. *The Orthodox Church: New Edition*. London: Penguin Books, 1997.

Weigel, George. *The End and the Beginning: John Paul II—The Victory of Freedom, the Last Years, the Legacy*. New York: Doubleday, 2010.

———. *Witness to Hope: The Biography of Pope John Paul II 1920–2005*. New York: Harper Perennial, 2005.

Weisbrode, K. *Old Diplomacy Revisited: A Study in the Modern History of Diplomatic Transformations*. New York: Palgrave Pivot, 2016.

Wellerstein, Alex. *Restricted Data: The History of Nuclear Secrecy in the United States*. Chicago: University of Chicago Press, 2021.

Westad, Odd Arne. *The Global Cold War: Third World Interventions and the Making of Our Times*. Cambridge, UK: Cambridge University Press, 2007.

Wilkenfeld, Jonathan, Kathleen Young, David Quinn, and Victor Asal. *Mediating International Crises*. London: Routledge, 2005.

Willey, David. *The Promise of Francis: The Man, the Pope, and the Challenge of Change*. New York: Gallery Books, 2017.

Wimmer, Andreas. *Nation Building: Why Some Countries Come Together While Others Fall Apart*. Princeton, NJ: Princeton University Press, 2018.

Woodward, Kenneth. *Making Saints: How the Catholic Church Determines Who Becomes A Saint, Who Doesn't and Why?* New York: Touchstone Books, 1990.

Wynn, Wilton, *Keepers of the Keys: John XXIII, Paul VI and John Paul II: Three Who Changed the Church*. New York: Random House, 1988.

Zartman, I. William. *Cowardly Lions: Missed Opportunities to Prevent Deadly Conflict and State Collapse*. Boulder, CO: Lynne Rienner, 2005.

Zartman, I. William, ed. *The Negotiation Process Theories and Applications*. Thousand Oaks, CA: Sage Publications, 1978.

Zartman, Ira William, and Maureen R. Berman. *The Practical Negotiator*. New Haven, CT: Yale University Press, 1992.

Index

Abbas, Mahmoud, 308
Abdullah II, King of Jordan, 249
ad limina meetings: Benedict XVI
 with Colombia (2012), 232; Francis
 with Kenya (2015), 209; with South
 Sudan (2018), 302; with Ukraine
 (2015), 162
Aeterni Patris (On the Restoration
 of Christian Philosophy, 1879), 101
Aid to the Church in Need, 302
al-Shabab, 206
al-Tayeb, Grand Imam Ahmed, 133–35,
 372n76
Alexander VI, Pope, 52
Alexy II, Patriarch of Moscow and all
 Russia, 166, 171
Ambrose, Saint, 51
American Jewish Committee, 184
Anastasiades, Nicos, 265
Anderson, Carl, 193
Anderson, Jon Lee, 190
Anglican Communion, 39, 95, 179, 217,
 303, 308, 309, 438n51
Annan, Kofi, 115, 207
Aoun, General Michel, 250, 262–63,
 264–66, 268, 269
Aparecida text (CELAM, 2007), 137,
 149, 232, 373n88

Apostolic Palace: 61, 69, 84, 85, 97,
 98, 100, 110, 168, 191, 260, 273,
 300
Araujo, Robert, SJ, 96, 356n7
Arinze, Cardinal Francis, 208
Aristotle, 81, 87
Armand Jean du Plessis, Duke of
 Richelieu (Cardinal Richelieu), 68,
 119, 121, 122, 198
Armed Forces of the Colombian
 Revolution (FARC), 221, 223–24,
 231, 232–33, 235–36, 239–42,
 243–44, 401n19, 401n22, 403n51,
 404n56, 405n65, 409n114
Armenian Catholic Church, 257, 259–
 60, 416n65
Arteaga y Betancourt, Cardinal Manuel,
 195
Ashworth, John, 306, 315, 316
Asia Times, 288, 421n3
Assad, Bashar al-, 5, 249, 251, 252,
 257, 261, 263–64, 410n7
Athenagoras, Ecumenical Patriarch of
 Constantinople, 90, 165, 253
Aung San Suu Kyi, 133, 150
Auza, Archbishop Bernardito, 25, 130
Ayuso Guixot, Cardinal Miguel Angel,
 31–32

452　　　　　　　　　　　　　　　　　Index

B'nai B'rith, 184–85
Balestrero, Archbishop Ettore, 233–34, 404n64, 427n47
Balvo, Archbishop Charles Daniel, 208, 213, 214, 218
Barreto Henriques, Miquel, 229–30
Bartholomew, Ecumenical Patriarch of Constantinople, 169–71, 173–74, 176, 186, 308, 380n20
Batista, Fulgencio, 195
Bay of Pigs invasion, 195
Becciu, Cardinal Angelo, 148, 162, 188, 337n84, 389n32
Benedict XVI, Pope, 12, 20, 21, 28, 29, 34, 61, 118, 136, 142, 152, 184, 186, 194, 203, 233, 252–53, 335n71, 343n51, 380n18; Bergoglio, relationship with, 137; China, 271, 279, 280–83, 285, 289, 294–95, 423n13; Colombia, 221, 231–33; ecumenism, 169–71; election of, 325n16; history, theology of, 88–89; Latin America as future, 232; 404n54; loyalty of, 375n3; Middle East, 252, 253–54, 257, 266, 409n3, 410n7, 412n31, 413n36, 414n47; politics, view of, 124; Regensburg address and Muslim relations, 133, 247–48, 331n24; resignation, 13, 22, 145; Russia and Russian Orthodox Church, ties to, 3–4, 11, 169, 172–3, 176, 177; Ukraine, 381n29; US, frustration with, 3; visits Aparecida, Brazil, 137, 232; visits Turkey, 170–71
Benedict XV, Pope, 26, 62, 77–78, 90–91, 102–03, 105, 122–24, 336n80, 360n62, 361n64, 361n76
Beran, Cardinal Josef, 196, 293
Bergoglio, Jorge: Aparecida report, 137, 149, 232; Argentina, politics in, 8, 376n6, 376n8; Asia, early interest in, 283; Benedict XVI, runner up to, 319, 325n16; character assassination of, 708; culture of encounter,

120, 129, 152, 186; election as pontiff, 32, 323n5; geopolitical independence, 4, 12–13, 153, 390n44; grandparents, 283; history, view of, 152–53; installation, 173; intellectual influences, 132, 346n102, 371n56, 376n11, 377n22; interfaith commitment, 248; Jesuit education, 11, 120, 149, 152; manager, experience as, 146–48; Mary Untier of Knots, devotion to, 310, 439n57; missionary disposition, 150–51; Parolin, selection of, 118; pastor, role as, 11–12, 145; Roncalli, similarities to, 66; Shevchuk, friendship with, 159
Bertone, Cardinal Tarcisio, 253, 282–83, 331n24, 375n3, 389n32, 404n64, 427n47
Betancourt Pulecio, Ingrid, 231, 242
Betancur Cuartas, Belisario, 223
Bidi Bidi Refugee Settlement (Uganda), 302
bin Abdul Karim al-Issa, Mohammed, 266
bin Abdulaziz Al Saud, King Salman, 265
bin Fahad Al Eidan, Abdullah, 266
bin Salman, Crown Prince Mohammed, 264–65
bishops, 36, 57, 70, 198, 336n82; authority of, 34–35, 46, 57, 196; as diplomats, 51, 54; diplomats, selection of, 70; Francis' perception of, 29, 34, 150, 189, 207, 209–10, 218, 233–35, 252; national conferences, 17, 33, 35, 39, 41, 53, 80, 140, 147, 162, 205, 212–14, 230–32, 255, 275, 300–02; network of, 12, 35–36, 147; nuncios and, 23, 62, 65, 72, 140; selection of, 119, 125, 289–91, 295–96; state, relationship to, 55, 108, 117, 286; Synod of Bishops on Youth, 296
Bo, Cardinal Charles, 133, 150

Borghesi, Massimo, 152, 186, 371n56, 376n11, 377n22
Boris III of Bulgaria, 64
Bourj el-Barajneh, Lebanon, 257–58
Boutros-Ghali, Boutros, 79
Bouvier, Virginia, 233
Brazil-Argentina conflict: 1990 accord, 138–39
Brenes, Cardinal Leopoldo, 131
Brzezinski, Zbigniew, 422n9
Budapest Memorandum (1994), 158
Buddhism, 126, 289
Burundi, 26–27, 300, 309
Buryadnyk, Father Mykola, 159–60, 161
Bush, George H. W., 2, 15–16, 17, 198, 277, 342n50
Bush, George W., 2, 3, 134, 180, 247, 249, 343n50, 390n37, 434n4
Byrnes, Timothy, 107

Caccia, Archbishop Gabriele, 257–59, 415n52
Camilleri, Monsignor Antoine, 118, 295, 429n66
Capovilla, Cardinal Loris, 2, 85–6, 324n5
captive popes, 98–99
Capture of Rome (1870), 97
Caravaggio's *The Calling of St. Matthew*, 130
Caritas Internationalis, 38, 128, 302
Caritas, Beirut, 256–57; Caritas Cuba, 198
Carlucci, Frank, 422n9
Carneada Rodríguez, Jose, 197
Casaroli, Cardinal Agostino, 19, 53, 56, 182, 268
Castrillón Hoyos, Bishop Darío, 225
Castro, Fidel, 183, 185, 189, 191, 193–94, 195–96, 197–98, 199, 201, 294, 390n44, 392n58
Castro, Raul, 176, 183, 184, 187, 188, 189–90, 192, 193, 194, 201–22, 204, 237

Castro Espín, Alejandro, 185–86, 189, 191
Castro, Mariela, 237
Cathedral of the Virgin Mary of the Immaculate Conception (Havana), 201
Catherine the Great, 174
Catholic Church, 70, 80, 83, 115, 146, 277, 353n76; bilateral ties, value of, 44; charity and, 57, 66, 103, 127–29; criticism of, 6, 8, 85, 324n6; double nature of, 43; Eastern Catholic Church, leadership of, 31, 245–47, 250–53, 255–56, 259–60; ecumenism and, 171–77, 308–09, 312; expressive power of, 109–10, 129, 357n99; foreign leaders, attitude toward, 19; Holy See, government of, 13, 16; in China, 273–76, 281–82, 284–86, 366n1, 427n48, 430n70; Colombia, 219–22, 225–31, 233–44; in Cuba, 188–204, 391n48, 392n58; in Kenya, 205–06, 207–10, 214–18; in Korea, 140–43; in Russia, 166–67, 171–73; in Saudi Arabia, 266; in South Sudan, 299, 300–04, 315–16; in Ukraine, 158–163; inter-faith respect and, 89–90, 261–62; just war theory and, 90–1; organization of, 11, 28, 34–5, 355n7; peace building and, 91; principles of, 17, 86–9, 120–29, 178, 350n39; properties of, 24, 68, 166; political power, views on, 123–26; religious personnel, 36; sovereignty of, 93–108, 332n39, 356n8, 357n14; social network, as, 12
Catholic Peacebuilding Network, 232
Catholic Relief Services, 302, 389n37
Catholic Social Thought, 80, 82–83, 100
Catholic University of South Sudan, 301, 206, 435n10
Ceausescu, Nicolae and Elena, 18, 422n9
Celli, Archbishop Claudio, 274–75, 280, 283, 285, 287–88, 291, 296, 429n66

454   Index

Center for Research and Popular Education (CINEP), 230, 403n42
Central African Republic, 38, 258, 415n60
Central Intelligence Agency (CIA), 1, 10, 15, 18, 85, 86, 190, 198, 328n45
Cepero, Harold, 203
Chalmers, Rev. John, 308, 310, 312, 437n45
Chane, Bishop John Bryce, 3, 389n37
Chamseddine, Imam Mohammad Mehdi, 262; Ibrahim, son of, 262
Chiang Kai-shek, 273, 369n26
China, 10,123, 272, 274, 277; 1982 Constitution, 272; Belt and Road Initiative, 429n64; Hebei Province, 119, 278, 294, 295 illicit bishops, 274, 276, 290, 291, 293, 367n2, 424n17, 425n28; persecution of Christians, 119, 275, 285, 290, 319n18, 366n1, 392n58; Protestantism in, 272; State Administration on Religious Affairs (SARA), 284, 429n66; underground, or unregistered, Church, 6, 117, 128, 273, 275, 278, 283, 290, 291, 293, 296, 423n16, 427n47; underground, or unregistered, clergy, 118, 276, 279, 281, 291, 296, 367n2, 426n38, 427n47, 431n86; United Front Work Department (UFWD), 429n66
China-Vatican relations: 101, 103, 128, 195, 197, 271, 273, 274, 275, 283, 286–87, 289, 348n17, 422n10; bishop selection, negotiations, 6, 118, 119, 126, 280, 282, 287, 295; bishop selection, signed agreement (2018), 119, 295–96, 367n2; bishop selection, agreement renewal (2020), 297, 367n6; Sino–Vatican working group, 288; US criticism of, 5, 6
Chinese Catholic Patriotic Association (CCPA), 117, 274, 276, 280, 281–82, 284, 289, 422n11, 427n47; national seminary, opening of, 280, 426n37

Chinese Philharmonic Orchestra, 282
Chrism Mass in Mindong, 118, 294, 432n94
Christian Liberation Movement (MCL), 199–201, 203
Christiansen, Father Drew SJ, 84
Chrysostom, Saint John, 60, 169–70
clash of civilizations, 177, 258, 266
Claver, Saint Peter, 238, 243
Clement VII, Pope, (1769–1774), 94
Clement XI, Pope (1700–1721), 68–9
Clement XIII, Pope (1758–1769), 69
Clement XIV, Pope, 174
Clinton, Bill, 79, 389n37
Clinton, Hillary, 184
Clooney, George, 305
CNN, 8, 290–91
College of Cardinals: 32–33; diplomatic roles of, 12, 57, 135–38
Columbus, Christopher, 51–52
Comboni missionaries, 31–32, 302, 312, 437n39
Comboni Missionary Sisters, 303, 435n18
Comboni, Saint Daniele, 303
Commission for Truth, Coexistence, and Non-Recurrence, 243
Common good, 12, 46, 59, 74, 83, 87, 88, 89, 120, 124, 130, 146, 211, 215, 300, 352n58
concordats, 54–55, 105, 108, 343n52, 353n76, 355n91, 362n84
Congregation for the Evangelization of Peoples, 30, 33, 118, 283, 287, 294
Congregation for the Oriental Churches, 30, 33, 259
Congregation for the Propagation of the Faith, 30, 62, 334n61
Congregation of the Immaculate Heart of Mary (CICM), 273, 421n7
Congress of Vienna (1814–5), 75–76, 95, 113, 120, 333n51, 348n20, 349n25, 349n27, 357n15, 369n27
Consalvi, Cardinal Ercole, 55, 75–76, 98, 333n51, 348n20, 349n25, 355n91

constitutive theory, 98
Cooke, Cardinal Terence, 189
Socialist Renewal Current (CRS), 226–27
Council of Trent, 99
Courtney, Archbishop Michael, 26–27
Cousins, Norman, 84–5, 353n69
Craig, Greg, 188
Creagan, James, 16–17, 330n12, 419n100
Crimea, 158, 379n13, 379n14
Cuban Five, 184, 189, 190
Cuban Missile Crisis, 84, 91, 113
Cuban National Assembly, 199
Cuban National Ecclesial Encounter (ENEC), 200
Cultural Revolution, 117, 272–74, 279
culture of encounter, 11–12, 21, 91, 118–120, 129–33, 137, 142, 152–53, 175, 179, 181, 186, 240, 243, 253, 258, 288
Custody of the Holy Lands, 251
Cyprus, 24–25, 37, 247, 265

Daesh, 255, 266, 414n46; Beirut bombing by, 257–58; defeat of 263–64; Shia Muslims, attitude toward, 261
Dalin, David, 124, 369n30
Damaskinos of Athens, Archbishop, 63
Dau, Bishop Dr. Isaiah, 312
Daughters of Mary Immaculate, 125
Davidian, Bishop Sarkis, 260, 416n61, 416n62, 416n65
Davis, Kim, 35
de Callières, François, 76, 121–22
de Gasperi, Alcide, 106
de Roux, Francisco, SJ, 228–30, 243
Deng Bul Yak, Archbishop Daniel, 307
Deng Gai, Taban, 311, 437n46
Deng Pufang, 276–77
Deng Xiaoping, 272, 274, 366n1, 421n6
Dennis, Marie, 227
Dias, Cardinal Ivan, 283

Dicastery for Promoting Integral Human Development, 136–37, 334n58, 373n86
Dinka, 299, 301, 314, 316
diplomatic precedence, 95, 349n25
Dominus ac Redemptor (1773), 174
du Rosier, Bernard, 120
Durbin, Dick, 187
Dziwisz, Bishop Stanisław, 168

Eastern Orthodox Church Synod, Crete (2016), 31
Ecclesia in Medio Oriente (Church in the Middle East, 2012), 252, 412n31
Echeverri, Father Dario, 234–35
Ecumenism (ecumenical dialogue), 90, 165, 169–70, 177, 179, 312, 365n129
Eisenhower, Dwight David, 5, 85, 353n76
el-Sisi, Abdel Fattah, 265
Emperor Constantine, 47
Emperor Theodosius, 51
Episcopal Conference of Colombia (CEC), 231, 234, 236, 239, 241; educating voters, 237; Minimal Proposals for Reconciliation and Peace in Colombia, 235; victims, brought to Havana peace talks, 235
Escobar, Pablo, 223, 225, 226
Etchegaray, Cardinal Roger, 125
European Union, 5, 157, 219, 229, 244, 252, 257, 413n40
Evangelii Gaudium (On the Proclamation of the Gospel in Today's World, 2013), 30, 128–29, 131, 134, 149, 155, 175, 186, 371n56, 373n88

Fang Jianping, Bishop Peter, 294
Fang Xinyao, Bishop Johan, 289
Farrell, Bishop Brian, 31
Fatimah al-Zahra, 260–61
Ferguson, Niall, 36, 38
Filioque Clause, 171

First Vatican Council, 99, 333n47
Fitzgerald, Cardinal Michael, 22, 134, 331n24
Food and Agriculture Organization (FAO), 112, 364n111
France, 28, 48, 54, 64, 69, 75–6, 77, 85, 95–6, 101, 102, 103, 110, 120, 123, 164, 174, 225, 256, 259, 267, 336n76, 349n24, 353n76, 355n91, 360n53, 381n23, 385n72, 427n47
France 24 TV, 253–54
Francis, Pope. See also Bergoglio, Jorge Mario: al-Tayeb, relationship with, 132–35; anti-war position, 4–5, 141, 144, 153–54, 180, 236, 245; Bangladesh, visit to, 132; brother bishops, deference to, 178, 252–53; charity, 61; China, appreciation for, 272, 283–84, 285, 288, 415n3; China diplomacy, new approach to, 118–19, 272, 283–85, 288–90, 292, 294–95, 297; Chinese faithful, communication with, 296; collaboration with global religious leaders; 132–35, 173–74, 179, 306–09, 314; common good, 12, 124, 129, 186, 258; concrete diplomatic steps, promotion of, 118, 120, 122, 133–34, 142–43, 147, 149, 152–53, 205, 210–11, 219, 257–59, 262, 266, 302; culture of encounter, 21–22, 91, 129–31, 142–43, 152–3, 175, 181, 186, 198, 240, 259–60, 309–10, 315; diplomatic personnel, deployment of, 29–33, 115, 135–140, 300–01, 306–08; diplomatic practice, 11–13, 27, 116, 119–22, 129–134, 153, 155, 177–78, 186, 221–222, 233–36, 238–44, 245–47, 249–50, 254–55, 265–66, 283–86, 287–97; diplomatic rules of thumb, 131–135, 155, 179–80; evangelizing Church, 40, 128–29; G20, letter to, 249; humility in diplomacy, 132, 136, 150, 178; interfaith diplomacy, 188, 247–48, 256, 258, 260–62; ideological colonization, 56; John XXIII, admiration of, 66; John Paul II, continues policies of, 12; Kenya, reconciliation in, 207–10, 212–14, 217–18; Kirill, meeting with, 155, 175–77, 186, 309; Kirill, joint declaration with; 177–78; Lebanon, day of fasting, for, 269; Leo XIII, consistent with, 83; Lunar New Year greetings; 421n3; Matthew 25, 131–32; moral example, 181; Myanmar, visit to, 132; non-Western European outlook, 264; partisan politics, 25, 35, 124, 154; peacebuilding in Colombia, 219, 221–22, 233–36, 238; presidential mediation, 239–40; visit, 241–44; peripheries, promoting from, 27, 32–33, 136, 150–51; sciatica, 311; slander against, 8; South Sudan leaders, kissing feet of, 299, 310–313; sciatica: 311; Ukraine's "fratricide," 159–60, 162–65; US-Cuba mediation, 181–82, 187, 190–91, 194, 203; visit to Cuba, 194–95; visit to Holy Land, 253–55; visit to Kenya, 210–212, 218; visit to Korea; 141–42; visit to US, 286–87; Zen, understanding of, 292
Franco, Massimo, 162, 323n1
Franco-Prussian War (1870), 100
Freeman, Jr., Charles W., 164, 271, 420n1
French Revolution, 54–5, 75

Gallagher, Archbishop Paul, 27, 135, 240, 297, 309, 337n84; Burundi, nuncio to, 27; Parolin, relationship with, 27; South Sudan, visit to; 300, 306–07
Garagni, Abbot Pietro, 68
Garang, Rebecca, 308, 311, 312, 313, 314
Garfias Merlos, Archbishop Carlos, 136, 138–39

Gasparri, Cardinal Pietro, 103, 106, 361n76
Gaudium et Spes (The Church in the Modern World, 1965), 84, 91, 114, 352n62, 365n129
Geagea, Samir, 262
Gerbillon, Father Jean-Francois, 73–4, 348n17
Germany, 7, 24, 38, 49, 56, 63–4, 67, 77, 86, 101, 105, 108, 120, 123–24, 162, 170, 221, 247, 341n36, 353n76, 359n37, 365n122, 368n24, 385n72, 439n57
Gingrich, Callista and Newt, 203
Girelli, Archbishop Leopold, 24–5
Global Times, 119, 294, 433n101
González, Archbishop Roberto, 197
Good Samaritan parable, 130, 131
Gorbachev, Mikhail, 56, 158
Gore, Al, 79, 350n41
Greene, Father Jim, 305–06
Gregory Peter XX Ghabroyan, Catholicos-Patriarch of Armenian Catholic Church, 259
Gross, Alan, 182–85, 187–88; Judy, wife of, 184
Guangqing, Bishop Dong, 274–75
Guardini, Romano, 132,186, 371n56
Gudziak, Archbishop Borys, 159–61
Gullickson, Archbishop Thomas, 162,164, 381n29

Hamas, 127
Hammarskjöld, Dag, 113
Hanoi seminary, 125
Harada, Ken, 45
Hariri, Rafic, 250, 263
Hariri, Saad, 245, 263, 264–66
Harvey, Cardinal James, 19–20
Havana Accords, 236–40, 243–44; voters' rejection of, 239
Havana, 4, 182, 185, 187, 190, 192, 195–98, 201, 203; Colombia peace negotiations, location of, 232–33, 235–36, 240; Francis-Kirill meeting location of, 155, 175; Francis, visit to, 194; Jewish community in, 183; Payá and, 199–200; US negotiations with, 181
Hebblethwaite, Peter, 85, 346n95
Hereford Cathedral, 49
Heyndrickx, Father Jeroom, 273, 276, 280, 421n7, 421n8
Hezbollah, 255, 257, 261, 262–63, 264, 266, 268–69, 417–18n79, 418n82
Hiiboro Kussala, Bishop Edward, 302, 304, 306
Hilarion (Alfeyev) of Volokolamsk, Metropolitan, 173, 176, 178
history, Catholic theology of, 49, 88–89, 129–30, 152–53, 194, 292
Holy See. See also Vatican, Vatican diplomacy: absolute monarchy, 11, 28; diplomacy, purpose of, 33–34, 49; as empire, 271; Francis' leadership of, 11; as global network, 36, 38, 41, 57–58, 127, 146; government of Catholic Church, 1, 13, 16, 93–94; Iraq invasion, opposition to, 2–3; neutrality of, 18–19, 35; organization of, 28–29, 33–36; papal authority, 28; Roman Curia, 29; secrecy and, 19–20; United Nations, membership in, 111–116; Vatican, distinction from, 13
Hon Tai-fai, Archbishop Savio, 283, 427n46
Hong-Soon Han, Thomas, 138
Hu Jintao, 281
Huang Bingzhang, Bishop Joseph, 291
human dignity, 3, 82, 87, 89, 112, 123, 125, 161, 208, 214, 229, 390n44
Huntington, Samuel, 258
Hwang Jang-yop, 423n12

Innocent III, Pope, 48
Intergovernmental Authority on Development (IGAD), 300
International Atomic Energy Agency (IAEA), 21, 112, 331n28

458 *Index*

International Conference on Population and Development (ICPD), 78–80, 350n37, 351n46
International Law Commission, 93
international personality, 96, 104, 356n8, 358n33, 361n67
International Telegraph Union (ITU), 110, 364n104, 364n110
Iran, 31, 79, 175, 247, 249, 257, 259–60, 389n37, 410n7, 416n61, 416n62, 416n65; geo-strategy and, 255, 257, 263–65; nuclear weapons and, 21; Shia Islam and, 247, 260–62, 410n68; US nuclear agreement with, 4, 7, 180, 262
Irish Sisters of Loreto, 301
Israel, 24, 110, 126, 183, 210, 257, 263, 268, 308; barrier wall, Francis' prayer at, 5, 254–55; Francis' itinerary (2014), 253–55; Jerusalem, status of, 5, 413n40; Maronite community, Raï visit to, 247, 253–54, 413n36; Neve Shalom, 316; South Sudan, arms sales to, 305, 436n29; Yad Vashem, 64, 255
Ivereigh, Austen, 129, 186, 346n102, 371n56, 376n6, 376n8, 376n11, 439n57

Jackson, Robert, 94
Japan, 123, 141, 219, 389n37; Bergoglio's interest in, 283–85; bombing of, 10, 144, 154; diplomatic recognition by Holy See, 1, 43–6, 339n5
Jaramillo, Alma Rosa, 228
Jeanbart, Archbishop Jean-Clément, 264
Jesuit missionaries, 36–37, 337n90; in China, 73–4, 272, 295–96, 348n17; in South America, 174, 238
Jesuit Relief Services, 302
Jesus Christ, 2, 27, 28, 43, 46, 47, 49, 54, 57, 74, 78, 81, 86, 90, 125, 129–30, 137, 149, 178, 229, 240, 254, 259, 278, 295–96, 311–12, 351n51, 416n68
Jin Luxian, Bishop Aloysius, 275–76
Jincai, Bishop Guo, 294
Jinde Charities, 278
Joan of Arc, Saint, 103
John X, Patriarch of Antioch and All the East, 250–51
John XXIII, 39–40, 56, 62, 88–89, 100, 195, 335n71, 346n96, 346n101, 377n21; CIA, clash with, 1–2, 91; Cuban missile crisis and, 84–85, 113; Francis, reminiscent of, 12, 66; Khrushchev, relationship with, 85; Ostpolitik, 56, 355n92; Second Vatican Council, convened, 83–4, 86, 177
John Chrysostom, Saint, 60, 169, 170
John Paul II, Pope, 20, 31, 38, 59, 69, 136, 138, 147, 152, 225, 233, 267, 334n59, 360n49, 381n29, 363n103, 419n100, 422n9; anti-communism of, 11, 294; Beagle Channel mediation, 52–4; Bergoglio and, 147; China, attitude toward, 271–2, 273–4, 275–76, 421n6, 423n13, 424n20, 426n38; Chinese saints, canonization of, 279; Cuba, and, 191, 193–94, 196–99, 200–201, 390n44; diplomacy and, 79, 88, 111, 115, 125, 145, 151, 221; diplomats, view of, 61; inter-faith dialogue, 126, 165–67; Iraq invasion, opposition to, 2; 124, 179–80, 247, 249, 342n50; Left-wing politics, hostility toward, 222–23; Muslims, relationship with, 133, 247, 262, 369n31, 410n6; Orthodox Church, and, 166, 169–70, 173, 177, 383n41; Ostpolitik and, 156; Panama, crisis in (1989), 16, 19; Reagan, relationship with, 1; recentralized papacy, 34; Russia, and, 167–68; Sant-Egidio, and, 39–40; United Nations membership,

115–16; United Nations speech, 364n105; visits Colombia, 223; visits Holy Land, 253–55, 413n38; visits Puebla, Mexico, 222; visits, Mozambique, 38; Visits Damascus, Syria, 126, 415n60
Joint Commission on Theological Dialogue, 178
Jones, James, 203
Jubilee Party, 213–14, 218
just war vs. just peace, 90–1, 233, 234, 404n59

Kangxi Emperor (1661–1722), 73
Kasper, Cardinal Walter, 168
Kenyan Conference of Catholic Bishops, 208, 211–13, 217–18
Kennedy, John F., 7, 84–5, 273
Kenyatta, Uhuru, 205, 207, 210–13, 214–17
Kerry, John, 187, 188, 191–92, 212, 239, 249, 389n37
Khrushchev, Nikita, 1–2, 84–5, 91, 158, 353n69, 355n92, 379n14
Kibaki, Mwai, 207
Kiir, Salva, 299–300, 305–08, 311, 312–14, 315, 434n4, 437n46, 439n63
Kim Dae-jung, 144
Kim Hee-jong, Archbishop Hyginus, 140–41
King Henry VIII, 94
King Victor Emmanuel III, 64, 97, 108, 110
Kingdom of Italy, 97, 333n47, 362n84
Kirill, Patriarch of Moscow and all Russia, 164–5, 171–73, 249, 384n56
Knights of Columbus, 193, 202–03, 381n29, 391n52
Koch, Cardinal Kurt, 31, 171, 176
Kondrusiewicz, Tadeusz, 166–67
Korean Demilitarized Zone (DMZ), 139
Korean Peninsula Peace-Sharing Forum, 135
Korir, Bishop Cornelius, 213–14, 216
Koterski, Joseph, 101

kulturkampf, 100–101
Kuron Peace Village (Holy Trinity Peace Village), 316

L.F.L. Oppenheim, 98, 356n8, 358n33, 358n34
La Civilta Cattolica, 123, 359n37
Laboa, Archbishop Jose Sebastiano, 15–19, 330n12
Ladies in White (*Damas de Blanco*), 193, 200, 202, 203
Laghi, Cardinal Pio, 2, 247, 277, 324n8, 324n9, 342n50
Lamb, Christopher, 325n18, 376n5
Lateran Accords (1929), 98, 106–08, 332n39;financial settlement, 110, 363n101; Mussolini, motives of, 104–06; neutrality required, 123; signing of, 110; symbolism of, 109–10
Latin American Episcopal Council (CELAM), 12, 150, 222, 399n8, 400n10; Aparecida, Brazil, meeting in (2007), 137, 147, 149, 232
Lavrov, Sergei, 249
Law of Guarantees, 97, 105, 358n30
Law, Cardinal Bernard, 194, 196–98, 277
Leahy, Patrick, 187–88
Lei Shiyin, Bishop Paul, 290
Lenin, Vladimir, 10, 55
Leo the Great, Pope, 47
Leo XIII, Pope (1878–1903), 69–70, 323n1, 335n72; diplomatic prowess, 100–01; neutrality and, 123; *Rerum Novarum*, 100–02; social teaching and, 82–3; Thomism, elevation of, 101
Leuven University, 273
Levin, Carl, 187
Li Baofu, 278
Li Shan, Archbishop Joseph, 282
liberation theology, 222, 224, 402n40
Liu Bainian, Anthony, 276–77, 280, 424n19, 426n37

Lokudu Loro, Archbishop Paulino, 304, 436n24
Londoño, Rodrigo (aka Timochenko), 239, 241, 242, 409n114
López Trujillo, Cardinal Alfonso, 223, 226–27; homosexuality, 399n8; liberation theology and, 222; office targeted, 223; Pontifical Council for the Family, 226
Loreto Rumbeck School, 301
Luttwak, Edward, 134

M-19, 223, 234, 400n12
Ma Yinglin, Bishop Joseph, 287, 292
Machar, Riek, 299, 305, 306, 308–09, 311–12, 313–15, 436n30, 437n46
Machiavelli, Niccolò, 120, 368n11
Mack, Eitay, 305, 436n29
MacNutt, Francis, 70–1, 347n10
Macron, Emmanuel, 265
Maglione, Cardinal Luigi, 44, 107, 340–41n5
Maidan Square (Ukraine), 157–61, 381n23
Maluwa, Tiyanjana, 104, 363n97
Mao Zedong, 272, 295, 420n1
Marino, Archbishop Joseph, 2, 71, 267, 420n101
Maritain, Jacques, 93, 111–12, 364n109
Maronite Church, 245, 247, 250, 262, 267
Martino, Cardinal Renato, 6, 79, 350n37, 351n45
Mattingly, Garrett, 49–50, 340n19
Mazarin, Cardinal Jules, 68, 347n5
Mazur, Bishop Jerzy, 166
McCann, James, SJ, 178
McCarrick, Theodore, 189–90, 389n35, 389n37
McCone, John, 85
McDonough, Denis, 187, 189–90
Meir, Golda, 20
Menendez, Bob, 187
von Metternich, Prince Klemens, 76, 348n20

Mickens, Robert, 375n3
Mindszenty, Cardinal József, 55–6, 196, 292–93, 431n83
Minsk agreements, 175, 382n31, 385n72
Miracle on the Vistula (Poland), 26
Mission de Vie (Mission of Life), 257
missionaries, 32, 35–38, 62, 103, 140, 167, 174, 218, 331n24; China, activities in, 73–4, 101, 103, 272, 276, 278–80, 283, 289, 295, 424n18, 424n19, 425n29; South Sudan, activities in, 301–03, 435n10
Montini, Giovanni, 44, 111, 352n64
Montoya, Laura (Madre Laura), 233
Moon Jae-in, 135, 139–41, 142–43
Morlion, Father Felix, 84
Mother of God of Kazan icon, 167–68
Mother Teresa of Calcutta, 36, 133, 167, 276–78, 287, 301, 424n18
Moynihan, Robert, 168
Mugabe, Robert, 58–9
Muhammad, Prophet, 22, 48, 206, 248, 261, 410n7, 416n68
Muheria, Archbishop Anthony, 210, 218
Mukonori, Fidelis, SJ, 58–60
Munich Security Conference, 297
Murphy, Father Lawrence, 273–75, 277, 423n12,
Murphy, Bishop William, 197–98
Mussolini, Benito, 104–06, 108–10, 332n39, 339n1, 361n72, 361n76
Myanmar, 128, 132–33, 150

Napoleon Bonaparte, 28, 54–5, 75–6, 95, 333n51, 343n53, 348n20, 357n14,
Napoleon III, 96–7
Nasrallah, Hassan, 264
National Catholic Register, 8, 134
National Liberation Army (ELN), 223–24, 228, 231, 234, 241, 400n18, 401n19, 401n22, 404n56
natural law, 46, 80, 81–2, 86, 87, 88, 94, 111, 122, 359n48, 365n129

Index

Nazianzen, Saint Gregory, 169–70
New York Post, 99
New York Times, 8, 10, 79, 99, 104, 225, 239, 242, 249, 295
Nicaragua, 131, 330n12, 431n83
Nicene Creed, 171
Nicolson, Harold, 121, 368n24
Ninth National Assembly of Chinese Catholics, 289–90
Njue, Cardinal John, 207–08, 209, 212–13, 214, 216–17
Nobel Prize Committee, 239
non expedit, 108
Noriega, General Manuel, 15–19
Nostra Aetate (In Our Time, 1965), 31, 89, 260
Nuer community, 299, 309, 314
Nugent, Archbishop Eugene, 23
Nuland, Victoria, 157
Nuzzi, Gianluigi, 13
Nye, Joseph, 109, 371n55

O'Connor, Cardinal John, 197, 276–77, 424n20
O'Malley, Cardinal Sean, 188, 287, 392n64
Obama, Barack, 181, 182, 184–85, 187–88, 190–92, 208, 249 286, 411n15
Obama administration, 4, 158, 180, 181, 388n15, 389n37
Odama, Bishop John Baptist, 310
Odom, William, 8
Odinga, Raila, 205, 207, 210, 212–13, 215–18
Okoth, Archbishop Zacchaeus, 207–210, 215–17
Organization of American States (OAS), 18, 131
Orobator, Agbonkhianmeghe, SJ, 310
Ortega, Cardinal Jaime, 176, Castro regime, mediating for, 182, 193–197; Cuba-US negotiations, 187, 189–90, 390n41, 393n73
Romero, Saint Óscar, 136, 138
Ostpolitik, 56, 195, 324n6, 343n57

Otunga, Archbishop Maurice, 209–210
Our Lady of Lourdes, 110
Oves Fernandez, Archbishop Francisco Ricardo, 196, 293

Pacelli, Eugenio (Pope Pius XII), 105, 123–24, 353n76, 369n29, 369n30
Pacelli, Francesco, 105
Pacem in Terris (Peace on Earth, 1963), 84–6, 88, 89, 91, 113, 195
Palestine, 5, 24, 31, 63–4, 253–4; "State of Palestine," 254–55
Palestine-Vatican relations, 255, 413n38, 414n44
Panama, 185, 197, 230; US invasion and standoff at nunciature (1989), 10, 15–19, 72, 329n2, 330n6, 330n12
papal infallibility, 100, 359n37
Papal States, 12, 28, 69, 75–6, 95, 96–7, 100–01, 333n50, 333n54, 343n53, 357n14, 359n39
Paris, 45, 49, 51, 65, 68, 71, 75–6, 77, 97, 102, 104, 111, 123, 250, 259, 263, 265, 333n51, 343n53, 353n76, 417n72
Paris Peace Conference (1919–1920), 77–8, 104, 122–23, 349n29
Parolin, Cardinal Pietro, 27, 29, 115–16, 284, 337n84, 343n58, 428n50; China diplomacy and, 6, 118, 279–80, 282–85, 290, 292, 296, 426n38, 427n46, 433n104; Colombia diplomacy and, 234, 238, 240; Cuba-US mediation, 187–88, 191–92; Korea diplomacy and, 140, 143; Middle East diplomacy and, 265, 268–69; Russian Orthodox Church, diplomacy with, 164; South Sudan diplomacy and, 309; undersecretary for relations with states as, 21, 127, 258, 415n56, 431n83; Vietnam diplomacy and, 125–26, 370n42
pastoral diplomacy, 59–60
Paul VI, 2, 20, 31, 32, 56, 60, 84, 90–1, 113–14, 165, 209, 253, 255,

268, 309, 324n6, 334n58, 335n68, 336n77, 352n64, 354n90, 365n119, 380n18, 438n51
Pax Christi Netherlands, 198, 225–6, 230, 403n43
Payá Sardiñas, Oswaldo, 199–202, 203–04; Francis, family's meeting with, 204; Ofelia Acedevo, wife of, 200, 203, 204; Rosa Maria, daughter of, 200, 204
Peace of Westphalia (1648), 68, 95, 122
Pereira, Thomas, SJ, 73, 348n17
Peres, Simon, 308
Peter's Pence, 100
Petro, Nicolai, 172, 328n51, 384n59
Petro Urrego, Gustavo, 235–36
Philippines, 1, 34, 44, 84, 208, 232, 323n1, 347n10, 415n52, 429n64
Pierre, Archbishop Christophe, 33, 35, 57, 336n76
Pius VI (1775–1799), 28, 69, 75, 174, 333n51, 355n91
Pius VII (1800–1823), 75–6, 174, 333n51, 343n53, 369n27
Pius IX, Pope (1846–1878), 96–8, 107–08; First Vatican Council, 99, 333n47
Pius X (1903–1914), 102
Pius XI (1922–1939), 26, 43, 45, 62, 88, 339n1, 361n65; Lateran Accords, negotiation of, 104–110, 332n39, 362n79
Pius XII (1939–1958), 7, 46, 60, 86, 112, 123, 149, 209, 222, 274, 333n47, 353n76, 364n106, 364n113, 422n10; World War II and, 1, 43–5, 63, 91, 124, 329n5
Plokhii, Serhii, 157
political authority as moral force, 74, 86–7
Pontifical Council for Christian Unity, 30–1
Pontifical Council for Interreligious Dialogue, 30–1, 248, 329n5, 419n94, 437n39

Pontifical Council for Justice and Peace, 125, 197, 334n58
Pontifical Ecclesiastical Academy (*Accademia*). Founded as Pontifical Academy of Ecclesiastical Nobles (1701–1939). 2, 18–19, 24, 120, 131, 267, 285, 347n7, 347n8, 347n10, 404n54; career path, 27, 32; case studies, examples of, 73–80; curriculum, 25, 30, 71–72, 114–15; demographics, 69; papal graduates, 60–61, 69–70, 100–102, 102–03, 123–24; origins, 67–69; Pontifical Academy of Ecclesiastical Nobles, 68; students, selection of; 70
Pontius Pilate, 81
Poroshenko, Petro, 157
Porta Pia, 97
Preadicate Evangelium (Preach the Gospel), 29, 334n56, 334n59
Program for Development and Peace in the Magdalena Medio region (PDPMM), 228–30, 402n40
Putin, Vladimir, 158, 172; Middle East, engagement in, 249–50, 264, 411n72; Ukraine, 158, 161, 374n15; Vatican, relations with, 3, 164, 173–75
Pyatt, Geoffrey, 157
Pyongyang Joint Declaration (2018), 142

Quadragesimo Anno (On Reconstruction of the Social Order, 1931), 88
Quintana, Archbishop Pedro Lopez, 23

Raï, Cardinal Béchara Boutros, Maronite Patriarch of Antioch and All the East, 163, 245, 247, 269; Holy Land, trip to (2014), 253–55; Saudi Arabia, trip to (2017), 245, 264–66; Syria, trip to, (2013), 250–51
Ramsey, Archbishop Michael, 309, 438n51

Rasoul al-Azam (Mighty Prophet) Hospital, 257
Ratti, Achille (Pope Pius XI), 26, 332n39, 361n65
Ratzinger, Joseph, 11, 28, 88–9, 148, 325n16, 401n28, 425n38
Reese, Father Thomas, 28–9, 34
Religion of the Lord of Heaven (Catholicism), 272
religious extremism, 11, 124, 133–34, 176, 257–58, 266
religious freedom, 22, 33, 46, 84, 72, 74, 82, 85, 89, 275, 281, 288, 337n84, 425n31
Ren Yanli, 282
Republic of Florence, 28, 120
Rerum Novarum (Of New Things, 1891), 82–3, 88, 100–01
Revolution of Dignity (Ukraine), 159–60
Rhodes, Ben, 185–86, 188–92, 411n15
Ricci, Matteo, 73, 272, 421n3
Rigali, Cardinal Justin, 70–2
Risorgimento, 97, 359n39
Rohingya people, 132, 150
Roman Curia, 20, 28, 29, 70, 147, 352n62, 375n3, 383n41
"Roman Question," 98, 105–09
Romania, 18, 55, 64, 86, 108, 134, 166, 353n76, 381n25, 383n41, 422n9
Roncalli, Angelo, 62, 66, 83, 111–12, 346n95, 346n102; Bulgaria, 62–3; France, 65, 353n76; Greece, 63; Jews, protection of, 63–5, 346n96; Turkey, 34, 63–5
Rooney, Francis, 21, 29, 36, 247, 284, 333n54, 428n50
Roosevelt, Franklin D., 1, 44–5
Ros-Lehtinen, Ileana, 202
Rosa Chavez, Cardinal Gregorio, 135–38, 139
Rota Graziosi, Monsignor Gianfranco, 280, 285, 287, 296, 425n31, 427n47
Rotta, Archbishop Angelo, 63–4
Rouhani, Hassan, 260–61

Rubio, Marco, 187
Rugambwa, Archbishop Novatus, 22–3
Russian Orthodox Church: 166, 172, 383n40, 384n59 protecting Middle Eastern Christians, 135, 250; Holy See, relations with, 6, 11, 165–66, 167–69, 171–73, 175, 179; Ukraine and, 165, 176, 380n20

Sacred Scripture (Bible), 17, 57, 76, 80–1, 208, 287, 311–12, 363n100
Sáenz, Archbishop Pedro, 230–31
Salazar Gómez, Cardinal Rubén, 232–33, 234–35, 239
Salesians of Don Bosco, 283
Samorè, Cardinal Antonio, 52–4, 342n43
San Carlos and San Ambrosio National Seminary (Cuba), 193
Sandri, Cardinal Leonardo, 259
Sant'Egidio, 38, 133, 440n67; Mozambique and, 39–41; South Sudan and, 313–14
Sarraff Trujillo, Rolando, 189–90, 390n41
Sarros, Peter, 268, 342n42
Saudi Arabia, 23, 255, 261, 263–64, 420n1; guest workers, 419n97; Hariri and, 245, 247; Iran, rivalry with, 410n7; Raï, 2017 visit, 245, 264–66
Saudi–Vatican relations, 23, 266–267, 329n5
Scherer, Cardinal Odilo Pedro, 136–39
Schism of Christianity (1054), 90, 165, 382n38
Second Vatican Council, 12, 31, 34–35, 60, 66, 80, 83, 86, 89, 91, 114, 165, 222, 255, 260, 276, 333n47, 336n82, 352n62, 352n64
Self Defense Units of Colombia (AUC), 228
Seton Hall University, 274, 287
Shevchuk, Major Archbishop Sviatoslav, 159, 162–63, 380n18
Sigler, Ariel, 202

Simonis, Cardinal Adrianus, 226
Sin, Cardinal Jaime, 34
Sixth Summit of the Americas, 184
Slipyj, Major Archbishop Josyf, 293, 353n69
Sodano, Cardinal Angelo, 14, 331n23, 425n31
Solidarity with South Sudan, 301, 305–06
Solidarność, 201
Soroka, Archbishop Stefan, 161, 381n25
South Sudan Council of Churches (SSCC), 306, 308, 313, 437n39
South Sudan Opposition Movements Alliance (SSOMA), 313
South Sudan Relief Fund, 301
sovereignty of Holy See: 93–110, 356n8, 358n29, 359n37, 363n97
Spellman, Cardinal Francis, 189
Sprizzi, Archbishop Marco, 140, 142
St. Elie and St. Gregory the Illuminator Armenian Catholic Cathedral (Beirut), 259–60
St. George Cathedral (Beirut), 263
St. Jude's Church (Hong Kong), 293
St. Theresa's Cathedral (Juba), 307
Suarez, Father Francisco, 94–5, 356n11
Subsidiarity, 56, 87–8
Sunni-Shia rivalry, 263, 410n7
Suu Kyi, Aung San, 133, 150
Sweig, Julia, 187, 387n15, 388n17, 390n41, 391n47
Sylvester I, Pope, 47
symphonia, 172

Taban, Bishop Paride, 304, 316, 436n24
Taiwan, 273, 279, 369n26
Tauran, Cardinal Jean-Louis, 329n5; Panama, diplomacy in, 16, 330n12, 419n100; Pontifical Council for Interreligious Dialogue, 31, 134, 248, 258; Requiem Mass for, 267; Saudi Arabia, diplomacy in, 266–67, 419n94; Serbia, diplomacy in, 420n101

Teoctist, Patriarch of Romanian Orthodox Church, 166
ter Laak, Jan, 225–26
The Mission, 174
Thirty Years War (1618–1648), 67–8, 95
Thomas, Gordon, 20, 85
Tillerson, Rex, 217, 265
Tittmann, Jr., Harold, 44
Tomasi, Archbishop Silvano Maria, 261, 417n71
Tong Hon, Cardinal John, 288, 290, 293, 423n13
Treacy, Sister Orla, 301, 313
Treaty of Nerchinsk (1689), 73–4
Treaty of Versailles (1919), 77–8, 122–23
titular sees, 57

U Thant, 113–15, 365n115, 365n119
Uganda, 216, 299, 302, 305–06, 310, 315
Ukrainian Autocephalous Orthodox Church, 380n20
Ukrainian Greek Catholic Church, 158–63, 176, 380n18, 381n23, 381n27, 381n29
Ukrainian Orthodox Church—Kyiv Patriarchate, 160, 161, 380n20
Ukrainian Orthodox Church—Moscow Patriarchate, 160, 380n20
Umayyad mosque, 124, 410n6, 415n60
UN—UN High Commissioner for Human Rights, 307
UN General Assembly, 18, 151
United Nations, 13, 22, 23, 78, 84, 88, 91, 93–4, 111–116, 123, 130, 192, 262, 350n36, 364n104, 364n105, 364n110, 413n40, 414n44, 415n52
UNESCO, 112, 364n109
Unitatis Redintegratio (Restoration of Unity, 1964), 90, 165
United Arab Emirates (UAE), 5, 135
United Nations Fund for Population Activities (UNFPA), 78, 350n36, 351n44

Universal Postal Union, 110, 112, 364n110
Urbaniana University (Rome), 118
Uribe Vélez, Álvaro, 221, 232, 236, 238–40, 242, 403n51, 404n56
USAID, 183, 415n51
US Conference of Catholic Bishops (USCCB), 4,35, 261, 273, 392n58
US military, 5, 17–8, 72, 144, 177
US militarized foreign policy, Vatican critique of, 3–5, 13, 18, 144, 179–80, 424n20
US-China relations, 277
US Institute of Peace, 227, 233, 303
US–Iran nuclear disarmament agreement, 261–62
US-Vatican relations, 2, 30, 33, 113, 249, 314, 323n1, 324n8, 353n76, 428n50; abortion and, 78–80, 350n37; Bergoglio and, 4, 8–9; Biden and, 7, 10–11; China and, 6, 274, 286–87, 422n9, 423n12, Cuba and, 181–82, 187–88, 190–95, 202–03; Francis and, 5–6, 13, 150–51; humanitarian collaboration, 127; Iran and, 4; Iraq and, 2, 25;Japan, wartime disagreement, 43–45; Middle East and, 249–51, 257, 267–68, 413n40; Obama administration and, 4; Panama and, 15–18; Russia and, 3–4, 6; Soviet Union and, 1–2; Wikileaks and, 20–22, 431n83; World War I and, 77

Valenzuela, Arturo, 203
Varela Project, 199–200, 201, 202
Vatican diplomacy: Beagle Channel dispute, 52–54; Benedict XVI, approach to, 231–32, 247–48, 279–83, 375n3, 412n31; broken world, ministry to, 45; cardinals, utilized by, 32–33, 135–39; China, 117–19, 283–86, 287–97, 427n47; collegiality, 20–21; Colombia, 219–244; continuity between pontiffs, 12; Cuba and, 181–82, 187–88, 190–93, 204; Cuban Missile Crisis and, 84–86; dialogue, commitment to, 11, 21–22, 31–32, 61, 86, 90–91, 125–28, 134, 138, 141, 152–53, 165, 170–71, 174, 177–79, 191, 198, 201, 204–05, 211–15, 218, 228–29, 233–34, 240, 243, 248–49, 260–62, 265, 272–73, 279–80, 283–85, 288, 292, 296, 307–10, 355n91; dictators, 195–96, 353n69; discretion and secrecy of, 12, 24–25; duality of, 43; efficiency, 22–24; evangelization, 46, 56–58; as global network, 12; hearts, conversion of, 19, 91, 300–01, 315; history of, 46–52, 62–65, 67–71, 73–79, 94–109, 111–116, 329n1, 333n51, 339n5; inter-state system, functioning within, 11; Iraq invasion opposition, 2, 25; Iran, 260–62; Israel and, 255; Japan, 44; John Paul II approach to, 219, 222–225, 272–76, 279; Korea, 135–43; Lebanon, 255–260, 262–66, 267–69; mediation, 46, 359n44; moral authority, 192–93; Mozambique, 39–41; natural law tradition, 46, 359n48; nuncios, 12, 23; impartiality of, 18–19, 46, 316; organization, 27–38; Orthodox Church representatives and, 166–67,173–77; Ostpolitik, 56, 195–96, 324n6, 343n57; Palestine, 254–55, 414n44; Panama and, 15–19; papal diplomats, 69–70, 100–109, 145; partisan politics, avoidance of, 35, 124–26, 201; pastoral techniques, 19, 58–62, 66; priestly cadre, 26, 57, 58–62, 66, 70–71; preservation, 46, 54–56; principles, 18–19, 80–83, 86–91, 120–29; representation, 45–46, 46–50; Russia, 171–73; Saudi Arabia, 266–67; Second Vatican Council and, 83–84, 90, 165, 352n64, 365n129; Secretary of State, 16, 19, 21, 29, 33, 44, 53,

55–56, 75, 103, 107, 114, 118, 145, 253, 279, 282–84, 309, 331n24, 333n54, 337n84, 339n5, 343n58, 349n25, 360n53, 375n3, 404n64; South Sudan and, 300–01, 306–14; sovereignty and, 93–116, 356n8; United Nations and, 111–116; US militarism and; 3–4, 18, 144; wide network, 25; World War I and, 77–78, 86, 90, 122–24; World War II and, 43–46, 91, 102–04, 107, 123–24
Vatican diplomats, 13, 300; dedication, 26–27; education of, 71–74, 76, 78, 80; as priests, 26, 59–62, 66, 70–71; "spiritual worldliness" risk of, 66; vow of secrecy, 19–20
Vatican City State, 1, 13, 93, 107, 110, 112–3, 123, 271, 308, 339n1, 355n5, 356n8, 362n84, 363n97, 421n2
Verbitsky, Horacio, 4, 7–9, 327n34
Viaene, Vincent, 100
Vienna, 23, 97, 331n28, 360n52, 419n94
Vienna Convention on Diplomatic Relations (1961), 20, 33–4
Vietnam-Vatican relations, 125–26, 128, 365n119, 370n41, 370n42
Vietnam War, 2, 18, 113, 114
Vigano, Archbishop Carlo Maria, 35, 337n84, 337n85
Vitral, 193
Vladimir, Saint, 165
von Humboldt, Wilhelm, 95, 357n14
von Papen, Franz, 64–5, 346n95
von Ribbentrop, Joachim, 107

Wahhabism, 261
Wang Chao, 119, 295
Wang Yi, 297
Wang Zuo'an, 430n70
Welby, Archbishop Justin, 303, 307, 308–10, 312, 314, 438n51
Wellerstein, Alex, 144
Wells, Archbishop Peter, 23–4
Wikileaks, 128, 173, 325n13, 410n7; Bergoglio, information on, 325n16;

US–Vatican consultation, 20–1, 127, 415n56
Women religious, 22, 36, 63, 213, 233, 278, 291, 301, 333n53
World Bank, 229, 355n5
World Council of Churches, 171
World War I (Great War), 23, 77–8, 83, 90, 102–04, 105, 122–23, 368n24
World War II, 7, 25, 43, 55, 86, 91, 107, 123–24, 379n14
World Youth Day, 13, 130
Worthley, Fr. John, 276–77, 286–87, 292, 424n18, 429n64
Wu Qinjing, Bishop Joseph Martin, 285

Xi Jinping, 118, 283–84, 285–86
Xijin, Bishop Guo, 118, 291, 367n2
Xuan Loc, Vietnam, 125
Xuereb, Archbishop Alfred, 140, 142

Yanukovych, Viktor, 157
Yeltsin, Boris, 166
Yeom Soo-jung, Cardinal Andrew, 139, 141
Yeung Ming-cheung, Bishop Michael, 293
Youssef III Younan, Patriarch of the Syriac Catholic Church, 251–52

Zacchi, Archbishop Cesare, 195–96
Zapada Tamayo, Orlando, 200
Zartman, I. William, 295
Zen Ze-kiun, Cardinal Joseph, 126, 280, 283, 288, 290, 292–93, 296, 430n75, 431n83, 432n88, 433n104
Zenari, Archbishop Mario, 27
Zhan Silu, Bishop Vincenzo, 118, 291–92, 294, 367n2
Zhang Shijiang, Father John, 278
Zhang Yinlin, Father Joseph, 286
Zhuang Jianjian, Bishop Peter, 291, 292
Zimbabwe, 58–9
Zuckerberg, Mark, 286
Zumpolle, Liduine, 225–27, 244, 404n56
Zuniga, Ricardo, 185, 187, 189–90, 191

About the Author

Victor Gaetan, PhD, has served as international correspondent for Catholic News Service and the *National Catholic Register*. He contributes to *Foreign Affairs* and *America* magazine. For over twenty years, he has filed stories from countries in turmoil: Bosnia-Herzegovina, Cuba, Lebanon, Kosovo, Peru, Turkey, and Ukraine as well as from Hong Kong, Korea, and Taiwan. He received numerous awards from the Catholic Press Association of North America and has written for publications ranging from *Art & Auction* to *Le Figaro*. Gaetan graduated from Sorbonne University in Paris with a license in Byzantine and Ottoman studies. He has a PhD from Tufts University in ideology in literature and a masters in International Law and Diplomacy from the Fletcher School. More information can be found at: victorgaetan.org.

Printed in Great Britain
by Amazon